Culinaria Germany

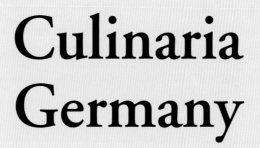

Culinaria
Germany

Christine Metzger
Editor

Ruprecht Stempell · Christoph Büschel · Saša Fuis
Photography

Peter Feierabend
Art Director

Michael Ditter
Coordination and Layout

h.f.ullmann

Abbreviations and Quantities

1 oz	= 1 ounce = 28 grams
1 lb	= 1 pound = 16 ounces
1 cup	= 8 ounces * (see below)
1 cup	= 8 fluid ounces = 250 milliliters (liquids)
2 cups	= 1 pint (liquids)
8 pints	= 4 quarts = 1 gallon (liquids)
1 g	= 1 gram = 1/1000 kilogram
1 kg	= 1 kilogram = 1000 grams = 2¼ lb
1 l	= 1 liter = 1000 milliliters (ml) = approx 34 fluid ounces
125 milliliters (ml)	= approx 8 tablespoons = ½ cup
1 tbsp	= 1 level tablespoon = 15-20 g * (see below); = 15 milliliters (liquids)
1 tsp	= 1 level teaspoon = 3-5 g * (see below) = 5 ml (liquids)

Where measurements of dry ingredients are given in spoons, this always refers to the dry ingredient as described in the wording immediately following, e.g. 1 tbsp chopped onions BUT: 1 onion, peeled and chopped. The weight of dry ingredients varies significantly depending on the density factor, e.g. 1 cup flour weighs less than 1 cup butter.

Quantities in ingredients have been rounded up or down for convenience, where appropriate. Metric conversions may therefore not correspond exactly. It is important to use either American or metric measurements within a recipe.

Quantities in recipes
Recipes serve four people, unless stated otherwise.
Exception: Recipes for drinks (quantities given per person).

© 2004/2007 Tandem Verlag GmbH
h.f.ullmann is an imprint of Tandem Verlag GmbH

Studio photography:	Food Foto Cologne – Brigitte Krauth, Jürgen Holz
Food stylist (studio):	Stephan Krauth
Food stylist (on location):	Ursula Virnich
Photographic assistance (on location):	Martin Kurtenbach, Sonia Büschel
Picture research:	Regine Ermert
Recipe editor:	Ingeborg Pils
Layout assistance:	Birgit Beyer
Maps:	Astrid Fischer-Leitl
Cover design:	Peter Feierabend, Claudio Martinez
Front cover photo:	Ruprecht Stempell
Back cover photo:	© Tandem Verlag GmbH

Original Title : *Culinaria Deutsche Spezialitäten*
ISBN 978-3-8331-1030-6

© 2008 for this English edition: Tandem Verlag GmbH
h.f.ullmann is an imprint of Tandem Verlag GmbH

Special edition

Translation from German:	Anthea Bell, Mo Croasdale, Karen Green, Martin Pearce, Judith Phillips, Elaine Richards in association with First Edition Translations Ltd.
Editing and typesetting:	First Edition Translations Ltd., Cambridge, UK
Project Management:	Birgit Dietz and Béatrice Hunt for First Edition Translations Ltd.
Project Coordination:	Nadja Bremse

Printed in China

ISBN 978-3-8331-4908-5

10 9 8 7 6 5 4 3 2
X IX VIII VII VI V IV III II

www.ullmann-publishing.com

Contents

To eat is to live, but if by that we simply mean to sustain life, we are stating the obvious. Of course we have to eat if we are not to starve. Having ensured the basics of life, we can extend the idea: eating is more than taking in nourishment; it is life in all its dimensions. Not a day passes without asking, "What shall we eat today?" Not a social event occurs without the vital question of what food is to be served. From birth to death, every stage of life is marked by time-honored and established dishes, more observed in the past than the present. Germany has its birthday cakes, its goose at Christmas. Food features in literature – any writer describing everyday life or celebrations is bound to mention it.

Composers wrote *Tafelmusik* as music to dine to; ceramic artists, vessels and fine china to adorn the table. When food is more scarce, it becomes a central topic of conversation. During the Cold War, an entire city – Berlin – was fed by the airlift. Food and drink reflect the facts of political, historical, and social life: riots occurred when the price of beer or bread rose; the desire for spices on the part of people in the Middle Ages led to the discovery of the New World. Various factors influenced which dishes became the local specialty of a given region: the produce of its soil, and the degree of prosperity. The effect of a region's neighbors could be distinctive: Bohemian and Austrian cuisine made its mark on Bavarian cooking, while in the north of the country, the influences came from Scandinavia and Britain. The basic produce available in the lands of Germany, from the northern coasts of the North Sea and Baltic to the southern range of the Alps, was essentially the same, so the variations in German cuisine lie in the detail. There is, for example, a huge variety of potato dishes, reflecting the inventiveness of those who had to live on potatoes for most of the year. The aim of this book has been to snap up "morsels of knowledge" from the people of this country, exploring every aspect of the fascinating subject of food.

Christine Metzger

Hamburg
Schwerin
Bremen
Berlin
Hanover
Magdeburg
Potsdam
Düsseldorf
Dresden
Bonn
Erfurt
Wiesbaden
Mainz
Saarbrücken
Stuttgart
Munich

ULLA RETTIG
Thuringia

Rarely did Johann Wolfgang von Goethe repeat himself but, when faced with the wonderful scenery in the area around Ilmenau in the Thuringian forest, words almost failed him. "Magnificent! Magnificent!" he cried, and on the slopes of the Kickelhahn wrote "Wanderers Nachtlied": "Over all the peaks lies rest…" There is a good reason why Thuringia is renowned not just as the land of steamed dumplings, cakes, and sautéed sausages, but also as the green heart of Germany. Anyone who has ever completed the Rennsteig walk knows why. For decades the best-known hiking route in Europe was criss-crossed by army patrols. The Rennsteig stretches for 105 miles (168 kilometers) along the spine formed by the Thuringian Forest, the Franconian Forest and the Schiefer mountains. Yet the Kyfferhäuser mountains, the Eichsfeld and the Rhön biosphere reserve are charming too.

Around half of the Free State of Thuringia is used for agriculture. In the Thuringian Basin, with its rich weathered limestone soil, and on the fertile loess soil of east Thuringia wheat, rape and sugarbeet flourish; highly prized Thuringian barley for brewing is harvested in the foothills. Vegetables grow around the regional capital, Erfurt, as well as on the western edge of the Thuringian Basin. In east Thuringia cauliflower, white cabbage, broad beans, onions, and cucumbers are grown.

This territory, the eleventh biggest Federal state, once disparagingly called a "patchwork of principalities," has also helped to shape European history. Martin Luther translated the New Testament on the Wartburg mountain, near Eisenach. Hegel, Fichte, and Schelling taught at the University of Jena. Bach made music in Weimar, and in the 18th century, at the time of Goethe and Schiller, the city of Weimar became the center of German Classicism.

In 1919 the German National Assembly promulgated the Weimar Constitution in the town.

Weimar has also made an impression in culinary terms. It is said that Napoleon Bonaparte's troops took away with them the recipe for Weimar onion tart, which was then transformed into the now famous Quiche Lorraine.

Left: "No other forest on this Earth is as beautiful as the Thuringian Forest. It lies there like a separate world, raised up high under the sky, oppressively gloomy or cheery in a mantle of white snow."

Martin Andersen Nexö

Dumplings with ...

Thüringer Topfbraten
Thuringian pig meat stew
(Illustrated)

2 pig kidneys
½ pig head
1 pig tongue
1 pig heart
Salt
2 large onions, each peeled and spiked with 1 bay leaf and 3 cloves
Bunch of fresh parsley, roughly chopped
5 peppercorns
Generous ⅓ cup/100 ml wine vinegar
3½ oz/100 g honey cake or rich fruit cake
1 tbsp plum purée
1 tsp cornstarch
Pinch of sugar
White pepper
Slices of lemon to garnish

Wash the kidneys, cut them in half horizontally, and remove the ureters. Soak the kidneys for 15 minutes. Wash the pig head, tongue, and heart. Bring 12 cups/3 liters of water to a boil with 1 teaspoon of salt, the onions, parsley, peppercorns, and vinegar. Place the pig head in the liquid and boil it for 1 hour. Then add the remaining pig meat and simmer on a low heat for another hour. Take the meat out of the stock and strain, reserving the stock. Bring 2 cups/½ liter of reserved stock to a boil, then add the crumbled honey cake or rich fruit cake, and stir in the plum purée. Simmer the sauce for 10 minutes. In the meantime, skin the tongue, and take the lean meat off the pig head. Cut the meat, tongue, heart, and kidneys into strips. Blend the cornstarch with a splash of water, and stir into the stock. Add the strips of meat, season to taste with salt, sugar, and pepper, and allow the flavors to develop for a few minutes. Before serving, garnish with the lemon slices. Serve with Thuringian dumplings.

Thuringian pig meat stew

Thüringer Rotkohlwickel
Thuringian red cabbage parcels

1 red cabbage
Salt
4 tbsp wine vinegar
2 cloves
1½ tbsp sugar
2 tbsp dry breadcrumbs
2 tbsp butter
3 oz/80 g slab of bacon, diced
2 onions, roughly diced
2 oz/50 g mushrooms, sliced
12 oz/350 g lean ground beef
Grated rind of 1 lemon
1 egg
White pepper
2 tbsp clarified butter
1 cup/250 ml red wine
Scant 1½ cups/350 ml meat stock
1 tbsp crème fraîche
1 tsp flour

Wash the red cabbage and remove the stalk. Bring
6 cups/1½ liters of water to a boil with 1 teaspoon of salt,
3 tablespoons of vinegar, the cloves, and 1 tablespoon of
sugar. Put the red cabbage in the pan and simmer for
15 minutes. Lift the red cabbage out of the liquid, drain,
and take off 8 large leaves. Melt the butter in a skillet, and
sauté the bacon until crisp. Add the onions and
mushrooms to the skillet, and sweat for 5 minutes. Take
the skillet off the heat, and leave to cool. Knead together
the ground beef, lemon rind, breadcrumbs, bacon
mixture, and egg. Season to taste with salt and pepper.
Divide the meat mixture between the cabbage leaves.
Wrap the cabbage leaves around the mixture and tie
them up with kitchen string. Melt the clarified butter in a
roasting pan, and seal the cabbage parcels all over.
Deglaze the pan with the red wine and stock, then add
the remaining vinegar and sugar. Cover and braise in a
preheated oven at 425 °F/220 °C for ¾ hour. Blend
together the crème fraîche and flour. When the cabbage
parcels are cooked, remove them from the pan, and use
the crème fraîche mixture to thicken the juices.
Serve with bread dumplings.

Thuringian dumplings

Mutton stock and gherkin liquor

"The value which he (Goethe) placed on good food
and drink, and the upset and hurt which he suffered
if he felt he had been neglected in that regard, are
part of this humorous picture of bourgeois life, as is
the fact that Zeltner regularly provided him with his
particularly cherished dish of glazed turnips with
bacon, which doubtless stood his friendship with
Goethe in good stead. There is extensive testimony
to the fact that meals at the table of his Excellency
J.W. von Goethe were exceptionally delicious, and I
am unfailingly reminded of a little story which,
curiously enough, brought home to me the nature of
the man much more vividly than many accounts of
more significant matters. The Icelandic explorer and
man of letters Martin Friedrich Arendt was staying in
Weimar, a man whose somewhat strange
appearance and rather unsophisticated habits
reflected his bohemian lifestyle. He was invited to
lunch at Goethe's house, where he entertained his
host and a group of his close friends with travellers'
tales and accounts of research into ancient books,
enjoying a delightful meal as he did so. There was
braised mutton with cucumber salad, and after
eating several servings Arendt could not bring
himself to leave the mutton stock which had mixed
with the cucumber juices. He took hold of his plate
with both hands and raised it to his mouth, but at
the last moment he froze and glanced towards his
host for permission. At this the great man, with his
abundance of good manners, showed total
sympathy for the enthusiasm of his guest; with the
greatest bonhomie and sincerity, he invited him not
to be at all embarrassed, and while his guest was
slurping at his plate Goethe sustained the
conversation, lest a sudden silence should perhaps
disturb Arendt's enjoyment as he ate. He spoke,
expounding with the greatest enthusiasm upon the
wonderful taste of such a mixture of stock and
cucumber juices, and his oration provided the bon
vivant with the opportunity to satisfy his desire. Try to
imagine Goethe speaking, and looking as he does in
the painting by George Dawe executed in 1819, a
picture which I have always felt to be particularly true
to life, with eyes full of the fire of youth mixed with a
depth of life experience, a knowing benevolence for
all things human. Imagined like this, the happy
incident is brought fully to life and you can share in
its emotions."

(From: Thomas Mann, Essays, 1932)

Dumplings – unthinkable without sauce

Frau Holle was obviously not just an expert bed maker, she was also expert at creating national dishes. At any rate, she is the person the Thuringians have to thank for their instructions on how to make delicious dumplings from potatoes. Frau Holle showed them how to grate, and squeeze, and shape – placing considerable physical demands on a frail, old woman – and then gave them the recipe with the words "Hier hast du es. Hüt' es!" ("Here you are. Keep it safe!"). Consequently, in south Thuringia, the raw dumplings are called *Hüts* or *Hütes*. In west Thuringia, Frau Holle gave the same cookery lesson, then handed over her recipe with the sound advice to "Heb' es auf" ("Tuck it away safely"). It is therefore etymologically quite clear why the dumplings are called *Hebes* there …

Whether you call them *Hütes*, *Hebes*, or Thüringer Klösse – to the locals they are the best invention of regional cuisine. In the center of Germany they say that a Sunday without dumplings is no Sunday at all. A juicy, tasty roast becomes a mere accompaniment to these little round delicacies, but it still has its uses, because it provides the gravy that doubles the pleasure of eating dumplings.

There is no such thing as a "basic" dumpling recipe in Thuringia. Many different instructions for preparing dumplings circulate in the Free State, passed down from mother to daughter through the generations. The recipes vary from region to region, and family to family, just as much as the names for them do.

Dumplings are primarily made from raw and/or boiled potatoes, but also include white bread, semolina, or flour. Floury potatoes are best. You should not use a food processor to make them – connoisseurs swear that "hand grated" is best – so making the dough is hard work and, in many families, a Sunday chore for the man of the house. Generally speaking, the dumplings are cooked in gently simmering, salted water. Under no circumstances should they be boiled, otherwise they collapse.

Some dumplings are traditionally baked in a cake pan or a skillet, hence the name *Pfannenklösse*, (pan dumplings). These include, for example, *Rohe Detscher*, which can be sweet or savory, and the *Aschkloss*, where potato dumpling mixture is covered with slices of bread. *Flockzammet* consists of blobs of potato dumpling mixture sautéed on a layer of diced bacon.

Thüringer Klösse
Thuringian dumplings

3½ lbs/1.5 kg large, floury potatoes
Vinegar
Salt
1 dry bread roll
1 tbsp clarified butter

Wash and peel the potatoes. Grate ⅔ of the potatoes into a large bowl with some lukewarm water and a splash of vinegar. Change the vinegar water twice. Transfer the grated potato to a dish towel, wrap it around the mixture, twist up the ends, and thoroughly squeeze the liquid out of the mixture into a bowl. Leave the mixture in the dish towel until required. Remove the crust from the bread roll. Cut the roll into cubes and sauté in the clarified butter until golden brown. Boil the remaining potatoes in salted water until tender. Drain them, reserving some of the liquid, then mash them with the liquid until a runny purée forms. Bring the purée to a boil. Put the grated raw potato in a bowl with a pinch of salt, and the starch from the grated potatoes, which should have settled out on the bottom of the bowl of liquid. Knead these ingredients together, then using a hand-held electric mixer, gradually beat in the boiling potato mixture. Continue beating the mixture until it comes away from the sides of the bowl. Wet your hands, and shape the potato dough into even-sized dumplings. Press a sautéed bread cube into the center of each dumpling. Place the dumplings in simmering, salted water and cook on a low heat for about 20 minutes, or until cooked.

Raw and boiled potatoes, and sautéed croutons – these are the ingredients for Thuringian dumplings.

The raw potatoes have to be grated by hand – it's a lot of work, but you can taste the difference.

A job for the strong – the grated raw potato has to be squeezed out hard.

The grated raw potato is combined with the mashed, boiled potato to make a dough.

The golden-brown croutons are pushed into the center of each Thuringian dumpling.

The dumplings have to steam in simmering water. They are cooked when they rise to the surface.

Diebichen is the name given to dumplings made from flour, milk, eggs, salt, and sugar. They are shaped using two spoons. Pitted prunes, or raisins, can also be kneaded into the dough, and the dumplings may be cooked in milk rather than simmering water.

Fauleweiberklösse (Lazy wives' dumplings) come in various forms: they can be made of equal parts of raw, grated potato and boiled potato, or boiled potato mixed with potato starch and semolina.

Gemengte Klösse (Stärkemehlklösse, Gemengte Hüts) (Mixed dumplings) are made from potatoes boiled in their skins, peeled, and mashed, to which semolina, flour, and potato starch are added. The mixture is combined with hot milk and eggs.

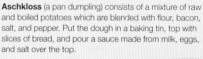

Halbseidene Klösse consist of boiling moist potato purée, combined with potato starch, salt, and nutmeg. They may also be made with potatoes cooked a day in advance, which are mashed with flour, eggs, and potato starch.

Hefeklösse (Mahlhüts) (Yeast dumplings) are shaped from yeast dough and steamed for about 20 minutes over boiling water. A dishcloth is spread across the saucepan and the dumplings are placed on top. The cloth should not touch the water.

Seidene Watteklösse are prepared from a mixture of bread cubes sautéed in butter, and mashed, boiled potatoes. Kneaded together with eggs, potato starch, and nutmeg.

Aschkloss (a pan dumpling) consists of a mixture of raw and boiled potatoes which are blended with flour, bacon, salt, and pepper. Put the dough in a baking tin, top with slices of bread, and pour a sauce made from milk, eggs, and salt over the top.

Serviettenkloss (Cloth dumpling) is made from cubes of bread beaten together with milk. The mixture is wrapped loosely in a dishcloth and suspended in boiling, salted water for about 40 minutes. The dumpling is traditionally sliced using a piece of strong thread.

Thüringer Klösse (also known as Kindsköpfe, Rohe Klösse, Hütes, Hüts, Ruahne Hütes, or Hebes) consist of two parts raw, grated potato with the starch squeezed out, and one part mashed, creamed potatoes.

Braids of gold

Thuringia's biggest folk festival would move you to tears, yet despite this, or indeed because of it, some 300,000 visitors flock to Weimar's onion market, which is held on the second weekend in October. From afar they can smell the aroma of onion soup and freshly baked onion bread. They sample onion tart and meat stews rich in onions, and await with bated breath the crowning of the Onion Fair Queen, or enjoy a leisurely stroll around the 500 stalls that are set up between the National Theater and Frauenplan.

Many families are on the lookout for the most attractive braid of onions as a decoration for their home. The choice is vast: 40,000 hand–tied bulbs are offered for sale, mostly produced by about 130 families from the little town of Heldrungen. Their trade is traditional: on October 4, 1653, their forebears carted onions and other vegetables to the "Cattle and Produce market" in Weimar, 30 miles (50 kilometers) away, for the first time.

The onion braids were subsequently invented by shrewd farmers, who wanted to bring as many bulbs as possible to market. The piquant vegetables are cleaned, graded for size, and twisted by hand around a hank of straw, to tempt people to buy in large quantities, because each braid contains on average 60 onions of the "Yellow Stuttgart Giant" variety, or the "Brunswick Dark Blood Red" variety.

What is different about the Thuringian braid is that the smallest onions are at the top, and the biggest at the bottom. The longest onion braid that Weimar had ever seen measured 17 feet (5.14 meters) and hung from the town hall tower in 1995. It was made by gardener Gert Müller, naturally a citizen of Heldrungen.

Before the re-unification of Germany, the Weimar onion market officially became a Socialist harvest festival. Behind the scenes, however, it is amazing how little things changed. The many small onion-growers in Heldrungen were exempt from the collectivization which took place in the late 1950s, for the simple reason that on average they each owned less than half an acre (2000 square meters) of land. If they owned more than four acres (1.6 hectares), they would have had to join the collective. In this way they benefited from the fact that the government wanted to give those who only had a little land, such as industrial workers and their families with smallholdings, an opportunity to earn some extra money. They also received subsidies: for onions which they contributed to the state-run Fruit, Vegetables, and Potatoes Board (the O.G.S.), the small-scale gardeners were paid the retail price.

Everything has its place: in the case of Thuringian onion braids, the smallest are at the top and the biggest at the bottom.

"Yellow Stuttgart Giants" and "Brunswick Dark Blood Red" onions in braids and in bags.

Onion know-how

Of all the varieties of onion, the yellow domestic or culinary onion is most important. Culinary onions keep well and are particularly piquant. They are suitable for hearty dishes, such as onion soup.

Scallions, the young bulbs from the yellow onion, taste best raw or braised. The green parts are used in salads or as a garnish.

The yellow or white Spanish onion has a less powerful flavor than the culinary onion, and is much larger. Spanish onions are used for onion tart; they are also popular raw, on an open fish sandwich, for example, or in a mixed salad.

Red onions may be hot or sweet, depending on the variety. They are popular for use in salads.

Hazelnut-sized pearl onions, also called silverskin onions, are usually pickled in vinegar.

Little egg-shaped shallots, which are also members of the onion family, along with garlic, leek, and chives, are used as both a vegetable and a seasoning. They are mild and especially suitable for sauces and fish dishes.

Onions are an extremely healthy food, and are regarded as a vegetable antibiotic. In addition to protein, vitamins B, C, E and provitamin A, they also contain the minerals calcium, potassium, phosphorus, and zinc, as well as trace elements such as selenium, which is known to protect against cancer. The essential oils in onions also have a cleansing effect on the blood; they prevent heart attacks and help to relieve coughs and sore throats. The same oils, however, are also responsible for the tears which flow when you slice an onion. It may help if you peel the onion, then place it in cold water for a few minutes before slicing it.

When buying onions, you should make sure that they are firm, and feel dry. They should not have any green shoots.

Onions should be stored in a cool, dry place, preferably in a basket or net, but never in a plastic bag. Unlike culinary onions, Spanish onions should be consumed within eight days.

Green Thuringia

The traditional vegetable-growing area in Thuringia lies around Erfurt. Cauliflower in particular (about 740 acres/300 hectares), kohlrabi (37 acres/15 hectares), broccoli (37 acres/15 hectares), and cabbage (red, white, and savoy, a total of 25 acres/10 hectares) grow around the regional capital. But vegetables are also cultivated in other parts of the state. One of the specialties of the Mühlhausen region is pickled gherkins, which are preserved according to traditional recipes. Good quality onions are also grown in the Thuringian Basin, helped by low summer rainfall. Domestic asparagus, with its powerful flavor, is also prized. It mainly grows around Hersleben, Weissensee, on the edge of the Fahner Höhen and near Kindelbrück; the latter two areas also play an important role in fruit growing. However, although the mostly heavy soil does not provide optimum conditions for growing asparagus (currently around 198 acres/80 hectares), the area being cultivated is to be extended as a result of increasing demand. Cultivated mushrooms from the mountain caves at Nordhausen are also increasing in popularity.

Cultivation of vegetables under glass centers around Laasdorf, near Jena. Cucumbers, tomatoes, lettuce, and many other vegetables flourish on about 12 acres (five hectares) of land there. After Bavaria, Thuringia is the second most important area for the cultivation of medicinal and herbal plants. At one time herb growers from all over Germany came to the "peppermint town" of Kölleda in order to study cultivation on site. Trains from Kölleda were recognized by the garlands of peppermint which decorated them.

If the "Heiligenstadt Carrot Kings" are mentioned, though, this has nothing to do with vegetable growing. Legend has it that the people of Heiligenstadt got their nickname of "carrot kings" because they once barred the town gate with a carrot, when no wooden bolt could be found, to fend off enemy hordes. They didn't reckon on the appetite of a large billy-goat, however, who simply ate the carrot…

Zwiebelsuppe
Onion soup

Generous 1 lb/500 g onions
3½ tbsp/50 g butter
1 apple
1 tbsp flour
4 cups hot meat stock
½ cup/125 ml lager
Salt and white pepper
½ tsp dried rubbed marjoram
Bunch of fresh chives, snipped
5 tbsp/75 g grated Emmenthal cheese or 2 tbsp croutons

Peel, halve, and slice the onions. Melt the butter in a saucepan and sauté the onions in it until translucent. Peel, quarter, and core the apple. Slice it thinly. Stir the apple into the sautéed onion, allow to sweat for a few minutes, then sprinkle over flour. Add the stock and beer, season to taste with salt, pepper, and marjoram, and simmer over a medium heat for about 20 minutes. Just before serving, sprinkle the soup with snipped chives and grated Emmenthal, or croutons.

Gebackener Blumenkohl
Deep–fried cauliflower

1 cauliflower
Salt
3 eggs
White pepper
¼ tsp grated nutmeg
4 tbsp flour
½ cup white breadcrumbs
Oil for deep frying

Rinse the cauliflower, trim, then divide into florets. Cook the florets in boiling, salted water for about 10 minutes, until just tender. Strain the florets, refresh in cold water, and drain well. Beat the eggs with the salt, pepper, and nutmeg. Toss the cauliflower florets first in flour, then dip them in the beaten egg, and finally toss them in the breadcrumbs. Fry batches of cauliflower in the hot oil, and drain on kitchen paper before serving.

Schnippelsuppe
Vegetable soup

1 leek
2 carrots
Generous 1 lb/500 g potatoes
1 tbsp butter
1 onion, peeled and finely diced
Scant 4½ cups/1 liter meat stock
Bunch of fresh marjoram, chopped
Salt and pepper
4½ oz/125 g bacon

Wash and trim the leek and carrots. Peel the potatoes. Slice the leek, carrots, and potatoes thinly. Melt the butter in a saucepan, and sauté the diced onion until translucent. Add the sliced vegetables, sauté briefly, and add the stock. Season to taste with marjoram, salt, and pepper, and simmer for 15–20 minutes. Cut the bacon into small dice, and sauté in a dry skillet. Just before serving the soup, stir the lardons and bacon juices into the soup. The soup may be thickened with beaten egg if desired.

Game and wild produce

In Germany, Thuringia is regarded as a traditional hunting area. Even today some 1.3 million acres (535,000 hectares), or one third of the total area of the State is covered in forest. But up to a few years ago, the average man in the street could only dream of game. In the days when Thuringia was part of the former East Germany, the State foresters delivered the slaughtered animals to a meat cooperative. Game was a delicacy which was only rarely available in stores. Even the foresters were only given a piece of game by officials on special occasions. The meat was reserved for the privileged few, supplied to hotels, or exported.

The Thuringian Forest and neighboring Schiefer mountains provide particularly good opportunities for hunting red deer, whilst it is primarily the tracks of fallow deer and moufflon (wild mountain sheep) which cross the Thüringer Holzland. The Schleizer Oberland features stocks of red and roe deer; the southern Harz mountains are known for red deer and moufflon. Roe deer and wild boar occur throughout Thuringia, but especially in the hilly and mountainous region of Rhön, in the deciduous woods of the Hessberge, von Hainich and Hainleite, Ohmgebirge and Kyffhäuser, Hoher Schrecke and Leinawald. Hare, rabbit, pheasant, duck, and other wild animals are fair game, on the other hand capercaillie, black cock, and pheasant are protected. Wild mushrooms such as chestnut mushrooms, porcini, chanterelle mushrooms or blusher mushrooms are a delicious complement to meat and game dishes. Mushrooms themselves are

a healthy food, although you should not eat too many because of the high level of harmful substances they contain.

Formerly, people gathered mushrooms for their own consumption, for a tasty mushroom bake, for example. This is based on strong-flavored mushrooms which are combined with ground meat, or bacon, onions, and other ingredients, and baked. Berries, on the other hand, were formerly gathered for sale. Up to the 1960s, people from the forest villages still earned a little extra money by gathering and selling berries.

Blueberries, cranberries, raspberries, and blackberries have in the meantime also tempted numerous city-dwellers to take a walk in the woods. Blueberry compote tastes superb with dumplings, and a blueberry cake is the highlight of any Thuringian coffee morning.

Gulasch mit Pilzen
Goulash with mushrooms

1¾ lbs/750 g stewing beef, cut into strips
2 tbsp clarified butter
14 oz/400 g onions, roughly diced
2 tbsp tomato paste
1 cup/250 ml lager
1 tbsp medium hot chili powder
Salt and pepper
1 tsp dried thyme
7 oz/200 g mixed wild mushrooms
Bunch of fresh parsley, chopped
Scant ½ cup/100 g crème fraîche
Pinch of sugar

Seal the stewing beef quickly in the hot clarified butter. Add the diced onions and sauté until translucent. Stir in the tomato paste, and cook briefly, then deglaze with the beer, and season with chili powder, salt, pepper, and thyme. Cover and braise on a medium heat for 1 hour, or until the meat is tender. Wipe and slice the mushrooms. When the meat is cooked, stir in the mushrooms, and parsley, and simmer for another 10 minutes. Fold in the

crème fraîche, and season to taste with salt, pepper, and sugar. Serve with boiled potatoes.

Rehgulasch mit Dörrobst
Venison goulash with dried fruit

9 oz/250 g dried fruit
7 oz/200 g slab of bacon
2 lb 3 oz/1 kg venison, cut into strips
4 onions, finely diced
2 bunches of soup vegetables (4 carrots, 2 leeks, 4 celery stalks, parsley)
2 cups/500 ml stock
1 cup/250 ml red wine
½ cup/125 ml wine vinegar
1 tsp dried thyme
1 bay leaf
1 tsp coriander seeds
1 tsp juniper berries
1 tsp peppercorns
2 cloves
Salt
2 tbsp redcurrant jelly
1 tbsp tomato paste
Sugar
½ cup/125 g cream
1 tsp cornstarch

Soak the dried fruit in a little cold water. Cut the bacon into thin strips and dry-fry in a large skillet. Add the strips of venison to the skillet, and fry to seal. Add the onions, carrots, leeks, celery, and parsley. Sauté them with the meat. Deglaze the skillet with the stock, red wine, and wine vinegar, then add the herbs, spices, and ½ teaspoon of salt. Cover and simmer for 1½ hours. After an hour, add the dried fruit to the skillet. After 1½ hours, stir the redcurrant jelly and tomato paste into the sauce, and season to taste with salt, pepper, and sugar. Whisk together the cream and cornstarch, stir the mixture into the sauce, and bring to a boil again. Serve spätzle, boiled potatoes, or dumplings with the venison goulash.

Meat dishes from Thuringia

Kindstaufschüssel
Baptism Stew
(Illustrated right)

2 lb 3 oz/1 kg breast of veal, boned
Salt and pepper
2 tbsp clarified butter
2 bunches of soup vegetables, roughly diced (4 carrots, 4 celery stalks, 2 leeks, parsley)
1 cup/250 ml dry white wine
1 large onion, spiked with 1 bay leaf and 2 cloves
1 tsp allspice
⅓ cup/75 g raisins
2 tbsp flour
2 tbsp butter
2 tbsp capers
Juice and grated rind of 1 lemon
1 tsp chopped almonds
Scant ½ cup/100 g cream
Sugar
1 tbsp chopped parsley

Rinse the breast of veal, pat it dry, and rub it with salt and pepper. Seal it all over in the hot clarified butter. Add the carrots, celery, leeks, and parsley, and sauté with the veal for a few minutes. Deglaze the pan with the white wine, add 7 cups/1½ liters of water, and add the spiked onion and allspice. Simmer the breast of veal for 1 hour, or until tender. Lift the veal out of the stock. Strain the stock and reserve it. Allow the meat to cool a little, remove the fat, and cut the veal into bite-size dice. Soak the raisins in a splash of hot water. Sauté the flour in the butter until it foams and turns golden, add 2 cups/500 ml stock, stirring all the time, and simmer for 10 minutes. Then stir the capers, drained raisins, lemon juice and rind, and chopped almonds into the sauce, and add the diced veal. Simmer the meat and sauce for 10 minutes. Stir in the cream and season the sauce to taste with salt, pepper, and sugar. Sprinkle over chopped parsley before serving.

Heldrunger Sauerbraten
Heldrung Marinated Braised Beef
(Illustrated left)

½ cup/125 ml red wine
½ cup/125 ml red wine vinegar
2 bay leaves
1 lemon, sliced
8 juniper berries
4 allspice berries
1 tsp peppercorns
Soup vegetables, roughly diced (2 carrots, 1 leek, 2 celery stalks, parsley)
2 onions, roughly diced
2 lb 3 oz/1 kg piece of beef (rump or topside)
Salt and pepper
4 oz/100 g slab of bacon
Scant ¼ cup/50 g clarified butter
14 oz/400 g root vegetables (onion, celeriac, carrot, leek), chopped
Scant ¼ cup/50 g butter, chilled
4 tbsp sour cream

To make the marinade: in a saucepan combine the red wine, vinegar, 2 cups/500 ml water, the bay leaves, lemon slices, juniper berries, allspice, and peppercorns, and bring to a boil. Add the diced soup vegetables and onions to the marinade, then leave it to cool. Rinse the beef, pat it dry, and remove any fat, sinews, etc. Put the beef in a dish, pour over the marinade, then cover and leave to marinate in a cool place for 2–3 days. Before roasting the beef, take it out of the marinade, pat it dry, and rub it with salt and pepper. Dice the bacon and sauté it in the clarified butter. Quickly seal the beef all over in the clarified butter, add the root vegetables, sauté briefly with the beef, then add the marinade. Cover the beef, and braise on a medium heat for 2 hours, or until the meat is tender. Take the beef out of the pan and keep it warm. Pass the gravy through a sieve, return it to a saucepan, and simmer until it has reduced a little. Stir nuts of chilled butter into the gravy, stir in the sour cream, and season to taste with salt and pepper. Cut the beef into slices of even thickness, arrange on a warmed serving dish, and serve the gravy separately. Serve with Thuringian dumplings and red cabbage.

Heldrung Marinated Braised Beef

If you find a mushroom such as this on your search, consider yourself lucky. Porcini are one of the most prized culinary mushrooms.

Schusterpfanne
Herring and liver bake
(Illustrated center)

2 salt herrings
1½ lbs/600 g potatoes
Salt
5 oz/150 g piece of prosciutto, diced
1 tbsp butter
1 large Spanish onion, roughly diced
10 oz/300 g calf liver
Butter for the dish
1 cup/250 g sour cream
1 egg
Pepper
2 tbsp breadcrumbs

Soak the salt herrings in water. Wash the potatoes, put them in a pan with salted water, bring to a boil and simmer for 15 minutes. Drain the potatoes, leave them to cool, peel, and slice them. Sauté the diced ham in the butter, add the onions, and allow them to sweat until translucent. Cut the liver into strips. Skin, fillet and dice the herrings. Butter an ovenproof dish. Cover the bottom with a layer of potato, then a layer of ham and onion, herring, and liver, finishing with a layer of potato. Beat together the sour cream and egg, season with salt and pepper, and pour the mixture over the potato. Sprinkle the breadcrumbs on top and bake in a preheated oven at 350 °F/180 °C for about 30 minutes.

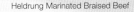
Herring and liver bake

Baptism stew

Sausages with pizzazz

"Fetch a plate," the butcher instructs his assistant, and he runs off diligently. The minute he returns with the desired article, an inflated pig bladder is placed on the plate and cut open, "to let the air in!" Such jokes, and even cruder ones, are popular with Thuringian butchers, because they know at least as much about seasoning their sausages as they do about teasing naïve employees.

From around St Martin's day (November 11), when the animals are brought in from the meadows, butchering begins on Thuringian farms. Steamed, scalded, and cured sausages are all produced, and there's a hearty sausage soup especially for friends and neighbors.

Cured sausages are either spreadable, such as *Mettwurst* (dry-cured pork and beef sausage) and *Teewurst* (smooth pork and beef sausage), or they are hard cured, such as salami and cervelat. The latter category includes *Eichsfeld Feldkieker*. Its name is thought to be derived from the fact that, in the past, it was taken out into the fields, and peeked (kiekte) out of the pannier. *Feldkieker* are made from top quality pork (e.g. fillet), and seasoned with pepper, salt, and garlic. It is important for the meat to be processed immediately after slaughter, and packed whilst still warm into a casing made from a pig intestine, about 2 feet (60 centimeters) long, or a calf bladder. This type of process is typical for Eichsfeld, as is the subsequent natural curing. The butcher uses salt as a preservative, and schnaps and sugar to cure the sausage. When manufactured and stored under optimum conditions, a *Feldkieker* will keep for up to two years. *Feldkieker* are air dried for at least six to eight months, preferably in a mud hut, where the temperature is kept at a constant 60 °F (15 °C). Traditionally the sausage is eaten with bread and cream.

In other parts of Thuringia, most cured sausages are smoked. This applies to Greussen salami, which traditionally is made from lean pork, beef, and fatty bacon. Other versions also contain turkey or venison. The climate in the Greussen Basin is perfect for six-week maturation of the smoked salami, which is known for its slightly peppery flavor.

Scalded sausages, such as the famous *Thüringer Rostbratwurst* (finely chopped pork and veal sausages), are scalded in water heated to 175 °F (80 °C) after the casings have been filled.

Steamed sausages include liver sausage and blood sausage, for example, which use meat which has been pre-cooked. The sausages themselves are then heated up again, or boiled. In Thuringia, *Presskopf*, a large molded pork brawn which has blood added, is also classed as a steamed sausage. The fame of *Thüringer Rotwurst* (blood sausage), also called *Garwurst* in Eichsfeld, has spread beyond the boundaries of Thuringia. It consists of pork, bacon lardons, and blood, is seasoned with pepper, salt, nutmeg, cayenne pepper, and marjoram, and is packed into natural casings.

Opposite: Thuringian butchers are masters of seasoning, and proud of the quality and variety of their produce.

Thüringer Rotwurst includes ground, boiled pork rind.

Cooked, diced meat is also used. The blend of seasonings is the butcher's own secret recipe.

The ground pork rinds are added to the sausage mixture and folded in using a mixing machine.

Before adding to the sausage mixture, the blood has to be stirred with a wooden spoon to prevent it coagulating.

The butcher tastes the finished sausage mixture before it is packed into hog casings. The seasoning is adjusted if necessary.

The hog casings are threaded onto string and tied off at one end. The other end remains open.

The butcher stuffs the sausage mixture into the casings through this opening. He uses a special syringe.

Two assistants tie up the end of the sausage and shape it into a link, so it can be hung up.

When the sausages have cooked for two to three hours they are taken out of the vat.

They are immersed in a vat of cold water to cool, where they stay for about half an hour.

Ready for the smoke room. The Thüringer Rotwurst hangs there in the cold smoke for about six to eight hours.

When the sausages cool the gelatinous mass sets and the blood protein hardens, so the sausages can be sliced.

Thüringer Mettwurst is a spreadable cured sausage.

Thüringer Leberwurst is a steamed sausage.

Also a steamed sausage: the popular Thüringer Rotwurst.

A different kind of Rotwurst: in a bladder instead of a casing.

Dishes with sausages

Blutwurst mit sauren Linsen
Fried blood sausage with spicy-sour stewed lentils

Brotsuppe mit Leberwurst
Vegetable soup with black bread and diced liver sausage

Eichsfelder Weckewurst mit Pellkartoffeln und grünem Salat
Potatoes cooked in their skins, a green salad, and a coarse sausage made of ground pork, onions, white bread, pork rinds, fat, and seasonings

Salami auf Sondershäuser Schärpplätzle
Sour dough rolls filled with salami

Stolzer Heinrich
Thüringer pork sausages in a sour sauce with capers and lemon

Topfwurst-Sauerkraut
Various types of sausage heated through with braised sauerkraut

Mühlhäuser Schlachtfestsuppe
A typical meal on the day animals are butchered: a spicy sausage soup with vegetables, liver sausage, and blood sausage

Thüringer Leberwurst, sauer
Coarse spreading sausage dressed with a spicy liquor made from vinegar and oil, onions, chives, mustard, pepper, and salt

Erfurter Kachelwurst
A "sausage dish" which doesn't contain any sausage. Fresh goose or pig's blood is mixed with milk, breadcrumbs, finely chopped onions, and spices, and baked in the oven until a crust forms on top.

Thuringian pork sausages must be hot and hearty. Eating them with a knife and fork is taboo. Traditionally they are placed between two halves of a bread bun.

A sausage for every occasion

Thuringian sausage

If "Thuringian incense" is wafting across back gardens, then it must be Sunday – or just a warm summer's evening when friends and neighbors are having a get-together, because this "incense" has nothing to do with religious ritual; there is no need for priests and ministers. All that is required is an expert who knows how to conjure glowing coals from charcoal and firelighters, who uses beer and water beneficently, so that the smoke rises and the delicious aroma of Thuringian sausages cooking outdoors on a barbecue unfolds.

Every barbecue expert has his own tricks. Some grease the grill rack with bacon rind so the sausages won't stick. Others turn the sausages often and swear by a beer baste, while some baste with water. Some like their sausages dark brown and crisp, others take them off the fire as soon as they are delicately browned and striped.

There is little discussion, however, as to the best way to consume them. Connoisseurs eat their sausages without a knife and fork. They prefer to clamp it between the halves of a sesame seed bun which has not quite been cut in half. Potato salad (no bacon!), red cabbage, and sauerkraut are the preferred accompaniments to sausage. Many sausage fans scorn mustard, unless it is Born mustard from Erfurt, which has a strong,

exceedingly good mustard seed flavor. Although it is imitated throughout the world, Thuringians all agree that genuine Thuringian barbecue sausage only comes from their homeland. History bears them out: it has been proved that the tradition of this rustic meal dates as far back as 1613.

Thuringia's butchers do not all follow the same recipe, though. Lean pork from the belly and shoulder are used. Veal and beef are usually added too. These traditional ingredients are finely chopped, seasoned with herbs and spices, then bulking agents are added, and the mixture formed into a farce. This is packed into hog's or sheep's casings, and then sold either raw, or scalded. Raw sausages must be eaten on the same day, scalded sausages will keep in the refrigerator for up to four days; 14 days if shrink wrapped.

Salt gives the sausage meat its grayish color. The other ingredients – fresh garlic, caraway, and nutmeg – are carefully guarded family secrets. Some butchers add lemon to the mixture; others use marjoram, unless they live in Eichsfeld. The use of marjoram in "genuine Thuringian sausages" is, in fact, frowned upon there.

Facing page: Thuringian pork sausages taste best when grilled in the open air. The special flavor comes from a beer baste.

Thüringer Rostbratwurst
Thuringian pork sausages
Recipe for 20 sausages

16-20 feet/5-6 meters sheep's casing
2 lb 3 oz/1 kg lean belly pork
2 lb 3 oz/1 kg pork shoulder, derinded
2 eggs
3 tbsp salt
Heaped tsp white pepper
½ tsp ground nutmeg
½ tsp ground coriander
½ tsp ground caraway
2–3 tbsp rubbed dried marjoram
Grated rind of ½ lemon

Rinse out the casings with water, and soak them in lukewarm water for 15–20 minutes. In the meantime rinse the pork, pat it dry, and cut into large chunks. Grind the pork. Put it in a bowl with the eggs and seasonings, and knead them all together until thoroughly combined. Pack the farce into the casings, and twist into 6–8 inch/15–20 cm links.

Stolzer Heinrich

8 Thuringian sausages
2 tbsp butter
2 tbsp flour
1 cup/250 ml lager
1 cup/250 ml meat stock
1 tbsp vinegar
1 bay leaf
Salt
Pepper
1 tsp capers
Juice and grated rind of 1 lemon

Sauté the sausages in the butter until brown. Take the sausages out of the skillet, then sprinkle the flour on the hot butter and cook, stirring all the time, until the flour foams and turns golden. Add the beer and stock, stirring all the time, until the sauce thickens and there are no lumps. Add the vinegar and bay leaf, then simmer the sauce for 10 minutes. Season the sauce with salt, pepper, capers, lemon juice and rind. Place the sausages in the sauce, and simmer for another 5 minutes on a low heat, until the sausages are warmed through.

The charcoal burner and charcoal

Anyone who has ever forgotten to buy charcoal for a barbecue knows it is an essential part of any pleasant social evening around a barbecue. Without it, a barbecue is nothing. What is less obvious, however, is that the schnaps consumed after the sausages and burgers also owes its existence to charcoal, amongst other things. It is used during the filtration process in the form of activated charcoal. And if you have over-indulged, and take a charcoal tablet to calm your stomach, then you have charcoal to thank for the tablet's beneficial effect. To take things even further, charcoal also plays a role in manufacture of the steel for the barbecue itself.

Before charcoal was produced on an industrial scale, being a charcoal burner was a profession which regularly claimed men's lives. Building the man-high charcoal kilns was an art in itself and took weeks. The charcoal burners used split, well-seasoned beech wood, which was stacked in a circle around a wooden pole. This pole was later removed, thus creating a chimney. The beech wood was covered with brushwood, turf, and soil, then ignited.

During burning, temperatures of up to 1832 °F (1000 °C) would develop inside the kiln. Every two days the charcoal burner had to climb up on the kiln to add more wood from the top – an extremely dangerous task, because the charred wood constantly collapsed in on

itself. Even experienced charcoal burners died when the interior of the burning structure collapsed into glowing embers. Furthermore, the kiln had to be watched day and night to prevent a full-scale fire. After three to four weeks the charcoal process was complete. The result would be 1765 to 2825 cubic feet (50 to 80 cubic meters) of charcoal. Today the old earth kilns have been replaced by concrete kilns and steel retorts, enabling larger quantities of charcoal to be produced in two to three days, and the job of charcoal burning is much less terrifying.

Rostbrätel

Rostbrätel is a must at Thuringian folk festivals, as is Thuringian sausage. The basic recipe consists of pork spare ribs brushed with a mixture of salt, pepper, and beer, and grilled over charcoal until crisp. The spare ribs are basted with beer during cooking. The Rostbrätel is ready when it is still quite moist and the edges are slightly blackened from the charcoal. The strong flavors are complemented by hot mustard and fresh wholegrain bread, or potato salad. Rostbrätel can also be prepared in a skillet or it can be seasoned, and then marinated for several hours in oil, beer, mustard, pepper, garlic, and parsley, before being broiled or grilled.

Skat evening

When amiable Skat enthusiasts turn into bitter enemies because they can't agree on the rules, there is only one solution: an appeal to the Altenburg Skat Court, which has been the supreme body ruling on disputes from all over the world since 1927. The honorary judges have inside information, so to speak, because the fiendish game was invented in Altenburg around 1813. Moreover, playing cards have been manufactured in the town for more than 450 years.

Things get serious on Tuesdays and Thursdays in Altenburg's bars, when members of domestic Skat clubs thump the tables in frustration in a suitably decorated room. Food and drink are of no real consequence. The players' preferred snack is sautéed potatoes with brawn. Others enjoy open sandwiches or similar cheap snacks. The most important criterion is that it should be possible to consume the snack in just a few minutes, because during the frantic exchange of cards only the dealer has time to eat.

Skat was the result of playful tedium and anti-Napoleonic sentiment: the people of Altenburg no longer wanted to play Omber and Taroc for political reasons. Firstly they made do with the old German game of *Schafskopf*, a simple version of Skat, but it was too simplistic for them in the long term. Then the experienced card players of the Bromme'sche Abendgesellschaft – including the publisher F.A. Brockhaus – hit upon the idea of enriching *Schafkopf* with the rules and nuances of foreign games. Thus Scat was born. However, the "King of all German card games" had very little in common with the modern game. The most significant change was introduced by Leipzig students, who introduced number bidding instead of suit bidding and chicanery such as *Nullo* and *Grand*. But the guardians of the rules proved to be orthodox: it took decades, from the First German Skat Congress in 1886 in Altenburg, to the 11th Congress in 1927, for the exciting innovations to be recognized.

Since then, Skat has been spread across the world by German migrants. Deviations from the sole valid rule creep in, and so the Skat Court is always kept busy. If you want to prove you're right at the card table, we recommend you take lessons at the Altenburg Skat school.

Background: beer and little snacks – there is no time for anything else; because an evening of Skat depends on bidding, eating and drinking are just incidental.

German playing cards showing the suits and the royal cards of the king, queen, and jack.

The perfect snack for a Skat player. Spades, clubs, hearts, and diamonds – edible French delicacies.

It's just a game

Scrolled plague pillars, warlike knights on horseback, pensive poets and philosophers, mannekins relieving themselves into a fountain basin – these are all well-known sights in the market squares of German cities. But four boys fighting openly over a card trick: you will only find this image in Altenburg. In keeping with card players' jargon, the boys are known as the "Wenzels" (knaves), and their quarrel is taking place in the Skat Fountain. The present fountain is the second: the first, erected in 1897, was melted down by the Nazis in 1942. The people weren't supposed to play cards, they were supposed to fire guns, and for that they needed ammunition. But in 1954 the knaves resumed their quarrel, when the newly-cast fountain was completed and dedicated. The playing card museum suffered a much worse fate. When the Altenburg playing card factory (founded in 1832) was dismantled in 1946, the museum's exhibits were also removed to the Soviet Union. They are thought to be lost without trace. Yet since then it has been possible to assemble the world's greatest exhibition of playing cards. Exhibits include silk cards from the Baroque period, porcelain chips from the 19th century, printing relief plates, card tables, gaming machines, and gaming tables.

Dry or moist?

Nothing happens in Thuringia without cake. It decorates the breakfast table, it is the focal point of a coffee morning, and is served to party-goers as a late night snack. The Thuringians are true masters of the art of "dry" and "moist" traybakes. "Dry" cakes may be classic streusel cake or the cake which always causes a stir, *Prophetenkuchen*, which contains the same quantity of egg yolks and brown schnaps or rum as it does flour. It is usually baked around Easter time.

The moisture in "moist" cakes is supplied by the quark mixture which is spread over the dough, as well as fruit, and crème patissière. Over all this splendor, a glaze of sweetened cream, often enriched with eggs and sugar, is usually poured. Heartier versions, which are often made with bread dough, use onions and/or bacon to create a juicy consistency. These savory cakes are served warm, offset by a cool beer.

Kirmeskuchen is named after Thuringia's most popular folk festival. In many places it is also known as wedding cake. Characteristically it comprises a thin yeast dough base, a thick filling of crème patissière and fruit, and a topping of eggs, sugar, butter, and usually a splash of cream. When Thuringia was part of East Germany, there was Snow White cake and LPG cake. Snow White cake was so called because the dark dough and chocolate frosting represented Snow White's black hair, the red cherries were reminiscent of her lips, and the vanilla custard a reminder of her pale skin. LPG cake was topped with butter cream and butter biscuits, with brandy drizzled over and decorated with chocolate frosting.

In Thuringia it is still customary to prepare traybakes at home and then take them to the bakery. It is rare for anyone to leave the house with less than two trays. Baking usually starts several days before a special event, because it doesn't do the cakes any harm if they are stored for a couple of days – they taste even better then.

Tea with Anna Amalia

In 1775 he just came for a short visit and stayed, to the town's eternal fame. What kept Johann Wolfgang von Goethe in Weimar was not just his friendship with Count Charles Augustus, and his permanent position at Court which the latter offered him, it was also the intellectual atmosphere in the town, the tone of which was quite definitely set by Anna Amalia, the Count's mother. Interested in literature and herself a composer – she wrote the music to Goethe's *Erwin and Elmira* – she understood the importance of gathering the intellectual greats of the day at her "Court of Muses."

Weimar offered opportunities for displaying one's talents; in 1791 the Hoftheater opened; the Court supported artists, not least financially, and provided intellectuals with opportunities for intellectual exchanges and discussions.

The most important of many social circles in the royal capital were Anna Amalia's "round tables." Unlike her other tea and chocolate parties, where Madeira cake, petits choux, meringues, mazarins, mille-feuilles, apricot tarts, Hirsch-Zungen, Berliner Zuckerbogen, and other elegant pastries were served, Anna Amalia made sure her guests ate before the conversation really began. The round table was a showcase for the renowned skill as a pâtissier of the ducal chef, François Le Goullon, who later collated his knowledge in works such as "The elegant tea table" or "The new Apicius." Anna Amalia presided over these meetings in person. The nature of the round table, which was rooted in Court society, was determined by three of the four "Weimar giants": Christoph Martin Wieland, who was summoned to Weimar in 1772 to tutor the princes, Gottfried Herder, and of course Goethe, who dominated this group just as he did countless others. The fourth "giant," Friedrich Schiller, only became a guest after 1802. Visitors from far and near also found a place at the massive table in the reading and dining room at the ducal Wittumspalais, including Heinrich von Kleist, Jean Paul and Madame de Staël. Weimar became the cultural center of Germany, and an inspirational destination for intellectuals from all over Europe.

Readings were given from the latest works by writers and poets, there were discussions on scientific problems, people painted, played music, composed, or even acted in plays.

Goethe's *Iphigenia on Tauris* (1787) was premiered in Weimar, with Goethe himself playing the Orator, as well as all Schiller's dramatic masterpieces up to *The Maid of Orleans*.

Nowadays, the former Ducal Library in Weimar is named after the woman who contributed to all this, Anna Amalia.

There are no limits to the variety of Thuringian traybakes. A layer of quark spread over the dough ensures that "moist" cakes are moist, as well as a coating of cream, which is poured over the topping. The cakes are cut into small, rectangular slices and layered on top of each other in a cake mountain which is the crowning glory of any Thuringian coffee morning.

Thüringer Obstkuchen vom Blech
Thuringian fruit traybake

Yeast dough
½ cup/125 ml milk
⅓ cup/80 g butter
Scant ¼ cup/50 g sugar, Pinch of salt
Grated rind of 1 lemon
1 egg, 3 cups/375 g flour
1 ½ cakes/25 g compressed yeast
Quark mixture
4 cups/500 g quark
½ cup/125 ml milk
1 egg, 3 tbsp flour
Scant ⅓ cup/75 g sugar
½ teaspoon vanilla essence
2 tbsp lemon juice, 1 tbsp rum
Topping
2 lb 3 oz/1 kg fruit, e.g. apples, plums, rhubarb
Custard
2 cups/500 g sour cream, 2 eggs
1 tbsp flour, 2 tbsp sugar

Make a yeast dough according to the basic recipe. Mix the ingredients for the quark mixture and beat until the consistency is smooth and spreadable. Roll out the yeast dough on a shallow square baking pan lined with baking parchment. Draw the dough a little way up the sides of the pan. Spread the quark mixture over the dough. Arrange the prepared fruit on top of the quark. Whisk together the sour cream, eggs, flour, and sugar and pour the custard over the fruit. Bake in a preheated oven at 350 °F/200 °C for 30 minutes.

Tens of thousands of Martinshörnchen sweeten the birthday of religious reformer Martin Luther.

Martinshörnchen

St Martin's day is usually celebrated on November 11, in memory of the Bishop of Tours, canonized by the Pope. As a young soldier St Martin gave away half of his cloak to a beggar. But in Erfurt, Eisenach, Wittenberg and other "Lutheran towns," the celebrations start a day early when the Protestants celebrate "their" reformer Martin Luther, who was born on November 10, 1483.

Bakers in Erfurt are rushed off their feet, as they stock up on trays of hundreds of *Martinshörnchen*. The traditional pastry is served at least twice a day, usually at breakfast and dinner. Some bakeries even open as early as 5 a.m., so that people on the way to work can stock up on the crescent-shaped pastries. Rüger's bakery and cake shop on Gutenbergplatz alone makes 25,000 *Martinshörnchen*. The original recipe consists of a yeast dough or flaky pastry filled with jam or fruit preserve.

Modern variations on the traditional pastry include marzipan, plum preserve, or sultanas. Sometimes puff pastry is used instead of yeast dough. In the view of local experts, there is now very little connection between these and the original recipe. *Martinshörnchen* are not the only thing about this day which is special. During the day the citizens of Erfurt and their guests visit the great Martinsmarkt in the Cathedral Square, and in the evening people gather there for a church service, with well over 100,000 lanterns glowing in the darkness. Then, carrying their lanterns, the children walk through the streets to "*heischen*" or "*schnorren*" (beg), as it is called in Erfurt. They go singing from house to house and are rewarded with candy and other little gifts. This is an evening when lots of families gather together, and many a Martin's day goose is consumed later.

This all takes place on the birthday of Martin Luther, who received his doctorate from Erfurt University, and enrolled in the Faculty of Law there in 1505. In the same year he joined the Augustinian hermitage in Erfurt. It is also claimed that it was in this town that Luther looked at the Bible for the first time ever.

Background: St Martin's day in Erfurt. On the evening of November 10, the Cathedral square is transformed into a sea of light. Children feverishly await the moment when they can run off singing, and demand as many treats as possible.

ULLA RETTIG
Saxony

Foreign observers describe the Saxons as the "caffeine of the German nation," and not just for their proverbial preference for that stimulating drink. When the former East Germany was still in existence, it was obvious that "If Saxony has the sniffles, the whole Republic gets the flu." This was borne out in October and November 1989, when the peaceful Monday demonstrations in Leipzig started the movement towards reunification of Germany.

Leipzig, the old city of fairs, universities, and publishing is the economic heart of Saxony, but its showpiece is Dresden. Gradually the skyline of the regional capital, which was totally destroyed by bombing toward the end of World War II, is once more starting to resemble the Baroque "Florence on the Elbe": the Zwinger and Semperoper have been rebuilt; the Frauenkirche too has been reconstructed. At the start of the 18th century, August the Strong turned the city into a European artistic and cultural center. Johann Sebastian Bach worked as choirmaster in Leipzig, and in 1743 the Gewandhaus orchestra was founded.

The geographical backbone of Saxony is formed by the mountainous areas in the south. They stretch from the Vogtland, across the Erz mountains and Saxon Switzerland, almost to Lower Silesia. These stone walls did not, however, prevent Saxony from always being on the losing side during warlike conflicts, and having to cede almost half its territory to Prussia following the Battle of the Nations at Leipzig in 1813.

The highest point in the state, at 3982 feet (1214 meters), is the Fichtelberg, in the Christmas card scenery of the Erz Mountains. There is also "Easter scenery," the Oberlausitz, in eastern Saxony. Customs and cuisine there are marked by Sorbian traditions, whilst in the Zittau mountains of Lower Silesia the influence of Bohemian cuisine is unmistakable.

As far as food is concerned, Saxony is synonymous with Dresden *Stollen*, *Leipziger Allerlei* (Leipzig mixed vegetables), coffee, and a plethora of sweet cakes and pastries. To prevent these sweetmeats becoming too cloying, there is the "Leipzig Peppermill," a lively cabaret which, in the good old Leipzig tradition, adds its own spice to the political scene.

Left: the Saxon Switzerland is one of the main attractions in the Federal state. There is a wonderful panorama across the region from the Bastei, the 656-feet (200-meter) high rock which drops steeply away to the River Elbe below.

Coffee

"Mother likes a coffee brew, Grandma drank the same thing too, who now ticks off their sweet daughters? Saxons drink it as they ought to." ...so it is said in Johann Sebastian Bach's famous *Coffee Cantata*, which was written in the 1730s, when Bach's "Collegium Musicum" gave weekly concerts in Zimmermann's coffee house.

The term "coffee sisterhood" which came into being in Bach's day, and the comic literature of the 18th century which makes fun of the coffee morning and women's passion for the beverage, give the impression that only middle-class women were addicted to the black brew. Quite the contrary – coffee, which was introduced to Europe in the 17th century, was soon extremely popular with all classes of society and both sexes. It was welcomed by the ruling classes as the great "reviver," and replaced beer as the people's drink. It was only in the mid-18th century that this positive attitude to coffee on the part of the powers-that-be changed. Coffee was declared "un-Germanic" and a return to beer was promoted.

Prohibition of coffee was even promulgated, as in Prussia. The reason was economic: Germany, which did not possess any colonies, had to buy the beans from the French or Dutch, and consequently a vast amount of money flowed out of the country. During this period of anti-coffee propaganda, substitute coffees, made from cereals or chicory, were popular.

It is therefore doubtful whether the Saxon term "Blümchenkaffee" (flower coffee) refers to these substitutes, as some sources maintain, because the word was already known in 1729. In the *Dressdnischen Mägde-Schlendrian* (Dresden Maid's Inefficiency) published at that time, it says, "'Flower coffee' is the name given by the people of Leipzig to coffee which is so weak, you can see the flowers on the bottom of the coffee cup through it."

It is a source of constant irritation to the "coffee Saxons" that they are associated with "flower coffee." They may like their beverage sweet, but not, as they say "labberig," in other words weak. Fifteen coffee beans for 16 cups, the supposed formula for "flower coffee," is nothing to do with them, and their scornful term for a brew made from coffee grounds which have been used several

times is "Plempe" or "Lorke" – dishwater. On the other hand, they are proud that it was a Saxon woman who invented the now-famous coffee filter. In 1908 Melitta Bentz, an inhabitant of Dresden, punched holes in the base of a saucepan, and lined it with a sheet of blotting paper. Then she put ground coffee in it, and poured over boiling water. This new invention became a bestseller at the popular Leipzig Fair.

The city of Leipzig plays an important role anyway in Germany's story of coffee. Coffee was sold publicly here as early as 1694, with this being the customary way to enjoy the new drink in the early days – in public, in a coffee house. It was only later that coffee made its way to people's sitting rooms, where it would be served in the morning or afternoon in a tranquil and private surrounding. In Leipzig, the ancient fair and publishing city, and a center of German enlightenment, a quite distinct coffee house culture developed rapidly which, with very few exceptions, was unrivaled throughout Germany. Like their rather more famous predecessors in London or Paris, Leipzig's coffee houses provided both commercial and cultural centers of communication for the up-and-coming, rational bourgeoisie.

Iced coffee: cold coffee with vanilla ice cream, and whipped cream.

Black Forest coffee: cold coffee with one or two shots of kirsch, and crushed ice.

Spiced coffee: with cloves, cardamom, cinnamon, and whipped cream.

Dithmarsch coffee: coffee with egg yolk, rum, and cream.

The latest newspapers were read, news and gossip exchanged, deals done and last, but not least, politics discussed here. In the 18th century the Association of the German Book Trade was established in "Richters Caffee Haus," and as early as 1698 the newspaper which claims to be the first written in a German café appeared in Leipzig.

Initially women were barred from entry to the Leipzig cafés by decree, the reason for this being that prostitution was allegedly practiced on the cafés' premises. But women knew how to tackle this. From about 1715 the ladies organized private meetings within their own four walls, the coffee morning. This new fashion spread across the whole of Germany from Leipzig and Hamburg. Finally, in the 20th century, women gained access to the cafés which, to the sociologist Wolfgang Schivelbusch, represented "delayed revenge on the patriarchal coffee house culture."

Opposite: Coffee house culture is a tradition in the old fair city of Leipzig. Its beginnings were not as bourgeois and modest, though, as they appear here in a photograph taken in 1915, in the Café Panorama.

Poor Prussia: coffee sniffer

The measures which Frederick the Great announced in the *Vossische Zeitung* of 1780 against coffee, even though it was really a quite harmless pleasure were indeed draconian. By decree, the people of Prussia were to have the mere thought of enjoying a coffee driven completely from their minds. "You shall send our rich half-brothers of the German nation wood and wine, but no more money for coffee: all pans, elegant cups and common bowls, mills, roasting machines, in short anything to which the adjective coffee can be added, shall be completely destroyed, so that its memory be eradicated from the thoughts of our brethren. Whosoever dares to sell beans shall have his entire stock confiscated, and whosoever once again purchases crockery for the purpose of drinking coffee shall meet with punishment."

Frederick the Great, although himself a passionate lover of coffee, did not want too much currency to be spent on the foreign beans. Taxes were increased drastically. The coffee trade came under state control, private roasting of coffee was strictly forbidden, and henceforth only permitted in official roasting houses. Packets of coffee went on sale bearing official seals and stamps, at maximum prices which were no longer affordable for the average citizen.

In the opinion of the Emperor, people should content themselves with substitute coffees. Potato and rye coffee were extolled, and in particular chicory, whose roasted and ground roots were used to prepare false coffee, otherwise known as "mocha faux" or "Muckefuck," which was also called "Prussian coffee" or "German coffee" by the Huguenots. But once the people of Berlin had tasted coffee, they were not prepared to give it up. A flourishing black market trade in green beans grew up, which were then roasted in secret in private houses. In order to put a stop to the illegal trade, the Emperor took special measures. He appointed veterans of the Seven Years War as coffee sniffers. They strode the streets and alleys of the town in their old uniforms and tricorne hats, sniffing in every corner, house doorway, and square in order to detect the illegal aroma and catch the cheeky offender in the act.

The triumphal march of the coffee bean could not be stopped, however, even in Prussia. After the death of Frederick the Great in 1786, the state monopoly was withdrawn. Forty years later the Viennese Georg Kranzler established another milestone in the history of coffee consumption when, in 1825, he opened his café on the corner of Friedrichstrasse, which later became famous throughout the world,. The second café, which he opened on the Kurfurstendamm, is still a popular meeting place today.

The flour, butter, sugar, egg, salt, and brandy are kneaded quickly together to make a dough.

After it has rested the pastry is rolled out on a floured work surface.

The pastry is laid over the top of the muffin tins and carefully pressed in.

The muffin tins are filled with the prepared almond mixture and the top is leveled off.

Narrow strips are cut from the remaining pastry.

The pastry strips are placed on top of the almond mixture in the shape of a cross.

When they have been baked the muffin tins are turned out.

Finally the "skylarks" are released from the tins.

Free as a bird: Leipzig skylarks

"The small worm eats the sprouting seed.
And feeds the youthful lark along,
And as I too am here to feed.
I consume the songbird's song."
What a good thing that Johann Wolfgang von Goethe was no longer alive in 1876, because from then on there was no more "Consuming the songbird's song," as the nature conservationists banned the hunting of skylarks. Up until then each year hundreds of thousands of the birds landed in the kitchens of Saxony and further afield – studded with spices, wrapped in slices of bacon, and then roasted. Leipzig vendors even sent the plucked and stuffed birds as far as Moscow and Spain. "Stuffed breast of skylark with truffles" was one of the delicacies served at the Saxon court. In reply to critics who spoke of "barbaric eating habits," the Electress Anna is reputed to have said that

fawns, piglets and calves were also lovely creatures, but were still eaten. Anyway, she could not persuade her husband to turn vegetarian.
Perhaps the Electress should have urged the pastry chefs to try and change her husband's mind, because after the ban on skylark hunting came into force, they managed to find a guaranteed bird-free substitute for the roast skylarks which is still popular today – the *Leipziger Lerche*, or "Leipzig skylark," a shortcrust pastry tartlet with marzipan filling. They sent these "skylarks" out into a world which eagerly awaited the delicious birds. The pastry distantly resembles a bird's belly. Two strips of shortcrust pastry which form a cross on top of the tartlet are supposed to symbolize the nets which trapped the real larks in the past. Everyone was happy with this solution – gourmets and larks alike. The latter could now soar unhindered into the sky once more, to be praised by poets, not eaten by them.

Leipziger Lerchen
Leipzig skylarks

Pastry
2 cups/250 g flour
½ cup/125 g butter, softened
⅔ cup/85 g confectioner's sugar
1 egg
Pinch of salt
1 tbsp brandy

Filling
½ cup/125 g butter
1 egg yolk
Scant 1½ cups/170 g confectioner's sugar
Scant ½ cup/100 g ground almonds
2 tsp almond essence
⅔ cup/75 g flour
1 tbsp cornstarch
3 egg whites
Flour for the work surface
Butter for the muffin tins
Beaten egg yolk for glazing

Sift the flour onto the work surface, and make a wide well in the center. Add nuts of softened butter, the confectioner's sugar, the egg, salt, and brandy. Knead all the ingredients together to form a smooth dough. Shape the dough into a ball, and put it in the refrigerator to rest for at least 30 minutes. Meanwhile prepare the filling. Beat together the butter, egg yolk, and confectioner's sugar until light and fluffy. Gradually fold in the almonds, almond essence, flour, and cornstarch. Whisk the egg whites until very stiff and fold them carefully into the almond mixture. Roll out the pastry on a floured work surface until approximately ¼ inch/½ cm thick. Butter the muffin tins and line them with the pastry. Prick the base of each tin several times with a fork. Fill the muffin tins with the almond mixture and smooth off the top. Cut the remaining pastry into thin strips, and use these to make a cross on top of each tartlet. Brush the tartlets with egg glaze and bake in a preheated oven at 350 °F/180 °C for about 35 minutes.

The cake-loving Saxons

Saxony is Germany's bakery. The cake-loving Saxons have proved to be extremely inventive in the matter of devising and perfecting more and more new tastebud ticklers. And they have developed their own particular way of savoring their cakes and pastries: they "ditsch" or dunk them in their "Scheelchen Heessen," their cup of coffee.

It is not simply by chance that the "cake-loving Saxons" are the very same "coffee-loving Saxons," for there is a historical explanation. When the new hot drinks of coffee, chocolate, and tea reached Europe in the 17th century, they first entered aristocratic circles as a luxury item, and there were combined with another delicacy to which the Court had had access since the 16th century – sugar. Coffee, tea, and chocolate were taken with sugar, although the example of other countries shows that this approach is far from obvious. Here is just one example: in northern Scandinavia, where there was no Court to set an example, coffee was taken with salt. Furthermore the Court established the practice of serving cakes and pastries with coffee, tea, or chocolate. At the same time as the bourgeoisie adopted the products, they also took on the nobility's eating habits: coffee, sugar, and cakes were the big three. Thus, the coffee-loving nation of Saxony became a cake-loving nation too.

It is only possible to mention just a few of the wealth of cookies, cakes, and pastries here: *Dresdner Eierschecke* with its delicate brown topping over juicy quark and yeast dough, or the numerous variations on streusel cake and poppy seed cake which betray obvious Bohemian and Silesian influences.

The Saxons are just as inventive in naming their baked goods as they are in creating them. "Bäbe" is the name for a yeasted sweet bun, in which raisins are the essential ingredient. "Leipziger Räbchen" are plums filled with marzipan which are coated in a batter of flour, oil, and sugar, then deep fried. As a finishing touch they are dusted with a coating of cinnamon sugar. The name *Meissner Fummel* conceals a light choux pastry which looks like a big sesame seed roll. Elector August of Saxony caused this pastry to be made for the first time in 1710, for a particularly "boozy" courier.

The oldest porcelain maker in Europe

For almost 250 years it has graced the tables or windows of bourgeois households. If it breaks, then there are tears. If someone inherits a piece, then there is great rejoicing. The topic under discussion here is Meissen porcelain, or more precisely, the famous "onion pattern" Meissen. It has been on sale since 1739 and has not only survived generations of plate-smashing serving maids, and crockery-eating dishwashers, it has also survived changing tastes in the last few centuries. It does not seem to bother lovers of the classic design that the "onion pattern" does not show an onion, but pomegranates and peaches which, when combined in this way, look like onions. Both fruits are supposed to symbolize fertility and longevity, and the products from the porcelain factory in Meissen have indeed achieved the latter. The factory was founded on the Albrechtsburg in 1710 by Elector August the Strong. August had won the race to find the secret of manufacture of the "white gold," although by not very elegant means. In those days a man by the name of Johann Friedrich Böttger was on the run, and he maintained he could make gold. When he sought protection in Saxony from the King of Prussia, August imprisoned him and kept him there until his death, because he wasn't likely to let a man such as Böttger go free. He did not discover how to make gold in Saxony, but he did discover white European hard paste porcelain. Thus Europe was finally in a position to make porcelain itself. Gone were the days when quality crockery had to be imported from the Far East for a king's ransom!

In 1865, the factory moved to the Triebisch valley, near Meissen. Since 1991 the former state-owned business has belonged to the Free State of Saxony. Even today though, the Saxon trade mark of the crossed blue sabers stands for glowing colors and precious decoration. The cobalt blue "onion pattern" and the "full green vine garland" are the best known designs from the cradle of Saxony. But services from the "Staatlichen Porzellan-Manufaktur Meissen" (Meissen State Porcelain Factory) are also decorated with flower patterns, Chinese fables, dragons, and fairytale figures. The most comprehensive is the Swan Service with some 2000 pieces. The entire Meissen collection comprises more than 20,000 pieces, including thimbles, vases, candelabra, figures, and animals. Some 3000 of them are on display in an exhibition which changes regularly in the manufacturer's own exhibition rooms. In the works themselves, visitors can admire craft skills, because at Meissen every piece is still produced by hand, even today.

Henceforth the tippler had to dispense with his glass of wine, because in order to get the crumbly "Fummel" back in one piece from Meissen to the Elector, he needed all his wits about him.

Flowers and blossoms

It seems natural nowadays to decorate the dining table with flowers. You will find them even in basic cafés – the inevitable carnation in a narrow vase – whilst at luxurious buffets the table is frequently crowned by an impressive floral arrangement. The custom of putting fresh flowers on the table is not more than 150 years old, however. In the Middle Ages the most important decorative elements on a table were splendid vessels of gold and silver.

At the start of the Renaissance, when sugar became available in aristocratic circles and those who could afford it were ostentatiously wasteful with the expensive product, it became a major design medium. Sugar cooks worked it – drew it, spun it, whether white or colored; shaped into figures, trees, and flowers, it crowned the festive ducal table.

In the 18th century, when it became possible to manufacture porcelain in Europe, sugar and marzipan figures were replaced with ones made from porcelain.

Lavish decoration on plates and dishes – lots of flower patterns – satisfied the esthetic needs of those seated at table. Cut flowers were not used in table decorations because they symbolized mortality and death.

People have always used blossoms and flowers as a food though. The Persians made an early form of marzipan from rose water, crushed almonds, and sugar. Travelers from the Orient also told stories of preserved cherry blossom, rose petals on rice, and other floral delights.

The Romans cultivated massive violet and rose plantations, in order to have adequate supplies for festivals. They gave their heroes bouquets of roses rather than medals, and they sprinkled rose petals on guests' wine. They ate violets in sugared, roast, or deep-fried form. Saxony's crafty sugar confectioners sprinkled rose water on perfumed cheesecakes and ices, and on deep-fried sprays of elderflower, or they experimented with orange blossom, and the blossoms from other fruit trees. Candied roses, violets and other flowers still decorate cakes and desserts today, and they are furthermore accepted as a decorative addition to teas and liqueurs. Violet cream is also a popular filling for candy, and rose jelly adds a delicious flavor to chocolate cake.

Candying is a laborious process which also requires a certain instinctive feeling and sensitivity. The blossoms are dipped in sugar syrup, using a pair of tweezers, or coated in a thin layer of beaten egg white and then sprinkled with sugar. They then have to dry until they are rock hard and can be stored. But flowers not only lend emphasis to sweet dishes. They can be used to round off salads and other appetizers, garnish soups and sauces, flavor teas, wines, and liqueurs. In spring, daisies, for example, lend a pleasant nutty flavor to salads; in summer, yellow sunflowers or red and orange nasturtiums have a role as a garnish. The list of flowers which are suitable for decorations is long. They range from dahlias via chrysanthemums, to violets, and dandelion flowers. But take care, because some plants are poisonous. Gathering edible flowers is just as much of a science as picking wild mushrooms.

1   **2**

3   **4**

5   **6**

7   **8**

9

1 Dog rose
2 Elderflower
3 Daisy
4 Jasmine
5 Nasturtium
6 Pumpkin
7 Dandelion
8 Marguerite
9 Violet

Himmeltorte
Strawberry meringue

Decoration
8 sprays of elderflower, just opened
6 egg whites
3¾ cups/750 g sugar

Meringue
6 egg whites
3 cups/300 g confectioner's sugar
2 tbsp lemon juice

Topping
Generous 1 lb/500 g fresh strawberries
3 tbsp sugar
1 envelope of cake glaze
1 cup/250 g heavy cream

Four days before you want to bake the cake, rinse the elderflower sprays under running water. Stand them in water and leave the blossoms to dry. Whisk together the egg whites and 8 tablespoons of cold water with a fork, Do not let a froth form. Dip the elderflower sprays in the egg white, swishing them around carefully. Then sprinkle sugar evenly and not too thickly on the top of the spray, then on the bottom. Unbend a paper clip so that it forms a hook, spear the stalk of the spray on the paper clip, and hang it up to dry. Leave the elderflower sprays to dry for 4 days. On the day you want to bake the cake, whisk the egg whites until stiff, gradually add the confectioner's sugar and lemon juice. Line an 11-inch/28-cm springform pan with waxed paper. Put the meringue mixture into a pastry bag fitted with a round nozzle and pipe an even spiral on the waxed paper. Then, using a star shaped nozzle, pipe rosettes at regular intervals around the edge. Bake the meringue base for 1 hour on a very low heat. The base should not brown. Lift the meringue off the waxed paper whilst it is still warm. Shortly before serving, arrange the washed and drained strawberries on the meringue base, then sprinkle sugar on top. Prepare the cake glaze according to the instructions on the packet and pour it over the strawberries. Leave the glaze to cool. Whip the cream until stiff and add sugar to taste. Pipe rosettes of cream around the edge of the gateau. Decorate the gateau with the candied elderflower sprays.

You only need a few ingredients to candy flowers, but you do need a certain amount of instinctive feeling.

First beat together the egg whites and water with a fork, avoiding the formation of any froth.

Now dip the elderflower sprays in the egg white and swish them backward and forward carefully.

When the spray has drained a little, sprinkle it with sugar from the top and bottom.

A paper clip which has been prised open is a perfect hook for hanging up the sprays.

The blossoms must be left to dry hanging up for 4 days before they can be used as a decoration.

Dresden Stollen

Saxony's most famous culinary specialty is presumed to have been created in the 14th century as a meager Christmas cake, a dry white bread made from flour, yeast, and water, whose dough had to make do with oil rather than butter, because the churchmen in Rome had prohibited butter as part of the Advent fast. It was easy for them to ban butter when they were based in Italy where there is delicious olive oil – the Saxons had only rape oil, and God knows that was not suitable for making fine cakes and pastries edible. The oil, and the situation, must have stunk to high Heaven, such that the Elector intervened. The Pope allowed the Elector to persuade him to give way on the question of butter; a considerable sum towards the construction of Freiburg Cathedral made the decision a little sweeter for the Holy Father. And so he permitted the Saxons, "by power of this letter, that you, your wives, sons, and daughters and all your true servants and domestics may use butter instead of oil without any penance and fittingly."

The Saxons could now work at enriching their *stollen* "without penance"; although it is dubious if they always went about it in a "fitting" manner. The ingredients became more and more luxurious; the richer a region was, the more refined their Christmas cookies and cakes. After the competition had finally degenerated into "stollen wars" between rival towns, the people of Dresden finally got a firm hold on their position in the market. In the 17th century they managed to obtain an order that only Dresden producers could sell their wares at the Christmas market which took place in the town every year.

The "Dresdner Striezelmarkt" has been in existence since 1434 and is therefore the oldest German Christmas market. *Strutzel* or *Striezel* is the Middle High German word for a long piece of yeast dough. The term *die Stolle* or *der Stollen*, which is used in many Saxon districts comes, according to the *German Etymological Dictionary* from a "comparison with a post, log," in other words the supports which were used during the construction of mining galleries!

Dresdner Stollen

3 cups/600 g sultanas
4 tbsp rum
8 cups/1 kg flour
2 cups/500 ml lukewarm milk
2 cakes compressed yeast
1 cup/200 g sugar
Pinch of salt
Grated zest of 1 lemon
Ground nutmeg
2 cups/500 g butter
¾ cup/100 g ground or chopped almonds
1 cup/150 g candied lemon peel, finely diced
¾ cup/100 g candied orange peel, finely diced
Butter for brushing
Confectioner's sugar for dusting

Soak the sultanas overnight in the rum. Prepare a yeast dough using the flour, milk, yeast, sugar, salt, and butter. In turn work the almonds, lemon peel, orange peel, nutmeg, and sultanas into the dough, kneading well after the addition of each ingredient. Leave to rest for 1 hour. Then knead the dough again, divide in half, shape into stollen, and bake in a preheated oven at 350 °F/180 °C for 1 hour. Whilst the stollen is still warm, brush it with melted butter and dust thickly with confectioner's sugar.

The sultanas must be soaked overnight in rum.

A yeast dough is prepared from flour, milk, yeast, sugar, salt, and butter.

The ground or chopped almonds are added.

Knead the dough to distribute the almonds evenly.

Add the orange and lemon peel, then knead the dough again.

Finally add the macerated sultanas to the dough.

Knead again very thoroughly to disperse the sultanas.

Then shape the dough into a stollen shape.

After it has rested, the dough is pressed flat.

The flattened dough is rolled up to give the stollen its final shape.

The house of the gingerbread maker Tobias Thomas in the old gingerbread town of Pulsnitz.

"A Dresden Childhood"

"When I was a young boy, I used to traipse over to the shop in the Grenadierstrasse before school. "A liter and a half of fuel and a fresh four-pound loaf, second grade," I said to the assistant. Then I sped away with the change, the discount vouchers, the bread, and the fuel sloshing about in the can. The snowflakes danced against the twinkling gas-lamps. The coldness of the frost pinched my nostrils and left them tingling. Now I was off to Kiessling, the master butcher. "A quarter-pound of home-made blood and liver sausage, half and half!" After which it was Frau Kletsch in the greengrocer's. "A slab of butter and six pounds of potatoes. Greetings to everyone, and away before we all freeze to death!" And then I was off back home, carrying my bread, fuel, sausage, butter, and potatoes! My breath spilled in a white mist from my mouth, like the smoke from a steam-ship on the river Elbe. The four-pound loaf which was still warm started to slip from under my arm. The coins clinked against each other in my pocket. The fuel slopped about in the can. The net bag holding the potatoes slapped against my knee. The house door squeaked. Then the stairs, three steps at a time. The bell on the third floor, with no free hand. A shoe kicking the door. The door opens. "Can't you use the bell?" "No, mother – what with?" She laughs. "You haven't forgotten anything?" "What, me?" "Come right on in, young sir." And then, at the kitchen table, there would be freshly ground coffee with Karlsbad extract of figs, and with it the still-warm crust of the bread, the "heel," spread with fresh butter. And all the while my schoolbag, packed and ready to go, stood in the hallway… ."
(from: Erich Kästner, When I was a young boy, 1957)

Pfefferkuchen

Gingerbread is known as "Pfefferkuchen" (pepper cake) in Germany, but every child knows that it doesn't taste of pepper. Nevertheless, the most expensive and hottest spice in the Middle Ages gave its name to the aromatic sweetmeat. "Pepper" became a collective term for all exotic spices which were imported from distant lands. As far as gingerbread was concerned, these were primarily cinnamon, cardamom, mace, anise, cloves, nutmeg, ginger, coriander, cayenne, fennel, almonds, citrus fruits, vanilla, black and white pepper, and many more. Rye and wheat flour, as well as honey and syrup, subsequently sugar too, formed the basic components of the beloved cake.

Before these ingredients could be shaped into golden brown gingerbread hearts, triangles or square "cobblestones," the starter dough often had to ferment for years in massive containers. A master baker from the "gingerbread town" of Pulsnitz in the Westlausitz claimed that he prepared a starter dough on the occasion of the birth of his son, and only used this when he handed the business over to his son.

The people of Pulsnitz have had the privilege of baking gingerbread since 1558. For generations they had passed down their secret recipe by word of mouth. Today there are still eight small businesses and a limited company ensuring that the aroma which awakens memories of Christmas wafts over the town.

If you want to take a look behind the scenes, you can do so in Weissenberg's "Old Gingerbread Shop" museum in the Oberlausitz. The hallway which is used as a bakery and domestic work room houses an old German baking oven with the family stove and cooking kettle in front. Supplies of ingredients and the so-called starter dough were once stored in the cooler rooms.

To make gingerbread, the baker warmed the dough, and kneaded it in a wooden trough. This consisted of a chopping board and a serrated chopper, which buried itself heavily in the hard mass. Depending on the recipe, doughs of different ages were mixed with fresh dough, and then worked in the warm bakery.

Gingerbread was also regarded as a medicine due to its healthy ingredients. As recently as the 1930s, worm gingerbread, which was supposed to treat the annoying intestinal parasites, was still being made in the Erz Mountains.

Above: old and new cutters which are used to shape gingerbread.

All kinds of green

The "sweet Saxons" prove that they don't just live on coffee and cakes with a recipe which has earned a reputation for itself, even if it is partly a sad one, because it would be difficult for an intrinsically delicious dish such as *Leipziger Allerlei* (Leipzig mixed vegetables) to sink any lower. Carrots, peas, and asparagus, canned and tipped out onto a plate, sometimes thickened with a little flour *roux* – this was very popular in Germany in recent decades, in mediocre restaurants, and with busy housewives.

Luckily, growing health–consciousness has once again placed the spotlight on vegetables, and thus Leipzig mixed vegetables is once more respectable. It was originally an early summer dish and even cheap, at one time, because in the past the rivers were full of crayfish and the woods full of morel mushrooms. Nowadays you have to dig deep in your pockets to make *Leipzig Allerlei* according to the original recipe, but it is worth it!

Leipzig Allerlei obviously originated in a traditional vegetable-growing area. In the fertile Elbe Valley of Saxony, between Riesa and Pirna, lettuces flourish, together with kohlrabi, cucumbers, tomatoes, and culinary herbs. But tasty "Saxon green" also sprouts in great quantities in the area around Zittau, as well as south of Leipzig, and around Torgau. In addition to peas, beans, spinach, white cabbage, and red cabbage, horseradish, leeks, asparagus, tomatoes, and radishes are now increasingly grown. More and more of the 1100 Saxony vegetable growers are focusing on integrated, ecologically controlled cultivation.

Background: Around four million Germans are lucky owners of green allotments.

The garden gnome – the best loved symbol of German allotment culture.

Leipziger Allerlei
Leipzig mixed vegetables

1 oz/30 g dried morel mushrooms
9 oz/250 g asparagus stalks
9 oz/250 g baby carrots
½ small cauliflower
2 cups/500 ml meat stock
3½ tbsp/50 g butter
Salt
Pinch of sugar
1 ½ cups/200 g frozen petit pois
1 tbsp flour
½ cup/125 g cream
2 tbsp/30 g crayfish butter (puréed crayfish tails in butter with chives, celery, and parsley)
White pepper and nutmeg
10 oz/300 g cooked crayfish tails

Soak the morels in ¾ cup/200 ml water for 1 hour, then drain them and reserve the liquor. Trim and wash the asparagus stalks, carrots, and cauliflower. Cut the asparagus and carrots into 2 inch/5 cm chunks. Divide the cauliflower into florets. Bring the stock to a boil with 1 tablespoon of butter, salt, and a pinch of sugar. Add the carrots and simmer for 5 minutes. Add the cauliflower, and asparagus, then simmer for another 8 minutes. Stir in the peas and morels, and cook for 10 minutes. Drain the vegetables, reserving the stock. Sweat the flour in the remaining butter, stirring all the time, until golden brown, then add the reserved stock and mushroom liquor. Stir in the cream and crayfish butter. Boil the sauce until it has reduced a little. Add the vegetables and crayfish tails, and heat through, but do not boil. Season to taste with salt, pepper, and grated nutmeg.

A summer house for special occasions, and beds for flowers and vegetables are all part of an allotment.

Doctor Schreber's gardens

The lower middle class gardens which are named after him were never seen by Dr Daniel Gottlob Moritz Schreber (1808–1861). When his friend Ernst Innozenz Hausschild founded the first "allotment association," which was at that time still an educational association, in Leipzig in 1864, the doctor had been dead for a good two years. And to be quite frank it was association member Karl Gesell who had the idea of allotments, not Schreber. They first appeared in Leipzig in 1870. But the impetus came from Schreber, and that was enough. He also called for children's playgrounds to be set up in the open air. It was on the edge of such a playground that children's gardens first appeared, in 1886, for the "physical education" of the young. These developed into family gardens, because without parents' help the plants did not do so well, and the aforementioned allotments came later.

Their purpose is twofold: they enable city dwellers to grow fruit and vegetables for their own use, and create a restful place for their entire family in the fresh air. The allotments are now indispensable, especially in built-up areas. Today four million Germans indulge in allotments. Their plots are usually between 180 square yards (150 square meters) and 480 square yards (400 square meters). Paths, play areas, and club houses are all used jointly. So much for the benefits which people associate with Schreber. The Leipzig doctor's educational views are the subject of heated discussion, as are the methods by which he pursued his studies of public health. It is alleged that his own children suffered as a result. In order to inculcate a "good attitude" in them, he used means which seem like torture techniques from the Middle Ages. Schreber's oldest son later committed suicide. The younger spent many years in psychiatric institutions – and became a subject of research by Sigmund Freud.

Count Pückler ice cream

Hermann, Count Pückler-Muskau (1785–1871) was a daredevil Saxon bon viveur. He used all his wealth to create superb country parks, and as a sideline he wrote fascinating travel journals.

It is not quite clear how this cool refreshment came to have Pückler's name. One source says that the Count brought the recipe home with him from Arabia; another that he created the ice cream bombe himself, and a third that the Lausitz master confectioner Schulz dedicated the chilly treat to the aristocratic gourmet. Anyway, Pückler used the ice cream recipe as the basis for a passionate love letter to the landlord's daughter Caroline.

"For good temper
take chocolate,
for physical pleasure – sugar,
For curiosity – raspberry jelly,
Macaroons for the desire to travel,
Ice for joie de vivre,
For faithfulness take white gelatin,
Vanilla sugar for spiritual affection
Here you have the recipe for my
but recently composed ice cream."

Caroline is supposed to have cried a great deal at the time, because Pückler's faithfulness seemed extremely wanting – he had only allowed for less than a teaspoonful (4 grams) of gelatin! His escapades with women on the one hand are balanced on the other by Pückler's true love – his plans to create one of the loveliest country parks in Europe, in the English style, at Muskau in the Oberlausitz. He set about the work in his princedom in 1815, but his money ran out just a year later, and this was the reason why he married the wealthy countess, Lucy of Pappenheim. He truly succeeded in conjuring a paradise from the sandy and loamy soil, with artificial lakes and waterfalls, hills, and more than 3000 species of trees and shrubs, some of which were purchased as mature specimens from other gardens. The 1482 acre (600-hectare) park showed nature "at its finest." In 1845 Pückler, deep in debt, had to sell Muskau, but just a little later he designed a new garden at Branitz, near Cottbus. His heart is buried there, in a 60-foot (18-meters) high pyramid in the center of a lake.

Fürst Pückler Eis
Count Pückler ice cream

5 oz/150 g strawberries
¾ cup/125 g superfine sugar
4 oz/100 g almond macaroons
5 tbsp maraschino
2 cups/500 g heavy cream
3 oz/75 g grated chocolate

Wash, hull, and drain the strawberries. Purée them in a blender with a scant ¼ cup/50 g superfine sugar. Crush the macaroons and soak them in 2½ tbsp maraschino. Whip the cream until stiff, gradually trickle in the remaining sugar, then divide the cream into three equal portions. Fold the puréed strawberries and ⅓ of the macaroons into ⅓ of the cream. Transfer the mixture to a bombe mold and freeze for 10 minutes. Combine the second batch of cream with the remaining maraschino and ⅓ of the macaroons, spread over the strawberry mixture, and return to the freezer for another 10 minutes. Fold the chocolate and remaining macaroons into the remaining cream, and transfer to the mold. Cover the mold and freeze for 4 hours. Before serving, dip the mold in hot water, and turn the ice cream bombe out onto a serving dish.

The basic types of ice cream

The basic ingredients for ice cream are milk, cream, and butter, to which is added sugar and fruits in the form of fruit flesh, essence, or juice. Coffee or cocoa, a shot of alcohol (rum, brandy, wine, kirsch, etc.) lend a special flavor, as do hazelnuts, almonds, vanilla, raisins, and many more. In Germany there are seven basic types of ice cream:

Dairy ice cream must contain at least 70 percent milk.
Cream ice cream contains at least 60 percent heavy cream.
Ice cream is made with a milk fat content of 10 percent or more.
Only 8 percent is needed for fruit ice cream.
Basic ice cream has a milk fat content of at least 3 percent.
Premium ice cream contains at least 9½ oz (270 grams) of whole egg or egg yolk per liter of milk.
Fruit ice cream consists of 20 percent or more fresh fruit, fruit flesh or essence. For lemon ice cream it must be at least 10 percent of lemon oil or juice.
Artificial ice cream may, contrary to other types of ice cream, contain non-harmful artificial colors and flavorings, but many ice cream manufacturers voluntarily dispense with them.

In the park which he created in Branitz lies the heart of Count Pückler-Muskau, buried in a lake pyramid.

Hermann, Count Pückler-Muskau – Saxon bon viveur, inspired garden designer, and ice cream inventor.

The Sorbs

Between the Spree Forest and Lausitz Bergland, the traveler enters a different world. Place and street signs are bilingual, and the inhabitants greet you with a cheery "dobry dzen!," which roughly means "Good day."

This is the home of the Sorbs, the Slavic people with the smallest numbers, and supposedly the smallest race in Europe. They once made the Spree Forest cultivable and also helped Count Pückler to construct his country park in Muskau.

Some 60,000 members of the western Slavic race preserve their own language, and culture as well as cuisine in the Oberlausitz, Saxony and Niederlausitz, Brandenburg. With their colorful regional folk costumes, with the splendid bonnets, and their folk festivals, they have made their mark on the whole region.

The Sorbs' cultural center is now Bautzen. The young children attend Sorb and bilingual kindergartens, then move on to Sorb high schools, and can ultimately complete their education at a Sorbian-speaking college or university. There are a few Sorb newspapers, Sorbian radio and television are part of daily life, as well as Sorb dance and theater groups.

This is a unique multicultural phenomenon for Germany, when one thinks that the Sorbs ("Serby," "Serbya") have never been protected by their own state borders. Yet for more than a thousand years they lived in a largely peaceful manner with their German neighbors, without separatist leanings. Despite repeated attempts to stamp out the spoken Sorbian language, they even developed (around 1700) their own writing system. "A thought-provoking area in many respects" was also the opinion of the author Arno Schmidt about

the "Wasserpfütze" (water puddle), as the Lausitz is known in German.

The Sorbs were brutally oppressed by the Nazis though; their umbrella organization "Domowina" was banned as early as 1937. They were no longer allowed to speak their language and important Sorb personalities were driven from their homeland, or assassinated. Furthermore there were plans to rehome the Sorbs after the "final confrontation." During the Communist regime in East Germany, the Sorbs were used as an example to demonstrate a tolerant nationality policy. The Sorbs were better off then, though, than they were under the Nazis, provided that they toed the political line.

Today most Sorbs are Catholic or Evangelical, which is reflected in their rich culture – the Easter rites for example, or the Bird's Wedding, a children's festival which is celebrated on January 25, predominantly in the Bautzen/Kamenz/Hoyerswerda area. As on St Nicholas' Day, the children put plates on the window sill or outside the door. The magpie and her bridegroom, the raven, then put candy on the plates, especially *sroki*, little magpies made from milk dough rolls with sugar frosting and raisins for eyes, as well as baked birds' nests and meringue birds.

Later in the day the children dress up as birds or wear their traditional costumes and celebrate a wedding. The procession, dance, and wedding feast are all essential components. The celebratory procession through the village is traditionally lead by a "Hochzeitsbitter" (a messenger who issues invitations to the wedding) wearing tails and a top hat, followed by the bride and bridegroom, two female sponsors, the bridesmaid and the rest of the company. Whilst the children celebrate their bird's wedding banquet with candy, and nothing else, a "genuine" Sorbian wedding breakfast also awaits with numerous typical hearty regional dishes.

Easter customs

Hot wax, goose feather quills, knives, files, fire, and corrosive acid – are these really used for decorating innocent white hens' eggs? The Sorbs use them, and with wonderful success. Sorbian Easter eggs are amongst the most exquisite products of German folk art. Traditional decorations are geometric and symmetrical patterns. Rows of triangles are known as "wolf's teeth." Lines radiating out from a circle are known as a "pin wheel" or "bundle of rays." More recently flowers and sprays, names, greetings, and short proverbs are applied to these oval symbols of fertility.

No two eggs are alike. This is ensured quite simply by the four different production methods: etching (with a goose quill and hydrochloric or nitric acid), delicate scratches (with a knife or file), the colorful wax reserve technique (the egg is subjected to several color baths, with wax being applied in a pattern to more and more parts of the egg's surface), and the wax embossing technique (where wax remains as a decoration on the already dyed or natural colored egg). Visitors can admire every aspect of this splendor in the round at the Easter Egg Markets in Kamenz, Weisswasser, and Bautzen. The Oberlausitz has not just acquired its reputation as the "Easter country" because of the art of painting eggs. The Easter rites are equally famous. On Easter Sunday, in the Catholic Sorb area, nine processions wend their way between Bautzen, Kamenz, and Wittichenau to bring the neighboring parishes the news of the Resurrection of Jesus. Up to 1300 riders in frock coats and top hats set off, mounted on horses, proceeded by bearers of the church banners and the cross. The horses' coats shine under embroidered white silk trappings, garlands of flowers, and braided manes and tails. The bridle is sewn with white cowry shells or mussels. The tradition of the Easter procession is based on the pagan tradition of beating the bounds. It still takes place nowadays in Ostro, early on Easter morning, and so even on Easter night many Sorbs steal through the woods and fields with a "carbide gun." The deafening noise made by the home-made shot fired from an old tin can containing some carbide, and with a rubber lid will surely drive away even the most obstinate evil spirits.

The wedding is an opportunity for Sorbs to don their traditional costumes.
The children imitate the adult world with the Bird's Wedding.

Sorbian Wedding Breakfast

Mohnkuchen
Poppy seed cake
(Illustrated below right)

Yeast dough

Generous 4 cups/500 g flour
1 cake compressed yeast
1 cup/250 ml lukewarm milk
¼ cup/50 g sugar
1 egg
Pinch of salt
Butter for the baking sheet

Topping

1 vanilla bean
4 cups/1 liter milk
1 cup/150 g semolina
2 cups/250 g ground poppy seeds
¼ cup/50 g sugar
2 eggs, separated
Grated rind of 1 lemon
Confectioner's sugar for dusting

Prepare a yeast dough using the flour, yeast, sugar, egg, and salt. Butter the cookie sheet, then press the yeast dough onto it. Leave to rise until doubled in size. To make the topping: split the vanilla bean in half, and bring it to a boil with the milk. Then stir in the semolina and leave it to swell. Take the vanilla bean out of the mixture, and fold the poppy seeds into the hot semolina. Leave the poppy seed mixture to cool. Whisk together the sugar, egg yolk, and lemon rind to form a thick cream, then fold this into the poppy seed mixture. Whisk the egg white until stiff and fold it carefully into the poppy seed mixture. Spread the mixture over the dough base and bake in a preheated oven at 350 °F/180 °C for about 40 minutes. Before serving, cut the cake into slices and dust with confectioner's sugar.

Sorbische Biersuppe
Sorbian beer soup
(Illustrated below left)

1 cup/250 ml lager
1 cup/250 ml malt beer
2 cups/500 ml milk
2 tbsp flour
Scant ½ cup/100 g cream
Sugar
Pinch of salt
1 egg, beaten
½ cup/100 g raisins

Mix the beers together and heat them through. In another pan, bring the milk to a boil and pour it into the beer. Blend the flour and cream together and use the mixture to thicken the soup. Bring to a boil again and season to taste with sugar and salt. Take the pan off the heat and stir in the beaten egg. Pour the soup into soup cups and sprinkle the raisins on top.

Rindfleisch mit Meerrettich
Beef with horseradish
(Illustrated above left)

2 lb 3 oz/1 kg beef (in one piece)
2 marrow bones
Soup vegetables (2 carrots, 1 leek, 2 celery stalks, a bunch of parsley)
1 onion, spiked with a bay leaf and 2 cloves
1 tbsp butter
1 tbsp flour
2 eggs
½ cup/125 ml milk
½ cup/100 g freshly grated horseradish
Salt and pepper
4 tbsp melted butter

Rinse the beef and the bones. Bring 8 cups/2 liters water to a boil with the soup vegetables and the spiked onion; add the beef and marrow bones; cover, and simmer for about 2 hours. Take the beef out of the stock, and drain the stock, reserving it. Melt the butter, sweat the flour in the butter, stirring all the time, then add 1⅔ cups/400 ml stock. Simmer the sauce until it thickens a little. Beat together the eggs and milk. Take the pan off the heat and stir in the egg and milk mixture, and horseradish. Season to taste with salt and pepper. Cut the beef into even slices, arrange on a warmed serving dish, and pour over the horseradish sauce and the melted butter.

Beef with horseradish

Poppy seed cake

Sorbian beer soup

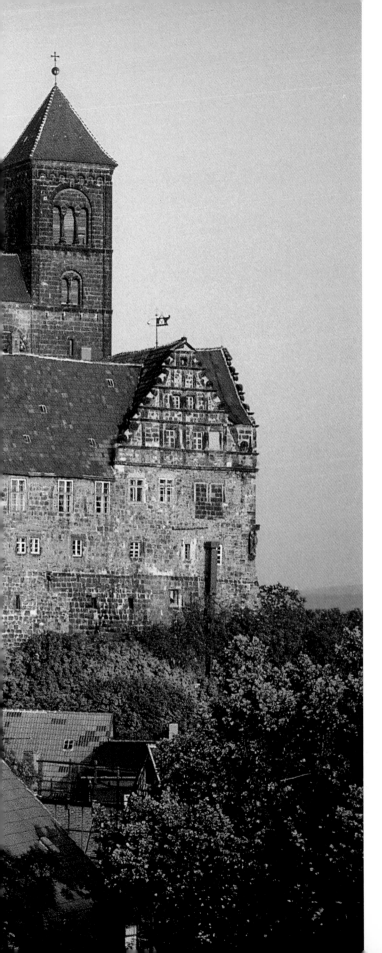

ULLA RETTIG

Saxony-Anhalt

The young Federal State of Saxony-Anhalt has a marvelous heritage of history and fable. Kings, artists, and nonconformist thinkers have shaped a whole nation from this strip of land. All the same, the locals have not found it easy to establish a common identity. After all, the people of the Altmark, the Harz Mountains, and their neighbors in the regions Halle-Saale-Unstrut, Anhalt-Wittenberg, and Elbe-Börde-Heide have only been reunited as Saxony-Anhalt since October 14, 1990. Before this, Saxony-Anhalt existed only briefly as a political and administrative unit between 1947 and 1952.

This is nothing but a blink of the eye in comparison with what has happened here in previous centuries. In 919 the Saxon ruler Henry was crowned King of Germany in Quedlinburg. Later in the 10th century Magdeburg grew under Emperor Otto I to become one of the greatest Christian centers on the globe, while the great theologian of the Reformation, Martin Luther, shook the whole Christian world when he nailed his *95 Theses* to the door of the Wittenberg Schlosskirche. Saxony-Anhalt has also played host to a whole procession of the finest writers and musicians to come out of Germany, including Goethe, Heine, Fontane, Telemann, Bach, Handel, and Schütz.

Nevertheless, the best way to awaken a feeling of community is to appeal to the palate. The people of Saxony-Anhalt are united in their pride over the fruits of their soil: sugar and cereals from the fertile plain around Magdeburg, the Börde, onions from Calbe, asparagus and milk from the Altmark, apricots and wines, still and sparkling, from the Saale-Unstrut area, cheese from the Harz Mountains. Inventive chefs are also doing their best to give the food of the region a higher status once again, consulting old recipes and using them as the basis for the preparation of nourishing, hearty dishes.

This reawakened feeling of confidence became especially evident in 1996. In a reversal of the CARE aid program run by the Americans and Canadians during the Cold War, the people of Saxony-Anhalt sent hundreds of thousands of food parcels containing *Rotkäppchen* sparkling wine, *Halberstädter* sausages, and other typical regional specialties to West Germany. The campaign made history: two of the parcels even ended up in the German Historical Museum in Berlin.

Left: The ancient city of Quedlinburg with its castle and the Stiftskirche church. With more than 1600 half-timbered buildings, the old center of the city is one of the most important conservation areas in Germany.

Between 1870 and 1965 the silhouettes of the steam plows dominated the landscape of the Magdeburg Börde. They would work in pairs along the opposite edges of a field, pulling a balance, or throw-over, plow backward and forward across the field between them with cable winches. The plows had sets of shares and turned over the heavy soil to a depth of up to 15 inches (40 cm). The 70-150 hp steam plows managed up to 9 hectares per day.

A "Klump" in the Oven

"Kale and Klump fill the farmer's belly," according to an old saying from the Magdeburg Börde. Hardly any meal was set on the table without this side dish. Originally *Klump* was a layer of yeast pastry laid like a lid over the food and then cooked in a coke breeze oven. Sometimes the dough was used to make dumplings called *Löffelklump* that were added to soups and stews.

There are many different types of *Klump*, such as *Jestklump* (made with yeast), *Mehlklump* (with flour), *Bollenklump* (with onions), *Kartoffelklump* (with potato), *Schotenklump* (with peas) and *Zwiebackklump* (with rusk), which is also known as *Kleine Klump* and used as a dumpling in vegetable soups. *Jestklump* was sometimes sweetened with sultanas, candied lemon peel, or orange rind and served as a biscuit with coffee.

Apart from "Kale and Klump," "Bratgen und Klump" was a particularly popular Sunday dish. Dried plums, apples, or pears – *Bratgen* – were cooked for several hours with raisins in either bacon or pork fat. Then the *Klump* was laid over the mixture, the iron pot placed in a coke breeze oven, and ashes piled on top of the lid.

The oven used was fired with a special kind of granular coke made from lignite known as coke breeze. These iron ovens were sometimes built into the wall and were practically air tight. Straw and branches or coke breeze glowed around the pot for several hours. The heat retained by the oven was used to dry fruit overnight. Potatoes have now largely replaced *Klump*, and there are hardly any ovens burning coke breeze left in the Börde.

The riches of the Börde

Sugar and cereals

The widow Haberhaufe from Eickendorf became one of the proudest widows in the land that day in the 1930s when the government's agricultural assessors dug on her fields. She was awarded a full score of 100 points, the official confirmation that her fields in the Magdeburg Börde were perfect agricultural land. The high fertility of the loamy loess soil, combined with the superb transport connections of the widow's property, set standards for all the other arable farms in Germany.

There are many other superlatives associated with the approximately 360 square miles (930 square kilometers) of the Börde. It is one of Germany's largest granaries and the most important center of sugar beet cultivation in the country. Thriving crops have been grown all over the world using beet seeds from Klein Wanzleben. As early as 1914 one in every three sugar beet came from cultivars that originated in the Börde.

Today cereal fields make up 62 percent of the area cultivated. Wheat, barley, and oats flourish here, and rye is grown on the edge of the Börde for *Burger Knäckebrot*, the famous crispbread that has been produced in the town of Burg since 1931. Sugar beet only takes up 10 percent of the area cultivated, but has played an important role in the history of the Börde. With the construction of the sugar factories in the second half of the 19th century the region experienced a massive economic boom. The steam plows that were employed from 1870 on had originally been developed for work in the cotton fields overseas. They revolutionized sugar beet cultivation, which was as hard a job as can be imagined when it was all done by hand, and made a considerable contribution to increasing yields.

The new riches also influenced the architecture of the region, with the building of what were known as "beet palaces." In many ways these magnificent mansions, with their fine ladies', gentlemen's, and music rooms, were typical of the villas constructed during the boom of the early 1870s that followed the establishment of the German Empire.

However, the Börde farmers remained faithful to their substantial, nourishing regional food, especially the sauerkraut they loved so much. One local saying sums the matter up: "What made him strong and stout? – Magdeburg sauerkraut." One extremely popular meal was a combination of knuckle of pork, pease pudding, and sauerkraut, known popularly as *Bötel, Lehm und Stroh*, which translates as "Wether (a castrated male sheep), Clay and Straw." Meat, which was often on the menu in the prosperous Börde, was salted in large quantities. Pork rib, bacon, and ham were preserved in separate smokehouses and stored in the kitchen fireplace.

Many traditional Börde dishes are still eaten today. Others, such as warm salad: lettuce dripping with a sour, warm flour sauce, have not survived the changing tastes of later generations. Nowadays warm salad is no longer eaten as an accompaniment to pancakes, and with good reason. By 1900 experts were of the opinion that the "modern stomach is completely incapable of digesting" greens treated in this way.

Braunkohl mit Klump
Kale with Klump

2 lb 3 oz/1 kg curly kale	
salt	
1 ¾ lbs/750 g pork	
1 onion, diced	
1 tbsp clarified butter	
pepper	
4 pears	
1 ¾ lbs/750 g potatoes	
1 large whole onion	
2 eggs	
6 tbsp/100 g butter	

Strip the kale leaves from the thick stalks, wash thoroughly and blanche in salt water for 2 minutes. Drain and leave to cool for a few minutes. Chop the kale coarsely. Dice the pork. Fry the onion lightly in 1 tablespoon of clarified butter. Briefly fry the meat with it, add the kale and pour on 4 cups (1 liter) of water. Season with salt and pepper and cook for 30 minutes with the lid on. Quarter and core the pears, and add them to the kale. Cook for another 15 minutes. Peel and wash the potatoes, then grate them coarsely with the large onion. Wrap in a tea towel and press out all the moisture. Place immediately in a bowl and mix with the eggs and salt. Put the cabbage mixture into a heatproof dish and spread the potato and onion over it. Scatter flecks of butter over the topping and bake for approximately 40 minutes until golden in an oven preheated to 345 °F (175 °C).

Bötel, Lehm und Stroh
Wether, clay and straw

Wether (knuckle of pork)
2 salted knuckles of pork weighing 14 oz/400 g each
1 onion spiked with 2 cloves and a bay leaf
soup vegetables (2 carrots, 2 celery stalks, I leek, 1 bunch of parsley)
1 tsp peppercorns and whole allspice

Straw (sauerkraut)
1 onion, diced
1 tbsp clarified butter
1 lb/500 g sauerkraut
5 juniper berries

Clay (pease pudding)
12 oz/350 g yellow split peas soaked overnight in water
1 onion, diced
2 potatoes, peeled and diced
soup vegetables (2 carrots, 2 celery stalks, I leek, 1 bunch of parsley), diced
salt and pepper
1 tsp rubbed marjoram
5¼ oz/150 g rashers of bacon, diced

Rinse the knuckles of pork. Bring 12 cups (3 liters) of water to the boil in a large pot. Add the knuckles, spiked onion, soup vegetables, and peppercorns and allspice, cover with a lid, and cook over a low heat for 1½ hours. Take out the knuckles and sieve the stock. To cook the sauerkraut, fry the diced onion lightly in hot clarified butter until it is transparent, add the sauerkraut and crushed juniper berries, pour on 2 cups (500 ml) of the stock in which the knuckle was cooked, and simmer for 1 hour. During the last ½ hour put the knuckle in to cook with the sauerkraut. While it is cooking, bring the drained peas to the boil with 2 cups (500 ml) of stock, the onion, potatoes, and soup vegetables. Season with salt, pepper, and marjoram. Cover with a lid and cook over a medium heat for 1 hour. Finally press the peas through a sieve. Fry the bacon in a dry pan and scatter over the pease pudding and sauerkraut. Serve with the knuckles of pork.

Whitefish

At seven in the morning, fisherman Wilfried Kagel puts out onto the water. He is hunting a fish that is to be found nowhere else in Saxony-Anhalt, the European whitefish. Tensely, Kagel and his colleague, Sabine Schultze, pull their drift nets up from a depth of 30–65 feet (10–20 meters). They can be happy with today's catch: there are hundreds of fish hanging by their jaws in the nets.

The whitefish (*Coregonus albula*) is a member of the Salmonidae family, which includes both salmon and trout. They all have a noticeable adipose dorsal fin. Whitefish are freshwater fish that grow up to 10 inches (24 centimeters) long and live off zooplankton. They usually do not survive for more than three years, and are ready to reproduce in their second year.

The fish are found mainly in the clear, deep lakes of Mazuria in Poland, but have also taken up residence in Schleswig-Holstein, Mecklenburg-West Pomerania, and Brandenburg. They arrived in the Arendsee over 110 years ago, when a fisherman brought them with him from Schleswig-Holstein. Since then the whitefish has become the principal commercial fish in the lake, which is 1300 acres (530 hectares) in area and up to 170 feet (52 meters) deep, and was formed as a result of subsidence in the earth's crust.

On the lake shore Kagel puts part of the catch onto spits and smokes the fish for about half an hour over alderwood. He seasons them with salt and herbs, but will not give away the precise combination.

In the summer the most popular place to eat the fish by the lake is at the "Marienhof" restaurant. A slice of bread is quite sufficient accompaniment. "Some customers buy the fish fresh and fry or pickle them at home," says Kagel. Kagel is the fifth generation of his family to work as a fisherman. About 30 years ago fate led him from the River Havel to the Arendsee, a place associated with numerous legends. He has been there ever since. After the G.D.R. collapsed he took out a lease on the water. Kagel was therefore extremely interested, in 1995, when the Leipzig/Halle Environmental Research Center (the U.F.Z.) began a completely unprecedented experiment in lake cleaning on his very doorstep. The aim was to put a stop to the excessive growth of blue algae in the water. About 74,500 cubic yards (57,000 cubic meters) of clay were extracted and pumped into the lake through pressurized pipes. This was intended to reduce the phosphate content of the water and remove the nutrients on which the blue algae live. The first results suggest that the project has been a success.

By contrast, the situation is much more difficult in the Elbe, which is home to 33 of a total of 40 species of fish living in Saxony-Anhalt. Since 1989 all commercial fishing has been banned in the river where it runs through Saxony-Anhalt. Research had shown that the fish were contaminated by pollutants that included mercury, hexachlorobenzene, D.D.T., musk compounds, and heptachlor. However, developments in recent years have given grounds for hope. The quality of the water has improved considerably since sewage has been treated more effectively and a number of major industrial polluters close to the banks have been closed down. Now the ministry responsible hopes that professional fishermen will be allowed back onto the Elbe in the year 2000.

Maräne
Whitefish

4 whitefish, cleaned for cooking
juice of 1 lemon, salt
8 sprigs of Italian (flat-leaf) parsley
½ cup/125 g butter
7 oz/200 g flaked almonds
2 tbsp parsley, chopped
slices of lemon to garnish

Rinse the whitefish under running water and pat dry. Drizzle with lemon juice and sprinkle with a little salt. Allow to marinate for 20 minutes. Place a sprig of parsley into the stomach cavity of each fish. Melt the butter in a large skillet and fry the whitefish on each side until golden brown. Remove the fish. Fry the flaked almonds lightly in the butter. Return the whitefish to the skillet and turn once. Serve on warmed plates. Sprinkle with chopped parsley, pour the butter left in the skillet over the fish, and garnish with lemon slices.

Nature gets a helping hand here to maintain whitefish stocks. The roe (fish eggs) and the milt (sperm) are taken from the fish, insemination takes place in a bowl, and the fish hatch in glass containers.

Salt

"Ye are the salt of the earth," Jesus told his disciples, and continued, "but if the salt have lost his savour, wherewith shall it be salted?" His question meant the equivalent of "how could we live then?" for salt has important functions in the human body. It is essential to the maintenance of muscle tone, regulates the water metabolism, ensures that muscles and nerves respond properly, supports the formation of bones, and is an important component of a number of elements in the digestive juices.

The deliberate intake of salt became important for humans when they settled in one place. Our ancestors began to eat less meat, and more fruit and vegetables, which do not contain enough salt for human requirements. The Celts were operating salt mines as early as 1000 B.C. Roman legionaries received part of their wages in salt and, like the French *salaire*, "salary" is derived from the Latin word *sal*. In ancient times there was a network of salt roads running throughout Europe. The cities on these routes prospered, and soon the powerful secured monopolies and raised salt taxes. There were salt wars and salt rebellions. Anyone who owned supplies of salt became rich, the poor "could not even afford to salt their soup." In Germany bread and salt are still presented as gifts when someone moves house. They are basic foodstuffs in the sense of the German word *Lebensmittel* – the means by which we live.

Until the invention of artificial cooling and freezing methods salt was not just important as a seasoning, but also for the preservation of foodstuffs. Of the salt produced in pre-industrial times 50 to 60 percent was used for this purpose, and there has been a flourishing trade in salted fish ever since the Middle Ages.

'Als, pronounced "hals," was the Greek word for salt, and place names that include "hall" indicate an association with the salt trade. One example is Halle an der Saale, where salt was being extracted by 1000 B.C. Halle had four large saline springs and developed into one of the most famous salt producing cities in Europe by the Middle Ages. The white gold was sent out along twelve salt roads, and the Saale and Unstrut rivers were also used as transport routes. On the return journey the carters brought butter, eggs, and cheese from the Electorate of Saxony, cereals from Bohemia, or iron and linen from Silesia.

In 1582 the people of Halle agreed a special contract with Elector August of Saxony, according to which they would exchange salt for wood, of which there was a great shortage in Halle. Massive quantities were required for open pan evaporation, which was carried out in small pan houses called *Kothen*. There were about 100 of these pan houses crowded into the valley where the springs were found. The salt workers, known as *Halloren*, stood at large iron pans measuring 6 feet by 9 (2 meters by 3), in which the saline was

Hallorenkugeln: the sweets with the salty past

It is ironic that the most famous food named after the Halle salt workers is a sugary, sweet praline: the round *Hallorenkugel* with its luscious filling of tempting, calorific cream and cocoa fondant hidden within a coating of fine chocolate. The sweet is a relatively recent invention of the oldest chocolate factory in Germany. The company history of the "Halloren Schokoladenfabrik GmbH Halle" goes back to 1804. During the 1950s the sweetmakers were inspired to create a round praline by the silver buttons the salt workers wore on their traditional costume.

For many G.D.R. citizens the sweets from Halle were the definitive pralines. After reunification production reached 100 million *Hallorenkugeln* for the first time in 1996. Alongside sweet-toothed Germans, people in Eastern Europe, Scandinavia, the U.S.A., and Japan now enjoy the sweets with the salty past. The original *Hallorenkugeln*, with its creamy cocoa fondant filling, has been joined by a strawberry yogurt version, while the company's latest creation, the *Graf Metternich Praline*, is a champagne jelly with *Marc-de-Champagne* truffle in the center.

boiled. After the fire had been lit, 21 or 22 buckets of salty water were poured into the salt pan. Next came a bowl full of cattle blood or dye, and another 14–17 buckets of brine. The blood or dye was believed to accelerate evaporation and purify the salt. After any impurities had been skimmed off, crystallization took place as the salt was precipitated from the saturated solution. The saltmakers drew the salt to the edge of the pan as it settled and put it into baskets.

The collection of silverware owned by the salt workers shows how lucrative the salt trade was. The Brotherhood of Salt Workers in the Valley at Halle still owns 83 beautifully decorated drinking vessels, a jug, and two chain belts.

Hallorenkuchen is a culinary tradition left over from the times when the salt trade dominated the life of the city. It was baked on feast days for the wife of the Salzgraf, the official in charge of salt production and the salt workers' court. Special beer was drunk in huge quantities at these festivities, there was dancing, and the salt workers played a game on the river in which the aim was to push one's opponent off his boat with a long pole. When the celebrations were over, the Salzgraf was accompanied home by one of the salt workers and his wife, who carried a glass tankard of strong beer and a *Hallorenkuchen* covered with raisins, almonds, and other nuts.

Soleier
Pickled Eggs

10 eggs
3 tbsp salt

Boil the eggs for 7–8 minutes until hard. Cool them in cold water, then knock them lightly several times so that the shell cracks but does not fall off.
Boil the salt in 4 cups (1 liter) of water.
Place the eggs in a glass or earthenware container, then cover with the salt solution and allow to marinade overnight.

Pickled eggs taste particularly good with coarse bread and beer.

Hallorenkuchen
Saltworkers' Cake

8 oz/250 g raisins
5 oz/150 currants
½ cup/125 ml rum
1 cup/250 g butter
1 cup/200 g sugar
4 eggs
grated rind of 1 lemon
1 tsp cinnamon
1 tsp cardamom
½ tsp mace
1 lb 10 oz/750 g fine wheat flour
5 level tsp baking powder
2 cups/500 ml milk
5 oz/150 g ground almonds
3 oz/100g candied lemon peel, finely diced
fat to grease the pan
confectioner's sugar to dust the finished cake

Wash the raisins and currants, drain, and soak in the rum. In the meantime, cream the butter with the sugar. Mix in the eggs, lemon rind, cinnamon, cardamom, and mace. Gradually work in the flour, baking powder, and milk until the mixture is smooth. Drain the rum from the raisins and currants, then mix in the ground almonds, diced candied lemon peel, and soaked fruit. Grease a cake pan, spoon in the mixture and bake for approximately 1 hour in an oven preheated to 400 °F (200 °C). Turn out the finished cake onto a cooling rack, allow to cool, and dust thickly with confectioner's sugar before slicing.

The king of cakes

Baumkuchen

Standing close to the fire baker Achim Lehnig often finds himself dripping with sweat. At a room temperature of 176 °F (80 °C) the employee of the "Erste Salzwedeler Baumkuchenfabrik Oskar Hennig" makes cylindrical *Baumkuchen* (literally "tree cakes") according to a patented traditional recipe. The sweet delicacy is built up skillfully on a rotating beechwood roller over an open flame.

It is the fault of Luise Lentz that Achim Lehnig has to sweat so much. She was the person who bequeathed the "King of cakes" to the people of the Altmark. Originally the secret recipe came from her grandfather Ernst-August Gardes, who had worked as head chef under King Frederick-William II, but it is his granddaughter who we have to thank that his instructions did not molder away for ever in a packing case. In 1808 she dug out the recipe and set to work, serving up the results to the customers at the "Schwarzer Adler," the restaurant run by her parents in the cellar of the Salzwedel town hall. The response was rapturous.

His Majesty Frederick-William IV was delighted in 1841 when he first tried the wonderfully light cake on a visit to the town on the River Jeetze. He had a sample packed up for his wife straight away. At his royal recommendation the orders came flooding in from Berlin, St Petersburg, and Vienna. In 1865 King William I also discovered the sweet delicacy for himself when he traveled to Salzwedel with Otto von Bismarck. At that time confectioner Andreas Fritz Schernikow was the leading *Baumkuchen* baker in the town. His cakes and pastries tasted so good that he rose to become a supplier of the royal household. Soon Salzwedel was famous as the "home of *Baumkuchen*." The sweet specialty, which was soon available with chocolate icing, developed into a major factor in

the local economy. Deliveries were sent off to cafés and private customers all over Germany. *Baumkuchen* squares and tarts also created a stir. At the moment there are four Salzwedel *Baumkuchen* makers competing for the favor of customers at home and abroad. Oskar Hennig's products, for example, even decorate the table of the noble Thurn and Taxis family.

What actually goes into a real *Baumkuchen* continues to remain a secret: the master bakers will only let an outsider see so much. As in years gone by, when there were no artificial raising agents available, it is large quantities of egg white that make the mixture rise – 40 eggs are used for each 11½ pound (5 kg) cake, along with creamed butter, sugar, spices, wheat flour, and semolina.

After the mixture has been creamed and heated, it is applied to the wooden roller in 12 or 13 fine layers. This gives rise to the characteristic "year rings" in a piece of *Baumkuchen*. As the process continues, protruding rings of cake begin to take shape, creating the unique outline of a real *Baumkuchen*. "Salzwedel *Baumkuchen* really grows wild," Hennig says proudly.

After about 20 minutes the cylindrical cake is complete. It is finished over an open flame in order to give it a golden brown sheen on the outside. The cake has to cool for one day. Only then is it coated classically with white icing or, for more modern tastes, with dark, milk, or white chocolate. The cake tastes best when fresh, but cunning *Baumkuchen* addicts freeze it in order to have a piece at their finger tips "just in case."

Baumkuchenspitzen
Baumkuchen Squares

1 cup/250 g butter
8 ½ oz/250 g sugar
½ tsp of vanilla essence
5 eggs, separated
2 tbsp rum
grated rind of one lemon
½ tsp cinnamon
½ tsp ground cardamom
⅛ tsp ground allspice
5 oz/150 g flour
3 oz/100 g cornstarch
3 tsp baking powder
white icing and dark coverture

Cream the butter with the sugar and vanilla essence. Add the egg yokes, rum, lemon rind, cinnamon, cardamom, and allspice. Gradually stir in the flour, cornstarch, and baking powder. Beat the egg whites until they are very stiff and carefully fold into the mixture. Line a deep baking pan with greaseproof paper and spread a thin layer of cake mixture onto it. Bake in an oven preheated to 375 °F (190 °C) for ten minutes until light yellow. Spread a second layer of cake mixture over this and bake for another ten minutes at a slightly lower temperature. Continue in this way until all the cake mixture has been used up. It is important that each layer is baked for ten minutes and that the heat is reduced each time a new layer is added. Turn the finished cake out onto a cooling rack and allow to cool. Cut into equal-sized squares and coat half with white icing, half with dark coverture.

A surfeit of Baumkuchen

In his memoirs Hans Fallada (1893–1947) tells a story that illustrates how any delicious food can become a punishment if consumed in excessive quantities. While their parents were dining with guests, he and his brother went to the pantry, found the dessert for the dinner party, broke off all the rounded lumps from two large Baumkuchen, and ate them.

"The next morning came; our parents were still sleeping. For breakfast we boys were given Baumkuchen, while our sisters got bread and butter. They wanted to protest … Charlotte simply said that our father had given instructions for this to be done. When we unpacked our morning snacks at school, we found not sandwiches, but Baumkuchen. At lunch mother remained rather cool towards us, but did not mention Baumkuchen. All the same, we had to eat it, nothing but Baumkuchen, while the others enjoyed the wonderful food left over from the night before…

"At dinner and supper our menu remained unchanged: Baumkuchen. The next day: Baumkuchen! At lunch, while the others ate potatoes in meat stock with beautiful green parsley and lean beef, we had Baumkuchen. We found it ever more difficult to satisfy our hunger with Baumkuchen. We felt that Baumkuchen was an overrated cake. Soon we discovered that we hated Baumkuchen!…

"A third day arrived – Baumkuchen! Would these two awful Baumkuchen never come to an end? And the places where the lumps had been broken off continued to stare at us accusingly. We did not dare complain. We did not even dare ask… We chewed on our Baumkuchen with aching jaws…

"And the worst of it all was that no one ever uttered a word about our rather monotonous round of meals. It seemed the most natural thing in the world that we alone were fed Baumkuchen. It had always been that way, and it always would be…

"O God, how happy Ede and I would have been if we had received a good beating like other boys! But my father did not believe in either beating or shouting. All things violent and loud went against his nature. He punished us with terrible precision in the very area where we had sinned. He punished our desire for Baumkuchen with a surfeit of Baumkuchen. …

"And finally the Baumkuchen was finished. That lunch, I remember it well, there were sweet and sour Westphalian broad beans with smoked meat, a meal to which I had always been averse till then. I ate it like a starving man."

Garlic provides effective protection against vampires. Wild garlic, often known as bear garlic, is also thought to help fend off witches.

The witchcraft of the Harz

"The witches fly to the Brocken, the stubble is yellow, the crops are green," sings the choir of witches, while Mephisto and Faust climb up the mountain to spend Walpurgis night on the *Blocksberg*, as the Brocken, at 3711 feet (1142 m) the highest mountain in northern Germany, is known in legend and folklore. In *Faust*, published in 1790, Goethe made the myth of the Brocken and its flying witches riding on their brooms famous throughout the world. What he wrote came only partly from his own imagination. When he set about tracing the footsteps of the sorcerer Dr Johannes Faustus (born *circa* 1480), who is himself supposed to have flown through the air, the poet also did research into traditional folk magic.

Goethe had to be "very secretive" when he did this work. And who can wonder? After all, the widespread persecution of witches had only just come to an end. A woman had been executed in Kempten for witchcraft as recently as 1775, and before her, millions had fallen victim to the inquisition set in train by the Catholic Church during the 13th century. The *Hammer of the Witches*, published in 1486, gave detailed instructions on how witches were to be identified and punished.

In ancient times wise women had been highly esteemed for their healing powers. They worked as midwives and healers, and knew methods of contraception and abortion. The Church interpreted these skills as the work of the devil. The final twist was given to the paranoid persecution of these women in Germany by the Leipzig magistrate Praetorius. He described ritual ceremonies, probably fertility rites, which had been taking place on the Brocken since pre-Christian times, as "satanic orgies" in his work *Blocksberg Ceremony, or a Detailed Geographical Report on the High, Ancient, and Famous Blocksberg, Including Descriptions of Flying Witches and Witches' Sabbaths Supposed to be Performed by Demons from All Germany*. As a result, the women who officiated at these ancient ceremonies came to be regarded as witches, while holy stones became the "Devil's Pulpit," or the "Witches' Cauldron."

Goethe mentions a magical ointment, saying that, "it gives the witches courage." There is no doubt that such an ointment was really in use. Various tinctures caused the users to hallucinate that they were flying, or believe that they had been transformed into owls, cats, or other animals. Narcotic drugs like these enabled wise women to escape from their everyday lives for a short while.

Apart from fat, various ingredients were used in the ointments. They included highly toxic wolfsbane (a member of the buttercup family) and plants of the Solanaceae family, such as mandrake, deadly nightshade, henbane, and thorn apple, which are also poisonous. Sometimes fly agaric was mixed in as well. Toad tongues, bat wings, and other non-vegetable ingredients must have been less effective. The ointment was rubbed into the armpits or onto other sensitive parts of the body. Experiments such as those carried out by the Göttingen folklore expert Will-Erich Peukert, who has tried these potions himself, have confirmed that the witches'

ointments contained alkaloids that caused the users to go into trances, hallucinate that they were flying, or fall into fits of uncontrollable laughter. Many of those affected were later convinced that their visions had been real. After drug-induced experiences of this kind other herbs were supposed to have a calming effect, such as Valerian, which was used by the wise women for this purpose. In fact, this herb was often praised for its power to repel witches.

And today? All that is left of the stories of the Blocksberg is a fascinating popular festival that takes place each year during the night of April 30 to May 1 on the Brocken. Since the opening of the border the occasion has attracted tens of thousands of tourists each year to Schierke, Thale, Ilsenburg, and other villages in the Harz Mountains. Witches and goblins, humpbacked toads, and wily magicians get up to all sorts of mischief on the streets and squares, and at midnight performers imitate the flight of the witches – but without the notorious ointment.

Stinkmorchelkompott
Stewed stink horns

A dish to cure hopeless wimps, foul moods, and lovesick lady-killers

1 lb/500 g stink horns
4 cups/1 liter crocodile tears
125 g sweet wood shavings
10 plaited troll hairs
1 tsp ground helebore
250 g cream of curdled lizard milk

Wipe the skin off the stink horns and cut them into fine strips. Bring them to the boil with the crocodile tears, wood shavings, and troll hairs, and stew for 10 minutes. Have a virgin drain them with a silver sieve and mix in the lizard cream widdershins. Enjoy cold.

Since the fall of the G.D.R. the witches of East and West Germany have been reunited and celebrate together.

All those endowed with magical or musical powers come together on the Brocken on the night of 30 April.

A young warrior in a hopeless situation. The witches always have the upper hand on Walpurgis night.

Even witches need a square meal from time to time, such as oat pancakes topped with herb cheese or edam.

No one cares if the oat pancakes have gone out of shape. In the end, things are all a bit askew on the Brocken.

Wise women would learn about the healing powers of plants from books of herbal lore like this one.

Bernburg onion stew

Meat Dishes

Bernburger Zwiebelklump
Bernburg onion stew
(Illustrated above)

1 lb/500 g mutton
3 large onions, chopped coarsely
2 cloves of garlic, finely diced
salt and pepper
1 tsp caraway
1¾ lb/750 g potatoes
1 tbsp cornstarch
2 eggs
2 tbsp croutons

Cut the mutton into bite-sized pieces and boil with the onions, garlic, salt, pepper, and caraway in 8 cups (2 liters) of water with the lid on for approximately 1 hour. While the meat is cooking, peel and wash the potatoes, then grate them coarsely. Wrap the grated potato in a tea towel and press out all the moisture. Put the potato into a bowl straight away and mix with the cornstarch, eggs, and a little salt. With wet hands form the potato mixture into small dumplings. Press a crouton into the center of each dumpling. When the meat is cooked, take it out of the stew and keep warm. Let the dumplings cook through in the stew. Return the meat to the stew, reheat, and serve piping hot.

Harzer Wurzelfleisch
Harz beef with root vegetables
(Illustrated on opposite page, bottom)

2 lb 3 oz/1 kg brisket of beef
1 onion spiked with 2 cloves and a bay leaf
soup vegetables (2 carrots, 2 celery stalks, 1 leek, 1 bunch of parsley)
2 sprigs of marjoram, salt
5 peppercorns
1 lb/500 g root vegetables (carrots, celery, leeks), cut into matchsticks
2 onions, cut into thin slices
2 tbsp butter
1 tsp sweet paprika
2 tbsp vinegar
½ bunch of diced parsley
1 tbsp of freshly grated horseradish

Wash the brisket and set it to cook in 8 cups (2 liters) of water with the spiked onion, soup vegetables, marjoram, salt, and peppercorns. Bring to a boil and leave covered to simmer for 2 hours over a low heat. When it is cooked, lift the meat out and sieve the stock. Keep the meat warm in a small amount of stock. Cook the root vegetables in the stock until they are al dente. While the root vegetables are cooking, fry the onion slices in the butter until they go transparent, salt lightly, dust with paprika, and add vinegar. Cut the brisket into slices approx. half an inch (1 cm) thick, spread the vegetable matchsticks and onion rings on top, and sprinkle with parsley. Serve with freshly grated horseradish.

Altmärkischer Tiegelbraten
Altmark beef in aspic
(Illustrated on opposite page, top)

Serves 6
2 lb 3 oz/1 kg beef
1 lb/500 g belly
4 marrowbones
2 onions, diced
2 cloves of garlic
soup vegetables (2 carrots, 2 celery stalks, 1 leek, 1 bunch of parsley), coarsely chopped
salt
1 tsp whole allspice
½ tsp peppercorns
½ tsp ground ginger
2 bay leaves

Rinse the beef and belly, and put them on the heat with the marrowbones, onions, garlic, and soup vegetables in 8 cups (2 liters) of water. Bring to a boil and cook for one hour. From time to time carefully remove any foam that has formed on the surface of the water. When the meat is cooked, lift the beef, belly, and marrowbones out of the stock and allow them to cool a little. Sieve the stock. Cut the beef and belly into bite-sized pieces, press the marrow out of the bones. Put the meat and bone marrow back into the stock, add salt and the other spices, then reduce over a low heat. Pour the broth into an earthenware dish and leave to cool. Cut into slices before serving.

Köthen cobblers' hot pot

Altmark beef in aspic

Harz beef with root vegetables

Köthener Schusterpfanne
Köthen cobblers' hot pot
(Illustrated center)

2 lb 3 oz/1 kg potatoes
4 stewing pears
1¼ lb/600 g pork belly, cut into slices approximately an inch (2 cm) thick
1 tsp caraway
1 tsp mugwort
salt and pepper

Wash and peel the potatoes. Peel the pears. Cut the potatoes into slices. Quarter and core the pears. Cut the pork belly into strips approximately 1½ inches (4 cm) wide. Layer the ingredients in a casserole, first covering the bottom with half the potatoes, then adding half the pork belly, followed by the pears. Cover the pears with the remaining meat, then lay the rest of the potatoes on top. Season with caraway, mugwort, salt, and pepper, and pour in just enough water to cover everything. Simmer covered for 20 minutes, then place the casserole into an oven preheated to 430 °F (220 °C) and cook until the potatoes are crispy. The dish can be served decorated with a slice of fried pork belly.

The first canned sausages in the world

A new development from Halberstadt revolutionized the meat market in 1896. The first ever canned sausages were put on sale just in time for the inauguration of the Kyffhäuser monument – 40,000 of them. The inventive entrepreneur Friedrich Heine from Halberstadt had succeeded in preserving his fresh, beech-smoked *Halberstädter* sausages in such a way that they could be kept for months. All the same, he must have been biting his nails in the run up to the launch, because before this Heine had endured a number of embarrassing failures. In 1895 an entire batch of sausages went off before he could deliver them to the excited Duke of Wernigerode. The problem was how to heat the sausages to a temperature over 212 °F (100 °C) without the skins splitting. Eventually it was decided to copy the procedure used to can asparagus, which proved a success.

So business began to flourish. Around the turn of the century *Halberstädter* sausages were to be found on the menu in almost every railway station restaurant in Germany. By 1913 Heine's company had become the largest meat processing factory in Europe. In 1930 his

premium product won the Grand Prix at the World Exhibition in Antwerp. Other prizes followed. In the G.D.R. *Halberstädter* sausages were regarded as highly desirable meat products. If you were traveling on the train between Halberstadt and Stralsund known as the "Sausage Express" you might be lucky enough to persuade the *Mitropa* catering staff to give you a can. The sausages were sold in West Germany until 1971, when the G.D.R. government stopped exports to "the non-Socialist economic area" due to supply problems. After the collapse of the G.D.R. the former export earner was one of the first East German products to penetrate the West German market. *Halberstädter* sausages in natural gut are unique in Europe because they are still smoked in Heine's original smoke house as they always have been, before maturing for 24 to 36 hours under conditions of closely controlled air humidity and room temperature.

Of course, the exact recipe is a commercial secret. The only clues we have to go by are the ingredients given on the label: pork, beef, bacon, freshwater, nitrite curing salt, milk protein, stabilizer E 331, spices, sugar.

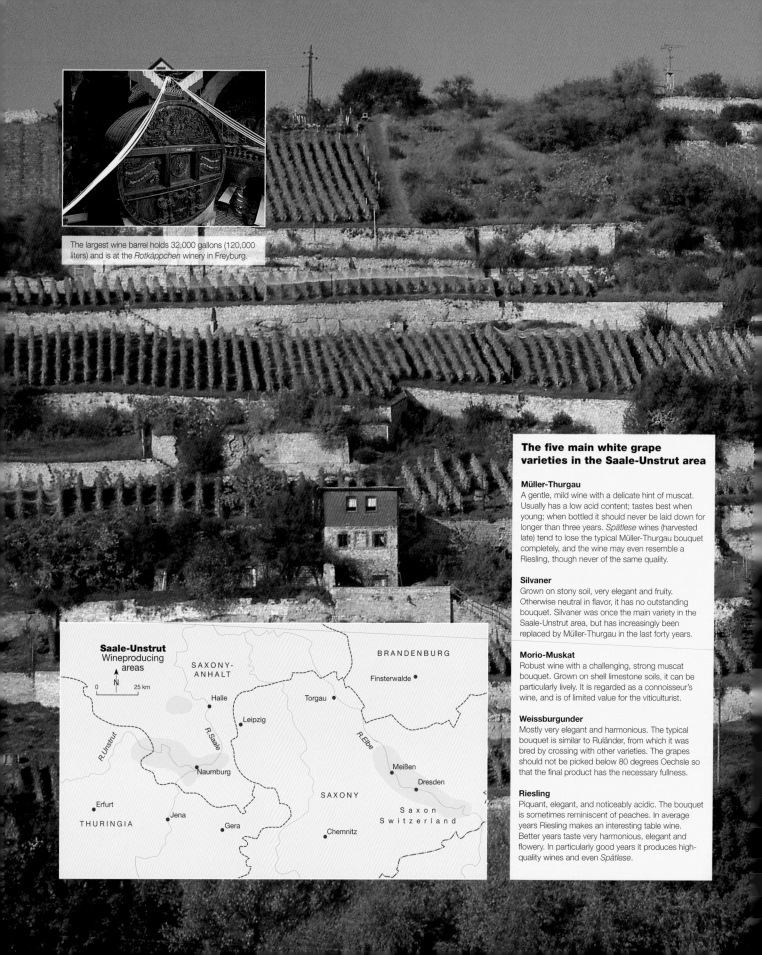

The largest wine barrel holds 32,000 gallons (120,000 liters) and is at the *Rotkäppchen* winery in Freyburg.

The five main white grape varieties in the Saale-Unstrut area

Müller-Thurgau

A gentle, mild wine with a delicate hint of muscat. Usually has a low acid content; tastes best when young; when bottled it should never be laid down for longer than three years. *Spätlese* wines (harvested late) tend to lose the typical Müller-Thurgau bouquet completely, and the wine may even resemble a Riesling, though never of the same quality.

Silvaner

Grown on stony soil, very elegant and fruity. Otherwise neutral in flavor, it has no outstanding bouquet. Silvaner was once the main variety in the Saale-Unstrut area, but has increasingly been replaced by Müller-Thurgau in the last forty years.

Morio-Muskat

Robust wine with a challenging, strong muscat bouquet. Grown on shell limestone soils, it can be particularly lively. It is regarded as a connoisseur's wine, and is of limited value for the viticulturist.

Weissburgunder

Mostly very elegant and harmonious. The typical bouquet is similar to Ruländer, from which it was bred by crossing with other varieties. The grapes should not be picked below 80 degrees Oechsle so that the final product has the necessary fullness.

Riesling

Piquant, elegant, and noticeably acidic. The bouquet is sometimes reminiscent of peaches. In average years Riesling makes an interesting table wine. Better years taste very harmonious, elegant and flowery. In particularly good years it produces high-quality wines and even *Spätlese*.

Saale-Unstrut
Wineproducing areas

0   25 km
N

SAXONY-ANHALT

BRANDENBURG

Finsterwalde

Halle

Torgau

R. Saale

Leipzig

R. Elbe

R. Unstrut

Naumburg

Meißen

Dresden

SAXONY

Saxon Switzerland

Erfurt

Jena

Gera

Chemnitz

THURINGIA

Auerhahn und Rotkäppchen

A toast from the east

During the 1990s the capercaillie has become something of a star in the world of advertising. This relative of the grouse features prominently on the label of Hasseröder Premium Pils, which has risen in just a few years to become one of the most successful East German beer brands. The cool, golden foaming beer from the foot of the Brocken may have been regarded as a secret tip for many years by G.D.R. citizens, but the new management team can hardly have reckoned on a boom of such proportions after German reunification. This subsidiary of Gilde Brauerei AG Hanover now produces nearly 53 million gallons (two million hectoliters) of beer a year and is on the way to conquering the whole German market.

This is a fantastic story at a time when the German brewing industry as a whole is stagnating, the Germans are tending to drink less beer, and major management consultants are advising radical restructuring in the industry. Nevertheless, *Hasseröder* is not an isolated success. "East German brewers see off competition," the newspapers were saying at the end of 1996. The companies there seem to be on the right track with their belief in "going back to traditional brewing." After all, the Wernesgrüner Brauerei in Vogtland (Saxony) can reflect on a history that goes back to the year 1436. And the first Pilsner-style beer brewed in Germany comes from Radeberg near Dresden. All the same, all the traditional brewing methods have not been taken over. Today *Pubarschknall* from Quedlinburg no longer has dire effects on the digestion, as its name suggests, because the popular brown beer now comes onto the market fully fermented.

Apart from this, drinkers can also experiment with new products, such as mix drinks like *Potzblitz* (beer and lemonade) from the Garley Spezialitäten Brauerei in Gardelegen. Other novelties include creations like the light, sweet Christmas beer made with a special kind of malt by the Stadtbrauerei Olbernhau in the Erzgebirge; while in Leipzig people are toasting each other again with good old *Gose*, a top-fermented wheat beer.

It is not just the brewing sector that has experienced a renaissance since the fall of the wall, but also the most northerly winegrowing area in Europe. Since the reunification ever more small and large winegrowers have been setting to work on the gentle hills that skirt the Saale and the Unstrut rivers. They are continuing a thousand-year-old year old tradition that began in 998 and saw its first great flowering with the founding of the Cistercian monastery at Pforta in 1137.

The growing demand from throughout Germany is

proof that the wines from Bad Kösen, Freyburg, Naumburg, and the surrounding areas have been successful in widening their appeal. The only problem is the limited supply: the entire area of land covered with vines is just 480 patchwork hectares (1185 acres). The extensive use of terraced slopes ensures the quality of the wines, and average production is around 40 to 50 hectoliters per hectare (425–535 gallons per acre). Traditionally almost all the wines produced are dry whites. One third of the vines are *Müller-Thurgau*. However, the white grapes Weissburgunder, Silvaner, Riesling, Bacchus, Gutedel, Traminer, Morio-Muscat, and the reds Portugieser, Spätburgunder, André, Dornfelder, Lemberger, and Zwiegelt are all cultivated in the Saale-Unstrut area.

The shell limestone and sandstone soils, and a particularly favorable microclimate on the slopes of the river valleys, create the unmistakable character typical of the Saale-Unstrut wines. Nevertheless, every harvest remains a risk if the winegrowers are aiming for more than average results. "We are not in the Palatinate here," emphasizes vintner Uwe Lützkendorf from Bad Kösen, "The continental climate hits us pretty hard." This is why it is necessary to make use of every last ray of sunshine. If there is any doubt about the grapes, the harvest may start as late as November. *Auslese* and *Beerenauslese* wines made from exceptionally mature grapes are a rarity.

The Saale-Unstrut vintners were kept on a short leash by the G.D.R. authorities, just like their colleagues in Saxony. There were no private vineyards, and amateur winegrowers made wine for their own requirements or delivered their grapes to a vintners' cooperative. It was difficult to obtain rootstocks, and even the state vineyard at Bad Kösen (founded in 1899 as the *Staatliche Weinbauverwaltung Naumberg* by the Prussian government), which produced about 500,000 liters (130,000 gallons) of wine a year, had to work with decrepit, antiquated machinery.

G.D.R. citizens were seldom able to savor Saale-Unstrut wines. The supermarket in Bad Kösen stocked locally made wines almost only on special occasions. However, it goes without saying that foreign guests staying in the exclusive Interhotels were able to enjoy these delights, for hard currency only. Those days have long gone. Today the association representing the winegrowers in Freyburg/Unstrut alone has about 750 members. The state vineyard was taken over by the Federal State of Saxony-Anhalt in 1993 and renamed the Landesweingut Kloster Pforta. What is more, about 15 new private vineyards have been established, some of them with great success.

These triumphs appear almost modest, though, in comparison with the huge turnover achieved by the Rotkäppchen winery in Freyburg. Just a few years after the collapse of the G.D.R. it had established itself as the fourth largest producer of sparkling wines in Germany. Rotkäppchen sparkling wine has been fizzing away for a hundred years.

The cheese that lives

"They're mad in Wurchwitz," opine sensitive gourmets when they learn for the first time of the most peculiar cheese in Saxony-Anhalt. However, it is not the 350 inhabitants of this small village near Zeitz who do the hard work on real *Würchwitzer Spinnenkäse*, but tiny relatives of the domestic dust mite (*Tyrogliphus casei L.*) one hundredth of an inch (0.3 mm) long. Hundreds of thousands of these creatures crawl cheerfully over balls of quark, turning them into a gourmet delicacy over the course of a few months. The eight-legged invertebrates receive poor thanks for all their labors. When their work is done they are simply eaten along with the cheese.

Such rough manners are part of a tradition that goes back a good 500 years. For 30 years the biology teacher and trained farmer Helmut Pöschel was the only person in the village to offer the "cheese mites" a home. There are now plenty of other people in the village who share his passion.

The recipe: Take a wooden case full of cheese mites, feed them every day with rye flour, and give them dried organic quark made without preservatives. The mites' excretions permeate the cheese by diffusion. The enzymes they contain cause the cheese to ripen. After about a month the outer skin turns yellow; after three months it is reddish brown. However, lovers of the cheese wait a whole year for it to become a black lump, and only eat it then.

The taste is described as similar to the cheeses produced in the Harz Mountains, but with a more bitter flavor. The cheese can be tasted every year at the Würchwitz Mite Cheese Festival in June. It is served with bread, and beer or cocoa. In earlier times the fully ripened cheese was sucked like a sweet. These morsels are so rich in protein that one is even claimed to have saved the life of a Stalingrad veteran. Recently biochemists have also taken an interest. According to Pöschel it is noticeable that people who acquire a taste for *Spinnenkäse* never suffer from allergies caused by house dust. "The cheese acts as an oral vaccination," concludes the biologist.

With the aim of keeping the animals healthy Helmut Pöschel has established contacts with cheese producers who use the same method in the northern Spanish city of Oviedo. Now German and Spanish mites are to be crossed to "introduce some fresh blood," opening the way for the mighty Euro-mite!

The mites have exacting standards. They are only interested in high quality organic quark.

The demanding mites have to be fed with fresh rye flour every day.

After three months the cheese is ripe and is eaten along with the tiny invertebrates.

Spinnenkäse can be sampled every year at the mite cheese festival in June. Many lovers of the delicacy prefer to drink cocoa with it instead of beer.

The secret of mite cheese viewed through a microscope. Hundreds of thousands of these mites turn quark into Würchwitzer Spinnenkäse.

CHRISTA WACHENFELD

Berlin

The opinion expressed by the ethnologist Georg
Forster when he wrote about the city at the end of the
18th century was hardly flattering: "Berlin is certainly
one of the most beautiful cities in Europe. But its
inhabitants! Hospitality and refined enjoyment –
corrupted into extravagance, bad taste, and, I should
venture to say, gluttony."
With its magnificent boulevards, historic buildings, and
extensive areas of parkland, Berlin is certainly still
beautiful. As far as the gluttony is concerned, Forster's
verdict is surely out of date. What the visitor does notice
about the Berliners is their inclination to have a little
snack now and then between meals, because, as the
writer Kurt Tucholsky said, a Berliner has no time. Berlin
food is simple and wholesome: solid, basic fare that
betrays influences from a variety of different cuisines
introduced by different immigrant groups over the years.
Berlin has been giving refuge to victims of religious
persecution from other countries for centuries: fifty
Jewish families driven out of Vienna in 1671 and
thousands of French Huguenots after 1685. Their salads,
vegetable varieties, and sausage and fricassee recipes
have permanently enriched the city's cuisine.
When the German Empire was founded in 1871, the
Prussian royal capital rose to become the capital of all
Germany. The spectacular rate at which the city's
industrial base was growing attracted people looking
for work from all areas of the country, particularly
from Pomerania and Silesia. It is often said that all real
Berliners can trace their roots back to Breslau (now
known by its Polish name Wroclaw).
The city's cultural life flourished during the 1920s. It
developed into a Mecca for the avant garde, and the
"Romanisches Café" became a legendary meeting
place for artists and intellectuals. This era came to an
end in 1933. On January 30, 1933 a torchlight parade of
Nazi troops marched through the Brandenburg Gate.
After the Second World War the city was divided. The
construction of the Berlin Wall hermetically sealed the
eastern part of the city from the west until 1989, when
the G.D.R. government lifted border controls. In 1991
it was decided that Berlin was to be the Federal capital.
Most of the German Federal Government moved there
in 1999, and the city is now well on the way to
regaining its international role.

Left: The Berliners call the Victory Column *Goldelse* (Golden Else). It was
opened in 1873, and has 285 steps leading to the viewing platform at the
top, from where visitors can look out over the city and the many new
government buildings.

The birthplace of the Currywurst

The spice of life

The whole world seems to have fallen in love with it. The man and woman in the street cannot get enough of it, though they occasionally think about the calories with a shudder of guilt. Many of the rich and famous have also revealed themselves to be among its innumerable fans. It has even starred in a popular television series about three women running a snack bar. Serious politicians show that they are in touch with modern trends by talking of it with confident reverence and admitting frankly to an uncontrollable desire, what the Berliners call *Jieper*, for a *Currywurst*. However, the story that, when he was Mayor of Berlin, the former Federal President Richard von Weizsäcker spontaneously dragged the American President George Bush

from the Schöneberg City Hall to the closest Currywurst stall is nothing but a rumor.

It all began in a small snack bar on Stuttgarter Platz on September 4, 1949. It was raining cats and dogs, and there was not a soul in sight. In order to pass the time, and because she liked eating spicy food, the owner of the sausage stall Herta Heuwer started experimenting. She mixed and tasted, played around with all kinds of spices, then added plenty of tomato puree, pouring the resulting concoction over a fried sausage cut up into bite-sized chunks. The first Currywurst was ready. The proud inventor's signboards were soon boasting of her shop's unique place in culinary history: "1st Currywurst sellers in the world," and, "We invented this Berlin specialty!"

In Berlin a real *Berliner Currywurst* is not just a *Dampfwurst* (steamed sausage) or a simple *Brühwurst* (scalded sausage), as in other parts of Germany, but, according to a definition given by the State Office for Veterinary Medicine and Food Safety, "a fried, scalded sausage with a fine texture that has been prepared to be served with curry sauce." Very few snack bars use an exclusive,

homemade mix of spices. The sausage is usually served with a processed tomato sauce based on ketchup. The original mixture still remains a secret. The mother of the Currywurst had her successful recipe patented as "Chillup Sauce."

There is no way of avoiding the fact that it is impossible to indulge in this apparently simple pleasure without first having answered the most important question of all: with or without? Sausage with gut or without? This may appear a trifling point, but it is almost a matter of faith for devoted Currywurst lovers.

The counterpart to the Currywurst at Berlin snack bars is the ever present *Currybulette*, a rissole served with the same curry sauce. All these establishments also serve Wiener ("Viennese") sausages, which, despite their name, are, in fact, real Berliners. Then there is the *Bockwurst*, another Berlin original. A group of thirsty students who had gone out drinking one evening ordered a publican at the Görlitzer Bahnhof station to serve a basket full of round, thick sausages with a strong beer known as Bockbier – hence the name.

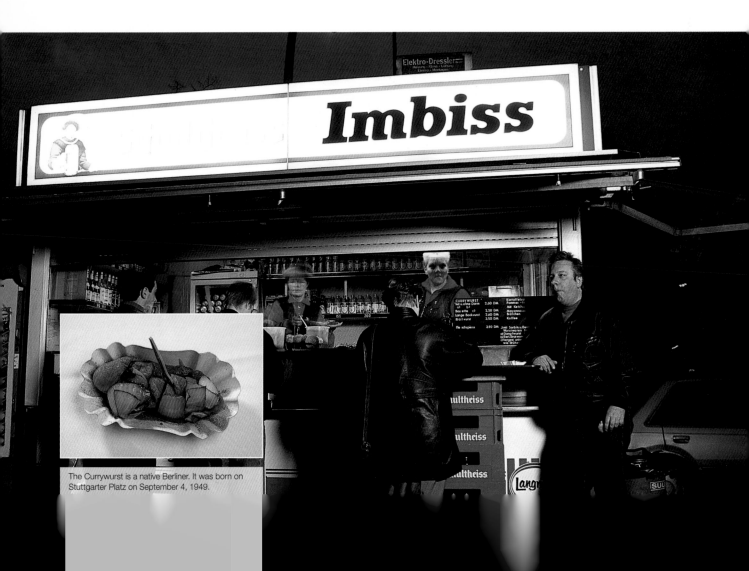

The Currywurst is a native Berliner. It was born on Stuttgarter Platz on September 4, 1949.

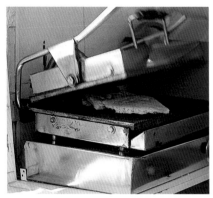
Doner kebab is not served with a normal bread roll. The finely cut slices of meat from the turning spit are served in white, unleavened bread warmed on the grill.

Every kebab shop has its own way of preparing the kebab. Some spread a garlic sauce directly onto the bread, others garnish the assembled doner with tsatsiki.

Thin slices of roasted meat are carefully shaved from the column with a sharp knife while the spit continues to turn.

These pieces of meat are laid onto the warmed bread to form the heart of the kebab. Kebabs can be of lamb, veal, beef, or even chicken.

There is plenty of scope for creativity when it comes to the salad garnish: this shop serves doner with finely sliced onions, iceberg lettuce, and grated cabbage.

Finally, the kebab is topped with tomatoes. Now the whole thing is rolled up – and eaten with such skill and grace that only half of it falls onto the floor!

A new favorite from Kreuzberg

The doner kebab

In January 1995 the German newspaper *Bild* reported from Berlin on a new trend in the fast food industry in its usual breathless fashion: "Snack Wars: Doner Skewers Bockwurst."

Indeed, since then the doner kebab has won the competition against the Currywurst and now occupies the top of the fast food hit parade with nearly 100 million doner portions served each year, compared to roughly 70 million Currywurst. There were about 200 kebab shops operating in Berlin in 1983; now their numbers have expanded to about 1300 outlets, which sell about 25 tons of "rotating roast," as *doner kebab* translates into English, every day. The annual turnover of all the kebab shops in Germany is about 2 billion Euros, which is more than the combined takings of McDonald's, Burger King, and the German fast food chain Wienerwald.

Things did not look so rosy for the kebab industry in the doner capital Berlin only a few years ago. It looked then as though the success story that began in 1971 with the first vertical, rotating spit in Kreuzberg might be heading for an unhappy end. Sales had fallen by more than 20 percent at a time when overheads were rising.

The opening of the Berlin Wall and German reunification brought a happy turn in events for the kebab shops of Berlin, threatened with bankruptcy as they were. The Turkish fast food specialty evidently appealed to the taste buds of the new citizens of the German Federal Republic, who consume about 450,000 doner kebabs every day.

The doner kebab had already been in the headlines of the Berlin newspapers towards the end of the 1980s, when the less salubrious side of the success story was brought to light. Quantity did not mean quality, and as sales increased, more and more shortcuts were taken by the kebab shops. Instead of using layers of veal, beef, or lamb piled on top of each other to form a substantial, rounded column, a large proportion of ground meat was added, and padded out with flour and diphosphates. This was a case for the German regulations on ground meat, to which the doner kebab was made subject from 1984. In the end, a joint commission of Turkish and German experts met to discuss how to restore respectability to the doner kebab. On June 1, 1989 they issued a definition of "doner kebab" appended to the city of Berlin's consumer goods regulations, stipulating the proportion of ground meat in a doner kebab should be no greater than 60 percent.

Kebab shops serve their wares either in sliced pocket-shaped pita breads or in unleavened bread that is first warmed and then rolled up with the meat inside. The bread is also filled with lettuce, tomato, gherkin, onion, and yogurt-garlic sauce.

Opposite: A snack stall. Hurried passers-by fortify themselves while neighbors meet to gossip over a Currywurst.

Meat dishes

Königsberger Klopse
Königsberg meatballs
(Illustrated left)

1 stale bread roll
½ cup/125 ml hot milk
1 lb/500 g mixed ground meat
1 small onion, finely chopped
4 anchovy fillets, finely chopped
1 egg
salt and pepper
4 cups/1 liter meat stock
1 tbsp/15 g butter
2 tbsp flour
3 tbsp capers
2 tbsp lemon juice
1 pinch of sugar
2 egg yolks
½ cup/125 g cream
1 tbsp chopped parsley

Cut the bread roll into slices and soak for 15 minutes in the hot milk. Then knead the bread together with the ground meat, onion, anchovy fillets, and egg, seasoning with salt and pepper. Form the mixture into small meatballs. Bring the meat stock to a boil, add the meatballs, and cook for 15 minutes. Remove them with a skimmer and sieve the stock. Melt the butter and sweat the flour. Pour on 3 cups (750 ml) of stock, stirring all the time, and mix in the capers. Reduce for 10 minutes. Reheat the meatballs in the sauce (which must not be allowed to boil again) and season with lemon juice, salt, pepper, and sugar. Whisk the egg yolk with the cream and stir into the sauce. Sprinkle with chopped parsley and serve immediately.

Schnitzel Holstein
Escalopes of veal
(Illustrated top)

4 escalopes of veal, weighing about 6 oz/150 g each
salt and pepper
oil for frying
4 pieces of sliced bread
1 tbsp/15 g butter
4 sardines in oil
4 small slices of smoked salmon
8 anchovy fillets
1 small jar of caviar (½ oz/15 g)
4 eggs
gherkins and lemons to garnish

Season the escalopes with salt and pepper, then fry for four minutes on each side in the oil. While the meat is cooking, toast the bread, spread thinly with butter, and cut each slice diagonally into four triangles. For each portion spread one triangle of toast with a sardine, one with smoked salmon, one with two anchovy fillets, and one with caviar. Place the cooked escalopes on warmed plates and keep warm. Fry 4 eggs in the meat juices, season with salt and pepper, and place on top of the escalopes. Arrange the triangles of toast around the escalopes, and garnish with gherkins and slices of lemon.

Berliner Kalbsleber
Berlin calf liver
(Illustrated bottom)

4 small onions
2 cooking apples
8 tsp/40 g butter
4 slices of calf liver, weighing about 6 oz/150 g each
flour
8 tsp/40 g clarified butter
salt and pepper

Slice the onions into fine rings. Core and peel the apples, then cut them into slices, but not too thinly. Heat the butter, and fry the onion rings and apple slices. While the onion and apple are cooking, coat the calf livers in flour. Knock off any excess flour and fry the livers in hot clarified butter for 3–4 minutes on each side. Season the livers with salt and pepper, and place on warmed plates with the onion rings and apple slices. Serve with creamed potatoes.

Escalopes of veal

Königsberg meatballs

Berlin calf liver

Eisbein mit Kraut
Knuckle of pork with sauerkraut

4 pickled knuckles of pork, weighing about 14 oz/400 g each
3 onions
4 bay leaves
5 white peppercorns
5 whole allspice berries
sugar
1 tbsp/15 g clarified butter
1¾ lbs/800 g sauerkraut
5 juniper berries

Rinse the knuckles of pork. Bring 12 cups/3 liters of water to a boil in a large pan and put in the knuckles. Peel and quarter 2 onions, and add to the knuckles with 2 bay leaves, the peppercorns, whole allspice berries, and ½ teaspoon of sugar. Put the lid on and cook for 1½ hours over a low heat. Remove the knuckles and sieve the stock. Chop the remaining onion finely, and fry until transparent in clarified butter. Add the sauerkraut, crushed juniper berries, and the remaining bay leaves, then pour on 2 cups (500 ml) of the stock. Place the knuckles of pork on top of the sauerkraut and cook for a further 40 minutes with the lid on. Serve with boiled potatoes or pease pudding.

In loving memory

Egon Erwin Kisch is one of the classics of German journalism. His best known work, *Der rasende Reporter* ("The racing reporter"), was published in 1924 in Berlin. Its title became a byword for the literature of the "New Objectivity." Kisch was born in Prague in 1885, trained as a journalist in Berlin and lived in the German capital from 1921 to 1933. As a Jew, a Communist, and an Antifascist, he was forced to leave Germany in 1933.

In the 1920s Kisch came across a curious tradition on his wanderings through Berlin. On slaughtering day the butchers placed stools with white aprons laid over them at the entrances to their shops. According to an old Berlin custom this signaled to the customers without the need for any other announcement that "today there is fresh *Blutwurst* (blood sausage) and Leberwurst (liver sausage)." "The racing reporter" gave an amused account of the origins of this marketing ploy, which dated back to the 18th century. It originated with a butcher and *Budike* (see page 68) owner called Friebel on the Molkenmarkt. Every Friday, after he had finished his slaughtering, he would step out in front of his shop wearing a gleaming white apron in order to catch a little fresh air and, at the same time, to announce by this act that there was now fresh Blutwurst to be had. When Friebel fell ill and became paralyzed, his wife continued his work. On slaughtering day she would settle her husband in a chair in front of the shop. After his death she placed an empty chair by the door, complete with a white apron. The aproned chair was copied by the competition and soon came to be used by all the butchers in the city. To a certain extent, bars and restaurants selling *Eisbein* are continuing this tradition when they hang up white banners outside with red slogans praising the meat dishes on the menu.

Kasseler mit Kraut
Kasseler with sauerkraut

4 raw Kasseler ribs, weighing about 7 oz/200 g each
1 onion studded with 1 bay leaf and 2 cloves
soup vegetables (2 carrots, 2 celery stalks, I leek, 1 bunch of parsley), coarsely chopped
5 peppercorns
1 tbsp/15 g clarified butter
2 onions, chopped
1¾ lbs/800 g sauerkraut
1 pinch of sugar
½ tsp coarsely milled pepper
½ cup/125 ml white wine

Rinse the Kasseler ribs. Bring the studded onion, soup vegetables, and peppercorns to a boil in 4 cups (1 liter) of water. Add the ribs, cover, and simmer over a low heat for 30 minutes. While the ribs are cooking, heat the clarified butter, and fry the chopped onion until it is transparent. Add the sauerkraut, season with sugar and pepper, and pour on ½ cup (125 ml) of the stock in which the ribs have been cooking. Finally, stir the white wine into the sauerkraut. Serve the sauerkraut and ribs on warmed plates with boiled potatoes.

Eisbein and Kasseler

It was love at first bite in the cellar bar "Zum strammen Hund," "a piece of real Berlin that had crawled underground" at the end of Friedrichstrasse, where the Swabian student Theodor Heuss, a future President of the Federal Republic of Germany, first tasted *Eisbein* (knuckle of pork), a robust flavor that he would continue to enjoy for the rest of his life. *Eisbein* with pease pudding and sauerkraut is the meal that every Berliner loves. Marlene Dietrich, who was born in Berlin, claimed that it was her favorite dish. As the name suggests, *Eisbein* (literally, "ice-leg"), is associated with the coldest time of the year, when lakes and rivers freeze over. In earlier times, when

metalwork was still at a primitive stage, the blades of skates were made from the most resistant bone of the pig, the shin, which, according to the food historians, was first pickled in the 19th century at a Budike not far from the Görlitzer Bahnhof station and served by the landlord as *Eisbein*.

Before the days of refrigeration and freezing, the need to conserve food was a spur to inventiveness. At around the same time a butcher called Cassel with a shop on Potsdamer Strasse was experimenting with his own pork creation. He smoked a large piece of pork loin and left it to mature in brine: the famous *Kasseler* had been born. This style of meat preparation was not invented in the city of Kassel, as most people assume, but in Schöneberg, which was an independent village beyond the gates of Berlin at the time. Traditionally, salting the meat was a lengthy business, but "time is money," and the meat is now injected with salt to speed up the whole process.

Hoppelpoppel

1 lb/500 g boiled or roasted meat (leftovers)
2 onions, chopped
4 tbsp clarified butter
1½ lbs/750 g potatoes boiled in their skins
1 tsp caraway, coarsely chopped
salt and pepper
8 eggs
1 bunch of parsley, chopped

Cut the meat into thin strips and fry quickly with the onions in 2 tablespoons of clarified butter. Cut the potatoes into slices, put them into another skillet, and fry with the caraway, salt, and pepper in the rest of the clarified butter until golden brown. Mix the meat in with the potatoes. Whisk the eggs, pour over the meat and potatoes, and sprinkle with parsley. Carefully stir until the eggs set, then serve immediately with green salad.

Pubs and Bars

The model for the typical Berlin *Eckkneipe* (street corner bar) was London, where cheap porter pubs began to spring up in Westminster towards the end of the 18th century. They soon became a common sight on the street corners of the newly developed working class areas. In place of the small serving hatches common till then, they had long bars, at which the thirsty customers could stand to chat over a beer or drain a swift glass of gin. Half a century later, as industry began to develop in Germany, the first *Eckkneipen* with modern bars were opened in proletarian Berlin. There was a terrible shortage of living space in the city. Working families would rent places to sleep to unmarried colleagues in their often damp, unhealthy apartments. It was not unusual for these lodgers to share a bed on a shift system. For men forced to live in such circumstances it was an obvious step to go to the local *Kneipe* (bar) and use it as a public living room. It became part of the everyday working-class culture and functioned for many people as a substitute family. There were about 13,000 *Eckkneipen* in Berlin at the end of the 19th century. On average almost every building in the working-class quarters had a bar.

One remarkable institution at the beginning of the 20th century was the *Bulljong-Keller* (bouillon, or broth cellar), which only opened at 10 o'clock in the evening and, apart from bouillon, had nothing but alcohol-free drinks on the menu. However, when the regulars ordered a "cold broth," all became clear. There was no need for them to go without their beer and schnaps chaser after all.

Of the approximately 3000 *Kneipen* in existence today, about half are located on street corners. However, their numbers are in constant decline. Many landlords can no longer bear the rental costs, which have risen steeply in recent years. Chic designer bistros, with their exorbitantly priced champagnes and cocktails, banks, retailers, and fast food chains occupy desirable locations and are prepared to pay the highest prices.

The words *Kneipe* and *Pinte* are not Berlin expressions, but are generally used throughout Germany. *Kneipe* comes originally from the student slang of the 19th century, when student fencing fraternities flourished in Germany. The members of these groups would throw themselves passionately into fierce duels and manfully cross swords with each other, only to meet afterwards on the friendliest of terms for a communal drinking session, or *Kneipabend*. *Pinte* derives from the Latin verb *pingere*, meaning "to paint," and refers to the painted oaken boards used as signs outside bars. *Budike*, *Destille*, and *Kaschemme* are all original Berlin expressions. *Budike* comes from the French word *boutique*, meaning "shop" or "bar." *Destillen* had the right to distil schnaps and sell it on the premises. *Kaschemme* denotes a seedy, third-class drinking hole and comes from the thieves' cant of the criminal underworld.

No old Berlin pub is complete without a *Hungerturm* ("hunger tower"), an open glass case displaying pickled eggs, rissoles, rollmops, pickled gherkins, ground pork rolls, and boned pork chops in aspic. Today the case must close and have a built in cooling system if it is to comply with statutory regulations.

Zille's Berlin

"From the back of the house the children peep out. Pale and uncombed, some with shirts, some without. . . That was his milieu, that was your milieu. Every Kneipe and Destille knows good Father Zille." These are the words of a song sung by the legendary Berlin street ballad singer and vaudeville performer Claire Waldoff in memory of her friend of many years, the draftsman and caricaturist Heinrich Zille (1858–1929).

Zille's milieu was the Berlin of the workers, *Destillen* and *Kaschemmen*, drinkers, prostitutes, and paupers. His drawings depicted the living conditions in the slum quarters with great realism and a shot of black humor: the cramped conditions in the overcrowded apartments, the dark rear courtyards, the tenement blocks, and the misery of the children who had to grow up there.

In Zille's day Berlin had more tenements than any other city in the world. Due to massive influx of migrants from rural areas the population had grown from 450,000 in 1855 to about two million in 1905. Blocks of apartments with side wings, lateral extensions, and up to five rear courtyards were thrown up overnight in the most cramped spaces. The first tenement blocks were built in the early 19th century close to the Hamburger Tor in "Vogtland," as the settlement was known after the region where the migrants came from. Each building housed about 2500 people, who lived crammed together in 400 one-room apartments. In 1843 Bettina von Arnim attacked the inhuman conditions in this poverty-stricken district in her book *This Book Belongs to the King*. She illustrated the misery of Vogtland's inhabitants by giving detailed accounts of their financial problems, explaining the situation of a family with a monthly income of six and a half *Talers*, of which two *Talers* went on rent.

In 1847 the harvest failed, and the price of the main foodstuff, potatoes, spiraled upward with

The lives and living conditions of Berlin's workers were the themes of the artist Heinrich Zille. His work *Der späte Schlafbursche* (*The Late Lodger*) shows the suffocating, cramped conditions endured by many people in the 19th century.

Porridge, one of the oldest foods known to mankind, is eaten by the poor around the world.

shocking rapidity. There were disturbances that spread into the center of the city, and only when the military intervened and a maximum potato price was set were the authorities able to pacify the revolt. Just like the food riots in the Paris markets before the French Revolution in 1789, the "potato troubles" were an early warning of the 1848 revolution.

One person who sought to alleviate poverty in Berlin was the women's rights activist Lina Morgenstern, known popularly as "Suppenlina" (Soup Lina). In 1866, during the Prusso-Austrian war, when food was short and much more expensive as a result, she founded the *Volksküchen* (people's kitchens), which drew on the ideas of the cooperative movement. The start-up capital came from calls for donations published in the *Vossische Zeitung* newspaper, after which the project paid for itself. The intention was not to relieve the poor by simply giving them alms. Rather, the food was purchased at lower prices by buying in bulk. Middle-class women volunteered to prepare the meals and sold them at cost price. Whole families gathered around the wooden tables at Lina's soup kitchen. It was not just that working-class households were short of money, there was simply not enough time to cook, as most women had to work in the factories. When she was attacked by conservative critics, who claimed that the *Volksküchen* would destroy domestic family life, Lina Morgenstern argued that it was not the soup kitchens, but social conditions, that would have to be changed.

In 1883 the journalist Konstantin Liebich founded a center to provide breakfasts for the homeless and needy. Each person received two bread rolls and a cup of *ersatz* coffee. The Inner Mission, a Christian group based in Wedding, later continued Liebich's initiative and went down in the history of Berlin charity as the "bread-roll church."

Today, at the beginning of the 21st century, over four million unemployed present Germany's affluent, modern society with serious problems. The numbers of homeless and needy are increasing, and the gap between the poor and the rich is growing ever wider. Aid is provided by the German Red Cross and schemes run by charitable organizations, churches, and volunteer groups. For example, there is the soup kitchen in the Franciscan monastery at Pankow, which serves a meat dish once in the week, stews on the other days. They give out 400 to 500 meals a day in summer, and half as many in winter – during the colder months many homeless people find lodgings in hostels where they can get food and a bed for the night.

Founded in 1993 and modeled on the example of a New York volunteer group, the *Berliner Tafel* bridges the gap between those who are in need and those who have food to spare, such as supermarkets, wholesale suppliers, industrial catering providers, and restaurants. The donors give fruit and vegetables a little past their best and groceries just before their sell-by date, which are collected and distributed to appropriate welfare projects. Each month the 70 volunteers work a total of 1400 hours and handle over 40 tons of food.

Soups and stews

How can she feed the rich uncle from Silesia, the impoverished major's widow asks herself in Fontane's novel *Die Poggenpuhls* (*The Poggenpuhls*) (1895–1896). Her pragmatic daughter knows what to do: "Well, I'd say: wheat beer soup with sago, he enjoyed that so much the last time." As this extract shows, beer soup is enjoyed by rich and poor alike.

Since the Middle Ages beer soup has been a common dish in Germany, and has generally been consumed in the morning for breakfast. It once used to be thickened stodgily with flour so that it made a filling meal. It has, however, been refined over the centuries with the addition of lemon peel, cinnamon, sugar, and raisins, as well as egg yolk, which combine to give the soup the final, stylish touch.

With the exception of *Bouillon mit Markklösschen* (bouillon with bone marrow dumplings) the typical Berlin soups are not starters. They are made to keep body and soul together. In fact, they are really stews. Like his subjects, the last German Emperor, a notoriously fast eater, loved potato soup made with ham bones. However, while the ordinary people had to content themselves with sausages as an accompaniment, William II had his favorite dish served with brisket of beef.

Pea soup was sometimes eaten with pig's ears and snout, sometimes with Kasseler or bacon. In the 19th century it was a popular way to end a night on the town, and revelers would spoon it in the gray of dawn. It also inspired Heinrich Heine to a little poem while he was living in Berlin:

> I wish that all my love songs
> Were flowers by the score:
> I'd send them, sweet and fragrant,
> To my darling's door. …
>
> I wish that all my love songs
> Were little peas galore:
> I'd make a pea soup of them –
> A tasty one, what's more.

Manna from heaven

"You people of the world, you people of America, England, France, Italy! Look upon this city and know that you must not abandon it or its people, that you cannot abandon them!" The speech that Ernst Reuter gave at a demonstration of 300,000 Berliners during the Berlin Blockade has gone down in legend. In response to the extension of the economic reforms already introduced in the Western Zones of Germany to the Western Sectors of Berlin, the Soviets imposed a blockade on June 24, 1948, cutting off the western part of the city from its transport connections by land and water. Stalin wanted to force the Western Allies to give the city up by starving its population. He achieved the complete opposite: the triumphal victory of the West in the first great struggle of the Cold War. Following an order given on June 25 by the city's American Military Governor, General Clay, the air bridge was opened officially on June 26. Two days later Great Britain also announced that it would be taking part. Feeding the city's almost 2.2 million inhabitants by air was a unique logistic operation in the history of aviation. The Tempelhof and Gatow airports were extended. 19,000 Berlin workers labored to build a new airport in Tegel at record speed within three months. The increase in capacity was massive. The 500 flights flown in the first month carried just 1404 U.S. tons (1273.6 tonnes) of supplies, but at the high point of the operation 27,718 flights carried 250,740 U.S. tons (227,532 tonnes) in May 1949. 67 percent of all the loads were coal, 24 percent foodstuffs, and 9 percent industrial supplies and other goods. At peak times the planes were taking off and landing at 90 second intervals. There was a constant, unwavering drone of engines in the skies over Berlin. With their native wit the Berliners thankfully christened the transport planes *Rosinenbomber* ("raisin bombers"). The children's hearts were conquered by the *Schokoladenflieger* ("chocolate flier"), a lieutenant who scattered a rain of chocolate bars on handkerchiefs knotted into tiny parachutes as he was flying in to land. On May 12, 1949 the Soviet Military Administration admitted defeat. The blockade was lifted.

A "raisin bomber" flying in to land at Tempelhof Airport. In 1948/49, during the Berlin Blockade, the Western Powers supplied the city via an air bridge.

Pea soup
with bacon

Green beans
with mutton

Berlin potato soup

Berliner Kartoffelsuppe
Berlin potato soup
(Illustrated bottom)

1½ lbs/750 g floury potatoes
soup vegetables (2 carrots, 2 celery stalks, l leek, 1 bunch of parsley)
1 mild onion
1 tbsp clarified butter
4 cups/1 liter hot meat stock
1 tbsp rubbed marjoram
salt and pepper
½ cup/125 g cream
2 pieces of sliced bread, diced into croutons
4 oz/100 g lean bacon
2 tbsp butter
1 tbsp chopped parsley

Wash and peel the potatoes, then dice them finely. Dice the soup vegetables and the onion. Melt the clarified butter in a large pan, and fry the onions and soup vegetables until the onions are transparent. Add the potatoes and fry briefly with the other vegetables. Pour on the meat stock, season with marjoram, salt, and pepper, and boil for 20 minutes. Stir in the cream and blend the soup. Dice the bread and bacon finely. Fry the bacon in the butter. Add the croutons and fry until golden. Scatter over the soup, sprinkle with parsley, and serve straight away.

Grüne Bohnen mit Hammel
Green beans with mutton
(Illustrated center)

1 lb/500 g mutton (breast or loin)
1 tbsp clarified butter
1 clove of garlic, diced finely
1 onion, diced
4 cups/1 liter meat stock
1 lb/500 g fresh green beans
1 lb/500 g potatoes
salt and pepper
1 tsp savory
1 bunch parsley, chopped

Dice the meat into bite-sized cubes. Heat the clarified butter in a large pan and start frying the meat. Fry the garlic and onion briefly with the meat, then pour on the meat stock and boil for 30 minutes. While it is cooking, clean the beans, and peel, wash, and finely dice the potatoes. Add the vegetables to the stew, season well with salt, pepper, and savory, and cook for a further 20 minutes. Sprinkle with chopped parsley before serving.

Erbsensuppe mit Speck
Pea soup with bacon
(Illustrated top)

14 oz/400 g split peas
9 oz/250 g breakfast bacon, unsliced
2 onions, coarsely chopped
1 carrot
1 parsley root
¼ celeriac root
1 small leek
9 oz/250 g potatoes
salt and pepper
1 1/4 tsp rubbed marjoram
½ tsp savory

Soak the peas overnight in 2 liters of water. The next day bring to a boil in the same water, and add the bacon and the onions. Cover and simmer for 1 hour over a medium heat. Clean the root vegetables and leek, and chop coarsely. Peel the potatoes and dice finely. Mix the vegetables in with the peas and season with the salt, pepper, marjoram, and savory. Boil the stew for another 20 minutes. Take out the bacon before serving, chop finely, and mix back into the pea soup.

Fish

"The Havel is an unusual river. The blue of its water and its innumerable bays – it is really a series of lakes – make it unique among its kind." Though it may have been true in Fontane's day, no one would now describe the Havel Lakes of Berlin as blue. However, they are still an ideal environment for the pike-perch, or zander, a predatory fish that grows up to 3 feet (1 meter) long and hunts mainly in large lakes and the lower reaches of rivers. The most popular way to enjoy the delicate flavor of Havel zander in Berlin is simply to fry it light brown in butter and sprinkle it with a little lemon juice. In this case the subtlety of the cooking lies in its simplicity.

Berlin carp is a traditional Christmas and New Year dish. It is originally a Polish recipe, and no one knows quite how this festive feast came to Berlin. Was it an ancient dish cooked by the Slavic Wends in the old fishing village of Coelln? Or was it migrant workers from Silesia who got Berliners hooked on the taste? Mirror carp used to be purchased alive, and many of them passed their last days in a bathtub. When it was killed, the blood was collected and used to enrich the sauce, which was also flavored with beer and *Lebkuchen*.

Day trips to the countryside enjoyed great popularity in the 19th century. On fine Sundays whole families of Berliners would set off by steamer, by train, or in a rented *Kremser*, a horse-drawn buggy with several seats under a canopy, streaming out to the beer gardens in the countryside. They always had one aim in mind above all else: *Immer Richtung Aal jrün* ("set course for fresh eels") was their motto. The tasty fish was always served with gherkin salad sprinkled generously with chopped dill.

Fish, whether from domestic, or foreign, waters has always been a favorite meal in Berlin. Over 100 years ago the gourmet restaurant "Borchardt" presented its customers with the dilemma of choosing from a vast menu that included a bewildering array of 60 different sole dishes. Herr von Czako in Fontane's *Stechlin* knew why fish were so good for the health: "Fish are also said to contain plenty of phosphorus, and phosphorus originally meant something that makes things 'bright'." Perfect food then for the witty Berliners, who have always been known as bright sparks!

Havelzander mit brauner Butter
Havel zander with brown butter

4 slices of zander fillet, weighing about 7 oz/200 g each
salt and pepper, lemon juice
flour
10 tbsp butter
sprig of curly parsley to garnish

Wash the zander, pat it dry, season with salt and pepper, and sprinkle with lemon juice. Marinade briefly, then coat lightly in flour. Melt 3½ tbsp (50 g) of butter in a skillet and fry the fillets on both sides over a medium heat for about 3 minutes until golden brown. While the fish is cooking, brown the rest of the butter. Place the zander on warmed plates and garnish with parsley. Serve the brown butter separately.

Karpfen Polnisch
Polish carp

1 carp, weighing approximately 3 lb/1.5 kg, cleaned
salt and pepper
lemon juice
4 carrots
2 onions
butter for the dish
3 cups/750 ml dark beer
2 bay leaves
1 clove
1 tbsp sugar
½ cup/125 ml wine vinegar
2 cups/100 g crumbled Lebkuchen

Wash the carp, and cut into portions. Season each piece with salt and pepper, then sprinkle with lemon juice. Marinade for 15 minutes. In the meantime cut the carrots into thin strips and dice the onions finely. Layer the carrots and onions in a heatproof dish greased with butter. Place the pieces of carp on the onions and carrots, and pour the beer over them, adding the bay leaves and the clove. Cover with aluminum foil and bake in an oven preheated to 430 °F (220 °C) for about 15 minutes. Take out the carp and keep warm. Fry the sugar in a dry skillet until it goes brown. Pour on the vinegar and mix in the Lebkuchen. Add the cooking liquor from the dish and reduce the sauce a little. Pass the sauce through a sieve and season again with salt, pepper, and sugar. Place the portions of carp on the sauce and serve with boiled potatoes and green salad or red cabbage.

Aal grün
Fresh eel

1¾ lbs/750 g fresh eel, boned and skinned
salt
juice of 1 lemon
soup vegetables (2 carrots, 2 celery stalks, l leek, 1 bunch of parsley)
1 onion spiked with 1 bay leaf and 2 cloves
½ cup/125 ml mild wine vinegar
6 peppercorns
2 tbsp butter
2 tbsp flour
½ cup/125 ml white wine
pepper
1 pinch of sugar
1 scant cup/200 g cream
2 egg yolks
3 tbsp finely chopped dill

Wash and dry the eel, then cut into portions. Salt the eel and sprinkle on the lemon juice. Marinade for 10 minutes. Bring the soup vegetables to a boil in 4 cups (1 liter) of water with the spiked onion, vinegar, and peppercorns. Add the pieces of eel and cook over a low heat for approximately 20 minutes. Once they have cooked, remove the eel and drain. Sieve the fish stock. Melt the butter, stir in the flour, and fry until light golden. Mix in 2 cups (500 ml) of fish stock and the white wine, then season with salt, pepper, and sugar. Simmer for 5 minutes, then take the sauce off the heat. Whisk the cream with the egg yolks and mix into the sauce to thicken it. Stir in the dill and return the eel to heat in the sauce, but do not allow it to boil. Serve with potatoes boiled in their skins.

Cut the prepared carp into portions.

Place the fish and the vegetables in the dish and pour the beer over them.

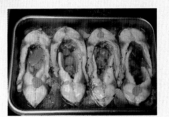

When the fish is cooked, take the portions out and keep warm.

Caramelize the sugar for the sauce in a skillet.

Pour on the vinegar, then add the *Lebkuchen*.

Pour the cooking liquor from the dish into the skillet to enrich the sauce.

Pass the sauce through a sieve and season with salt, pepper, and sugar.

Serve Polish carp with boiled potatoes and green salad.

The art of sugar

Those were the days, when Berlin confectioners celebrated the artistry of their craft and, in addition to their wide range of tarts and cakes, created elaborate sculptures made of icing, which they displayed in their cafés. This was all part and parcel of the competition between the city's master confectioners. One of them, Fuchs, created a furore in 1822 when he presented a court party modeled realistically in icing to mark the visit of the Russian Grand Duke Nicholas. The public could marvel at this piece of sugary art in a magnificent mirrored room at Fuchs's premises. Heinrich Heine was among those who made the trip, but were unable "to see anything of this wonder at Fuchs's because the lovely ladies' heads formed an impenetrable wall in front of the icing sculpture."

Traditional Berlin sweets are not made merely for display, but to eat. The most famous are *Berliner Sandkuchen* (a type of sponge cake) and the much loved *Berliner Pfannkuchen*, a doughnut that is eaten at New Year and Carnival time. According to legend they were first made by a Berlin soldier who was drafted into the artillery in 1756 at the beginning of the Seven Years War, but proved unfit for service on the front and was posted to the army bakery. To show his relief, he formed small cannonballs of yeast dough and so created the famous *Berliner Pfannkuchen*.

Berlin air with summer fruit sauce

Poor knight

Apple boats

The young Theodor Fontane would enjoy a picturesque scene in the autumn months: huge cargo barges, richly loaded with baskets of fruit, crowded in tight rows along the banks of the Spree. The air was filled with the fragrance of the apples and pears that were sold direct from the boats: "Every morning we schoolboys had to pass their mooring between the Hercules and Frederick Bridges, and all we can remember is walking along unable to take our eyes off the long row of Werder barges to our right." In Fontane's youth, during the first half of the 19th century, Berlin's fruit was still mainly supplied by water. The *Äppelkähne* ("apple boats"), as the Berliners called the heavily laden barges, came not just from nearby Werder, but also from Lusatia, and even from distant Bohemia. They sailed to Berlin and dropped anchor in the center of the city for days or weeks on end to sell their fruit wholesale or direct to the public.

When the urban rail network was constructed toward the end of the 19th century, the delivery routes became quicker. The "apple boats" fell victim to rationalization, but are still a presence in Berlin dialect. The spontaneous cry, "Mensch, is det'n riesiger Äppelkahn!" (Man, that is one big apple boat!), which expresses amazement at the imposing size of a passing freight barge, is still heard, though the boats are no longer carrying apples on board.

Berliner Luft mit Beerensauce
Berlin air with summer fruit sauce
(Illustrated above right)

1 oz/30 g gelatin
⅔ cup/125 g sugar
½ tsp vanilla essence
5 fresh eggs, separated
juice of ½ lemon
½ tsp cinnamon
1 lb/500 g mixed berries (for example: strawberries, raspberries, blackcurrants, blackberries)
⅓ cup/75 g sugar

Cream the sugar with the vanilla essence and the egg yolks. Mix in the lemon juice and cinnamon. Heat the gelatin in the white wine until it dissolves, then stir in the creamed egg yolks and sugar. Place in the fridge until the mixture begins to set. Beat the egg white very stiff and fold into the wine creme with a whisk. Spoon into a dessert dish and leave in the fridge for at least 3 hours to set. In the meantime bring the fruit and sugar to a boil with a little water, pass through a sieve, and allow to cool. Serve separately with Berlin air.

Armer Ritter
Poor knight
(Illustrated above left)

1 cup/250 ml milk
3 eggs
1 tbsp sugar
grated rind of 1 lemon
8 slices of stale white bread
6 tbsp white breadcrumbs
5 tbsp/75 g clarified butter
cinnamon and sugar mixture

Whisk the milk with the eggs, sugar, and grated lemon rind. Dip the bread slices in the batter, turning several times, then coat with breadcrumbs. Heat the clarified butter in a large skillet and fry the coated bread slices on both sides until golden brown. Sprinkle with cinnamon and sugar, and serve immediately.

The cool blonde

Even the beer experts do not know how the world-renowned Berliner Weisse came to be brewed on the banks of the Spree. All that is certain is that it originated in foreign lands. Whether it came from England or the Czech city of Plzen (known in German as Pilsen), the beer became popular first in northern Germany, and was then taken up in Berlin. In 1575 it was mentioned for the first time as "Hamburg wheat beer." It is now the German capital's most famous beer, and is known affectionately by the locals as *die kühle Blonde* ("the cool blonde").

Today wheat beer is bottled in a mechanical filling plant and dispatched around the world like any other product, but it has its own unique history of craft brewing and commercial inventiveness behind it. Like the equally famous South German wheat beers, Berliner Weisse owes its dominant flavors to malted wheat and barley – though the brewers on the Spree use only a quarter of malted wheat – and the secondary fermentation that takes place in the bottle. By contrast with the beer's southern relatives the bottle fermentation stage is promoted by the addition of a strain of *lactobacillus*. Nevertheless, it is above all the combination of this fermentation agent with the Berlin water that creates the special, slightly tart, spicy flavor appreciated so much by Field Marshall Wallenstein for its refreshing effect.

The immigrant Huguenots called the foaming drink they enjoyed so much the "Champagne of the North." The Great Elector was delighted by the popularity of this drink in the 17th century, because it gave him the opportunity to top up the empty state coffers by raising a special tax on the brewing of wheat beer.

Cunning Budike owners soon found a way of using the beer's secondary fermentation to improve its

Enjoying a "cool blonde" with a view over the Wannsee is one of the great Sunday pleasures in Berlin.

Berliner Weisse is served in a deep goblet with a high stem. Drinkers regard it as an excellent way to still their thirst.

flavor, as well as increasing their profits. They filled stone jugs with wheat beer and sealed them with corks, which they bound firmly to the bottle necks with string for extra security, and buried them deep in the sand piled in their cellars so that they did not explode. After a year or more in storage they could then be served to the expectant customers as Sandweisse (sand wheat beer), for a correspondingly higher price, of course. The most ingenious wheat beer brewers added another process. The naturally cloudy wheat beer was poured carefully into a second jug, leaving the yeast residues behind in the first. The result, the height of wheat beer refinement, was called "Champagnerweisse."

Berliner Weisse has been, and still is, combined with other ingredients in innumerable ways. Caraway schnaps came into fashion in the 19th century. It was served in long, narrow glasses that immediately reminded the Berliners of the string on the jugs of wheat beer, which was known in Berlin dialect as *Strippe*. A glass of wheat beer with caraway schnaps poured into it was called a *Weisse mit Strippe* and is still popular today. Hot wheat beer with lemon juice and slices of lemon is supposed to be an effective remedy for colds. Pretentious designer bars have been known to make cocktails by mixing wheat beer with various liqueurs and flavors.

Originally, Berliner Weisse was served in tall straight glasses with colored lids. In the 19th century it was supped from a footless bowl weighing 3 lb (1.3 kg). The head of the beer had to be exactly level with the glass's white rim, so that the customer knew that he had been served an

honest measure. The popular tongue called this monstrosity a *Klauweisse*, because, firstly, the filled bowl could only be raised to the mouth with both hands, known in Berlin dialect as *Klauen*, and, secondly, the more than three pints (two liters) it held were usually too much for one drinker, so other customers would refresh themselves from the glass and stole (*klauten*) the beer. These huge bowls were replaced by a shallow goblet with a short foot, before the current glass, a deep goblet with a high stem, became generally accepted.

Tourists are often keen to sample wheat beer red (with raspberry) or green (with woodruff), though people whose palates are unaccustomed to the flavor may require some time before they learn to love it. As a young man, the artist Heinrich Zille worked as a guide, conducting visitors round the city for a small fee. He reported their reactions to the pleasures of wheat beer. Most of them, so he wrote with a suppressed grin, found it "too sharp, too sour – so I would drink it up to preserve the 'cool blonde's' reputation."

Beer for the masses, wine for the few

The Quadriga and the Brandenburg Gate decorated with vines and grapes – this is not an aspect of official Berlin with which most people are familiar. Should we forget our romantic notions of magical, green landscapes covered with vines where peaceful rivers meander lazily between gently sloping hills?
It seems that we should, because, unbelievable as it may sound, in bustling Berlin a wine of the city's own is being produced. The capital city's vineyard extends along the southern slope of the 66-meter (214-feet) high Kreuzberg Hill in the middle of this great, grimy city, where the vines grow as if at the bottom of a barrel, surrounded by the facades of high rise apartment blocks. In fact, there is a tradition of winegrowing here, and grapes were cultivated on this site up until the 19th century. What the Berliners thought of the product is shown by an old saying: *Den musste in die Strümpe jiessen, der zieht de Löcher zu!* ("You should pour it into your socks, it'll mend the holes!").
Despite this verdict, in 1968, seven years after the city was divided, the people of Kreuzberg made a brave new start. Their partner city, Wiesbaden, had given the district a present of five vineroots. More followed, and there are now over 300 vines. And there the grapes hang, ripening in the life-giving city air, soaking up the glorious Berlin sun. However, once harvested, they are sent away to the Rhine. The Kreuzbergers are not able to make wine without the help of outside experts and the Berlin grapes are taken to Wiesbaden and Ingelheim am Rhein to be pressed. They return in bottles labeled "Kreuz-Neroberger Riesling" and "Kreuzberger Blauer Spätburgunder."
Eleven bottles were produced in 1970, just seven in 1971. Today the Kreuzbergers get about 1000 bottles each year to lay down in their cellars. These bottles are never put on sale, so no ordinary citizen knows what Berlin wine tastes like and whether it is good for anything other than mending socks. The Kreuzberg district council hoards the rarity and guards its stocks jealously, only presenting bottles to official guests and local people celebrating their hundredth birthdays.

Foreign pleasures

America was in. Anything that seemed in the slightest way connected with the New World exerted a magical fascination and was eagerly adapted, copied, and consumed by young West Germans in the years after the war. The bitter opposition of a generation of parents whose backbones had been stiffened by traditional German food had little effect. For all their grumbling and complaining, in the end, there was no way of keeping the ketchup bottle off the table. For teenagers in stylish outfits wearing skintight riveted jeans and turtleneck pullovers with whipping ponytails or short haircuts, what could be trendier than lounging lazily at the counter of a milk bar? When they sucked a banana or pineapple milkshake devotedly through a straw,

they were paying tribute to the "American way of life." And there was no way of avoiding Coca Cola: the global concern's all-pervasive advertising campaign made sure of that long before American fast food chains swamped whole continents with hot dogs, spare ribs, and hamburgers.

Travel broadens not just the mind, but also the palate. The growth of tourism to the sun-drenched countries of southern Europe that started in the 1950s introduced the Germans to culinary pleasures of which they had been ignorant till then: pasta, pizza, paella, gyros pita, feta cheese, paprika, eggplant, and zucchini. The immigrant workers recruited from Italy, Spain, and Greece to cover labor market shortages from the mid-1950s on did the rest. Having settled permanently, many of them opened grocery shops, pizzerias, and restaurants, so that the Germans would not have to go without foreign culinary delights as they reminisced about their holidays on their home

turf. The world has become a village. Beyond the culinary borders of Europe there are more and more restaurants offering food from Central and South America, Asia, and Africa to please the discriminating palates of a multicultural society. According to a survey conducted on December 31, 1996, of the three and a half million people living in Berlin, 444,112 are foreign citizens, far more than the entire population of the former German capital Bonn. About one third of the foreign population are Turkish citizens – the largest group by a long way. After the construction of the Berlin Wall on August 13, 1961 companies in West Berlin lost all their employees from the surrounding areas and East Berlin at a single stroke. The agreement on recruitment signed by Turkey and the F.R.G. on October 30, 1961 was intended to close this gap by encouraging Turks to look for work in Germany. In the meantime the German capital has become the largest Turkish city outside Turkey.

Yugoslav pljeskavica, a spicy grilled patty of ground meat.

Cevapcici, a thumb-sized grilled sausage of ground meat from the former Yugoslavia.

Stuffed vine leaves, a Turkish specialty. They are filled with rice, or mutton and rice.

Minestrone, the best known Italian vegetable soup.

Greek salad with olives, red onions, tomatoes, cucumber, and feta cheese.

There are many varieties of pizza. This one is topped Sicilian-style with tomatoes, mozzarella, black olives, and oregano.

Tsatsiki, a Greek starter and side dish made of yogurt with fresh cucumber and garlic.

The famous Spanish rice dish paella contains meat, seafood, and a variety of vegetables.

A gyros pita, a Greek version of the doner kebab.

The most famous pasta dish of all: spaghetti bolognese with a sauce of tomato, meat, and onion.

Tiramisu, the Italian dessert that has conquered the buffet tables of Germany. Sponge fingers with liqueur, coffee, and mascarpone cheese whipped with cream.

Italian lasagna is a baked dish of pasta sheets layered with a meat and tomato sauce and topped with béchamel sauce.

Hamburg
Schwerin
Bremen
Berlin
Hanover
Potsdam
Magdeburg
Düsseldorf
Bonn
Erfurt
Dresden
Wiesbaden
Mainz
Saarbrücken
Stuttgart
Munich

MAREN HOFFMANN
Brandenburg

"Anyone who wishes to travel in the Mark of Brandenburg must first of all bring with him a love of the land and its people, or at least have no prejudices. He must have the goodwill to see the good in it instead of killing it with critical comparisons," demanded the great writer Theodor Fontane, who was famous for the accounts he wrote of his wanderings through the area. Extensive pine forests and huge lakes, long tree-lined roads, and villages of brick houses dominate the image of this flat, thinly populated Federal State. According to official statistics, there are only 86 people to the square kilometer (226 per square mile), while Potsdam, Brandenburg's capital, has barely 137,000 inhabitants. Brandenburg was the core of Prussia. Potsdam was its most important garrison town, but was given cultural significance by Frederick II when he built the Sanssouci Palace. Other highlights include the gardens near Cottbus designed by Count Pückler-Muskau and the idyllic town of Rheinsberg, which was made a place of pilgrimage for lovers by the humorous writer Kurt Tucholsky. Traditions of quite a different kind are maintained in Lower Lusatia, which includes the Spreewald forest. This is the homeland of the Sorbs, a Slavic minority with their own language and cuisine. After reunification the people of Brandenburg successfully insisted that the land between the Rivers Elbe and Oder should be reconstituted after being divided between three administrative districts for nearly forty years. The borders of Brandenburg have changed again and again in the course of history – in 1815 the Altmark was lost to Saxony, and after World War II large parts of Brandenburg to the east of the Rivers Oder and Neisse went to Poland. All the same, the Brandenburgers have maintained a sense of identity. At any rate, they had no desire to merge with Berlin and voted against a fusion of their flat, rural State with the new capital city in 1996.

All the same, the kitchens of Brandenburg and Berlin have much in common: after all, the surrounding areas have always provided the city with fish, game, fruit, and vegetables. Quark with linseed oil and potatoes is one of the native specialties of the region, and Teltow turnips, Spreewald gherkins, and Beelitz asparagus are all famed far beyond its borders.

Left: "Instead of a footpath, a smooth waterway; with foliage stretching over our heads like a vaulted roof we float along the water..." Thus did Theodor Fontane travel through the Spreewald, "a network of waterways woven out of the innumerable arms of the Spree and its many canals..."

Ostalgie

"For certain reasons we wish to inform customers that the bowl of southern fruits is not suitable for consumption," a sign warns visitors to the "last East German grocery," a relic from the days of the G.D.R. when exotic fruit was still a rarity. The daily world of the G.D.R. shopper is preserved by a museum in Lenzen (Elbe) in the Prignitz area. However, nothing in the little shop is for sale any more. The certificate awarded to a "retail outlet of exemplary sales culture" for "outstanding performance in Socialist competition" is today a historical artifact.

Most visitors come from East Germany, and their reactions are mixed. Some remember with horror mushy rice and Cuban oranges that could only be used for pressing juice. Others would love to fill their cupboards again with practical Tempo lentils, baking mixes from the VEB Backmehlwerk Halle, and the affectionately remembered powdered chocolate desserts that disappeared with the "workers' and peasants' state." Rare goods were known as *Bückware* because they were kept under the counter and the shop assistant had to bend over – *bücken* (to bend) – to retrieve them for favored customers. These rarities lie about openly in the museum: lemon juice, tomato ketchup, real honey, boil in the bag rice – a selection that none of the shops had on offer during the G.D.R.'s existence. Many who grew up in the G.D.R. now miss one thing more than any other: the bread rolls. However, there is little call for jars of pickled green tomatoes, crumbly cakes of starch for thickening sauces, or ginger in syrup.

The yearning for the western goods that were once only available at inflated prices in the *Intershop* and *Delikat* chains has now been satisfied, and many people in the new Federal States are beginning to appreciate some of the foods they grew up with. The word *Ostalgie* was coined by combining the words *ost* (east) and *Nostalgie* (nostalgia) to refer to a longing for the lost G.D.R. lifestyle, but it does an injustice to many products. Some of them have been on sale since long before the G.D.R. was founded, such as the Rotkäppchen sparkling wine that was ridiculed by West Germans for many years as cheap bubbly. It has been made for more than a hundred years by the Freyburger Sektkelterei in Saxony-Anhalt, while Hallorenkugeln come from Germany's oldest chocolate factory in Halle. Other long established brands, such as Köstritzer black beer, Nordhäuser Doppelkorn schnaps, Spreewälder gherkins, Werderaner ketchup, Burger Knäckebrot crackers, and Salzwedel Baumkuchen have regained their places on the shelves of the west, though many producers have gone through serious crises or been taken over by western groups.

The Burgmuseum in Lenzen displays items that were never available in the shops while the G.D.R. still existed.

Glossary of terms used in the G.D.R.

Broiler: a factory farmed chicken from a K.I.M. (see below). Premium chickens were sold as *Goldbroiler*.

Bückware: rare goods that were hoarded by the sales staff under the counter and sold only to a privileged group of customers.

Delikat: a chain of shops selling high quality goods at high prices: basic foods were provided by *Konsum* supermarkets.

Erichs Krönung: ("Erich's coronation"): derisive popular name for a mixture of ersatz and real coffee produced for a short period under the Honecker regime.

Grilletta: the East's answer to the hamburger. In essence, it was the same as its western competitor: a round, flat meat patty in a bread roll with sauce and garnish.

Jägerschnitzel: (hunter's schnitzel): in the G.D.R. this was not an escalope of pork or veal, but a fried slice of Jagdwurst (smoked sausage).

Kali: a sickly sweet coffee liqueur.

Ketwurst: comparable to the American hot dog: a sausage came in a bread roll with a ready-made hole and was topped with ketchup.

KIM: abbreviation for "Kombinate industrieller Mastproduktion," the factory farms where broiler chickens were kept.

Kiwi: a liqueur often ordered in bars and described as "cherry whisky."

Nudossi: a chocolate-hazelnut cream.

Sättigungsbeilage: potatoes, rice, bread, vegetables, all of which would be described in West Germany as *Beilage* (side dishes). The use of *Sättigung* ("repletion") in this compound word states the aim of the side dish with a directness that sounds curious to western ears.

Schlagersüsstafel: cheap imitation chocolate made of vegetable fat, a little cocoa, and peanuts.

Tempo-Linsen: tinned lentils. Peas and beans were also available under the Tempo brand.

Zückli: an artificial sweetener that was advertised with the slogan "Süssen ohne Sorgen" (sweeten without a care).

Potatoes
for Germany

The farm hands on the estate at Sorau in Lower Lusatia were not to be persuaded: they had no intention of putting the strange tubers on their tables. Leopold, the farm manager, could not even convince the pig girls to let the pigs try the potatoes he had brought from the Erzgebirge. This was in 1730. *Pappas americanorum* had already been in Europe for more than 150 years, but was not yet widely known among the populace.

In the 16th century the Spanish had brought back potato plants from Peru and Chile, where they had been used by the local populations as a foodstuff for hundreds of years. In Europe the botanical newcomer first found a home in medicinal herb gardens and the pleasure gardens of the aristocracy. Some doctors even hoped that the "Indian sugar-root" would "strengthen marital performance." On the whole, however, the *Tartuffel*, as it was known, was grown for its pretty flowers. For example, in 1649 Elector Frederick William had potatoes planted in his Berlin pleasure gardens. Gradually they found their way into the court kitchens. The Elector's personal physician, Johann Sigismund Elsholtz, noted in 1682 in his *Newes Tischbuch*: "These Tartuffel are eaten partly for pleasure and diversion, partly as a nourishing food, since they have now become quite common among us."

By the middle of the 17th century the potato had become accepted as a food by the lower classes in the Palatinate and, slightly later, in Vogtland. In the 18th century many Saxon priests, the so-called *Knollenprediger* ("tuber preachers"), used their sermons to urge their parishioners to grow potatoes. Those who followed this priestly advice found earthly reward soon enough: the potato proved what a blessing it was in the famine of 1719. Frederick the Great pressed ahead with large-scale potato cultivation in Germany. He recognized that it offered an opportunity to prevent famines caused by poor cereals harvests. On March 24, 1756, he issued an order to all his rural administrators and government officials: "In other provinces We in Our Highest Person have been recommended most seriously to plant in our lands the so-called *Tartoffeln* as a very useful root vegetable serviceable in many ways to both people and animals."

These decisive words were needed. Twelve years earlier the King's attempt to interest farmers in potatoes on a voluntary basis had failed. He had potatoes distributed free to the farmers of Pomerania after the great famine of 1743/44, but they threw the strange things to their dogs, who refused to touch them. Something that even dogs did not want to eat could not really do people much good, they reasoned. The practicality of the

No one wanted to eat the new tubers at first. Later they were seen as a panacea for famine.

tuber was demonstrated shortly after Frederick's "potato order." During the Seven Years War (1756–1763) the potato made a decisive contribution to keeping the Prussian army well fed and in high spirits. In 1774 the King tried again and instructed the governing council of the Mark of Brandenburg to ensure that "potato cultivation is encouraged as much as possible and is not neglected." The ruler's persistence bore fruit. By the end of the 18th century potatoes were among the most profitable arable products in Brandenburg. In 1794 one *Morgen* (as much land as a man could plough in a morning) of potatoes brought in a net profit of 36 Reichstaler – more than many craftsmen earned in six months.

In the late 18th century the potato finally became widespread among the ordinary people and replaced cereals as a staple food almost completely in many regions, particularly in northern Germany. What had once been grown by princes as a decorative plant now became sustenance for the poor. For a large part of the year the families of impoverished agricultural workers were fed almost solely on potatoes. As a result, the great famine of 1846/47 was caused by the very plant that was supposed to have prevented such catastrophes. The total dependence on potato cultivation meant that there were serious shortages in both years due to plant diseases.

During the 1950s potato cultivation became a matter of state of the highest importance again in the G.D.R.. The struggle against the Colorado beetle was conflated with crude political propaganda during the Cold War. American planes were claimed to have deliberately dropped the six-legged class enemy onto collective farm fields in order to sabotage the economy, and millions of Ostmarks were invested in the fight against the "Yankee beetle."

All about potatoes

Shoppers accustomed to the dismal selection in the supermarkets might not believe as much, but over 150 different types of potato are grown in Germany. It is true, however, that some of them are not intended for human consumption. What are known as economic potatoes are used exclusively for the production of starch and alcohol, others are bred specially for ready-to-eat potato products.

Eating potatoes are classified according to when they are harvested as first early, second early, maincrop, late, and very late varieties. The harvest runs from the end of May to the end of October.

First earlies: the most common include Arkula, Atica, Berber, Christa, Gloria, Hela, Karatop, Leyla, Rosara, and Ukama. The first potatoes from German fields arrive on the market at the beginning of June. They ripen under polythene sheeting and are regarded as particular delicacies. These new potatoes are not peeled, but scrubbed in water before cooking. Only a few of the first early varieties are suitable for storage.

Second earlies: the most common varieties include Arnika, Cilena, Cinja, Forelle, Karat, Rikea, and Sieglinde. They are on the market from the beginning of June to the middle of August and can be stored until the autumn.

Maincrop varieties: The most common include Adretta, Agria, Exquisa, Grandifolia, Granola, Hansa, Koretta, Likaria, Linda, Liu, Nicola, Quarta, Roxy, Secura, Selma, Solara, and Solina. Maincrop varieties are the most important potatoes in Germany. They are harvested from the middle of August to the beginning of October and possess good characteristics for storing.

Late and very late varieties: the best known is Aula. These varieties are harvested from the middle of September to the end of October. They are grown for storage, but are decreasing in importance as so few households have large storage space.

The starch content and composition of the different potatoes vary widely. The higher the levels of starch in a potato, the lower the moisture content, and the more floury it will be. The earlier potatoes are harvested, the less starch they will have produced, and the firmer they will be when cooked. According to the German regulations defining the different classes of eating potatoes, they are categorized in the following groups: *festkochend* (waxy), *vorwiegend festkochend* (mainly waxy), *meligkochend* (floury).

Waxy varieties: the most common include Cilena, Exquisa, Exquisita, Forelle, Hansa, Linda, Nicola, Selma, and Sieglinde. They do not split when boiled and are particularly good for use in salads, frying, and boiling.

Mainly waxy varieties: the most common include Agria, Arkula, Arnika, Atica, Berber, Christa, Cinja, Gloria, Grandifolia, Granola, Hela, Karat, Karatop, Koretta, Leyla, Liu, Quarta, Rikea, Rosara, Roxy, Secura, Solara, Solina, and Ukama. They only split a little when boiled and are good for boiling, frying, and making Rösti and fries.

Floury varieties: the most common include Adretta, Aula, and Likaria. They split when boiled and are perfectly suited for soups, stews, creamed potatoes, and potato dumplings.

Opposite: Potatoes originate from South America. This oil painting by W. Guntermann dating from 1950 shows them being passed on in a symbolic gesture.

The introduction of the potato was not the only service performed by Frederick the Great (1712-1786) for Prussia. He gained a new province for his land without even having to fight for it. Starting in 1747, he had dykes dug in the Oderbruch, which had always suffered severe flooding. This area on what is now the border with Poland was drained and settled, and is still one of the most important agricultural districts in Brandenburg.

Agria: mainly waxy, flat eyes, yellow skin, yellow flesh.

Anni: slightly floury, flat eyes, veined skin, yellow flesh.

Aula: floury, deep yellow flesh.

Berber: one of the first early potatoes, mainly waxy.

Cilena: pear-shaped; fine, mild flavor, regarded as a delicacy.

Cinja: early variety, mainly waxy, flat eyes, dark yellow flesh.

Dobra: smooth skin, flat eyes, and therefore easy to peel.

Exquisa: particularly fine, recently bred variety, yellow flesh.

Grandifolia: maincrop variety, good for storing.

Granola: veined skin, yellow flesh, maincrop variety.

Linda: outstanding eating potato, oval tubers, yellow flesh.

Nicola: widely used salad potato with yellow flesh, stores well.

Tubers at a glance

They sound like exotic beauties: Rosara, Ukama, Cilena, Cinja, and Likaria. But their flowery names are deceptive. They are of modest appearance, dull even, are round or oval, and sometimes a bit flat. Some have deep eyes, they are usually brown, and are often smeared with earth. However, beneath the skin, Christa, Gloria, and their fellows are unbeatable: they are easy to cook, full of flavor, and rich in proteins, minerals, and vitamins.

In fact, all these beauties are potatoes, which are still one of the most important basic foodstuffs in Germany, even if they have become much less important in the last few decades. Until 1914 Germany was one of the largest potato producers in the world, and between 1900 and 1904 per capita consumption was almost 630 pounds (286 kilos) a year. After World War II a hundredweight of potatoes was a desirable asset that could be used for barter or sold on the black market, but as the German "economic miracle" began to take off, the tuber became less popular. In 1950/51 the Germans ate 409 pounds (186 kilos) each, but by 1983/84 the figure had sunk to just 154 pounds (70 kilos). In the 1990s consumption rose again a little to 160 pounds (73 kilos) per head. At the same time consumption of processed potato products, such as chips, fries, dehydrated creamed potato, and the like has increased massively. In 1992/93 every German consumed more than 68 pounds (29 kilos) of these products, in 1953 consumption was less than 2 pounds (1 kilo) per head.

As the potato was almost exclusively a food of the lower classes during the 18th and 19th centuries, it is no wonder that potato dishes play a major role in traditional regional cookery. They had greater importance in the north of the country than in the south, and were more often on the menu in poor regions than in rich ones. Where people are on short commons, need often seems to be alleviated by imagination. The number of German potato recipes is legion and the names for the same dish vary from one area to the next. Potatoes are the basis for many filling stews, are used in soups and salads, formed into dumplings, pureed, sweetened, combined with other flavors, and eaten as main, or side dishes.

Background: The potato is easy to cook and grows even on poor ground. For hundreds of years it was a "secret weapon" in the fight against hunger.

Arkula: mainly waxy, flat eyes, slightly yellow flesh.

Atica: mainly waxy, yellow flesh, fine texture.

Bettina: yellow, smooth skin, flat eyes.

Christa: very popular variety with yellow flesh.

Clivia: well known storing potato, waxy consistency, deep yellow flesh.

Désirée: red skin, light yellow flesh, mainly cultivated in southern Germany.

Forelle: strong flavor, regarded as a gourmet potato.

Gloria: first early variety, mainly waxy.

Grata: golden yellow flesh, late variety.

Hansa: waxy, main variety grown in northern Germany.

Selma: waxy, particularly popular in Bavaria, smooth skin, flat eyes.

Sieglinde: tried and tested early variety, waxy, delicate, mild flavor.

A thousand and one variations

Potato salad

The best opportunities to conduct field studies on the topic of potato salad arise at parties when the thrifty hosts have invited guests to "bring something for the buffet" without taking the trouble to coordinate the various contributions. As a result, Petra, Juliane, Ingrid, and Paul all arrive with enormous bowls of potato salad to add variety to a buffet that otherwise consists of five different versions of pasta salad. With a bit of luck this lack of organization may at least serve as a conversation starter, as all the guests discuss how potato salad should be made, how someone's grandmother from Silesia used to make it, and how someone once ate it in Bavaria – with fresh cucumber instead of pickled gherkin. Then they try the salads on the table and discover that all four of them taste quite different, though Petra, Juliane, Ingrid, and Paul all definitely come from the same part of the country.

Only the authors of cookbooks have the audacity to set down just one recipe for each region and call it "Hamburg, Lusatian, Harz, or Swabian, potato salad." In this way they may indicate certain regional preferences, but not the whole variety. The fact is that in Germany there are about as many recipes for potato salad as there are people with the surnames Müller, Schmidt, Schmitz, Schmied, Schmitt, Maier, Meier, Mayr, Mair, and Mayer.

The common factor in all these recipes is the potato, and the potatoes have to be boiled – all are in agreement on that point. This is where things start to get complicated. Some people use waxy potatoes, others prefer mainly waxy varieties, that absorb the dressing better. Some swear that the potatoes should have been cooked the day before, others suggest that they should be boiled in their skins and made into salad straight after the skin has been removed and they are still warm. Then there are the finer points of the vinaigrette... or the mayonnaise... or the meat stock. At this point it becomes impossible to keep track of the various additional ingredients: gherkins, onions, wild garlic, apples, white cabbage, leek, egg, bacon, fish, or sausage – the possibilities are endless. The only thing that is out of the question is the pale imitation of potato salad served on paper plates at German snack bars. The people who made potato salad a fast food did their best to destroy one of the greatest wonders of German cooking.

Ingeborgs Kartoffelsalat
Ingeborg's potato salad

As there are at least as many potato salad recipes in Germany as there are people who cook, Ingeborg Pils, who is responsible for the recipes in this book, has given us her own personal recipe, which betrays certain influences from Bavaria and Baden-Württemberg.

2 lb/1 kg small waxy potatoes
2 tsp caraway
salt
2 mild onions
1 scant cup/200 ml hot meat stock
4 tbsp white wine vinegar
1–2 pinches of sugar
freshly milled black pepper
2 tbsp good quality vegetable oil
2 bunches of rocket
6 oz/150 g breakfast bacon

Wash the potatoes. Place in salted water with the caraway and boil for 25 minutes until cooked. Drain, rinse with cold water, and allow to cool a little. Peel the potatoes and cut into thin slices. Place in a salad bowl. Peel the onions, chop finely, and stir into the potato slices. Mix the meat stock, vinegar, salt, sugar, pepper, and oil to make a dressing and pour over the salad. Stir thoroughly and keep covered at room temperature for at least 2 hours so that all the flavors blend. Wash the rocket, shake dry, and cut away the stalks. Tear into small pieces and fold into the salad. Dice the bacon finely and fry in a dry pan. Scatter over the salad and serve immediately.

Twelve typical potato dishes

1 **Thüringer Klösse:** (Thuringian potato dumplings, recipe on page 16) are among the culinary glories of Thuringia. They are also popular in Bavaria, where a Sunday roast without bread or potato dumplings is unthinkable.

2 **Grossbottwarer Kartoffelkuchen:** (Grossbottwar potato cake): an example of the mix of flour and potatoes that are so prized in Baden-Württemberg. The dough is leavened with yeast, and mixed with eggs and bacon fat.

3 **Kartoffelsuppe mit Speck und Backpflaumen:** (potato soup with bacon and prunes), as it is known and loved in Mecklenburg-West Pomerania. The potatoes are boiled and pureed, then soaked prunes and fried bacon are added.

4 **Hunsrücker Kartoffelwurst:** (Hunsrück potato sausage) contains pork belly and beef. The meat is put through a mincer, mixed with seasoned potato, then used to fill sausage skins. The sausages are scalded in hot water.

5 **Buttermilchgetzen:** (buttermilk pancake): a variation on the potato pancake that is eaten everywhere in Germany. This version comes from the Erzgebirge, where the batter is prepared with buttermilk, eggs, onions, and bacon.

6 **Himmel und Erde:** (heaven and earth): a mixture of creamed potato and apple puree eaten in the Rhineland with Blutwurst. In Mecklenburg, pears are used instead of apples.

7 **Saures Kartoffelgemüse:** (sour potato vegetables): a Bavarian dish in which potatoes are cooked with other root vegetables and seasoned with sugar and vinegar to give a sweet and sour flavor.

8 **Hoppelpoppel:** the Berlin method of using up leftovers. Meat is cut into fine strips and fried with onions, potatoes, and eggs.

9 **Reibekuchen:** a crispy baked potato cake known under various names in different parts of Germany. The best known version is from the Rhineland (recipe on page 227).

10 **Kerschder:** is the word for fried potatoes in the Saarland (recipe on page 304). In the rest of the country they are known simply as *Bratkartoffeln*.

11 **Schleizer Bambser:** (Schleiz sweet potato noodles): a specialty from Thuringia. A dough of boiled potatoes, chopped apple, eggs, and sugar is formed into noodles that are fried lightly in a skillet then baked in the oven with cinnamon sugar.

12 **Pellkartoffeln mit Leinöl und Quark**, (potatoes with curd and linseed oil): the yellow oil extracted from flax seeds is the most important component of this dish. The people of the Spreewald swear by the combination, saying, "What makes the Spreewälder strong? Potatoes, linseed oil, and curd."

Background: this lady at her stand in the Munich food market specializes exclusively in potatoes.

The first stage of industrial gherkin production is steam cleaning the barrel.

Two men work on the conveyor belt. One fills the barrel . . .

. . . the other keeps the supply of washed gherkins coming.

A view from above into the well-filled barrel before the spices are added.

A special spiced vinegar mixture is used to preserve the gherkins.

The gherkins are removed from the barrel and taken to the filling plant.

Gurkensuppe mit Pökelrippchen
Cucumber soup with salted rib

| 4 raw Kasseler ribs, weighing 7 oz/200 g each |
| 1 onion spiked with 1 bay leaf and 2 cloves |
| 5 peppercorns |
| 2 cucumbers |
| 4 onions, diced |
| 3½ tbsp/50 g butter |
| 1 tbsp sugar |
| 2 tbsp flour |
| 1 scant cup/200 g cream |
| white pepper |
| ½ bunch of parsley, finely chopped |
| 2 tbsp croutons |

Bring the Kasseler ribs to a boil in 6 cups (1½ liters) of water with the spiked onion and peppercorns, and cook for 1 hour. While the meat is cooking, peel and halve the cucumbers, remove the seeds, and cut the flesh into slices. Fry the onions in butter until transparent. Sprinkle with sugar and caramelize gently. Stir in the cucumber, sweat briefly, and dust with flour. Pour on 2 cups (500 ml) of the meat stock and cook for 10 minutes. Then mix in the cream and vegetables, and season with salt and pepper. Before serving sprinkle with chopped parsley and croutons. Serve the ribs separately.

Gherkins and cucumbers

In Germany bacon is used to catch mice, but they can also be driven away with cucumbers and gherkins: "mice will not touch anything that has been sprinkled with the powder of a cucumber," wrote a German author in the 16th century. Cultivation of gherkins and cucumbers began in the Spreewald at around the same time, and the people there had much better things to do with the curved fruit than pulverize them for use against pests. Flemish clothworkers originally brought to the region to improve linen production introduced these green relatives of the pumpkin to the area, which is ideal for their cultivation on account of its plentiful supplies of water. It was recognized early on that, not only was *Cucumis sativus* perfect in salads, soups, and sauces, it could also be used as a remedy for the painful consequences of a night's drinking: "Was klärt den Kopp bei Mann und Frau? Saure Gurken aus Lübbenau!" (What clears the head of man and wife? Pickled gherkins from Lübbenau!), as they say in the Spreewald. The Berliners were more than willing to believe this and soon began to share a liking for the flavor ". . . of pickled gherkins alone, which the town itself consumes in unbelievable quantities. They deliver many thousands of Thalers worth to Berlin; indeed a few years ago they made this sum from peeled gherkins alone," marveled the travel writer

Bernouli, who visited Lübbenau in 1779. Nearly a hundred years later, in 1874, the Lübbenau salesman Schulz discovered a small, but important, culinary trick. The pickled gherkins had to be pricked to stop them becoming hollow and collapsing. In 1932 the way was opened up for production on an industrial scale when it first became possible to pickle sterilized gherkins.

As far as the spices were concerned, every family had its own jealously guarded combination. Even today the companies in the region keep their special recipes secret. One classic recipe was recorded by Auguste Wilhelmine Fontane: "For the gherkins that are to last until the next crop, select the finest without any spots, wash them clean, and layer them in a barrel with vine tendrils, cherry leaves, and dill. Then pour salted, boiled water onto them. When it has cooled down, boil the same water and pour it over the gherkins again. Do this three times. The third time cover the barrel immediately, however hot it is, seal it, then store it in the cellar, where it must be stirred every day." It is important that the gherkins are not taken out of the brine by hand, as this would impair the remaining gherkins' shelf life. It is best to fish them out with a gherkin fork.

After a bad patch following German reunification, the Spreewald gherkin, which used to be exported to Bavaria by the G.D.R., has now started to recover some of its former success. Pickled gherkins are certainly good business: at peak times daily output of the largest pickling plant in the region is up to 450,000 jars of *Sechsneuner* a day. Every day the factory uses more than 3 tons of dill, 2 of mustard seeds, and 5 of onions. Fennel, basil, and bay leaves are also used in some styles of pickled

gherkins. Traveling gherkin addicts can even buy them in America. 316 acres (128 hectares) of land are devoted to the cultivation of the green "Spreewald bananas." They are harvested from the beginning of July to the middle of September with *Gurkenflieger* (literally "gherkin airplanes"), so called because the long side arms of the tractors look like wings. Thirty-four seasonal workers lie on their stomachs on each wing to pick the gherkins. In Golssen they are processed to make jars of classic spiced gherkins, sweet and sour sliced gherkins, gherkin spears, and gherkins with onions.

Spreewälder Dillgurken
Spreewald dill gherkins

4 onions, cut into rings
4 cups/1 liter white wine vinegar
9 bay leaves, 9 cloves
2 tbsp sugar
½ cup/100 g salt
6½ lb/3 kg pickling gherkins
10 fresh vine leaves
1 bunch of flowering dill

Bring the onions to a boil in 3 liters of water with the white wine vinegar, bay leaves, cloves, sugar, and salt, and then allow to cool completely. Brush the gherkins thoroughly, rinse under running water, and drain. Cover the base of a large ceramic pot with 5 vine leaves and half of the dill. Put in the gherkins and pour on the cold brine. The gherkins must be completely covered. Top with the rest of the dill and vine leaves. Lay a clean board over the pot. Store in a cool place for at least 4 weeks.

Below: the gherkins are put into jars at the filling plant. The jars are topped up by hand if they are not completely full.

Vegetables for soups and stews

From garden to pot

Brandenburg is vegetable country. Every year Brandenburg's farmers produce more than 80,000 tons of vegetables, including ever more carrots, cucumbers, and asparagus. The fierce competition on the market has led to a reduction in the use of expensive methods of cultivation, such as growing under glass. On the other hand, many farmers are trying to create new sales opportunities by means of direct marketing and are growing small amounts of niche products in order to be able to offer as wide a variety as possible.

With its complex river systems and network of canals, the Spreewald is famous above all for cucumbers, gherkins, and horseradish. This area to the south of Brandenburg is the main center of horseradish cultivation in Germany outside Bavaria. The thick, fleshy roots of horseradish (*Armoracia lapathifolia*) contain allyl isothiocynate compounds. When the flesh of the root is broken down, these compounds form mustard oils, essential oils that irritate the skin and produce a hot, spicy flavor. In addition to the Spreewald, the area around Beelitz has also made a name for itself on the culinary front as an asparagus-growing area. The "Queen of the vegetables" has been cultivated there since 1861 and is honored each year with an asparagus festival.

Pumpkins are also grown in the Spreewald, many in the vegetable patches of Brandenburg's 160,000 amateur gardeners. Pumpkin is regarded as a "typically German" vegetable. Support for this view is provided by the fact that even Goethe mentions it: he once called someone who wished to reprimand him a "pumpkin," meaning that he was a dimwit. The sheer size of the pumpkin satisfies the strong desire felt by all gardeners to outdo their neighbors. Pumpkins can weigh up to 220 pounds (100 kg) and therefore attract the competitive horticulturists whose triumphant photographs appear in local newspapers under such headlines as "One Man and his Giant Pumpkin." Cooks tend to pickle pumpkin or use it in soups.

A great many of the numerous vegetable varieties grown in Brandenburg were originally introduced by the French Huguenots, who settled there in the middle of the 17th century. The Edict of Potsdam (1685) granted them freedom of worship and economic support. Apart from new vegetable varieties, such as endives, chicory, and artichokes, they brought modern agricultural techniques with them and introduced tobacco to the Uckermark, which, thanks to its high air humidity and slightly loamy soil, is still the largest single area devoted to tobacco cultivation in Germany.

Teltow turnips

The Pope had several barrels sent to him each year, Goethe had them delivered to Weimar by mailcoach, and innovative traders exported them to Portugal. The town of Teltow to the south of Berlin is "the true home of tasty turnips" enthused one author in 1740. The secret of this early agricultural brand name was that the roots grew more slowly on the sandy soil of the Mark of Brandenburg than elsewhere. It took longer for them to ripen, but they were wonderfully tender as a result. They are expensive to grow, and their cultivation has been in decline over recent decades, but one agricultural cooperative has shown itself willing to experiment and has been sowing them on a large scale since 1996.

Turnips can be fried and served with a light roux, or glazed by caramelizing them with sugar and butter before pouring on meat stock, and cooking them until the fluid has evaporated.

Gänsesuppe mit Bohnen
Goose soup with beans

1lb/500 g dried white beans
1lb/500 g goose meat
1 tbsp/15 g clarified butter
4 oz/100 g bacon
salt and pepper
3 sprigs of marjoram
1lb/500 g potatoes
flour and butter for the roux
sugar and vinegar

Soak the beans overnight. Bring them to a boil with the water in which they have been soaked. Dice the goose meat. Heat a little clarified butter and fry the bacon. Fry the goose meat briskly in another skillet with the rest of the clarified butter. Add the bacon. Mix everything in with the beans; season with salt, pepper, and marjoram. Cover with a lid and cook for about 1½ hours over a low heat. While the soup is cooking, peel the potatoes, and dice finely. Boil in salted water. Add the diced potato to the soup. Make a roux with the flour, butter, and a little of the soup. Add to the soup, and season with sugar and vinegar to give a sweet and sour flavor.

Kürbissuppe
Pumpkin soup

1lb/500 g pumpkin flesh
2 tbsp butter
1 tbsp sugar
mace, ground cloves
2 cups/500 ml vegetable stock
2 cups/500 ml milk
salt and pepper

Halve the pumpkin and remove the seeds. Peel the pumpkin, dice the flesh, then fry it in melted butter. Sprinkle with sugar. Add the spices, milk, and vegetable stock. Cover with a lid and simmer for approximately 30 minutes. Blend the soup and season with salt, pepper, and sugar.

Bring the soaked beans for the goose soup to a boil.

Dice about 1lb (500 g) of goose meat.

Heat clarified butter and fry the diced goose briskly.

Fry bacon in another skillet, then add to the goose.

Hirsekohl
Millet cabbage

1 small white cabbage
9 oz/250 g smoked pork belly
1 onion, finely diced
salt
1 tsp caraway
14 oz/400 g millet
1–2 tbsp linseed oil

Clean and quarter the cabbage, then cut into strips.
Dice the pork belly and fry in a pan. Add the onion
and fry with the meat until transparent. Add the
cabbage and pour on a little water. Season with salt
and caraway, then fry lightly. Wash the millet and
simmer over a low heat for about 15 minutes.
Combine the millet with the cabbage and add linseed
oil to taste.

Märkischer Topf mit Teltower Rübchen
Brandenburg stew with baby turnips

1½ lbs/750 g baby turnips
½ cup/60 g butter
1 tbsp sugar
½ cup/125 ml hot meat stock
11 oz/300 g fresh mushrooms
2 shallots, finely diced
salt and pepper
1¼ lbs/600 g fillet of beef
2 tbsp oil
1 tbsp flour
1 scant cup/200 g sour cream

Clean and halve the turnips. Melt half the butter, mix in
the sugar, and caramelize. Add the turnips and pour
on the stock. Cook for 20 minutes over a low heat.
While the turnips are cooking, clean the mushrooms
and cut into pieces. Fry the shallots until transparent
in the rest of the butter. Add the mushrooms, season
with salt and pepper, and fry for a further 10 minutes.
Cut the fillet of beef into fine slices, fry briskly in the oil,
then sprinkle with flour. Mix in the sour cream, then
combine the turnips and all the cooking liquids with
the mushrooms. Season well with salt and pepper,
and serve with creamed or boiled potatoes.

Mix everything in with the beans,
season, cover, and cook.

Make a roux while the potatoes are
cooking.

Add the potatoes and the roux to the
soup and bring to a boil again.

Season the goose soup with sugar
and vinegar for a sweet-sour flavor.

**German
vegetables**

Blanched celery

Celeriac

Dwarf bean

Broad bean

Cucumber

Runner bean

Peas

Spinach

Carrots

White winter
radish

Red winter radish

Black salsify

Radishes

Asparagus

Leek

Red beet

Swede

Teltow baby turnip

Onion

The carrots are ready to be harvested. It is time to start the machines, grab the vegetables by their tops, and pull them from the earth.

Cauliflower

Pumpkin

Rhubarb

Kohlrabi

White cabbage

Pointed cabbage

Kale

Red cabbage

Brussels sprout

Swiss chard

Savoy cabbage

Broccoli

95

An anti-gelling agent is mixed into the strawberry must. It is stirred, then wine yeast is added.

The strawberry must is filtered, then poured into a fermentation jar through a funnel.

Sugar is dissolved in hot water, then added to the fermentation jar.

A fermentation lock is placed on top of the fermentation jar. This allows carbonic acid to escape.

Last of the summer wine

When the trees began to bloom in Werder, the clerks at the town's post office knew they were in for a hectic time. Four to five hundredweight of picture postcards from the idyllic town not far from Potsdam and Berlin had to be processed on *Blütensonntag* (Blossom Sunday). This was all on account of the fruit cultivator Wilhelm Wils. On March 13, 1879 he suggested to a committee meeting of the Werder fruit growers' organization that an announcement should be printed in all the Berlin newspapers when the blossom on the fruit trees was nearing its best. Nearly two months later the Berliners came in hordes on special trains to drink the famous Werder fruit wine and get a little tipsy under the blossoms of the peach, apple, and pear trees. The sweet, fruity flavor of the wine disguised its treacherous character, and, for obvious reasons, it came to be known as *Bretterknaller* ("the hammer"). It often gave the police extra work during the blossom festival. Though things are somewhat less rowdy nowadays, Werder still celebrates the coming of the blossom every year, electing a "Blossom Queen" at the beginning of the celebrations. Fruit is cultivated on 6200 acres (2500 hectares) of land in the Havelland, which is more than half the total acreage devoted to fruit growing in the entire Brandenburg region.

Until the middle of the 18th century winegrowing and fishing were the main ways that the people of Werder made their livings. The monks at the Lehnin Cistercian monastery had begun growing vines in the 13th century, and in 1740 there were 130 vineyard owners. The end came suddenly when *phylloxera* insects destroyed all their vines, so the winegrowers turned to fruit cultivation. By 1900 there were 3575 acres (1448 hectares) around Werder planted with fruit.

The fruit growers used the produce they could not sell to make a range of wines. And what a range: strawberry wine, apple cider, cherry wine, blackcurrant wine, gooseberry wine, raspberry wine, apricot, peach, and plum wines.

The exact recipes are family secrets, but anyone who goes to Werder for the blossom festival is more than welcome to sample a few. Not only that, for the last ten years even the Werder vineyards have been seeing a renaissance. The Werderaner Wachtelberg amateur winegrowers' club now administers the local winegrowing area and fills as many as 20,000 bottles every year.

The Duchesse de Paris and her entourage

Pears

"Herr Ribbeck lived on Ribbeck in Havelland, / In his garden a pear tree did stand," begins a famous poem by Theodor Fontane about old Herr Ribbeck, who gives the children pears during the "golden autumn time." When he dies he has a pear laid in his grave. In time it sprouts and grows into a pear tree, which calls on the children to taste its fruit in autumn, speaking the same words as the old man before he died.

The old man of Ribbeck's famous pear tree is no longer standing. On February 20, 1911, a hurricane knocked over the rotten trunk by the church wall of the village of Ribbeck once and for all. Modern children, accustomed to sweeter food, would probably have taken little pleasure in its fruit. Historical sources prove that the old tree was a wild pear and bore only *Kodden* (sour pears) all its life.

Happily, sweeter varieties also flourish in the orchards of Brandenburg. The abundance of traditional dishes, such as the many different regional variations on dumplings with pears, shows that the fruit has long been popular in the region's kitchens. It is not only eaten as a sweet dessert, but also as a hearty main meal dish. *Salzbirne*, for example, are often pickled with fennel and dill, and preserved pears seasoned with cinnamon and cloves are eaten from the stone jug with relish as an accompaniment to roast meat and potatoes.

The pear was introduced to Germany from Persia and Armenia by way of Asia Minor and Italy. There are now 1500 varieties of pear grown in

Most of the pear varieties commonly found in Germany today were bred in France and Belgium during the 18th and 19th centuries.

Germany, only a fraction of which are cultivated in large quantities. Some varieties have very attractive names, such as Duchesse de Paris, the sweet Vereinsdechantsbirne ("association deacon pear"), and the Katzenkopf ("cat's head") pear, which is inedible when raw, but wonderful when cooked.

The flesh of the pear is rich in minerals, such as potassium, magnesium, calcium, and phosphorus. Pears do not keep as well as apples, and many are preserved, puréed, stewed, or used for making wines and liqueurs. A cookbook dating from 1724 gives the following recipe for fried minced pear: "Take peeled pears, cut them into small pieces, fry them in lard, put in a handful of raisins, sugar, cinnamon, a little toasted bread, mix all together well. Spread the pear quite thickly onto wafers."

Nordhäuser Winterforellenbirne.
A sweet dessert pear, stores well.

Beurre de Bosc.
A juicy dessert and stewing pear.

Alexander Lucas.
A juicy sour-sweet dessert pear.

Duchesse de Paris.
A late ripening dessert pear, stores well.

Pastorenbirne.
A dessert pear with yellow-white flesh.

97

Load the goulash cannon!

The Roman king, who later became Emperor Joseph I, ordered not less than two wagons of poultry and six of wine to accompany him in his baggage train when he set off from Vienna for the Rhine to take part in the siege of Landau in 1702. If only with regard to his own person, he had already taken to heart what the Prussian King Frederick II later expressed in the words: "Someone who wants to build an army must begin with the stomach, because it is the foundation on which he must build." Hardly any soldier has ever enjoyed the kind of luxury required by Joseph I, but provisions could decide between victory and defeat. Plundering was one way of feeding hungry soldiers, but the science of food logistics gradually became a focus of military thinking as mercenary armies began to be replaced by standing forces after the Thirty Years War. In 1714 Gottfried Wilhelm von Leibniz described his concentrated meat extract, which was intended to satisfy soldiers' hunger. The idea had been suggested to him by the inventor of the pressure cooker, the French physicist Papin. In 1784 a man by the name of Benjamin Thompson, who was in the service of the Bavarian court, gave thought to a soup for soldiers and wrote:

"It surprised me not a little to discover how a small amount of solid food, if it is prepared properly, can satisfy hunger sufficiently and maintain life and health, and with how little cost even a strong, hard-working man can be fed."

The "proper preparation" was as follows: a great deal of water, pearl barley, peas, and potatoes were boiled for three hours, then mixed to an even consistency. Finally, a little salt and vinegar, and a couple of slices of bread were added to this vitamin graveyard. At the court they were delighted, but what the soldiers who had to eat Thompson's soup thought, we do not know.

Highly concentrated food was essential, particularly in emergency rations, or "iron rations," as they are known. In the 19th century there were already many alternatives: "pea sausage" made of pea flour, bacon, spices and salt, Paman's Blutzwieback, a biscuit made of flour baked with blood serum, and Professor Knoblauchs Kleberbrod, what was known as a *Fleischmehltafel*, a biscuit made of pea flour and meat extract. Many discussions revolved less around the nutritional properties of the foods than the costs involved. A "book of advice for managing military messes" calculated in 1882 how it was possible to make savings when cooking

In the 1871–72 war 1200 people were employed making pea sausage, which was mixed with water to make soup. Daily, more than 225 cwt of bacon, 450 cwt of pea flour, 28 bushels of onions and 40 cwt of salt were used to make 75,000 pea sausages, each weighing over a pound.

Kommissbrot (military bread) is made of rye flour. It was invented for Wallenstein's troops at the Siege of Stralsund in 1628. It is highly nutritious and keeps well.

Mobile field kitchens are known as "goulash cannons" in German military slang. They are also used to feed the crowds at large outdoor events.

Highly concentrated foods, such as meat extract, are essential emergency rations. They have been in production since the 19th century.

potatoes: "When they are peeled by the soldiers of the troop, 30 to 40 percent waste is to be expected, when women peel the potatoes only 15 to 25 percent." The author found it lamentable that many soldiers posted to kitchen duties were people "whom their commanders wanted to remove from the front for some reason or other." Instead of this, he felt it would be better to employ cooks who at least knew a little about cookery. This was important if only because suppliers often resorted to tricks in order to increase their profits. Rotten smells were disguised with chamomile tea, and meat was painted with aniline to make it appear fresh. Flour was adulterated with gypsum or chalk, and coffee powder was sometimes found to contain traces of wood from cigar boxes. In spite of these disgusting findings many young men were better off in the army than they were at home. Statistics show that most new recruits put on weight during their first months in uniform.

In the wars of the 20th century the standard foods, such as the coarse army bread made almost entirely of rye, meat extract, and military biscuits, were joined by new synthetic additives, such as Vitamin C. The *Gulaschkanone* ("goulash canon"), as mobile field kitchens have always been known in German military slang, was often a hastily improvised arrangement. One book for field mess officers describes how a kitchen can be built using a barrel as a fireplace, several food cans as a chimney, and pans made from captured British metal canisters. "The quality of the mess sergeant showed in how close to the front line he dared to take his pots," wrote Erich Maria Remarque in his novel *All Quiet on the Western Front*, which described conditions at the front during World War I. Even when the cooks were brave, soldiers still suffered from hunger. The book begins with a cynical description of soldiers at last enjoying a good meal. The only reason there is so much food for them is because the kitchen has cooked for 150 men, but only 80 have returned from the front.

Germany's modern peacetime army is fortunate in having lesser worries, such as how a vegetarian can get through military service without eating meat. This is not a problem, says the *Bundeswehr* (the army of the F.R.G.). The military recruitment agencies have been instructed to send vegetarians to units that offer modern "modular provisions," which allow each individual to assemble his or her own menus. Every army unit has a mess committee that takes part in consultations about what the soldiers should be given to eat. About 225,000 soldiers and civilian workers currently partake of military food every day in the German army. The goulash cannons are still in used, but now they are described officially as modern "integrated field kitchens with 250 men and equipment on trailers," and are able to boil, fry, and even bake.

Opposite: Soldiers queuing for food. Since the transition from mercenary armies to standing forces food logistics have been a military topic.

December 1812, The retreat from Moscow

"I found myself close to the French, one of whom went around the people sleeping by the fire to steal their food. He came back happily with a small sack of flour. What joy! I offered a piece of money if I could have part of his soup, which was now to be made. Soon the work began, and the flour was fried with horse fat in a small casserole, though we were worried that we might have to pay for it with our lives because a crowd of poor wretches collected around us who all wanted to have some. We had just decided to defend the soup at any cost when some of the flour went up in blue flames. It was sulfur and not flour! In my mind I had already eaten my share of the yellow brew, and now had no food at all. A fine way to greet the morning!"

(From: Carl Sachs, *Diaries, 1812*)

Wild boar

Wild boar do have rather wild manners. They root around in carefully tended front gardens, dig up despairing farmers' meadows, and search out every last maize seed that has been sown in the fields. The omnivorous razorbacks have become a real problem in some areas of Brandenburg, such as the outskirts of the Federal State capital Potsdam that border on the forest. Some difficulties arise because people like to feed the cute little young boar and are then amazed when the pack returns fully grown. On account of the huge expanses of unbroken arable land and forest inherited from the G.D.R.'s collective farms and the many areas of unused land at former military bases, the animals can move around more or less unhindered in many places. Stocks of wild boar in Brandenburg are estimated to be around 30,000, and hunters are permitted to kill 40,000 of them each year. The numbers only appear to be contradictory. On average a population of wild boar will grow at between 150 and 180 percent a year.

The European wild boar, which bears the fine Latin name *Sus scrofa scrofa* and, as readers of the Asterix books know, likes to say "oink oink," is a shy, nocturnal animal. The males, which grow to a maximum of 440 pounds (200 kilograms), are loners and only join the pack of sows and young during the mating season at the end of October. After bitter battles with its rivals in love, the victorious male goes off to mate with its chosen partner. The mating habits of wild boar are not exactly tender, and the females are left with large bites on their necks. Shortly before giving birth the female leaves the pack and keeps her four to twelve new-borns hidden for the first few days of their lives.

Obelix is certainly the most famous "historic" figure to have been obsessed with roast wild boar, but the Gauls were by no means the first to appreciate the animal's tasty meat: bones and cave paintings found by archeologists have proved that boar were being hunted in the Stone Age. They began to be domesticated around the middle of the 6th millennium B.C., and the modern domestic pig is originally descended from the wild boar.

Today wild boar is esteemed as a great delicacy, and the neck and back give excellent joints for roasting. The meat has a strong flavor and is leaner than that of domestic pigs.

Meat and game dishes

Wildschweinbraten
Pot roast wild boar
(Illustrated left)

2 lb/1 kg wild boar leg
salt and pepper
1 cup/250 ml red wine vinegar
soup vegetables (2 carrots, 2 celery stalks, 1 leek, 1 bunch of parsley)
2 onions, coarsely chopped
2 bay leaves
4 cloves
5 whole allspice
1 lemon cut into slices
1 tbsp sugar
5 oz/150 g streaky bacon, diced
1 tbsp clarified butter
1 cup/250 ml red wine
2 tbsp black breadcrumbs

Wash the leg, pat dry, and rub with plenty of salt and pepper. For the marinade, bring the vinegar briefly to a boil with the soup vegetables, onions, bay leaves, cloves, allspice, lemon slices, and sugar, then allow to cool. Pour the marinade over the meat and leave covered in a cool place for 1–2 days. Before roasting take the meat out of the marinade and drain well. Fry the bacon in hot clarified butter, then add the boar and turn it so that it is coated completely with butter. Pour on the red wine and the marinade. Cover and leave to cook slowly over a low heat for approximately 1 hour. When it is cooked, take the joint out of the pot and keep warm. Thicken the juices with the bread. Carve the joint and serve with the sauce, boiled, or creamed potatoes, and red cabbage or sauerkraut.

Pot roast wild boar

Meerrettichlende
Loin of beef with horseradish
(Illustrated right)

1¼ lbs/600 g loin of beef
salt and pepper
3 tbsp oil
9 oz/250 g onions cut into rings
1 cup/250 ml stock
2 large apples
1 tbsp butter
1 tbsp flour
scant ½ cup/100 g cream
1 cup/200 ml milk
2 tbsp red currant jelly
½ small root of horseradish, freshly grated
1 tbsp lemon juice

Wash the loin, pat dry, and rub with salt and pepper. Fry briskly in oil, turning frequently. Add the onion rings, fry them briefly with the meat, and pour on the stock. Cover and cook over a medium heat for approximately 1 hour. Peel, quarter, and core the apples. Cut them into pieces and fry in the butter. Mix the flour with the cream and the milk, combine with the apple, and simmer for a few minutes, stirring all the time. Mix the red currant jelly and horseradish into the sauce. Take the loin out of the casserole and pour the juices through a fine sieve into the apple sauce. Season the sauce with salt, pepper, and lemon juice. Cut the loin into slices and serve on warmed plates with the sauce and boiled potatoes.

Brandenburger Kohlrouladen
Brandenburg stuffed cabbage
(Illustrated center)

1 white cabbage
salt
1 stale bread roll
5 oz/150 g breakfast bacon, finely diced
13 oz/350 g ground meat
1 egg
2 tbsp diced black bread
salt and pepper
7 oz/200 g bacon, cut into slices
1 can of plum tomatoes
1¼ cups/300 ml meat stock
scant ½ cup/100 g sour cream
1 tsp sweet paprika
1 bunch of parsley, finely chopped

Clean the cabbage, cut out the stalk, and place in boiling salty water. Simmer for 20 minutes, then remove, and drain. Soak the bread roll in hot water for 10 minutes, then press the water out. Mix the ground meat thoroughly with the egg, the bread roll, diced breakfast bacon, and the diced bread, and season with salt and pepper. Strip the eight outer leaves from the cabbage and fill with the ground meat mixture. Fold the leaves around the stuffing and tie up with kitchen thread. Fry the slices of bacon in a metal casserole dish. Place the parcels of stuffed cabbage on top, and keep turning them as they fry. Dice the tomatoes and add to the stuffed cabbage. Pour on the meat stock, cover with a lid, and bake for approximately 1 hour in an oven preheated to 355 °F (180 °C). When they are cooked, take the parcels of stuffed cabbage out and keep warm. Mix sour cream into the sauce and season with salt, pepper, and paprika. Pour over the stuffed cabbage and sprinkle with parsley.

The joys of the chase

With 5.7 million acres (2.3 million hectares) of hunting land and large stocks of almost all kinds of game, Brandenburg is one of the richest hunting areas of the Federal Republic of Germany. 113,000 roe deer, 18,700 fallow deer, and 16,000 red deer were estimated to live there in 1996. Not far north of Berlin is one of the oldest and largest hunting grounds in Europe, the Schorfheide heathland. In 1962 the G.D.R. declared the area around the Werbellinsee lake a heavily guarded state hunting area.

The approach was not always sporting. On occasion the Chairman of the State Council Erich Honecker and similarly privileged comrades would shoot from their car, closed seasons were ignored, and little attention was paid to the finer points of hunting etiquette. The stocks of red deer were kept artificially high so that Honecker's trigger-happy guests could always find something to blast away at. The effects of this short-sighted management have been devastating. Shortly after reunification severe damage was found to have been done to the woodland in the Schorfheide, and there was hardly any heather left – there were simply too many animals. Shooting quotas have now improved the situation again.

Since 1996 new regulations have been in force that make poaching more difficult. They are also intended to protect people who like eating game from inferior goods. All hunters have to label the game they shoot with numbered tags before selling it on, and when a carcass is bought, the buyer is obliged to enter its tag number in special game registers. This means that the authorities can always trace its origins.

Loin of beef with horseradish

Brandenburg stuffed cabbage leaves

101

Hamburg

Schwerin

Bremen

Berlin

Hanover

Potsdam

Magdeburg

Düsseldorf

Dresden

Bonn

Erfurt

Wiesbaden

Mainz

Saarbrücken

Stuttgart

Munich

MONIKA ALBRECHT

Mecklenburg-West Pomerania

"We have found our little island in today's rather stormy world … when an airman flies over this part of the province of Mecklenburg he sees forests and lakes, lakes and forests," wrote the author Hans Fallada. Fallada retired to Carvitz, near Feldberg in 1933, when the times were stormy indeed. Even today, many decades and two political systems later, the landscape of Mecklenburg and West Pomerania conveys a sense of natural peace and tranquility. Its lakes and rivers, its Baltic coastline, the inlets from the sea and the freshwater lagoons known as the "Haff", right on the Polish border, make up ten percent of the entire territory of the province. However, the fertile land is cultivated by over 4000 farmers. Grain, potatoes, roots and fodder crops in particular flourish on its 3700 million acres (1.5 million hectares) of arable land. In early summer, when the oilseed rape is in flower, great expanses of the countryside glow brilliant yellow.

It is only since 1990 that Mecklenburg-West Pomerania has been a single province of Germany. It consists of what used to be the three northern administrative districts of Rostock, Schwerin and Neubrandenburg. Mecklenburg, with 1000 years of history behind it, became a Grand Duchy in 1815. Pomerania, on the other hand, was Prussian territory before Germany absorbed it. Frederick the Great valued his Pomeranians as "men of plain and upright disposition" with "something unaffected about them."

For centuries, the two landscapes have been notable for their contrasts. The Baltic coast, with such offshore islands as Rügen and Hiddensee, attracted poets and painters; the citizens of the Hanseatic towns of Wismar, Rostock, Stralsund, Greifswald, Demmin, and Anklam had a flourishing trade with Scandinavia which brought economic prosperity, yet serfdom was not abolished in rural areas until the 19th century.

For a long period, parts of the region were in the possession of Sweden, a fact that probably influenced its cuisine. Characteristic of the local food is a liking for sweet-sour flavors; in general, the cooking of the area can be described as nourishing and down-to-earth.

Left: 4374 kilometers (2734 miles) of roads in Mecklenburg-West Pomerania are tree-lined avenues, protected under the constitution of the province.

Chalk cliffs on Rügen, by Caspar David Friedrich, is a major work of Romantic painting.

Elizabeth on Rügen

"We arrived, therefore, at Stubbenkammer about six o'clock in a state of perfect concord, pleasantly tired, and hot enough to be glad we had got there. On the plateau in front of the restaurant – there is, of course, a restaurant at the climax of the walk – there were tables under the trees and people eating and drinking. One table, at a little distance from the others, with the best view over the cliff, had a white cloth on it, and was spread for what looked like tea. There were nice thin cups, and strawberries, and a teapot, and a jug in the middle with roses in it; and while I was wondering who were the privileged persons for whom it had been laid Gertrud came out of the restaurant, followed by a waiter carrying thin bread and butter, and then I knew that the privileged persons were ourselves.

'I had tea with you yesterday,' I said to Mrs Harvey-Browne. 'Now it is your turn to have tea with me.'

'How charming,' said Mrs Harvey-Browne with a sigh of satisfaction, sinking into a chair and smelling the roses. 'Your maid seems to be one of those rare treasures who like doing extra things for their mistresses.'

Well, Gertrud is a rare treasure, and it did look clean and dainty next to the beer-stained tables at which coffee was being drunk and spilt by tourists who had left their Gertruds at home. Then the place was so wonderful, the white cliffs cutting out sheer and sharp into the sea, the huge folds filled with every sort of greenery – masses of shrubby trees, masses of ferns, masses of wild flowers. Down at the bottom there was a steamer anchored … quite a big, two-funnelled steamer, and it looked from where we were like a tiny white toy."

From: Elizabeth von Arnim, *The Adventures of Elizabeth in Rügen*, 1904.

The cuisine of the islands

Rügen is Germany's largest island, a whole landscape in microcosm with its coast, moorland, forest, salt meadows, fields, cliffs, and even a chain of hills known as the "Alps." The fertile land, the sea, and the waters of the inlets made the islanders self-sufficient for centuries. They were fishermen and smallholders, and although not rich they had enough to live on: "Our poultry yard provided geese, turkeycocks, ducks, chickens, and pigeons,

and with his trusty gun my father brought down hares, partridges, wild duck, and the fine snipe with which the beach and the broad meadows nearby teemed," recollected the writer Ernst Moritz Arndt, born in Gross Schoritz on Rügen, in his childhood reminiscences written around 1765. Many traditional dishes of island cookery are the kind that people could make without too much laborious preparation after a day working in the fields, or on a fishing boat. They show the influence of Pomerania and Mecklenburg, and also Scandinavia, since Rügen and nearby Hiddensee belonged to Sweden from 1648 to 1815. Naturally, fish features prominently in island cuisine: Rügen has 170 miles (273 kilometers) of coastline. The inlets typical of the entire coast of Mecklenburg-

West Pomerania are particularly rich in fish. These inlets, for which the local word is *Bodden*, are irregularly shaped bays enclosed on almost all sides by land. As there is only a narrow opening from these inlets to the sea, the salt content of the water is so low that freshwater fish can live here. Inlet fish are more tender and tasty than fellow members of the same species from the sea or from fresh water. Among the delicacies of the islands are boiled cod with mustard sauce, Hiddensee eel soup, and braised eel. There are also a great many cabbage dishes: cabbage grows particularly well in the islands, which have moderate temperatures and plenty of sunlight. *Rügengeist* is offered with these traditional dishes: it is a high-proof mixture of grain spirit, sea buckthorn juice, and herbs, served very hot.

Rügener Aalsuppe
Rügen eel soup

1¾ lbs/800 g potatoes
4 cups/1 liter meat stock
1 large onion, finely diced
1 bayleaf
5 peppercorns
4 oz/125 g each carrots and celery
7 oz/200 g smoked eel
salt and pepper
½ tsp marjoram
1 bunch of chives

Peel the potatoes, wash and cut into cubes. Bring to a boil with the meat stock, onion, bayleaf, and peppercorns, and simmer for about 30 minutes. Then remove the bayleaf and purée the soup with a hand-held mixer. Cut the vegetables into thin strips and blanch them briefly. Cut the smoked eel into narrow strips, heat it and the vegetables in the soup, and season well with salt, pepper, and marjoram. Snip the chives finely and sprinkle over the soup before serving.

Opposite: Rügen is Germany's largest island and the chalk cliffs are its best-known feature.

Geschmorter Schweinekamm mit Backpflaumen
Braised pork fillet with prunes

12 oz/350 g prunes, stoned
2 oz/50 g sugar
2 tbsp grated gingerbread
1¾ lbs/800 g boneless pork fillet (from the neck)
salt and pepper
2 tbsp clarified butter
soup vegetables (2 carrots, 2 celery stalks, 1 leek, a bunch of parsley), coarsely diced
2 onions, finely diced
1 tsp tomato paste
1 tbsp cornstarch

Simmer the prunes with the sugar in 1 cup/250 ml hot water for 10 minutes. Stir in the grated gingerbread and bring to a boil again. Remove from the stove, and allow to stand for 1 hour. Rub the meat with salt and pepper and seal on all sides in the hot butter at high heat. Add the soup vegetables and onions and fry all together for a few minutes. Stir in the tomato paste, add 2 cups/500 ml water, and allow the meat to braise, covered, for about 1 hour. Take the meat out of the pan and keep it warm. Strain the liquid and bring to a boil again. Blend the cornstarch in a little water, add to the sauce and simmer for a few minutes. Meanwhile, reheat the prunes and cut the pork in slices. Arrange the meat on a warmed serving dish, pour the sauce over, and garnish with the prunes.

Filet vom Boddenbarsch
Fillet of bay perch

4 bay perch fillets, each weighing 7 oz/200 g
salt and pepper
5 tbsp flour
2 tbsp oil
1 onion, finely diced
½ cup/125 ml white wine
¾ cup/200 g puréed tomatoes
¾ cup/200 ml cream
7 oz/200 g crayfish tails

Wash the perch fillets, pat them dry, season with salt and pepper. Coat with flour and fry on both sides in the hot oil until golden brown. Take the fish fillets out of the skillet and keep them warm. Fry the diced onion gently in the contents of the pan, then add the white wine, the puréed tomatoes, and the cream. Season the sauce with salt and pepper, add the crayfish tails and perch fillets, and let them simmer gently in the sauce for a few minutes, but do not boil them. Serve with fresh buttered vegetables such as green asparagus and sugar snap peas.

A good catch of fish
Fresh fish

"A visitor to any part of the coastline, hearing family anecdotes told in cosy little cottages, taking his ease in a modern hotel, or enjoying the sun on the warm, sandy beach, must never forget that all the villages, meadows and pastures, woods and dunes have a dangerous neighbor – the water!" In his book *Zwischen Meer und Bodden* ("Between sea and inlet") Fritz Meyer-Scharffenberg describes the elemental forces that prevail on the Baltic coast, which is very different from the North Sea coast, where everything is ruled by the ebb and flow of the tide.

The fishermen become more closely acquainted than anyone with that "dangerous neighbor." They have gone out for generations to harvest the riches of the seas. Indeed, the sea has been so thoroughly exploited, particularly over the last few decades, that deep sea fishing is now in serious difficulties. Stocks of cod, the staple catch of the Baltic fishing industry, have been so severely reduced that the quota for German fishermen is set at only a few thousand tonnes. In addition, cheap imports from Scandinavia and Eastern Europe are flooding the market, undermining the basis of the native fishermen's very existence. Nor can they earn much from the herring which made many merchants rich in the past. Herring stocks have in fact improved again, but Baltic herring are smaller than North Sea herring and fetch lower prices.

About 600 deep sea and coastal fishermen work in Mecklenburg-West Pomerania. They catch over 100 species of fish in their nets, first and foremost herring, followed by cod, flounder, needlefish, turbot, whiting, sprats, plaice (summer flounder), dabs, haddock, sole, and hake. Fishing grounds for shrimp are Oderhaff, Peenestrom, Achterwasser, the Greifswald Inlet, Strelasund, the Darss inlet chain, the Bight of Wismar, and the coastal waters of the Baltic. The most common freshwater fish include perch, zander, roach, pike, eel, bream, houting, salmon and trout, and

laveret. Various fish species used for animal feed are also caught.

Fresh herring can be enjoyed in Freest, a fishing port which is becoming more and more of an attraction for gourmets. The herring season brings visitors early in the year, and they can come back for the eel season in late summer. In Rostock-Warnemünde, whole flotillas of trawlers put out to sea in February and March to catch herring. Chugging along, always two by two, they bring up the silver harvest of the sea, with flocks of gulls in their wake looking for easy pickings. In Rankwitz, on the island of Usedom, you can buy fish on the quayside, and indeed eat it on the spot. Fishing has been the main industry here since the end of the 19th century. Over a long period the Usedomer Feinfisch (Usedom Fine Fish) company has been a hot tip among people on vacation or a sailing trip; a small country restaurant attached to it serves salmon trout, *matje* herring and smoked eel to its own recipes, and there is a trout farm only a few meters away.

While the people of Rügen swear by their local cod, which lives in brackish water and is particularly tender, the people of Ueckermund claim that the best zander are caught in the "Haff" freshwater lagoons. The coastal dwellers have another speciality: the garfish (*Belone belone*). It is caught in May, and then the restaurants along the coast prepare garfish dishes. You get a surprise when you take the fish off its bones – they are bright green! But there is no need for alarm: vivianite, the mineral substance that produces the green color, is entirely harmless.

Kak't Dösch
Poached cod

4 cod steaks, each weighing 8 oz/250 g
salt and pepper
juice of 1 lemon
3 tbsp butter
soup vegetables (2 carrots, 2 celery stalks, 1 leek, a bunch of parsley), coarsely diced
1 onion spiked with a bayleaf
4 allspice berries
2 tbsp flour
1 cup/250 ml cream
3 tbsp hot mixed mustard
2 egg yolks
a dash of wine vinegar
a pinch of sugar

Wash the cod steaks, pat dry, and season with salt and pepper. Sprinkle them with the lemon juice, and let them stand for 15 minutes. Meanwhile, melt 1 tbsp of the butter, and gently fry the soup vegetables in it. Add 6 cups/1½ liters of water, the onion, and the allspice berries, and simmer for 10 minutes. Then add the cod steaks and cook gently over low heat for about 8 minutes. Lift the fish out and keep it warm; strain the liquid. Melt the remaining butter and add the flour, stirring. Blend with 1 cup/250 ml of the fish stock, stir in the cream, and simmer together for a few minutes. Mix the mustard, egg yolks, and wine vinegar together. Take the sauce off the stove, stir in the egg yolk mixture, and season to taste with salt, pepper, and sugar. Serve with boiled potatoes or buttered vegetables.

Gebratene Fischklopse Sassnitzer Art
Fried fishballs Sassnitz style

a generous 1 lb/500 g fish fillet
2 eggs
1 onion, finely diced
3 oz/75g breadcrumbs
salt, white pepper, and nutmeg
oil for frying

Put the fish fillet through the grinder and mix to a firm consistency with the eggs, onion, and breadcrumbs. Season with salt, pepper, and ground nutmeg, and shape into small balls. Fry in batches in the hot oil until golden yellow, then lift out with a slotted spoon, and allow to drain briefly on kitchen paper. Serve with potato salad, or with boiled potatoes and mixed vegetables.

To prepare cod fillets, first remove the backbone of the fish.

Then cut the fish into portions of about equal size.

Season with salt and pepper, sprinkle with lemon juice and allow to stand.

The fish must not boil, just poach very gently.

Eels

"The man in the longshoreman's cap ... stood firmly planted over the lump of horsemeat, from which small light-green eels were darting furiously. The man had trouble in catching them, for eels move quickly and deftly, especially over smooth wet stones. Already the gulls were screaming overhead. They wheeled down, three or four of them would seize a small or medium-sized eel, and they refused to be driven away, for the breakwater was their domain."

The scene observed in this passage by Oskar Matzerath, the hero of Günter Grass's *The Tin Drum*, is not very appetizing – the longshoreman has put a freshly killed horse's head into the water as bait – but luckily such methods of catching eels are no longer in use.

The eel that ends up in a smokehouse or the pot today has been caught either by professional fishermen or amateur anglers. In this province, which contains more areas of water than any other *Land* in Germany, 55,000 inhabitants hold an angler's license and look forward to the eel season in summer. The eel is a creature of darkness; it winds its way along the bottom, and is usually caught from boats by night, or as twilight falls. It is not always easy to get an eel to take the bait, so it should be offered some tempting morsel from its natural environment: worms, mollusks, shrimp, tiny fish. It is a proud moment for an amateur angler when he bears an eel home in triumph. Commercial fishermen cannot wait for such moments, but work with trawl lines or eel traps that guarantee a bigger catch. Since the eels pass through Danish coastal waters on the way to their spawning grounds, catches there are particularly good.

In former East Germany the eel was described as a three-colored fish: it was caught green, smoked brown, and sold black – that is, at a high price on the black market.

Besides its high protein and vitamin content, the eel has few bones, so people who find eating fish tricky can enjoy it without fearing they may choke. However, even those who like Japanese raw fish *sushi* dishes ought not to eat eels raw: they contain a strong neurotoxin (ichthyotoxin) which is destroyed only by smoking or cooking.

Amateur anglers seldom catch eels. Professionals use eel traps or trawl lines.

The journey of life

The surface of the waters of Lake Müritz, the largest lake in Mecklenburg, is turbulent: new tenants have arrived, about 70,000 of them. But there will be no underwater housing problems – the lake, 45 square miles (117 square kilometers) in size, can easily accommodate the little elvers, each weighing no more than 25–30 g (1 oz), placed there in special containers every year in the fall. Their new home will be in the reeds along the bank, where they will have natural protection from the predators of the water and the air. Their survival is in the interests of the fishermen of Lake Müritz, who want to maintain their stocks; conservation as well as catching fish is part of their job.

The elvers have a long journey behind them; they come from the tributaries of the Rivers Rhine and Maas. However, that is not by any means the longest journey they have made in their lives. The spawning grounds of *Anguilla anguilla*, the European river eel, are in the Sargasso Sea south of the Bermudas, some 2485 miles (4000 kilometers) from Europe. As soon as they have hatched, while still at the larval stage, the tiny eels begin their journey, which is literally child's play – they simply let themselves drift with the Gulf Stream. They do not mind that it is a slow journey: it will take them two or three years to reach the coasts of Europe and North Africa. By now they are the size of a matchstick and transparent, and are known as elvers or glass eels. Now the serious business of life begins for the eels, in the rivers. During this phase of growth they turn dark in color. They have to swim upstream along the rivers to find a new place to live, and since civil engineering works often make that impossible, they are caught and taken to new surroundings – eel farms such as Lake Müritz. However, some eels spend this part of their lives in brackish water. The age of sexual maturity depends on the food available and the water temperature, but on average it is eight to ten years old. "In densely populated brackish water or in captivity with other eels, eels tend to be male, remaining lethargic and short in length, 1 m/ 3 ft long at the most. But if they make the effort to struggle upstream alone, they become female, and can be up to 5 feet (1.5 meters) in length," writes Jörg-Uwe Albig in *Geo*.

On reaching sexual maturity the eels stop feeding. They feel the urge to return to the sea in September and October, and will often go through damp meadows if there are no waterways available. They now have silvery markings on the sides and belly, and are known as silver eels.

An exhausting journey follows on their way back to the Sargasso Sea – without assistance from the Gulf Stream this time. They have to swim, deriving nourishment from their thick cushion of fat. An eel can live up to four years without food. It is thought to take eels about six months to return to the spawning grounds.

When they have reproduced, the eels die. They are about ten years old. If eels are prevented from going back to spawn, however, perhaps because researchers keep them in aquariums, they can live to be 50 – although of course without ever seeing the seas of their youth again, or making the last part of the journey that sets the seal of success on the life of an eel.

Aal in Sauer oder Marinierter Aal
Pickled or marinated eel

a 2 lb/1kg fresh eel, cleaned and ready to cook
salt and pepper
1 cup/250 ml white wine vinegar
1 unwaxed lemon, sliced
1 tsp sage
2 onions, coarsely diced
2 bay leaves
1 tsp mixed allspice berries, mustard seed, and peppercorns

Cut the eel in pieces about 1½ in/4 cm long, season with salt and pepper and set aside for 20 minutes. Bring the vinegar to a boil with 2 cups/500 ml water, the sliced lemon, sage, diced onions, bay leaves, allspice berries, mustard seed, and peppercorns. Simmer for 10 minutes. Add the eel to the liquid, and simmer gently for 15 minutes. The eel can be served hot in its liquid, or allowed to cool in a dish with a well-fitting lid.

The eel fishermen's day begins early in the morning.

The eel traps are heavy; there may well be a good catch.

Such a weight could send him head first into the water!

What have we here? The contents of the eel pots are tipped out on deck.

Now they must be sorted quickly, since …

… the eels are packed into containers still alive.

The "three-colored fish" in its first stage: green.

It will be smoked brown in the smokehouse.

The eel leaves the smokehouse a gleaming golden brown.

Smoked eel is no longer sold on the black market.

A glass full of fire

The drinking habits of the people of Mecklenburg and Pomerania have changed a number of times over the centuries. Once their main beverage was a kind of weak beer called *Kofent*. When coffee and tea reached Europe in the middle of the 17th century, this weak drink fell out of favor. But the most popular drink was schnaps: it was warming and stimulating, and you could put it in a metal flask and take it out in the fields. Many people made their own schnaps from potatoes.

Although home distilling was forbidden, the Prussian state made sure that its population had enough to drink – a certain amount of apathy among the common people was politically useful, so during the 19th century distilleries were built at intervals of 30 to 60 miles (50 to 100 kilometers) to supply taverns and grocery stores. The best-known liquor manufacturer in the area is probably the Richtenberg distillery of northwest Pomerania, where schnaps has been made for over a century,

including the brands known as Pommernschnaps and Richtenberger Korn.

Sparkling elderflower wine and sloe wine are other typical local drinks, still made today by country people in the northeast of the region. Men and women alike go out to strip the fruit off the elder bushes and sloe trees growing beside the fields.

However, the climate is generally unsuitable for winegrowing, and it was not until the 18th century that wine became increasingly popular in the high society of Mecklenburg and Pomerania. It was shipped to the seaports in barrels, and was usually red Bordeaux from the Pyrenees. It had to be kept for at least three months before it was fit to drink, and was then put into carafes. Beer became popular again in the 20th century. Doctors and dieticians deplore the amount of alcohol consumed here, which is far greater than in other parts of Germany; the people of Mecklenburg and West Pomerania definitely hold the record, consuming 28 pints (16.1 liters) of pure alcohol per head a year. The average in Germany is 21 pints (12 liters) per head. Much of the amount drunk is high-proof liquor, and it is always possible that the high unemployment rate of up to 25 percent in many parts of the region is behind an increasing readiness to reach for the bottle.

Egg beer: either dark or light beer, mixed with sugar, ground ginger, egg yolk, cinnamon, and a little water.

Elderberry glühwein: wine made from elderberry juice is heated and flavoured with cloves.

Bilberry liqueur: freshly picked bilberries are mixed with sugar, schnaps, vanilla, and cinnamon.

Pomeranian punch: this mixture of bitter oranges, red wine and sparkling wine used to be served to army officers in the mess.

Sea buckthorn liqueur: sea buckthorn juice, sugar and spirits are the ingredients of this vitamin-rich drink.

Sloe wine: wine made from sloe juice fermented with sugar.

Rügengeist, a high-proof mixture of grain spirit, sea buckthorn juice and herbs, is served hot.

Desserts

Rhubarb compote in late spring, red fruit pudding with milk in summer, potato pancakes with fresh apples in early fall – these were the staple dishes eaten by the people of Mecklenburg and West Pomerania to sweeten their lives. In the old days, before the invention of preserving and bottling methods, dried fruit was used for compotes during most of the year. Housewives stocked up for winter by drying plums, apples, pears, and even cherries. Prunes were particularly important, as an essential ingredient in stuffings for roast duck or goose. Pears with dumplings, and puréed prunes often featured on the menu, along with red fruit pudding – *Rote Grütze* – cold sweet soups, and a "good semolina flummery."

Everything provided by nature or the garden was put to good use. People went into the woods to pick blueberries and raspberries, white elderflowers and black elderberries, and sloes after the first frosts. All kinds of fruit soups and liqueurs were made from these ingredients.

The fruit often went into cakes too. Although a 19th-century chronicler claimed that "we know little of cakes in these parts," many *Pottkauken* (cakes stirred in a pan over heat) and *Platenkauchen* (cakes cooked in the oven on a cookie sheet) were made. Countrywomen would mix the latter at home, put them on the cookie sheet and then take them to the village baker to be cooked, since their homes often had no ovens. These cakes included the yeast cakes still very popular today, and baked in large quantities for special family celebrations. *Pottkauken*, on the other hand, really were partly cooked in a pan, and later baked in a round earthenware mold.

Götterspeise
Fruit jelly dessert
(Illustrated right)

4 cups/200 g black breadcrumbs
2 tbsp cocoa powder
2 tbsp sugar
brandy
5 tbsp/150 g blackcurrant jelly
1 tbsp rum
¾ cup/200 ml cream
½ tsp vanilla extract
the zest of 1 lemon, grated

Mix the breadcrumbs with the cocoa and sugar, and stir in enough brandy to give the mixture a glutinous consistency. Allow to soak for 30 minutes. Stir the blackcurrant jelly with the rum until smooth. Whip the cream with the vanilla extract until it begins to thicken, and fold in the grated lemon zest. Arrange layers of the breadcrumb mixture, the blackcurrant jelly, and the cream in four glasses.

Brotpudding
Bread pudding

8 oz/250 g black bread
1 cup/250 ml red wine
4 oz/ 100 g raisins
2 oz/50 g currants
6 eggs, separated
½ cup/125 g confectioner's sugar
¼ cup/60 g butter
½ tsp cinnamon
4 oz/100 g nibbed or flaked almonds
pinch of salt
butter and white breadcrumbs for the mold

Crumble or grate the black bread finely, and soak in the red wine for 20 minutes. Soften the raisins and currants in a little hot water. Beat the egg yolk with the confectioner's sugar and butter until foamy, then stir in the cinnamon and almonds, the breadcrumbs, and the drained raisins and currants. Whip the egg whites with a pinch of salt until very stiff, and fold into the breadcrumb mixture. Butter a lidded mold, and sprinkle with the white breadcrumbs. Pour the pudding mixture into the mold, put the lid on, and let it cook in a *bain-marie* for an hour. Let it stand in the mold for another 20 minutes, to firm up. Turn the pudding out on a dessert platter, and serve with zabaglione sauce.

Birnen und Klösse
Pears with dumplings

a generous 2 lb/1 kg pears
the juice of 2 lemons
1 vanilla bean
1 cinnamon stick
4 cloves
1 cup/250 ml white wine

Peel, quarter, and core the pears. Cut into slices, and sprinkle with the lemon juice. Split the vanilla bean in half lengthways and simmer in the white wine for ten minutes with the cinnamon stick and cloves. Add the pears and 1 cup/250 ml water, and simmer for another 10 minutes. Strain the compote, reserving the syrup. Bring the syrup back to a boil, and simmer small dumplings in it until they are done. Put the pears back in the syrup and serve hot or cold, sprinkled with sugar and cinnamon.

A flock of goslings. Soon after they have hatched, their feathers dry out and they look like little balls of down.

Geese

Martina was the name of the gosling adopted by the animal behaviorist Konrad Lorenz soon after she hatched. In a fascinating book, Lorenz tells us a great deal about the social behavior of geese and the way they communicate. Martina was a graylag goose, the original form of our domestic goose. Mankind has probably kept geese ever since the New Stone Age, but the modern breeds have been developed only in the last 200 years. Among the old breeds that are now rare are the Emden goose, the Diepholz goose, and the Lippe goose. The goose most usually kept in northern Germany is the Pomeranian goose, which is also bred across the border in Poland, although mainly for export to Germany.

The goose is regarded as the best of all poultry, and was once sure to feature on the menu of a princely banquet, and for Christmas dinner in prosperous families. Once the old northeast German custom, whereby masters and men dined together, went out of fashion in the second half of the 19th century, ordinary laborers seldom tasted roast goose. The farmer and his farmhands used to eat from the same dish, but the new custom of separate dining also brought with it differences of social class in table manners and the kind of food served.

In the old days, the goosegirl or gooseherd used to lead the birds over the stubble fields, where they could fatten themselves up on the grain that had fallen to the ground, and they were known as "stubble geese." Before the invention of man-made fibers, goose feathers were of great economic importance, providing both warm stuffing for quilts, and quill pens for writing.

A free-range country goose is one of the culinary delicacies of northeast Germany. It cannot be too big, for there is a saying that: "A Pomeranian can stomach anything," and the people of Mecklenburg complain that a goose is "too much for one and not enough for two." However, if you serve a roast goose to guests with normal appetites you can expect it to feed five to six people very well. In Mecklenburg-West Pomerania the bird is, of course, stuffed with the culinary trio of prunes, apples, and bread typical of the region.

Opposite: geese are good watchmen. In ancient Rome they saved the Capitol from attack with their loud cackling, and many ganders can be more dangerous than a watchdog. They like to attack people's calves.

Gänsebraten Pommersch

Pomeranian roast goose

Serves 6

8 oz/250 g stoned prunes
generous ½ cup/100 ml brandy
1 goose, weighing about 9 lb/4 kg
salt and pepper
a generous 1 lb/500 g apples
½ a bunch of thyme
3 tbsp dried black breadcrumbs
1 tsp cornstarch
½ cup/125 g cream

Soak the prunes in the brandy. Draw the goose (or remove the giblets if it is bought oven ready), clean it and pat it dry. Rub with salt and pepper outside and inside. Peel, quarter, core, and slice the apples. Mix them with the prunes and brandy, stir in the thyme and breadcrumbs, and stuff the goose with the mixture. Close the opening with toothpicks, and tie the bird up crosswise with kitchen string. Place the goose on a grid, stand the grid in a roasting pan containing 1 cup/250 ml of water. Roast in a preheated oven at 480 °F/250 °C for about 20 minutes, then pierce the goose below the legs with a skewer to make the fat run. Reduce the heat to 375 °F/190 °C, and roast the goose for another three hours. While it is roasting, baste it with a little water every 15 minutes. To make the gravy, skim the fat from the juices in the pan, add a little more water if necessary, and bring to a boil. Blend the cornstarch with the cream, and use to thicken the gravy. Serve with red cabbage and potato dumplings.

Regional goose specialties

Schwarzsauer von Gänseklein (Ragout of goose giblets with blood and vinegar)
Simmer the goose giblets until soft in salted water with some unsmoked, unsalted belly of pork, root vegetables, and a little seasoning. Strain the stock, and poach peeled, quartered pears in it until soft. Add some of the goose blood mixed with vinegar, ground cloves and allspice, pepper, and a little sugar. Bring the pears to a boil several times in the thickened stock, stirring. Place the meat in a dish, and pour the pears and their liquid over it.

Sauer eingekochtes Gänsefleisch (Preserved goose in vinegar)
Joint a goose. Add enough wine vinegar mixed with water to cover the meat. For 9 lb/4 kg of goose joints, flavor the stock with 5 or 6 bay leaves, 1 tsp each ground allspice and black pepper, 6 medium onions, and salt to taste. Simmer the meat until done in this liquid. For a more delicate flavor, add about 1 cup/250 ml of white wine. Once the meat is cooked, put it in a stoneware jar, and strain the stock over it through a sieve.

Gebratenes saures Gänsefleisch (Fried preserved goose)
Melt the jellied stock from the preserved goose over low heat, or wash it off with hot water. Sprinkle the meat with a little sugar, put it in a pan with very hot butter, and fry it briefly. Add the stock from the jar to the pan, and cook the meat for another 5 minutes, basting frequently with the sauce.

Karamelisiertes Gänsefleisch (Caramelized goose)
Joint the goose. Make a marinade of 3 cups/750 ml vinegar, 4 cups/1 liter water, 2 bay leaves, 4 allspice berries, 2 cloves, 2 onions, 1 tbsp salt, black peppercorns, a few mustard seeds, 1 leek, 1 carrot, and 1 parsley root if available, and bring to a boil in a large pan. Place the goose joints in the pan, bring to a boil again, and reduce the heat. Allow to simmer gently for 2 hours. Skim off the fat, put it in a lidded jar and let it cool (it can be used in red cabbage or sauerkraut dishes). Put the goose in a stoneware jar, and pour the skimmed stock over it. Seal with melted coconut fat or butter. The meat will keep in a cool place for about two months. Remove the coconut fat before preparing the caramelized goose. Take the goose joints out of the liquid, place in a pan with some of the reserved goose fat and some sugar, and fry over moderate heat until the sugar turns light brown and begins to form threads. Then take out the caramelized meat and keep warm. Boil up the juices in the pan with water and 4 to 5 tbsp of the marinade from the jar, and thicken with cornstarch or flour. Serve with boiled potatoes and red cabbage prepared with goose fat and blackcurrant jelly.

Gänseleber im Steintopf mit Sauerkraut (Potted goose liver with sauerkraut)
Slice an onion and soften it gently in butter. Add about 1¼ lb/600 g of sauerkraut and top up with water. A few juniper berries and bacon rinds can be simmered with the sauerkraut, if desired, and removed at the end of cooking. Meanwhile prepare the goose liver, season with salt, pepper and mild paprika, and braise gently for an hour in a covered casserole with ½ cup/125 ml white wine and good stock. When the sauerkraut is tender, season it with salt, pepper, and sugar, and thicken it with grated raw potato. Now peel and slice 2 apples. Put the apple slices in the bottom of an earthenware dish, with the sliced goose liver on top, and the sauerkraut on top of the goose liver. Braise gently in the oven for about 20 minutes. Stir some potato flour into the juices to bind, and adjust the seasoning.

Geriebener Gänsemagen (Ground goose gizzards)
Mix about 1¼ lb/600 g of salted goose gizzards with finely diced onions, aromatic vinegar, pepper, and thyme. Put the mixture through the grinder twice, and add piquant seasoning. Ground gizzards go well with potatoes boiled in their skins, or they can be eaten as a spread.

Gänseschmalz (Flavored goose fat)
Take a generous pound/500 g of uncooked goose fat, cut into large dice, and melt slowly in a pan with 4 oz/125 g pork flare (the fat from around the kidney). Add a whole apple, with the stalk and flower base removed, a large onion, and a sprig of thyme. Take them out when the onion has turned brown. Strain the fat through a sieve, and cool to a firm consistency in a stoneware jar.

Gänse-Weisssauer (Pickled goose)
Put about 3 lb/1500 g pig trotters or calves' feet in a pan with cold salted water, and simmer for an hour. Add about 5 lb/2500 g goose or duck meat, season with salt, and cook until the meat is tender. Add cleaned, diced root vegetables, a bay leaf, peppercorns, and vinegar or lemon, and allow to simmer for about another 10 minutes. Place the meat in layers in glass jars. Strain the liquid through muslin to remove the fat, and pour over the meat in the jars.

The festive goose

230 calories per 3½ oz/100 grams is quite a lot. Eating the same amount of roast chicken would put only half as much on your hips – and the scales. But who wants to welcome family and friends on the first day of Christmas with a skinny fowl? Goose goes with a festive meal, dumplings go with goose – and never mind the calories.

Traditionally, geese have their necks wrung on 11 November. According to a Christian legend, it is their own fault for betraying St Martin when he was hiding in a goose shed before being chosen as bishop. But no doubt the geese would not have escaped anyway, since they are ready for slaughter in November, and in fact are even better eating then than at Christmas, because they are leaner. St Martin's Day, or Martinmas, also used to mark the end of the farming year. The birds could no longer graze in the pastures, and slaughter made better economic sense than stall-feeding them.

Martinmas was an important date in the agricultural year. Work in the fields and gardens was over, and people prepared for the coming winter. The harvest had been brought in, and the cattle sold, so there would be money in the house. Bills could be settled, rent paid, and the servants received their wages. This was also the traditional day for servants to change their jobs, first taking a few days off and enjoying themselves at the Martinmas fairs.

The date was feared by those too poor to pay their rent: "If your rent you cannot pay, St Martin's is a dismal day," ran a country proverb, and people would threaten, "Wait until Martinmas!" On 11 November, village schoolmasters received a goose as payment in kind for school fees, and the day was generally observed as a good chance to eat and drink well before the fasting of Advent began. In winegrowing areas of Germany people drank "Martinmas wine" the first of the new vintage, and anyone who indulged too freely was mocked as a "Martin's man." Special pastries were baked in honor of the day, and as gifts for the children and servants: Martinmas horns, rolls, rings, and cakes.

As the date that marked the turn of the year, Martinmas was also important in fortune-telling and especially in weather forecasting. People would consult the roast goose for advice about the future. If its breastbone was reddish in color, then you were in for a hard winter, but if it was white, you could expect mild weather.

The inner life of German geese

Bavarian stuffing
Slice two stale rolls and let them soak in ¾ cup/200 ml hot milk. Squeeze excess liquid out of the bread and mix with two bunches of parsley, chopped, two onions, diced, the giblets of the goose, finely diced, 8 oz/250 g ground meat, three eggs, tarragon, chervil, and marjoram.

Rhineland stuffing
Soak a generous 1 lb/500 g of prunes, soften 4 oz/100 g raisins in rum. Peel about 2 lb/1 kg apples and cut into dice. Mix with marjoram, salt and pepper.

Mushroom stuffing
Mix together a generous 1 lb/500 g mixed mushrooms, thinly sliced, 4 oz/100 g diced bacon, 4 oz/100 g chopped walnuts, a diced onion, 4 tbsp white breadcrumbs, two eggs, chopped parsley, salt, pepper, and mild paprika.

Chestnut stuffing
Fry 4 oz/100 g peeled cooked chestnuts in butter with 4 apples, cut up small. Finely dice 6 oz/150 g chicken livers and the goose liver, add to the pan and fry gently for 5 minutes. Season to taste with salt, pepper, cinnamon and armagnac.

Apple and onion stuffing
Dice 4 sharp apples and fry in butter for 5 minutes with 8 oz/250 g shallots. Season highly with dried marjoram, tarragon, salt, and pepper.

When the goose has been stuffed it must be sewn up with kitchen string.
It is easier to do this if you close the opening of the body first with toothpicks.

No longer the food of the poor

Herrings

There used to be an old dialect saying in the area, when some very ordinary meal was being prepared: "Runner von'n Disch, Mudeer kaakt Fisch," meaning: "Get down from the table, mother's cooking fish." For in the past most people's main meal was fish, usually herring, because it was the cheapest.

Unlike its North Sea counterpart, the Baltic herring is particularly suitable for curing, being smaller but fatter. As a result the fish sold inland until the middle of the 19th century were mainly Baltic herring. At the beginning of the 19th century, as a result of the second great period when herring flourished (1748–1808), these fish were especially cheap. A document from Rostock dated 1807 tells us that: "Herring are cheaper than any other fish, and are very frequently eaten by the common man in spring; some are also dried, and exported in that form, but they are not salted."

It is surprising that salt was not used in Rostock at the time, for salting had been the most usual way of preserving herring for centuries. In 1820 the Prussian state even provided economic support for fishermen by allowing them untaxed salt. "Salt houses" were set up all along the Baltic coast: brick buildings thatched with reed, standing near the shore, where the fishermen stored their salt. Most of these buildings were destroyed by the storm tides of 1872 and 1874, and only six of them still stand. One of them, in Koserow on Usedom, is now a mini-museum.

Herring tastes best freshly caught, and can be bought straight off the fishing boats from February to May, the main herring season. Housewives once had to deal with buckets full of herring at this time of year. They were fried fresh, or preserved in vinegar, and provided a range of different dishes for a large family.

Today herring make up two-thirds of the entire catch in Mecklenburg-West Pomerania. These days, however, fishermen have to face a considerable drop in their profits, since conditions of supply and demand for Baltic herring are poor. Because of international maritime law, the German fishing fleet has been drastically reduced since the beginning of the 1970s. The deep sea fisheries now operate only 17 vessels. In addition, cheap imports from countries outside the EU represent serious competition. The provincial government of Mecklenburg-West Pomerania supports the fishermen by encouraging investment, but it cannot compensate for all the losses.

The herring (*Clupea harengus*) is divided into several sub-species. The most important in the East Atlantic are the White Sea herring, the Murman herring, the winter-spawning Norwegian herring, and the smaller Baltic herring. The Norwegian herring is the most important to the fishing industry. Shoals of herring are located by means of echo-sounding devices which also provide data to help in estimating size of the shoal. Stocks of herring have decreased drastically in recent decades, not least because of the efficiency of such fishing methods. Within only a few years, stocks of North Sea herring sank to one-tenth of what they used to be. The fact that herring is still the most popular fish among German customers does not help; herring is the market leader, with a figure of 25 percent, followed by Alaska sea salmon. However, herring is no longer good business. The days when it was still a kind of currency, and cities like Amsterdam and the Hanseatic ports of Rostock and Greifswald could grow rich and powerful from the herring trade, are gone for ever.

Not a job for late risers. Fishermen have to be up at dawn to put out the nets, which should fill with fish over the next 24 hours.

A good catch, but not as good as in the past. Stocks of herring over the last few decades have fallen drastically.

When the fishing boats come into port, the people whose job it is to free the herring from the mesh of the net are waiting for them.

Grüne Heringe gebraten
Fried fresh herring

8 fresh herring, ready to cook
salt and pepper
6 tbsp flour
5 oz/125 g diced bacon
6½ tbsp/100 g butter

Clean the herrings thoroughly, pat dry, and season inside and outside with salt and pepper. Allow to stand for 10 minutes, then toss the fish in flour, shaking off any excess. Melt the diced bacon in a large skillet. Remove the bacon from the skillet, add the butter, and fry the herrings for about 5 minutes on each side until golden brown. Arrange on a warmed serving dish. Reheat the diced bacon in the fat in the skillet, and arrange it over the herrings.

Fishermen will not grow rich on these herring: falling prices and small catches have led to a drop in profits.

Herring products

Salt, oil, vinegar, aspic, gherkins, hardboiled eggs, cream, beetroot, tomatoes – no other fish goes so well with such a variety of vegetables and flavorings, or can be prepared in so many different ways. You can buy herring smoked, as buckling, in jars and cans, as a snack or a salad. Cured in salt, it used to provide the people of inland regions with delicious dishes for fast days over the centuries, and many drinkers have found it good for a hangover the morning after. It even brought added fame to the great 19th-century politician, Chancellor Bismarck of Germany. His name was given to a herring fillet cured in mild, spiced vinegar. Bismarck himself prophesied that : "The Bismarck herring will immortalize me."

A fish cure for Bismarck

"He was tall, and in his youth lean, but became fat later, since he ate and drank large quantities, and his expressive round eyes took on the damp gleam induced by alcohol." This is the portrait painted by the historian Golo Mann, son of the novelist Thomas Mann, of Otto von Bismarck, the "Iron Chancellor" and "first statesman of Europe," who was instrumental in determining the policy and history of Germany in the last decades of the 19th century.

Otto von Bismarck was born in 1815 in Schönhausen on the River Elbe, and was Chancellor of the German Empire from 1871 to 1890. Although he spent a good deal of time at court, where he enjoyed the best French cuisine, he enjoyed regional, country cooking all his life. Not for nothing does the Bismarck herring bear his name. There is a story that the great Prussian politician said: "If herring were as expensive as lobster, they would be considered a delicacy too."

Bismarck ate both – lobster as well as herring. According to his personal physician, the founder of the German Reich would often eat as many as 16 eggs for breakfast. He frequently consumed a variety of foods at once. At the Berlin Congress of 1878, for instance, he was observed "stuffing shrimp into his mouth with one hand, and cherries with the other." Scarcely any other politician gave himself up to the pleasures of the table with as little restraint as this famous Prussian nobleman. At an early date, Bismarck realized that good food can be an elegant means to political ends.

Over the years, however, the Iron Chancellor was forced to take a thorough look at his life style, and at one point his physician prescribed him a diet of herring. The diet obviously worked, for Bismarck said later: "Those herrings cured me."

Bismarck herring is marinated in vinegar and salt, and preserved with spices.

Fried rollmops, a fried herring rolled up around the same stuffing as rollmops.

Rollmops, half a herring marinated in vinegar and rolled around a pickled gherkin.

Herring in cream: matjes herring fillets in a cream sauce are very tender.

Fried herring: a fresh herring coated in flour, fried, and preserved in vinegar.

Herring in aspic: herring fillets set in aspic jelly with slices of hardboiled egg.

Sild are cured in the same way as Bismarck herring, but are very young fish.

Kippers are mildly salted herrings, cold-smoked with their skins on.

Matjes are young herring caught before they are mature enough to spawn. The main catch is in May and June.

Hotchpotch

Mangkokt-Äten (hotchpotch) is typical of the cookery of Mecklenburg-West Pomerania. It is a kind of meat and vegetable one-pot dish, usually consisting of turnips, carrots, and white cabbage, and it often included peas or other pulses. Green cabbage with grits remained a popular dish on the menus of farmers and day laborers, even after the introduction of the potato. In winter a large pot would be made in advance, and this green cabbage dish would be served several times a week, often three times a day. This was the kind of dish that helped to make the supply of cereals last the winter. The threshers who had the hardest work to do during the grain harvest ate green cabbage and grits first thing in the morning, to fortify themselves for the day's work. The German political economist Wilhelm Roscher said, around 1890: "A day laborer from Mecklenburg eats almost twice as much as a Thuringian, but then he does almost twice as much work." A solid, nourishing, calorie-rich diet, containing plenty of carbohydrates, was good country fare. Once the potato had become the food of the common people, people of the urban lower middle class began to serve potatoes, vegetables, and meat separately on plates, no longer mixing them up in a "hotchpotch." In the country, however, no separate vegetable dishes were prepared even in the second half of the 19th century; everything went into the same pot. The day laborer placed the big dish on the table, just as he had done for centuries, and everyone at table helped himself from it. These social classes did not use individual plates of their own until the beginning of the 20th century.

Pomeranian pea soup

Pommersche Erbsensuppe
Pomeranian pea soup
(Illustrated)

12 oz/350 g dried yellow peas
7 oz/200 g bacon
1 pig tail
1 pig ear
1 bunch of thyme
soup vegetables (carrot, celery, leek, and parsley), finely diced
1 onion, finely diced
a generous 2 lb/1 kg potatoes
salt and pepper

Soak the peas overnight in 8 cups/2 liters of water. Drain next day. Simmer the pig tail, pig ear and bacon in 8 cups/2 liters lightly salted water for about 1 hour. Add the peas, thyme, soup vegetables, and onion, and simmer for 40 minutes. Meanwhile wash, peel, and slice the potatoes. Put the pieces of potato in the pea soup and simmer for another 25 minutes. When the peas and potatoes are done, take the thyme, meat, and bacon out of the soup. Cut the meat and bacon into bite-sized pieces, and return to the soup. Season well with salt and pepper.

Kliebensuppe
Sweet custard soup

4 tbsp flour
4 tbsp sugar
3 egg yolks
a pinch of salt
8 cups/2 l milk
½ vanilla bean

Sift the flour into a bowl, stir in the sugar and egg yolks, then add the pinch of salt and 2 tbsp milk. Mix with a fork to a firm, crumbly dough (this dough is the "Klieben"). Bring the rest of the milk to a boil with the vanilla bean, gradually add the crumbly mixture, and allow to simmer for a few minutes. Remove the vanilla bean before serving.

Fliederbeersuppe
Elderberry soup

a generous 1 lb/500 g elderberries
½ cup/75 g sugar
½ tsp vanilla extract
1 pinch of salt
2 large, sharp apples
1 tbsp cornstarch

Bring the elderberries slowly to a boil with 4 cups/1 liter water, the sugar, vanilla extract, and salt. Pass the soup through a sieve. Peel, quarter, and core the apples. Cut them up, not too small, and simmer them in the soup until they are just soft but not mushy. Blend the cornstarch in a little water, and use it to thicken the simmering soup. Take the pan off the stove, taste, and add more sugar if necessary. Serve small dumplings floating in the elderberry soup.

Fischsuppe
Fish soup

8 oz /250 g potatoes
3 carrots
1 leek
½ small celeriac root
2 onions
2 tbsp butter
1 cup/250 ml white wine
salt and pepper
a generous 1 lb/500 g fillet of white fish, such as pollack or cod
½ bunch of dill
½ bunch of parsley

Wash, peel, and finely dice the potatoes. Clean the leek, carrots, and celeriac, cut them into cubes, and finely dice the onions. Melt the onions in the butter until transparent, then add the potatoes and vegetables, and cook all gently together for a few minutes. Add the white wine and 4 cups/1 liter of water, season with salt and pepper and simmer for 15 minutes. Meanwhile clean the fish fillets, divide into fairly large pieces, and season with salt. Put the pieces of fish into the soup, and allow to simmer gently for 10 minutes. Stir in the dill and parsley before serving.

Schweriner Suppe (Sommersuppe)
Schwerin soup (summer soup)

1 cucumber
2 onions, finely chopped
2 tbsp butter
6 oz/150 g young green peas, podded
8 oz/250 g sugar snap peas
4 lettuce hearts
4 cups/1 liter stock
1 tbsp each chopped parsley, chervil, and salad burnet
½ tsp ground ginger
salt and pepper
1 tsp cornstarch
3 egg yolks

Peel the cucumber and cut into dice. Melt the onions in the butter until transparent, add the cucumber, green peas and sugar snap peas, and simmer all together. Cut the lettuce hearts into strips, add to the vegetables, and pour in the stock. Mix in the herbs, season with salt and pepper, and simmer for 10 minutes. Blend the cornstarch with a little water, add to the simmering soup, and bring to a boil again. Take the pan off the stove, and thicken the soup with the whisked egg yolk. Serve with boiled potatoes or croutons.

Cookbooks of the East German period: Mother Schulten

Who exactly is Mother Schulten (or in the local dialect, Mudder Schulten)? Every child in Mecklenburg-West Pomerania knows the answer. She was a real historical character popularized by Fritz Reuter (1810–1874), the dialect author, someone with whom the Mecklenburgers are happy to identify. In his book *Dörchläuchting* (a dialect form of *Durchlaucht*, "Serene Highness"), Reuter described a meeting in the Neubrandenburger market place between Adolf Friedrich IV, Duke of Strelitz, who reigned over the state of Mecklenburg-Strelitz from 1752 to 1794, and Mother Schulten, the baker's wife. She reminded him that bakeries were among the establishments supplying goods to the ducal court, and pointed out that it was five years since his Serene Highness had paid his bills. At the time, of course, it was unheard-of for an ordinary working woman to make such a protest to her sovereign. However, the brave baker's wife found the right words for the occasion, and was regarded as a popular heroine.

Mother Schulten's name is still known today, through the good offices of the 70-year-old actress Inge Schumacher of Neubrandenburg. At the end of the 1960s she appeared in a play by the East German writer Franz Freitag, describing a journey taken by Mother Schulten and his Highness through modern Neubrandenburg. Inge Schumacher, who was born in Ziethen, still loves appearing in the part, and the local people enjoy visits from "their" Mother Schulten, who travels around telling stories and reciting rhymes. She knows a great deal about Fritz Reuter, and indeed about the region in the present day, for in the last few decades Inge Schumacher has become a notable figure in Mecklenburg-West Pomerania, a position she uses to maintain local traditions, including culinary traditions. Under the East German régime, she was behind the publication in Neubrandenburg of nine "Mother Schulten" cookbooks, containing recipes handed down by mothers, grandmothers and great-grandmothers. These books were bestsellers at the annual meetings of journalists, and were usually snapped up at once.

Inge Schumacher also has a training in home economics and hotel management, and says, of the local cooking: "Mecklenburg-West Pomerania used to be the most backward part of Germany, as described by Fritz Reuter in his *Kein Hüsung* ("Nowhere to live"). There were two kinds of cookery, one for the poor and one for the rich. While the former had to make something out of every scrap, the latter could draw on a wide range of recipes, experimenting with dishes from foreign countries." She is an enthusiastic cook herself, but finds it hard to choose a favorite dish. "A good plum soup or a tasty fish soup is better than most joints of meat," she says. For a festive occasion she might suggest a menu such as this: to start, a clear fish soup made of three carps' heads, with carrots, leeks, onions, and a few noodles. Main course: cured pork shoulder, braised with plenty of onions, no cream in the sauce. The same joint of meat can be marinated in beer for two days before cooking, and will taste excellent. She would serve it with red cabbage cooked with a piece of bacon, and redcurrant jam and apples to give a sweet-sour flavor. A dessert of semolina flummery, or black bread pudding with rum, adds the crowning touch to this typical local meal.

Meat as a Sunday treat

Tollatsch – a fall specialty

The slaughtering of livestock in fall was often a festive occasion in the villages of the region, and the typical Pomeranian dish known as *Tollatsch* was made to celebrate it. *Tollatsch* is a kind of sweet black pudding made with pig's blood, raisins and sugar. The word itself is Slavonic and means "round cake." Although there are variants of the dish closely resembling each other in Mecklenburg and West Pomerania, it is scarcely known in the western and southern parts of Mecklenburg. In West Pomerania, several butcheries have turned to making this specialty in recent years, producing it all the year round and not just in fall, the traditional season. *Tollatsch* is eaten sliced, fried, and sprinkled with sugar, usually accompanied by a big pot of black coffee.

In this rather poor area of Germany, meat used to be served only on Sundays or for special celebrations: a hundred years ago, for instance, livestock would be slaughtered for weddings on the Monday before the great day. The wedding breakfast usually consisted of chicken soup, a large pike with brown butter, fresh roast pork, and a red fruit fool. Or it might be eel soup, roast duck, and finally a creamy pudding.

Gebackener Schinken auf mecklenburgische Art
Baked ham Mecklenburg style

2 1/2 lb/1.2 kg cured leg of pork, without rind but with the layer of fat in place
cloves
salt
1 cup /150 g dried breadcrumbs
1 tsp ground cloves
2 tbsp sugar

Score the fat on the joint with a sharp knife, making 8 to 10 large diamond shapes. Put a clove in each cut. Sprinkle with salt, put the pork on a grid in a roasting pan containing 1 in/2 cm of water. Bake for about 2 hours in a preheated oven at 400 °F/200 °C, adding hot water from time to time. Mix the dried breadcrumbs with the ground cloves and sugar. When the meat is done, take the pan out of the oven and remove the cloves. Sprinkle the breadcrumb mixture over the meat, and put it back in the oven to form a good crust. Let the joint rest for a little while before carving, then carve it into slices. Serve with glazed carrots and onions, and with potatoes too if desired.

Rügenwalde sausage and other sausages

In the 19th century the butchers' guild of Rügenwalde in East Pomerania used to meet once a week for tea, talk, and schnaps. One day a guild member brought along what he said was a failed cervelat sausage, but when his colleagues tasted it they liked it. This was the origin of the *Rügenwalder Teewurst*, Rügenwalde tea sausage. The secret of the original recipe is carefully preserved and handed on. One recipe for making these sausages is as follows: Mix about 4½ lb/2 kg fat belly of pork, diced, with a generous 2 lb/1 kg lean meat, finely ground. Season each 2 lb/1 kg of the meat mixture with 1 oz/32 g salt, a pinch of saltpeter, a small pinch of ground white pepper, and a small pinch of mild pink paprika. Mix well with the meat, then grind the mixture finely with a sharp blade. Pound the mixture well, then put it into cellophane sausage skins. The sausage must first be cured for two or three days in moderately hot smoke before it is finally cold-smoked until golden brown.

The farmers made sure that nothing was wasted when an animal was slaughtered. The heart and lungs, for instance, could be made into a dish known as "hash", but lung sausage and liver sausage were prepared first, with the typical local seasoning of herbs such as thyme and marjoram. A cookbook dated 1797 from Stettin gives the following helpful hint: "When you prepare sausages, you must make sure that they cook very slowly and with plenty of space around them, and there must be no wood at the center of your fire, directly under the pot, or they will easily split."

The quality of the meat is very important for baked ham.

It must have a thick layer of fat, scored in a diamond pattern.

Put a clove in the intersections of the cuts.

Bake on a grid over some water in a roasting pan.

When it is cooked, remove the cloves.

Sprinkle dried breadcrumbs over the meat.

Bake again to firm the crust, and carve the meat into slices.

A picture from the old days of the DDR: a demonstration in favor of progress in beet growing in March 1963 at a rally in East Berlin.

Gestowte Wruken
Stewed rutabagas

1½ lb/750 g belly of pork
salt
1 onion, spiked with a bay leaf and 2 cloves
soup vegetables (carrot, celery, leek, and parsley), finely diced
5 allspice berries
a generous 2 lb/1 kg swedes
1 onion, finely diced
1 tbsp clarified butter
1 tsp cornstarch
½ cup/125 g cream
pepper
1 tsp marjoram leaves
½ bunch of parsley, chopped

Bring the belly of pork to a boil in 4 cups/1 liter cold water with 1 tsp salt, the onion spiked with the bay leaf and cloves, the soup vegetables, and the allspice berries. Simmer, covered, for about 1 hour. Meanwhile peel the swedes, remove any woody parts, and cut into pieces about 1½ in/4 cm long. Melt the diced onion in the clarified butter until transparent, add the swedes, and enough of the liquid from the pork just to cover them. Braise the vegetables for about 20 minutes. Blend the cornstarch with the cream, stir it into the simmering vegetables, and season with salt, pepper, and marjoram. Bring to a boil again, and add the chopped parsley. Serve in portions on warmed plates, adding a slice of belly of pork to each plate.

Rutabagas: the burden of history

The winter of the rutabagas

The rutabaga, known by the dialect name of *Wruke* in this area, is among the typical local products of the northeast. It is made into one-pot dishes of *Gestowte Wruken* ("stewed rutabagas"), dishes that are among the local specialties of this region. Studying regional recipes, cooks have rediscovered the rutabaga, and are trying to find a place for it in gourmet cookery.

However, it is difficult for the rutabaga to win recognition as an elegant vegetable. After the "winter of the rutabagas" in 1916/17, it was banished from many families' kitchens, for during the famine caused by the First World War, rutabagas with potatoes and water were often the only food, served not only for dinner, but for breakfast and supper too. At that time, hunger drove the workers out into the streets; they went on strike in Rostock, chanting the slogan: "Oh, Deutschland hoch in Ehren, du kannst uns nicht ernähren!" ("Great Germany, you need us, but oh, you cannot feed us.")

Of all the turnip family, sugar beet is the most important for Mecklenburg-West Pomerania. It is one of the largest local crops, for the often heavy soil offers excellent conditions for growing sugar beet. In addition it is good animal feed. For over 100 years, sugar beet has been mechanically cultivated. After the reunification of Germany in October 1990, only two of what had once been a large number of sugar factories remained active in the northeast: the Güstrow factory, and the factory in Anklam on the Peene in West Pomerania. The latter is one of the most modern sugar factories in Europe, and also one of the largest in Germany. At the beginning of the 1990s a Danish company took over the old plant and invested over 320 million Deutschmarks to modernize the firm, which can look back at over a hundred years of existence in Anklam. With an annual production standing at around 152,000 tons (150,000 tonnes) of sugar, the Anklam plant is one of the most efficient in the north. During the sugar beet campaign, around a million tons of beet are brought from Rügen to Prenzlau in a period of 100 days and nights. Around 200 specialists set to work to make it into refined white sugar.

Schwerin
Hamburg
Bremen
Berlin
Hanover
Potsdam
Magdeburg
Düsseldorf
Dresden
Bonn
Erfurt
Wiesbaden
Mainz
Saarbrücken
Stuttgart
Munich

**JUSTUS STEIDLE • VERENA VON FUNKE
RENATE SCHOBER**

Schleswig-Holstein

Centuries were to pass before Schleswig-Holstein acquired its hyphen – although a vow had been taken as long ago as 1460 that it would remain "up ewig ungedeelt," meaning "undivided for ever." It was not until 1946, however, that the state lying between two seas achieved political unity.

Before this, times had been confused, characterized by wars, voluntary partitions, and foreign domination. The Danes ruled for a long period, followed at a later stage by the Prussians, and even Austria and the Hanseatic city of Hamburg became involved. Many cities, such as Lübeck and Flensburg, profited from this political intrigue, but the state remained poor, with agriculture and fisheries providing the sole basis for survival. This naturally left its mark on the cuisine. The produce served at table was almost exclusively local, but in great abundance, and in the form of robust, rich dishes – stews, hams, huge dumplings, and fish of all kinds. For back in those times people needed a great deal of fuel in view of the harshness of the climate, and hard labor in the open air.

Yet, in spite of the hyphen, something resembling a border does divide the state. Contrasts are evident in the people as well as the landscape: between the formality of the people of the Isle of Sylt and the informality of the rustic Angles; the taciturnity of the eastern Friesians and the openness of Lübeck or Flensburg people; between Theodor Storm, the provincial poet from Husum, and Thomas Mann, the man of the world from Lübeck; between the tempestuous North Sea, and the comparatively calm Baltic.

The state of Schleswig-Holstein resembles, or so it has been written, a ham with fat on both sides. The fat symbolizes the two coasts with their new tourist industry. In the center, along the Geestrücken, the sandy moorlands forming the backbone of the state, life remains for the most part rustic and deeply traditional. Churches here are still full, and any excuse, from a christening to a funeral, is used to put on a festive spread. It is here too that the cuisine proves most down to earth, even though, like everywhere else, the fat content has been reduced a little and the fare has become lighter. Yet this too – in keeping with the hyphen in Schleswig-Holstein – is a successful partnership.

Left: Sylt, with its vast beaches, is one of the most popular holiday destinations on the North Sea coast.

Delicacies from the Gold Coast

Kiel sprats

There is an old rhyme in the local dialect, "Da plagen sich de Lüd herum mit luder leege Saken. In Eckernför verstaht de Lüd, ut Sülwer Gold to maken." Elsewhere, it says, people waste their time on trivial pursuits; the people of the Bay of Eckernforde, on the other hand, have learned how to turn silver into gold. In order to perform this miracle of alchemy, the inhabitants of the small Baltic seaport have no need to call upon a magician. Their medium is "*Clupea sprattus*," the shiny silver sprat, which is a member of the herring family measuring between 4½ and 6 inches (12 to 15 centimeters), whose principal habitat is the Baltic Sea.

Sprats are mostly caught in the Bay of Eckernforde, nearly 19 miles (30 kilometers) north west of Kiel, off the Fehmarn Peninsula and the Danish coast. The main fishing season is during the winter months, when the fat content of the fish is highest. As recently as the 19th century, sprats were poor people's fare, as they were cheap and high in calories. Today the stocks have been much depleted and are in jeopardy as a result of overfishing. The same applies to the herring, a relative of the sprat; both species of fish are normally caught in the same net, because they live at about the same depth.

Sprats would not really be much of a delicacy if they were not refined by smoking. And on the east coast of Schleswig-Holstein special recipes for this exist, handed down from generation to generation, which are closely guarded secrets in the smokehouses. Only freshly caught fish are suitable for processing, so the sprats are delivered directly to the smokehouse, where they are first cleaned and then soaked for half an hour in weak brine. Then they are threaded on skewers, one by one, through the gills and gullet. Forty of these steel skewers, each holding between 25 and 30 sprats, fit into a frame, which is then suspended in the smoking oven; this can accommodate several thousand sprats.

This is where the art of the master smoker begins. The first stage involves drying, and a beech log fire is kindled for this purpose. As soon as the skin of the sprats crinkles slightly, they are dry, and the smoking process can begin. Alder wood, with the occasional addition of a little oak at the end, is added to the burning beech log. The wood is dampened beforehand, so that it produces the right amount of smoke. The refining process takes about an hour, and must be stopped at exactly the right moment to prevent the sprats becoming hard. The secret lies in the correct mixture of smoke and heat (140–175 °F/60–80 °C.) This is what transforms the silver skin of the fish into gold.

Since it is now clear that the Eckernforde people mastered the art of "making gold," the question remains as to why the smoked sprats are known as "Kiel sprats." The misnomer arose because the fish used to be dispatched from the railway station at Kiel. As a result the goods, traditionally packed in wooden crates, were stamped with the name of the station of dispatch, "Kiel," and thus quite undeservedly acquired the brand name "Kieler Sprotten," or Kiel sprats.

Those who are not squeamish eat Kiel sprats whole, including the head and tail. Others fillet them and eat them served on a plate, with scrambled egg, for instance. Regardless of how they are eaten, however, the best accompaniment is always wholesome black bread and a cold beer.

Opposite: Packed in layers in the crate and seasoned with a pinch of salt, the sprats are ready for their journey.

Fish specialties

Scholle mit Krabben
Plaice with shrimps

4 plaice halves	
Juice of 1 lemon	
Salt	
5 tbsp flour	
3 eggs	
Scant ½ cup clarified butter	
9 oz/250 g shelled shrimps	

Wash the plaice and pat dry. Sprinkle with the lemon juice, rub with salt, and leave to stand for 10 minutes. Then pat dry again using kitchen towels. Whisk the eggs and dip the plaice first in flour, then in egg. Fry in the butter for 5 minutes on each side until golden brown. Lift out the plaice and keep warm. Heat the shrimps in the butter and scatter over the plaice before serving.

Matjes mit grünen Bohnen
Young herring with green beans

2 lb 3 oz/1 kg new potatoes	
Salt	
2 lb 3 oz/1 kg green beans	
½ bunch savory	
8 fillets of young herring	
7 oz/200 g bacon, cut in small cubes	
1 tbsp butter	
2 small onions, finely chopped	
Pepper	

Wash the potatoes and boil for about 20 minutes in salted water. Clean the beans and cook with the savory for 15 minutes in a little salted water. Soak the young herring fillets briefly under cold running water, pat dry, and keep chilled. Fry the bacon in a dry pan until the fat runs, add the butter and cook the onions gently until they are soft and transparent. Drain the potatoes and beans and rinse briefly in cold water. Remove the potato skins if desired, or serve with the skins on. Pour the bacon and onion mixture over the beans and serve with the chilled young herrings.

Pfannfisch
Pan-fried fish

2 lb 3 oz/1 kg potatoes, boiled in their skins	
4 oz/100 g bacon	
2 onions	
2 tbsp clarified butter	
Salt and pepper	
Generous 1 lb/500 g cooked fish, e.g. cod or pollack	
1 bunch parsley, chopped	

Slice the potatoes thinly, cut the bacon fat into strips, and the onions into rings. Heat the clarified butter in a large pan and fry the bacon in it until the fat runs. Add the potatoes and onions and fry briskly. Season well with salt and pepper. Shred the cooked fish into bite-sized pieces, mix carefully with the potatoes, and fry the mixture briefly. Scatter the parsley on top and serve with pickles.

After they have been caught, the fish are threaded through the gills onto skewers.

The frame about to be placed in the smoking chamber holds about 1000 sprats.

The produce of the Gold Coast is still packed in wooden boxes, according to tradition.

Protein from the North Sea and the Baltic

Fishing grounds

An example taken from historical linguistics illustrates the extent to which man regards his environment as a source of nutrition. Etymologists argue that the western Indo-Germanic word for "fish," the root form of which is also cognate with "food" in some languages, was originally used to signify food exclusively. "Fish" was synonymous with "dietary supplement" and it was not adopted as the generic term to refer to creatures that live in water until later.

Fish and crustaceans provided a rich source of protein for hunters and gatherers, who erected barriers on the coast to trap fish and used spears to catch them. The fisherman's hook is one of man's oldest tools, and bast nets were already in use in Stone Age times.

Although salting and drying were familiar methods of preserving food from time immemorial, fish only had a small nutritional role in Central Europe for centuries. The salt cod and salted herring which could be obtained relatively cheaply inland were mainly served during periods of fasting. Saltwater fish was only a staple food for coastal populations, where it did much more than supplement the diet – if the catch was a good one, the highly perishable wares were sold at giveaway prices, and then even poor people had fish for days on end, especially herring.

This situation did not change until the 1880s, when as a result of expansion of the road system and the invention of new preserving methods, such as canning or refrigeration (the first ice houses were built in the large cities around 1870), it became possible to supply saltwater fish inland too. The demand there had greatly increased. Industrialization and urbanization had led many farmers to relinquish their land, with the result that they could no longer be self-sufficient. In addition, many stretches of water were drained, and rivers were straightened and diverted, thus restricting the habitats of freshwater fish.

Hand in hand with industrialization, the population in Germany increased by leaps and bounds from 1870 onwards. Laborers could not afford meat, and so the availability of saltwater fish was seen as a solution to the food problem. Technical advances and the use of steam-powered trawlers equipped with mechanical winches to wind in the nets enabled the fishing grounds to be expanded and the catches to be increased. As a result, advertisements in around 1900 were able to claim that "factory workers in all the states in Germany are now able to have what was impossible in Lucullus' time – fresh saltwater fish provide the animal constituent of our diet every week, even for those in our prisons."

Today Germans consume approximately 33 pounds (15 kilograms) of fish per head annually, only four pounds (2 kilograms) of which are freshwater fish. Catches from German national waters, however, have fallen drastically since the 1970s: 85 percent of the fish landing on German plates is imported. On the one hand this is due to developments in maritime law – many profitable fishing grounds were lost as a result of the introduction of the 200-mile fishing zones – but on the other hand it is also due to the fact that the North Sea and the Baltic are quite simply being overfished. In the North Sea, for example, catches of cod have fallen by 74 percent, pollack by 70 percent, sole by 17 percent, plaice by 35 percent, herring by 56 percent, and mackerel by 99 percent.

This is due not least to fishing methods. Because of the fine meshes of the nets (just over ½ inch/1.6 centimeter mesh), many other species of fish are caught in addition to the main catch, and young fish in particular. The "incidental" catch is either thrown back into the sea – Greenpeace claims that each pound of fish is caught at a cost of 6 pounds of dead sea creatures – or processed to make fish meal and fish oil. The method of trawling that involves regular plowing of the sea bed with heavy chains also creates huge problems. The fishermen's aim in doing this is to startle the flat fish that live on the sea bottom; the side effects, however, include serious damage to marine flora and fauna, resulting in the extinction of certain species. In addition the incidental catch is particularly high with this method – up to 80 percent of the total catch. Will full nets result in empty seas? Man's view of his environment merely as a source of food and profit has serious implications.

Buying fish – the test of freshness

It is easy to tell how fresh fish is – regardless of whether it is saltwater or freshwater fish – from the five indicators below. The flesh of fish that are caught and die out of the water is generally firmer.

The eyes must be clear, bright and shining; if the fish has been on ice for too long, the eyes become glazed and dull.

The gills must be bright red and firm; in fish that have been stored for too long they appear pale and sticky.

The indentation made when a fresh fish is pressed with the finger remains visible only for a short time; if the imprint stays visible for any length of time, the fish is no longer fresh, nor is the flesh any

The entrails are quite distinct in fresh fish and can be clearly separated; the longer the fish has been dead, the more difficult it is to distinguish the outlines.

The layer of mucous on the skin of freshwater fish is a sign of freshness; if the skin appears dull, the fish is too old. Fish with scales do not have a mucous layer.

Blue ling. Ling have an elongated body and can grow to a length of over 4½ ft (1.5 m). Blue ling is also available salted and dried.

Dogfish. The stomach flesh of the dogfish, cut into strips and smoked, known as "Schillerlocken", is considered a great delicacy by gourmets.

Codfish. Young cod is the staple of the Baltic fishermen. It is very versatile in the kitchen, and can be eaten boiled, steamed, or fried.

Brill. Brill resembles turbot, but is thinner. Although in culinary terms it is not of such high quality as turbot, it is nevertheless also a great delicacy and is cheaper than turbot.

Herring. Herring live in huge shoals and were once so common that no great value was placed upon them. Despite this, they are a delicacy – fried, smoked, or pickled.

Salmon. Most salmon on the market today is farmed. It is available smoked, or it can be poached, broiled, fried, or used to make mousses and pâtés.

Mackerel. Mackerel often swim in shoals near the surface of the sea. The flesh is relatively oily. They are smoked whole, or fried, or broiled.

Conger eel. In appearance the conger eel is distinguished from the freshwater eel by its dorsal fin, and in terms of quality by the fact that its flesh is less oily and less tasty.

Whiting. Whiting is often caught in drag nets alongside herring and shrimps. Its flesh is tender and full of flavor, and is best poached.

Red mullet. It is not difficult to work out how this fish acquired its name. It can be broiled, fried, or cooked in foil, but is unsuitable for poaching.

Witch flounder. This is a flat fish that grows to a length of around 12 in (30 cm). Its flesh is not of the same quality as that of sole, but it is prepared in similar ways to sole.

Plaice. Plaice is one of the most important fish, and lives, like other flat fish, on the sea bed. It is either fried whole or filleted before cooking.

Lumpsucker. This bizarre-looking creature belongs to the lumpfish family. The roe, which is black in parts, is marketed under the name "German caviar."

Sole. This oval, elongated flat fish lives on sandy or silty sea beds. It has firm, white flesh that is easy to roll up, and for this reason it is frequently rolled and stuffed.

Turbot. This can grow up to 3 ft (1 m) long, but in the Baltic it rarely exceeds 18 in (50 cm). This is a very good fish to eat. It is either filleted or fried whole.

Saurel. Also known as horse mackerel, saurel are prepared like sardines, and are sold fresh or smoked. The flesh is relatively oily.

The oyster bank – a good investment

Hard shell, soft center

While excavating in Denmark, archeologists were astonished to discover prehistoric kitchen refuse containing huge quantities of oyster shells. This provided proof, not only that our ancestors had refined tastes, but also that they ate healthily, since oysters have a high nutritional value and are low in calories. While their protein content is 10 percent, their carbohydrate content is only 4 percent, and their mineral and vitamin content is between 1 and 2 percent, as is their fat content; the rest is essentially water. In addition – and this is more important to modern man than it was to prehistoric man – the low fat content minimizes contamination with harmful substances, since these only accumulate in fatty tissue.

Oysters are hermaphroditic sea creatures, which change sex according to the season and the temperature, and are alternately male and female. They reproduce by laying eggs, which turn into larvae that swim free and then, about two weeks later, attach themselves to stones or empty mussel shells and begin to form their typically slate-like shell. It often takes between four and five years until oysters are fully grown, depending on the water temperature and availability of food. They live on the minutest of floating particles, phytoplankton, which they filter out of the water. An oyster can process up to 4½ gallons (20 liters) of water an hour.

Collecting oysters from a depth of between 15 and 30 feet (5–10m) was once a difficult enterprise. Transporting the perishable seafood was also a problem. It was because of this that Canute the Great, King of Denmark and also of England and Norway in the 11th century, had the idea of cultivating oysters. As a result oysters were taken by the shipload from England to the coast of the North Friesian islands, including Sylt, which then belonged to Denmark, where they were cultivated. This venture, the first oyster farm in the North Sea, was a significant source of income for Sylt for a long time; the oysters were packed in brine in wooden barrels and were sent to Bremen and Hamburg, and even to the Danish court.

Until problems arose, that is. The method of harvesting using metal rakes dragged across the sea bed by boats, which was the normal method of catching oysters even back in the 13th century, ruined entire banks of oysters. While in Sylt in 1870 there were still 47 banks yielding around 5 million oysters annually, commercial oyster fishing had to be practically abandoned there only 12 years later. The end finally came before the Second World War.

A number of attempts to re-establish oysters on Sylt failed, until the German Federal Ministry for Fisheries tried an experiment. In the mid-1970s they tried using the more highly resistant Pacific rock oyster instead of the native oyster, and were successful. At first, five small businesses were involved in the venture, which was subsidized initially. Following the withdrawal of financial support, only one company remained – Dittmeyer's, of List on the island of Sylt, an oyster company well known among connoisseurs. The renaissance of the German oyster is due to this company and its marine aquaculture operation. When oysters are cultivated, the procedure is as follows: they are placed in plastic sacks known as "*poches*," which are roped to steel racks anchored in the tidal shallows along the low water line, at the point where the tide turns. The oysters flourish here, and can be harvested without difficulty. The sacks, each holding between 33 and 55 pounds (15–25 kilos), are opened, and the ripe oysters, which weigh between 2½ and 3 ounces (70–90 grams), are removed and sorted. This sounds simple, but is in fact an arduous task, especially in cold weather, when Dittmeyer's employees are obliged to stand in the water for hours on end. The job is also hard before the onset of winter – in order to protect them from ice drifts, which would destroy the oyster beds, all the "*poches*" are brought into special pools filled with seawater inshore of the dyke. At the beginning of spring they are then returned to the tidal shallows, where the "Friesian oysters" continue to thrive. As befits their status, they are known as "Sylt Royals" and have performed extremely well in blind tastings, even when compared with the classical varieties from France. One in four oysters now consumed in Germany is from Sylt, a total of approximately 25 tons annually.

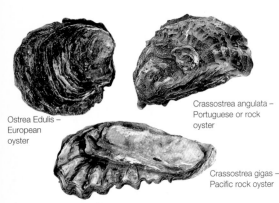

Ostrea Edulis – European oyster

Crassostrea angulata – Portuguese or rock oyster

Crassostrea gigas – Pacific rock oyster

Of the classical varieties of oyster, the Pacific rock oyster, which is particularly resistant and is also cultivated in Sylt, is in the ascendant.

Right: a delicacy rich in protein, to which oyster enthusiasts also ascribe aphrodisiac properties.

The oysters are stored in sacks under about 20 in (50 cm) of water.

The sacks are stacked on steel racks, and anchored in the tidal shallows.

After the sacks have been emptied, the oysters are cleaned.

The ripe oysters, weighing between 2½ and 3 oz (70-90 g), are sorted.

Sylt oysters begin their journey packed in wooden cases.

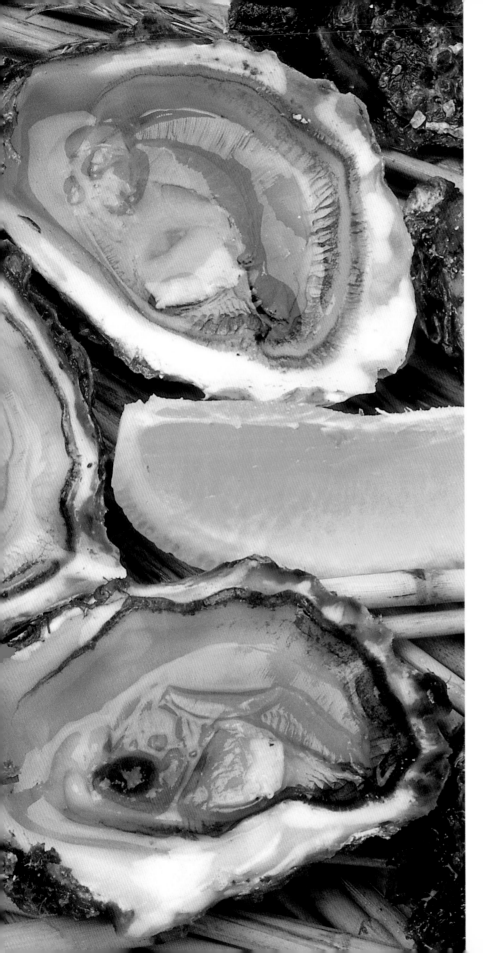

In order to reach the soft inside part, the hard shell must first be opened with a sharp knife.

The wearing of a protective glove is recommended. The correct rotational movement of the knife is also important.

Success! Now the oyster is exposed in the lower shell, but it cannot be freed yet.

The muscle has to be cut through with the knife; then the oyster is ready to eat.

129

Brachyura

"*Brachyura*" means "short-tailed crustacean," or just "crab." There are over 4,000 varieties of these decapods, most of which live in the sea; the shrimps are a sub-species, and include the North Sea shrimp known to biologists as "*crangon crangon*" and to the natives simply as a "*Granat,*" meaning garnet, the common term for the red shrimp. The shrimps themselves do not ascribe much importance to these specialist terms, but are far more concerned with good quality water, which they find in the vast tidal shallows of Büsum, where water temperature and salt content fluctuate violently.

About 115 cutters are still plying the North Sea coast of Schleswig-Holstein between Friedrichskoog and Hörnum fishing for shrimps. The North Friesian fishermen know exactly which conditions are the best for a good catch. Success is guaranteed under cover of darkness or if the current is strong, by clouding the water so that it is impossible for the prey to recognize the opening at the mouth of the net and take evasive action.

In the fishing ground, devices known as "metal trees" are lowered to the left and right of the boat and the nets are let down onto the sea bed. The shrimps living on the sea floor are startled by the noise of the nets dragging along the bottom, and are trapped in their fine mesh. The depth of the

The shrimp must be shelled to reach the delicious meat.

This is done by grasping the shrimp by the head and tail.

The deft twist of the right hand requires a bit of practice.

Once this is mastered, the shell around the tail can easily be pulled off.

This only exposes part of the tasty shrimp flesh, however.

The remainder is still hidden inside the head and needs to be freed.

This is a relatively simple task; hold the head firmly and pull the tail.

Only the middle part is edible. The rest ends up in the garbage can.

water in the fishing ground varies between 12 and 40 feet (4–13 meters). The cutter never sails faster than 2.5 knots, and trails the nets behind it on drag lines over 50 yards long. Although sonar, satellite navigation aids, or even day-vision radar can simplify work on board, even the latest technology cannot guarantee a good catch.

When the nets are eventually hauled in, the sight is an astonishing one – only 10 percent of the catch consists of shrimps. And even these do not look very appetizing, since they resemble gray, transparent woodlice. It is not until they have been

boiled for ten minutes in sea water on board ship that these unprepossessing decapods are transformed into the well-known red, hooked, appetizingly aromatic "*Granate*", which are basically stronger in flavor than their relatives, the pale pink North Sea shrimps and giant shrimps. Only a proportion of these delicious sea creatures are shelled in Germany. In addition to the professional shelling operations, which are primarily to be found in Poland, five crab shelling machines operate in Friedrichskoog alone. True connoisseurs, however, prefer to shell their shrimps themselves.

The "metal trees," from which the nets are suspended, are hauled in.

The mixed catch from the sea bed poses an ecological problem.

Only about 10 percent of the catch consists of the required shrimps.

The shrimps are now given a cold shower after their hot bath.

The basket containing the shrimps is hung from the railing to drain.

Locals and tourists are already queueing up for the fresh sea creatures.

Seafood dishes

Krabben in Dillsauce
Shrimps in dill sauce
(Illustrated below)

1 small onion, finely chopped
2 tbsp butter
4 tbsp flour
2 cups chicken or vegetable stock
1 pinch sugar
Salt and pepper
Ground nutmeg
4 puff pastry shells
14 oz/400 g shelled shrimps
1 bunch dill, finely chopped
2 egg yolks
½ cup/125 g cream

Fry the onions gently in the butter until soft and transparent. Add the flour and cook gently, stirring constantly. Pour in the chicken stock and season with sugar, salt, pepper, and nutmeg. Simmer the sauce for 15 minutes. Meanwhile, warm the puff pastry shells in the oven. Add the shrimps and dill to the sauce, allow to simmer briefly and season again with the spices. Whisk the egg yolk with the cream. Remove the shrimp sauce from the hob, stir in the egg yolk mixture, and fill the pastry shells with the mixture. Serve immediately.

Sylter Muschelsuppe
Mussel soup, Sylt-style
(Illustrated bottom)

3¼ lbs/1.5 kg mussels
½ lb/250 g carrots
1 parsley root
¼ celeriac root
2 onions
5 tbsp butter
4 cups/1 l white wine
Salt
2 tbsp flour
1 tsp red paprika pepper
1 tsp tomato paste
½ tsp coarsely ground pepper
1 pinch sugar
1 small red pepper, finely chopped
2 shallots, finely chopped

Wash the mussels thoroughly several times, brush and remove the beard. Wash the carrots, parsley root, and celeriac, clean and dice them finely, and chop the onion. Melt 1 tbsp butter in a large pan and cook the vegetables slowly until soft and transparent. Add the mussels, cover and allow to sweat for a few minutes, then add the wine. Add a little salt and soak for about 6 minutes until the shells have opened wide. Drain the mussels, reserving the mussel stock, and remove the mussels from their shells. Melt 2 tbsp butter, add the flour, and cook gently, stirring constantly, and pour in the mussel stock. Season with paprika, tomato paste, pepper, and sugar, and simmer for 15 minutes. Meanwhile, cook the red pepper and shallots gently in the remaining butter until they are soft and transparent. Add to the soup and cook the mixture briefly, then add the shelled mussels, and reheat them in the soup. Scatter garlic croutons over the mussel soup before serving.

Helgoländer Hummer mit Schnüsch
Helgoland lobster with vegetables in a cream sauce
(Illustrated below)

Serves two

4 oz/100 g fresh peas
4 oz/100 g young shell beans
4 carrots
1 bunch scallions
1 kohlrabi
7 oz/200 g turnips
Soup vegetables (2 carrots, 1 leek, 2 celery stalks, parsley)
½ tsp caraway seeds
Salt
2 small live lobsters
1 cup reduced lobster stock
1 generous cup/300 g cream
3½ tbsp butter
1 tbsp chopped parsley

Cook the vegetables separately until just tender. Bring a pan of water to a boil and add the soup vegetables, caraway seeds, and salt. Plunge the lobsters head first into the boiling water and simmer for 10 minutes. Remove from the water, release from the shell, and set aside in a warm place. Reduce the butter, lobster stock, and cream a little, add the vegetables and reheat them in the sauce, then arrange in a circle on the plates. Place the lobster in the center, or cut up into medallions and arrange around the outside. Finally scatter the chopped parsley over the vegetables.

Shrimps in dill sauce

Lobster with vegetables in a cream sauce

Mussel soup Sylt-style

131

Cabbage

80 million cabbages are lifted yearly in Dithmarschen, the largest cabbage-growing region in Europe.

Since cabbages are extremely sensitive to pressure, they are mostly harvested by hand.

Laid end to end, the 80 million or so heads of cabbage harvested each year in Dithmarschen, the "cabbage center" of Germany, would reach from the North Pole to the South Pole. A total of around 264 million pounds (120 million kilos) of white cabbage, red cabbage, Brussels sprouts, and cauliflower, as well as Savoy cabbage, are produced annually on approximately 7400 acres (3000 hectares) of land, the largest cabbage-growing area in Europe.

The area around Dithmarschen on the west coast of Holstein has always been regarded as a fertile region. It is, however, only a little more than a hundred years ago that the flat marshy terrain with its humid, warm climate was recognized as being outstandingly well adapted to growing cabbages. In 1889 Eduard Lass, a gardener from Wesselburen, planted the first cabbage field. The harvest was so successful that many farmers followed suit. Dithmarschen became very important for the German agricultural economy in the lean years at the end of World War I.

Cabbage has always been poor man's fare – it was eaten as an accompaniment to cereal broth by the lesser orders back in Roman times, and was a staple ingredient of stews alongside beans and legumes – and as a result it did not enjoy a particularly good reputation. "All types of fruit and all types of cabbage are nutritionally poor, because they make bad blood," wrote a doctor in the 13th century. Today nutritional scientists take a different view: cabbage lowers cholesterol levels and is rich in minerals, especially iron. Its vitamin C content is approximately equal to that of citrus fruits, and it is a rich source of vitamin B as well as calcium. It is an important source of fiber, and although each 3½-ounce (100-gram) serving has on average only 30 calories, it is very satisfying.

In the wake of increasing awareness of nutritional matters, the image of the cabbage has also undergone a transformation. The various varieties of cabbage now have their place, even in "haute cuisine." *Sauerkraut* in particular has retained its universal popularity, and therefore a large proportion of the white cabbage harvested in Dithmarschen goes to be processed and canned.

In Dithmarschen cabbage thrives almost without the use of pesticides. One reason is that mono-culture has been rejected as an option and cabbage is planted as part of a proper crop rotation sequence, alternating mostly with cereals. The other reason is that the nearly constant westerly wind provides a natural defense against pests. The harvest, primarily from September to November, is hard work. Since cabbage heads are extremely sensitive to pressure, manual lifting is best. Most of

These cabbages have been lifted, trimmed, cut and await collection.

They are loaded up carefully and then taken away immediately to cold stores or factories.

The cabbage festival is held during the first half of September in Dithmarschen.

Everything revolves around cabbage, and naturally all kinds of cabbage specialties are on offer.

the harvest (except for the early variety of cauliflower) is put into huge cold stores, where it is "put to sleep" at a temperature of 3 to 4 °F (2 °C) above freezing. As a result, cabbage from Dithmarschen is available as a fresh vegetable nearly all the year round.

Above: What is good enough for a winegrowing district is good enough for a cabbage-growing area – here a "cabbage queen" has been chosen.

Sauerkraut with oysters?

"The dish known as sauerkraut, with which everyone is familiar, is made by salting and fermenting finely shredded white cabbage, preferably using the late flat-leaved varieties. A barrel in which white wine has been stored will start the cabbage fermenting gently and will also impart a pleasant flavor of wine vinegar. To produce the same effect in a new barrel, a few crushed grapes are scattered in the bottom. Sauerkraut often accompanies fish, oysters, and other foods eaten during periods of fasting. Yet it seems to me that it is at its best when eaten in hearty German style with a broth made from potatoes, white beans, or yellow peas, and with an accompaniment of salt pork."

(Karl Friedrich von Rumohr, 1822)

Gefüllter Kohlkopf
Stuffed cabbage

1 large white cabbage
Salt
1½ lbs/750 g smoked bacon
1 onion, spiked with 1 bay leaf and 2 cloves
A few allspice berries and peppercorns
2 tbsp butter
2 tbsp flour
Scant cup/200 g sour cream
Salt and pepper, nutmeg
1 pinch sugar

Remove the wilting outer leaves and the stalk of the cabbage and steam the cabbage in plenty of salted water for 10 minutes. Lift the cabbage out of the water, drain and cut in half. Remove the inner leaves and hollow out the two halves. Pass the bacon through the coarse blade of the meat grinder and use to fill the hollows in the middle of the cabbage. Put the two halves of the cabbage back together and secure with kitchen string. Bring the cabbage water back to a boil with the spiked onion and the spices, lower the stuffed cabbage into the water and cook over a low heat for at least 1½ hours. Melt the butter in a pan, add the flour and cook gently until it turns golden brown, stirring constantly. Pour in 2 cups of the cabbage water and simmer the sauce for 10 minutes. Finally stir in the sour cream and season the sauce with salt, pepper, ground nutmeg, and sugar. Lift the cabbage out of the water, drain, remove the kitchen string, and arrange the stuffed cabbage halves on a warmed plate. Serve the sauce separately.

Kohlrollen
Cabbage rolls

9 oz/250 g flour
Salt
1 pinch baking powder
9 oz/250 g quark (see p. 137)
1 cup butter
1 lb/500 g cabbage, cut into fine strips
⅛ tsp ground caraway seeds
1 lb/500 g ground meat
2 large onions, coarsely chopped
5 oz/150 g grated cheese, e.g. Gouda
2 eggs
1 tbsp tomato paste
2 tbsp breadcrumbs
Pepper
½ tsp rubbed marjoram
1 tbsp chopped parsley
2 egg yolks, ½ cup milk

Make a quark pastry dough using the flour, 1 pinch salt, the baking powder, quark, and butter, and leave to chill for several hours. Blanch the strips of white cabbage briefly with the caraway in salted water, drain and leave to cool. Knead the ground meat, onions, cheese, eggs, tomato paste, and breadcrumbs together well, season with salt, pepper, marjoram, and parsley, and mix in the white cabbage. Divide the dough into two pieces, roll out each half thinly and cut into 6 rectangles. Place some of the ground meat and cabbage mixture on each piece, roll up and place with the seam side down on a lined cookie sheet. Whisk the egg yolk with the milk and brush the pastry rolls with the mixture. Bake in a pre-heated oven at 430 °F/220 °C for about 35 minutes until golden brown.

Salt meadow lamb

The sight of sheep grazing on the salt pastures of the dykes – yellowish white balls of wool against a dark green background, with the blue-gray sea in the distance – is one that is enjoyed by everyone who takes a vacation in North Friesland. From March and April onward, at the height of the lambing season, the north-western coast of Schleswig-Holstein, the Halligen and other islands are populated by innumerable ewes, each with one or two lambs. In total, over 100,000 sheep are kept here.

One of the purposes of grazing on the dykes is that it affords coastal protection. It has been proven over the centuries that cultivation of the soil and turf strengthens it, making it more able to withstand storms and floods. The other purpose, which is also an important economic factor in the region, is to provide meat from the lambs kept on the dykes, also known as salt meadow lamb. This is held in particularly high esteem because it comes from animals who have spent their entire lives in the open air. As soon as the lambs are able to follow their mothers, usually two or three days after they are born, they are put out to graze. They are fed only on their mother's milk, and later on the unfertilized grass of the dykes. The grass, however, does not grow very long on the windswept dykes. The lambs must move around a great deal within the vast tracts of land fenced off on the dykes in order to find enough food. Their development is therefore rather slow, which in turn improves the quality of the meat, since the proportion of fat it contains is unusually low.

Lambs kept on the dykes are usually a cross between German white-headed sheep and the Dutch Texel breed. The cross-breed is particularly robust, which is essential in view of the raw North Sea climate. The lambs are ready for slaughter after three to six months, depending on how fast they have grown. Their mothers, however, stay out in the pastures all the year round. They spend only the last two or three weeks of their five-month gestation period in the stalls. Shortly before the onset of winter the animals are brought in to pastures on the landward side of the dyke.

Sheep were once kept primarily for their wool, which yielded twice the profit that could be made from selling the meat. Now the profit from wool barely covers the costs of shearing. The market for mutton, like that for the meat of castrated rams, which is not to everyone's taste owing to its very strong flavor, is nevertheless small in Germany. The demand, which is increasing, is only for lamb, that is to say the meat from animals less than one year old. The seal of quality – "fresh quality lamb from Germany" – is only awarded by the German trade association for lamb provided that the animals are of German origin, and that they are no more than six months old and no heavier than 48 pounds (22 kilos) when slaughtered.

What are the distinguishing characteristics of meat from lambs kept on the dykes? It is leaner and perceptibly more tender than that from other lambs. It also has a milder flavor, although at the same time it is distinctly richer and spicier, but by no means saltier. Connoisseurs liken the taste of it to fresh sea air. Its virtues are evident when it is being prepared: the meat hardly shrinks at all when braised, roasted, or broiled, and very little juice escapes from the meat.

Naturally, lamb plays a major role in North Friesian cuisine. Lamb chops, lamb stew with white cabbage, breast of lamb stuffed with lamb's liver, lamb goulash with green beans, or roast lamb in a herb crust – all these and many other dishes are best tried locally, for example during the "North Friesian lamb festival" which is held for two weeks in May every year, and features some delicious specialties.

Lammrücken mit Kräuterkruste
Loin of lamb with a herb crust

2 lb 3 oz/1 kg potatoes
Salt and pepper
1 cup/250 g cream
3 lb 5 oz/1.5 kg loin of lamb
Oil for frying
½ cup butter
2 egg yolks
1 tsp hot mustard
2 cloves of garlic
2 bunches Italian (flatleaf) parsley, finely chopped
2 oz/50 g fresh chervil leaves
2 tbsp breadcrumbs
1¾ lbs/800 g green beans, cut in pieces
6 oz/160 g bacon, diced
2 tbsp crème fraîche
½ jar quince jelly
7 oz/200 g fresh button mushrooms, very finely sliced
1 tbsp clarified butter

Slice the potatoes and season with salt and pepper, arrange in a baking pan, pour over the cream and cook in the oven for 40 minutes at 250 °F/120 °C. Meanwhile wipe the loin of lamb and season with salt and pepper, fry on all sides in oil for about 20 minutes until golden brown, then leave to cool slightly. To make the herb crust, beat the butter with the egg yolks and mustard until foaming; press the garlic and add to the mixture, and stir in the herbs and breadcrumbs. Brush the paste over the loin of lamb and bake in a moderate oven for 15 minutes. Cook the beans in salted water. Cook the bacon in a dry pan until the fat runs, add the cooked beans and stir in the crème fraîche. Strain the juices from the roasting pan into a clean pan, stir in the quince jelly and season the sauce. Fry the button mushrooms in hot clarified butter and use to garnish the loin of lamb before serving.

Opposite: The sheep grazing on the dyke also protect the coast. Cultivation of the soil and turf strengthens the land and makes it more able to withstand storms and floods.

Salzwiesenlamm mit Thymian, Schnippelbohnen und Heide-kartoffeln
Salt meadow lamb with thyme, green beans and moorland potatoes

1 shoulder of lamb, boned
Oil for frying
Salt and pepper
2 sprigs thyme
2 bunches of soup vegetables (4 carrots, 2 leeks, 4 celery stalks, large bunch of parsley), coarsely chopped
1 onion, chopped
1 tbsp tomato paste
2 cloves of garlic, chopped
4 cups meat stock
2½ lbs/1.2 kg small potatoes
1 large noisette of lamb, taken from the leg
1 tbsp hot mustard
Generous 1 lb/500 g green beans, cut into pieces
2 sprigs savory
2 cups Béchamel sauce
2 oz/50 g bacon, finely diced
4 oz/100 g sugar
Clarified butter for frying
6 lamb chops
3 cloves of garlic, crushed

Season the shoulder of lamb with salt and pepper, place the sprigs of thyme in the middle, roll up and secure. Fry well in the oil, remove the meat, and fry the soup vegetables and onions in the juices left in the pan. Stir in the tomato paste and add the garlic, pour over the meat stock, add the shoulder of lamb, cover, and braise in the oven for 45 minutes. Meanwhile cook the potatoes in salted water until tender, peel and leave to cool. Lift out the shoulder of lamb and set aside in a warm place. Purée the sauce with a hand-held blender and season with salt and pepper. Rub the noisette of lamb with mustard, salt, and pepper, fry well on all sides in oil, and roast in the oven for 15 to 20 minutes at 480 °F/250 °C, until pink. Boil the beans in salted water with the savory. Cook the bacon in a dry pan until the fat runs. Add the bacon and beans to the Béchamel sauce and leave to stand to absorb the flavors. Heat the sugar in a pan until it turns brown, quench with 1 cup water and boil until caramelized. Fry the potatoes in the clarified butter, pour over the caramel, toss and add a little salt. Rub the lamb chops with the crushed garlic. Fry in hot oil for 2 minutes on each side, and season with salt and pepper. Arrange 1 slice of the noisette, 1 slice of the shoulder, and 1 chop on some sauce on each warmed plate and serve with the beans and potatoes.

Lammkoteletts
Lamb chops

Serves two

6–8 milk-fed lamb chops
3 cloves of garlic, crushed
Salt and pepper
Clarified butter for frying
1 tsp thyme, finely rubbed

Rinse the chops and pat dry. Rub on both sides with garlic, season with salt and pepper. Heat the clarified butter in a pan and add the chops. Fry for 1½ to 2 minutes before turning. Scatter the thyme over the cooked side, then turn and cook on the other side for 1½ to 2 minutes. Serve on warmed plates. Roast potatoes or delicate vegetables such as steamed spinach or green beans go well with this dish.

The best cuts of lamb

Leg: Whole, for roasting or braising; sliced for steaks; cubed for kebabs, goulash or for fondue.

Loin: Whole, for roasting; for double or single loin cutlets. The part of the loin containing the fillet is a good cut for rolling and roasting. Lamb chops, slices of between 1 and 1½ inches (3–4 centimeters) thick suitable for quick frying, are also cut from the loin, as are fillets of lamb, which are taken from the rear part of the loin. Noisettes of lamb, which are just under an inch (2 centimeters) thick, also come from the fillet or the loin.

Shoulder: Whole, for roasting, boned or with the bone in; it is important to remove the outer covering of fat. Shoulder meat is also used in stews and goulash.

Neck: This cut is most suitable for stews and ragouts or for quick frying (neck chop).

Breast and flank: The breast has relatively little meat and more fat than the other cuts; the flank is similarly thin with quite a high proportion of fat. Breast and flank are cheap and suitable for ragouts or stews.

The long journey from udder to glass

Milk

Germany is supplied with around 29 million tons of milk a year from nearly 5.2 million cows. Schleswig-Holstein plays an important role in this, contributing about one tenth of the total. Milk is also an important economic factor in this federal state, accounting for more than a third of agricultural earnings.

Cows are a characteristic feature of the landscape, above all in the central and northern part of Schleswig-Holstein – green meadows, frequently stretching out as far as the horizon, with black and white animals resembling stones in what appears to be a constantly changing mosaic. Here in the north the black and white Friesian breed predominates, with the red and white breed that is more typical of southern Germany accounting for only a third of the total cattle population.

This idyllic impression of cattle husbandry in Schleswig-Holstein is, however, a little misleading,

since this is one of the most modern dairy industries in the whole of Europe. Although farms with dairy cows are becoming fewer and fewer, those that remain are larger and therefore more efficient. In the past 20 years the milk yield per head has risen from 9300 pounds (4200 kilograms) to nearly 12,600 pounds (5700 kilograms) annually. High-yield cows can produce as much as 22,000 pounds (10,000 kilograms) or sometimes more per year. (The unit of measurement for milk is the kilogram; one liter (2.2 pints) of milk weighs 1030 grams/36 ounces.) The dairies are also organized in terms of a market economy: fifty years ago there were still 550 dairies in the state, whereas today there are only 26 large dairy co-operatives. This concentration not only improves market opportunities – two-thirds of production has to be sold outside Schleswig-Holstein – but also guarantees the quality of the milk, for which Schleswig-Holstein enjoys an outstanding reputation nationwide. In addition to testing the milk in accordance with the federal regulations, even the cattle feed is checked on a monthly basis. The result is the seal of quality "produced and tested in Schleswig-Holstein."

Further processing of raw milk in the dairy is an expensive business. After the milk has been filtered, ventilated, and chilled to a temperature of 39–46 °F (4–8 °C) on the farm, it is transported in special tankers to the dairy. Before it enters the tanks there, it is first tested for freshness, fat content, absence of bacteria, specific gravity, and odor. Only when it has passed these tests is the milk given clearance for the procedures that follow. The milk is next chilled to around 39 °F (4 °C) in the collection tank before it is purified and separated into cream and skimmed milk in a large centrifuge called a separator. At a speed of between 6000 and 8000 revolutions per minute the globules of dairy fat (2/1000 to 6/1000 of a millimeter in diameter) accumulate around the axis of the centrifuge, while the heavier skimmed milk is hurled by centrifugal force against the outer walls. Most milk sold for consumption has its fat content precisely regulated (the information appears on every bottle or pack). This is achieved by the further addition or removal of a corresponding amount of cream.

In the subsequent homogenization process the milk is forced through narrow tubes under

In the north, the black and white native Friesian cattle are a favorite breed. As well as supplying milk they contribute a significant proportion of agricultural earnings.

Milk products

Sour milk products

To make sour milk products the milk is first heated to eliminate bacteria. Then certain lactic acid microbes are added to start the fermentation process that converts part of the lactose in the milk to lactic acid; this causes the casein, a milk protein, to coagulate. The result is thickening of the milk.

Yoghurt: mostly produced by the addition of "*lactobacillus bulgaricus*" and "*streptococcus thermophilus*." The acidification process at 107–113 °F (42–45 °C) takes two to three hours, and is halted by chilling. Yoghurt is available with different fat contents: creamy yoghurt contains at least 10% fat, regular yoghurt at least 3.5%, low-fat yoghurt between 1.5 and 1.8%, and yoghurt made from skimmed milk a maximum of 0.3% fat. Regular yoghurt is soured in vats, drinking yoghurt in large tanks. Many varieties are available with fruit added. "Bioyoghurt" is produced using different bacteria cultures and has a particularly mild flavor.

Kefir: a sour milk drink of Caucasian origin, with a slightly frothy, acidic taste. Kefir contains very small quantities of alcohol, but seldom more than 0.1%. Fermenting yeasts (kefir fungus) are used in addition to lactic acid bacteria. Like yoghurt, kefir is available with four different fat contents and with various fruits added.

Dickmilch: milk that is thickened and soured by the addition of bacteria cultures. It is available either set or runny, and is also marketed with a choice of four different levels of fat.

Buttermilk: a by-product of butter-making. It has a high protein content and also contains a great deal of calcium and lecithin, but has very few calories and is low in fat (maximum 1%). A distinction can be drawn between the thicker "pure buttermilk" and regular buttermilk, to which skimmed milk and water may be added. It is also available with added fruit.

Cream products

These are produced from the cream that is separated from the milk in the centrifuge. Ultra-heat-treated and sterilized products, which can basically be stored for longer, are sold in addition to fresh products.

Single cream: contains a minimum of 10% fat.
Whipping cream: contains a minimum of 30% fat.
Extra thick whipping cream: contains a minimum of 36% fat.
Heavy cream: cream containing approximately 43% fat.
Crème fraîche: slightly acidic, 30 to 40% fat.
Schmand: a soured cream product, usually produced by ultra-heat treatment, with a fat content of about 24%, also marketed as "set sour cream."
Sour cream: produced by acidification of cream using lactic acid bacteria, and subsequent homogenization. The fat content is between 10 and 15%.

Cream cheese products

Cream cheese production also involves the acidification and consequent thickening of pasteurized milk with lactic acid bacteria. Rennet, a fermenting agent obtained from the stomachs of calves, is often added. Because of the varying quantities of water in these products, the fat content is given as a percentage of the dry mass, and therefore the actual fat content of all these products is less than the fat content indicated would suggest.

Quark: milk thickened by acidification, centrifuged a second time to remove more whey. It is then strained and enriched by the addition of cream if required. There are three varieties: very low fat (less than 10% of the dry mass); half-fat (20% of dry mass), and regular (40% of dry mass).

Cream cheese: made from cream and soured, thickened milk. A longer period in the centrifuge gives it an even stiffer consistency than quark. Regular cream cheese has a fat content of 50% of the dry mass, while cream cheese made from double cream has between 60 and 85% fat as a proportion of the dry mass.

Cottage cheese: to make cottage cheese, quark acidified using rennet is cut up and reheated, resulting in the formation of small, solid granules. Cottage cheese usually has a fat content of 10% or 20% of the dry mass.

---

enormous pressure: between 2200 and 3000 pounds per square inch (150 – 200 bar); this breaks up the fat globules so that they no longer rise to the surface and separate out as cream. At this stage they are so minute that they are distributed throughout the milk as a suspension. As well as imparting a full-bodied flavor, this also makes the milk more easily digestible.

Milk is a highly perishable foodstuff and can also contain germs. For this reason the law requires all milk processed in the dairy for consumption, or for the manufacture of other milk products, to be heat-treated. Three methods are used:

Pasteurization: gentle heating brings the milk to a temperature of 161–167 °F (72–75 °C) for 15 to 30 seconds. The nutritional value is preserved, and neither flavor nor odor are affected. After the heat treatment, pasteurized milk is immediately chilled again and then bottled. It will keep in a refrigerator for at least six days. Milk is available with three different fat content levels: full-cream milk with 3.5 percent, low-fat with 1.5 to 1.8 percent, and skimmed with 0.3 percent fat.

Ultra-heat treatment: this process (heating for 3 to 10 seconds to a temperature of 275–302 °F/ 135–150 °C) eliminates germs almost completely, but largely preserves the nutritional value. The resulting U.H.T. milk, which is likewise marketed with three different fat content levels, is immediately chilled again and bottled under sterile conditions. It can be kept unopened for up to six weeks, even at room temperature.

The natural product must undergo a whole series of processing and monitoring procedures in the dairy before a glass of cold milk like the one above reaches the table.

Different types of milk

Raw milk: untreated milk fresh from the cow, which has simply been filtered to remove particles of dirt. Raw milk is sold straight from the farm and must be boiled briefly before drinking. Fat content 3.5–4.5%.

Premium quality milk: untreated raw milk from strictly controlled farms, where it is bottled. The fat content is around 3%.

Full-cream milk with natural fat content: purified and tested in the dairy. The fat content is at least 3.5% and cannot be adjusted; it is often somewhat higher, however, depending on the season and the cattle feed used.

Full-cream milk with regulated fat content: the fat content is adjusted in the dairy and is usually 3.5%. Partially skimmed milk (low-fat) milk has a fat content of 1.5–1.8%. Enrichment with milk protein is permissible.

Skimmed milk (milk from which the cream has been removed): has a maximum fat content of 0.3%, and can be enriched with milk protein.

Sterilization: following this procedure, which is only rarely used nowadays, milk can be kept for up to a year. It is heated in bottles that have already been sealed to a temperature of 230-248 °F (110–120 °C) for 10 to 30 minutes and is thus completely free of germs. The nutritional value and flavor are, however, considerably affected as a result.

Meat dishes

Lübecker National
Traditional Lübeck gammon

1½ lbs/750 g raw, lightly smoked gammon, without bones
Salt
1½ lbs/750 g turnips
2 onions, coarsely chopped
1½ lbs/750 g small potatoes
1 tbsp cornstarch
1 cup/250 g cream
Salt and pepper
½ bunch parsley, chopped

Place the meat with 1 tsp salt in 6 cups cold water, bring to a boil and simmer for 30 minutes. Meanwhile, peel the turnips and cut into bite-sized pieces. Add the turnips and onions to the smoked gammon and cook for another 30 minutes. Wash and peel the potatoes, cut into pieces and boil in salted water until just tender. Lift the meat out of the stock and set aside in a warm place. Whisk the cornstarch with the cream and stir into the root vegetables. Simmer for a few minutes, then season with salt and pepper. Scatter the parsley over the potatoes. Serve the gammon and salted potatoes separately from the root vegetables.

Schwarzsauer
Sour pork

2 lb 3 oz/1 kg pork (pig trotters, collar meat, snout)
4 cups sausage or meat stock
1 onion, spiked with 1 bay leaf and 2 cloves
Salt and pepper
5 allspice berries
⅖ cup plus 1½ tbsp/100 ml wine vinegar
2 cups/½ liter pig blood

Cut the pork meat into bite-sized pieces. Bring to a boil in the stock with the spiked onion, salt, pepper, allspice berries, and vinegar. Cook over a low heat for 1½ hours until tender. Lift out the meat and set aside in a warm place. Strain the stock and bring back to a boil. Stir in the blood and boil to reduce the sauce until it has thickened. Season again with salt, pepper, and vinegar, and pour over the meat. Serve with salted potatoes or dumplings and dried fruit.

Husumer Ochsenkuchen
Husum oxtail pudding

1 oxtail
Salt and pepper
2 tbsp oil
1 onion
1 carrot
½ root celeriac
2 tbsp tomato paste
¾ cup/200 ml red wine
2 cloves of garlic
1 bay leaf
7 oz/200 g poulard meat
10 tbsp/150 g cream
½ oz/50 g each finely diced baby carrots, celery, and leek
1 tbsp chives, finely chopped
1 pig caul
Clarified butter for frying

Divide the oxtail into individual joints, season with salt and pepper and fry in hot oil. Chop the onions, carrot, and celeriac and fry for a few moments with the oxtail. Stir in the tomato paste, pour in the red wine, add the crushed garlic cloves and bay leaf, and add enough hot water to cover the pieces of meat. Braise in a covered pan for approximately 2 hours, adding a little more water from time to time. Then lift out the pieces of oxtail, drain and leave to cool. Meanwhile cut the poulard meat into small pieces and process in a blender with the cream, pepper, and salt until the mixture is smooth. Blanch the diced vegetables briefly in boiling water and add to the mixture with the chives. Remove the bones and gristle from the oxtail pieces, wet the pig caul thoroughly and spread the meat on it. Add the stuffing mixture, roll back into shape and completely wrap in the pig caul. Fry the stuffed oxtail gently in a little clarified butter, then skim the fat off the braising juices and add these to the pan. Braise for approximately 20 minutes until tender. Serve with creamed Savoy cabbage and potatoes with parsley.

Brooken Sööt

What happens to a southern German when confronted with certain north German specialties is seen in Thomas Mann's novel *Buddenbrooks*. The daughter of the family, Tony, has married a Munich man and serves her husband some of her local dishes, on this occasion sorrel with currants – with the result that her husband does not speak to her for the rest of the afternoon.

Pears and beans with bacon, pork ribs, with prunes, and eel with rhubarb compote are just some of the dishes that are typical of Schleswig-Holstein. The term used to describe such combinations, *"Brooken Sööt"* – which literally means "broken sweet" – means more than "sweet and sour." It conveys the combination of robust flavors with fruity sweetness. Why this preference for sweet and sour should have established itself in the north, while the south firmly rejected it, remains a mystery, even in view of the Viking predilection for eating meat and fish with berries and fruit. This is simply the way things are. And there should be no arguments, or even theorizing, in matters of taste.

A *"Büdel"* or *"Grosser Hans"* in Schleswig-Holstein refers to a dumpling, found here in a huge variety of shapes and sizes depending on the region, and made with eggs or beaten egg white, without raising agents. A dumpling can be a meal in itself, served with potatoes and gravy, and is served for dessert with compote or dried fruit, or it can appear as an accompaniment to meat dishes – always large enough to mop up every last drop of the delicious sauce, so none is wasted. It was also once the custom to make dumplings from left-over bread.

The fine art of smoking

Ham – a cottage industry

Black Forest ham comes from the Black Forest, Westphalian ham from Westphalia – so what about Holstein ham? From a cottage. These cottages are small houses belonging to farmers or agricultural workers, with untiled, thatched roofs that are just as much a feature of the Schleswig-Holstein landscape as the black and white cattle. From the outside, the age of these small houses – over a hundred years – is not apparent, but many of the interiors reveal that smoking has been practiced there for generations: the walls of the low-ceilinged rooms are sooty, almost black, and hams – Holstein cottage-smoked hams with their slightly spicy flavor – hang in profusion from the beams.

Of course, Holstein ham is no longer smoked exclusively in cottages. It owes its characteristic flavor to the knowledge and experience of the master smokers as well as to the quality of the meat, which in turn depends on the age of the pigs and, in particular, the way in which they have been reared. Only half of all hindquarter legs of pork find their way into the smokehouse: following the slaughter, the animal is hung by one leg, as a consequence of which the muscle fibers are torn. This results in "rubbery ham," which is extremely unsuitable for the top quality home-smoked Holstein product.

Before it is smoked, the master smoker salts the hams, dry and on the bone, with a special mixture of salt, herbs, and mustard seeds, scorches them, and finally rinses them under running water for 36 hours. Only then is the ham allocated its place in the smoking cottage, where it acquires its full, delicately spicy flavor from cold beechwood smoke at a temperature of 64–68 °F (18–20 °C). A ham may hang in the smoke for up to 13 weeks; if smoking is still in progress in a cottage, it is essential to ventilate it every evening during this period for the duration. The choice of wood determines the flavor of the ham; alder and beech are extremely good, while pinewood spoils the taste. Dry beech logs are usually used rather than shavings. For obvious reasons, wood shavings do not inspire confidence; the wood – three full washtubs of which are burned daily – is frequently impregnated with substances, even toxic ones.

The skill of regular and prompt repositioning of the hams according to their size to vary the temperature at which they are smoked also forms part of the art of smoking in Holstein. Finally the smoked hams are moved to the highest possible position, where they acquire their exquisite, incomparable flavor. Smoking takes place in the winter, between 15 October and 15 May. According to the smoking experts, the importance of salt, as well as that of smoke and air, should not be underestimated; an excess of salt has a marked effect on the quality of the ham.

Birnen, Bohnen, Speck
Pears and beans with bacon

2 lb 3 oz/1 kg bacon joint
3 lb 4 oz/1.5 kg green beans
Salt and pepper
2 sticks savory
4 firm pears

Boil the bacon for approximately 1½ hours until tender. Remove the meat and set aside in a warm place. Cook the green beans in half the stock with the salt, pepper, and savory. Halve the pears, remove the cores and steam the pears in another pan in the remaining stock. Slice the bacon. Arrange the beans on warmed plates, and lay the meat and pears on top. Serve salted potatoes separately as an accompaniment.

A flight that ends on the table

Game birds

In broad terms, "game birds" can be taken to mean all feathered creatures that may be hunted – gallinaceous birds (chicken, turkey, partridge), pigeons, geese, and ducks, wading birds and gulls, cranes, birds of prey, sparrows – in other words, anything that flies and falls to the ground when peppered with shot.

The periods during which various birds are free to circle the skies undisturbed are determined by laws that specify the close seasons. The capercaillie, for instance, is protected all the year round in Germany, and thus escapes the fate of being stuffed and hung on the wall as a trophy, or roasted for an exotic meal. Other birds live happily ever after because nobody wants to eat them anyway, at least in times of prosperity. It was once common practice in poor districts, for instance, to roast crows. Songbirds are no longer eaten in Germany, either. In the 19th century larks were still considered a delicacy, but even then the animal conservationists were sabotaging the connoisseurs' roast dinners.

Although it is really a contradiction in terms, most wild game birds these days are reared, and are therefore commercially available all year round. Generally speaking the wild varieties, whether geese, ducks, or pigeons, are stronger flavored and more robust than their domestically reared counterparts. The pheasant is especially popular with gourmets and huntsmen alike. Connoisseurs enjoy roast pheasant, stuffed and wrapped in bacon, which provides a feast for two people;

huntsmen no doubt love the pheasant because it is so beautiful – the male in particular, with its colorful plumage, is magnificent to behold in the field – and because its swiftness on the wing makes shooting it a sporting challenge. They do not appear to be worried by the fact that what happens before the shoot is not very sporting. Since the pheasant population is in constant decline due to the changing landscape and environment, the birds are raised in large-scale breeding operations, under conditions which could not possibly be described as appropriate, and are then released for huntsmen to shoot in the wild. Under German law the birds must have enjoyed freedom for a minimum of six weeks before they can be shot.

The pheasant originated in Asia and has established itself over a wide area, from the Black Sea to Korea and Japan. It is said that the Greek argonauts captured pheasant in the Caucasian country of Colchis and took them back home to Greece. The name "pheasant" is derived from the bird's place of origin, from the river Phasis between Asia Minor and Colchis.

The breeding, hunting, and eating of pheasant are European traditions. Pheasant was a welcome sight on Greek and Roman tables, and it is said that Charles the Great dined on it regularly. For decorative reasons, roast pheasant were brought to the table at royal banquets still decked with their brightly colored plumage. The magnificent bird is a recurrent motif in still-life paintings and hunting pictures.

From the 13th century onward, royal courts had "pheasant gardens," where pheasants were kept as an object of beauty and where, like peacocks, they were greatly revered. Pheasants were not hunted as game birds until after the Thirty Years War.

Wildentenbrust mit Schmorkohl
Breast of wild duck with braised cabbage

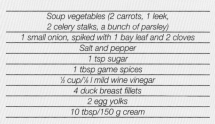

Soup vegetables (2 carrots, 1 leek, 2 celery stalks, a bunch of parsley)
1 small onion, spiked with 1 bay leaf and 2 cloves
Salt and pepper
1 tsp sugar
1 tbsp game spices
½ cup/⅛ l mild wine vinegar
4 duck breast fillets
2 egg yolks
10 tbsp/150 g cream

Place the soup vegetables, spiked onion, spices, and vinegar in 4 cups water and bring to a boil. Add the duck breast fillets and simmer gently over a low heat for 20 minutes until tender. At the end of the cooking time lift the duck breasts out of the stock and set aside in a warm place. Pour the stock through a sieve into a casserole and boil until reduced by half. Whisk the egg yolk with the cream and thicken the sauce with the mixture, without boiling. Cut the duck breast fillets into pieces diagonally and arrange them on warmed plates with braised cabbage and potato paste. Serve the sauce separately.

The guinea fowl grows almost as large as the domestic chicken.

On his travels through Germany, Goethe ate two partridge daily.

Woodpigeon gather together in large flocks to confuse their enemies.

The mallard is the most common duck in Europe.

Quail, the smallest game bird, is only available commercially reared.

Gefüllter Fasan
Stuffed pheasant

1 oven-ready pheasant
Salt and pepper
5 oz/125 g button mushrooms
3 oz/75 g cooked ham, diced
1 egg
1 tbsp breadcrumbs
½ tsp rosemary
1 tbsp chopped parsley
2 slices fatty bacon
2 tbsp clarified butter
1 cup/¼ l stock
¾ cup/200 ml red wine
1 tsp cornstarch
6½ tbsp/100 g cream

Wash the pheasant, pat dry and rub with salt and pepper. Clean the button mushrooms and chop finely. Mix them with the diced ham, egg, breadcrumbs, rosemary, and parsley, and stuff the pheasant with this mixture. Wrap the pheasant in the slices of bacon, securing with kitchen string. Place the pheasant in a roasting pan. Heat the clarified butter and pour over the pheasant. Roast in a preheated oven at 425 ºF/220 ºC for approximately 40 minutes, occasionally basting with a little stock. At the end of the roasting time lift the pheasant out of the roasting pan and set aside in a warm place. Add the remaining stock to the juices in the roasting pan, strain through a sieve into a clean pan, skim off the fat, pour in the red wine, and bring to a boil. Whisk the cornstarch with the cream, stir into the sauce, and season with salt and pepper. Slice the pheasant with the stuffing on to a warmed serving dish and serve the sauce separately.

Left: Pheasant have been reared in Europe since the Middle Ages. Noblemen also kept them in "pheasant gardens" for decorative purposes.

Canola oil: cholesterol-free; high vitamin content.

A gas station in the field

Cars are running on environmentally friendly biodiesel. Industry is using biodegradable lubricants and hydraulic oils. Houses are heated with vegetable oil. Cattle are eating cake instead of animal meal. This utopia is not so very far away. Sustainable raw material is already being grown in fields in Germany – in the form of canola. By adding methanol, canola oil is converted into rape methylester (RME), in other words, biodiesel. The benefits of this are 100 percent less sulphur dioxide, 80 percent less carbon dioxide, 52 percent less soot, 22 percent less hydrocarbons, and 17 percent less particulate matter. Canola oil can also be used for heating: electricity and heat are generated simultaneously in what are known as biomass block-type thermal power stations. Diesel engines capable of running on vegetable oil generate electricity, and heat generated by the engine is recovered. Lubricants and hydraulic oils based on canola have excellent properties. Up to two-thirds of "wasted lubricants," in other words oil that is lost to the environment in use, can already be replaced by environmentally friendly canola oil products. Canola oil cattle cake and pellets are already playing an important role in animal foodstuffs and provide a natural, healthy alternative to cereal-based feed. The textile and leather industries also use canola oil, and it is even frequently to be found in washing agents, ointments, plasters, cosmetics, bath and dental products.

Canola

In Schleswig-Holstein people speak of the "fluorescent yellow season" at the beginning of May, when the canola comes into flower and the fields are transformed into carpets of golden yellow. This magnificent sight may bring to mind sweet canola honey, or clear oil flowing over fresh lettuce leaves – hardly anyone associates it with throbbing diesel engines, or even lubricants. And yet, the raw material for biodiesel and other alternative industrial products also flourishes in Germany's most beautiful oilfields.

However, to concentrate on the nutritional aspect, canola is the most important oil seed cultivated in Europe, ranking third on the list of fruits from which oil is produced worldwide. It contains 45 percent oil and is extremely high in protein. Because of its composition, canola oil is among the most valuable culinary oils. Its fatty acid profile, with nearly 60 percent simple saturated oleic acid and over 30 percent polyunsaturates, is particularly important for diets promoting a healthy heart and circulatory system.

Because of its physiological nutritional properties and neutral flavor, refined culinary canola oil is extraordinarily well suited to food processing. It is used in the manufacture of margarine, mayonnaise, or even highly refined salad products. Cold-pressed canola oil is now available from refineries and delicatessens.

Canola is a cruciferous plant. A distinction can be drawn between winter canola and summer canola: the latter, which accounts for only 0.6 percent, is of lesser importance. For some time now 00-rape, the erucic acid and glucosinolate content of which is practically zero, has been the only variety in cultivation.

Bees also enjoy a romp in the canola fields.

Desserts

"Experience shows that all poets enjoy eating cake," wrote the poet Theodor Storm, a native of Husum, who left a literary monument to his birthplace in the form of the novella "*Der Schimmelreiter*" ("The Ghost Rider"). Storm speaks of sweet things "putting him back on his feet" when he feels "half dead." The same appears to apply to many natives of Schleswig-Holstein, for whom life without a decent portion of dessert is scarcely imaginable.

A particularly popular dish is *Rote Grütze*, called "*Rode Grütt*" (red groats) in the local dialect, which has now conquered dessert trolleys throughout Germany. Its name betrays its origins – the usual barley or oat gruel was refined by cooking it with the juice of bottled blackcurrants, raspberries, or even cherries or blackberries. Today fresh or frozen fruit is preferred. Fruit also forms the basis of many other desserts, for example the "peasant girl with a veil," a combination of finely sliced apples, crumbled black bread, and cream. The preference for sweet and sour is not, moreover, excluded from the dessert course – pears and bacon are combined in a baked pudding known as "Birnenbeschlag." Proximity to England has also resulted in the appearance on the table of puddings, the most famous of which is the "Plettenpudding" that was held in such high esteem by Thomas Mann. Theodor Storm, by contrast, preferred the "Förtchen," or petits fours, the only example of baking with lard in the Schleswig-Holstein dessert repertoire, or the ring-shaped pound cake, and cakes baked with butter that were often eaten with afternoon tea – the English influence is again apparent here.

Background: berries of all kinds find their way into Rote Grütze, which is served with custard.

Rote Grütze
Red fruit compote

8 oz/250 g blackcurrants
8 oz/250 g bitter cherries
8 oz/250 g raspberries
1 cup blackcurrant juice
1 cup cherry juice
1 cup raspberry juice
3 oz/75 g cornstarch
2 tbsp sugar
½ tsp vanilla essence

Pick over the fruit and clean it, removing the currants from their stalks and pitting the bitter cherries. Bring the blackcurrant juice to a boil with the cherry juice and raspberry juice. Whisk the cornstarch with a little cold water and stir into the fruit juices. Add the sugar and vanilla essence and bring back to a boil. Carefully stir in the fruit. Pour into a dessert bowl and chill, stirring several times at intervals to prevent it setting. Cold custard or whipped pouring cream are suitable accompaniments.

A variety of red berries and fruits, fruit juices, and syrups form the basis of Rote Grütze.

All the berries must be washed and their stalks removed, and the cherries are pitted.

The fruit juices and syrup are brought to a boil and cornstarch, dissolved in cold water, is added.

After the sugar and vanilla essence have been added, the liquid is brought back to a boil.

Finally, the prepared fresh fruit is stirred in carefully, making sure it is well coated.

The Rote Grütze is poured into dessert bowls. It is served cold with custard or cream.

Food for
the intellect

"Lübeck was not amused." The upper social strata of this free city of the Holy Roman Empire struggled, not entirely successfully, to keep its composure, the most undignified expressions were voiced behind the façades of stately patrician family houses, and even the pleasures of the table, which held ritual significance for the inhabitants of the Hanseatic city, suffered an outrage: someone had spat in their soup. In the summer of 1901 the Berlin publishing house Fischer had published "*Buddenbrooks*," a wide-ranging novel of more than a thousand pages on the subject of commerce, for which the author was to be honored in 1929 with the Nobel Prize. This was a literary phenomenon, and as such was of no importance to Lübeck, for people on the banks of the Trave had from time immemorial displayed more inclination to devote time to book-keeping than to the fantasies of some scribbler or other who had just arrived on the scene. Unfortunately, however, the author of "*Buddenbrooks*" was a scribbler who had left the scene. Born in 1875 in Lübeck, the second son of a highly respected important

businessman and senator, he had access to inside information that endowed his novel with the authenticity of a book of accounts. It had to be taken seriously; this was no fantasy, but reality, embodied in the "exploiting appetite of the poor relations," as well as in the sad fate of the diabetic senator James Möllendorpf, who succumbed to his fatal passion for gateaux in a cheap hotel not in keeping with his position: ("…and there too they found the deceased, his mouth still full of half-chewed cake.")

People recognized themselves, and from then on the author was considered a deserter, who had fouled his own nest and betrayed his ancestry. Part of this was quite true; Mann had indeed fled the narrow confines of his native city. In 1894, at the age of 19, he had moved to Munich, where in 1893, following the early death of his father, his mother and siblings had already found a new home. Here, in a series of Swabian lodgings, "*Buddenbrooks*" was written. The attitude to life of the writer, who had actually been destined to inherit the family firm, was at that time one of "indolence, a bad bourgeois conscience and certain conviction of his latent abilities."

However, the bad bourgeois conscience was soon to be a thing of the past. "I am going to have my photograph taken," wrote the 26-year old, when the novel was successfully completed and had been accepted. The picture has survived: we see a serious young man of good breeding, who has just

Thomas Mann in the 1930s. By then he was living in Munich and had become well-known as a writer.

Many restaurants in Lübeck reproduce the so-called "Buddenbrooks Menu," starting with a herb soup made with robust meat stock.

Ham, Lübeck-style: "A colossal, brick-red ham appeared, coated in breadcrumbs, smoked, boiled, accompanied by a brown, tart shallot sauce," wrote Thomas Mann.

"The gourmet of the written word," as Thomas Mann was called, relished good food and drink and was not averse to fillet of sole.

In "*Buddenbrooks*" he also describes the delicious "Plettenpudding" as "a layered mixture of macaroons, raspberries, biscuits and custard …"

demonstrated that achievement is a privilege not confined to sober men of action and accountants. And also – this was quite important – that artistic achievement could also be honored by society. Basking in the rays of "public favor and esteem," he was now finally able to establish ties with the patrician ancestry he appeared to have betrayed. While Lübeck foamed at the mouth with rage, Thomas Mann drew up a "constitution" for himself in Munich. Despite his homosexual inclinations, in 1905 he married the beautiful, intelligent Katja Pringsheim, who enjoyed high social standing, with whom he conceived one child after another, establishing himself and his family in increasingly aristocratic accommodation. He felt secure in this environment, and "worthy and bourgeois" values gave him a firm anchor.

Life at the Mann residence was civilized – which naturally entailed a reasonable standard of catering. Guests to the house at 1, Poschingerstrasse, like the guests in "*Buddenbrooks*," could always expect a "decent bite to eat," in other words an average of five courses according to the old Lübeck custom. And although the man of the house constantly complained of indigestion and stomach pains, he ate heartily all his life, as his diaries show. A breakfast consisting of "hors d'oeuvres, noodles, roast veal, cheese, and strawberries" was not unusual, and when a "light snack" is mentioned the reader should picture a series of substantial titbits. Good food was one of the few permitted sensual pleasures in the life of Thomas Mann, and in this respect he could count on the approval of his Hanseatic forebears.

And as far as his Hanseatic contemporaries were concerned, they became increasingly mellow with time. The scribbler who had run away had made something of himself, his lifestyle was respectable and his market value, if one converted the Nobel Prize into hard currency, appeared not inconsiderable. Although the recognition accorded to him mounted, a penalty had to be paid: it was not until May 1955, three months before his death, that Mann was given honorary citizenship of his native city of Lübeck.

An episode related by Katja Mann shows that, even before this, Lübeck had occasionally displayed understanding of the alienating needs of the writer. Some years after their marriage, as she recounts in her "*Unwritten Memoirs*," they had visited Lübeck together for the first time, and, having inherited an estate from the Mann family, had even been tempted to settle there. Whereupon a long-established great-nephew of her husband, having considered the matter, had protested, "Oh, but I think you would find that you missed intellectual food."

Left: A scene from the film "*Buddenbrooks*" (directed by Alfred Weidenmann): Gerda and Thomas are celebrating their marriage; the family toasts the health of the couple and the growing prosperity of the dynasty.

Marzipan

Thomas Mann called it a "sumptuous burden on the stomach." He probably had no idea that in earlier times it was prized as a medicine, to treat ailments specifically including an "upset" stomach, as is shown by a prescription for a cure at Karlsbad dating from the year 1571.

The concept of marzipan as a medicine may be linked with the fact that, up until the 18th century, it was mainly pharmacists who sold expensive sugar and produced confectionery, marzipan, and other goods made with sugar. Making cakes and confectionery was regarded at that time as a "free art" and was therefore not subject to the privileges conferred by the laws relating to the guilds.

The art of making marzipan from almonds and sugar is over a thousand years old and has its origins in the Near East, from where it spread with the Arab conquerors to Spain and the rest of Europe. Marzipan then made rapid advances as a highly desirable dessert at royal tables, for the extremely high price of sugar meant that only the wealthy could afford such expensive delicacies. It was not until sugar was obtained industrially from sugar beet at the beginning of the 19th century that marzipan became affordable to any extent. This was also the time which marked the beginning of Lübeck's history as the "capital city" of marzipan. It is closely associated with the name of Johann Georg Niederegger, who in 1806 took over the confectioner's shop on the market square and began the first factory production of marzipan shortly afterwards. At that time, however, marzipan was still a seasonal product, bought principally to indulge a sweet tooth as a Christmas treat.

The raw materials for marzipan production are sweet almonds and sugar. Firstly, what is termed the "raw mass" of marzipan is made. This process is fully automatic today. The almonds, which come mainly from the Mediterranean region, pass through cleaning and sorting machines; they are then scalded to remove the skins, are washed and passed through several rollers that chop them into progressively smaller pieces until a mass resembling a paste is obtained. Very small amounts of rosewater or similar ingredients are added, the precise nature and quantities of which remain a secret, closely guarded by each manufacturer. Next, the raw mass is heated for approximately 45 minutes to a temperature in excess of 210 °F (100 °C). This melts the sugar, improves the cohesion of the almond and sugar paste, intensifies the flavor and enables the marzipan to be kept for longer (six to twelve months, depending on the product.) After a cooling period in special vats the raw marzipan leaves the machine in blocks between 12 and 16 inches (30–40 centimeters) wide and 10 inches (25 centimeters) high. It can now be shaped and kneaded and the refining procedure can begin. Sifted confectioner's sugar is now added to the raw mass. In Lübeck marzipan, which is a protected brand name, a maximum of 30 parts confectioner's sugar to 70 parts raw mass is permissible, and for fine marzipan the maximum is only 10 percent.

The market leader, the Niederegger company, itself produces up to 30 tons of marzipan a day. The automated belts that carry the molds in which the marzipan is transformed into a wide variety of shapes, and on which it is then cooled and finally packaged, are over 76 yards (70 meters) long.

Right: the products formed from the raw mass must dry out before they can be processed further.

Almonds and sugar are passed through several rollers where they are chopped ever more finely.

Lübeck marzipan is a quality product that is marketed throughout the world.

The paste-like mass is stirred in copper vats and various flavorings are added.

There are more than 200 marzipan products. Here, loaves are being coated with chocolate.

Nimble fingers and concentration are essential for rolling nice round marzipan apples.

200 varieties of marzipan

White marzipan loaves, black ones coated with chocolate, potatoes rolled in cocoa powder, a wide range of pralines, little parcels flavored with pineapple, raspberry, strawberry, apple, apricot, cherry, ginger, walnut, hazelnut, pistachio, mocha, cappucino, rum, or red wine – this is just a selection of more than 200 variations of Lübeck marzipan. There are motifs and figures to suit every occasion and every season: lucky pigs and chimney sweeps, Easter eggs, Easter bunnies and chicks, cockchafers, trolls, bears, monkeys, and elephants. Marzipan replicas are particularly popular – apples, pears, oranges, peaches, bananas, lemons, carrots, tomatoes, and much else besides, all life-sized and deceptively real in appearance. For a very long time Christmas has been regarded as the peak period for marzipan, so snowmen, nutcrackers, Father Christmases, cinnamon stars, as well as angels for the Christmas tree and marzipan *Stollen* – a traditional tea bread – are indispensable. Tourists visiting Schleswig-Holstein, who may take marzipan souvenirs home with them, are also catered for, with seals, starfish, eels, and other fish, as well as the famous Lübeck Holstentor gate in the form of a marzipan cake. Another traditional type of marzipan is also produced in Lübeck, the famous Königsberg variety – tiny marzipan balls, which have been deliberately scorched.

Rum

"Fifteen men on the dead man's chest/ Yo ho ho, and a bottle of rum!/ Drink, and the devil had done for the rest/ Yo ho ho, and a bottle of rum!" bawled the captain in Robert Louis Stevenson's "*Treasure Island*," and sea captain Hans Hinrich Pott probably sang a similar song on his crossing from the Danish West Indies, while he enjoyed sampling the rum carried on the ship. This drink must have tasted so good to him that he started producing rum in 1848 outside the northern city gate of Flensburg. This is how the legend of "good old Pott" began.

The first Flensburg ship, the "*Neptunus*," sailed to the Danish West Indies in 1755. The city had belonged to the Danish kingdom since 1460, and had brought it considerable wealth. Its ships sailed under the "Danebrog," the Danish flag, which meant that it could carry cargo unmolested, even in time of war. In 1755 the Danish king allowed his subjects to participate in the lucrative trade with the West Indies, as a result of which the city continued to prosper. In the last quarter of the 18th century the Flensburg fleet tripled in size, and the population of the city rose between 1796 and 1803 from 6,800 to 10,700.

At first, rum was only declared as a secondary cargo on the sailing ships that loaded up with sugar, tea, coffee, tobacco, cotton, and precious wood. The brandy distillers in the old part of the town, which already numbered 150 independent businesses in 1794, lost no time in transforming the unpalatable pure rum into an exceedingly popular drink, a refining process in which the quality of the water in Flensburg played a decisive role.

The pure rum was produced immediately after the sugar cane harvest on the Caribbean islands. Rapid processing of the sugar cane was important, since the juice spoiled easily. Therefore the cane was brought into the plantation's own sugar cane mills, on the day of harvest if possible, where it was passed through rollers. The juice flowed along a channel into the sugar house, where it was heated to thicken it. The syrup produced in this way dripped through barrels with holes in the bottom into a pool of molasses. The brown cane sugar accumulated at the bottom. The colonial masters of the British Caribbean islands usually shipped the molasses and distilled the rum in what is now the northeast of the U.S.A. This served as a valuable exchange commodity. In Africa, slaves were obtained in exchange for rum; they were then shipped to the Caribbean, where they were exchanged for molasses. This was what was known as the three-cornered trade that had enormous economic importance for the colonies, as a result of which an entire continent was robbed of its population. The pure rum that arrived in

Flensburg had been produced on the islands. Molasses, sugar foam, and the residues from previous distillation processes were prepared as a wort for the rum and then distilled. The beverage produced in this manner had not yet earned the name rum, however; it was practically undrinkable. There was no change in this situation until the Atlantic crossing; in those days the voyage took months, and the rum had the opportunity to mature in the barrels and develop its flavor. The art of refining – the blend of rum is basically achieved by the addition of water, pure alcohol, and various flavorings – was then left to the people of Flensburg.

Egg nog: yolks and sugar are beaten until frothy, then a small glass of rum and some hot water are added.

Icebreaker: a glass is filled two-thirds full with boiling water. Sugar, red wine, and rum are then added.

Pharisee: strong, hot coffee is poured into a special glass. Sugar, rum, and whipped cream are added.

Lemonade, ice, and rum are the ingredients of the cold drink known as Anglermuck.

There are five ingredients in punch: rum, lemon or orange juice, sugar, various spices, and wine.

Tea punch: black tea, orange and lemon juice, spices (cloves, cinnamon, vanilla beans) and of course rum.

The pastor and the Pharisee

"Unless you have drunk a Pharisee, you do not know Nordstrand!" So say the natives of the Isle of Nordstrand, near Husum. They like to entertain their guests with the story of how the delicious drink with the light cream topping was invented.

A child was christened in 1872, and a celebration followed, to which the pastor was naturally also invited. As was the custom then, strong coffee with whipped cream was served, at least ten or twelve cups of which had to be drunk in order not to offend the host. It was well known, however – and this was a thorn in the side of the pastor – that the population of Nordstrand enjoyed drinking. They would dearly like to have had a "proper drink" to mark the event in a fitting manner – but the presence of the man of God prevented this. There was coffee to drink, and nothing else.

The pastor, in turn, saw in this occasion a good opportunity to give his flock a lecture, the gist of which was "it is possible to enjoy oneself, even without alcohol," and entertained his parishioners with jolly anecdotes – evidently with some success. The guests were growing visibly more relaxed and happy. What had escaped the notice of the priest, however, was that the host had instructed the kitchen staff to add sugar and rum to the coffee and cover it with a particularly generous topping of cream so that the pastor would not smell the alcohol. Care was also to be taken that the pastor was given only the right coffee and not a cup of the highly alcoholic drink.

The guests enjoyed this game, and the atmosphere became increasingly merry, especially when the initiated met one another's gaze with knowing looks. The new creation was also extensively tested in the kitchen, with eventually disastrous results – the pastor was given coffee containing alcohol. He noticed the deception immediately, sprang up and cried, "You hypocrites! You Pharisees!" The story spread like wildfire, and everyone wanted to try the new invention, with the result that the "Pharisee" became the national drink of the population of Nordstrand.

Rumtopf

It takes a whole summer to prepare this delicious drink, just as long as it takes for Mother Nature to ripen the fruit. A successful *Rumtopf* requires, in addition to patience, a stoneware or glazed pottery container with a lid (available from specialist stores), fruit, sugar, and rum containing a minimum of 40 percent alcohol by volume. Since fresh fruit is not cheap, it is worth buying good quality rum as well, rather than economizing.

A simple rule of thumb applies to setting up a *Rumtopf:* half a pound (250 grams) of sugar should be added for each pound (500 grams) of fruit, with enough rum to ensure that the fruit is always covered. As fruits that rise to the surface can go moldy, a plate should be laid on top of the fruit. While the *Rumtopf* is waiting for other fruit to ripen, it should be kept covered in a cool, dark place. The *Rumtopf* should be left to stand for at least another two months after the last variety of fruit has been added.

The fruit should be fully ripe, but still firm and unblemished, if the *Rumtopf* is to keep well. *Rumtopf* can be served with lightly whipped cream, but it also tastes very good with vanilla ice, custard, or semolina flummery.

Rum terminology

Pure rum: the clear, colorless pure rum shipped to Flensburg in barrels has been imported for the past 100 years, mainly from Jamaica. It is a spirit with a high percentage of alcohol (of the "German flavored rum" type) amounting to between 76 and 80% by volume, obtained exclusively from the fermentation and distillation of molasses or sugar cane syrup.

Rum blend: if another type of alcohol is mixed with rum, it must be labeled a "rum blend." The proportion of rum in the alcohol contained in the finished product must be at least 5%, while the minimum alcohol content is 35% by volume. The Flensburg distillers developed the rum blend at the end of the 19th century. By mixing water, pure alcohol, and flavorings, the manufacturers refined the still undrinkable pure rum and developed their own branded products. The additives used for refining in each case remain a closely guarded trade secret.

Original rum: only a product imported from abroad that has not been subjected to any domestic processing can be called original rum.

Genuine rum: genuine rum is original rum, the strength of which has been reduced for the domestic market. If it is a mixture of rum from various sources, an all-embracing geographical term must be used to describe it, for instance "genuine overseas rum."

White rum: white rum is a light rum that has been stored in stainless steel tanks, and whose strength has been reduced. By contrast with the other types of rum, which obtain their brown color from the addition of sugar coloring or caramel, it is marketed without coloring.

Vanilla pudding with Rumtopf

Hamburg
Schwerin
Bremen
Hanover
Berlin
Magdeburg
Potsdam
Düsseldorf
Dresden
Bonn
Erfurt
Wiesbaden
Mainz
Saarbrücken
Stuttgart
Munich

STEFAN SIEGERT

Hamburg

Despite the fact that it is a port, Hamburg lies some distance from the sea. The River Elbe, on which it is situated, runs for more than sixty miles (one hundred kilometers) beyond the city before beginning to widen into the river mouth. Gradually broadening, the estuary eventually reaches a width of nine miles (fifteen kilometers). Hamburg's distance from the coast, and its position between the North Sea and the Baltic, gives it more than one outlet to the sea. Hamburg is a city of 1.6 million inhabitants, one of the historic Hanseatic League of trading cities. It has a lake at its heart, the dammed inland waterway, the Alster, and boasts more canals than Venice. Historically, its connections were as much with the Baltic as the North Sea, though the latter has been of more importance in recent times, providing a dynamic communications route with the world.

This contact has influenced the character of Hamburg's citizens ever since the Emperor Barbarossa granted them shipping privileges in 1189. A free city of the Empire, Hamburg became a Hanseatic city in 1321. Its merchants developed their contacts with London, the leader in world trade, to such an extent that Hamburg, more than any other German city, was able to share in exploiting the resources of the world in the early days of colonialism.

The sailing ships of the East India Company delivered spices, tea, coffee, and tobacco; Hamburg's own four-masted vessels and broad, high-sided Hanseatic trading ships brought not only goods from around the world, but information about distant lands, and recipes from afar. The people of Hamburg reveled in the flavors, and they became oriented toward the wider world, not least in culinary matters, despite a certain unbending reputation that has persisted to this day.

This reserve has traditionally marked the attitude of Hamburg's plutocracy toward culture. In Germany's classical past, Lessing tried in vain to establish a German national theater on the Gänsemarkt; Bach had little success in finding a position here, as did Brahms, a native of the city. When it came to good food and drink, the purse-strings were distinctly more relaxed.

"In Hamburg, one can dine in the English, the French, and the German fashion." This old quotation in praise of the city continues: "yet overall, it is always in Hamburg fashion that one dines."

Left: Tea, tobacco, coffee, spices – these are the imports that made Hamburg rich. They used to be stored in the city's warehouse quarter.

The crowd gathers in amazement, not so much at the sight of the smoked fish being plied for sale as at hearing the salesman's patter, sometimes distinctly uncensored.

The rows of stalls cluster around the fish auction hall. Early risers and night owls come here, either in search of food to start the day or to round off a long night.

Meat is no longer off the menu at the fishmarket. Among the salespeople crying their wares here are those selling sausages. The language is as salty as in the fish section.

Fish cannot possibly come any fresher than this. The sales counter is the boat itself. Mackerel, plaice, sardines, and other tasty fish head straight for the bags.

Hamburg's fishmarket

"Twelve Euros (sixteen dollars) – tweeelve Eurooos, everyone!" bellows a voice. Everyone looks round. "And another eel, and another!" The diminutive old man in the grubby white overall slaps one smoked fish after another onto the piece of paper spread out in his left hand, shouting at a volume that makes him seem at least six feet (two meters) taller. "And another couple of flat fish, and" – in a reference to the reputed aphrodisiac qualities of smoked trout – "a boost for your potency – the whole lot for twelve Euros, tweeeelve Eurooos, everyone!" People laugh, stop and turn. A few at the front pull out their purses, hand over the money, receive a plastic bag with two months' supply of smoked fish, and squeeze their way onward through the press of the crowd. Over 100,000 people gather at Hamburg's fishmarket every Sunday morning between five and nine-thirty.

A short distance away, bananas fly through the air. Second only to the fishmerchants as the stars of the market are the salespeople at the truck loading area where boxes of bananas and crates of pineapples and oranges are stacked. The sheer energy and entertainment value of their patter is enough to sell crates of oranges and grapefruit even to buyers allergic to citrus fruits. Wherever they hail from, be it Seoul, Helsinki, Rome, San Francisco, or closer to home in Hamburg-Emsbüttel, the clientèle is neatly divided into two groups: the night owls and the early birds. The former are easily recognizable by their crooked ties and disheveled hair, the latter by their fresh morning faces and shining shoes. Their buying habits differ, too: the one group maybe lugging a teddy bear or a huge indoor plant, the other tucking a garden gnome or a rabbit under their arm. As a mere bonus to all this, delicious *matjes* herring, smoked turbot, filled shrimp rolls, and salmon are on sale, with all manner of other foods. The fishmarket has long since become a tourist haunt. The market sells almost everything, from all-purpose cleaning materials to "Jesus loves you" sweatshirts, and from sheepskin slippers to budgerigar food. This is sold at the very top of the sloping triangle between the red brick houses that make up the fishmarket itself. That is where the stalls of the pet dealers can be found very soon after cock crow.

Hamburg's fishmarket is, strictly speaking, the Altona fishmarket. The location where the market is held lies in Altona, which, unlike Hamburg itself, was a Prussian possession until 1938. Long after the first fishmarket was opened in 1703, there were two landing stages and two marketplaces on the Elbe. Rivalry was intense until the period of industrial expansion in the 1870s. At that time, sail

This is how the fish auction hall at Hamburg's fishmarket in Altona used to look.

gave way to steam power in the fishing fleet, and the invention of canning gave a great boost to fishing and the trade in fish. The sale of fish straight from the trawlers was replaced by large-scale fish auctions. The auction hall was built, and the Altona fishing harbor became the main landing place for the German North Sea fishing fleet and ocean-going vessels.

Today, during the hours when the fish market is operating, a glance through the windows of the fish auction hall will reveal the tireless Saturday night partygoers exchanging their last kisses and addresses. Around the hall, curious onlookers push their way between the rows of stalls. In the midst stands the diminutive old man in the white fishmerchant's overall. "And a goldfish for you, 14 carat gold plated," he cries, adding a kippered herring to a pile of smoked eel. Beside his stall stands an open container full of fish heads. Above them in the Hamburg skies the seagulls circle in patient anticipation.

And another eel, and another! Soooo cheap!

Acting talent is a necessary qualification to sell your wares here. Putting on a show is an essential part of proceedings at the Hamburg fishmarket.

Good things from afar

Through all the ups and downs of Arab-Israeli relations, the stability or tumult of the political situation in Ecuador, there is hardly any aspect of world trade that is as directly affected by Hamburg's legendary openness to the world than that in tropical and subtropical fruits. Bananas, kiwi fruit, carob, and pineapples must all reach the market in fresh condition. The importers are strictly bound by this necessity; time is money in the fruit trade, more than in any other. It is no coincidence that the exotically named fruit cargo ships entering the port of Hamburg have more elegant, racing lines than the massive container ships. They need above all to be fast. The sensitive cargo in their refrigerated holds has to make the continent-to-continent journey to Hamburg in record time.

In 1995, a total of 146,331 tons (132,751 tonnes) of fruit arrived in Hamburg. Apples and pears are the most important of these on the German market. Of the 533,349 tons (483,981 tonnes) of tropical and subtropical fruits sold, 80 percent consisted of oranges, clementines, lemons, and bananas.

The import opportunities existing today mean that all fruit varieties are available all year round. There is, however, a noticeable difference in flavor between the raspberries imported from New Zealand in December and the local ones grown in Vierlande, which reach the market in June.

Mass production, the only economic option for export, has resulted in a loss of flavor. Tomato plants, for example, once stood no higher than 4 feet (1.2 meters); now are double the height and bear correspondingly more fruit. There are varieties developed especially for export, which must have particularly good keeping qualities to cope with long transportation times and long periods of storage in refrigerated warehouses and on supermarket shelves. Anyone who has ever eaten papaya or figs in the locality where they are actually grown would willingly do without the small, unripe products of the large plantations sold as papaya and figs here.

Kiwi fruit originates from New Zealand. It is rich in vitamin C.

Guavas are exotic fruits. They are rich in phosphorus and calcium.

The Japanese persimmon contains vitamins A and C as well as calcium.

Star fruit grows mainly in the Canary Islands. It makes a beautiful decoration for desserts.

Pomegranates contain delicious, bright red seeds.

Chirimoya comes originally from the Andes. The fruit is eaten raw, or made into a sweet liqueur.

Prickly pears are the fruit of the South American Opuntia cactus.

Lemons are much used in cooking, especially for salad dressings and fish marinades.

Pineapples that are harvested when ripe have an unrivalled sweetness of flavor and aroma.

The main types of melon are the watermelon and sweet melon (shown here).

Medlars are held to be very digestible and easy on the stomach.

Today, even in northern climes, tropical fruit is in the stores all year round. But fruit that has made the long journey to the port of Hamburg and on to the stores can never taste as good as in its country of origin – in this case, Malaysia.

Papaya is particularly rich in enzymes that aid digestion (papain).

Beneath the unprepossessing skin of the passion fruit lies exceptionally delicious flesh.

Tea

The *Preussischer Adler* or "Prussian Eagle" appears in the records of the tea trading company G. W. A. Westphal & Son for 1848. This is the name of a sailing ship, and it had unloaded 8,065 boxes of fragrant tea from Canton, for the storerooms of the company in Hamburg. This was the time when tea consumption in Germany was rising. The first mention of tea in Germany was in the middle of the 17th century. It could be bought from the apothecary for use as medicine. From 1722 to 1772, the tea imported into Germany increased from one variety to sixty. The main reason for this large increase was the "Königlich-preussisch-asiatische Handelskompanie zu Emden" (the Royal Prussian-Asiatic Trading Company of Emden), which Frederick the Great of Prussia (1740-1786) hoped would yet enable him to obtain a slice of the large colonial cake. Only four years later, this Prussian version of the East India Company fell victim to the Seven Years War. Despite this, tea consumption in Germany grew. The poet, Heinrich Heine, commented on this development in his *Buch der Lieder* (The Book of Songs) "They sat at the tea table, drinking, and talking of love a great deal. The gentlemen all were aesthetic; the ladies with tenderness feel..."

From the end of the 18th century onward, Bremen and Hamburg were the main centers of import and transshipment of tea in Germany. This ties in with the hegemony of Britain and Holland in tea-growing, transportation, and tea-drinking. The Dutch East India Company enjoyed equality with the British as long as the tea continued to come mainly from China, its country of origin. Once the British began to grow tea in India, which was a British colony – using seed from China – Holland fell behind, eventually losing the competition. Tea was first grown in Assam in 1830, and, from 1870, in Darjeeling. Westphal & Son's record-keeper noted in 1880 that the bulk of the firm's imports now came from India and Ceylon, today called Sri Lanka. This major change in tea imports was associated with the first signs of a change in tastes, from green tea to black; the British produced only black tea in their colonies. The Hamburg tea traders, who had just moved into the new warehouse quarter of the city, compensated for this change in local tastes by exporting green types of tea to Arab countries. In Hamburg itself, the "Hamburg mixture" (*Hamburger Mischung*) became popular. This was a blend of green and black teas.

The leaf color is the result of different production processes. Black tea is withered, rolled, fermented, and dried after picking. Then, finally, it is sorted according to leaf size. Between rolling and fermentation, the British inserted a further stage: the leaves are torn into pieces and the leaf veins removed. Such tea is called "broken." This process results in a stronger tea. In the preparation of green tea, which has been produced and drunk for thousands of years, mainly in China, but also in smaller quantities in Japan, the leaves are not fermented. Instead, in China, they are heated in special pans. In Japan, they are treated with hot steam. This neutralizes the enzymes in the leaves. Green tea retains its vitamins and polyphenols, as well as the stimulant caffeine. As a result, green tea is more refreshing than black. It is still little used in Germany, despite press reports of the health-promoting effects of green tea.

The company Westphal & Son is no longer in existence, but the warehouse quarter is still standing, and most of Hamburg's tea importers have their warehouses there. A few also have more spacious ones on the edge of town. The warehouse quarter was built between 1882 and 1888. During the boom years of industrial expansion following Hamburg's customs union with the German Empire, this quarter grew to become, within 25 years, "the largest integrated warehouse complex in the world." Today, the conversion of the beautiful old warehouse buildings to boutiques, design centers and bistros is taking place. Any tea found there is used strictly for drinking, maybe for pleasure, but no longer for professional purposes.

More than 25 percent of the tea imported into Germany comes from India. It is harvested by hand.

Senators' mixture tea cookies

Buttermürbeteigmischung
Butter shortcake

10 cups/1.2 kg flour
3¼ cups/800 g butter
3½ cups/400 g confectioner's (icing) sugar
½ tsp vanilla essence
Pinch of salt
4 egg yolks
2 eggs
Zest of 1 lemon, grated
Flour for dusting work surface

Sift the flour onto the work surface, and make a well in the middle. Cut the butter into cubes, bring it to room temperature, and add it to the well in the flour, along with the other ingredients. Knead quickly to a smooth dough. Place the ball of dough in the refrigerator to rest for 30 minutes. Preheat the oven to 400 °F/200 °C. Roll out the dough to a thickness of about ¼ inch/5 millimeters. Cut out the cookies using a heart-shaped cutter for half the mixture, and a flower-shaped cutter for the rest. Bake in the preheated oven for about 10 minutes, until golden.

Filling for flower-shaped cookies

3½ tbsp/100 g peanut butter
Scant 1 cup/100 g confectioner's sugar
Scant ⅓ cup/75 ml lemon juice

Beat together the peanut butter and confectioner's sugar, adding the lemon juice gradually. Spread the mixture onto half the cookies, and sandwich together with the other half. Decorate with yellow frosting or other garnish.

Filling for heart-shaped cookies

3½ tbsp/100 g blackcurrant jelly

Pass the jelly through a sieve, and spread onto half the cookies. Sandwich together with the other half. Decorate with pink frosting.

Eigelbmakronen
Egg yolk macaroons

1 lb 10 oz/750 g marzipan
5½ oz/160 g egg yolk
1¼ cups/150 g confectioner's (icing) sugar
½ tsp vanilla essence
Pinch of salt
Refined sugar for frosting
10½ oz/300 g dark chocolate couverture

Crush the marzipan thoroughly with a fork, and blend to a smooth mixture with the egg yolk, gradually adding the confectioner's sugar, vanilla, and salt. Preheat the oven to 500°F/260°C. Line a baking sheet with parchment. Pipe small rings of the mixture onto the baking tray, using a piping bag and nozzle. Sear the cookies in the preheated oven, and frost them by sprinkling them with refined sugar while they are still hot. Melt the chocolate couverture. Dip the bottom of the macaroons into the chocolate, and cool them on a cake rack.

Buttersandmasse
Butter Cookies

3¼ cups/800 g butter
3 cups/320 g confectioner's (icing) sugar
1 tsp vanilla essence
Pinch of salt
Zest of 1 lemon, grated
4 egg yolks
2 eggs
8⅓ cups/1 kg flour
1 cup/300 g apricot jelly
7 oz/200 g dark chocolate couverture

Preheat the oven to 400 °F/200 °C. Cream together the butter, confectioner's sugar, vanilla, salt, and lemon zest until frothy, gradually working in the egg yolks, eggs, and flour. Line a baking sheet with parchment, and pipe portions of the mixture onto it, using a piping bag with a star nozzle. Bake for 10 minutes, until golden. Leave to cool. Sieve the apricot jelly, and spread over half the cookies. Sandwich together with the other half. Melt the chocolate couverture. Dip the ends of the cookies in the chocolate, and leave to cool on a cake rack.

Makronen
Macaroons

A generous pound/500 g of marzipan
¾ cup/360 g egg white (about 12 eggs)
2½ cups/500 g sugar
3½ tbsp/100 g nougat (confectioner's cocoa-flavored almond paste)
3½ tbsp/100 g peanut butter
1 lb/500 g milk chocolate couverture
Pistachio nuts to garnish

Blend the marzipan to a smooth mixture with the egg white, gradually adding the sugar. Line a baking sheet with parchment. Preheat the oven to 350 °F/180 °C. Pipe the mixture onto the baking tray, using a piping bag and nozzle. Bake the macaroons in the preheated oven for about 10 minutes, until pale brown. Leave to cool. Beat together the *nougat* and peanut butter until slightly frothy. Using a piping bag and nozzle, pipe a round of this mixture onto each macaroon, just a little smaller than the macaroon itself. Melt the milk chocolate couverture, and cover the tops of the macaroons. When the coating is nearly set, garnish with half a pistachio.

Teecreme
Tea cream

1¼ cups/150 g sultanas
½ cup/125 ml rum
1 oz/20 g powdered gelatin
4 tbsp black leaf tea
⅔ cup/150 ml milk
½ a vanilla bean
½ cup/100 g sugar
3 egg yolks
¾ cup/200 ml whipping cream

Soak the sultanas in the rum. Soak ¾ of the gelatin in about 3 tablespoons of cold water. Brew the tea by pouring on ½ cup boiling water and letting it stand for 3 minutes. Then strain half the brewed tea into a saucepan with the milk and the vanilla bean. Bring to a boil. Remove from the heat, and take out the vanilla bean. Beat the sugar together with the egg yolks until frothy. Stir it into the tea and milk mixture, together with the gelatin. Cool the mixture, and place in the refrigerator until it begins to set. Meanwhile, whip the cream stiffly. Then fold the whipped cream into the tea mixture. Drain the sultanas, reserving the rum. Stir a generous half of the sultanas into the mixture, and replace it in the refrigerator until set. Cut the remaining sultanas in half, and scatter over the top of the chilled tea cream. Sprinkle the remaining powdered gelatin over the rum in a small saucepan, and warm gently, stirring, to dissolve. Do not allow to boil. Pour the rum and gelatin mixture over the sultanas. Keep the tea cream refrigerated until it is to be served.

Trüffel
Truffles

1½ cups/350 ml heavy cream
30 oz/850 g milk chocolate couverture
confectioner's (icing) sugar for decoration

Bring the cream to a boil. Cut 12 oz/350 g of the chocolate couverture into small pieces, and stir these into the hot cream until melted. Leave to cool, then beat until sightly frothy. Pipe strips of the mixture onto baking parchment, using a piping bag. When fully cold, cut the strips into 1¼ inch/3 cm long pieces. Melt the remaining chocolate couverture, and use to coat the pieces of truffle. When the coating is almost set, toss the truffles gently in confectioner's sugar.

Eel soup

Ask any citizen of Hamburg which dish they consider a typical local specialty, and the reply will probably be prefaced with a scratch of the head and a puzzled frown. The answer will come: eel soup. The list begins and ends there; eel soup is the only Hamburg specialty whose fame stretches beyond the bounds of the city. It is rich in ingredients and in history, and not uncontroversial. It is said to have been made entirely from fish in the 18th century, but other accounts claim that it takes its name not from "eel" but from the Hamburg dialect word for "all." This refers to the considerable number of other ingredients – meat, vegetables, fruit, and spices – which overwhelm the eel itself. An "eel soup" without eel, called *sure Supp* (sour soup), is supposed to have come to Hamburg in earlier times from Schleswig-Holstein. It was the fishermen's wives of Finkenwerder who first added slices of eel to this soup; fish was, after all, constantly on their minds, and an ever-present ingredient in their cooking. This change was evidently taken up so enthusiastically in Hamburg that the soup is called *verlorene Aalsuppe* (lost eel soup) if there is no eel in it.

In Hamburg, it is not only the origins and etymology of eel soup that are steeped in controversy, so are the ingredients. Some local cooks extend the list of vegetable ingredients to include two leeks, sliced into thin rings, 10 ounces (300 grams) of diced asparagus, and some diced swede; others flavor it not with sugar, but with unsweetened redcurrant juice. The soup tastes just as good if smoked eel is used instead of fresh eel (7 ounces/200 grams per person). Although the usual method is to serve the eel in the soup, the 16th edition of Sophie Charlotte Hommer's *Grosser Hamburger Kochbuch für alle Stände* ("Big Hamburg Cookbook for all Classes of Society") recommends that the fresh eel, once skinned and salted, be doused in hot vinegar. They are to be left in this marinade for an hour before boiling, and served separately with the soup, a little of the cooking stock being poured over them. Frau Hommer demonstrates the care that can be shown in attending to every detail of such an eel soup: "Having sorted a generous quantity of parsley, washed it repeatedly, and plucked out the selected leaves, chop it finely; proceed likewise with the other herbs, viz. thyme, marjoram, tarragon, and celery leaves, then pass the bouillon through a sieve, stand and allow to separate, pouring the clear, separated bouillon into a sufficiently large vessel to cook the soup to completion."

Aside from these variations, one indispensable accompaniment to eel soup is dumplings (*Schwemmklösse* or *Mehlklösse*), which are served in the soup.

Aalsuppe
Eel soup
Serves 6

1 ham bone
1 onion, studded with 1 bay leaf and 2 cloves
4 pints/2 liters meat stock
1¾ lb/800 g fresh eel
Salt
1 lemon
1 lb/450 g dried fruit (prunes, apple rings, and pears)
¼ lb/125 g each of carrots, leek, and asparagus
½ lb/250 g frozen peas
½ bunch parsley, chopped
2 tbsp butter
4 tbsp flour
Sugar and white pepper

Set the ham bone to boil in the meat stock, together with the onion. Cook for about 1½ hours. Skin and clean the eel and cut into bite-size pieces. Sprinkle with salt and the juice of the lemon, and allow to infuse. Soak the dried fruit in hot water for 15 minutes. Meanwhile, wash, clean, and dice the vegetables. Place the eel in another saucepan, and cover with meat stock. Simmer on a low heat for 10 minutes, and keep hot. Add the dried fruit, vegetables, peas, and parsley to the ham stock, and boil for 15 minutes. Then take out the ham bone. Scrape off the meat from the bone, returning the pieces of meat to the soup. Knead together the butter and flour, and use to thicken the soup. Add the pieces of eel. Season the soup to taste with salt, sugar, and pepper. Serve with dumplings.

Each family has its own recipe for the Hamburg specialty, eel soup. The ingredients vary accordingly.

Prepare the eel and soak the dried fruit while the ham bone is boiling to make the stock.

Cover the pieces of eel with the meat stock, and simmer no more than briefly, on a low heat.

Add the prepared vegetables to the stock with the ham bone, and boil just long enough to cook them.

Add the dried fruit to the vegetables. Then add the meat from the ham bone, and the eel.

In the best English manner

Until very recently, gentlemen in bowler hats and carrying umbrellas were quite the norm in the city district of Hamburg. The town's most elegant club spells its name the English way with a "C"; hockey and tennis are played; society ladies appear dressed in green, blue, and yellow tartan pleated skirts; the gentlemen sport blazers with brass buttons. Hamburg has a traditional liking for all that is in the "best English manner."

The first official sign of this came in the powerful "Merchant Adventures Guild," which opened its Hamburg office in 1611. British trade links enabled the Hamburg merchants to participate, to some degree, at least, in the flourishing colonial trade in tea, silk, pepper, and porcelain. During the Biedermeier period in the mid-19th century, powerful Hamburg patricians such as Caspar Vogt had extensive parks laid out in the English fashion around their houses on the Elbchaussee. Peter Godeffroy, known for the fact that a complicated Hamburg recipe for lobster was named after him, furnished his entire house – called the "weisses Haus" (white house) – in the elegant district of Blankenese with English Chippendale furniture.

It comes as no surprise that such love of all things English entered the kitchens of Hamburg. Dishes such as oxtail soup, roast beef, plum pudding, and the Hamburg "snack" have enjoyed special respect here for generations. To cook a steak in the way that used always to be called "English" is to cook it in the way we now call "medium." The cut of meat served as steak in Hamburg is not necessarily fillet; it is often the less tender but more substantial cut from the extended part of the rump, in the fold of the leg.

In Hamburg, plum pudding makes its traditional major entrance as part of the New Year celebrations. The mixture for this heavy pudding is made from beef suet, breadcrumbs, flour, raisins and currants, sugar, salt, lemon peel, bitter almonds, nutmeg, cardamom, cinnamon, ginger, cloves, eggs, rum, and cream. The pudding is boiled in a cloth or pudding basin, and served with punch sauce. Rum is poured copiously over the pudding and ignited, so that the pudding is served flaming. It provides a solid start to the year, indeed, substantial enough for the new millennium.

The genteel lifestyle has a long tradition in Hamburg, where the local merchants nurtured close trading contacts with Great Britain, following the English fashion in manners as in much else.

The sad career of the "Hamburger" steak

The hamburger has achieved what other members of the meatball family, such as the *Bulette* or the *Fleischpflanzerl* have not: it has had a worldwide career. The reason may be that Hamburg's particular ground meat preparation was always seen as more refined than its cousins from southern and eastern Germany. The traditional recipe uses pure beef steak and egg yolk, and contains no satiating or cheap bulking additives, such as ground pork or breadcrumbs from the local bread rolls, *Schrippen* or *Semmel*, used in Berlin or Bavaria.

Beef began to gain economic importance in America in the 19th century. However, it took until the 1960s for it to gain a larger share of the market than pork, which today plays an important role only in the regional cuisine of the southern states. Large-scale beef farming began on the Great Plains, an area where thousands of herds of bison once roamed. After the white newcomers had exterminated the bison, and in doing so deprived the native Americans of their livelihood, huge expanses of grazing land became available, ideal for cattle.

The meat processing industry established itself in the mid-west, and Chicago assumed the role of the nation's slaughterhouse.

The hamburger is thought to have originated in the mid-west, in Ohio. That is its history according to McDonald's, who should know. They do, after all, have the closest and most financially rewarding connections with the hamburger. Toward the end of the 19th century, apparently, a seller of snacks in Ohio ran out of sausages to serve inside milk rolls, and put a "hamburger" steak between the two halves of the roll. There it has remained to this day, known all over the world as a hamburger. The item that now goes by this name is greasy and flavorless. Beef steak and egg yolk are mere history.

Roast beef

Generous 2 lb/1 kg roasting joint of beef
Salt and pepper
3 tbsp butter
1 cup/250 ml meat stock

Preheat the oven to 400 °F/200 °C. Rub the meat thoroughly with salt and pepper. Melt the butter, and brown the meat on all sides to seal. Place in the preheated oven to roast for about 1 hour. Baste the meat periodically during the cooking period by spooning over the juices. Let the meat rest for at least 5 minutes before carving.

Seafood

Hamburg's "lobster mile" lies to the west of the Altona fishmarket. A mere remnant of the once huge fish processing and trade sector continues to make a living there from the import and sale of the finest seafood: caviar, oysters, sturgeon, spiny lobster – and lobster.

The European and American lobster, *Homarus gammarus* and *Homarus americanus*, one of the oldest living creatures, favors the jagged coasts of northern Europe, Icelandic and Irish waters, the Norwegian and Danish coastlines, Canada, and the United States. It is occasionally, but more rarely, found in the Mediterranean. It seldom occurs in Germany as a consequence of overfishing. It was driven away from Helgoland by British weapons testing in the early 1950s, but has since begun to return in small numbers.

It is to the satisfaction of gourmets the world over that the lobster has no bones; it needs none, for its skeleton is outside its body, in the form of its shell. Roughly once a year, when this protective shield becomes too small for it, the lobster casts its shell, easing out of the old one at a joint between its rear body and upper carapace. At this stage, the new shell has already formed underneath. The lobster will retain it until its body has once more increased in size by 15 percent and by 50 percent in weight, and must again cast its old shell. It is possible to tell whether a lobster has just gone through such a change, if the lobster purchased has a softer shell than usual, which is not yet filled with meat to its extremities.

When buying freshly cooked lobster, in order to avoid upsetting squeamish family members, it is best to order it the day before. When cooking it at home, boil plenty of water with caraway or a little dill. Plunge the live lobster quickly into the vigorously boiling water head first. Never cook a dead lobster: they smell unpleasant, the meat flakes, and it could endanger health. If the lobster is to be broiled, three minutes in boiling water is enough, until the shell turns red. Then place it under the broiler or on the open fire. If it is to be cooked in the pot, boil a European lobster for 20 minutes per pound (500 grams); a Canadian or American Maine lobster needs 15 minutes per pound (500 grams).

Fervent disagreement has existed among experts ever since people began to eat lobster: is it the tail or the claw meat that tastes best? It is a matter of individual preference. So too is the choice of sauces and accompaniments. Cold or warm, lobster tastes best with home-made mayonnaise or a light hollandaise sauce with plenty of lemon. Lobster "Godeffroy" calls for a sauce made of green onions and sliced mushrooms fried in oil and butter, with white wine, fresh herbs, cream slightly thickened with cornstarch, and chopped

1 Lobster
2 Red abalone
3 Vongole; Venus clam
4 Langoustine; Dublin Bay shrimp
5 Caviar
6 Oysters

sardines tossed in butter. The lobster meat is removed from its shell, the sauce poured over, and the dish served with boiled rice.

Caviar, the rich man's egg dish

Russian caviar, those tiny, round, firm, mild, and very fragrant eggs, is seen as the food of the gods. The "gods" of Hamburg, rich merchants and shipyard owners, have known this for centuries. They gathered in Schümann's or Cölln's oyster bars – places still to be seen on the Jungfernstieg – to take their *déjeuner* or fork buffet or to enjoy a small *souper* below ground, or in Ehmke's Biedermeier restaurant on the Gänsemarkt. This no longer stands, having fallen victim to a short-sighted piece of town planning in the 1970s. There, with ceremony and great pleasure, they consumed the eggs of the sturgeon. That is to put it crudely. "Roe" sounds better; "caviar," being a foreign word, sounds better still. The term was borrowed from the Turkish "havyar" in the 17th century.

The sturgeon is a long, bony fish with a tapering head. It can reach a length of up to 29 feet (9 meters). It is found in the Caspian Sea and in Siberian lakes and rivers. More accurately, it was found there, but has been driven almost to extinction by pollution and overfishing. Its flesh, seen as a delicacy, and its roe have been its downfall.

There are around 25 species of sturgeon, three of which are in particular demand: firstly, the sturgeon, whose name is in fact shared by the entire genus. It is also known by its Russian name *osetr*, and its roe appears on the market as osetr-caviar. It is brownish in color, the eggs some ⅛ inch (3 millimeters) across. The sevruga or Caspian sturgeon, which provides sevruga-caviar, is smaller than the osetr sturgeon, which can weigh up to 440 pounds (200 kilograms). The caviar is smaller and darker in color. It measures about ⅒ inch (2.5 millimeters) across. The most expensive caviar comes from the beluga, the giant among sturgeons. The adult can attain 29 feet (9 meters) in length and 3300 pounds (1500 kilograms) in weight. Its eggs, likewise larger, are pale gray. They measure ⅛–⅙ inch (3–4 millimeters) across. Whatever the type of caviar preferred, toast is too mundane an accompaniment; it should be eaten with *blini*, the golden, Russian buckwheat pancakes made with yeast. These should be brushed with hot butter, and the heavenly caviar set on top, nestling on a white bed of slightly soured cream.

Dumplings and savory molds

"Hüt Klüt, morgen Fisch, vergnögt gaht wi to Disch" – "Dumplings today, fish tomorrow, with eager contentment we come to the table." Such are the words in which the Hamburg writer, Gorch Fock, described the everyday diet of the fisherfolk of Finkenwerder in his 1913 novel, *Seefahrt ist not!* ("To sea we must go"). Poor people on the other bank of the Elbe ate much the same way. Fish was cheap in those days. In the early years of the 20th century, it was even served in the poorhouses of Hamburg. Dumplings were made of potato, flour or semolina, and water, with egg or fat as available. *Kartoffelklösse* (potato dumplings) and *Fettklösse* (fat dumplings) were served as a main dish, or as an accompaniment to fish. *Mehlklösse* (flour dumplings) or *Schwemmklösse* (floating dumplings) were served in fish soup, and also with stewed dried fruit. *Griessklösse* (semolina dumplings) were served in elderberry and blueberry soup. *Schwemmklösse*, unlike *Mehlklösse*, are made from a dough for which the flour is stirred into milk over a low heat, then enriched with egg and nutmeg.

Well-heeled merchants found such fare too frugal. Their cooks or *"Kochmamsells"* made lobster and oysters into dumplings and savory molds, and shrimp into croquettes. These were served as appetizers, entrées, or elaborate accompaniments to meat or game.

Rauchfleischklösschen
Smoked meat dumplings
(Illustrated right)

4 slightly stale bread rolls (or white bread)
½ cup/ 125 ml hot milk
Fat for frying
13 tbsp/200 g butter
2 eggs
4 egg yolks
4 tbsp flour
7 oz/200 g Hamburg smoked meat, finely diced
1 bunch of parsley, chopped
Salt, pepper, and nutmeg

Slice two bread rolls, pour on the hot milk, and leave to soak for 10 minutes before squeezing out. Dice the rest of the bread rolls, and fry in a little fat until golden. Knead the butter, eggs, egg yolks, soaked and squeezed out bread, and flour into a dough. Finally, mix in the smoked meat, diced bread, and parsley, and season with salt, pepper, and nutmeg. Shape with wet hands into small dumplings. Place in boiling salted water and simmer over a low heat for about 15 minutes until cooked through. Serve with browned, melted butter and cabbage.

Hummerpudding
Lobster mold
(Illustrated left)

2 small boiled lobsters
4 egg yolks
2 cups/100 g breadcrumbs
10 tbsp/150 g butter
Salt, white pepper, and nutmeg
8 egg whites
Butter and breadcrumbs for the mold

Remove the claw and tail meat from the lobster and chop finely. Bring the butter to room temperature, and knead together with the egg yolks and breadcrumbs. Then add the lobster meat. Season with salt, pepper, and ground nutmeg. Beat the egg whites with a pinch of salt until stiff. Fold gently into the lobster mixture. Grease a lidded, sealable mold with butter, sprinkle in breadcrumbs, and turn to coat the inside of the mold. Transfer the mixture to the mold, to fill it to at least ¾ of its height. Close the mold and steam it in a bain marie for about 1½ hours. Then place it momentarily in cold water before opening and turning out the mold onto a warmed plate.

Granatkroketten
Shrimp croquettes
(Illustrated center)

1 finely chopped onion
1 tbsp butter
3½ oz/100 g left-over boiled potatoes
14 oz/400 g shrimp meat
Salt, white pepper, and nutmeg
1 tbsp finely chopped parsley
1 tsp finely chopped dill
3 tbsp milk
2 cups/100 g breadcrumbs
3 eggs
Fat for deep frying

Sweat the onion in the butter until translucent. Pass the potatoes through a potato ricer, and mix thoroughly with the onion and shrimp meat. Season with salt, pepper, and ground nutmeg. Knead in the chopped herbs and the milk. Rest the mixture for 15 minutes to absorb flavors, then shape into cork-shaped croquettes. Toss them first in breadcrumbs, then in beaten egg, and finally in breadcrumbs once more. Deep fry them in batches for about 4 minutes until uniformly golden. Lift out with a slotted spoon, and drain briefly on kitchen towels before serving.

Bacon is an important ingredient in making Finkenwerder plaice.

Toss the plaice in flour, and fry in butter until golden.

Sweat the bacon in another skillet, and fry with the onion.

Plaice and smelt

Hamburg streets such as "Stintfang," "Bäckerbreitergang," "Lämmersieth," "Brodschrangen," and "Caffamacherreihe," whose names refer to fish, bakers, lamb, bread, and coffee, remind us how important food is to the city's inhabitants. Its best-known town squares also echo the edible theme: "Gänsemarkt," "Fischmarkt," and "Hopfenmarkt" are named after geese, fish, and hops.

Fish still features extensively on Hamburg's menus, even though fishing no longer takes place on the "Stintfang," and the "Fischmarkt" is no longer a fishmarket. For a long time now, Finkenwerder plaice has come by refrigerated truck from Denmark, mild *Matjes* from Holland, cod all the way from Greenland or Iceland. The best that can be said is that in Hamburg, the fish is at least much fresher than it would be after making the journey on down to the frozen food compartments of stores in southern and western parts of Germany.

Edible freshwater fish from the Elbe are once more available, as water quality in the river gradually improves. Smelt, salmon-like fish up to 8 inches (20 centimeters) long, are once more making their way upstream to their spawning ground in the upper reaches of the river, though no longer in such numbers as before, when they were an everyday item in the diet of poor people in northern Germany. Only small, residual numbers of smelt are found, and their significance as food fish is negligible. They do still have their place in the language, however. There is an old expression that translates as "to rejoice like a smelt." A braggart is called a "Stint" (smelt). Someone who has an unexpected stroke of luck is said to have "set out to catch a smelt and caught a salmon."

The denizens of the sea are boiled, broiled, and grilled in Hamburg. A local dish, Finkenwerder wherry-boat plaice, has found its way into the cookbooks. The plaice is tossed in flour, then fried in butter. Diced bacon, fried with onion, is scattered over the fish. The fish can be coated in egg and rusk-crumbs or flour to keep it especially moist. This is not the traditional recipe, but tastes very good. In Hamburg, in times past, fish was often enhanced with an elaborate sauce. Shrimp sauce, for example, was made with chopped shrimp meat, flour, butter, white wine, cream and green onion – delicious served hot, poured over sole. Caviar sauce involved stirring 2½ ounces (75 grams) of caviar carefully into a sauce made of ½ cup (125 grams) well-creamed butter and six egg yolks. This was seasoned with two teaspoons of lemon juice and a little salt.

Finkenwerder Scholle
Finkenwerder plaice

4 fresh, gutted plaice
Salt
Juice of 1 lemon
7 oz/200 g bacon
1 onion
8 tbsp flour
8 tbsp butter

Wash the plaice, pat dry, and sprinkle with salt and lemon juice. Leave to infuse for 10 minutes. Meanwhile, dice the bacon and the onion. Pat the plaice dry again, toss in flour, and shake off the excess. Heat the butter in a large skillet. Fry the plaice one at a time on both sides, until golden. Keep hot while the remaining fish are being cooked. Preheat the plates for serving. Sweat the bacon in another skillet, add the onion, and fry both together. Serve the fish light side uppermost, with the diced bacon scattered over it. Potato salad makes a suitable accompaniment.

A Hamburg menu – local and adopted specialties

"Restaurateurs, refraîchisseurs, and Swiss eating houses have set up their establishments here; below ground, cellars have opened, ice cellars, and Italian cellars; above ground, Chinese coffeehouses." This was said back in 1805, long before it became the fashion to go to a Greek or Turkish restaurant or steakhouse. Hamburg's cosmopolitan attitude was not limited to absorbing ideas from far afield; dishes which probably originated in neighboring regions – Holstein, Mecklenburg or Lower Saxony – were also assimilated into the Hamburg repertoire:

Bickbeersuppe mit Klüten (blueberry soup with dumplings): Blueberries, boiled in water, the juice thickened slightly with cornstarch. Served with *Griessklösschen*. Elderberry soup is made in a similar way. In Hamburg, this is called *Fliedersuppe*.

Birnen, Bohnen, Speck (Pears, beans and bacon): Smoked bacon, boiled with French beans, summer savory, and round, tasty pears, Bergamotte pears. Served with boiled potatoes.

Hamburger Rauchfleisch mit Kohl: (Hamburg smoked meat with cabbage): Smoked meat, set to boil in cold water with spices. Coarsely chopped white cabbage is added, and bound with a light white sauce before serving. The meat is served, diced, on top of the cabbage.

Hamburger Stubenküken: Young chicken from Vierlande, with a stuffing of chicken liver, boiled ham, cream, and egg. It is wrapped in bacon and roasted, and served with a cream, brandy and Madeira sauce.

Labskaus (Seaman's hash): a mixture of diced salt beef (corned beef) and mashed potatoes. Served with beetroot and pickled gherkins, sometimes also with pieces of *Matjes* (cured herring) or Bismarck herring and a fried egg per person.

Plockfinken: A stew of root vegetables with diced smoked meat with a dash of vinegar, thickened with a roux and served with *Fettklösschen*.

Plumen un Klüten (Plums and dumplings): Boiled streaky bacon with prunes in a slightly thickened sweet-and-sour sauce with *Schwemmklösschen* or *Fettklösschen*.

Quetschmadam: Rice milk pudding with pears cooked in sugar, cinnamon, and lemon peel, and served with thickened strawberry juice. This is a typical local dish. The name comes from the pear variety *Quisse Madame*, introduced in the 18th century.

Snuten un Poten (Pickled pig's snout): Pickled pig's snout (*Snuten*) and trotters (*Poten*), and sometimes pig's ears, boiled until tender. Served with sauerkraut, boiled potatoes, and pease pudding.

The addiction that changed the world

Spices

The age when spices filled the vaults, catacombs and storerooms of Hamburg's warehouse quarter with their costly aroma is slowly drawing to a close. The massive brick walls of the old warehouses breathe, and provide excellent storage conditions for the sacks of pepper, thyme, allspice, curry, cardamom, and other flavorings from distant lands; however, all the work of stacking and transportation has to be done by hand here, because of lack of space. Capacity is frequently inadequate. Storage in modern corrugated iron and cinderblock-constructed warehouses is therefore much more economical, despite the occasional damp, and less than ideal preservation of flavor.

Most of the 30,000 tons (27,000 tonnes) of spices imported into Germany each year still pass through the port of Hamburg. The majority of these sacks, chiefly from Brazil, Indonesia, China, India, and Turkey, now go to large-scale centers within the region of the city for storage, instead of the warehouse quarter. The spices are sometimes transported onward immediately to customers in the east and south of the country.

The first spice to create history was pepper. Mention of it dates back to the early period of migration of peoples across Europe and Asia. In 410 B.C., Alaric, king of the western Goths, demanded not only 5000 pounds of gold, 30,000 pounds of silver, 4000 silk garments, and 3000 purple carpets from the capitulating Romans, but also 3000 pounds of black pepper.

Spices, then, were a sought-after commodity, brought from India to Constantinople by long and arduous trade routes. There, they fetched accordingly high prices. It was following the Crusades that the real hunger for spices in the Christian West began. As a result, the Orient became "a palpable presence" in Europe, as Wolfgang Schivelbusch put it in his *Das Paradies, der Geschmack und die Vernunft* ("Paradise, taste and reason"). Silk, velvet, damask, carpets, and spices were among the oriental luxury goods with which the upper strata of European society surrounded themselves at that time. Spices became a status symbol. The whole of the high Middle Ages is characterized by the unrestrained use of spices in food. Some historians explain this phenomenon by pointing out that with the lack of refrigeration, meat easily became spoiled. Pepper was used to improve its keeping qualities, or, alternatively, hot spices were added to mask the tainted flavor. This theory falls down when we remember that pepper was far too expensive to be used as a preservative. Further, overseasoning came to an end in the 17th century, yet no other

methods of preservation had been found. The theory put forward by Schivelbusch sounds more likely: he believes that intensely fragrant spices, especially pepper, symbolized the advance of Central European culture, beginning with the Crusades. Until that time, it had been something of a backwoods culture. It received a boost from the high culture of the Orient; people who were able to enjoy the consumption of pepper acquired, we might say, "good taste." Spices became practically an addiction. In the days before tea, coffee, chocolate, and sugar existed, pepper fulfilled many roles: stimulant, status symbol, official state gift, and currency.

Addiction causes dependency: on the dealers, the spice traders, who set astronomically high prices, and on the suppliers, the Orient. Addiction creates wealth – there is a link between the period in which Venice flourished and the spice trade. When, in the 15th century, the price of pepper rose thirty-fold, and supply stagnated as demand increased, people looked for alternative ways: the sea route to India.

"We seek Christians and spices," wrote Vasco da Gama, the first European to round the Cape of Good Hope, in 1498. This was the first step into the modern era, and the incentive to take it came from pepper, with all its potential for addiction and for profit. The period of European colonialism had begun, with all its unpleasant side effects for the countries that produced these much sought-after commodities.

The center of the spice trade now shifted from Venice to Lisbon. At the beginning of the 17th century, the Dutch seized the hegemony in the world spice trade from the Portuguese. Amsterdam now dictated the prices. Given favorable winds, a good sailing ship could reach Hamburg from Amsterdam in less than two days.

The monopoly was held by the United Dutch East Indies Company. It demonstrated what is truly meant by a monopoly, destroying the opposition by permitting the cultivation of nutmeg and cloves only on a few of its islands, and keeping prices artificially high by having huge quantities of cinnamon or nutmeg burned.

Today's centers of the international spice trade are Singapore, New York, Rotterdam, and Hamburg. The United States and Germany lead the world as importers of spices.

Despite the significant growth in interest in foreign foods and dishes over recent decades, the Germans' loyalty has stayed with their three favorite herbs and spices: pepper, paprika, and parsley. When vanilla flavor is called for, they still content themselves with the powdered, synthetic variety, rather than the intensely fragrant pulp of black vanilla beans from Central America; when they want cinnamon, most still opt for the ocher-colored powder. They little imagine how much richer the flavor of cinnamon would be if they were to use the dried bark of the Ceylon cinnamon bush instead.

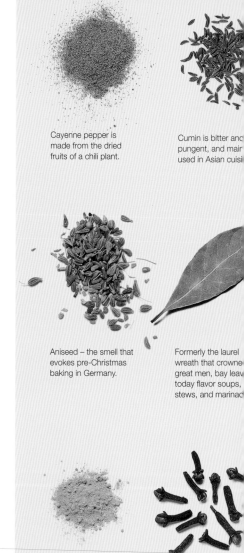

Cayenne pepper is made from the dried fruits of a chili plant.

Cumin is bitter and pungent, and main used in Asian cuisi

Aniseed – the smell that evokes pre-Christmas baking in Germany.

Formerly the laurel wreath that crowne great men, bay leav today flavor soups, stews, and marinad

Curry powder comes from India. The main ingredient in this mixture of spices is turmeric.

Cloves are the dried flower buds of a tree the myrtle family.

Star anise has a stronger flavor than aniseed. It is used to flavor stewed fruit, Christmas cookies, and punch.

Saffron is the costlie all spices. It gives a golden color to soup sauces, and rice dis

Paprika – there are several degrees of intensity, from mild to hot.

Cardamom is one of the spices in curry powder. It is also used to flavor cookies, and sausages.

Nutmeg – the stone inside the fruit of the tropical nutmeg tree.

Mace is used in clear soups, fricassées, foods made with meat, and cookies.

Pepper was used as currency in times past. Today, it is on every table.

Allspice is the dried berries of the *Pimenta* tree. It is used to flavor baked dishes and sausage.

The spicy flavor of juniper berries complements game, sauerkraut, and ham dishes.

Cinnamon, the bark of the cinnamon tree. The best comes from Sri Lanka (also called Ceylon cinnamon).

PETER SCHULZ

Bremen

The Bremen saying "een beten veel un een beten good" – a typical understatement meaning "good food and plenty of it" – indicates a love of plenty where food and drink are concerned. This is something of a paradox, for the people of Bremen have a reputation for thrift. But the fact is: tables are well laden, whether the occasion is a large-scale feast such as the *Schaffermahl*, a small family celebration, or an ordinary meal, and whatever the time of day.

There is an unmistakable bent toward companionable comfort in this city, combined with a taste for good food. Bremen is a city of seafarers and merchants, with an openness to the world and a long history: it has been the seat of a bishop since the year 787. From 1947 onward, the two towns of Bremen and Bremerhaven have formed a single German state. The proximity of the sea produced a love of fish; close connections with the surrounding countryside a liking for rustic fare. Trade provided contacts with the wider world, and a readiness to try new, delicious and exotic foods.

Trade is the key here. It is to trade that Bremen owes its prosperity, always valued on a par with independence by the self-assured patricians of the city. The stone statue of Roland in the market square was erected in 1404. It has stood ever since as an emblem and symbol of the city's independence, declaring its *vryheit*, its freedom from ruling princes and bishops.

In contrast, Bremen's councilors and merchants took a penny-pinching approach to the arts. Painters, musicians, and eminent literary figures generally bypassed the city, for flourishing as it was, it lacked artistic patrons, free-spending rich landowners or bishops. It was a place where oil drums were more highly valued than oil paintings, and banknotes meant more than manuscript notes.

Nevertheless, in their steady local fashion, the citizens of Bremen have a flair for living, a cosy hospitality centering around the pleasures of the table. All is done with the utmost dignity, exemplified in the respectable merchants of Bremen, who exhibit the same earnest pride in their dark blue suits as naval captains in the still darker blue of their uniforms. They still celebrate a successful deal with a bottle or two of wine in the Ratskeller restaurant under the City Hall. Not exuberantly – God forbid – in quiet contentment… in the Bremen style.

Left: The stone statue of Roland in the market square symbolizes the city's freedom and independence.

The Schaffermahl

Residents of Bremen may not attend; thus states a strict rule of the "Haus Seefahrt" (the Seafarers' Foundation). Every year on the second Friday in February, at three in the afternoon, the traditional *Schaffermahl* takes place in the imposing upper hall of the Rathaus (City Hall). When this happens, the people of Bremen, whatever their real or imagined importance, are excluded. Guests are summoned with the words: *"Schaffen, schaffen, unnen un boven schaffen."* The word *schaffen* is seaman's slang from the days of the old sailing ships. It meant that the ship's cook had "served up" the meal, and all hands below and above deck *(unnen un boven)* ran to eat as soon as they heard it. Today, *Schaffer* refers to the three men who provide the meal, that is, who pay for it. The 300 men attending (only men are admitted to this huge and illustrious hall!) are their guests. However, at the end of the meal, a salt cellar is passed around for donations, and everyone puts in a generous contribution. The money collected is used for charitable purposes by the Seafarers' Foundation, which continues to this day to support distressed seamen and their families.

This practice dates back to 1545, so the *Schaffermahl* is thought to be the oldest such communal meal of a fraternity in the world. It was in fact the farewell meal held by merchants and shipyard owners for the captains of their ships as they put to sea again after the springtime thawing of the ice. Before their departure, they all met to enjoy a good meal, consult each other, sort out social and financial affairs – seafarers risked their lives in their profession – and check the financial health of the Seafarers' Foundation.

Sea captains still number among the guests. Over the years, however, increasing numbers of influential, respected figures from the worlds of politics, economics, and culture have joined them. It is a once-in-a-lifetime honor to receive this highly prized invitation. The Federal Republic of Germany's first President, Theodor Heuss, is the only person to have attended a *Schaffermahl* twice. He invited himself – and the President, as the most important person in the country, can hardly be refused. The mayor, who presides as host, and those who have acted as *Schaffer* in the past, are among those who attend every year. The event takes place beneath the historic ships that hang from the ceiling of the City Hall, and diners wear naval uniform or full evening dress. The traditional menu demands a strong digestion. The dishes placed on the long tables (arranged in the shape of Neptune's trident) were once deemed "simple Bremen fare." They are hearty, heavy, and rich in everything imaginable. The meal lasts five

hours, punctuated by weighty speeches about the fatherland, Bremen, and seafaring. It begins with a white and a brown soup, the one chicken, the other, ox loin. Dried cod in mustard sauce follows, accompanied by brown seamen's beer in silver tankards, passed round from guest to guest. This is a thick, malt beer, no longer on the market. It used to be drunk as a way of preventing scurvy during a long sea voyage. It is now brewed just once a year, specially for the *Schaffermahl*, by Haake-Beck's brewery in Bremen. Apart from this, red and white wine accompany the meal.

The guests wipe their knives and forks between courses with paper towels; to have enough cutlery to change would have been a luxury on board ship. Curly kale with smoked meat, Bremen *Pinkel* sausage and chestnuts follow, then roast veal with poached apples and prunes. The meal ends with Chester cheese, cream cheese, tongue, and smoked flounder – which still carries the name of the city of Riga, the place that used to provide it – then fruit and coffee. Lastly, long, clay tobacco pipes are lit and handed round, the final touch of companionship in this gentlemen's gathering.

When all the courses have been consumed (and not before!) the gentlemen may rise, and transfer themselves, somewhat heavily for the most part, to join the ladies who await them in the neighboring rooms of the City Hall. Ancient custom decrees that these rooms are the only ones that ladies are permitted to enter. They are also the place where the men can at last obtain a decent glass of beer.

"Schaffermahl" recipes to eat at home

Kalbsbraten mit Selleriesalat, Katharinenpflaumen und gedämpften Äpfeln
Roast veal with celeriac salad, prunes, and poached apples
(Illustrated right)

4 oz/100 g prunes (unpitted)
8 cloves
Rind of 1 lemon
4 sticks of cinnamon
Sugar
2 small celeriac roots
Salt
Oil and vinegar
Salt and pepper
2 onions, finely chopped
4 dessert apples
4 cups/1 liter white wine
Juice of 1 lemon
Generous 2 lb/1 kg roasting veal
Clarified butter for frying
Few veal bones
Soup vegetables (2 carrots, 2 celery stalks, 1 leek, and a bunch of parsley)
1 tsp rosemary
1 cup/250 ml veal stock or natural gravy
1 tsp cornstarch
1 cup/250 ml cream

Soak the prunes 2 days in advance. On the second day, boil the liquid from the prunes together with the cloves, lemon peel, cinnamon, and a little sugar. Pour it back over the prunes, and leave to soak for one more day. Peel and slice the celeriac, and boil it until just cooked, but still firm to the bite. Drain, then cut into strips. Make a salad dressing with the oil and vinegar, adding a little salt, pepper, and sugar. Place the strips of celeriac in a bowl, pour over the salad dressing, and leave to infuse. Peel, halve, and core the apples. Bring the white wine, lemon juice, and a little sugar to a boil, and poach the apples until soft. Leave in the cooking liquid to cool. Preheat the oven to 300 °F/ 150 °C. Rub the veal with salt and pepper. Melt the butter in a robust, fireproof roasting pan, and brown the meat on all sides. Lift out the meat, and fry the veal bones, soup vegetables, and rosemary in the same butter. Pour on a little water, and replace the meat in the roasting pan. Roast for about 40 minutes until tender then remove from the pan, and stir in the veal stock. Strain. Whisk the cornstarch into the cream, stir into the gravy, and heat to thicken.

Bremer Hühnersuppe
Bremen chicken soup
(Illustrated below left)

1 fresh boiling fowl
1 piece of beef bone for stock
1 onion, spiked with 1 bay leaf and 2 cloves
Soup vegetables (2 carrots, 2 celery stalks, 1 leek, and a bunch of parsley)
Salt
3 egg yolks
2 cups/500 ml cream
2 tbsp crayfish butter (puréed crayfish tails in butter with chives, celery, and parsley)
Cooked asparagus tips and green peas to serve in the soup
Pepper
White wine to flavor
1 tbsp chopped parsley

Rinse and clean the chicken. Place in a large saucepan with 8 cups/2 liters lightly salted water, the beef bone, the studded onion, and the soup vegetables. Bring to a boil, cover, and simmer for about 1½ hours. At the end of the cooking time, lift out the boiling fowl and strain the stock. Take the chicken breast meat off the bones, and dice it. Discard the skin. Whisk the egg yolks into the cream, and stir into the chicken stock, along with the crayfish butter. Add the asparagus tips, peas, and diced meat. Reheat the soup, without boiling. Adjust seasoning with salt, pepper, and white wine. Sprinkle with parsley before serving.

Stockfisch, Senfsauce und Salzkartoffeln
Dried cod, mustard sauce, and boiled potatoes
(Illustrated below)

1¾ lbs/800 g dried cod (stockfish)
Fish bones and trimmings for stock
Soup vegetables (2 carrots, 2 celery stalks, 1 leek, and a bunch of parsley)
2 bay leaves
Salt and pepper
5 whole allspice berries
1 leek, cut into thin strips
2 tbsp flour
1 tbsp butter
2 tbsp German mustard
1 cup/250 ml cream

Ask the fishmonger to soak the dried cod for 36 hours and fillet it. Place the fish bones and trimmings, soup vegetables, bay leaves, salt, pepper, and allspice in 6 cups/1½ liters water, and bring to a boil. Cover and boil for ½ hour, then strain the stock. Cut the fish into strips. Simmer it gently with the leek in 4 cups/1 liter of the stock until cooked. Meanwhile, make the mustard sauce. Make a roux with the flour and butter, blend in the remaining fish stock, and cook gently for 10 minutes. Season with mustard, salt, and pepper. Whip the cream stiffly, and fold into the sauce. Serve the fish with plain, boiled potatoes, passing the sauce separately.

Dried cod with mustard sauce

Bremen chicken soup

Basket of fruit

Celeriac salad

Roast veal with prunes and poached apples

173

Bremen's "Ratskeller"

When he visited the Ratskeller, the (wine) cellar beneath Bremen City Hall, the Federal Republic of Germany's first Chancellor, Konrad Adenauer, praised the Rhine wine: "Excellent, this Assmannshausen!" The President, Theodor Heuss, voiced similar enthusiasm; his special request for a wine from his own region "Would you happen to have a Württemberg wine?" was likewise fulfilled without a moment's hesitation.

Well in excess of 700 different German wines – Main, Moselle, Rhine, Saale – are stocked in the cellars of Bremen's Ratskeller. Karl-Josef Krötz, who has charge of the cellars, can respond confidently to the most unusual requests. He can offer his customers the most comprehensive wine list in the whole of Germany, with a range and variety greater than any visitor could expect.

The centerpiece is the vast hall, built in 1404, lined with impressive casks. In the shadow of these casks, visitors sit companionably drinking a measure or two of wine at long, wooden tables. They nibble a snack of pretzels with sticks of young Gouda cheese, called *Steckrüben* (swedes). It was a wise foresight on the part of the councilors to build the cellar, to which the *Bacchuskeller* (Bacchus cellar) was added in the 17th century. The city's wine monopoly ensured substantial revenues. This was for centuries the only place where the highly regarded wines of the Rhine and Moselle were allowed to be served; consequently the duty monies flowed as freely as the juice of the grape.

The Ratskeller and the associated cellar trade are still in city ownership. The gastronomic side was transferred to a private enterprise, though it still has to observe two "iron rules": In "the delightful and pleasant vaults below Bremen City Hall," to quote Matthias Merian in his *City Chronicle* of 1650, vile beer is frowned upon. The second is the "golden rule": to serve only wines produced in German vineyards.

Anyone requesting a Bordeaux will be disappointed, though fine French wines have been finding their way into German carafes through Bremen since the 17th century. Bremen's wine importers took up the Bordeaux trade at that time, thus establishing the leading market position they have maintained to this day. Bremen is the headquarters of many famous wine companies. The Ratskeller is, however, the ideal place to request a fruity Moselle, an earthy Franconian wine, or a rich-berried Württemberg variety. The choice offered by the full wine list is overwhelming. It need not be the 1727 Hochheimer Apostel or the 1653 rosé from Rüdesheim, the oldest and greatest treasures of

Wine cellar poets

For centuries, the Ratskeller has attracted poets, painters, and musicians to drink, draw, and philosophize in the dim light of its vaults. Fontane, Slevogt, Brahms, and others appreciated the wines, praised the atmosphere, and delighted in the special charm of these historic halls. The poet Wilhelm Hauff, unhappy in love, created their most beautiful literary memorial when he wrote his *Phantasien im Bremer Ratskeller* ("Fantasies in the Bremen Ratskeller"). Unable to win the heart of the charming Bremen girl, Josephe Stolberg, the young Swabian poet conquered his heartache through work by writing this maudlin fairy tale in 1826. Hauff dedicated the following lines to the Ratskeller, whose delights he had copiously imbibed: "Of all the castles of our time, I praise the one in Bremen; its noble halls so broad and high no emperor would shame." The poem *Im Hafen* ("In harbor") in Heinrich Heine's cycle of poems *Buch der Lieder* ("Book of Songs") has almost the quality of a hymn, opening with the words: "Happy the man who is safe back in harbor, leaving behind him the sea and the storms. And now sits, warm and all at peace, in the good Ratskeller in Bremen."

In a very different mood, Friedrich Engels wrote a letter to his friend Wilhelm Graeber in 1839, in which he described himself as the "foremost poet in Bremen's Ratskeller and privileged drinker," admitting that "the evening before last, I had a great soak in the wine cellar with two bottles of beer and two and a half bottles of 1794 Rüdesheim wine." The humorist Joachim Ringelnatz was another who did not shun the cost. He wrote one of his *Reisebriefe* ("Travel letters") in the Ratskeller in 1924. His homage to Bremen begins: "Here I'm of no esteem, yet wish to earn a share: this is a genuine, honest town, and genuineness is rare."

Bacchus has every reason to rejoice: wine stocks in Bremen's Ratskeller will not easily be exhausted. The revelries here are not in any other respect Bacchanalian; Hanseatic decorum reigns.

the cellar, though these are now collectors' items only. Their pronounced acidity, and their bouquet reminiscent of an old Madeira, have long since rendered them undrinkable. They are also unaffordable: it was calculated in the 1950s that a single drop would cost over \$21,000 (EUR 20,000), when everything is taken into account.

These treasures are stored in the Rosé Cellar and the *Apostel* Cellar, which are opened to visitors only during official guided tours. It is however, always possible to glimpse inside the triple-aisled Bacchus cellar, where a chubby figure of the god sits, riding with evident pleasure on an enormous, ornate wine cask.

The Hauff Cellar and Bacchus Cellar are only open to serve guests for large party bookings, but small alcoves around the main hall are available, and offer a genuine taste of the wine cellar atmosphere. Called *Priölken*, these snug, hidden niches are often used for confidential conversations. They even have closable doors. They are no use as love nests, however; the head waiter keeps a half-serious, stern eye out when a couple is inside, to make sure that the doors are not closed!

There is one more piece of protocol for the guest to be aware of: within these august vaults, "wine, women, and song" do not belong together in the way the world in general thinks. Any attempt at a drinking song will be frowned on, and may even earn a reprimand. Hanseatic prudence and respectability reign in the Ratskeller, even on exuberant occasions. It is a constant characteristic of Bremen's citizens. Only once a year do they relax their composure: in the second half of October, when the *Freimarkt* takes place. This is a festival that combines aspects of the Cologne *Karneval* as well as the famous Munich *Oktoberfest* in true north German fashion.

175

"Stubenküken"

Meaning literally "living room chickens," this typical Bremen chicken stew has been a favorite here on the River Weser for generations. It has to be mouthwateringly tender, so that traditionally, among housewives in the upper echelons of Bremen and Hamburg society, the delicate meat of very young chicken is the preferred basis of the dish. An almost 200-year-old recipe also calls for equal quantities of lemon, chestnut, and crayfish butter (puréed crayfish tails in butter with chives, celery and parsley).

There is a history behind the tiny chickens in this stew. On the farms in the countryside around Bremen, grandmothers are said to have had the task of rearing the fluffy chicks in the springtime, nursing them in a box by the warm stove in the family living room – the "Stube." This was not always successful, so they made the best of things. Then as now, they made do with chicken breast fillet for the chicken stew. One indispensable ingredient was calf sweetbreads, another, a good stock made from lean beef, the lower mouth and palate of an ox, and pig's ears and tongues. The traditional list of ingredients also included fine and expensive vegetables, such as artichokes, asparagus, and pistachio nuts.

The modern list of ingredients for this dish mentions not only calf sweetbreads and tongue, but also cocktail sausages.

Bremer Kükenragout
Bremen chicken ragout

2 young chickens, 1¼ lb/600 g each
1 calf tongue, 1 calf sweetbread
1 onion
Soup vegetables (2 carrots, 2 celery stalks, 1 leek, and a bunch of parsley)
Salt
8 dumplings made of veal sausagemeat
5 oz/150 g button mushrooms
9 oz/250 g asparagus tips
3 tbsp butter, 2 tbsp flour
1 cup/250 ml white wine, Lemon juice
Pinch of sugar, Salt and pepper
½ cup/125 ml cream
2 egg yolks
Puff pastry crescents for garnish

Rinse and clean the chickens and the calf tongue. Boil the tongue for about 20 minutes in salted water with the soup vegetables. Then add the chickens and sweetbread, and continue to boil for another 40 minutes. At the end of the cooking time, take out the tongue, chickens, and sweetbread. Cool a little. Strain and reserve the cooking liquid. Remove the skin from the tongue. Lift the breast meat off the bones of the chickens, and skin. Skin the sweetbread. Dice the tongue, chicken breasts, and sweetbread. Cook the dumplings in the stock. Clean the mushrooms and asparagus. Melt the butter, stir in the flour, and cook the roux until crumbly in appearance. Add 2⅖ cups/600 ml of the stock, stirring to blend in thoroughly to a smooth sauce. Then bring to a boil, and cook the mushrooms and asparagus in the sauce. Add the diced tongue, chicken, and sweetbread. Season with white wine, lemon juice, sugar, salt, and pepper. Whisk the egg yolks and cream together, and stir into the sauce. Serve the stew, garnished with puff pastry crescents.

Curryhuhn
Curried chicken

1 fresh roasting chicken
2 tbsp oil
Scant ½ cup/100 ml yoghurt
Scant ½ cup/100 ml sour cream
¾ cup/200 ml coconut milk
Salt
1 tsp ground cumin
1 tbsp curry powder
1 tsp finely chopped red chili peppers
1 clove of garlic, finely chopped
½ bunch of parsley or coriander leaves, chopped

Rinse and clean the chicken inside and out, pat dry, and joint into 8 pieces. Brown well on all sides in the oil. Stir together the yoghurt, sour cream, coconut milk, and spices. Pour over the chicken pieces. Cover, and simmer over a low heat for ½ hour. Sprinkle with chopped parsley or coriander before serving, with rice to accompany.

Calf sweetbreads are an ingredient of Bremen chicken ragout, also calf tongue, and veal sausagemeat dumplings.

Remove the transparent skin, slice and then dice the sweetbread.

Boil the dumplings in the cooking stock used to boil the other ingredients.

For the sauce, blend the flour into the melted butter to make a roux. Cook until crumbly in appearance.

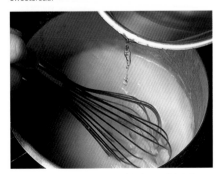

It is important to stir constantly while the stock is being added, to avoid creating lumps.

A dash of white wine adds a touch of elegance to the sauce. Season with lemon juice, sugar, salt, and pepper.

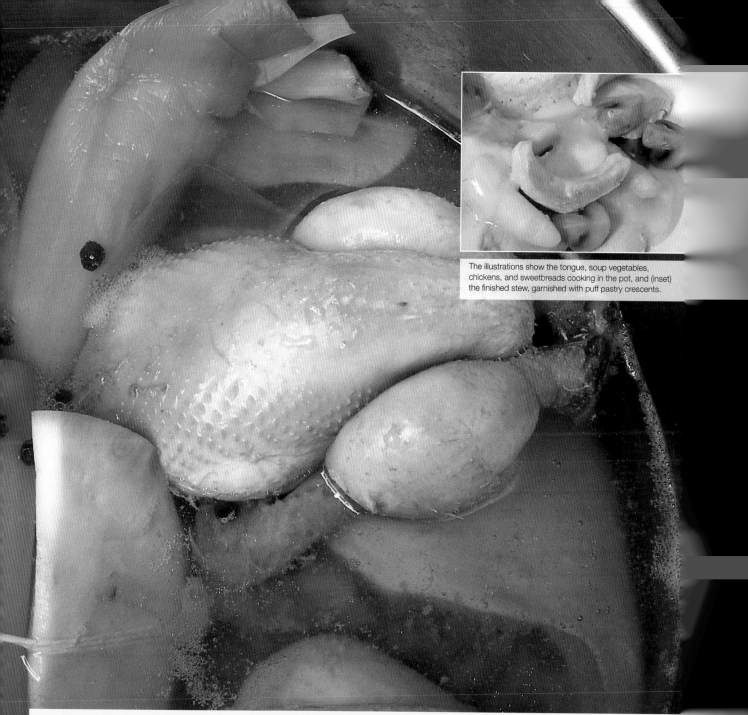

The illustrations show the tongue, soup vegetables, chickens, and sweetbreads cooking in the pot, and (inset) the finished stew, garnished with puff pastry crescents.

A Bremen menu – a guide to local dishes and names

Braunkohl und Pinkel: (Curly kale with *Grützwurst* sausage): From just before Advent until spring starts again, hordes of people can be seen at Bremen's main station on Saturday evenings, evidently bent on amusement. They can be recognized by the kale stalk tucked under their hatbands, and the liquor glass hung round their necks. They are headed for a restaurant outside the city where, after a fair walk, generous portions of the national dish, curly kale with *Grützwurst*, a sausage made with cereal grits, can be consumed.

Bremer Klaben or Kloben: (Bremen Klaben – or Kloben – cake): A rich, heavy, baked specialty containing raisins, plenty of butter, almonds, and lemon peel.

Butterkuchen: (Butter cake): Bremen's favorite cake is made from a rich yeast dough with plenty of butter. It is spread with a mixture of cream, butter, and chopped almonds.

Curry: (Curried dishes): Sea-going merchants popularized the use of curry for chicken, duck, and beef dishes.

Gedünsteter Schellfisch: (Poached haddock): The fish is served in a thickened sauce, with boiled potatoes.

Granat: (shrimp): Fresh shrimp, best peeled by hand, layered onto buttered black wholewheat bread, and topped with a fried egg.

Hedwigs or Heisswecken: (bread rolls in milk): Bread rolls with raisins. The center is hollowed out and filled with a knob of butter, and hot milk then poured over them.

Knipp: (pork and oatmeal fry): A dish born of pure need: Poor peat-cutters made ground pork go further by mixing it with coarse oatmeal. It is highly seasoned and very greasy, fried and thoroughly seared, and served with fried potatoes and pickled gherkins.

Rote Grütze: (Red fruit dessert): A traditional dessert. In Bremen, it is made with raspberries, redcurrants, cherries, and strawberries, and served with a thick vanilla sauce.

Stinte: (Smelt): These small fish, about a hand's breadth across, were once part of the everyday diet of poor people. They are tossed in rye flour, fried in butter (see page 165), and served with potatoes and a green salad.

Matje herring

The perfect herring for *matjes* is glistening silver, an immature fish at least a hand's breadth long, with tender flesh, and no hint of red near the bone. Its fat reserves should not yet have been used up in making the milt and roe; the fillets must contain at least 16 percent fat. The fish should still retain the salty tang of the sea.

The name *matje* comes from Holland, where this maritime specialty was invented. The key feature in producing them is the method of gutting the freshly caught fish, called "gibbing." This is done through a cut just below the gills, leaving only the pancreas inside. After a few days, the enzymes, in combination with a little salt, turn the herring into a *matje* cured herring.

Dutch fishermen brought *matjes* herring to Germany in the 18th century. Emden, Glückstadt, and above all, Bremen-Vegesack became the most important locations for the import and trade in this herring.

Around a quarter of a century ago, Vegesack was the home port of most of the German herring drifters. In those days, the fishing grounds of the southern North Sea still provided an economic reward for this laborious work. The crews were known as *Logger-Jantjes.*

Herring are still fished today, mainly off the Shetland Isles and the coast of Norway, though E.U. fishing quotas mean that the market is now led by well equipped Dutch vessels.

Another change has been in consumer expectations of a good *matje* cured herring. These are mainly sold in the form of a double fillet. In the past, the herring fillets used to be ripened in barrels of salt for 35 days ("hard cure"), after which they had to be soaked before eating. Today, once the herring have been gibbed, the process of light curing is preferred. Today, too, the *matjes* have to be frozen to a temperature of -4 °F (-20 °C) for at least 24 hours to kill off any parasites (nematodes) that might be present. It is therefore important to serve *matjes* herring within a few hours of buying. If refrigerated, they should be kept no longer than a day.

A feature that has remained unchanged is the high proportion of unsaturated fatty acids in *matjes*. These have protective effects against degenerative diseases like arthritis, arteriosclerosis, high blood pressure, and heart disorders. Hardly any other fish is as rich in omega-3 fatty acids as herring, so it is possible to say that *matjes* help guard against heart attacks!

A luxury lunch on board ship

In 1883, the journalist and correspondent of the newspaper *National Zeitung,* Paul Lindau, sailed from Bremen to New York aboard the Lloyd steamer *Elbe.* Unlike the 904 unfortunate passengers who traveled "steerage," he was a cabin passenger, so able to enjoy opulent meals. "At twelve o'clock, the gong summons us to the first meal. We can tell from the terminology that we have left our homeland behind, for what we would call "breakfast" at home is now termed "lunch." It is known in the widest of circles that the catering for first class passengers on board these steamers is quite superb, and it would be a crying injustice to utter the slightest word of criticism of the excellent dishes. The combination, however, I may timidly venture to say, occasionally seems a little adventurous. I can hardly recommend lunch aboard the *Elbe* as a sequel to a visit to the Karlsbad health spa. The following dishes usually appear on the menu: salmon, lobster, lampreys, smoked eel, cucumber salad, fresh blood sausage and liver sausage; the accompanying hot dishes being sauerkraut and peas with pig's trotters and other delicacies for those with an ailing stomach. But we are still sailing on fresh water, our appetites are still keen, the ship is traveling so smoothly that we can scarcely tell whether we are moving or no; the ship is so well ventilated that our noses are not yet assailed by the indescribably offensive smell that we are told will be so unpleasant to us later."

From: Paul Lindau: Aus der Neuen Welt ("From the New World"), 1884

Food from the galley

Joachim Ringelnatz, creator of the seafaring character "Kuddel Daddeldu," knew the sea well. A former seafaring man himself, he wrote: "Sailing is a hard profession, but an honest one." He discovered the delights of Bremen's Ratskeller in 1924 ("being lazy and feeding myself up," he wrote), including its cuisine, which has close similarities to traditional seaman's fare.

That fare had, above all, to be nourishing and filling, because strenuous work in harsh weather at sea makes people hungry. The ship's cook had to put a good, square meal on the firmly secured tables of the sailors' mess. Achieving this may often have caused the cook more upheaval than the motion of the ship. The fresh foodstuffs taken on board before they left port would have been used up quickly, or spoiled through lack of refrigeration. The commodities available in the galley during an ocean passage that might last for months were usually bacon, dried cod (stockfish), and barrels of salt meat – supplies which were all certainly nutritious, but limited in their edibility.

If, however, this meat – heavily salted to preserve it – was mixed with mashed potatoes and pieces of fish, the result was an unremarkable-looking but pleasant-tasting meal, steaming in the wooden bowls. It had the added advantage that it was easy to eat with simple metal spoons. This stiff-textured mash somehow acquired the name "Labskaus." Today, it is regarded as the typical seafarers' dish, although it can be embellished to appeal to the gourmet as well. Its visual appeal improves, once this sailors' staple is topped with a fried egg, and accompanied by a couple of herring fillets. On Thursdays, the "seafarers' Sunday," the menu offered better fare, and might have featured *pluckte Finken* ("plucked finches"). This is in fact a stew, consisting of various ingredients. It can be traced back to the whalers who used to set out for Greenland from their home port at Bremen-Vegesack until the 19th century, to hunt for whales. If they met with success, the whale blubber was cut (*pluckt*) into large chunks (*Vinken*), and stored in barrels as reserves. The "V" somehow became an "F," hence the misleading name. The chunks of blubber were boiled with potatoes, beans, and onions, until the liquid was no longer thick and cloudy, but fairly clear. At that stage, it could be seasoned with a generous dash of vinegar. Modern versions of this delicious stew (of which there are many) do not, of course, use whale blubber, but fat bacon or smoked meat.

Dried cod, which was once the traditional Friday dish in Bremen, would not have provided much variation in the monotonous diet on board. It was served with carrots, in a thick, pale, flour-based sauce – a leathery mass that not everyone would have found appetizing.

This insight into the Christian seafarers' bill of fare shows that the food was neither varied nor healthy. Symptoms of deficiency were inevitable; the dreaded scurvy was as much part of life at sea on the clippers and schooners as the wind and waves. Attempts were made to counter it by use of the high calorie, brown seamen's malt beer, which to its credit, tasted better than the brackish water, drawn from barrels that might previously have been used for transporting molasses or petroleum. It was not only hardened sailors, but emigrants, too, who had to contend with these harsh living conditions. Many crossed the "pond" via the port of Bremerhaven during the 19th century. Beginning at around 30,000 per year (1848), the numbers grew, reaching up to 75,000 per year (1864-1874). Having paid for their tickets as steerage passengers, they went on board with what was often the last of their savings. They had to take their own provisions for the journey, usually potatoes, salt meat, and ship's biscuits, and to do their own cooking. Hunger was not unusual on the ocean-going steamers; the rations might have been miscalculated, and food also spoiled.

Labskaus
Seaman's hash

4 salt herrings weighing 7 oz/200 g each
A generous pound/500 g potatoes
A generous pound/500 g salt beef (or corned beef. Note: corned beef should not be boiled)
2 onions, chopped
1 tbsp drippings
7 oz/200 g preserved beetroot (from a jar)
4 pickled gherkins
1 tbsp mustard; pepper
4 fried eggs

Rinse the salt beef and boil in water for about ¾ hour. Clean and fillet the salt herrings, and soak for ½ hour. Wash, peel, quarter, and boil the potatoes. Dice the herrings, potatoes, and salt beef, and pass through a meat grinder. Fry the onions in the drippings until translucent, add the meat mixture, and heat through, stirring. Dice and add half the beetroot and gherkins. Season the Labskaus with mustard and pepper. Divide it into four portions, serving on individual plates, each topped with a fried egg. Garnish with the remaining beetroot and gherkins. An alternative to the fried egg is a salt herring.

In the days before refrigeration, feeding the crew was quite a problem for the ship's cook, and he needed plenty of imagination to solve it. Dishes were usually monotonous and not very tasty.

The smell of coffee pervades the city

Beans from across the sea

If your mind's on coffee, you must be in Bremen already. Coffee is as much part of the town's history as the statue of Roland or the City Hall. The truth of this statement, which has long been uttered with conviction by Bremen's honest patriots, has recently been confirmed: the first, and so the oldest coffee house for which records exist in any German-speaking country, was opened in 1673. This predates those in Hamburg (1677) and Vienna (1683), previously credited with having had the first cafés.

This discovery is the work of the young historian Petra Seling-Biehusen. It confirms beyond doubt that the Senate of Bremen granted the right to serve coffee to a certain Jan Jantz van Huesden on "23 Augusti Ao 1673." A Dutchman, he had humbly entreated the "high and noble lords," with all the respect due, to grant him permission to deal in "foreign Indian drinks, to wit *coffi, schokolati,* and the decoction of the herb *herbathe* (tea)." The stern authorities of the City Council graciously granted it.

It was only one year earlier that the first coffee house had opened in Paris, so the Bremen of that time might rightfully have felt itself to be a European metropolis. Only London (1652) and Venice (1645) can boast earlier dates for the appearance of coffee drinking.

Bremen's coffee tradition remains unbroken to this day. Statistics show that every second cup of stimulating coffee drunk each day in Germany is made from beans produced by Bremen coffee roasters. Bremen is also the center of Europe's decaffeinating industry, dating from Ludwig Roselius' striking discovery of a successful process in 1905. The huge profits from his company, Kaffee-HAG, still prominent today with its trademark of a red lifebelt, served to finance the building of Böttcherstrasse, a Bremen landmark in warm red brick.

The port of Bremen has maintained its position as the leading German place of import for raw coffee beans since the 19th century, despite stubborn opposition. This fact can be experienced, or, rather, inhaled, daily in Bremen. A walk along the quays or *Kajen,* or along the River Weser, soon tells the passer-by that there is "something in the air." They will be enveloped in an aroma that breathes warmth and comfort.

Bremen coffee merchants have built up the trade in these precious beans, which were at first

The sacks of coffee arriving at the warehouse are weighed, and a sample is taken.

Beans from all over the world pass through Bremen's warehouses on their way to the consumer.

A few beans from each consignment are test-roasted as a means of ensuring quality.

On completion of the roasting process, the beans are removed from the roaster.

Professional coffee tasting

A noisy slurp; the taster plunges a hand into a bowl of unroasted beans; spits out; enters a couple of crosses on the control sheet. A coffee taster's day follows the rhythm: slurp, feel, spit, cross.

Up to 180 cups of coffee per day are tasted in this way, mouthful by mouthful, samples of consignments from all over the world. In matters of quality, the tasting experts with their sensitive taste buds and long years of experience have the last word. The roasting has long been controlled by computer. Coffee being a natural product, it is subject to many influences, and thus varies in quality. The

Slurping is part of the task of coffee tasting.

slurping professionals with their fine sense of taste are responsible for overseeing the correct composition of the blends, to ensure that consumers of a particular variety experience consistency of flavor. The coffee maestros also poke their noses into brown paper bags of the various blends, to sniff and evaluate the aroma. In this job, even a slight cold can render them unfit for work.

The blends ordered by large wholesale purchasers are made up at the warehouse.

The coffee beans have changed color from green to brown, and smell irresistible.

Coffee making methods

Great-grandmother did not beat about the bush: she simply put a couple of measures of ground coffee into a pot, poured on boiling water, and waited. Five to ten minutes later, after the grounds had settled, she poured the coffee through a strainer into the cup. This is what is meant by "brewing" coffee.

Generations of coffee drinkers endured the inconvenience of muddy coffee grounds until, in 1908, a housewife by the name of Melitta Bentz invented the coffee filter. This boon was enthusiastically adopted across the country, wherever there were people who could afford the expensive brown beans. Malt or acorn coffee served as substitutes at times of national emergency, or when the coffee ran out. These contained secret ingredients, which at least gave them a deep black hue. All modern coffee machines operate on Frau Bentz's principle, though connoisseurs still swear by the "hand filtering" method: medium ground coffee (best for releasing the flavoring substances) is placed in the coffee filter, together with a pinch of salt. Rapidly boiling water is poured on, just enough to barely cover the coffee. After pausing to let the coffee settle, more water is added, bit by bit, pouring slowly and evenly. Filtering cannot be done well in a hurry. To keep the pot warm during this process, which can take six to eight minutes, it is placed in a container of hot water.

available only in drugstores, and mainly came from Arabia. Later, cultivation began in Java, Surinam, and Martinique. Ever greater quantities of coffee were soon reaching Bremen via London, Amsterdam, and – mainly – Bordeaux.

Following the French Revolution, ships crossing from North America or the West Indies came direct to Bremen and docked in the town harbor. Shortly after the Napoleonic Wars, a Bremen trading company opened its own first foreign branches in Brazil, and from there shipped coffee direct to its distant home. There, the coffee sector became an established part of commercial life, along with tobacco and cotton. Bremen importers soon extended feelers into other coffee producing countries, such as Colombia, Malawi, and India. They continue to ensure that the major share of the raw coffee, over 10 million sacks per year, reaches the German market.

In a parallel development, Bremen coffee roasters and shipping companies helped substantially to establish and confirm the city's good reputation in coffee matters. The main companies continuing that Bremen tradition today are Kraft Jacobs Suchard, Eduscho, and Melitta. They are among the market leaders in Germany, and contribute significantly to the fact that, of the over 1 billion dollars (DM 2,000 million) in coffee taxes paid into the state coffers, around half is collected in Bremen.

BARBARA SCHNABEL

Lower Saxony

The variety of landscape in Lower Saxony is one of its strengths: a mere stone's throw from the delightful hills of the Weserbergland lie the dark forests of the Harz. The Lüneburg Heath is a delight to nature lovers even when it is not decked in late summer flowers. East Frisia and Ammerland in the green northwest are enough to convince even critically minded devotees of the south that a region lacking in respectably sized hills need not be a desert. Finally, there is the austere charm of the North Sea and its islands, which have for some two hundred years been a chosen destination for those in search of rest and refreshment. The most delightful of half-timbered houses are to be seen, notably – though not only – in the beer town of Einbeck and the town of Celle; many a village is still graced with picturesque thatched roofs; churches and the houses built by burghers of old are frequently works of art in deep red brick. Richly decorated buildings in the style of the local Weser Renaissance bear witness to the prosperity of the towns which grew along with the trade in grain.

The traditional specialties of the region between the rivers Ems and Elbe are simple and hearty: kale with *Pinkel* sausage, Harzer cheese, and sausage from the Brunswick area. Such specialties, with their time-honored link to the locality, correspond in character to the local national anthem, in which the people of this land sing of themselves as "stormfast and firmly rooted in the soil." It is a characteristic that brings to mind the fighting spirit of the 12th century Heinrich der Löwe (Henry the Lion), probably the most striking character of the Guelph Dynasty which ruled this region for centuries. Their castle in Hanover, the capital of Lower Saxony, and world-renowned for its trade fairs, now houses the regional parliament, and, in 1734, one of the dynasty founded Georgia Augusta university in Göttingen, providing the region with an academic center. The town remains proud of its many prominent intellectual figures, such as the liberal "Göttingen Seven," whose members included the Brothers Grimm. Newcomers to areas where *platt* (Low German) is still spoken, and where the inhabitants are people of few words, often complain of the locals' stubbornness. They are, however, obliged to confess that trust once given is enduring, and goes far beyond the shared drink of schnaps that is enjoyed all over Lower Saxony.

Left: The Lüneburg Heath has not only its impressive landscape of juniper bushes to offer, but extensive areas of woodland, broad meadows, peatland, and small lakes.

Taking tea

Tea is as much part of life in the sparsely populated extreme northwestern corner of Germany as the wide expanse of sky above the flat land, and the stiff breeze: a quarter of German tea imports are consumed in East Frisia – almost as much per head as in Britain. But, following the arrival of the first shipment of tea to Europe in 1610, it took some time, even in East Frisia, for the new drink to replace beer, the "people's nourishment," which was drunk even at breakfast. The rich farmers of the fertile coastal fens were able to buy the expensive green tea, as well as coffee and chocolate. Poorer people shared the preference for tea, choosing it before coffee, because it was more economical. They drank black tea, which was cheaper. Tea was drunk at all times of day, always with plenty of sugar, to provide much-needed calories. The teapot was repeatedly replenished with hot water, causing Heinrich Heine, who knew the North Sea, to write in 1827 that the local tea differed from seawater in name only. Guests were not given this dilute brew; they received the first pouring of freshly made tea as we know it today.

When the British custom of the tea party became fashionable in Germany in the early 19th century, it had already existed for some decades in the East Frisian town of Aurich. Tea was taken with dainty cakes and cookies, the whole accompanied by genteel conversation, entertainment on the piano, and cards. From about 1880, there developed what might be called the East Frisian "tea culture," across all sections of society. Central to the occasion is black tea; there is a distinguished blend called "Ostfriesische Mischung" (East Frisian blend), a mixture of at least 15 types, primarily from Assam. Experienced tea tasters work to ensure consistency of quality.

There are do's and don'ts here as with any ritual. The teapot, for example. Woe betide anyone who uses it for anything but tea, or who commits the sacrilege of cleaning it out with washing up liquid! The pot is carefully warmed, then a teaspoon of loose tea added for each cup, plus "one for the pot." Freshly drawn, rapidly boiling water is poured on. The tea is left to infuse for five minutes; if a stimulating brew is required, just three minutes. To enjoy its soothing effect, the tea should stand in the pot for ten minutes.

The cups now appear on the tea table. They are delicate, thin-sided cups, in the Chinese fashion, decorated with the East Frisian rose. This decoration was brought to the region around 1820 by a family from Thuringia. Ritual demands that the *Kluntjes*, (lumps of white "candy sugar" that makes a satisfying crackle when it comes in contact with the hot liquid) are placed in the cups before the tea is poured. The crowning addition is a spoonful of fresh cream. Rich (30 percent fat content minimum), unwhipped pouring cream is used, so that it floats on top. It must not be stirred. Connoisseurs claim that this is the only way to enjoy the threefold combination of flavors: the bitter tea, the gentle sweetness of the sugar, and the cool cream. The deep existential significance accorded to tea by the East Frisians is expressed in the old saying: "Hebben wi keen Tee, mutten wi starven," "If we have no tea, we must die."

East Frisian tea – as it should be served

The *Kluntjes* (white candy sugar) are placed in the delicate cup with silver sugar tongs. Frequently these were made in Emden or Aurich.

The *Kluntjes* crackle when they come into contact with the hot, bitter tea. The tea must have been left in the pot to draw for at least three minutes.

The teapot and sugar bowl are traditionally of silver, as is the spoon used to skim the rich top layer of pouring cream.

The cream slides around the edge of the cup, and rises from the bottom to form a "cloud" on the surface. It should never be stirred.

Tea tasting is an exact science: each measure of tea weighs 1/10 oz/2.75 grams.

Tea tasters throughout the world use the same traditional white china.

Each set consists of a cup and a lidded container in which to brew the tea.

On the second pouring, the lid catches the tea leaves.

The color and brilliance of the tea are examined in natural daylight.

The aroma, too, provides a guide to the tea's strength, bitterness, and flavor.

The tea is tasted. The sample is then spat into a bowl.

The taster also examines the spent tea leaves, to help form a judgment of the tea.

Tea is taken in style in East Frisia. Traditionally, the china is decorated with the East Frisian rose. It is accompanied by a wide choice of cakes and cookies: *Knedewaffeln* (waffles), *Spekulatius* (spiced cookies), East Frisian *Schneckenkuchen* ("snail cake") with raisins, *Pepernöte* (gingerbread cookies), and other regional specialties.

The traveling cookie

A product from Lower Saxony attracted much attention at the World Exhibition in Chicago in 1893. It was to become one of Germany's best known branded products: *Leibniz Keks*, a new type of cookie. They were created by Hermann Bahlsen in 1891 in Hanover, and made to a secret recipe. At that time, the name was still "Leibniz cakes," and the Hanover factory called the "Hannoversche-Cakes-Fabrik": Bahlsen had brought the idea from England. The name was Germanized to "Keks" in 1911.

Even at the outset, about a million "cakes" a week were manufactured, and licenses granted in North America and Moscow. At first, the cookies were sold loose over the counter, with no form of protection against moisture or the aroma of cheese or herring. In 1898, however, the company had the revolutionary idea of packing them in an airtight, dustproof wrapping, printed with the syllable TET, the ancient Egyptian symbol for "eternal, lasting." Broken cookies were a thing of the past. The cookie with the crenellated edge remained crisp, and its neat, rectangular shape could be packed into a format that was easy to carry.

Soon, no-one set out on a journey without slipping a packet of these cookies into their supplies – on station platforms, eager sales personnel in TET uniforms saw to that. They had the memorable slogan: *"Was isst die Menschheit unterwegs? – na selbstverständlich LEIBNIZ-CAKES!"* ("What do people eat on a journey? LEIBNIZ CAKES naturally!") Germany's first fluorescent advertising sign on the Potsdamer Platz in Berlin proclaimed the crunchy snack from Hanover in shining letters three feet (1 meter) high. In 1912, 90 centners (5 tons) of *"Reisekeks"* (travel cookies) per day were produced, using production line technology that was innovative for Europe at that time. Production declined during the two world wars, rising only during the 1930s. After 1948, *Leibniz* cookies again went on sale. In 1956, the company developed a new, thermoplastic packaging, which guaranteed the purchaser still higher standards of freshness – oven freshness – a claim which was impressively demonstrated in the water under a fountain. There have been many imitators, yet the *Leibniz* cookie is synonymous with butter cookie to this day the world over – not only because it was the first branded product of its type to be registered, but also because of the quality of the Bahlsen recipe, and skillful marketing. The man after whom Bahlsen named his cookie, with the intention of underlining his significance to Hanover, thoroughly deserved the honor, though he is famous in his own right: Gottfried Wilhelm Leibniz (1646–1716), the brilliant philosopher, mathematician, historian, and philologist. He is often described as the "last universal scholar." He entered the service of the court at Hanover in 1676, at first as librarian, but was soon entrusted with a host of other duties. His technological inventiveness helped the profitable mining of ore in the Harz; this enabled the ruling princes in Hanover to complete the summer residence of Herrenhausen, outside the city, designs for which had been laid out in 1666. Leibniz advised on the operation of the magnificent fountains in the baroque gardens. These gardens were a favorite of the Elector's wife, Sophie. These tall fountains serve as reminders of him here, as do the Leibniz Room in the Gallery Building, and the Leibniz Temple, containing a marble bust of the philosopher, in the nearby Georgengarten (George Garden).

Riches of the Altes Land

Lying just beyond the gates of Hamburg, the "Altes Land" has every right to call itself "Germany's largest orchard." Admittedly, the region around Lake Constance produces a greater quantity of fruit, but it is grown over a more scattered area than here, where it is concentrated between the Kehdingen country to the northwest and the Elbmarsch, around the town of Winsen to the southeast. This region was colonized by settlers from Holland and Saxony, and fruitgrowing has existed here since the 14th century. Today, its cultivation occupies an area of about 26,700 acres (10,800 hectares). Apples account for 87 percent of production, primarily the red-cheeked Elstar, followed by Jonagold and Boskoop. The Knubberkirsche cherry is popular, and accounts for 5 percent. The fruits are large, and not only sweet, juicy and crisp to the bite, but sure to be free of maggots, because the climate in the Altes Land does not suit the cherry fruit fly. Further down the list come pears, morello cherries, and the different classes of plum. About 1500 acres (600 hectares) are given over to soft fruit.

Germany's largest orchard lies just outside Hamburg. Apples account for almost 90 percent of the fruit grown.

Hanover Chamber of Agriculture's fruitgrowing research station (O.V.A.) and the fruitgrowing testing ring (Obstbauversuchsring), both centrally located in Jork, have played an important role in the development and quality of fruitgrowing in the Altes Land. The apple variety Gloster, a cross with good storage qualities, was bred by the O.V.A. in 1969. As well as supplying the fruit wholesalers, many of the 1200 businesses of the Altes Land preserve the tradition of direct marketing across a wide area, so that it is possible to buy fruit from the region at a stall as far away as the south of the Lüneburg Heath. It is sometimes possible to pick up experienced advice at the same time, from a farmer's wife maybe, on how to make a fruit-filled cake with crumble topping, a soufflé apple bake, or a fruit sauce.

Blossom time, when innumerable apple trees are in flower, is celebrated with a festival in Jork. The tasteful regional costume of the Altes Land is a sight to behold. It illustrates the prosperity of this fruitful fenland region. If overnight frost is forecast while the trees are in blossom, they are protected by spraying, which covers them in a sheath of ice, and heightens their charm as they sparkle in the spring sunshine. Sprinklers have been installed, easier here than in other fruitgrowing areas, because it boasts not only a system of dykes, but of drainage ditches, dating back to the Middle Ages.

Apple varieties

Auralia (Tumanga): medium size eating apple; delicate sweet acidity; fairly aromatic

Baumanns Renette: pleasantly mild flavor; good, firm apple

Erwin Baur: elegant flavor with wine-like acidity; stores well

Freiherr von Berlepsch: excellent eating apple; crisp and juicy

Boskoop: acid flavor; suitable for stewing and baking

Geheimrat Breuhahn: sweet, with delicate acidity. Keeps until February or March

Idared: aromatic eating apple with pleasant acidity. Keeping qualities less good

Jonagold: zesty, aromatic flavor. Early ripening; keeps well

Juno: combines aromatic wine acidity and pleasant sweetness. Stores well

Kaiser Wilhelm: large, firm apple with a lovely, rich quality. Keeps well

Wobers Rambour: very old variety; spicy, acid-sweet flavor

Rubinette Wintercox: highly aromatic, fine-tasting eating apple

Zwetschgen im Strudelteig
Deep fried plum strudels
Serves 6

Generous 2 cups/250 g flour
A pinch of salt
2 tbsp oil
1 egg
Generous 2 lb/1 kg firm plums or damsons
4 oz/100 g uncooked marzipan paste (see page 148)
2 tbsp ground almonds
2½ tbsp plum brandy
2 tbsp melted butter
Fat for deep frying
Cinnamon and sugar for dusting

Knead the flour, salt, oil, and egg to a smooth dough with ½ cup water. Shape into a ball. Rest the dough in a warmed bowl for 30 minutes. Meanwhile, wash the plums, slit them lengthwise, and remove the pits. Mix the marzipan, ground almonds, and plum brandy thoroughly. Stuff the plums with this mixture, close and reshape them. Roll out the pastry into a rectangle on a well floured kitchen cloth. Pull it carefully by hand until thin. Brush with melted butter. Cut squares from the pastry, and use to wrap the plums individually. Press the ends together to seal. Heat the fat in a deep fryer to 350 °F/175 °C. Fry the plums in batches until golden. Lift out and drain on absorbent kitchen paper, and keep hot until all are cooked. Then serve immediately, sprinkled with cinnamon and sugar. Vanilla sauce or plum sauce are suitable accompaniments.

The distance from producer to consumer is short: many businesses in the Altes Land sell their produce direct.

Pfannkuchen mit Kirschen
Cherry pancakes

1¼ cups/150 g wheat flour
A pinch of salt
4 eggs, separated
½ tsp vanilla essence
Grated zest of 1 lemon
8 oz/250 g morello cherries
Scant ⅓ cup/75 g brown sugar
½ cup/125 ml red wine
4 tbsp butter
Confectioner's (icing) sugar for dusting

Sift the flour into a bowl, and mix with the salt, egg yolks, vanilla, lemon zest, and 1 cup/250 ml water to a thick batter. Rest for 15 minutes. Meanwhile, wash and pit the cherries. Heat the sugar in a dry skillet, stirring, until melted and lightly caramelized. Pour on the red wine, stirring to mix, and let them cook together briefly. Then add the cherries, poach for 2 minutes, and remove from the heat. Whip the egg whites very stiffly, and fold gently into the batter. Heat 1 tbsp butter in a cast iron skillet. Put ¼ of the batter into the skillet, and begin to fry the pancake. Scatter ¼ of the cherries over the top of the pancake, cover, and continue to cook on a low heat until the surface is set. Fold over the pancake, and keep hot on a warmed plate until all the pancakes have been cooked. Dust with Confectioner's sugar before serving.

Above: Large, outspread fenland farm houses with thatched roofs are typical in the Altes Land.

187

Kale with Pinkel

North Germans whose fate has exiled them to one of the southern German states might be tempted on frosty days to enthuse over the *Grünkohl mit Pinkel* (kale with *Pinkel* sausage) they so much miss. They can expect a puzzled response. Kale in fact comes from the south, from the Mediterranean area, but for some time it has only been grown on a large scale in the north. *Brassica oleracea*, to give it its botanic name, is sometimes affectionately called *Oldenburger Palme* (Oldenburg palm), because one type grows particularly tall.

Another reason for this mystification may well be the term *"Pinkel."* There is an anecdote about a housewife whose husband was denied his favorite dish for years because his wife did not dare utter the word when shopping for food. *Pinkel* is simply a type of smoked, cereal meal containing sausage, made with *Speck* bacon, belly of pork, onions, and spices. The skin is made from the end of a cow's large intestine, which is also called *Pinkel* intestine. The dish also calls for a type of boiled sausage called *Kochmettwurst*, cured smoked pork (*Kasseler*), and fat bacon, added during the final hour of the long, slow cooking process.

Boiled, or sometimes fried, potatoes are served with it. Slow cooking eventually turns the kale brown, so it is called *Braunkohl* (brown kale) in Bremen.

Kale tastes best after it has had the frost on it. This turns the starch to sugar, and gives the dish a subtle sweetness. If the weather does not oblige, people resort to using a kitchen deep freeze; everyone in this region between the Ems and the Elbe longs for the season of this kale dish (which lasts from November through to March). Associations, firms, and groups of friends all organize "kale outings." Countless rooms and meals are booked. A long walk is taken as part of this ritual outing. The participants hang a liquor glass with a handle round their necks for a drink along the way. They also take with them a hand cart, carrying a few bottles of *Korn*. Music-making accompanies the outing, and they work up an appetite through bowls competitions, often using natural twig brooms. The meal lasts a long time, and everyone helps themselves repeatedly; the person who eats most is elected king or queen of the occasion, receives the "order of the pig," gives a speech, and stands a couple of rounds of drinks. The time is spent drinking beer and *Korn*, dancing, and playing cards, until the hired bus arrives to take its cheery passengers home.

In Oldenburg, the tradition of "kale outings" goes back over a hundred years, though its present format took shape only in recent decades. The town began to organize its annual *Gröönkohl-Äten* in Bonn in 1956. At this event, leading politicians enjoy this north German specialty, and do not count the calories.

Kohl und Pinkel
*Kale with **Pinkel** sausage*

3¼ lb/1.5 kg curly kale
Salt
6 oz/150 g smoked fat bacon
1 tbsp drippings
2 large onions and 1 bay leaf
4 slices of cured smoked pork (Kasseler)
1½ cups/350 ml meat stock
6 oz/150 g belly of pork
4 Bregenwurst (Pinkel) sausages
Pepper and nutmeg

Remove the wilted leaves and tough stalks and veins from the kale. Wash thoroughly. Blanch for 2 minutes in boiling salted water. Drain and chop coarsely. Cut up the onions and dice the bacon. Heat the bacon in the drippings in a large saucepan until the fat runs. Add the onions and the bay leaf. Then add the kale and the cured smoked pork. Pour on the meat stock, cover, and cook for about 1 hour. Add the sausages and belly of pork, and extra water as necessary. Cook together for a further 1 hour, stirring the kale repeatedly to prevent it from burning at the bottom. At the end of the cooking time, remove the sausages and keep hot. Season the kale with salt, pepper, and nutmeg. Serve with the meat and sausages.

The kale tastes best after the first frost, when the starch has turned to sugar. A spell in a deep freeze may be necessary if the weather is mild.

The kale is blanched in boiling water, because it contains bitter substances. It is then chopped, and added to the pot with the sweated bacon.

Cured smoked pork, bacon, and Pinkel sausages are the ingredients for a hearty Grünkohl mit Pinkel. And a nip of Korn to follow.

The wooden trays used to prepare and serve *Lüttje Lage* are three feet (1 meter) long.

The glasses are lined up side by side. The smaller ones are filled with *Korn*.

The beer glasses hold just over 3⅓ fl. oz (0.1 l) so that both drinks can be held in one hand.

The atmosphere of cheer inside the tent increases, and trays of *Lüttje Lage* do the rounds.

Korn

One in four of the spirits sold in Germany is a measure of *Korn*. There are about 500 *Korn* distilleries, mainly north of the River Main. A 1909 Purity Law decrees that the spirits may only be called *Korn* if they are produced from pure rye, wheat, buckwheat, oats, or barley, and not mixed with any other alcohol or flavoring additives. People were less fussy in the 15th century, when the distillation of spirits from grain began. The first written record of this dates from 1507. The popularity of this powerful beverage grew so quickly that – if the historians are to be believed – people working in the fields refreshed themselves with it out of pitchers holding some three pints (1.5 liters). Towns levied taxes on spirits, and it became necessary to issue edicts forbidding the distillation of grain in times of famine.

There are several steps in the process of turning a field of waving corn into a "nip of something good." First, the grains are heated and wetted for two hours at high temperature to release the starch contained inside. The temperature is reduced, and ground malt is added to the warm mixture of grain and water, called the mash. The quantities must be precisely controlled, because the enzymes in the malt convert the starch to sugar. Next, yeast is added, and a process of fermentation begins. This turns the sugar to alcohol and carbon dioxide. Fermentation takes about three days. Then the mash is heated in the distillation still, to separate out the alcohol. This

Hanover's *Schützenfest* is the best known, but similar events also take place in small towns, such as Alfeld on the River Leine. There is much jollity, and *Korn* is drunk.

The marksmen and their guests march onto the scene. After the procession, they all meet in the festival tent.

process exploits the fact that alcohol has a lower boiling point than water. It collects in the upper part of the still. From there, it is condensed and transferred to another vessel, connected to the

first. The resulting raw spirit is not only far too strong; it contains undesired, indigestible components, which are removed by means of a second distillation, called rectification. This produces the refined spirit, which is then diluted with pure water to the desired strength. For *Korn*, this is 32 percent by volume; for *Doppelkorn*, 38 percent. The designations *Edelkorn* and *Altkorn* may be used if the spirits have been matured for at least six months in wooden casks. *Korn* should be stored in cool conditions. The accepted way to drink it is at a little above freezing point. Connoisseurs never "knock back" a *Korn;* they sip it to enjoy it.

A *Lüttje Lage*, should you be offered one in Lower Saxony, is a beer and a *Korn* (a glass of each). This custom has become quite widespread; traditionally, it involved holding both glasses together and pouring both into the mouth with a continuous twist of the wrist. It is a knack still much practiced in Hanover, especially at the annual marksmen's festival, called the *Schützenfest*.

There is some dispute in the northwest of Germany about the origin of the *Löffeltrunk*. For this, two drinking companions face each other, each holding a metal spoon of *Korn* in their left hand. The traditional dialog, in Low German dialect, begins: *"Ick seh di!"* ("I see you") and *"Dat freit mi!"* ("I am glad"): the mutual assurance that the two drinkers, despite having imbibed, can still focus on each other, and are pleased to do so. When they have drunk the contents of the spoon, they lick it clean and turn it upside down. If the slightest drop lands on the tablecloth, that decides who is to pay for the next round.

Bock beer

Germany holds the world record for beer consumption, and beer is usually associated with Bavaria, and the Hofbräuhaus in Munich. There, too, after the annual tapping of the strong beer in late winter, the popular Bock beer flows copiously into the tankards. Many a self-confessed Bavarian might splutter over his drink to hear that this beer in fact comes from "Prussia," brought to the realm of the River Isar by an incomer, a *"Zuagroaster."* This is the background to the story:

The small town of Einbeck in the south of Lower Saxony has a continuous tradition of beer brewing going back over 600 years. In the Middle Ages, here as elsewhere, it was the norm for every "full" citizen – every house-owning burgher or estate owner, that is – to be allowed to brew beer for the household's own use. The town made available a public brew-kettle with the liquid brew which was brought to the house by the brew-master. The town had the right to buy up and sell any surplus beer. The brewers' art as practiced in Einbeck soon won recognition even outside the region. The oldest surviving receipt for beer, dated 1378, is lovingly preserved. It records the purchase of over two tons of beer by Duke Albrecht of Saxony and Lüneburg in Celle. Toward the end of the 15th century, Einbeck was exporting its beer, through

the trading links of the Hanseatic League, as far afield as Stockholm, Riga, and Reval using the port of Lübeck, and westward to Utrecht and Amsterdam via Hamburg. Einbeck beer, called *"Einpökisch Bier,"* was consumed with equal pleasure in the *Ratskeller* of the large cities and the privileged courts of princes. The dukes in Munich enjoyed it from 1545 onward. When, in

1612, skilled personnel were needed for the newly built Hofbräuhaus, a master brewer from Einbeck was "head-hunted." It was he who brought the Lower Saxon beer recipe to Bavaria.

Bavarian dialect turned *"Einpökisch"* into *"Oanpock,"* and eventually *"Bock"* beer. This richly flavored beer continued to be brewed in Einbeck, too, and the town's 700 or more breweries began to unite as early as the 17th century, first, to create the *Genossenschafts-brauereien* (brewing cooperatives), then, in 1794, the *Städtische Brauerei* (town brewery). From 1851, bottled beer was sold. Bock beer is a strong lager, with an alcoholic content of 5.2 percent by volume; double bock has 5.8 percent.

The Urbock produced today by the Einbecker Brauhaus A.G., with an original wort of around 16 percent, is the leader among the bock beers available in Germany. Their range also includes Brauherren-Pils, with a delicate bitterness, a mild Pilsener, and Mai-Ur-Bock, whose arrival in spring is eagerly anticipated by beer-lovers. The brewery's slogan is "Ohne Einbeck gäb's kein Bockbier" ("Without Einbeck, there would be no bock beer"), and they are proud to recall that Martin Luther is reputed to have made a rhyme about it at the Imperial Diet of Worms: "Den besten Trank, den einer kennt, der wird Einbecker Bier genennt" ("The best drink known to human ken is Einbecker beer, such is its name.")

Bregen, Pinkel: sausage lore

The artist Wilhelm Busch wrote enthusiastically in a letter describing Christmas Eve 1873 that his hosts were feeding five people, but provided "enough ham for six and enough sausage for twenty-five." He does not mention whether it was all eaten, though we can be certain that Busch ate copiously. He had a great liking for the sausages of his native Lower Saxony, and had them sent to him regularly by his sister-in-law while he was living in Frankfurt.

Lower Saxony has a host of sausage specialties to offer, particularly boiled sausages. *Pinkel* is the best known, partly on account of its odd name, and partly because the dish *Kohl und Pinkel* has made it famous. The recipe varies from place to place, as with all the regional specialties. In the case of *Pinkel*, there is *Fleischpinkel* ("meat Pinkel"), *Friesischer* (Frisian), and *Ammerländer/Oldenburger* (Ammerland/Oldenburg). The feature common to them all is that they contain cereal meal and onions.

Another sausage known beyond the bounds of Lower Saxony is *Bregenwurst* or *Brägenwurst*. Its name comes from the fact that this sausage used to contain brains *(Bregen)*. This is no longer so; all *Bregenwurst* arrives on the market "brainless." It, too, exists in many variations. It is widely manufactured from raw pork, rind, onions, nitrous curing salt, pepper, and allspice. The sausage is smoked when raw, and then boiled.

Other regional specialties include *Hannoversche Fleischwurst*, originally a boiled sausage, though now mainly sold to be heated in water before eating; *Göttinger Bierwurst*, known and popular all over Germany; *Hannoversche Schmorwurst*; *Harzer Schmorwurst*; *Hannoversche Weisswurst*; and *Knappwurst*. The Eichsfeld butchers made a particular name for themselves on account of their fine tradition of using spices. One of their specialties is called *Feldkieker*, which is also found in Thuringia (see page 22); part of Eichsfeld lies in today's Thuringia.

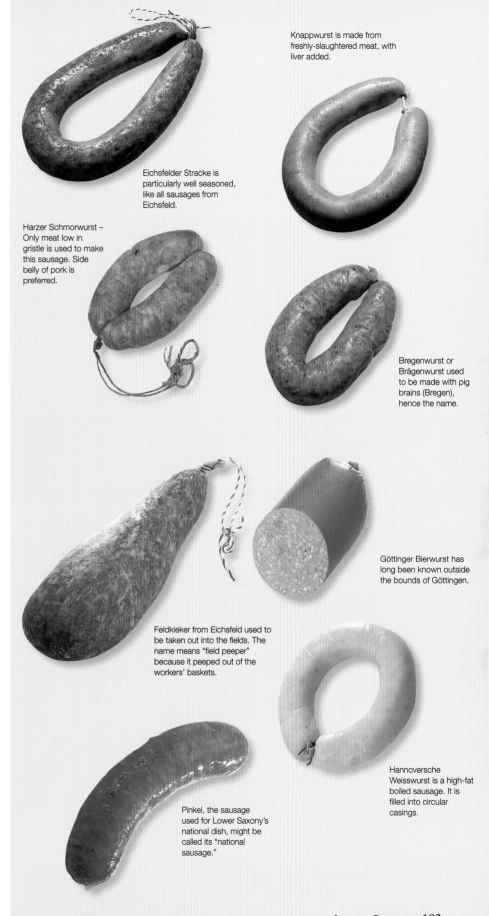

Knappwurst is made from freshly-slaughtered meat, with liver added.

Eichsfelder Stracke is particularly well seasoned, like all sausages from Eichsfeld.

Harzer Schmorwurst – Only meat low in gristle is used to make this sausage. Side belly of pork is preferred.

Bregenwurst or Brägenwurst used to be made with pig brains (Bregen), hence the name.

Göttinger Bierwurst has long been known outside the bounds of Göttingen.

Feldkieker from Eichsfeld used to be taken out into the fields. The name means "field peeper" because it peeped out of the workers' baskets.

Hannoversche Weisswurst is a high-fat boiled sausage. It is filled into circular casings.

Pinkel, the sausage used for Lower Saxony's national dish, might be called its "national sausage."

Meat dishes

Hannoversches Zungenragout
Hanover tongue stew
(Illustrated center)

Generous 2 lb/1 kg beef tongue
Salt
3-4 stock bones
Soup vegetables (4 carrots, 4 celery stalks, 2 leeks, and 2 bunches of parsley)
1 onion, spiked with 1 bay leaf and 2 cloves
1 finely chopped onion
2 tbsp butter
2 tbsp flour
Pepper and nutmeg
A pinch of sugar
2 tbsp Madeira
½ cup/125 ml red wine

Dumplings
10 oz/300 g ground pork
1 egg
½ cup/50 g breadcrumbs
3 green onions
1 tbsp butter
6 oz/150 g button mushrooms, sliced
4 oz/100 g cocktail sausages

Place the tongue and stock bones into a saucepan containing plenty of salted water. Bring to a boil and skim. Then add the soup vegetables and the studded onion, and simmer for about 2 ½ hours. At the end of the cooking time, lift out the tongue and strain the stock. Cook the onion in butter until translucent, then sprinkle with flour and brown. Pour on 2 cups/½ liter of the stock. Boil for 20 minutes. Season with salt, pepper, ground nutmeg, sugar, Madeira, and red wine. To make the dumplings, knead together the ground pork, egg, and breadcrumbs. Shape into small dumplings. Bring the remaining stock to a boil and cook the dumplings in this. Meanwhile, cook the green onions and button mushrooms in the butter. Dice the tongue. Transfer the cooked dumplings, mushrooms, tongue, and cocktail sausages to the red wine sauce, and bring back to a boil. Serve with boiled potatoes or rice and a green salad.

Knipp
Knipp meat loaf
(Illustrated right)

2½ cups/250 g oatmeal
8 oz/250 g pork rind
Generous 1 lb/500 g pork cheek
8 oz/250 g belly of pork
1 pig heart
4 pints/2 liters meat stock
Salt and pepper
1 tsp rubbed marjoram
5 allspice berries
2 bay leaves and 2 cloves
4 diced onions
Oil for frying

Soak the oatmeal overnight. Place the pork rind and meat in the stock and bring to a boil. Season with salt, pepper, marjoram, the allspice berries, bay leaves, and cloves, and simmer for 1 hour. Lift out the pork rind and meat. Strain the stock, and bring it to a boil in a clean saucepan. Pass the pork rind and meat through a meat grinder. Dice the belly and heart finely. Replace all the meat in the stock, add the diced onions, stir in the oatmeal, and cook for a further 1 hour. Transfer the cooked mass to a bowl. Keep in a cold place. Cut off a slice or *Schlag* of *Knipp* as required and fry it in hot oil in a skillet.

Oberharzer Pritschewerk
Oberharz sausage scramble with potatoes
(Illustrated left)

1½ lbs/750 g small potatoes (that remain firm when cooked)
Salt
3½ tbsp butter
1½ lbs/750 g Harzer Schwarzwurst (blood sausage)
6 eggs
4 small tomatoes
¼ bunch parsley, chopped

Preheat the oven to 430 °F/220 °C. Wash and scrub the potatoes thoroughly under running water. Sprinkle each potato with salt, place a knob of butter on top, and wrap it in aluminum foil. Bake in the preheated oven for about 35 minutes. Meanwhile, squeeze the sausage out of its casing into a skillet. Add ½ cup/125 ml water and bring the mixture to a boil. Then stir in the eggs and continue until the eggs set. Arrange on a plate with the potatoes, quartered tomatoes, and chopped parsley. Serve with a green salad tossed in a cream salad dressing – whipping cream, with a little lemon juice thoroughly stirred into it, and seasoned with salt and pepper.

Oberharz sausage scramble with potatoes

Knipp meat loaf

Hanover tongue stew

Heathland heathen grain

Buckwheat

Buckwheat is often called the "grain of the heath." This could be thought to go back to the significance it once had for the heathland farmers of Lower Saxony. In fact, the name comes not from "heath" but from "heathen," for the plant comes from distant, "heathen" Asia. The name is misleading in itself; although its grains, which resemble beech nuts, are the equal of any food grain in nutritional value, it belongs to the knotweed family. It is a "pseudo-grain." Whether it was the Tartars, the Turks, or the Moors who brought buckwheat to Central Europe, it became established there from the 16th century onward, colonizing areas where crops had to be grown on poor, sometimes acid soil. Within Germany, it was grown not only on the Lüneburg Heath, but also in regions of high hills such as the Taunus, Eifel, and Spessart. It had the advantage of good resistance to pests and a short growing season: sown at the end of May, buckwheat can be harvested in early September.

On the heath, better fertilizing methods meant that, from the late 19th century on, rye, oats, potatoes, and sugar beet could be grown, and buckwheat retreated. Much forestation was also taking place, as the region's trees had been sacrificed in the interests of Lüneburg's salt production since the Middle Ages. Attitudes have changed: today, the Lüneburg Heath is a popular tourist area, beloved through the books and songs of Hermann Löns. Formerly, travelers passing through it saw only charmless desolation. Heinrich Heine (1797–1856) even used it as a comparison, criticizing the bosom of a lady as being as flat and bleak as the Lüneburg Heath.

For the heath's inhabitants, buckwheat long formed part of the daily diet, whether as grain, grits, semolina, flour or coarse meal. Every bowl of porridge, every pancake, delivered excellent nutrition, for buckwheat contains particularly high value protein, and is rich in vitamins and minerals. It was also used as animal feed, fields of buckwheat were valued by beekeepers for their bees, and boiled buckwheat size was woven into linen cloth, to make it smooth.

Traditional specialties of heathland gastronomy have been revived. In Bispingen, there is once more small-scale cultivation of this ancient crop. Sowing and threshing are done by hand, making it into a tourist attraction. Favorite dishes that are back on the menu include various types of cheese and vegetable bake made with coarse buckwheat meal, buckwheat dumplings with vegetables, buckwheat waffles, and sweet milk puddings made of buckwheat, with milk or buttermilk, honey and nuts in the old style.

The grains need to be rinsed in hot water before

Wilhelm Busch (1832–1908)

The character Schmöck, husband of pious Helene, choked on a fish bone. She herself departed this life as a result of uncontrolled consumption of liquor. Max and Moritz robbed Widow Bolte of her nicely cooked poultry, and Herr Aktuar experiences a highly dramatic midday meal on discovering a long hair in his soup... Food and drink play a not insignificant role in the work of the satirist, artist and writer, Wilhelm Busch. The same is true of his memoirs and letters.

Born in 1832 as the son of a grocer in the village of Wiedensahl near Hanover, Busch was the eldest of seven children. He never suffered want, but family circumstances were modest, as they were for their farming neighbors, who grew their own food. By no means every day did they have sausage to add to the vegetable stew they ate. The established staple food, buckwheat, was already being challenged by the potato. In the Busch household as in others, they all dunked their portion in the *Pannenstippelse* (melted bacon fat) in the center of the table. They could also help themselves to onions. Beneath the edge of the table rested wooden spoons for more soup-like dishes. The spoons were always licked very clean – a labor-saving touch! Busch occasionally said himself that he liked to eat something "especially good," but he was normally more than satisfied with simple fare. He dedicated rhymes to the versatile egg, and even a "recipe poem" to such a solid country delight as pancakes with salad. A bachelor, Busch often put bread and sausage on the table when catering for himself. He praised the ones from Wolfenbüttel. For a long time, female relatives provided for Busch's culinary needs, and he often praised skill in the kitchen as a feminine virtue: "The art of cooking good roast meat/ Is justly judged a good, kind deed ... One who makes a good meat roast/ Has a good heart as well." He was not averse to roast hare, venison, or game birds, though the summons to the hunt otherwise made him shudder. The country practice of pig slaughtering always upset him, yet the pig is the best source of the sausages he loved so much. He therefore wrote with insight of his own and mankind's weakness: "The knife gleams sharp,/ The pigs all squeal,/ We have to make use of them,/ The whole world thinks: What are pigs for,/ If people do not scoff them?"

cooking, to avoid exciting any allergy to the fagopyrin in the membrane. If used for baking, buckwheat flour should be mixed with another type of flour, because of its lack of gluten. The plant is cultivated on a large scale in the former Soviet Union, Canada, and Poland. Imported buckwheat is also roasted and sold under the name of *Kasha*, further increasing the range of dishes that can be made from this nutritious "heathen corn."

In the past, buckwheat was valued highly by farmers, as it does not make great demands on the soil.

A tale to tell

"In the year 1284 in Hamelin, a strange-looking man appeared…" Thus begins the story of the Pied Piper as recorded by the Brothers Grimm in 1816. It is a story every child knows, one of the legends that has spanned the world, and inspired literary figures from Goethe to Carl Zuckmayer. In its most popular version, the story runs as follows: The town of Hamelin (Hameln), like others on the River Weser, prospered by the grain trade, but was visited by a plague of rats. Then a man appeared, offering to solve the problem. He charmed the rats by playing his pipe, led them to the river, and drowned them all. The magistrate ought then to have paid the man his promised reward, but showed no intention of keeping to the bargain. The music-maker, being of a trade that was not "honorable" and not eligible to join a guild, was consequently without rights, and was to leave empty-handed. But he returned and took something worth more than money, the most precious and dearest thing they had: the children. They followed him and disappeared, never to be seen again. The whole next generation, the town's future, had gone.

The men of literature were mainly fascinated by the social and historical aspect of the story; narrative researchers see it as the prime example of a "historical legend." Legends differ from fairy tales in that they expect to be believed. The brothers Grimm wrote: "The fairy tale is more poetic, the legend more historical; the former stands almost solely in its own right, in its natural flowering and perfection; the legend, possessed of less variety of color, has yet this special feature, that it holds to something familiar and conscious, a place or a name endorsed by history."

In the case of the Pied Piper, there is not only a place but a date, June 26, 1284. The probability that a true story lies behind the legend therefore seems great. If the legendary elements are eliminated – rats do not drown: they are excellent swimmers; a total stranger cannot enter a fortified medieval town and leave with 130 children, entirely unnoticed – the core remains: the departure or total disappearance of the children.

Various sources show that, at this point, the legend is probably handing down an actual historical event, known and passed on by word of mouth for generations, and only embellished with legendary elements once the connection was lost. Various theories have been put forward since the 16th century to try to explain what really happened, and what catastrophe led to the disappearance of a whole generation of young citizens of Hamelin. The theories range from tarantism, children's journeys, and children's Crusades, to the Plague and the battle of Sedemünde. None of these seems plausible if we remember that, in the story, it is repeatedly stressed that the parents do not know

Creating a delicious dish from "rat tails" calls for a large number of ingredients.

"Rat tails" need to be browned in butter to achieve the right flavor.

Season with salt and pepper, and flambé them. This overcomes the ratty flavor.

The "rat tails" are ready when all the ingredients have been combined. It is a simple dish, though the meat component can be difficult to obtain.

where their children are: "The boys' mothers ran from town to town and found nothing"; "soon, therefore, careful search and enquiry was made on land and water in all places."

Recent interpretations have tended to see the Pied Piper as a *Lokator*, a man sent to seek young settlers to occupy new territories in the east, who was lost at sea with them. This theory will probably never be fully proven. Folklorists are glad, however, to have been able to trace the historical core of a legend, and so to prove the words of Lutz Röhrig, the great 20th century narrative researcher: "Behind many apparently pseudo-historic and anachronistic legends there lies a core of reality, and beside all the historical inaccuracies of interpretation, folk transmission also demonstrates an enormous capacity for remembrance."

The people of Hamelin exploit the story in their own way: the Pied Piper is a highly marketable character, and a good advertisement for their pretty medieval town. The event has left its culinary mark, too: Hamelin is the only town where you will find "rat tails" on the menu.

Rattenschwänze
Rat tails

1¾ lbs/800 g fillet of pork, cut into thin strips
Generous ¾ cup/200 g butter
2 tbsp Calvados
Salt and pepper
2 onions, finely diced
Scant ½ cup Rhine wine
Scant ½ cup red wine
10 pimento-stuffed olives, sliced
20 button mushrooms, sliced
8 miniature corn on the cob, sliced
4 tomatoes, diced
2 "Tomato" capsicums (or 1 red bell pepper), cut into thin strips
2 cups/500 ml meat gravy
1 tsp each mild German mustard and tomato paste
Tabasco; Worcester sauce
3½ tbsp/50 ml cream
1 tbsp port

Fry the pork strips in half the butter, then flambé with the Calvados. Season with salt and pepper. Melt the rest of the butter in another skillet, and cook the onions until translucent. Pour on the red and white wines, and reduce to ⅓ quantity. Then add the olives, mushrooms, miniature corn on the cob, tomatoes, and "Tomato" capsicums or bell pepper. Cook gently, covered. Next, stir in the meat gravy, and season with mustard, tomato paste, Tabasco, Worcester sauce, salt, and pepper. Stir in the cream, add the port, transfer the pork strips to the sauce, and allow to infuse for a moment. Separate-grained rice and fresh salads accompany this dish.

Tales of Baron Münchausen

He pulled himself out of the mire by his own hair, rode through the air on a cannon ball, tethered his horse to the church steeple, and climbed a beanstalk to the moon, reporting from there, among other things, on the eating habits of the inhabitants: "They are not called the human species, but 'the cooking animals,' for they all dress their food by fire, as we do, but lose no time at their meals, as they open their left side, and place the whole quantity at once in their stomach, then shut it again till the same day in the next month; for they never indulge themselves with food more than twelve times in a year, or once a month. All but gluttons and epicures must prefer this method to ours." We conclude that Baron Münchausen was no lover of food himself: no more than can be expected of the old war horse, adventurer and daredevil he pictures himself to be. Münchausen is not a legendary figure, however

fantastical his stories: he really existed. Hieronymus Karl Friedrich von Münchhausen was born in Bodenwerder on the River Weser in 1720. He probably took part in the Russian-Turkish war, and in the war against the Swedes. At the age of 30, he retired to his estate, devoting himself to hunting and storytelling. Anecdotes about him began to appear in print in 1781, though they achieved popularity by the roundabout route of the English version published in 1786. This provided the framework for Gottfried August Bürger (1747–1794), who enlarged it with some stories of his own, and published it anonymously in Germany in 1786. It thus brought him neither economic success nor literary fame.

A famous story about Baron Münchausen is the one about his flight on a cannon ball.

Harzer cheese

Harzer cheese is often called *Harzer Roller* in Germany as a whole, but never here. The inhabitants of this area associate something quite different with that name, something with no culinary connections whatever: the region's canaries, whose eloquent trilling fills their breeders with such pride. Harzer cheese, on the other hand, is a sour milk cheese. As such, it is one of the oldest types of cheese. It was traditionally made in the home: when milk had become sour and thickened, because the protein in it had coagulated, the curd or quark was spooned out, carefully shaped into small cakes by hand, and laid out to dry by the kitchen range. The names *Handkäse* (hand cheese) and *Bauernhandkäse* (farmers' hand cheese) are still in use today. The Harz region was one where the produce of the dairy cow was processed in this way. At the end of the 18th century, a family from Switzerland established the first large-scale production of this strongly flavored cheese. In the 19th century, numerous cheese dairies arose in this low mountain area, using sour milk quark as the basis for their cheese. They laid the foundations of Harzer cheese's honorable reputation as a thoroughly local specialty. Working from the base product, milk, specially cultured micro-organisms are used today in cheesemaking to separate the desired sour milk quark from the liquid whey: lactic-acid bacteria convert the milk sugar into lactic acid, which precipitates the milk proteins as

Sour milk cheese

Today, Lower Saxony produces about 75 percent of all sour milk cheese. Hessen is also a significant production area. There, attention has mainly concentrated on "Gelbkäse," a style of cheese ripened by treatment with red bacterial cultures. An early form of the Hessen cheese we know today as "Mainzer" apparently first went on sale in 1820, when a farmer's wife from Gross-Gerau, near the town of Mainz, took some to the town's weekly market. Sour milk cheese is often sold in cylindrical format: the best known of these is "Olmützer Quargel," distinguished by the fact that the portions are already marked out with ridges. It is said to come from Olmütz in what was called Mähren (now in Czechoslovakia), and to have been popular as long ago as the 11th century. "Bauernhandkäse" occurs in various sizes, and is usually rectangular. This may be either a "Gelbkäse" (yellow cheese) or "Edelschimmelkäse" (cheese produced using mold). "Korbkäse" is round, again available in both styles. It used to be made in a basket, in which it was taken to market once it had matured. Round mini-cheeses look attractive, and can be eaten to accompany a beer at the bar, for example. The wide range of sour milk cheeses also offers plenty of choice for those who like caraway.

quark. This quark is granular, and is ground before adding salt or caraway (or similar) with the double purpose of contributing flavor and causing the cheese to mature. The cheeses are then shaped, by machine, according to the variety. *Gelbkäse*, the market leader among the sour milk cheeses, with a market share of 60 percent, is transferred to the "sweat room," where the conditions of high temperature and humidity begin to develop its pungent flavor. The cheeses are treated with a coating of red bacterial cultures before spending a period in the ripening room, which has a lower temperature. The much milder *Harzer Edelschimmelkäse* and *Halbschimmelkäse* also develop their flavor there. They are shaped and treated with white or blue-green mold cultures before transfer to the ripening room.

Harzer cheese is health-promoting and sustaining, since it is made from skim milk, and so has a fat content below 1 percent, combined with a protein content of 30 percent. It contains the minerals present in milk, such as potassium, magnesium, and calcium, and also provides the important vitamins B1, B2, and nicotinamide. The fat content of Harzer cheese served *mit Musik* ("with music"), that is, in a dressing of vinegar, oil, pepper, and onions, is somewhat higher, but, served with wholewheat black bread and goose drippings in the good old Lower Saxon tradition, this delicacy is still extremely low in calories. The cheese should be removed from the refrigerator an hour before serving, to allow it to develop its full flavor. It can be kept for about two weeks under refrigeration. It should be remembered, however, that *Gelbkäse* in particular has a very pungent odor.

Korbkäse mit Edelschimmel ("Basket cheese" with mold) is one of the milder sour milk cheeses

Mainzer is very popular, especially with those who like caraway

Harzer cheese is also known as *Harzer Roller*, but this name means "canary" in the Harz itself

Korbkäse ("Basket cheese") without mold used to be made in small baskets

Bauernhandkäse is treated with mold cultures

Olmützer Quargel was eaten by the Olmütz priests back in the 11th century

Stangenkäse has a distinctive shape

Honey

Humankind has had a weakness for the fruit of the bees' labors since time immemorial: the oldest pictorial record of a daring raid on a wild bee colony is a cave painting in Spain. The Egyptians and the Greeks prized honey as an ingredient for medicines; the Germanic peoples brewed strong mead from it. It was not until the middle of the 17th century that honey had a rival as a sweetener; then, expensive cane sugar became popular among the nobility. In the 19th century, the new rival was cheap beet sugar.

Forest beekeeping was therefore a respected profession in and around Germany for centuries, reaching its peak in the Middle Ages. Beekeepers adapted tree trunks to create a suitable home for a swarm of bees. They then collected the honey and wax from occupied trunks.

People also tried to tempt swarms nearer to human habitation. The straw basket as a place to attract colonies of bees has been known for about two thousand years. A prime example of its type is the hive called the *Lüneburger Stülper*. It represents the tradition of beekeeping on the heath, which was not only carried on by farmers: shepherds, teachers and ministers of religion often used to supplement their meager incomes that

"Real honey is like good medicine, and contains the full healing power of nature." Not a slogan by the Beekeepers' Federation, but said by the writer Theodor Fontane.

way. Candle wax often used to fetch a higher price than honey. The basic raw material from which bees make honey is either nectar from flowers – their "reward," as it were, for fertilizing them – or honeydew, produced by other insects after tapping the sap of broad-leaved or coniferous trees. Honey from honeydew is dark and richly flavored. The Germans have a name for it: *Waldhonig* ("forest honey"). Once the bee has collected its harvest in its honey sacs, it adds an enzyme-like secretion. In the hive, that mixture undergoes a process of transformation, dehydration and fermentation that turns it into honey. The bees seal the honeycombs with wax.

The word *Bienenhonig* on the jar indicates a mixed honey, originating from various plant types. The words *Sortenhonig* or *Trachtenhonig* may only appear if at least 51 percent comes from a single plant type. The popular north German *Heidehonig* comes from heather. It is red-brown, with a strong fragrance, and is rich in protein and enzymes. Its firm consistency means that it is often used as a pollen-rich pressed honey; it is jelly-like in honeycomb form, and the combs need to be sealed. The honey usually found on the market is strained honey, which is extracted using a centrifuge at room temperature, having first removed the wax. *Wabenhonig* (comb honey) is honey from newly constructed honeycombs with cell caps intact, that have never been incubated.

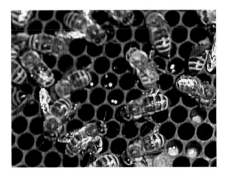

A swarm of bees: the old queen leaves the hive with her colony before the new queens are born.

The beekeeper usually installs the old queen in a new home (like this frame hive). The swarm follows her.

The bees have to travel 175,000 miles (280,000 kilometers) to produce just over 2 pounds (1 kg) of honey.

The swarm has to rebuild the whole structure of honeycombs by producing the wax caps.

The beekeeper has to inspect the hives regularly. If the brood spans all stages of development, all is well.

An uncapping fork is used to remove the caps sealing the cells. The honeycomb is then ready for extraction.

Heath maintenance on four legs

Heath sheep

The Lüneburg Heath and the *Heidschnucke*, or heath sheep, belong together. These animals are descended from the mountain sheep of Sardinia and Corsica, and were brought onto the continent of Europe around A.D. 1000. Travel brochures for this popular tourist area between the Rivers Aller and Elbe would be unimaginable without them, the smallest strain of sheep, standing among the juniper bushes and wide expanses of heather. This is not, however, the reason for the saying "without heath sheep, there would be no heath." This refers to the role of the sheep in preserving the area as it is. Deforestation (especially for the salt works in Lüneburg) and the keeping of cattle caused the gradual disappearance of the forests, and heather (*Calluna vulgaris*, a low-growing shrub native to the area for over 3000 years) colonized a landscape devoid of shade. The heath sheep feed mainly on heather, so farmers on this bare heathland were easily able to keep large herds. The constant grazing makes the heather grow more vigorously, instead of becoming woody and dying off. Its loss would be a disastrous one for tourism, for the great expanse of magnificent purple from late summer on attracts visitors in droves.

The sheep have other food, too: reforestation has provided them with young oak and beech saplings to nibble, and pine needles offer what is often their only green food resource in winter. Birches seed extensively, and the sheep tend the ground by biting off the shoots. There is an abundance of huckleberry, cowberry, and broom, as well as grasses such as sheep's fescue and wavy hair grass, and richly flavored herbs. Juniper has tough needles, and grows unhindered, pruned only slightly in spring when its soft, new shoots appear. The sheep move from one plant to the next, never pausing long over any. The name *Schnucke* is in fact a dialect word for "nibbler."

The heath once covered a vast area, and the farmers took a hand themselves in the management of those parts that were beyond the range of the sheep: heather burning was practiced to encourage new growth. Alternatively, large rootballs were chopped off. These could be strewn on the floors of the animal sheds, and later, when full of manure, scattered on the fields. Beekeeping also benefits from the sheep, since they destroy spiders' webs in the heather, which would otherwise spell danger to bees. The number of heath sheep grazing the Lüneburg Heath around 1860 was over 750,000; this declined massively until the 1970s, but numbers are rising again, currently standing at 15,000 or more. The sheep need tending daily. They must be brought in overnight, returning to their own sheds before evening – sometimes earlier, as they are sensitive to rain and fierce sun.

A shepherd's day is a long and strenuous one. There is much to do, and three years of training are needed. During this time, a shepherd learns not only to tend the sheep, but to be able to recognise diseases. Shepherding involves always keeping an eye open to avert any threat to the precious herd. The shepherd's dog is constantly at his side. German shepherd dogs are not the only breed used – mongrels are also in demand. The one important characteristic for a sheepdog is to have inherited the instinct to drive sheep. They learn how to make the sheep respect them without becoming alarmed while they are still puppies. The dogs have to keep the sheep moving, and bring stragglers into line with a warning, carefully judged bite. The shepherd has a crook, called a *Schippe*, to deal with stubborn sheep: the hooked end is used to catch the animal by the hind leg and bring it under control; the other end has a shovel-like attachment to dig up a little soil and throw it at the offender, startling it into returning.

The shepherd roams the heath within about a two-mile (three-kilometer) radius of the shed. Modern sheep farming involves giving extra feed, usually hay and barley straw. Licks are provided to guard against mineral deficiency, and pregnant ewes receive special care. The lambing season is between February and March; often, several ewes a day give birth. A few months later, there is a commotion in the herd, as sexual urges stir in the male offspring. It is by no means just any ram that is allowed to mate; that right is reserved for stud rams with a pedigree certificate. These come from the stud herds, which are strictly controlled.

The wool from heath sheep was economically important to the people of the area for a long time: in the middle of the 19th century, it was still producing about 200,000 centners (11,000 tons) of wool, which was sold as far afield as France. Eventually, however, this wool could not compete with cheaper imports from Australia. Today, only meat production is of any significance. It is mainly lamb that is sold.

Right: The Horned Gray Heidschnucke is most common on the Lüneburg Heath. The lambs are pitch black, becoming red-brown and then gray as they mature.

Heath sheep were also kept for their wool before Australian imports affected prices.

Juniper

Juniperus communis, or the common juniper belongs to the cypress family. Its slender, dark columns rise impressively across the Lüneburg Heath, nowhere more so than the area called the Totengrund, on the high point of the heath, the Wilseder Berg. Beauty is not all that juniper has to offer: the dried berries are used to flavor sauerkraut and game dishes; they also have antiseptic properties, as well as diuretic and sweat-promoting effects, making them a suitable ingredient for herbal teas to treat bladder and nervous ailments. As an embrocation, spirit of juniper is used to alleviate rheumatism and sciatica. It features in fairy tales, and was used for its healing properties by the Germanic peoples of old, who attributed magic powers to it. A sprig of juniper above the door is said to keep away evil spirits, while good spirits gather where juniper *schnaps* is drunk. It promotes digestion and warms the stomach before a cold beer.

Gefüllte Heidschnuckenhaxe im Wirsingmantel
Stuffed knuckle of heath lamb

4 knuckles of heath lamb
Salt and pepper
2 crushed cloves of garlic
4 tbsp oil
1 bunch of soup vegetables (2 carrots, 2 celery stalks, 1 leek, and a bunch of parsley), coarsely chopped
2 tbsp tomato paste
4 cups/1 liter heath lamb natural gravy or stock
1 bay leaf
1 clove
5 peppercorns
8 juniper berries
7 oz/200 g web suet (fine membrane from around organs, obtainable through traditional butchers)
12 light green Savoy cabbage leaves
10 oz/300 g pork sausagemeat
2 oz/50 g boiled ham, diced
4 tbsp/40 g fresh herbs, such as thyme, chervil, chives
1 cup/250 ml red wine

Preheat the oven to 350 °F/180 °C. Season the lamb knuckles with salt, pepper and garlic. Brown well on all sides in the hot oil. Add the soup vegetables and tomato paste, and cook briefly together. Deglaze by pouring on the gravy or stock. Add the spices. Braise for about 1 hour in the preheated oven. Then remove and cool the lamb knuckles. Keep the oven at the same temperature. Lift the meat off the bone, keeping the meat whole as far as possible, and reserving the bone. Strain the cooking liquid. Soak the web suet. Blanch the cabbage leaves for 1 minute in boiling hot water, then remove and dip them in iced water, and drain well. To make the stuffing, mix the sausagemeat, diced ham, and chopped herbs thoroughly. Spread a little of the stuffing onto the cabbage leaves, three leaves to each knuckle. Use the rest of the stuffing to fill the four pieces of knuckle meat. Reshape them, then wrap in cabbage leaves. Divide the web suet into four, and wrap around the outside of each to secure the package. Cut the bones shorter, then re-insert the knuckle bone by pushing the narrower, freshly cut end into the stuffed knuckle meat as in the illustration. Wrap the bone in aluminum foil. Replace the knuckles in the roasting pan, pour over the strained stock and the red wine, and braise for a further 20 minutes. Serve with young, fresh vegetables and mashed potato.

Anglers use "flies" to catch trout. These resemble the insects found in or just over the water, a favorite food of the fish.

Trout

The fish usually eaten by those who enjoy trout, whether it is boiled *au bleu*, baked, marinated, or smoked, is the rainbow trout, *Salmo gairdneri*. A hybrid of two North American trout species, its name comes from the rainbow stripes along its side. It arrived in Germany at the end of the 19th century. After carp, trout is the main freshwater fish species farmed in Europe, by the earth pond method. The tiny newly hatched fish spend their first four weeks in the hatchery tanks before being transferred to the fry ponds. At the end of the summer, they are moved on to deeper winter ponds, then, in the spring, to growing-on ponds. They are mainly fed on fresh and saltwater fish, as well as dry feed. Rainbow trout grow quickly, and reach "portion weight" (up to about half a pound/250 grams) between May and July. They are then sent to market, either deep frozen, on ice, or alive, in large water tanks.

The brook trout, *Salmo trutta fario*, is seldom farmed. Its ancestral home is the sparkling stream so charmingly evoked in Schubert's *The Trout*: in cool, well oxygenated waters up to about 8000 feet (2500 meters) above sea level. The Harz region of Lower Saxony offers ideal conditions, and the spring brooks of the Lüneburg Heath are also a congenial home. It is territorial, and defends its hunting beat against intruders. Overhanging banks and large rocks provide it with cover. It takes a good knowledge of the waters, patience, and much skill to catch these agile fish in what is probably the most efficient way: lying at the water's edge and grabbing them with lightning speed, as Wilhelm Busch used to do so well as a boy. Disciples of St Peter often employ artificial means: hooks with colorful "flies" made to look like insects in various stages of development, the food that the fish snap at in or just above the water, and shiny lures that look like tasty small fish. Trout bite at any time of day in the spring and fall, but mainly during the evening and night in the summer.

In large, deep Bavarian lakes, anglers find the lake trout, *Salmo trutta lacustris*; the Cut-throat trout, *Salmo clarki*, is a North American species farmed by a few European fisheries. The large, deliciously red-fleshed fish often sold as *Lachsforelle* (salmon trout) is not in fact a species in its own right: although trout belong to the same genus of fish as the salmon, the color comes from a pigment that they absorb from one of their favorite foods, freshwater shrimp – and fish farmers can work wonders by feeding the fish accordingly.

Opposite: Fishing for trout calls for skill, patience, knowledge of the fishing ground – and high waders.

Forelle blau
Trout "au bleu"

2 cups/500 ml white wine
½ cup/125 ml wine vinegar
Soup vegetables (2 carrots, 2 stalks of celery, 1 leek and a bunch of parsley)
1 onion, spiked with 1 bay leaf and 1 clove
Salt, ½ tsp peppercorns
4 fresh, ready-prepared trout

Bring 4 pints/2 liters of water, the white wine, and the wine vinegar to a boil with the soup vegetables, studded onion, 1 tsp salt, and the peppercorns. Simmer for 10 minutes. Rinse the trout and fasten them in a curve by attaching kitchen twine through the tail and lower jaw, and tying in place. Place in a spacious pan, and pour over the boiling hot vinegar stock. This turns it blue. Cover and simmer over a low heat for 15 minutes until cooked. Lift out the fish, remove the twine, and serve.

Forelle Müllerin
Trout "meunière"

4 fresh, ready prepared trout
Salt and pepper, Juice of 1 lemon
4 tbsp flour
6 tbsp butter; 2 tbsp oil
1 bunch of parsley, chopped

Wash the trout and pat dry. Season with salt and pepper, sprinkle with lemon juice, and leave for 5 minutes. Coat the trout in flour, shaking off any excess. Heat the oil in a large skillet with 2 tbsp of the butter, and fry the trout over a low heat for about 8 minutes each side. Brown the rest of the butter in a small saucepan. Place the trout on a warmed serving plate, sprinkle with parsley, and pour over the browned butter.

Trout *au bleu* – the lightest and most delicious method of preparation, which preserves the fish's true flavor.

Attach the kitchen twine to the lower jaw of the fish, and the tail. Pull, then tie the ends together.

Pour a hot stock made with wine vinegar and white wine over the trout.

Cover and cook for 15 minutes, ideally in a fish kettle or certainly in a roomy pan.

Remove the twine. The fish is now ready to serve, either whole or filleted.

Trout *au bleu* is served with boiled potatoes and melted butter – and perhaps a lettuce salad.

Fish "from the smokery"

Smoking as a method of conservation has been known since time immemorial. Our main interest in smoked foods today is for the flavor, as when a restaurant offers trout "fresh from the smokery." The great range of equipment now available means not only that restaurants can be self-sufficient, but that amateur anglers can smoke their catch on the river bank. Two methods of smoking exist for fish as for meat: hot smoking and cold smoking. The process of cold smoking is older. It involves temperatures not exceeding 86 °F (30 °C). In Germany, it is almost exclusively used for salmon and *Lachshering*, a type of semi-salted smoked herring. Cold smoking takes two to four days. Hot smoking is much more widespread. It demands temperatures of over 140 °F (60 °C). A small quantity of fish in a small smoke oven may be ready in a matter of minutes; larger quantities may take up to two hours. The hot smoking method is used for trout and mackerel, to produce the popular smoked herring called a buckling, and – a recently discovered delight – to smoke carp.

The fish (with the exception of sprats, which are left whole) are gutted and cleaned, and then salted. At this stage, herbs or spice mixtures can be added. Both methods begin by applying strong heat at first for a brief period, to ensure successful cooking and destroy any parasites. The next stage is to build up a large amount of smoke. This is responsible for the flavor and the golden color. Only natural wood shavings or sawdust, of hardwood from deciduous trees that contain no pitch, should be used. Sawdust made especially for the purpose is available, to create particularly aromatic smoke. Juniper wood and berries, and vine prunings, are also recommended.

At fishing festivals, smoking is still sometimes done in the old way, using barrels without ends set over a brick fireplace. Tiny smoked eel no thicker than your thumb, called *Bundaal*, are delicious served still warm from the smoke oven, and so small that they are sold tied together in a bunch. In Lower Saxony's best known eel country, around the two lakes, the Steinhuder Meer and Zwischenahner Meer, they are sold fresh, to be simply held and eaten in the hand. It is worth remembering the north German custom of accompanying them with a drink of *Korn*.

Background: Catching eel with a net by the Steinhuder Meer.

The eel is gutted immediately after it has been caught, and then washed.

Before going to the smokehouse, the eel is well salted and washed again.

The freshly smoked eel emerge from the smokehouse a golden color.

The fish taste best of all eaten "on the spot," gazing out over the Steinhuder Meer.

Types of smoked fish

1 Freshwater catfish – also delicious smoked
2 Sturgeon is popular for its roe (caviar) as well as for eating
3 Trout – no buffet should be without smoked trout
4 Buckling or pickling – herring is the traditional smoked fish
5 Mackerel – contains more fat than buckling. This makes it an excellent fish for smoking
6 Haddock develops its characteristic fine flavor when smoked
7 Cod roe – an unusual smoked specialty
8 Sprats or brisling go to the smokehouse whole and ungutted
9 *Schillerlocken* are hot smoked strips of belly wall from the dogfish
10 Salmon is one of the most popular smoked fish
11 Halibut – a flat fish which is usually boiled or fried, but is also good smoked
12 Ocean perch or redfish – its firm, fat flesh makes it an excellent fish for smoking

Duck

Duck count among their number some magnificent creatures, brilliantly colored, crested, and with iridescent plumage, ornamental species for parks and humid biotopes. The main reasons for keeping them, however, are those given by Wilhelm Busch when he said: "Firstly for the eggs that these birds lay; secondly, because a roast can be had now and again; thirdly, their feathers are also removed and used…"

Our concern here is mainly with the "roast, now and again." Duck eggs are larger and more nutritious than hens' eggs. They were once popular, but acquired a bad reputation after World War I, when they were responsible for an outbreak of paratyphus. They are in fact safe to eat if boiled for ten minutes, but their market role is no longer significant. Duck meat, on the other hand, is enjoyed. It is tender and – if eaten without the skin – low in fat. Who, though, would want to miss out on the skin? Roast, crisp duck skin is almost the best bit of all. The Chinese serve it to their guests, making do themselves with the remainder, the legs and breast – which we consider the best part.

The main species bred for food in Germany today are the white Peking duck and the muscovy duck, with the unmistakable warts around its beak. Its meat is dark, particularly tender and low in fat. The domestic duck is descended from the mallard, which is distributed across Asia, North America, and Europe. This wild duck species is found on ponds, lakes, and rivers with sufficient reed-beds, but also likes old trees, deserted large bird nests, even public parks, although ducks are more shy and timid than their relatives, the geese.

A stretch of water is essential for keeping ducks in a way that meets their needs. Ideally, the lake or pond should have running water. The birds will feed there by filtering the water through their beaks, and the mother duck will bring her day-old ducklings to the water. The duck breeder needs to supplement their food with plenty of grain, but the ducks will collect their own snails, worms, and greenery from the meadows.

Almost always, feeding ducks are sent to market as young birds, being slaughtered between seven and a half and eight weeks before the first non-juvenile plumage is due to appear. Oven-ready, they weigh about 3½ pounds (1600 grams). If they are older than one year at slaughter, the meat can still be used for stewing, for example, but the skin is no longer good to eat.

Roast duck should never be allowed to dry out. A juicy stuffing and repeated basting are to be recommended, and aluminum foil is also useful. This is removed for the last quarter of an hour of cooking time to allow the duck to brown. Spraying with cold salt water at this stage makes for a crispy skin. To carve, cut off the wings and legs at the joints. Next, divide the two halves of the breast by cutting the length of the bird, down as far as the cavity. Starting at the breastbone, make diagonal, downward cuts, to make slices a good ¾ inch (2 centimeters) thick, and lift them off the bone. This gives everyone a piece of breast meat. If catering for just one or two people, it is possible to buy and prepare just the breast, instead of a whole duck.

Vierländer Ente mit Birnen-Leber-Füllung
Vierlande duck with pear and liver stuffing

1 fresh duck weighing about 4 lb/2 kg
Salt and pepper
6 oz/150 g duck or chicken liver
3½ tbsp butter
3 medium pears
4 tbsp breadcrumbs
1 cup/250 ml stock
Scant ½ cup/100 ml cream
A pinch of sugar

Wash the duck, pat dry, and rub inside and out with salt and pepper. Pierce repeatedly on the legs and side of the breast. To make the stuffing, chop the liver finely and fry in 1 tbsp of the butter. Peel, halve, and core the pears. Slice them, then cook gently in the remaining butter for a few minutes. Mix together the liver, pears, and breadcrumbs. Stuff the duck, and sew up the opening with kitchen twine. Place the duck breast down in a lidded roasting pan, and roast for about 4 hours in a pre-heated slow oven. Place on a warmed platter and keep hot. Strain the meat juices, stir in the stock and the cream, and cook together briefly. Season with salt, pepper, and sugar. Serve the sauce separately with the duck, accompanied by buttered potatoes or other vegetables.

Right: The domestic duck is descended from the mallard, Europe's most common duck.

Cumberland sauce

This piquant sauce is served with game, both meat and poultry, and also goes well with cold chicken, pies, roast beef, and meat fondue. Despite its English name, it was invented in Germany, for the court of Ernst August (1845–1923), a prince of the Guelph Dynasty and only son of King George V of Hanover, who also had the right to bear the title Duke of Cumberland. This hereditary title has been held by the House of Hanover since 1799, and indicates the link with Britain: the regents of Hanover simultaneously combined this role with that of kings of Great Britain during the period 1714 to 1837. This state of affairs resulted from a decision of the London parliament, excluding the Catholic members of the Stuart Dynasty from the throne. Sophia of Hanover, a protestant and the granddaughter of King James I of England, thus became heir to the British crown, but her death meant that her son was the first member of the Guelph Dynasty to succeed to the throne. He became King George I of Great Britain and Ireland, though he showed no very sure political touch, a trait to some extent shared by his immediate successors, likewise named George. Hanover also attained the status of kingdom in 1814, but lost it in 1866, so that this distinction was not accorded to the gourmet Ernst August, whom we have to thank for Cumberland sauce.

These Guelph rulers paid scant regard to their German homeland once they became kings of Britain, yet the "English period" left its mark there, for example in fashions and furnishings. There is still an anglicized, early 19th century touch to certain respectable menus: it dates from Napoleon's Continental Blockade against Britain, which resulted in the rich farmers of Ammerland having to forego their highly prized turtle soup. They duly invented a substitute – a well seasoned veal consommé with finely chopped veal and mushrooms – and gave it an English name: "mock turtle soup."

DETLEV ARENS

North Rhine-Westphalia

North Rhine-Westphalia is a federal state by the grace of the Occupation forces, but nevertheless there are close historical ties between the two regions. The countryside in each is similar, although Westphalia has the higher peaks. At the south of Westphalia lies the Sauerland. Little towns with their own special character are dotted along the Weser river, and the delightful lake castles of the Münsterland. In the Rhine area the Siebengebirge is enshrined as a symbol of Rhine Romanticism, and the calm expanses of the lower Rhine lowlands also benefit from the presence of the mighty river. Yet this region's real attraction is the architecture of its towns, which stretches back to Roman times, and is epitomized by the architectural glories of Cologne cathedral and the minster in Aachen. The lively Ruhr area acts as a hinge between North Rhine and Westphalia. Historically, the Rhineland and Westphalia have had a close relationship, which has nevertheless had its problems. The studied Westphalians and quick-witted Rhinelanders are quick to ascribe regional characteristics to each other, and it is sometimes difficult to know whether this is meant in jest or not. Food customs are also a point of mutual distrust, because the regions are very alike, except from the culinary point of view. The Rhinelanders generally disparage the Westphalians for the heartiness of their fare, whereas the Westphalians criticize the Rhinelanders' fondness for sweet and sour combinations. Perhaps there is a grain of truth in these prejudices. The Rhineland's top fermented beer is popularly held up as proof of a light-hearted lifestyle. It doesn't take much pressure to draw it from the tap, and it is easy to knock back, whereas it takes a good eight minutes for the stronger Westphalian pils to fill a glass. The Westphalian cattle and grain farmers are at pains to point out that at least their cuisine is native, while the Rhinelanders have accepted external influences. Of course, this straight away adds fuel to the suspicion that, even in culinary matters, a Rhinelander is a bit of an adventurer.

Left: The Rur-Stausee is in the Eifel region, close to the ancient city of Aachen. In comparison with the Ruhr, which flows through the industrialized Ruhrgebiet, the Rur without an "h" meanders through the idyllic hills of the Eifel.

Sauerbraten

It may be difficult for Rhinelanders to admit, but there's no way round it – Westphalia has the more noteworthy cuisine. But there is one Rhineland recipe, a meat dish, which shines brightly in the heavens of German cookery, and that is *sauerbraten*.

The fundamental question "What do you need for a *sauerbraten*?" can be answered easily – lots of time. Under no circumstances does a *sauerbraten* pass directly from meat counter to roasting pan, but breaks its journey for two or three, preferably four or five days, in a marinade. This determines the tenderness of the meat; the acids in the marinade dissolve the collagen which is the component in the tissue responsible for texture and firmness. Just as important, if not more so, is the fact that tender meat makes for better eating. The marinade also makes a major contribution to the underlying flavor that gives the dish its name.

Sauerbraten is not just sour though. The sauce is created in a way which some critics refer to as "typically Rhinish." It acts as a counterpoint to the acidity of the meat, and its sweetness is responsible for most of the significant variations in the recipes for Rhinish *sauerbraten*. Usually a good handful of raisins is added, with flaked almonds often thrown in to enhance the flavor. Some cooks use sugar beet syrup, which is also fairly traditional. Others swear by *lebkuchen*, a sweet, spicy gingerbread-cookie, which tickles the tastebuds with a reminder of Christmas.

But that is far from all. The sweet counter-attack continues with the accompaniments. Stewed apple goes with a Rhinish *sauerbraten* as well as bacon goes with eggs. It seems remarkable that no one has thought to rename the dish "sweet sauerbraten."

Background: *Sauerbraten* is a Rhinish specialty which is famous far beyond the state boundaries. It gets its special flavor from the combination of sweet and sour. The marinade is prepared with vinegar, and *lebkuchen* or gingerbread is added during cooking.

Rheinischer Sauerbraten
Rhinish sauerbraten

1 cup/250 ml red wine
1 cup/250 ml wine vinegar
2 cups/500 ml water
2 bay leaves, 8 juniper berries
4 allspice seeds, 1 tsp peppercorns
Generous 2 lb piece of beef (top rump or brisket)
Salt and pepper
¼ cup/60 g clarified butter
Soup vegetables, roughly diced (2 carrots, 2 celery stalks, 1 leek, parsley)
Generous 1 cup/60 g crumbled lebkuchen or gingerbread
1 tbsp stewed apple, ½ cup/125ml sour cream
1 apple, peeled, cored, and diced
1 cup/150 g raisins, sugar

For the marinade: bring the red wine, wine vinegar and water to boil with the bay leaves, juniper berries, allspice, and peppercorns. Allow to cool, then pour over the beef. Allow the beef to marinate in a cool place for at least 2 days, turning frequently. Take the beef out of the marinade, pat it dry, and rub salt and pepper into it. Reserve the marinade. Heat the clarified butter until very hot and quickly seal the meat, browning well. Add the vegetables and sauté with the beef. Pour over the marinade and stir in the crumbled lebkuchen and stewed apple. Cover and braise over a medium heat for 1½ hours. Remove the beef and keep it warm. Strain the sauce, stir in the sour cream, and season to taste with salt, pepper, and sugar. The flavor should be sweet and sour. Add the diced apple and simmer for 10 minutes. Add the raisins to the sauce a few minutes before serving. Slice the meat, and arrange it on a warmed serving dish. Serve with stewed apple and potato dumplings.

Sauerbraten – originally horsemeat

"Wat maache mer mit dem Pääd, wat maache mer mit dem Pääd?" brood the citizens of Cologne during Carnival. If you look at the problem from the point of view of nutrition, it is obvious why they not only ask the question "What shall we do with the horse?" openly, but also in rhyme. Since Europe adopted Christianity, the horse has had a special place among domestic animals. In 732 consumption of horsemeat was banned, the only ban on food which the Catholic church has ever issued. "Amongst other things, you have also mentioned that some ate wild horses and even more ate tame horses. Under no circumstances, my brother in Christ, should you let the same thing ever happen again. Rather impose an appropriate penance on them such that, with Christ's aid, you will be in a position to prevent this happening again at any price, because this act is impure and abhorrent," wrote Pope Gregory III to the missionary Bonifacius.

The indignation which surrounds these words naturally did not stem from a sentimental love of animals on the part of the Pope. Some historians explain the ban by saying that it served as a means to weaken the heathen religion; to the Teutons the horse was the noblest sacrificial animal and a very special food. More probable, though, is the theory which Marvin Harris developed in his book *Good Taste and Revulsion*. He sees politics as being at the root of the Pope's involvement in the matter of horses. Europe, the stronghold of Christianity, was at that time threatened by mounted Islamic warrior hordes and needed horses as military weapons. Not without reason was the papal edict issued in the year in which

Charles Martel destroyed the Muslims in the battle of Tours and Poitiers. Horses were not butchered because they could serve mankind better first on the battlefield, and later as beasts of burden in the fields, rather than as a source of meat. In fact pigs, cows, and other domestic animals were far better than horses in this respect because they could be fattened more quickly and at less expense.

The actual reasons for prohibiting consumption of horsemeat have long been forgotten, but revulsion at the thought of eating horses spread throughout Christian Europe, and America. The ban became a nutritional taboo. Previously horses were slaughtered in times of poverty, when people ate rats and dogs too, and so today horsemeat is still regarded as a food for the poor.

Only in France are butchers who sell horsemeat commonplace; where one in three adults eats horsemeat. There are certain historical reasons for this too. After the French Revolution, the revolutionary forces decided to permit the consumption of horsemeat. The taboo on eating horsemeat was, they argued, determined by class-consciousness and superstition, and was contrary to the well-being of the workers. In order to make horsemeat socially acceptable, during the 1860s some exclusive Paris clubs issued invitations to elegant celebratory banquets of horsemeat. And it is surely not by chance that, since about 1860, the horse has been held in especially high regard in the French-influenced Rhineland because of one dish. To the question of what should be done with the horse, the people of Cologne traditionally give a pithy reply, "*Sauerbraten, sauerbraten* Hussar style."

The meat, which has spent a couple of days in the marinade, is thoroughly sealed.

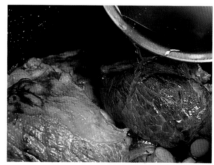

After the vegetables have been added, and briefly sautéed with the meat, the marinade is poured over.

After braising, the meat is removed from the sauce which is strained through a sieve.

The diced apple is cooked in the sauce, and raisins are added toward the end.

A final taste check – it is important that the sauce has the "typically Rhinish" sweet and sour flavor.

Meaty matters

"O hillige Graute-Baunen-Tid, O Buk, wärd mi noch mal so wit!" ("O holy fava bean time; O, that my stomach were twice as wide!") Many regional recipes are proof that this quick Münsterland prayer refers not only to fava beans themselves, but equally to their superb combination with a good piece of bacon. Bacon regularly brightens up life because it is available all year round.

Usually meat was the uncontested highlight, the true delicacy in a meal. A term such as "Sunday roast" expresses this with admirable succinctness.

Fat also previously played a much more important role; nowadays many a traditional meal is served without the once obligatory fat. When considering the history of recipes, it is striking how pork predominates over beef. This is hardly surprising, because it is much easier to feed omnivorous pigs throughout the year. Even city-dwellers frequently kept pigs.

Two dishes are outstanding examples of regional meat specialties: *Hämchen* in the Rhineland, and *Pfefferpotthast* in Westphalia. *Hämchen*, cured and smoked ham shank, which is served with sauerkraut and boiled potatoes, is cooked and served everywhere. It is lauded to the high heavens in Carnival songs almost as often it appears on Rhinish menus. *Pfefferpotthast*, a hearty beef dish, which was originally prepared from the less desirable cuts of beef, is very popular in Münsterland. The diced meat is braised in onions, stock, pepper, cloves, and bay leaves. The gravy is thickened with rye bread or fine dried breadcrumbs, and flavored with lemon juice.

Of all the sausages which find their way into the skillet, Cologne *Flönz* are worth a mention. Up to the 1920s, anyone ordering *Flönz* from the butcher would get all kinds of leftover sausages. They were cheaper, and therefore popular with the poor. Now *Flönz* means blood sausage, which is sautéed with or without a coating of breadcrumbs, and served with sauté potatoes. The term *Blotwoosch*, or blood sausage, on the other hand, indicates a smoked blood sausage.

Pannhas
Meatloaf

3½ oz/100 g fatty bacon, diced
3 onions, finely diced
12 oz/350 g liver sausage
12 oz/350 g blood sausage
6 cups/1 ½ liters meat stock
Salt and pepper
½ tsp ground cloves
1 tbsp rubbed marjoram
Generous 4 cups/500 g buckwheat flour
¼ cup/50 g clarified butter

Sauté the bacon in a dry skillet until crisp. Add the onions and sauté them in the bacon juices. Remove the skins from the sausages, and add the sausage meat to the skillet. Pour on the stock. Bring the mixture to a boil and season to taste with the salt, pepper, cloves, and marjoram. Add the buckwheat flour, stirring all the time, and boil for a further 10 minutes. Turn the heat down low, and allow the buckwheat to swell for a further 30 minutes. Transfer the mixture to a bowl, level off the top, and allow to cool. Turn the meatloaf out onto a plate and slice. Sauté the slices in the clarified butter until brown. Serve with parsleyed potatoes or rye bread rolls.

Münsterländer Töttchen
Münsterland veal stew

If you want to prepare the stew in a truly traditional manner, you should use calf's head, lungs, and heart instead of the shoulder of veal.

1¾ lbs/800 g shoulder of veal
1 onion, spiked with 1 bay leaf and 2 cloves
Soup vegetables (2 carrots, 2 celery stalks, 1 leek, parsley)
5 peppercorns
Salt
2 tbsp/35 g butter
1 Spanish onion, finely chopped
⅓ cup/40 g flour
¾ cup/200 ml dry white wine
Pepper
Pinch of sugar
1 tsp mustard

Simmer the shoulder of veal in plenty of water with the spiced onion, vegetables, peppercorns, and a pinch of salt for 1¼ hours, or until the veal is tender. Take the veal out of the stock. Strain the stock. Melt the butter and sauté the onion in it until translucent. Sprinkle over the flour, stirring all the time, and cook it until the flour foams and turns golden. Add the white wine and a scant 1¼ cups of stock, stirring all the time, and simmer for 20 minutes. In the meantime, cut the veal into bite-size pieces. Season the sauce to taste with pepper, salt, sugar, and mustard. Add the veal to the sauce and heat thoroughly. Serve with parsleyed potatoes or wholegrain bread.

Dicke Bohnen mit Speck
Fava beans with bacon

1¼ lbs/600 g smoked pork belly
1 onion
5 juniper berries
2 cloves
2 tbsp/35 g butter
⅓ cup/40 g flour
10 oz/300 g cooked fava beans
Salt and pepper
Pinch of sugar
1 tsp savory
Bunch of fresh chives, finely chopped

Bring the pork belly, onion, juniper berries, and cloves to a boil in 4 cups/1 liter of water, cover, and simmer for 1 hour. Take the pork out of the stock. Strain the stock. Melt the butter, sprinkle on the flour, stirring all the time, and cook until the flour foams and turns golden. Add 2 cups/500 ml of stock, stirring all the time, and simmer for 30 minutes. Slice the pork and keep the remaining stock warm. Add the fava beans to the sauce and heat them thoroughly. Season to taste with salt, pepper, sugar, and savory, and sprinkle with the chopped chives. Serve the beans with the sliced pork and potatoes.

Mixed whenever possible

Vegetables

The Rhineland's dominance in the cultivation of vegetables is clear from the statistics; 14,820 acres (6000 hectares) under cultivation in Westphalia compared with 32,110 acres (13,000 hectares) in the Cologne and Düsseldorf administrative districts. As far as the Westphalian figures are concerned, it should also be borne in mind that almost half of the area under cultivation is due to the presence of a large frozen food company; spinach is the main crop in the farms around its factory in the Münsterland.

The major consumer markets of the Ruhr and along the banks of the nearby Rhine are the main sources for the vegetable cultivation in the Rhineland. Nevertheless Rhinish vegetable growers have, in the past at least, lost many customers, especially the major ones, to their neighbors in the Netherlands. Yet this side of the border it has been possible to optimize marketing strategies. Lettuce, for example, is now washed immediately after harvesting, and the cut stem is placed in water. It keeps fresh longer, as long as it is not displayed in direct sunlight.

While we're on the subject of lettuce, cultivation of so-called colored varieties such as lollo rosso has increased greatly. The favorite is iceberg lettuce (around 12 million heads annually), but it is still no real rival for the inevitable round leaf lettuce, of which 62 million are sold. Cauliflower is also popular. Approximately 2700 acres (1100

hectares) are under cultivation, in the face of increasingly stiff competition from broccoli. Planting of kohlrabi has also been increased in recent years (to 1976 acres/800 hectares.) Recently Napa cabbage has joined the list of the top ten best-selling vegetables.

In the Rhineland asparagus plays an important role as a seasonal vegetable, with the main areas of cultivation being the lower Rhine and Vorgebirge/ Kölner Bucht. In the last decade endive has also achieved a certain importance, but in this case the Dutch and Belgian growers have the advantage. From the point of view of the vendors, an interesting new vegetable is blanched stick celery, as is mouli, which has also sold very well recently.

Stielmus
(Illustrated above left)
Kohlrabi in white sauce

2¼ lbs/1 kg kohlrabi
1 tbsp clarified butter
2 ½ oz/75 g sliced bacon, cut in thin strips
2 tbsp/30 g butter
4 tsp/20 g flour
1 cup/250 ml milk
Salt and pepper
Pinch of grated nutmeg

Roughly dice the kohlrabi. Melt the clarified butter and sauté the strips of bacon in it until crisp. Add the kohlrabi, cover, and sauté for 10 minutes, or until tender. Meanwhile melt the butter, sprinkle on the flour and cook, stirring all the time, until the flour foams and takes on a little color. Add the milk, stirring constantly. Simmer the sauce for 10 minutes. Add it to the bacon and kohlrabi, then season to taste with salt, pepper, and grated nutmeg. Serve as an accompaniment to potatoes boiled in their skins and smoked loin of pork, or Rhinish sausages.

Westfälisches Blindhuhn
(Illustrated below left)
Westphalian ham and bean stew

Generous 1 lb/500 g fresh fava beans
9 oz/250 g potatoes
9 oz/250 g carrots
2 tbsp oil
14 oz/400 g piece of bacon, roughly diced
Small bunch of fresh savory
6 cups/1 ½ liters meat stock
Salt and pepper
7 oz/200 g cooking apples
7 oz/200 g pears
7 oz/200 g frozen French beans
2 onions, finely diced
¼ cup/50 g butter
Small bunch of fresh parsley, chopped

Shell the fava beans. Peel and slice the potatoes and carrots. Heat the oil in a large saucepan and sauté the bacon in it. Then add the fava beans, potatoes, carrots, and savory. Add the stock, season with salt and pepper, cover and simmer for 20 minutes. Peel the apples and pears, cut in half, core and slice. Add to the stew with the French beans and simmer for another 15 minutes. Sauté the onions in the butter until golden brown, then add them to the stew. Adjust the seasoning. Before serving sprinkle with chopped parsley.

Pitter un Jupp
(Illustrated below)
Braised vegetables with pork and beef sausages

1 new season Savoy cabbage
1 leek
9 oz/250 g carrots
½ small celeriac
4 large/500 g potatoes
2 tbsp/30 g clarified butter
3 cups/750 ml meat stock
Salt, pepper, and grated nutmeg
Pinch of sugar
4 pork and beef sausages
Chopped parsley for garnish

Rinse the vegetables. Peel the carrots, celeriac, and potatoes. Cut the cabbage into quarters, and remove the stalk. Cut the leek and cabbage into ribbons. Dice the carrots and celeriac and cut the potatoes into small chunks. Melt the butter in a large saucepan and sauté the cabbage in the butter, stirring frequently. Add the remaining vegetables and stock. Season with salt, pepper, and nutmeg. Cover and simmer on a low heat for about 40 minutes. Place the pork and beef sausages in hot water for 10 minutes, but do not boil. Slice the sausages, add them to the stew, and cook for a further 5 minutes. Sprinkle with chopped parsley before serving.

Overground, underground

No, Eisenheim is not just any "settlement." It is the oldest iron, steel, and mining community in the Ruhr. The first houses were built as early as 1844, followed by more in 1865/66. The slightly more luxurious construction of the third phase of housing (built between 1897 and 1901) is evidence of the economic boom around the turn of the century. Eisenheim has been threatened with demolition for many years. Politicians deemed this way of life to be no longer in keeping with the times, but had not reckoned with stubborn local resistance. Finally even the politicians had to admit that the quality of life in Eisenheim, with its extant social structure, was far better than that on modern housing estates. Thanks to the preservation of Eisenheim, it has been possible to save another 40 mining communities.

Eisenheim remains a prime example of how company owners wanted their employees to be housed. Construction of these communities had no basis in romantic social ideals – it was determined by pure expediency. "Housing next to stables for our employees" was supposed not only to tie workers to their jobs, but also to ensure the lowest possible wages. If a family was largely self-sufficient, it could manage on less money. Besides, keeping a few animals and growing vegetables left less time for pursuing potential revolutionary plots. In any event, most of the miners and steel workers came from the country areas. After work they had the opportunity to maintain aspects of their familiar rural lifestyle, a lifestyle which, in the view of the authorities, kept the community in line. The miners usually kept a goat, also known as a miner's cow, in the shed; more often than not a pig too, and many kept chickens and rabbits. And what about racing pigeons, the "pitman's racehorses?" Obviously many a pigeon which didn't have the right turn of speed ended up in the cooking pot.

The other animals didn't fare any better, but they were only eaten on Sundays and holidays. The heat and high humidity underground were certainly not conducive to developing a hearty appetite. Meals were carried in cans, and the lovely story about a piece of marble cake between two slices of bread may not be apocryphal, but genuine testament to a wife's tender loving care. Hot meals came out of a billy can, frequently cursed for its ineffectiveness at keeping food hot.

The "stall," still an institution, started life as a "soda stall" outside the pit.

The more technical canteen, the "double decker," referred to the two sections which fitted into the canteen, and some models even had three. But recipes devised specially for canteens, that many a culinary storyteller claims to have discovered, never existed.

Opposite: Racing pigeons, the "pitman's racehorses." Besides acting as messengers, they also provided food.

"The working man's health spa" – pubs, stalls, and kiosks

The colliery site in Lünen–Brambauer has long since been razed and replaced by an industrial site. Only a round, dark green building is evidence of the traditional location, even if it is no longer directly outside the gates of the Minister Achenbach pit. There are only pale memories of the terrifying sight of wives turning up on pay day. This is where they came to collect their husbands, busy pouring a good part of the week's wages down their throats. Yes, this was men-only territory back then. In the very early days the pubs were allowed to dispense only mineral water. Of course working underground is thirsty work, and having a "soda stall" outside the pit gates made sense. In the past they were called "kiosks," a name which was originally reserved for Oriental summerhouses. Yet this pledge of freedom reached the district long before the first Turkish guest workers.

Despite the decline in the steel and mining industries, "dat Büdchen" can still be found in the area. Estimated to be some 18,000 in number, their varied wares range from nylon tights to canned pea soup, from shampoo to pistachio nuts. There is no law on shop hours so liberal that the stalls still can't flout it: many are open until nearly midnight. And the stalls, kiosks and pubs are still centers of communication. Their owners know where there are apartments to let in the area, and where relations are tense. But they won't breathe a word about any of this to outsiders.

Täubchen mit Linsen
Pigeon with lentils

2 oz/50 g diced bacon
¼ cup/50 g butter
1 leek, sliced
1 cup/200 g lentils
4 young pigeons
Salt and pepper
4 tbsp oil
1 cup/250 ml game stock
Generous ⅖ cup/100 ml red wine
2 tbsp vinegar
Pinch of sugar

Sauté the bacon in the butter, add the sliced leek and cook until translucent. Stir in the lentils and add 4 cups/1 liter of water. Bring to a boil and simmer for 30 minutes. Meanwhile rinse the pigeons, pat them dry, and rub them with salt and pepper. Fasten the wings and legs to the body. Heat the oil in a roasting pan and brown the pigeons all over. Deglaze the pan with the game stock. Return the pigeons to the roasting pan and roast in a preheated oven at 425 °F/220 °C for 20 minutes, basting them at least once. Take the pigeons out of the oven and keep them warm. Deglaze the pan with the red wine, and season generously with salt and pepper. Season the lentils with the vinegar, sugar, salt, and pepper, and serve with the pigeons. .

Zickleinkeule in Altbier
Leg of kid in dark beer

3¼ lbs/1.5 kg leg of kid goat, on the bone
Salt and pepper
2 tbsp butter
9 oz/250 g onions, roughly diced
9 oz/250 g tomatoes, diced
2 sprigs of thyme
2 cups/500 ml dark beer
1 tsp fresh thyme leaves

Rub the leg of goat generously with salt and pepper. Melt the butter in a roasting pan, sear the leg of goat in it until well browned all over, then take it out of the pan. Sauté the onions in the pan juices, add the diced tomatoes and thyme, then place the leg of goat on top. Pour 1 cup/250 ml of beer over the leg of goat, then roast in a preheated oven at 350 °F/180 °C for 1½ hours. Baste with the remaining beer during cooking. Take the meat out of the roasting pan and keep it warm. Strain the pan juices, and bring to a boil. Continue boiling until slightly reduced, then season to taste with thyme, salt, and pepper. Serve with mashed turnip or red cabbage with apples, and potatoes boiled in their skins.

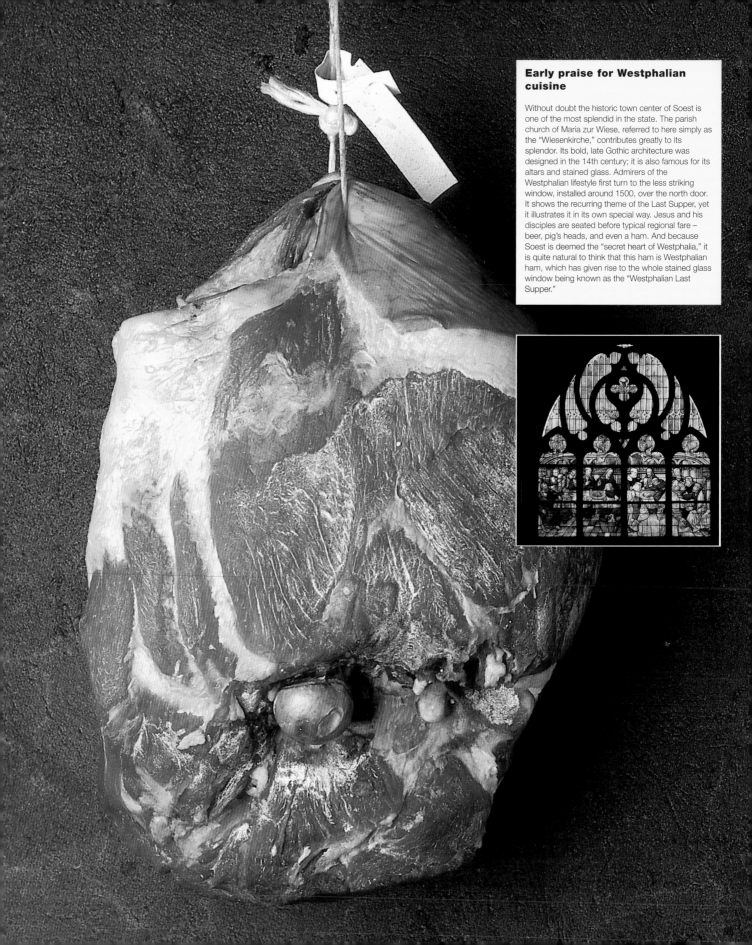

Early praise for Westphalian cuisine

Without doubt the historic town center of Soest is one of the most splendid in the state. The parish church of Maria zur Wiese, referred to here simply as the "Wiesenkirche," contributes greatly to its splendor. Its bold, late Gothic architecture was designed in the 14th century; it is also famous for its altars and stained glass. Admirers of the Westphalian lifestyle first turn to the less striking window, installed around 1500, over the north door. It shows the recurring theme of the Last Supper, yet it illustrates it in its own special way. Jesus and his disciples are seated before typical regional fare – beer, pig's heads, and even a ham. And because Soest is deemed the "secret heart of Westphalia," it is quite natural to think that this ham is Westphalian ham, which has given rise to the whole stained glass window being known as the "Westphalian Last Supper."

Westphalian ham

There is no doubt that Westphalian ham is a confirmed culinary great. Its fame has spread far beyond the national boundaries and is even reflected in literature. Although Emperor Sigismund (1368–1437) is supposed not to have had a good word for it, it still comes highly recommended. After all Johann Fischart (1546–1590) was already familiar with it, and the hero of Grimmelhausen's novel *Simplicius Simplicissimus*, published in 1669, also thought highly of it. Yet the authors do not explain what makes Westphalian ham so very special.

First of all it is raw ham, prized both for its tenderness and for its delicate flavor. Westphalian authors stress that the manner in which the pigs are fed plays a very important role. Nothing must be spared in the care of a young pig which must spend a year in the sty. A balanced diet is important – turnips, cabbage, and (later) potatoes must be included as well as clover, grass, and stinging nettles. An important aspect is special food to lay down winter fat. Acorns (later acorn flour) are recommended for this purpose, as they subsequently add to the ham's flavor. Connoisseurs expressly advise against pigs being driven though beech woods. Excessive consumption of beech mast makes the pig sluggish. In addition to the manner in which the pig is fed, the curing of the ham itself also determines quality. Of course it should not be placed in salt, or even better, brine, for too long, but it is the drying phase which is ultimately decisive. And this is where the historic differences start. There is no doubt that present-day Westphalian hams taste nothing like in the olden days. In the early days, the ham simply cured in the doorway of the house. Then came the triangular chimney hood, or smoke trap, over the open fire. This "trapped" the smoke, and had a certain concentrating effect. The sausages, hams, and sides of bacon hung there on frames.

This "black heaven," as Grimmelshausen called it, also survived the advent of the "cooking machine," in other words, the stove, at least in principle. The stove may have been connected directly to the fireplace, but the smoke continued to do its work in secret, in high smoke traps, diverted there by dampers. It was only with the irresistible advance of coal that this smoking process came to an end, because the rising smoke now contained poisonous gases. Thus came the day of the smoke room, and with it the possibility of directly influencing the flavor of the ham.

Consequently, Westphalian ham is really, or was originally, air dried. It would hang in the smoke chamber for almost six months before it was cut. The manner in which it is processed today (fast cured, sprayed with brine) is, out of respect for the ham, a story for another day.

Background: the famous Westphalian ham is cured on the bone and smoked.

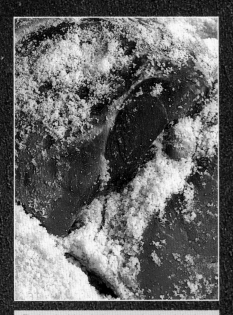

The length of time the ham cures in salt or brine is decisive in determining quality.

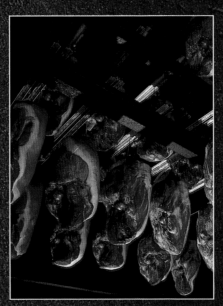

"Black heaven" was the term Grimmelshausen used for the smoke chambers where the hams hung.

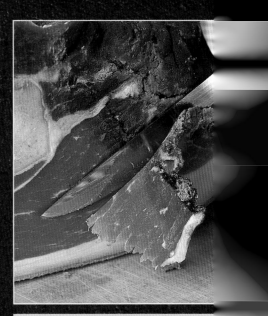

Bread baked in a clay oven and chilled schnaps – the perfect accompaniments to a nice slice of cured ham.

Pumpernickel

If you want to track down pumpernickel, you have to immerse yourself in the history of language, because one thing is certain – the word came before the bread. *Nickel* is the short form of Nikolaus (Nicholas), and *Pumper*, not to beat around the bush, means fart. Logically then, the name of the bread originally meant a foolish, coarse person. In *Weiberspiegel* (Wives' Mirror), by the ecclesiastical satirist Andreas Tharaeus (1570–1640), one of the ladies in question bemoans her subsequent choice of mate when her *Pumpernickel*, presumably a coarse, foolish man, leaves her. This isn't very encouraging, but in fact it was foreigners who first gave the bread this disrespectful name. The people of Westphalia themselves call it, quite simply, black bread. During the 17th century *pumpernickel* was used for the first time as army rations. This too is hardly indicative of an epicurean sensation and in his *War Songs* Ludwig Gleim (1719–1803) considered the consumption of pumpernickel a test of courage. He invents a "man of Münster" who, "filled with fear and hunger, took a prodigious bite of pumpernickel." But pumpernickel has long been regarded as an honorific, at least where the bread is concerned. It is made from whole rye grains and dark rye flour. The fact that a powerful starter dough is needed for such a heavy mixture goes without saying. Pumpernickel may be baked in several ways, but usually it is steam baked. The oven temperature is only moderate, but it is baked for at least 16 hours. During this time certain sugars are released and caramelized, giving the bread both its dark color and characteristic sweet taste. When sliced, pumpernickel is slightly sticky with almost no crust, which goes some way to making up for its heaviness and the fact that it is difficult to shape into loaves. At least it is not a hard bread.

The east Westphalian community of Steinhagen is the force behind the juniper brandy called *Steinhäger*. Its special characteristic is that it is double-distilled, first the juniper mash, then the alcohol. Anyone distilling in this way may call the resulting product *Steinhäger*. Alcohol produced in Steinhagen itself is known as *Echte Steinhäger*.

After 16 hours at a moderate heat in a steam oven, the *pumpernickel* is ready.

Pumpernickel contains whole rye grains and dark rye flour, but no sweeteners or caramelizing agents.

To give the bread its characteristic shape, the dough is fitted into long pans.

The surface has to be flattened and smoothed out before being sprinkled with rye meal.

Burg pretzels

Since 1989, in Burg an der Wupper, or more precisely Unterburg an der Wupperbrücke, there has been a monument to the pretzel merchants of Burg. With the high pannier on their back, the tall silk hat on their head, and trusty medlar staff in their right hand, these peddlers wandered across the country, selling the bread which was famous far and wide. Usually the peddler was also the baker, and thus had to deal with any complaints first hand.

Burg pretzels achieved their greatest fame at the beginning of the 19th century. During the 1920s, the uniquely shaped bread reached England, Spain, and America. Nowadays there are only a few pretzel makers left in and around Burg. Sometimes they will let visitors watch them as they work, and visitors are always keen to see the virtuoso swings with which the strands of dough are shaped into pretzels.

Another specialty of Burg pretzel makers was Zwieback. Only a couple of master bakers now know how to make these. The little loaves, which are baked twice (hence the name *Zwieback* – twice baked) are now sliced in half lengthwise after they have been baked for the first time, and spread with a sweet coating of chocolate, praline, or cracknel. Then they go into the hot oven again, where they achieve their final consistency.

A tried and trusted aid for dividing the dough, where the weighed pretzel dough is pressed flat.

When the lid is opened you can see just how precise the old machine is: 50 portions for 50 pretzels.

The art of the pretzel maker is in the swing. The strands of dough are swung and twisted at the same time.

The bread of those early years

"I had to learn the price of everything – because I could never afford it – when I came to the city on my own as a sixteen-year-old apprentice: hunger taught me the prices, and the thought of freshly-baked bread rendered me weak in the head. In the evenings I would often wander through the city for hours on end, with only one thought in my head: bread. My eyes ached, my knees were weak, and I felt a wolf-like longing in me – bread. I was addicted to bread, just as you can be addicted to heroin. I frightened myself, and I kept on thinking about a man who had once presented a slide-show at the apprentices' hostel about an expedition to the North Pole, and who had told us that they had torn apart freshly-caught fish and eaten them raw. Even now, when I have collected my pay and then walk around the city with my coins and notes, I am still often overcome with that wolf-like fear of those early days, and I buy bread which I see lying freshly baked in the bakers' shop windows: I will buy two which look particularly good to me, then another one in the next shop, together with small crispy brown rolls, far too many of them, which later I will put in my landlady's kitchen because I cannot eat even a quarter of the bread I have bought and the thought of all that bread going mouldy fills me with horror."

(from: Heinrich Böll, The Bread of those Early Years, 1929)

When sliced and packaged in plastic wrap, *pumpernickel* keeps for a long time. It is also popular in countries other than Germany.

Pretzels from Burg, formerly prized trade goods. They have been exported to England, Spain, and America.

The long road toward table manners

Spoon, knife, and fork

In the beginning was the spoon – and not just for those lucky persons born with a silver one in their mouths. As the tool we use to feed ourselves from infancy to old age, the spoon quite literally accompanies us from the cradle to the grave. Centuries ago, when everyone ate from a bowl, and this was customary even in middle-class circles up to the early 18th century, the spoon also served as a weapon in the struggle to survive. Perhaps this is why it was grasped with the fist until well into the 17th century. It was only then that the more civilized position came about, held in three fingers as is customary today. Anyway, the spoon was still the only implement which served to aid consumption of food. Historically the knife followed the spoon, but it always served other purposes as well. There were knives for many purposes and in every possible design, the fact that knives were a suitable status symbol surely being an additional reason for this. Staying with food, we know of priceless carving knives which date back to the 12th century. This is hardly surprising, because the person who carved the meat was very highly regarded in court circles. Accordingly, skilled knifesmiths were much sought after, and those from Solingen enjoyed an especially sound reputation.

The knife was used not just for cutting, but also for spearing. Thus, despite the many different knife designs, one development is striking – somewhere around the end of the 17th century, the tip of the knife became rounded. This is the moment at which an implement by the name of fork finally took cultural history by storm. While the spoon and knife were already known in antiquity, evidence of the existence of the fork first appears in the Middle Ages. It came from the land of fine living – not France, but Italy. Initially the many-pronged instrument was intended to hold meat still while carving – later it was no longer necessary for everyone to dabble their "five tined forks" in a common meal. This was regarded as progress, first establishing itself at court, as with any innovation in the field of table manners. In his story of Westphalia *Der Oberhof*, Karl Immermann (1736–1840) was still able to describe a 19th century wedding banquet as follows: "The farmers had taken their knives out of their pockets, each his own, knives which they knew well how to use without forks, and manfully addressed the roast chickens."

Now the so-called "table manners" obviously needed quite some time to filter down, to find their way from court circles, via the bourgeoisie, to the rural population. It can be deduced from the *Atlas of German Folklore* that as late as the 1930s, especially in southern Central Europe, the country folk still ate out of a common bowl.

The middle classes adopted court table manners during the course of the 18th century, at which time table etiquette reached its zenith. We have this century of fine living to thank for the existence of the terrine, the sauce boat, the sugar bowl, and the cream jug. It was at this time too that the fork acquired its bend. Hence it was no longer primarily a dagger, but a carrier. Food was pushed onto the fork and transported to the mouth.

It was much later that the fork took on its present form, and much later too that spoon, knife, and fork came together as flatware. While knife and fork occasionally appeared as a couple from 1550 onwards, it was only in the 19th century that the spoon was truly accepted as the third member of the trinity. In its later incarnation, flatware ceased to be tucked into the owner's belt, or carried in large cases. The custom of carrying eating utensils of one's own fell out of favor. Nowadays, those who can afford it keep several place settings available for guests.

1 Flatware, Hungary, Habaner work, 17th century, steel, gilded brass, mother of pearl.

2 Flatware, late 18th century, steel and silver.

3 Turned flatware in a leather case, late 16th century, ivory and leather.

4 Solingen flatware, around 1800, steel and bone, brown etchings of proverbs on the handles.

5 Silver flatware, Peter Fabergé, St Petersburg, around 1900, silver and steel.

Culturally advanced

Dining to music

In every culture and at every level of society where circumstances make it possible to regard dining as more than simply the consumption of food, aesthetics play a major role – both in the preparation of food and in its consumption. The beautifully laid table, the china, (frequently more expensive than the food served on it), and last, but not least, a certain behavior which is defined as "table manners," are all part of "dining culture" and are intended to facilitate a blossoming of pleasant sensations at all levels. We recognize the importance of presentation and yet we are so focused on the visual aspects, we quite forget the ear. Mankind has always known that gustatory and auditory pleasures are linked, combining in a masterpiece of all-round enjoyment.

There is proof on ancient Greek vases that meals were accompanied by music; you can see cheerful diners and behind them singing, lyre-playing musicians. In the Middle Ages bards and musicians traversed the land, making mealtimes more agreeable for the nobility, but also turning up at folk festivals and inns where, quite frankly, they were not always welcome. A decree by the city of Worms, dating from 1220, imposed a fine of 30 solidis on any landlord who gave entry to musicians against the wishes of his customers.

Like executioners, traveling players belonged to the "dishonored," those who did not possess any rights as citizens. They were accused of taking "money for gain." In other words they requested payment for the diversion they offered or, to put it another way, they made a living from their art. Moreover, they were prejudged in the same way as people of "no fixed address" are judged today. Still, if entertainment was required, traveling players were popular at court, and although they themselves did not belong to a guild, their presence was always required at celebrations by craft guilds and fraternities, and at weddings. When merchants or craftsmen celebrated, usually in a public building such as the town hall or the guild house, the wedding guests were seated separately, according to sex. In the background, on a musician's dais, were several lutinists, a viola player, and a fiddler. The musicians were obliged to play "quiet music," because the burghers "dined demurely." The number and type of instrument was determined precisely according to social rank. The type of music was not restricted in any way, so that anything guaranteed to cheer the spirits rang out, from street ballad to motet, from cheerful fanfare to organ crescendo.

During the 17th century, music joined wine in

The young Mozart also played to diners. This painting by Michel Barthelemy Olivier from 1766 shows him at the piano during afternoon tea with Prince Conti in the Four Mirror Room at the Temple in Paris.

accompanying luxurious celebratory meals both at court and in the houses of rich citizens. Soon, instead of sending for the musicians every time they were required, many courts established their own orchestras, with in-house composers. A repertoire devised exclusively for dining was created, and a new genre of music – "banchetto musicale" was the name given to it by the composer Johann Hermann Schein in 1617. In 1621 there was a "Table Concerto" by Thomas Simpson, and in 1672 Wolfgang Carl Briegel composed a "Table Confection consisting of lively discussion and concerts, from one to four voices and two violins in addition to basso continuo." A "divertimento di grassi" of 1681 describes the purpose of such music precisely in the sub–heading, "musiche da camera o per servizio di tavola," (music for chamber or service at table.) In the course of the 18th century, this evolved into the concept of "table music." Masters such as Bach, Haydn, and Mozart played such music as part of their service at court whereby, as musicians, they were also servants, ranked alongside gardeners and cooks. The composer Hans Eisler once remarked, tongue in cheek, that throughout secular Baroque music, in Haydn's early symphonies, and even in works by the young Mozart, and by Beethoven, one could hear the rattle of knives and forks, the clinking of glasses, and the chattering of the aristocrats, because it had practically been composed into the piece.

Georg Phillipp Telemann made table music famous in its latter stages, towards the end of the 18th century. Movement by movement, and measure for measure, his pieces are as carefully and sensitively constructed and chosen as one of the multi-course banquets at which they were performed. Telemann put almost as much thought into the ingredients in his music, the harmonic and atmospheric results, and devoted just as much craft and artistic skill to it as the virtuoso cooks working for his noble and patrician employers devoted to their soups, pastries, and meat dishes.

With a growing awareness of their civil identity, the musicians also demanded bigger and bigger audiences for their creations. Joseph Haydn, for example, responded dramatically to the ignorance of the nobility who talked over his music with their mouths full by including the famous second movement of his *Surprise Symphony*.

Like the people, the music also freed itself eventually from the courts. It made its way to the emerging public in the towns, and the privacy of drawing rooms. In the houses of the bourgeoisie during the Biedermeier period, the music room and dining room were usually located next to each other, music and dining took place one after the other, generally music first, followed by the meal (as recompense?). The music played in drawing rooms soon acquired the reputation of being banal and shallow, condemned as trumped–up salon graces by Robert Schumann. It established the fashion for mixing music, chat, and food which has persisted to this day.

Even if the bland piped music which is used in restaurants today to create atmosphere is regarded by many as the absolute nadir of music and food, when it is carefully chosen and as carefully composed as a well constructed meal with several courses, music can still contribute today to making a meal what it should be – a feast for all the senses.

A purely German invention

The open sandwich

When the Consul's wife in Thomas Mann's *Buddenbrooks* extends an invitation to "a sandwich," it is a euphemism which is not lost on her Bavarian guest, the hop merchant from Munich. " 'You've made yourselves comfortable here all right!' said Permaneder, as he seated himself and surveyed the choice of cold dishes on the table."

What caused Permaneder to come out with this – in Hanseatic circles – quite unsuitable, and familiar manner of address was not just the understatement used here, but as a south German, the sandwich itself was unknown to him, in the same way as the word *Abendbrot* or "high tea" had no place in his vocabulary. Spreading butter on bread and covering it with a topping is, as folklorist Günter Wiegelmann announced in 1996 via the German Press Agency, a "purely German invention," which conquered the Republic from the north down.

The first sandwich is mentioned in 1339 in the context of a festive meal held by the guilds of Bremen, the custom of topping it with cheese spread in the 17th century. In the 18th century sweet sandwich fillings became popular in central Germany. Even if the borders have become blurred today, it is still not customary in the south

and south-west of Germany to serve butter with bread. Crusty white bread rolls are not sliced in half and spread with butter, they are broken into pieces and served with ham, salami, or cheese. "Contrary to the custom in north Germany, bread plays a more independent role in the south," wrote Wiegelmann, and explains this by the various seasoning and flavoring traditions for bread. "In the north and north-western areas, where the tradition of seasoning or flavoring bread was largely absent, the custom of eating bread and butter had spread from the 15th century onward. If slices of bread were spread with the salty butter of north Germany, and usually topped with another spread (such as sweet purées and jams) or sliced meats and cheese, then a neutral–flavored bread provided a better base for the individual taste of the topping. It is hardly likely to be pure chance, therefore, that the areas where bread and butter, and various bread toppings, are consumed correspond exactly to the areas where plain bread prevails. Add to this the fact that coffee and tea were the beverages served daily with meals in those same areas of north-west Germany, in other words the hot drinks which had spread from the late 17th century onward, and were usually sweetened. They thus brought a marked flavor to meals which also did not go well with spicy or strongly flavored bread."

Right: in the early 1950s, when life in Germany was not yet as comfortable as it is now, the midday meal consisted of open sandwiches, as served here in a children's home in Freudenstadt.

Mett, finely ground pork, tastes good with raw onions.

Sandwich fillings – unusual variations on a theme

- Rye bread with blood sausage and onion rings, topped with a slice of sunflower seed bread covered with liver sausage and mustard, finished with a second slice of rye bread
- Rye bread with Pomeranian caviar (goose drippings)
- Rye bread with Pomeranian beet syrup
- Berlin wheat and rye bread with butter, horseradish, cold sliced potatoes, and slices of pickled gherkin
- Spelt flour bread with trout fillet
- *Döbelner Langbrot* (rye bread) with a spread made of cream cheese and puréed boiled ham
- *Eifeler Brot* bread with *Neuenahrer Rauchfleisch* – smoked meat with corn salad, and red grapes
- Barley bread rolls with prosciutto, strips of ham and salami in vinaigrette, chopped parsley, and pickled gherkins
- Herb bread with herb cheese in vinaigrette
- *Hamburger Rundstück* topped with slices of hot roast meat and hot gravy poured over

- Holstein wholegrain bread with scrambled egg and Kiel sprats
- Mecklenburg wheat and rye bread with smoked breast of goose
- Slices of mixed grain bread (sautéed in butter) with ham and fried egg, garnished with tomato, lettuce, and parsley (known as *Strammer Max*)
- Oldenburg black bread with a herring dip made from egg, gherkins pickled in brine, bacon, and finely diced herring
- Paderborn bread with cheese and quark mixed with ham and stinging nettles
- Black bread with quark and sugar beet syrup
- Black bread with boiled ham, Camembert, and fried egg
- Thuringian wheat and rye bread with bacon fat, topped with sliced blood sausage, liver sausage, and slices of Harz cheese
- Vogtland rye bread, or potato bread, with thinly sliced roast veal, anchovy fillets, and chervil
- White bread with small, thin squares of chocolate, or chocolate spread

Beloved throughout the land, bread topped with ham or salami.

Bread and cheese is also popular. Here with Camembert and hard boiled egg.

Children are not the only ones who like bread and jam for breakfast.

An egg sandwich. Not for people who have to watch their cholesterol levels.

Refreshing in summer. Quark with chives or other herbs.

Sugar beet syrup with quark is a popular spread in the Rhineland.

Bread and drippings, popular in bars, a good base for drinking lots of beer.

Bread with spreading sausage, in this case *Teewurst*, is good for picnics.

Potato pancakes

There are some dishes which cannot be improved by modern cooking fashions, and one of these, in and around Cologne, is *Reibekuchen* (potato pancakes) which in this area are known simply as *Rievkooche*. Almost everyone knows a catchy ditty about these delicacies, rhymes which perforce feature mothers heavily. "Mother, mother, get the pan, we want pancakes, hot from the pan," sang the Bläck Fööss, and the catchiest advertising jingle goes along the lines of "Nothing from a can, nothing from a packet, we want pancakes like Momma makes, fresh from the skillet."

The highest praise which can be accorded these admitted delicacies is that they taste like those your mother made. Mothers, though, tend to grit their teeth at the prospect of preparing potato pancakes. The smell of the oil clings longest to the cook, and is difficult to banish from the kitchen. Sensitive noses can still smell it for days even in the far corners of a house. Making potato pancakes at home is not, therefore, a popular activity. Bars in Cologne have potato pancake days, and there are also plenty of street stalls which sell them. The most famous one currently stands outside the main railway station in Cologne, and is an olfactory nuisance for many travelers.

Yet very few people dispute that potato pancakes are delicious, even when quite plain, rather than dressed up with smoked salmon, trout, or caviar as is fashionable nowadays. Into the bargain you don't have to bother your mother, although there are allegedly fathers in Cologne who, for once, have got to grips with the family stove just for this dish.

Waxy potatoes are best for making simple, delicious potato pancakes.

The potatoes have to be grated by hand, even if it's hard work and sometime you grate your fingers.

It's a matter of taste whether the onions are very finely diced or grated too.

Slices of the potato bread are sautéed in a skillet in plenty of oil or clarified butter.

French fries in the Rhineland

No, the French fry is not a Rhinish invention, but there are still good reasons to start singing the praises of potatoes in the Rhineland. The best reason is, of course, its immediate proximity to the home of the French fry. French fries came over the border from Belgium, the sundered kingdom in the west, and took Rhinish snack bars by storm. It goes without saying that not everyone has been able to master the art of making French fries which, with real potatoes and quality oil, requires expensive raw materials. Anyway, customers are much more interested in the accompaniments. Ketchup and mayonnaise are the most common – French fry fans order them using the shorthand "red and white." Quite by chance, these are also the city colors of Cologne and its most popular soccer team. What is important, however, is that the ketchup and mayo should be thick, so that they don't cover and soften the crisp fries. Mustard, which traditionally is most popular in the Aachen area, just across the border from Belgium, should of course have a similar consistency. Why this should be, no one knows. It certainly can't have anything to do with the contrasting colors.

Reibekuchen
Potato pancakes

8 waxy potatoes
2 onions, finely diced
2 eggs
1 tsp salt
Oil or clarified butter for sautéing

Peel the potatoes, wash them, and grate coarsely. Wrap them in a dish cloth and squeeze out the liquid thoroughly. Put the grated potato into a bowl immediately with the diced onion, eggs, and salt. Mix thoroughly. Heat enough oil to cover the bottom of a heavy-based skillet. Drop spoonfuls of the potato mixture into the hot fat, press down with the back of the spoon, and sauté on both sides until golden brown. Serve immediately.

Siegerländer Reibekuchen
Siegerland potato pancakes

Generous 2 cups/250 g wheat flour
1 tbsp salt
2 envelopes easy blend yeast
3 cups/750 ml lukewarm milk
6 waxy potatoes
Butter for the pan

Sift the flour and salt into a large bowl and make a well in the center. Dissolve the yeast in 1 cup/250 ml of the lukewarm milk, and pour it into the well. Sprinkle flour on top and leave to work at room temperature for 20 minutes.
Peel the potatoes, wash them, and grate them coarsely. Wrap them in a dish cloth and thoroughly squeeze out the liquid. Bring the remaining milk to a boil and add the potato. Add the potato mixture to the yeast mixture, and work together to form a smooth dough. Butter a loaf pan, shape the dough and place it in the pan. Bake in a preheated oven for 1 hour at 350 °F/180 °C.

Potthucke
Potato loaf

2 boiled potatoes
6 waxy potatoes
½ cup/125 ml milk
⅔ cup/150 g sour cream
4 eggs
Salt, pepper, and grated nutmeg
⅓ cup/80 g butter
2 tbsp clarified butter

Put the boiled potatoes through a potato ricer while they are still warm, and allow to cool. Peel the other potatoes, wash them, and grate them coarsely. Wrap the grated potato in a dish cloth and thoroughly squeeze out the liquid. Beat together the milk, sour cream, and eggs. Stir this mixture into the riced potato, add the grated potato, and knead together to form a smooth dough. Season with salt, pepper, and a pinch of grated nutmeg. Butter a loaf pan with some of the butter, shape the dough to fit, and place it in the pan. Dot the remaining butter on top of the dough, and bake in a preheated oven at 400 °F/200 °C for 50 minutes, or until golden brown. Allow to cool, turn out of the pan, and slice. Sauté batches of the potato loaf in hot clarified butter and serve with prosciutto and dark rye bread.

Pickert
Potato bread

4 waxy potatoes
2 cakes/40 g compressed fresh yeast
1 cup/250 ml lukewarm milk
3 eggs
Scant ⅓ cup/60 g sugar
Salt
8⅓ cups/1 kg flour
1 cup/300 g raisins
Butter and breadcrumbs for the pan
Butter for sautéing

Peel the potatoes, wash them, and grate them coarsely. Wrap the grated potato in a dish cloth and squeeze out the liquid thoroughly. Dissolve the yeast in the milk and add it to the potato. Gradually add the eggs, sugar, salt, and flour, and work until a smooth dough forms. Leave to rise at room temperature for 30 minutes. Rinse the raisins in hot water, drain well, and knead into the dough. Butter a large loaf pan and sprinkle the sides with breadcrumbs. Shape the dough, place it in the pan, and leave to rise for 1 hour. Bake in a preheated oven at 350 °F/180 °C for 1½ hours. Allow to cool in the pan, then turn out and slice. Before serving sauté the sliced potato bread in hot butter on both sides until pale golden brown, and serve for breakfast or with afternoon coffee.

From river and sea

If the topic of conversation in North Rhine-Westphalia is fish, then sooner or later Cologne gets a mention. The historic community has its centuries as a trade center for herring to thank for its wealth. Barrels of salted herrings bearing the brand of the city were proof of quality. And Carnival ensures that herring still has a safe place on today's menus, because herring is highly prized as a "lining" for the revelers' liquid nourishment.

But mussels are even more popular, both up and down the Rhine. They are traditionally eaten only in months with an "r," in other words between September and April. We are not talking about prestige delicacies such as the yuppie snack of oysters, but simple black mussels. As a food of the poor, they were always on the menu for the less well off, and of course nowadays a mussel dish is obligatory on a *Kölscher Foderkaat*, the menu in a Cologne bar.

In the past fish from the Rhine and its tributaries played an important economic role, but now the only stocks worth mentioning are trout. The lightning-fast robber still lurks in search of prey in the pure streams of the Mittelgebirge, and is also raised in fish ponds by fish farmers. It should, of course, be obvious that Eifel or Sauerland trout means the native brown trout, and not the rainbow trout, imported from North America.

Rheinische Muscheln
Rhinish mussels

4½ lbs/2 kg mussels
3 carrots
1 parsnip
¼ celeriac
2 onions
Parsley, thyme, and chervil
3 tbsp butter
4 cups/1 liter white wine
Salt
2 bay leaves
1 tsp coarsely milled pepper

Wash the mussels thoroughly several times, scrub them, and remove the beards. Wash, peel, and finely dice the carrots, parsnip, and celeriac. Peel and dice the onions, chop the herbs. Melt the butter in a large saucepan and sauté the vegetables until translucent. Deglaze the pan with the wine and season with a little salt. Add the mussels, along with the herbs, bay leaves, and pepper. Cover and simmer for 10 minutes, or until the shells have opened wide. Lift the mussels out of the pan with a slotted spoon and arrange them in a deep dish, discarding any unopened mussels. Pour the court-bouillon over the mussels. Serve with dark rye bread and butter.

Heringsfilet im Steintopf
Marinated herrings

8 herring fillets
1 apple
2 pickled gherkins
Scant 1½ cups/300 g sour cream
3 tbsp mayonnaise
2 tbsp wine vinegar
Pinch of sugar
Bunch of fresh parsley, chopped
Bunch of fresh chives, finely chopped
Lemon slices and fresh dill for garnish

Remove the bones from the herring fillets, soak them, and divide into bite-size pieces. Slice the onions very thinly. Peel the apple, quarter, core and slice thinly. Finely dice the pickled gherkins. Beat together the sour cream, mayonnaise, vinegar, and sugar to form a dressing. Fold in the parsley and chives. Divide the herring fillets between 4 ramekins, pour over the dressing, and leave to marinate. Garnish with lemon slices and dill before serving.

Rhine mussels can be prepared with few ingredients and without much trouble.

Before cooking the mussels must be washed thoroughly, and the beards removed.

The vegetables are finely diced and then sweated in butter until translucent. The pan is deglazed with wine.

The mussels must be covered in the stock and simmer for about 10 minutes until the shells open.

Salmon in the Rhine – just a historic memory?

"It is in fact maintained that the fish can no longer spawn since the river is never still because of the revolving propellers of so many ships. This much is fact, that the salmon fishermen of Cologne … have acquired free use of the steam boats to exercise their trade as compensation." In his bestseller *The Picturesque and Romantic Rhineland*, Karl Simrock recorded the beginning of the end in 1838. Even then stocks of salmon in the Rhine were under threat, even then the fishermen feared for their most important source of income. Development of the river into a waterway had already begun in 1817, and its pollution by industry soon followed. Finally massive locks and sluices cut off the salmon from its habitat and way of life. As a wanderer between the waters, between sea and river, such obstacles are especially difficult for the salmon.

By 1955 the fish in what had once been the most important salmon river in Europe had died out. After 1980, when the water in the Rhine became considerably cleaner, its inhabitants got a second chance. The salmon was chosen as a symbol of "ecological renewal." Using lots of biotechnology, and at great expense, the predator was re-established in the Rhine. Whether this will succeed in the long term remains to be seen. But one thing is certain, an epicurean delicacy such as the Rhine salmon will never again appear on our plates. "Salmon smells of money" claimed the fishermen in the olden days. We're just happy that it no longer smells of phenol.

Background: Rhine mussels cooked in a vegetable and wine court-bouillon are a delicacy which is traditionally enjoyed in months containing an "r," in other words from September to April.

Westphalia – land of beer

Dortmund – city of beer

One rarely comes across pils in the Ruhr area. The diminutive *dat Pilsken* is much more common. Because of the nickname, some people immediately suspect that it is a way of trivializing high consumption. But this is not so, the people of the area enjoy linguistic diminutives anyway; moreover the accusation of immoderate drinking applies to the "coal carts" as a whole just as much as to the Dortmunders in particular.

Dortmund can look back on a long tradition of beer brewing. It began in the Middle Ages, long before hops won the day in northwest Germany. Not for nothing in the dim and distant past was the Dortmund brewery immediately behind the Town Hall called *die Grütte*. *Grut*, or gruel, was a beer wort made of many kinds of ingredients, which differed from place to place, but which always included bog myrtle. This plant is nowadays quite rare and is a protected species, but at that time it was common throughout northern and north-western Europe. Contrary to the calming hop, bog myrtle is supposed to make drinkers pugnacious, which was presumably the reason why the authorities favored hops.

Such protectionism was not really necessary, however, because the advantages of hops in terms of digestibility, taste, and the life of the beer were too great. Eventually the Dortmund brewers realized this too. But their community only developed into a city of beer following the introduction of the Bavarian bottom fermentation method of brewing in 1845. And of course the industrialization of the area around the same time ensured sufficient consumers, especially the miners, who were especially thirsty after a shift underground. Thus not only Dortmund itself, but also its brewing industry, experienced enormous growth.

Adoption of the "Bavarian brewing method" certainly did not mean that the name "Pilsener" immediately appeared on the labels. No, Dortmund beer has its own character and, in "Export," its own name. It differs from Pilsener in that it has a slightly higher alcohol content, and is less bitter, in other words it is milder hopped. Thanks to its beer production, Dortmund leads all other beer-producing towns; no one else comes close to its enormous gallon (hectoliter) production. It should also be mentioned that recently sales of Export beer from the Dortmund breweries have fallen. Obviously the old clientele now prefers a drier beer. Nowadays the beers from the Sauerland and Siegerland lead the race. Their producers make the most of an "unspoiled nature," and in this respect advertising strategies are quick to use the term "mountain spring water." Obviously the more the environment is destroyed, the more triumphantly its resurrection is celebrated in advertising.

When the football fans celebrate a victory by their team in the bars of Dortmund, the beer flows freely.

The wise drinker orders the second round before his glass is empty.

It takes time to pour the beer, usually seven to eight minutes.

When the beer has been poured, wait until the froth settles …

then top it up. This gives the characteristic foamy white head.

Genuine *Köbes* and fake chicken

The Cologne brew pubs

Anyone who goes in search of the Cologne lifestyle will end up in a brew pub at some time or other. The souls of the people of Cologne are quite simply here, and the most soulful of all, the waiter, goes by the name of Jakob, or *Köbes* in the local dialect. No-one knows why he is called this and not by another name, such as *Herr Ober*, for example. But he ensures that the customers get their beer. In old photographs he is shown in a blue apron, with a change bag, and the *Köbes* wears the same apparel today. The only item he set aside, quite some time ago, is the flattering knitted waistcoat with two rows of buttons.

But never mind the knitted waistcoat or apron, the *Köbes'* most important attribute is the *Kranz*, or circular glass holder. It has eleven holes and a handle in the center. The *Stange*, a small glass holding 7 fl oz (200 ml) fits exactly into the hole,

and despite large quantities of beer being carried around in this way, it does not go flat, because a genuine *Köbes* ensures that empty glasses are replaced with full ones, without the customers having to ask, and indeed they rarely refuse. Everyone here likes *Kölsch*, and only customers from outside the area will need some time to get used to the *Köbes'* comments. Nowadays many a waiter hardly bats an eyelid if someone orders mineral water rather than *Kölsch*, although the *Köbes* famous and infamous comments on different drinking habits have made them a Cologne institution.

Although the *Köbes* still hurry between the tables, the *Thekenschaaf* or bartender has now almost completely disappeared. Whoever sat at the bar could see everything that happened, and doubtless the traditional trinity of bar in front, brewery behind, and hall, required a certain amount of supervision. The food also had to be carried from the kitchen past the bartender, and many landlords set the price for the braised ham shank after a personal inspection of it. From here the landlord or landlady could also keep an eye on the hall, where *Kölsch* was available straight from the barrel for customers in a hurry, and the *Köbes* fetched it for them. They bought it from the

landlord, and then sold it on to the customer, because every *Köbes* was self-employed. Even if the *Thekenschaaf* is a dying breed, he is still a credit to the bar, as in the "Malthouse." Otherwise the Cologne brew pubs are just as attractive as they ever were, because everyone tries to ensure a good atmosphere. Their attraction does not lie in the furnishings.

Although in the brew pub, everything revolves around liquid nourishment, solid food comes a close second. It is a known fact that drinking on an empty stomach makes the beer go to your head faster, which subsequently makes your head beg you to take it easy. Eating is also a means to an end (drinking). This is the reason why brew pubs don't serve scanty gourmet food, but plain, hearty cooking. In a real brew pub, the menu, or *Kölsche Foderkaat* will list nourishing Rhineland food, such as Rhinish potato salad, and *Hämchen* with sauerkraut and potatoes, which is essential. And of

Below: a full pub and a pleasant atmosphere in a traditional brew pub such as this one in Päffgen, Cologne. Even strangers will soon make friends here.

course the dishes whose names are so good at deceiving hapless foreigners simply have to be included – dishes such as *Halve Hahn* (half a chicken), which is in fact a dark, crisp rye bread roll filled with butter and a slice of medium Gouda cheese. Customers in pubs and bars never tire of this running gag between natives and *Imis*, or foreigners. The story goes that the *Halve Hahn* was invented after an internal dispute in Cologne. In 1878 a certain Wilhelm Vierkötter had it served, allegedly to get back at a woman customer. But he created a snack which became incredibly popular precisely because of its nickname. Vierkötter, however, was only following the tradition of giving a dish a name to make it sound better than it really was. Exactly the same applies to *Kölsch Kaviar*. Even with a vivid imagination, there is no way this bread roll topped with blood sausage is related to caviar. You also need a great deal of common sense to see what *Himmel und Äd* has to do with heaven and earth. In this dish, which consists of a mixture of puréed apple and potato, the potatoes represent the Earth and the apples Heaven, because as a fruit which grows on trees, it is nearer to heaven than the tubers which grow underground.

Kölsch and Alt – top-fermented beers from the Rhine

We don't really want to evoke centuries of history here yet again. Historically speaking, Cologne is still a wine-producing city, which to a considerable extent owed its wealth in the Middle Ages to the grape and not the grain. Yet even the long-time favorite beer of the people of Cologne is in fact a young beverage. *Kölsch* first flowed from the taps after the all-conquering Pilsener beer had swept all before it here too. Doubtless, however, the customary brewing process regained a little of its lost honor with the advent of *Kölsch*, around 1880. The variety of dark beer known as *Alt*, developed around the turn of the century, was understood to be a declaration of war intended to stress the value of traditional brewing. These beers are called top-fermented because the yeast floats on top of the tank. In the case of bottom-fermented beers it is deposited on the floor of the tank. Bottom-fermented beers are produced at lower temperatures. In the case of *Kölsch* and *Alt* the temperature is between 60 and 68 °F (15 and 20 °C). Both kinds established their own territories quickly and developed a committed group of devotees. Golden *Kölsch* dominates the upper Lower Rhine and the center of Cologne, the lower Lower Rhine is governed by dark *Alt*. For lovers of one or the other variety, it was a matter of honor to stay true to their preference. There was a clear border between *Kölsch* drinkers and *Alt* drinkers, which supposedly ran through Langenfeld. Rumor has it that the main street formed the demarcation line; on one side the landlords dispensed *Alt*, and on the other *Kölsch*. In the small, domestic market *Kölsch* and *Alt* have, to a certain extent, been able to keep their market share, even today, and their fans are no longer as irreconcilably opposed as before.

Brew pub recipes

There's no sign of meat in the half chicken, *Halve Hahn*, from Cologne. It's just a rye bread roll with butter and gouda cheese.

Essential on any *Kölsche Foderkaat*, *Hämchen* or braised shank of smoked ham. It is eaten with sauerkraut and potatoes.

Ätzesupp, a hearty pea soup, both a lining for the stomach before drinking, and afterwards a cure for excessive consumption.

Himmel und Äd, the dish made from a mixture of puréed apples and potatoes, is served with sautéed blood sausage in Cologne.

Rievkooche, or potato pancakes. If you eat them in a pub you are sparing yourself the job of grating the potato, and smelling hot oil in your kitchen.

No wonder this caviar is so cheap. It's *Kölsch Kaviar*, a bread roll spread with butter and topped with blood sausage.

Sugar

It is not only the dentist who warns of the dangers of sugar, but occasionally radio traffic reports too. It names it as a potential hazard, or the raw product anyway in the form of the sugar beets, and the debris which covers the roads when they are harvested. Rhineland drivers take it in their stride. They know that if the roads are dirty or even slippery toward the end of September, even if the weather is fine, then it's sugar beet time.

The sugar industry has a great tradition in the Cologne area, thanks to Napoleon's continental blockade. At that time no raw sugar reached the European mainland, and substitute raw materials were urgently sought. As early as 1747 Andreas Sigismund Marggraf, from Berlin, discovered the sugar beet as a source of sugar, and in 1798 Franz Carl Achard succeeded in putting this discovery to practical use. In 1801 he built the first sugar refinery in Cunern, Silesia. But production of sugar from sugar beet really took off when Napoleon heavily promoted the cultivation and processing of the beets.

At the end of the continental blockade it became apparent that this protectionist measure had lead to an illusory boom, but the Cologne refineries survived. First they processed cane sugar, as the raw product could be obtained easily and cheaply from Holland. In 1836 Cologne numbered 19

refineries. From the middle of the 19th century the sugar beet finally took over in the Rhineland. It was primarily the entrepreneur Eugen Langen who gave the local sugar industry definite impetus. Speedy development was also favored by geological conditions in the Cologne-Aachen Basin and the Lower Rhine. Sugar beet requires certain growing conditions, but in return it is one of, if not the most economic, crop for farmers. Cultivation of sugar beet is subject to quotas, but sugar beet farmers nevertheless always plant a few more rows than allocated, because sugar beet is also subject to attack, in particular by a virus which considerably reduces yields. The virus will soon be made harmless by gene technology, and genetically modified sugar beets will be available on the market in the foreseeable future.

For economic reasons it is worth processing the beets as near to the beet fields as possible. At harvest time between 10,000 and 14,000 tonnes of defoliated beets a day arrive at the factory, so transport costs are an important factor. From the end of September to the middle/end of December, the chopping machines, evaporators, and centrifuges are working flat out.

The beets are washed, sliced, and scalded and then placed in the extraction tower. Here the beets give off their sugar, the other substances which are released with them are bound with milk of lime. The clear juice is dehydrated until the sugar crystals form. The centrifuges spin off the syrup

and the drying removes the final residues.

Sugar is now available in all manner of forms, from confectioners' sugar and coffee sugar, to preserving sugar, and brown and white rock sugar. In Germany they all come from the refined end product; sometimes the different processed sugars look almost like the raw product again. A tasty Rhinish specialty is *Grafschafter Goldsaft* from Meckenheim. It consists of a thickened, not completely purified beet syrup, hence the golden color. A slice of dark rye bread with quark and golden syrup is regarded as a definite delicacy. Finicky gourmets spread the syrup on the bread first, although this place is really the quark's due. But when the viscous syrup is spread on the soft quark, it provides too little resistance, and turns the simple act of spreading a slice of bread into a game which exhausts the patience.

Thus the syrup remains hidden under the quark, a kind of Rhine gold whose camouflage does not prevent it from being eaten.

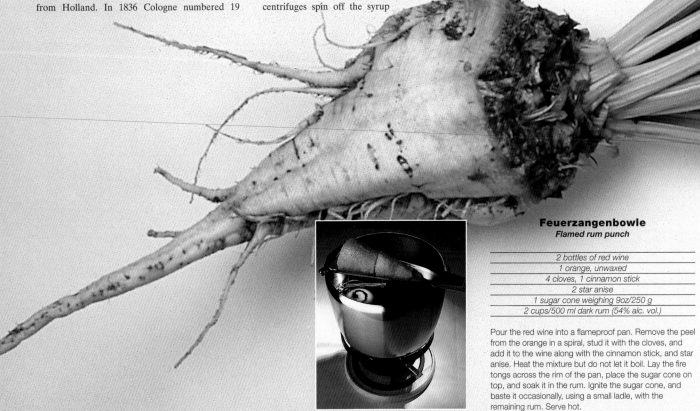

Feuerzangenbowle
Flamed rum punch

2 bottles of red wine	
1 orange, unwaxed	
4 cloves, 1 cinnamon stick	
2 star anise	
1 sugar cone weighing 9oz/250 g	
2 cups/500 ml dark rum (54% alc. vol.)	

Pour the red wine into a flameproof pan. Remove the peel from the orange in a spiral, stud it with the cloves, and add it to the wine along with the cinnamon stick, and star anise. Heat the mixture but do not let it boil. Lay the fire tongs across the rim of the pan, place the sugar cone on top, and soak it in the rum. Ignite the sugar cone, and baste it occasionally, using a small ladle, with the remaining rum. Serve hot.

The sugar beet harvest begins at the end of September. Here the beets are running to seed.

The harvesting is done by machines. 10,000 to 14,000 tonnes of beet a day are delivered to a factory.

If the beets are transported over land, the police warn of debris on the roads.

Golden-yellow *Grafschafter Goldsaft* consists of thickened, not completely purified sugar beet syrup.

Bergisch tea table

Even if the Bergisch tea table might occasionally seem a bit sparse, the *Dröppelminna*, or dribbling Minnie, is always luxuriant. In Bergisch the mighty urn with the spout had to be made out of pewter, long after pewter urns had gone out of fashion elsewhere. It lorded it over the set table in a dignified manner, its bellied fullness alone signifying warmth and comfort.

Such a powerful character would be forgiven its idiosyncrasies, and its name is really just a bit of teasing, because this Minnie would gush. But if the coffee grounds had blocked the valve, the coffee would only come out in dribs and drabs. The invention of the strainer brought an end to this nuisance, only to create a new one. Now the tap, which was rarely closed, dribbled because the coffee grounds no longer helped it to close …

The Dröppelminna is not an original Bergisch invention. Like many other constituents of the tea table, it hails from the west, from the Netherlands, with which lively trade relations existed in the 17th and 18th centuries. Even Bergisch beef cattle originally came from Holland. In return, the famous quality ironware from the Bergisch region was in great demand on the coast. The *Dröppelminna* came from Holland, though, and coffee came from there too.

Even the youngest scion of the tea table worked its way up the Rhine eventually, and by this we mean rice, or rice pudding in particular, as well as the other more or less solid fare offered by Bergisch Heaven. These include white currant bread, waffles and butter, as well as Bergisch dark rye bread, egg flans, quark, and occasionally extremely hearty delicacies such as liver sausage. Some visitors are little pleased by this difficult mix of sweet and sour, but a Bergisch tea table simply offers *Koffendrenken met allem dröm on dran*, or "Coffee to drink with all the trimmings."

The groaning tables of today might easily deceive one into thinking that coffee drinking might have been less prevalent in times of poverty, or in poorer households. If some had "genuine" coffee beans, the others drank "false mocha" made of malt and chicory. If the well-to-do sweetened their coffee with honey, the poor used homemade apple, pear, or sugar beet syrup. The waffles, which to most people are the pièce de résistance on the table, were originally made from oat flour. Even around 1900, only a very few could afford the luxury of making them from wheat flour.

Since the emergence of the tea table in the late 18th century, there have been many changes to the original recipes. For long-established tea table devotees, hot cherries and cream on one's waffles is still considered a new-fangled invention. On the other hand, everyone agrees that the *digestif* is a fitting conclusion. Traditionally made from korn schnaps and blackcurrants, it rounds off a rich meal at the Bergisch tea table in the best possible manner.

The chief personage at the tea table, the "dribbling Minnie."

Waffles
(Illustrated)

1 cup/250 g butter
½ cup/100 g sugar
6 eggs, separated
1 cup/250 ml milk
2½ cups/300 g flour
1 tsp grated lemon rind
Pinch of salt
Splash of oil

Beat together the butter, sugar, and egg yolks until foaming. Gradually beat in the flour and milk. Finally add the lemon rind. Whisk the egg whites with a pinch of salt until very stiff, and fold carefully into the batter. Brush a waffle iron with a little oil. Place portions of batter on the waffle iron and bake until golden brown. Dust the waffles with confectioner's sugar or brush them with jam. The waffles can also be topped with hot cherries and cream.

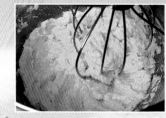

To prepare the waffle batter, beat the butter, sugar, and egg yolks until foaming.

Next gradually beat in the milk and flour, making sure there are no lumps.

The batter should be thick enough to cling to the whisk.

The waffle iron is lightly oiled and heated before the batter is spooned on.

The waffles are baked on the hot iron until golden brown, and served immediately.

Because the Rhineland has always had particularly close trade relations with the Netherlands, *Spekulatius* have to be included. Although the name for these flat, spicy Christmas cookies may originate from the Latin, it reached Germany via the Dutch language.

237

The sweet pleasures of Carnival

Candy

The cry *Kamelle*, or "candy," is reserved for the high point of Carnival, usually coming after the announcement *D'r Zoch kütt* or "the parade is coming." It springs easily to the lips of even foreign revelers, while the equally popular brief cry *Strüüsscher*, or little bouquets, does necessitate a certain command of Rhinish dialect.

From a historical point of view, candy is a late-comer to Carnival. The eve of Lent, or Shrove Tuesday, always had some connection with the so-called *Heischegängen*, or begging rounds. As early as 1403, the Cologne town council had to ban them, because the custom had developed into what was practically highway robbery. This is all irrelevant, because the first mention of a Cologne Carnival dates from 5th March 1341. Around 1500 a nun by the name of Anna wrote down the first Carnival song, and the term *Fastelovend*, or eve of Lent, became established in the 16th century.

The start of Carnival as we know it today dates back to 1823. After the French occupation and initial mistrust of the Prussian overlords, the citizens of Cologne made a fresh start which was simultaneously birth and rebirth. There was a *Festordnendes Comitee*, or celebrations committee, a procession on the Monday before Lent, and meetings and masked balls. The society cap was introduced in 1827, and it is still an indispensable part of the celebrations held by clubs and associations to this day. The first parades still parodied Prussian military drills. In the early days peasant and virgin appeared as representatives of agriculture outside the city walls, or as the symbol of the city (Colonia). The hero Carnival was the jocular fool who lead them all; it was only later that he was transformed into a prince – obviously a concession to the hierarchy of a court, perhaps the Prussian court. However, following the founding of the German Empire, in 1871, the parades stopped making fun of the military.

The years of poverty following both world wars have not succeeded in damping the spirit of Carnival. A festival committee was formed for the first time in 1947, in a Cologne which had suffered terrible destruction, and 25 societies took part. It has been the custom, since 1949, to start Carnival at 11 minutes past the hour of eleven o'clock on November 11. Each November the fools gather at the Alter Markt, not far from Ostermannplatz, named in honor of Willi Ostermann, the great reviver and songwriter of Carnival. Carnival Sunday also has a special highlight in the *Schull- und Veedelszöch*, a parade through the streets organized by local schools and the districts of Cologne. Since 1952, Shrove Tuesday also has a firm place in the festival calendar, because it was then that the first district procession took place in the district of Cologne-Kalk. From 1954 onward the Carnival activities of schools have played a special role in these processions. As if that were not enough, an alternative "ghost procession" has been established on Carnival Saturday. Those who are contemptuous of the "official" Carnival still follow this procession through the city center, making a great racket in their ghostly apparel.

Although, during the 1980s, abstinence from alcohol during Carnival was considered good form, the tendency to get "stinking drunk" has been increasing rapidly for quite some time. Those who once opposed drunkenness during Carnival do not oppose it quite so vociferously now, but the legendary pageantry to dress up in tails is becoming less and less popular.

Everyone unites, along the processional routes, and raises one voice in the cry for *Kamelle*. It is no longer just cream toffees though, which rain down on the revelers; instead they are showered with full-size candy bars and fine chocolate. Frankly, such large-scale shot no longer comes from the canons which are brought along. Things have been better and are better with the *Kamelle*.

Sweet finale

Let's not beat around the bush – even today no one knows why the *Weckmänner*, or bread men, hold their whitish pipes to their bodies like aprons. Generations of young men have smoked fresh ivy and/or dried chestnut leaves in them. In the Westerwald production of them supported a whole branch of industry (clay pipe makers), but how the pipes came to be part of a patterned pastry has remained their secret.

The *Weckmänner* (Rhinish), and *Stutenkerle* (Westphalian), are patterned pastries, or figure pastries. The tasty little figures mostly appear in cake shops around St. Martin's Day, historically the end of the old business year. Originally, though, and up until the turn of the century, they were given as a gift on St Nicholas Day; from the 16th century the saint was in charge of the gifts. At least this explains the male appearance of this popular delicacy. The real New Year also has its own cakes and pastries. In Westphalia they are called

Bollebäuschen, a pet name that could hardly be sweeter or fonder. Bollebäuschen, a type of doughnut, are made from yeast dough and deep fried in hot oil. Even today, older people think they are the most delicious thing on earth. What's right for the noisy New Year celebrations must be right for Carnival. Rhinish Shrove Tuesday doughnuts, though, have a puffier, lighter consistency, because they are made from a kind of choux paste. *Aachener Printen*, on the other hand, are much more solid. Yes, these cookies are also directly associated with New Year, and have the patterned pastries to thank for their existence. The word *Printe* stems, with the pastry itself, from the Netherlands, where *Prent* means "print." The molds for the cookie dough are now only brought out at Christmas. By 1860, though, the square molds were establishing themselves ever more firmly, because in the meantime *Aachener Printen* had acquired a very good reputation, and even foreign markets were embracing these fine cookies. The great distances involved demanded a standardized shape. In the form of a flat, square cookie, it was easier to transport, and also easier to circumvent the limited

business opportunities available at the end of the year. As the "brown gold" became increasingly popular, the cookies also acquired a value-added chocolate coating. Even today, one's teeth still encounter a thin layer of chocolate before doing battle with the hard cookie.

Weckmänner
Pipe men pastries

2 cups/500 g flour
⅓ cup/60 g sugar, 1 tsp salt
2⅓ cakes/40 g compressed fresh yeast
1 cup/250 ml lukewarm milk
¼ cup/60 g butter
2 eggs
⅛ tsp ground turmeric
Flour for the work surface, egg yolk for brushing
Raisins and clay pipes for decoration

Sift the flour, salt, and sugar into a large bowl, and make a well in the center. Crumble the yeast into the milk and allow it to dissolve. Pour the milk into the well, sprinkle a little flour on top, cover, and allow to stand for 15 minutes. Then add the butter, eggs, and turmeric, and mix together to form a smooth dough. Cover the dough and leave to rise for 1 hour. On a floured work surface shape the dough into figures. Line a cookie sheet with baking parchment and place the pastries on it. Brush the pastries with beaten egg yolk, use the raisins to make eyes, and push the clay pipe under the left arm. Bake in a preheated oven at 350 °F/180 °C for 20 minutes or until golden brown.

Ready-made and convenient

Some 35 percent of the 37.5 million households in Germany are one-person households, to the delight of industry. Doesn't every single person need a refrigerator, a mixer, and other items which are otherwise used by families with two or three members? Nutritionists, however, are not happy about this state of affairs. They have ascertained that people living alone eat less well than members of families, in other words they reach for convenience foods rather than preparing fresh vegetables and cooking meat.

Lifestyle magazines, on the other hand, see it as an opportunity to advise singles that they should visit their local supermarkets as a place to make friends with other singles, and in particular that they should frequent the sections where everything is available in convenience form. And of such products there is now an almost infinite range.

The industry which makes life easier for those who are on their own in the kitchen developed at a time when there was no mention of "isolation from society," on the contrary, a population boom was one of the problems in the second half of the 19th century. During this era immense technical, social, agrarian, and political changes took place in Germany. Although decreasingly fewer people worked in agriculture, the acreage under cultivation had increased due to the switch from a three-field system to crop rotation, and in many parts of Germany agricultural production increased by 40 percent. Release of the farmers from the feudal system ended their dependence, but also led to many farmers losing their land. A massive rural migration took place, because work was now needed in the towns and cities, where factories sprang up as part of the burgeoning industrialization. Thus it became impossible for many people to achieve what had been taken for granted in the country – self-sufficiency in food. The industrial workers in the towns had little choice but to relinquish previous nutritional habits, not least because in most workers' families the women also went to work in the factories and after a 12-hour working day had no time left to prepare elaborate meals. And it was not just time which was tight, money was lacking too. For families with many children and workers from the low-paid classes, meat was a rarity – the consequences were protein deficiency and resulting illness and high infant mortality.

The magic words which solved the problem were legumes and pulses. In other words peas and beans which could be planted in greater quantities due to improved agricultural production, which could be transported great distances thanks to improved transport routes, and which could be processed into protein-rich pea and bean flour in the newly-built factories.

The first person to use legumes in the mass production of a foodstuff was the Berlin cook Grünberg, who invented the pea meal sausage in 1872 (see page 98). It still contained a small proportion of bacon, and you could certainly tell by the taste, because soups which were made with legumes (marketed a little later by Knorr and Maggi) tasted horribly bland. The product only became palatable thanks to a trail-blazing invention by Julius Maggi – seasoning liquid. Maggi used the research results of Braconnot and Bercelius who, in 1820 and 1831 respectively, discovered that when protein was broken down into its components, products emerged which not only smelt like meat stock, they tasted like it too. This was the breakthrough. Although Maggi seasoning was made from vegetable protein, it tasted as though it was derived from meat, the very meat which the workers could generally not afford.

Of all the pioneers in the food industry in the 19th century, one man should be mentioned who also pioneered new developments – the chemist Dr August Oetker, the inventor of baking powder. Other people had tried to develop it, including Justus von Liebig, a pioneer in both agrochemicals and nutritional physiology. But Oetker, not for nothing the son of a baker, optimized the raising agent in 1891 and launched it on the market, packed in little envelopes and weighed out precisely for use with a specific quantity of flour.

Another discipline, which at that time was just emerging, also gained in importance with the industrial production and marketing of foodstuffs on a grand scale – advertising. Maggi and Oetker were among the first to recognize its importance. Enamel placards were used for advertising purposes. The advertisements totally complied with the claim of "honesty in advertising," for example, "One major factor in the preparation of Maggi soups is the addition of salt until the soup is tasty, and boiling until the soups are somewhat slimy, which with a fast boil should occur in about 15 minutes."

After this first attempt Julius Maggi left the writing of his advertising copy to a professional, a poor young man by the name of Frank Wedekind. And he now composed "I don't know why I should be so sad. Has a trusty friend deceived me without my knowledge? Is a threatening sword of Damocles hung above my head, or is the mailman approaching with an unlucky letter? I seem to be tortured by a memory, as if I have had a bad dream and my soul is still filled with its terrors. Look there, that's it! I had passed by a shop window and had seen Maggi's bouillon extract and Maggi's nourishing soups on display. I had often heard talk about both of them, but at the time I was short on time and money. Oh, there is help for me after all!"

Henriette Davidis (1801–1876)

She was born the tenth of 13 children in the vicarage at Wetter-Wengern. From 1841 the trained teacher ran a so-called girls' work school in Sprockhövel. "This sphere of activity," according to the *General German Bibliography*, "caused her to consider tending to the further education of young girls and mothers in the course of their daily work, by means of suitable written works." Henriette Davidis was not alone in this thought. A number of women felt impelled, in the mid-19th century, to teach other members of the female sex about household management. For bourgeois housewives during the Biedermeier era, cooking had become an outstanding virtue, and so several editions of books such as Lina's *The Cook as She Should and Must Be. Dedicated to the daughters and women of Germany* or Rosamunda's *The Cook Without Blemish or Reproach* were published. Neither Lina nor Rosamund, however, could compete with Henriette. Her *Practical Cookery Book for Commonplace and Refined Cuisine*, published in 1844, achieved its 39th edition in 1902, and its 76th during the 1960s. The work, which has been constantly updated and translated into many languages, has often had a change of heart under later editors, but the notorious "Take a …" beloved of cookery books has survived all innovation. This ingenious formula has ensured a firm place for Henriette Davidis on the pedestal of German utility literature.

Cigars

Admittedly, nowadays the cigar tends to convey contentment, but previously it could awaken feelings which were completely the opposite. In cartoons it was associated with a vulgar capitalist just as inevitably as a bowler hat and bag of money. Prior to 1848, however, the cigar was an accessory instead for a completely different sociological group. The hotheads of Vormärz clamped cigars between their teeth as a sign of their revolutionary fervor. Cigar in mouth, they announced their distrust of the pipe-smoking middle-class men whose preferred dress was the frock coat. And even the young Bertolt Brecht (1898–1956) discovered that, in his role as a scourge of the middle classes, a Havana in the mouth suited him rather well. Today, in largely smoke-free times, the cigar is enjoying a renaissance, not as a political statement, but as a status symbol.

The *Brockhaus Encyclopedia* of 1809 observed that "This behavior which is used in Latin America instead of the pipe is beginning to be very common, even in our region." This could only suit the town of Bünde. The cigar manufacturers migrated to the area around Ravensburg for several reasons, not least being the poverty of the local population, because making cigars is manual work, and manual work which does not pay much. In this region, with its weak infrastructure, there were plenty of unemployed people. Previously many had kept their heads above water by weaving linen, but they had been deprived of that living by cotton weaving in factories. They had no other choice but to enter into service with the cigar manufacturers. In addition to the factories in Bünde itself, the businessmen established numerous branches in the surrounding villages, in addition to a large number of homeworkers.

The homeworker's cigar-making table usually stood in the kitchen. It was called the "piano," due to its resemblance to that instrument which furnished better households. Here skilled hands rolled the top layer around the prepared wick, which usually came from the factories where the wick makers shaped by hand small pieces of leaves that had the stalk and ribs removed. These were held together by the enveloping layer, and several hours spent in the press.

In 1843 the first cigar factory was established in neighboring Ennigloh. At the start of 1856 the Wellensiek and Steinmeister Company took over production, marking the beginning of the success story. In 1864 the factories in Bünde employed 1000 workers, and another 2000 in the subsidiaries, but the number of home workers is unknown. They produced a total of 100 million cigars. Even today, after automation and restructuring, the town of Bünde still produces one third of all the cigars manufactured in Germany.

Even the state, which receives all the duty on tobacco, and which has always valued smoking as an important source of income, has honored the significant role of Bünde in its own way. In 1993 the Federal Republic of Germany chose the town for the head office of its central collection office for the so-called seal tax, which still contributes more than 10 billion Euros a year to the state's needy coffers. Bünde has thus become an administrative center, and so, in a way, is a capital city.

Naturally the community in eastern Westphalia realizes what it owes to the cigar industry. There is an (admittedly rather provincial) monument to the first two factories, and the brick tobacco store of 1896 is under a preservation order. And finally there is the German Tobacco and Cigar Museum in the beautiful Striedeckschen Hof on Fünfhausenstrasse. The Bünde giant cigar is on display there: 5¼ feet (1.60 meters) long, weighing 20 pounds (9 kilograms), with a smoking time of 600 hours. Doubtless an exhibit which would cause many a smoker's lung to tremble with delight.

Right: the cigar maker's table. Low-paid home workers rolled the top layers around the ready prepared "wick."

The top sheet, which is cut from a whole tobacco leaf, is placed around the wick.

It is wrapped around the pressed wick, which is made from leaves with the ribs removed and torn into pieces.

Experience and great skill are needed to roll the top sheet into a firm casing.

Finally the remainder of the top sheet is twisted into a tip.

This tip has to be capped …

… before the cigar is placed in its case.

Hamburg
Schwerin
Bremen
Berlin
Hanover
Potsdam
Magdeburg
Düsseldorf
Dresden
Bonn
Erfurt
Wiesbaden
Mainz
Saarbrücken
Stuttgart
Munich

KLAUS VIEDEBANTT
Hesse

A native of Hesse, the writer Rudolf Krämer-Badoni, is supposed to have said that "the people of Hesse, as a tribe, do not exist." This statement contains more than a grain of truth: the state was pieced together in 1946 from land which had formerly belonged to the ruling princes, the Church, and the free imperial city of the Holy Roman Empire. The people of northern Hesse, accustomed to poor soil and poverty throughout their history, have little in common with the people of southern Hesse, who have been spoiled by the sun and the fertile Rhine valley, and this difference is naturally also reflected in the cuisine of the various regions. Whereas the northerners tried to make the best of potatoes, the southerners were forever following trends introduced by the merchants traveling through the area. It comes as no surprise, therefore, that the two specialties that have put Hesse firmly on the culinary map – green sauce and Frankfurter sausages – originate from Frankfurt.

In ancient times the Limes, the line of fortifications marking the border of the Holy Roman Empire that split the world in half, followed the course of the River Main that divides northern from southern Hesse. The influence of the rich metropolis of Frankfurt and the city of Wiesbaden, the Roman spa town that became Hesse's capital, was constantly radiating southwards. The people in the north tend to be taciturn; the stereotype of the "chattering Hessian" only applies to those in the south. Northerners cultivated the traditional way of life – it was no wonder that the famous Hessian collectors of fairy tales, the brothers Grimm, were increasingly successful the further north they traveled. The other great intellectuals from this state gravitated towards the Frankfurt metropolis: Goethe and Büchner, the acerbic Georg Christoph Lichtenberg, Nobel prizewinners Otto Hahn and Adam Opel, to name but a few.

The feature that does unite Hesse is its landscape – forested uplands stretching from the Reinhardswald in the north to the Odenwald in the south. Hesse is richly endowed with forests, and is bordered to the west by fertile vineyards and to the east by the fascinating barren moorland of the Rhön. It is a state that offers a feast for both the eye and the palate.

Left: Hesse is a land of cherries; in the Witzenhausen region alone there are 160,000 cherry trees.

Cookery as a free art form

"Cookery is a medium that is equal in value to the other high art forms such as music, painting, or poetry." This is the thesis put forward with academic vigor by Peter Kubelka, who has been professor of "film studies and cookery as an art form" at the Städelschule, Frankfurt's academy of arts, since 1980. Kubelka, an occasionally roguish character, who was born in Vienna in 1934 and has a film industry background, can remember the era when the cinema had to fight for recognition as an art form. Now he is trying to achieve the same status for cookery. "Cookery," he says, "is the most ancient branch of the arts. Older than cave painting. Cookery is the mother of philosophy, of chemistry, of physics. Cookery is poetry, transformation."

As a result, his students not only learn about film, but cookery too. When funds are available, they sometimes even cook for the people of Frankfurt. To the annoyance of the painters, a studio in the venerable art institute has been converted into a kitchen, so the younger generation can learn the basics of the trade before moving on to elaborate free composition. "Anton Brückner was able to improvize on the organ because he was familiar with and could play everything in the organ repertoire. Anyone who does not know how long to cook a joint of beef, what it is exactly, and what should be eaten with it, will achieve nothing, not even shopping at the supermarket." Kubelka, the son of a musician whose grandmother worked as a cook for a parish priest, has no desire to produce gourmets. "It is a matter of complete indifference to me what vintage of red wine or white wine should be drunk with a salmon steak … we have to go back to the basic ingredients and get them right again." Who could seriously disagree with this opinion, so cheerily expressed?

The market gardeners of Oberrad ensure there is no seasonal shortage of salad vegetables in Frankfurt.

It is harvest time all the year round in the greenhouses. Parsley is the sole winter import.

Green sauce

"Which seven herbs are used to make *Grüne Sauce*?" is a favorite question in Frankfurt. The question is easily answered at the greengrocer's, for the secret ingredients are listed on the traditional white wrapping paper: borage, chervil, cress, parsley, burnet, sorrel, and chives.

So far everyone is agreed, but this is where the arguments begin. Is it permissible to add dill to *Grie Soss*, as this vitamin-packed delicacy is known in the local dialect? Yes, is the answer given in a pamphlet produced by the Palmengarten in Frankfurt, an institution recognized for its expertise on everything that is green and grows. No, say the market gardeners in the Oberrad district of the city – and they are the leading authority on *Grüne Sauce*, since they provide the herbs from their greenhouses all year round. Parsley alone has to be imported in the winter months, from France or Italy. Some people substitute young spinach in the appropriate season, while others regard this as the ultimate culinary sin. Which leads us to the question of the origins of this accompaniment to beef, fish, and boiled potatoes. On this point, for once, the various sauce factions in Frankfurt are united: the specialty comes from Italy, where it is marketed as *salsa verde*, a sauce made from herbs in vinegar and oil. Frankfurt people are not, however, prepared to tolerate Mediterranean frugality: they shake their vitamin cocktail using sour cream, with mayonnaise as an alternative for high days and holidays, and yoghurt for diet days. Egg is also an essential ingredient in this health-giving combination of herbs, either in the form of egg yolk, or – more frequently – hard-boiled and finely chopped, according to preference. The addition of diced gherkins is generally regarded as a lapse of taste, but the experts continue to debate the addition of onions at great length.

However, all this pales into insignificance when the vexed question arises as to whether or not the much-quoted "greatest son of the city of Frankfurt," Goethe, would have been familiar with *Grüne Sauce*. One camp is adamant that the "prince of poets" was extremely fond of it, especially the version prepared by his mother. This is nothing but idle supposition, counters the opposing faction, who maintain that *salsa verde* was first introduced to the Main region with the arrival of the Bolongaro family, a rich Italian mercantile dynasty, after Goethe's time. Before that, no cook had ever mentioned *Grüne Sauce* in a collection of recipes, not even Goethe's mother. But what is certain is that, even despite this argument, where *Grüne Sauce* and Goethe are concerned, the exchange of words is still far from reaching a conclusion.

The blend has to be exactly right: just seven herbs are used to make Frankfurt's specialty, Grüne Sauce.

Borage, chervil, cress, parsley, burnet, sorrel, and chives are the ingredients for Grüne Sauce.

The yolks of three hard-boiled eggs are passed through a sieve, and the egg white is finely chopped.

The egg yolk, mustard, and shallots are blended with vinegar, salt, pepper, and sunflower oil to make a sauce.

The finely chopped herbs are stirred into the chopped egg whites, crème fraîche, and sauce.

Grüne Sauce
Green sauce – Basic recipe

3 hard-boiled eggs
3 tbsp mild wine vinegar
1 tbsp medium hot mustard
Salt and pepper
Sugar
6 tbsp sunflower oil
1 cup/250 g crème fraîche
2 small shallots, finely diced
1 large bunch fresh herbs (sorrel, chervil, chives, parsley, burnet, cress, borage)

Press the egg yolks through a sieve and chop the egg whites finely. Make a sauce by mixing the wine vinegar, mustard, salt, pepper, sugar, and sunflower oil with the sieved egg yolks. Fold in the crème fraîche, and stir in the shallots and chopped egg whites. Wash the herbs, shake dry, and chop finely. Add to the sauce and leave to stand for 1 hour. *Grüne Sauce* tastes good as an accompaniment to cooked meat, hard-boiled eggs, jacket potatoes, pan-fried potatoes, and asparagus.

Grüne Sauce
Green sauce – an alternative version

⅔ cup/150 ml light cream
2 tsp hot mustard
Salt and pepper
Pinch of sugar
1 small onion, finely chopped
4 gherkins, finely chopped
2 hard-boiled eggs, chopped
1 bunch fresh herbs for Grüne Sauce

Mix together the mayonnaise, sour cream, and cream until smooth. Season with mustard, salt, pepper, and sugar. Stir in the chopped onion, gherkin, and egg. Wash the herbs, shake dry, and chop finely. Stir into the sauce and leave to stand for at least 1 hour.

The seven herbs

Borage: *Borago officinalis* is reputed to make people feel happy and to give them courage. For this reason the Crusaders were presented with a potion containing the sky-blue flowers of the plant before they set off.
Chervil: *Anthriscus cerefolium* contains vitamin C, carotene, iron, and magnesium. Chervil is highly prized in haute cuisine because of its flavor, which is reminiscent of parsley and myrrh.
Cress: *Lepidium sativum*, garden cress, is a cultivated form of watercress and has a more fiery taste than its wild relative.
Parsley: *Petroselinum crispum* was rated highly long ago by the ancient Greeks, although at that stage it was not yet used in cooking. It was used to crown victors and – according to Homer – as food for the horses.
Burnet: *Sanguisorba officinalis* is among the first green shoots to appear in spring. The young leaves have a slightly sharp taste, rather like cucumber.
Sorrel: *Rumex acetosa* grows wild on acid soils and is sour-tasting, as its Latin name implies.
Chives: *Allium schoenoprasum* belongs to the onion family and is said to have been brought to the West by Marco Polo.

Dishes that go with Grüne Sauce

Rhönforelle blau mit Grüner Sauce
Rhön trout with green sauce
(Illustrated below)

4 trout, ready for cooking
2 cups/½ l white wine
½ cup/125 ml wine vinegar
1 onion, studded with 1 bay leaf and two cloves
4 peppercorns
Salt

Rinse the trout under running water, leave to drain and tie in a semi-circle with kitchen string. Bring the white wine to a boil with 8 cups (2 l) water, the vinegar, the spiced onion, the peppercorns, and salt, and simmer for approximately 10 minutes. Place the trout side by side in a large pan, pour over the boiling stock, cover, and cook over a low heat for 15 minutes. Make the *Grüne Sauce* according to the basic recipe and serve separately. Potatoes boiled in their skins are a good accompaniment to this dish.

Spargel aus Lampertsheim mit Grüner Sauce
Lampertsheim asparagus with green sauce
(Illustrated below)

2 large bunches/1 kg asparagus
Salt
Pinch of sugar
1 tbsp butter

Wash the asparagus, peel, and trim the stems. Bring an asparagus pan full of salted water to a boil with a pinch of sugar and the butter. Place the asparagus in the boiling water and cook for approximately 20 minutes until just tender. Lift the cooked asparagus out of the water and drain well. Arrange on a warmed plate. Serve with the *Grüne Sauce* and potatoes boiled in their skins.

Tafelspitz mit Grüner Sauce
Boiled rump of beef
(Illustrated right)

2 lb 3 oz/1 kg boiled rump (haunch of beef)
2 marrow bones
1 onion, studded with 1 bay leaf and 2 cloves
5 peppercorns
4 allspice berries
1 tsp salt
Soup vegetables (2 carrots, 1 leek, 2 celery stalks, parsley)

Wash the beef. Place in a pot with the marrow bones and pour over sufficient cold water to cover the meat completely. Add the spiced onion, peppercorns, allspice berries, salt, and the soup vegetables. Bring to a boil and carefully remove the scum. Cover and cook until tender over a low heat for approximately 2 hours. Lift the cooked boiled rump out of the stock and slice, not too thickly. Serve with *Grüne Sauce*. Boiled or pan-fried potatoes are a suitable accompaniment to this dish.

Rhön trout

Asparagus

Gekochte Eier und Bratkartoffeln mit Grüner Sauce

Boiled eggs and pan-fried potatoes with green sauce

(Illustrated below)

8 potatoes, boiled in their skins the previous day
2 tbsp clarified butter
2 onions
Salt and pepper
8 eggs

Slice the boiled potatoes evenly. Heat the clarified butter in a heavy iron pan and sauté the potato slices in it for about 5 minutes. Peel the onions, cut in half and slice. Add to the potatoes and turn. Season with salt and pepper, and fry on all sides over a medium heat until golden brown. Boil the eggs until the yolks are just set. Serve the fried potatoes with the eggs and *Grüne Sauce*.

Food on the wing

It was Loriot who acquainted us with the fact that humans are the only living creatures that consume a hot meal in flight. And it is thanks to this that Hesse has become the home of the largest kitchen in Germany – the operation run by the Lufthansa subsidiary LSG/Sky Chefs. Approximately 70,000 meals are prepared daily, ranging from sandwiches for the hordes of tourists to caviar suppers for the first class passengers. Around 40 international airlines use the Lufthansa catering facilities every day to prepare food according to their own particular preferences, with the result that curry chefs from the Indian subcontinent cook in Frankfurt alongside Japanese sushi specialists. For their airborne menus, however, the latter are obliged to substitute marinated fish for raw fish, since every meal has to be prepared in such a way that it will not spoil in the interval between cooking and being served in the air. Around 80 percent of all dishes are cooked for economy class passengers, which means that they must be costed accurately to a tenth of a cent. In addition, the competition is stiff, so more and more depends on the imagination of the head chef. Although chicken is cheap, it is ubiquitous, and so it is increasingly important to cook it in interesting ways without driving the costs sky-high. Novel accompaniments are one option – this is how broccoli became a popular vegetable in Germany, for example. And it now seems quite probable that green asparagus will take to the air in a big way.

Green Sauce from Frankfurt

Boiled eggs and pan-fried potatoes

Boiled rump of beef

Riesling

The winegrowing area of Hesse consists of the Hessische Bergstrasse and Rheingau regions. The producers of the Rheingau account for only two percent of the total of German wine production. The Rheingau winegrowing area, which is located on the banks of the Rhine between Hochheim and Rüdesheim, and which includes the Lorch and Assmannshausen vineyards, is extremely small. However, the wines produced from the 6712 acres (2716 hectares) of vineyards, with such musical-sounding names as Schloss Johannisberg, Schloss Vollrad, Kloster Eberbach, and August Kessler, are true giants as regards bouquet and flavor – some of them rank among the best wines in the world.

Vines were already being cultivated by the Romans in the Rheingau district, where the flow of the Rhine from south to north is interrupted by one brief diversion from east to west nearly 20 miles (30 kilometers) in length. From the 11th to the 13th centuries, the slopes of the Taunus Mountains on the north bank of the Rhine were cleared under the direction of monks from the twelve monasteries in the Rheingau. The vineyards therefore lay in the lee of the cold north

winds, facing southward towards the sun. These conditions, combined with a long growth period, the dry and open soils based on gravel, sand, and slate, and the warmth provided by the Rhine, are ideal for cultivating Riesling grapes in particular.

The abbots of Johannisberg and Eberbach rationalized and perfected grape cultivation in the Rheingau at the beginning of the 12th century. The Cistercian monks in Eberbach created space for storage and for processing; they improved the quality by selecting grape varieties carefully, and their expertise in cellar management and preliminary commercial initiatives laid the foundations for the future high standard of wines from the Rheingau. It was only toward the end of the monastic era that the Benedictine monks of the Johannisberg monastery made their contribution: they introduced novel methods of harvesting grapes and making wine that are still familiar today, including concepts such as "Spätlese," (1775), meaning late harvest, "Auslese," (1787), meaning harvest of selected, very ripe bunches, and "Edelfäule" (noble rot).

The Rheingau winegrowers, who are well known for their obstinacy, remained loyal to these naturally sweet and dry wines, even when an international trend towards sweet white wines emerged after World War I. These thin, flat white wines, sweetened

with unfermented must or even sugar, which were marketed elsewhere in Germany as Riesling wines, taste like caricatures of Riesling wine and have done a great deal of damage to the reputation of German Riesling throughout the world. The tradition in the Rheingau of monocultural Riesling grape cultivation dates from 1720. Furthermore, by contrast with other regions, the Riesling grape has never been replaced in the Rheingau to any significant extent by grape varieties that are easier to grow, have higher yields, and therefore have greater commercial viability. The section of the river on the Rheingau river banks known as "Johannisberg" still grows the largest proportion of Riesling grapes (82 percent) of all the vineyards in Germany. In addition, the teaching and research institute at Geisenheim, having spent years breeding clones that are resistant to the vine weevil, became the largest promulgator of Riesling grapes in the Federal Republic of Germany.

The Rheingau, and in particular the vineyards around Lorch and Assmannshausen, also produces small amounts of very fine Spätburgunder wines made from the pinot noir grape, the strength and velvety texture of which are comparable with the best from the Côte d'Or. In any event, the top Rheingau Rieslings command record prices at wine auctions.

Sekt

"There you lie, in the subterranean gloom, and there in your depths the sparkling golden juice silently clears and ripens, destined to make many a heart beat faster and many a pair of eyes shine more brightly." These are the words of Felix Krull, the jolliest of Thomas Mann's heroes, as he surveys all the bottles of "Loreley Extra Cuvée" maturing in his father's champagne cellars. The most famous confidence trickster in world literature is in no doubt about the purpose of his father's stock – to spread "intoxication, light-heartedness, and desire." An advertising executive writing slogans for Sekt, the German name for champagne, might have expressed this rather differently, but the message would have remained essentially the same. As a native of the area between Eltville, Wiesbaden, and Hochheim, Felix Krull is the perfect ambassador for Sekt. Some of the best and most famous German sparkling wine cellars, of which there are more than a thousand, are found in this triangle, for example Fürst von Metternich, Henkell, Mathäus Müller, and Schloss Vaux. After the Rhineland Palatinate, Hesse is the second largest producer of Sekt in Germany, and has played its part in making Germany the largest producer of sparkling wines worldwide, outranking even France, the country of champagne. The producers have an impressively large domestic market to fall back on – Germans are the greatest drinkers of champagne-style wine in the world, with an annual consumption of just over 10.5 pints (5 liters) per person.

In view of this it comes as no surprise to find that there is a pipeline devoted exclusively to Sekt production that runs for 930 yards beneath the streets of Eltville, between the station and the building whose façade bears the curved twin letters MM, trade mark of the Mathäus Müller wine-producing establishment. Pure wine that has arrived at the station in railroad tankers flows through the pipeline. The wine used for Sekt production comes mainly from Italy, France, and of course Germany. Since the Riesling grape that flourishes in the Rheingau is particularly good for making Sekt, a sparkling wine production centre grew up here alongside the first German Sekt-producing operations around 1830. To produce sparkling wine, the wine has to undergo a secondary fermentation. This requires the addition of sugar and yeast, which together start the wine fermenting furiously, either in a large tank or in the bottle. The sweetness of the Sekt is then regulated by the addition of cane sugar and must, while the yeast is removed. The quality of Sekt is determined by the wines used to make it (although expensive wines alone do not necessarily guarantee good Sekt) and the skill of the cellar master. And many a connoisseur prefers a top German Sekt to champagne.

The carbon dioxide produced during secondary fermentation occurs as a result of adding yeast.

In order for the yeast to settle, the bottles must be stored neck-down. They are shaken and turned by hand.

The yeast that has collected in the neck of the bottle is frozen and shoots out when released.

After the addition of the replenishment "dosage" (sugar, wine or must) the bottle is corked and stored.

The ideal glass for Sekt has a tall stem and an elongated goblet. It curves slightly inwards at the top to capture the aromas.

Champagne breakfast with Sekt

Two things are essential for a "romantic weekend," as advertised by grand German hotels: a candlelit dinner, and a champagne breakfast – or so it would appear from the various brochures. But a private breakfast can also be enhanced by laying the breakfast table with champagne flutes alongside the marmalade jar.

No other alcoholic drink has managed to gain social acceptance at the breakfast table between the coffee and muesli milk, and be acknowledged as a good way to start the day: the effervescent liquid is regarded as a stimulant for the circulatory system, and thus practically qualifies as a medicine. How, then, can it be thought a sin, when an elderly aunt needs to drink a glass of Sekt in the morning after rising? According to the French system, the Sekt normally served with scrambled eggs and bacon is classified as "brut" (to which the maximum permissible amount of sugar added is six grams per liter); the other classifications are "dry" (maximum 35 grams), "demi-sec" (maximum 50 grams), and "doux" (over 50 grams). Here are a few more scraps of information to enliven the breakfast conversation: wine bearing the label "Deutscher Sekt" must be made exclusively from German wines. If the label also specifies a region, then the basic wines must come exclusively from that wine-growing region, and if a "Lagensekt" is promised, then at least 85 percent of the wine must come from a specific location and the rest from the same region. The 85 percent rule also applies to vintage Sekt, and Sekt made from a single grape variety.

However, the most important thing is that the drink taken with the first meal of the day should taste good.

Cooking with wine

Gestowtes Kalbfleisch

Pan-braised veal

(Illustrated left)

- 1⅔ cups/400 ml Rheingau Riesling wine
- 1 onion, studded with 1 bay leaf and 2 cloves
- Soup vegetables (2 carrots, 1 leek, 2 celery stalks, parsley), coarsely chopped
- Grated zest of 1 lemon
- 4 peppercorns
- 5 allspice berries
- 2 lb 3 oz/1 kg veal tenderloin
- Salt and pepper
- 2 tbsp lard
- 1 cup/250 ml cream
- ⅛ tsp ground nutmeg
- Pinch of sugar

To prepare the marinade, bring the Riesling to a boil with the spiced onion, soup vegetables, lemon zest, peppercorns, and allspice berries. Remove from the heat and leave to cool. Wash the veal tenderloin, lay in a dish and pour over the marinade. Cover and leave to stand overnight in a cool place. Next day remove the meat from the marinade, dry, and rub with salt and pepper. Heat the lard in a braising pan and brown the meat quickly on all sides. Pour in the marinade. Cover and simmer gently over a low heat for 1 hour. Then pour in the cream and season the sauce with nutmeg, sugar, pepper, and salt. Simmer for a further 20–30 minutes. Lift the meat out of the sauce and cut into slices. Press the sauce through a sieve and serve separately.

Winzersuppe

Vintner's soup

(Illustrated centre)

- 2 lb 3 oz/1 kg pork shoulder
- 2 tbsp lard
- Salt and pepper
- ½ tsp thyme
- ½ tsp caraway
- 1 bay leaf
- 4 potatoes
- Small bunch of celery, 2 carrots, 2 baby white turnips, 1 parsley root, 2 onions, and 1 leek, all sliced
- 3 cups/750 ml Rheingau Riesling wine
- 4 tbsp chopped parsley

Cut the pork shoulder into cubes. Heat the lard in a casserole and brown the meat quickly. Pour in 4 cups water and season with salt, pepper, thyme, caraway, and the bay leaf. Cover and cook for 30 minutes. Meanwhile peel the potatoes, wash and cut into slices. Add to the meat with the rest of the vegetables and cook for a further 20 minutes. Add the Riesling, bring back to boil and season with salt, pepper, and thyme. Pour into a rustic soup tureen and garnish with parsley.

Woihinkelche (Huhn in Wein)

Chicken cooked in wine

(Illustrated below right)

- 2 small roasting chickens
- ¼ cup/60 g butter
- 4 shallots
- 2 cloves of garlic
- 20 grapes, peeled and seeded
- 4 oz/100 g dried beef, cut into strips barely ½ inch (1 cm) thick
- 12 small button mushroom heads
- 1⅔ cup/400 ml Rheingau brandy
- 2 cups/500 ml Rhinegau Riesling wine
- Salt and pepper
- 2 sprigs rosemary
- 1 bay leaf
- 2 cups/500 ml cream
- ¾ cup/200 ml chicken stock
- 2 tbsp chopped chervil

Wash the roasting chickens, pat dry and cut into portions. Melt the butter in a heavy pan and brown the chicken pieces on all sides. Peel the shallots and garlic. Add to the chicken portions the grapes, dried beef strips, and mushrooms, and flame with the brandy. Pour in the Riesling and season with the salt, pepper, rosemary, and the bay leaf. Add the cream and the chicken stock. Simmer for 10–15 minutes. Lift the chicken pieces out of the sauce and set aside in a warm place. Boil the sauce to reduce it to the desired consistency. Arrange the chicken with the sauce on a warmed plate, garnish with chervil, and serve immediately.

Pan-braised veal

Vintner's soup

Rieslingsabayon
Riesling zabaglione
(Illustrated below)

4 egg yolks
4 tbsp sugar
1 cup/250 ml Rheingau Riesling wine
Grated zest of ½ lemon
⅛ tsp cinnamon

Beat the egg yolks with the sugar and a little hot water in a basin to form a smooth, white cream. Heat a little water in a pan and suspend the bowl containing the cream in the steam above the boiling water. Slowly pour in the Riesling and beat vigorously with a whisk until the cream is foaming and nearly stiff. Beat in the lemon zest and the cinnamon and remove the bowl from the pan of boiling water. Continue beating until the zabaglione is just lukewarm. Pour into dessert dishes and serve immediately.

Riesling zabaglione

Brandy

There is an old rhyme which goes something like this: "Hi-di-hi and hi-de-ha, brandy's good for cholera." Despite its grammatical shortcomings (brandy is supposed to act as an *antidote* to cholera), this rhyme is nevertheless historically accurate. Brandy was originally a medicine, thought to have originated in the monasteries as a result of the monks' efforts to concentrate wine in order to increase its healing powers. As the intoxicant medicine could also be distilled from other fruit, grain, and roots, all such products were referred to as brandy, even though the distillation vessel might not have contained a single grape. Brandy was termed "aqua vitae," the water of life. It was not drunk for pleasure in the Middle Ages, but was taken as a medicine, after those versed in the arts of healing had added herbs or other substances according to the nature of the affliction.

But of course it did not escape the notice of those members of the human race devoted to the pursuit of pleasure that enjoyment could be derived from this medicine without necessarily having to suffer first, and as a result – probably from the 14th century onward – innovative attempts at distilling were made using all kinds of plants to produce high-percentage alcohol products. The authorities did not approve at all of the wild carryings-on in disreputable establishments, since their subjects' productivity and respect for the ruling classes were reduced in equal measure.

It was not until cognac, the French cousin of distilled wine brandy, appeared on the scene that brandy was able to recover its stylish image. The winemakers on the Rhine were also quick to take up distilling. They soon discovered that a good wine does not necessarily make a good brandy, and for this reason German distillers use mostly Italian or French wines. Asbach, for example, which is surrounded by the vineyards of Rüdesheim, does not use local wines. Incidentally, it was Hugo Asbach who coined the German term for brandy, "Weinbrand," after the Germans were forbidden under the terms of the Treaty of Versailles in 1919 to call the brandy they produced "cognac."

Everything hinges upon the wine. Although the bouquet should be preserved during the distillation process, noxious alcohols and other undesirable substances should be virtually burned off. The classical production sequence consists of pre-heating, distillation, and cooling phases. During distillation, the most important phase, the wine mixture is heated carefully in copper vessels to a temperature of 173 °F (78.3 °C). Since alcohol evaporates at 172 °F (78 °C), but water does not evaporate until it reaches 212 °F (100 °C), the alcohol vapor can be collected and condensed again in a cooler. This process is repeated several times to produce the distillate. The art of the master distiller consists in preserving in the distillate the substances that impart a bouquet to the wine. In order that it can mature and acquire its golden brown color, the spirit is stored in oak casks. Brandy in small wooden casks must be stored for at least six months, in larger casks for a minimum of twelve months. Then the differently flavored distillates are blended to achieve the characteristic flavor of the various brands. The strength is then lowered to between 36 and 38 percent alcohol by volume.

Such casks never have a perfect seal, however, and a fair amount of the brandy is lost through evaporation while it matures. A large distillery would be able to fill about 1.5 million bottles a year with the brandy that evaporates into the air. Which means that if one breathes in deeply in a distillery, one is inhaling pure brandy.

Chicken cooked in wine

Frankfurter sausages

The people of Frankfurt regard some of the sausages sold around the world under their name – Frankfurters – as a disgrace: bland, of questionable origin and with dubious fillings, which at best bear some resemblance to "Wiener," or Viennese sausages. Genuine Frankfurter sausages are in fact a delicacy – sausages intended for boiling, made from pure, generously spiced pork meat and 30 percent strong-flavored back bacon. The filling is put into skins made from gut – fine sheep intestines – and the sausages are "cold" smoked until they are golden yellow. It was on account of this delicate smoky taste that the "calibre" or diameter of the sausages was reduced in 1890 to a maximum of just under an inch (24 millimeters) to permit maximum penetration of the smoke.

This leads us to consider the history of the global success enjoyed by the Frankfurter sausage. Its date of birth is unknown, but its birthplace was probably the "Schirn" district. This is first mentioned in 1268: it lay between the Römerberg and Dom districts and was the only place in Frankfurt where medieval butchers were permitted to sell their wares. We know from historical reports of the coronation of Maximilian II in 1562 that "Bratwerscht" was already being used as a stuffing for the coronation oxen roasted for the emperor and his people. At that time "Brat" – the German word for roast – signified any kind of sausage filling, and had nothing to do with the method of preparation. The name "Frankfurter" was bestowed by satisfied customers outside Frankfurt,

By chance, Frankfurter sausages inspired America's "hot dogs" – those sausages wrapped in a limp bread roll, with a flavor derived mainly from tomato ketchup and mild mustard. Because these supposedly German sausages reminded a consumer of the curved back of a German dachshund, or sausage dog, they became known as "hot dogs."

and the butchers were happy to adopt it. Success, however, attracted plagiarists, one of whom in particular made a name for himself: this was the butcher Johann Georg Lahner, who had learned his trade on the River Main and who in 1805 made his own sausages in Vienna, which were known as "Wiener," or Viennese sausages. But even there, sausages with a more refined taste continue to be called "Frankfurters."

Nothing changed as a result of the important victory won in 1929 by the butchers of Frankfurt before the Berlin Supreme Court, which stipulated that only sausages produced in the Frankfurt economic area can be called "Frankfurters." This ruling was confirmed in 1955 by the German Federal Supreme Court. Included in this area is the suburb of Neu-Isenburg, where the first

Frankfurter sausage factory was opened in 1860. Today most Frankfurters are still made in Neu-Isenburg. A further important date in the history of the "world star" – as local poet Heinz P. Müller calls the Frankfurter – is 1887, which marks the first successful attempt to preserve these slender sausages. Previously, in spite of light smoking, they could only be kept for a limited period of time and were therefore only eaten in winter. From 1887 on, Frankfurters were able to compete for honors at far-flung exhibitions. The gold medals won in 1893 at the world exhibition in Chicago were merely the prelude; awards in San Francisco, Paris, and other cities followed.

The sausages only develop their prize-winning taste, however, if they are cooked properly. After simmering in hot water for eight minutes they should be served with mustard on warmed plates. They are always served in pairs, and are eaten, not with a knife and fork, but with the fingers.

The beef sausage with a double-barreled name

Frankfurt was once called, with great respect, "Little Jerusalem," not just because the largest Jewish community in Germany lived there on the river Main, but also because the Jews always made decisive cultural and economic contributions, from the Rothschilds to Ludwig Landmann, who served his city as mayor for nine years before the Nazis hounded him out.

The Jewish way of life was always a part of everyday life in Frankfurt – and of course it also played a role in the economy. Frankfurt butchers were, however, unable to sell the popular Frankfurter sausages to Jews, as they were made from pork. When Karl Gref and Wilhelmine Völsing founded their butcher shop in 1894 in the old part of the city, near the Jewish quarter, they evidently also considered how they could entice their Jewish neighbors into their shop. A sausage that was as good as a Frankfurter, but made with beef instead of pork, was to provide the solution. The "Rindsworscht," or beef sausage, made from the best bull meat, became a success story for Frankfurt, losing none of its popularity even in the days when "mad cow disease" is constantly in the headlines. This was primarily due to Gref-Völsing, whose name is "world-famous in Frankfurt," according to the double-edged compliment that is typical of the area. These two butchers are remembered for the beef sausage that bears their name. Around 100,000 "Gref-Völsings" are produced daily and distributed to butchers' shops, restaurants, and snack kiosks in the Rhine-Main area. The traditional sausage business is now managed by the fourth generation of the founders' heirs and is established on the Hanauer Landstrasse, where blue-collar manual workers and Armani-clad advertising executives eat their beef sausages side by side in perfect harmony.

Although the special blend of spices remains a trade secret, the huge vat in which the sausage expert prepares his mixture is open to inspection. The beef must contain a maximum of 30 percent fat when it is minced – using dry ice, to preserve the protein in the mixture. Phosphates are frowned upon, as is deep-frozen meat – the bull carcasses always arrive fresh from the slaughterhouse.

A treat for the stomach

There is a saying in the Frankfurt dialect to the effect that the sausage known as "Schwartenmagen" has equal status among sausages as a king among princes, as a result of which the Frankfurt version of the sausage became known as the "Ferschte der Werschte," or "prince of sausages." It is no wonder, then, that Frankfurt's prince of poets should also have been particularly fond of the prince of sausages. Goethe had them sent to him regularly by his mother, Aja, who had a secret recipe – unfortunately lost – which she did not disclose to anyone, not even the countess of Weimar. A love of Schwartenmagen sausages was evidently one of the Olympian writer's most abiding passions. Only a month before the end of his life, the 83-year old native of Frankfurt, who remained devoted to the city of his birth only in culinary matters, asked Marianne von Willemer to send him some of the local specialty.

Schwartenmagen – the words mean "rind and stomach" – is found throughout Hesse, with slightly different variations in flavor. It originated from the slaughter of the pig, when the boiled rind was chopped up, mixed with sausagemeat, and heavily spiced, and the stomach of the pig was filled with the mixture. The sausage was cooked slowly until it was tender, then sliced and eaten hot with potatoes. If the sausages, which were usually spherical in shape, were to be kept for longer, they were either smoked or air-dried and eaten cold. Today these cold cuts are sold by every butcher in Hesse, and thicker slices are also eaten hot, fried in butter.

Brawn, or "Presskopf," is a close relative of the Schwartenmagen sausage, though it is made from cooked or boiled pig or calf heads. This meat was coarsely diced, mixed with rind and sausagemeat, and pressed into pig stomachs. The venerable German broadsheet newspaper, the *Frankfurter Allgemeine*, reporting on the economic problems of top chefs, ended its article with the words, "It is better to earn money from brawn than to enter the culinary record books with sea bass." Yet brawn was not always regarded as cheap food. When the new bishop made his inaugural visit to Speyer in 1466, the city was anxious to impress him with a banquet. In fifth place in the series of nine dishes was brawn in cumin sauce.

The general pattern with regard to menus in Hesse and the geographical distribution of prosperous areas is reflected in the sausages. The privileged south produced comparatively expensive sausages, intended for fast consumption, while in the barren north the sausages were "stretched" to save money, or made in such a way that they could be kept for a long time, even when only small pieces

Sausages hang from the skies in Hesse more delicate and expensive in the south, longer-lasting in the north.

were cut from them. It is unlikely that the potato sausage would ever have been produced in the south, but in the north, especially in the Alsfelder Raum and Dillgebiet areas, a fifth or even a quarter of the sausage filling consists of potatoes in their skins.

In the north of Hesse, typical sausages for keeping include the "Ahle Worscht," or old sausage, so called because it has to be kept until it is possible to cut it. It consists of pork meat and back bacon. The sausage is prepared using raw meat, and, depending on the region and the individual butcher, is seasoned with various spices, smoked using juniper wood, and then air-dried. Whether it is curved into a loop or left straight, the "old" sausage then needs to ripen for another six months or more.

Typical of the south of Hesse is the "Flaaschworst" – meat sausage – that is found all over Frankfurt and which can be obtained in butchers' shops at any time of the day. This chunk of meat sausage, eaten with mustard and a bread roll is the local patriotic response to the Bratwurst of other regions. The same was also once true of the yellow sausage colored with saffron, which, since it was lighter in texture than other sausages, was also called "Wöchnerinnenwurst" – a sausage suitable for women who had recently given birth.

"Freeloaders"

How unfair history can be. It just shows how one can fall into disrepute by providing hospitality and good food. "Nassauer" is a well known German term to describe scroungers who eat and drink but let others pay the bill. This is a painful slur on the citizens of the former dukedom of Nassau, most of which merged with Hesse, although they know that they are being done a great injustice. It came about because the wise rulers of Nassau had decided against building their own expensive university and had instead guaranteed Nassau children a place to study at the University of Göttingen. Thanks to their generous government, Nassau students were also able to eat there free of charge. However, a few Prussians would often slink in and gatecrash – hence the German verb "nassauern," to freeload. Of course there is an opposing view; some students of German maintain that the word entered the language, not because of the uninvited guests of the citizens of Nassau, but as a result of petty criminals. Their evidence is based on the fact that in the argot of tinkers and thieves, the word "nass" means "without money or means," and it is precisely from this that the German word for scrounging was derived. But the descendants of the citizens of Nassau find this laughable, and, hospitable as they are, allow everyone to share in the merriment.

Potatoes

The fact that Hesse is potato country is clear from the numerous and extremely imaginative potato dishes from this state in the center of Germany. This affection for the starch-filled tuber is not surprising, since for the most part Hesse was a poor state. And here, as in all poor households north of the Alps, the potato served as an affordable staple food, although when it was first introduced the new plant belonging to the poisonous deadly nightshade family was regarded with distrust by the peasants, as was the case throughout the rest of Europe.

It is not known for certain how the tuber arrived in Hesse: it was perhaps introduced by the botanists Philippe de Sivry and Carolus Currus, who bred potatoes experimentally and worked in Frankfurt from 1588 to 1593. There is also, however, the story of the Hessian Landgrave Karl, who at the beginning of the 18th century invited his suspicious peasants to a meal of salad at which he secretly served potatoes, which had previously been rejected. This convinced the peasants, who cultivated potatoes from that time onwards. The ruler's ruse is commemorated annually in Ziegenhain with a "salad fair."

The wide variety of potato dishes begins with soup, from "Waldeck potato soup," to which smoked bacon is added, to the delicate "Frankfurt partridge and potato soup." The dish called "Himmel und Erde," or heaven and earth, in which apples and potatoes are boiled to a pulp together, was once well known throughout Hesse, while "Kartoffelbloatz" is more often found in eastern Hesse. A "Bloatz" or salt cake consists of bread dough, rolled out thinly, covered in this case with a heavily spiced mixture of potatoes and eggs. Occasionally onions and "Schmand" – extra thick cream – are added to the filling.

In Hesse's unofficial capital the dishes may have been somewhat more elaborate. "Potatoes Frankfurt-style," the recipe for which was found in a Regensburg cookery book dating from around the middle of the 19th century, called for additional ingredients including ham, onions, butter, bay, thyme, and a generous shot of burgundy. But Hesse as a whole – like neighbouring Thuringia – was devoted to dumplings of all kinds. The most extravagant variation must be the "Beutelches" or "Beulches" from Vogelsberg: long dumplings made from raw and cooked potatoes and dried or salted meat. Finely chopped vegetables (carrot, leek, celery, and parsley) are frequently added to the mixture, which is boiled in small linen bags.

Sachsenhausen baker's potatoes

Potatoes cooked in stock

Kartoffelgemüs
Potatoes cooked in stock
(Illustrated left)

8 potatoes
Salt
2 onions
2 tbsp pork lard
2 cups/500 ml meat stock
1 bay leaf
1 clove
Pinch of sugar
Pepper
1 tbsp mild wine vinegar
1 bunch dill, finely chopped
½ bunch parsley, finely chopped

Wash the potatoes and boil them in their skins in salted water until tender but not too soft. Drain the potatoes, rinse with cold water and leave to cool a little, then peel and cut into thin slices. Peel and chop the onions. Heat the lard in a heavy iron frying pan and sauté the onions gently until soft and transparent. Pour in the meat stock, and add the bay leaf and clove. Stir in the potato slices and season with salt, sugar, pepper, and vinegar. Simmer until the potatoes have absorbed nearly all the stock. Garnish with the chopped herbs just before serving.

Sachsenhäuser Bäckerkartoffeln
Sachsenhausen baker's potatoes
(Illustrated left)

8 potatoes
2 onions
2 tbsp clarified butter
Fat for greasing the baking dish
Salt
Pepper
⅛ tsp grated nutmeg
3 eggs
Scant cup/200 ml cream

Peel the potatoes, wash, and cut into thin slices. Peel and chop the onions. Heat the clarified butter, add the onions and sauté until golden yellow. Grease an ovenproof baking dish and arrange the potatoes and onions in layers. Season well with salt, pepper, and nutmeg. Whisk the eggs with the cream and pour over the potatoes. Cook in a preheated oven at 390 °F/ 200 °C for approximately 50 minutes until the top is golden brown.

Fechenheimer Kartoffeltorte
Fechenheim potato flan
(Illustrated below)

4 boiled potatoes, cooked the previous day
3 eggs
6 tbsp butter, at room temperature
6 oz/175 g sugar
1 pinch salt
A few drops of almond essence
Juice and grated zest of 1 lemon
2½ cups/250 g flour
1 tsp baking powder
Fat for greasing the pan
2 tbsp breadcrumbs

Press the potatoes through a ricer. Separate the eggs. Beat the butter, sugar, and egg yolks together until foaming. Add the salt, bitter almond essence, lemon juice and zest. Stir in the flour and baking powder gradually. Stir the riced potatoes into the mixture. Beat the egg white until very stiff and fold gently into the batter. Grease a springform pan and sprinkle with breadcrumbs. Pour in the batter and smooth it level. Bake in a preheated oven at 350 °F/175 °C for about 1 hour.

Schmand (extra thick cream)

The German word "Schmand" has a rich and heavy sound. And this is exactly as it should be – the name, derived from the dialect of northern Hesse, signifies cream that is saturated with fat, either sweet or sour. Much use was made of the word in its original form, "Schmant," which is documented from the 15th century onwards, since cream was used frequently and abundantly north of the Taunus and Vogelsberg mountains to enhance mostly plain dishes. An example of this is "Schmandhering," filleted salted herring steeped in extra thick cream. Similarly typical of the cuisine of northern Hesse is "Duckefett," a mixture of crisply fried bacon, gently fried onions, and herbs and spices added individually, which is briefly boiled with Schmand and is eaten with potatoes. Also typically Hessian, and not just from the linguistic point of view, is the stew known as "Lumpe un Fleh," meaning rags and fleas. The rags are the shredded white cabbage leaves, while the fleas are the caraway seeds. The other ingredients in the stew are potatoes, onions, dried beef, or mutton, and stock to which Schmand is added. "Schnippche" on the other hand is eaten cold. The mixture of soured milk or quark and Schmand is seasoned with herbs and spices and is eaten with potatoes or spread on a slice of bread. Country desserts made with this thick cream include, for instance, "Schmandcreme," a creamy dessert resembling blancmange, and "Schmandkuchen," a cake which at its simplest consists only of a layer of Schmand with sugar and cinnamon on a yeast dough crust, the luxury version of which, however, consists of two or three layers of Schmand cream, fresh fruit, and meringue.

Fechenheim potato flan

"To make small Frankfurt pies…" begins the only recipe handed down from the gourmet von Goethe household. The writer's grandfather, Johann Wolfgang Textor, who was mayor of the city, made a note of it in his domestic records in 1730: beefbone marrow, a soft bread roll, nutmeg, lemon, a generous amount of butter, and plenty of beef formed the basis of the pie. Willy Berger, a Frankfurt gastronome and cookery historian, has revived the recipe. It is significant that this dish originated in Frankfurt, a rich city in which more people could afford meat than elsewhere in the state.

Fine meat dishes

Limburger Edelsäcker
Limburg meat parcels

4 oz/100 g bacon cubes
5 oz/150 g sausagemeat
4 oz/100 g spiced gherkins, finely chopped
5 oz/150 g sauerkraut
3 tbsp white bread croutons
Salt and pepper
¼ tsp ground caraway
2 lb 3 oz/1 kg loin of pork (ask the butcher to cut a pocket in this)
3 tbsp mustard
1 tsp caraway
1 pig caul
3 apples
2 tbsp/30 g butter
1¼ cups/300 ml apple wine
Generous cup/300 ml cream
Pinch of sugar
Pinch of ground ginger
2 tbsp calvados

For the filling, fry the cubes of bacon in a dry pan until the fat runs and mix with the sausagemeat, the spiced gherkins, the drained sauerkraut and the croutons. Season with salt, pepper, and caraway. Spread mustard on the inside surface of the pocket in the meat and fill with the stuffing. Sew up the pocket and season the pork with salt, pepper, and caraway. Wrap in the pig caul and roast in a preheated oven at 350 °F/175 °C for 30 minutes. Then reduce the temperature to 210 °F/100 °C

and cook for a further 30 minutes. Meanwhile cut the apple into segments (do not peel), remove the core, and fry gently in the butter. Remove the roast meat from the oven and leave to stand for a short while. Add the apple wine to the juices in the roasting pan and strain into a small pan. Pour in the cream, season with salt, pepper, sugar, ginger, and calvados, and boil briefly to reduce. Carve the roast meat into slices, garnish with the apple slices and serve with the sauce.

Frankfurter Pasteten
Frankfurt meat pies
(Illustrated above)

2 cups/300 g flour
⅔ cup/150 g butter
1 egg
Salt
4 oz/100 g beefbone marrow, cubed
1 small parsley root, 3 shallots, and 2 carrots
2 tbsp butter
1 lb/400 g ground beef
Juice and grated zest of 1 lemon
1 tsp ground mace
Pepper
Flour for the work surface
Fat for greasing the baking pan
Egg yolk for glazing

Make the pastry using the flour, butter, egg, scant ½ cup (100 ml) water, and a pinch of salt. Chill for 30 minutes in the refrigerator. Meanwhile, to make the filling, sauté the beefbone marrow and the root vegetables in the butter until soft and transparent. Add the ground beef, lemon juice and zest, mace, salt, and pepper, and sauté gently until the beef is crumbly. Remove the mixture from the stove and leave to stand until cold. Roll out the pastry dough on a floured work surface and cut out the bases and several rings for the sides. Assemble the pies and fill with the meat mixture. Brush the edges of the pastry with egg yolk. Cut out tops for the pies from the remaining pastry and lay on top. Prick small holes in the top of the pies, seal the edges firmly and brush with egg yolk. Chill for 1 hour. Bake in a preheated oven at 350 °F/175 °C for 40 minutes.

Fairytale forest

Once upon a time there was a giantess called Saba, who lived in a huge fortress deep in the forest. But her legend only lives on in the name of the castle in northern Hesse, the Sababurg. The story of the female giant has long since been eclipsed by the story of Sleeping Beauty who is said to have been awakened by her prince with a kiss in this castle. Today, in the castle hotel, one is woken in a more prosaic fashion – by telephone.

The long thorn hedge planted by Landgrave Wilhelm IV in 1571 for his zoological garden certainly provided the fairy tale with a definite location, as did the dense, "enchanted" Rheinhardswald forest that surrounded it. The zoological gardens have been re-established, and the aurochs, wild horses, and other endangered species are bred there. The forest still remains too; it forms part of the largest area of forestry in Germany, covering 81 square miles (210 square kilometers), 173 acres (70 hectares) of which are designated as a protected ancient forest, in which neither forest wardens nor forestry workers are permitted to interfere with nature.

The "fairytale forest" was also, if popular legend is to be believed, the place where Hansel and Gretel discovered their captivating gingerbread house. This is quite possible, given that the brothers Grimm collected many of their fairy tales in this stretch of countryside. The same is true of another fairy tale by the Grimm brothers, a story of three old men, which is also sometimes thought to be set in the Rheinhardswald forest. Because the good girl in the story shares her meager bread ration with the three old men, they use their magic powers to ensure that a piece of gold falls from her mouth with every word she utters.

The Rheinhardswald forest has always been particularly well stocked with game, and today it remains the territory of royal deer. Game was always the food favored by the princes – either roast, or in game pies, which were popular in the noble households of northern Hesse. These pies consisted of venison mixed with sausagemeat, covered with a layer of bacon, and flavored with sweet southern wine and spices, especially thyme and pepper. The simpler dish known as "*Dippehas*" was also formerly eaten by the masters rather than the peasants, and the same applied to an even greater extent to pheasant and partridge. Game birds fluttered through the forests and open fields in such abundance that the Rheinhardswald princes had no need of a pheasant reserve to ensure the survival of these birds.

However, the vast forest had yet another nutritional function: it was grazing land with acorns and beechmast that made pigs in particular grow fat and round and gave added spice to dishes such as "*Dippehas*." But the other domestic animals were also driven out to graze in particular areas in the forest – this is why the trees stood so far apart, so that the foliage and grass received enough light and air. Ancient trees, up to 1000 years old and measuring over six yards around the trunk, were able to grow in the forest as a result.

Dippehas
Hare cooked in red wine

1 onion, chopped
1 small celeriac root, cubed
1 carrot, cubed
1 small parsley root, cubed
3 bay leaves
1 tsp juniper berries
¼ tsp peppercorns
½ tsp allspice berries
1 clove of garlic, chopped
3 cups/750 ml Rheingau Spätburgunder (pinot noir) wine
1 hare, ready for cooking, in portions (ask the butcher to lard the back)
4 shallots
4 oz/100 g bacon, cut into strips
2 tbsp oil
3 lb 4 oz/1.5 kg bread dough
Flour for the work surface

Bring the root vegetables to a boil in a little water with the spices and garlic, and then leave to cool. When cold, add 2 cups (500 ml) red wine. Lay the hare portions in a dish, pour over the marinade, cover and leave to stand overnight in the refrigerator. Fry the bacon in a dry pan until the fat runs, add the peeled shallots and pour in the remaining red wine. Simmer for 10 minutes. Meanwhile remove the hare portions from the marinade and drain well. Heat the oil in a roasting pan and sauté the hare portions. Stir in the onions and red wine. Add the root vegetables from the marinade, cook until they begin to brown, and pour in the marinade. Roll out the bread dough on a floured work surface to a thickness of about 1 inch (3 cm), then, using the rolling pin to lift it, slide it on to the top of the roasting pan. Prick several times with a fork. Bake in a preheated oven at 390 °F/200 °C for 10 minutes, then reduce the heat to 320 °F/160 °C and cook for approximately 1½ hours. When it has finished baking, lift off the bread topping.

The marinated hare portions must be patted dry before they are browned in hot fat.

The shallots and vegetables from the marinade are added and sautéed. The marinade is then added to the pan.

The bread dough crust, rolled out to a thickness of about 1 inch (3cm), is lifted onto the dish using a rolling pin.

The topping is pricked several times with a fork and the dish then goes into the oven.

The apple wine is ready to drink in ten to twelve weeks. By the beginning of Advent, the year's supply of "Stöffche" is already in the cellar.

After delivery the apples are washed and any bruised ones removed.

Then the apples are roughly chopped into chunks.

Before pressing, the apple pulp is wrapped in thick cloths.

The cloths are stacked on top of one another, with plates between the layers.

The stack is then placed in the press and the apple juice runs out.

This is all that remains: the dry mass of apple inside the cloths.

Ebbelwoi

What is apple wine called in Hesse? Äppelwei? Ebbelwoi? Otto Rumeleit, the legendary Frankfurt innkeeper and apple wine expert, has the judgment of Solomon for this "dialectical" dispute: we should just call it "Stöffche." Most citizens of the Main town that is regarded as Germany's capital city for apple wine would agree. It is not known how the refreshing, mildly alcoholic "national drink" came to Hesse, and to Frankfurt in particular. An economic affairs journalist from Frankfurt, Frank Gotta, whose book *Aus einem goldenen Apfel* ("From a golden apple") is the standard work on apple wine, has convincingly refuted the erroneous reports still in circulation that apple wine was invented in 1754. At that time a gardener is supposed to have pressed his surplus apples to save them from spoiling. "Stöffche" has been widely available throughout Germany for centuries, and furthermore it was not confined to Germany. The Greek historian Herodotus described the production of wine from fruit as long ago as the 5th century B.C. and the Romans made frequent reference to apple wine. Historians also believe that the Germanic tribes were already familiar with apple wine before they adopted the more refined winemaking techniques of the Romans. Nevertheless, in medieval Frankfurt wine produced from grapes was much more popular than apple wine. At the beginning of the 18th century, as a result of changes in the climate, the grape harvests became increasingly poor and vineyards shrank in size (today the municipal horticultural authority still maintains a small vineyard at the edge of the city.) Only then did apple wine become popular in Frankfurt and southern Hesse.

Since then, "Stöffche" has become so popular that there are around 70 large pressing operations in Hesse, which press apple wine in large tanks using concentrate. Old devotees of apple wine grumble about the increasing industrialization of the process – traditional apple wine should, after all, be made from fresh fruit. However, apple juice concentrate allows large enterprises to continue the fermentation process all year round. Even when it is made on a large scale, however, apple wine is still one of the most naturally pure drinks: apart from the yeasts and minute amounts of sulphur it consists exclusively of apples.

The choice of apples largely determines the flavor of the apple wine – sour apples, owing to their higher acid content, are more suitable than sweet apples. Ordinary apples from scattered orchards are ideal, especially if the farmer considers them not sufficiently important to be sprayed with chemicals. Today, with the rationalization of agriculture, such apple trees are increasingly rare, and it is even necessary to import apples.

Yeasts are added to induce fermentation and convert the must.

A glass of apple juice is refreshing – it is thirsty work in the cellar.

Jugs and glasses

Shall we go to Hibbdebach or to Dribbdebach for some Ebbelwoi? If you have understood the question, you have earned your glass of wine, and if you can answer it, you deserve a whole "Bembel" – the name for the pitcher from which apple wine is served. The "Bach", or stream, is the Main; its northern bank is referred to as the "hibb," its southern bank the "dribb de Bach." Sachsenhausen is "dribb," on the south bank, and is without question the most famous district of Frankfurt. It owes its fame to the apple wine quarter, in the area around Klappergass and Affentorplatz – a small corner of the old city that survived the war. Discothèques and fast food outlets, however, have robbed it of its character. The few remaining establishments specializing in apple wine are few and far between and are firmly in the grip of the tourist industry. But even in Sachsenhausen, away from the leisure and tourist district, there are still traditional apple wine bars, such as the "Kanonesteppel" and the "Germania" in the Textorstrasse or the "Gemalte Haus" and "Wagner" on the Schweizer Strasse, where local

Everyone in Frankfurt has a favorite local apple wine bar, usually close to home, bearing out the local saying that "fallen apples are found close to the tree."

people are still in the majority. Away from the tourist routes we also find the traditional stamping grounds of the "Hohenastheimer," as apple wine drinkers in Frankfurt are called – in Bornheim (the "Eulenberg", "Zur Sonne", "Solzer"), and also in Seckbach or Bergen. Hesse's best known hostelry serving apple wine, however, was in none of these districts, but on the site once destined to house the new parliament when the Federal Republic was founded, before Adenauer cast his vote for Bonn as the new capital. Today, where the parliament buildings would have stood in the thwarted capital city of Frankfurt, there stands the state

broadcasting company, Hessische Rundfunk, home of one of the most popular comedy programs on German television, the *Blauer Bock*, featuring bar-room stories and jokes which increased national awareness and popularity of the apple wine drinker. Even the insignia of the apple wine culture became known beyond the borders of Hesse: the "Bembel," the "Rippenglas," and the "Deckel." The "Bembel" is the imposing, bulbous, salt-glazed stoneware jug in which the Ebbelwoi is brought to the table in traditional establishments, when it is not ordered by the glass. The "Bembel," which keeps the apple wine cool, evidently did not come into fashion until the late 19th century, or at least no mention of it has been found before that time.

The "Rippenglas" takes its name from the diagonal ridges on the glass, which form a diamond pattern and at the same time give a good grip. A full glass in Frankfurt is called a "Schobbe" and the guests are "Schobbepetzer" (the German word "petzen" means "to pinch"). In many apple wine bars the ribbed glass holds 1¼ cups (0.3 liters), but 1 cup (0.25 liters) is also quite common. It is not clear where the ribbed pattern comes from – Frank Gotta, the local authority on apple wine, is of the opinion that the glass ribs impart a certain sparkle to a drink which has a rather "tired" appearance in the glass.

The origins and age of the "Deckel," or lid, the mark of a true Ebbelwoi enthusiast, are similarly

Even though he may be gray at the temples, he is still known as the "pretzel lad." The name has long since become a generic term; if you sell pretzels in Frankfurt's apple wine establishments, you remain a lad for life. And even the range of wares on sale are tried and true: pretzel sticks and cheese straws for those who prefer savouries, and sweet "Makrönche" or "Hartekuchen" – flaky pastry with cinnamon and cloves – for those with a sweet tooth, are all found in the traditional basket fitted with a bicycle bell.

Types of apple wine

There are three stages in the life of apple wine from Hesse. It first appears as a "Süsser," a sweet drink, then a heady half-fermented "Rauscher," then finally a sedate "Stöffche," also known in Frankfurt as an "Alter," or old wine.

The "Süsser" is the equivalent of the must in other fruits; it is cloudy and brownish in color. It contains no alcohol and is a popular drink in September and October, although it is so sweet only a few glasses of it can be drunk. The same applies, for a different reason, to the "Rauscher," which is the equivalent of a new wine. It is still fermenting and already contains a considerable amount of alcohol, but this can hardly be tasted; this is why the "Rauscher" – meaning intoxicant – encourages one to drink more than is good for the head and legs.

Finally the "Alter," which varies in clarity depending on the individual press, is pale to golden yellow in color, and has a sharp, sour taste.

The "sauer Gespritzte," a drink in which apple wine is mixed with sparkling mineral water, is a well-established drink appreciated by drivers. The sweet version made from apple wine with lemonade, the "süss Gespritzte," is frowned upon, at least in apple wine strongholds. By contrast, the "Haasse," a hot "Alter," which must not, however, be allowed to boil, is acceptable in the cold winter months when colds and 'flu are rife. Different spices can be added, but cloves and cinnamon are customary, frequently with the addition of lemon juice. Sugar is added according to personal taste.

unknown. Wooden lids, which are becoming increasingly rare, have a carving or other decoration on the upper side, and serve to cover the glass. Why? Many Frankfurt people will say that it is because of the spray their drinking companions are inclined to generate when talking. However, it is more likely that the lids were introduced in the outdoor season and are intended to prevent small pieces of bark and twigs falling from the trees into the glass.

The locals who frequent the apple wine bars are known as "Ebbelwoi-Geschworene," or apple wine aficionados. The origin of this is not clear either, but perhaps derives from the time of the apple wine lodges, when "Stöffche" could only be enjoyed in private circles. Landlords were forbidden to press apples during World War I, since all the apples were to be used to produce food. It was at that time that the apple wine lodges were established; they had the apple wine pressed privately and gathered together to drink it at specified times, usually several times a week. After the war the lodges closed down. As well as the apple wine museum, visitors can also experience a tour of Frankfurt on the "Ebbelwoi Express," a colorfully painted old tram, and further tours include the "Apfelweinstrasse," a tourist route that naturally includes Frankfurt as a stopping place.

The "Rippengläser," or ribbed glasses, in which the apple wine is served, hold 1¼ cups or 1 cup (0.3 or 0.25 liters). Larger groups of people order a jug, or "Bembel."

"Rippche," salted and cooked ribs, a Frankfurt specialty, goes wonderfully well with Ebbelwoi.

Fruit flesh

The only flesh that even vegetarians are known to eat with relish is the flesh of fruit. Viewed in this light, vegetarians in Hesse are well placed. Firstly, the airport at Frankfurt guarantees availability of fruit all year round. Secondly, a great deal of fruit is grown in the state itself.

The apple undoubtedly has pride of place as the top fruit of Hesse. The orchards all over the state cover an area of over 1500 acres (600 hectares). Despite this, the apple growers are feeling the effects of foreign competition – of the original three million apple trees, only a million now remain. In second

place – covering an area of around 1,160 acres (470 hectares), and on the increase – are strawberries, and in third place are sweet and bitter cherries, grown on 1100 acres (450 hectares), mainly around Witzenhausen and in the Odenwald forest. Pear and damson growers vie with each other for fourth and fifth place, which shows that the nickname given to Hesse people – "damson eaters" – is only true up to a point. Damsons and other varieties of plum are nevertheless used a great deal in the form of dried fruit, a tradition stemming from the days when this supplied vitamins in the winter months. Examples are the lentil soup from upper Hesse, which contains dried damsons as well as potatoes and leeks, and the barley broth from the Main district, which contains prunes and a little cinnamon. Strawberries and cherries,

on the other hand, are used fresh, the best known recipe being "Kirschmichel," of which there are many variations, but which is usually based on left-over white bread cooked in a dish with milk, meringue and cherries.

Pears are frequently combined with potatoes, for example in "Stommsel," from the Taunus region, in which coarsely mashed potatoes are served with onion and pear compote, or in "Schnitz und Schnitz," in which dried pears and plums are softened and boiled with chunks of potato, sometimes with the addition of bacon. There are countless recipes for apples, from apples cooked in Rheingau wine (stuffed with chopped nuts, raisins, and spices, steamed in wine) to "Dippedotz" from the Dill region, in which potatoes, blood sausage, onions, and apples are stirred together and baked.

Apfelweintorte
Apple wine flan

For the dough
1½ cups/200 g flour
¼ cup/75 g sugar
5 tbsp/75 g butter
1 egg
1 tsp baking powder
Flour for the work surface
Oil for greasing the baking pan

For the topping
4 apples, of a variety such as Boskoop
1½ tsp vanilla essence
3 cups/750 ml apple wine
1 cup/200 g sugar
2 heaped tbsp cornstarch

Make a pastry using the flour, sugar, butter, egg, and baking powder, and chill for 30 minutes in the refrigerator. Then roll out the dough on a floured work surface. Grease a 10-inch (26 cm) springform pan and line with pastry, pressing the dough up around the sides of the pan. Peel, core, and quarter the apples. Slice the apples into the pastry case and sprinkle with 2 tsp vanilla essence. Mix the cornstarch and ½ tsp vanilla essence with the sugar and a little of the apple wine. Heat the remaining wine in a pan and pour it over the mixture. Return to the pan and bring to boil, stirring constantly, until it has thickened. Pour over the apples and bake in a preheated oven at 340 ºF/175 ºC for 1¼ hours. When baked, leave the cake in the pan to cool and then refrigerate.

Schnitz und Schnitz
Potato and dried fruit broth

8 oz/200 g dried pears
8 oz/200 g pitted prunes
4 potatoes, of a firm, waxy variety
4 cups/1 l meat stock
Salt and pepper

Soften the fruit overnight in 4 cups (1 l) water. Peel the potatoes, wash and cut into chunks. Place the dried fruit in a pan with the liquid in which they have been soaked, the potatoes, and the meat stock, bring to boil, cover, and cook for approximately 30 minutes. Season with salt and pepper before serving. If a more robust dish is required, smoked bacon or dried beef can be added.

Hutzelkloss
Fruit dumpling
Serves 6

3 cups/450 g flour
2 cakes/40 g compressed yeast
½ cup/80 g sugar
½ cup/125 ml lukewarm milk
6 tbsp/100 g melted butter
1 egg
Pinch of salt
½ tsp vanilla essence
Grated zest of ½ lemon
2 handfuls dried apple
2 handfuls dried damsons
1 stick cinnamon
1 clove
2 tbsp sugar

Sift the flour into a bowl and sprinkle with the sugar. Make a hollow in the center. Crumble the yeast into this, mixing it with a little sugar, flour, and milk. Cover and leave to stand in a warm place for the yeast to start working. Incorporate some of the flour in this mixture, then add the melted butter, the egg, salt, vanilla essence, and lemon zest, beating until the dough comes away from the sides of the bowl. Cover again and leave to rise until doubled in volume. Meanwhile, place the apples and damsons in a metal pan with the cold water, the cinnamon and the clove. Lay the dough on top, cover, and bake in a preheated oven at 300 ºF/150 ºC for 30–40 minutes. Then remove the lid, sprinkle the dough with sugar, and brown under a hot flame.

Cherries

Witzenhausen is only in bloom for a few weeks in spring, when the white blossom of the 160,000 cherry trees adorn the green meadows like a topping of whipped cream, but even after the beauty has faded, the little town in the Werratal valley in northern Hesse still has its cherries to fall back on. There are more of these heart-shaped fruits ripening here than anywhere else in the state – sweet or bitter varieties, butter-yellow or black, but mostly a luminous red. Although the cherries do not make the farmers rich – the work of harvesting them is too difficult and expensive – they are good for the tourist industry. It is no accident that Witzenhausen is the only town in the world where the tourist brochures give off a scent of cherries if you "scratch and sniff" a particular cherry.

Witzenhausen, a town of half-timbered houses on the "German fairy tale" tourist route, provides the best possible conditions for the plump fruit here known by the name "Kespern," since the highest mountain here, the Hohe Meissner at 2474 feet (754 meters), affords shelter from cold winds but does not keep off the sun. Lucullus is said to have been personally responsible for introducing the stoned fruit to Roman civilization from Cerasus on the Black Sea, from which the name "cherry" is derived. There had been wild cherries on both sides of the Alps before Lucullus' welcome import, but it was only with the arrival of the nobler fruit from the east that flavor became a significant factor.

Witzenhausen is practically the center of the German cherry culture, and has blue-blooded credentials: every year Witzenhausen crowns a cherry queen, a coveted title for which young women from various districts compete. One of the most distinguished duties of the monarch is to turn the "cherry fair," held on the second week in July when the cherry harvest is in full swing, into a glittering royal occasion. By then most of the crop has usually been harvested and is well on its way to being made into fruit compote, jam, juice, cherry wine, liqueur, or cherry schnaps. The latter, however, has to be distilled by the competition in the neighboring Black Forest, since Witzenhausen has enjoyed marketing rights since 1225, but has no licenced distillery.

The cherry blossom in Witzenhausen, the largest area in Germany devoted to the cultivation of cherries, is also a tourist attraction. The majority of cherries grown are sweet, and a cherry queen is crowned during the annual cherry fair.

Kirschenmichel
Cherry pudding

Mixture 1
5 bread rolls
2 tbsp/30 g butter
Generous 1½ cups/375 ml milk

Mixture 2
Generous 4 tbsp/70 g butter, at room temperature
⅔ cup/125 g sugar
4 egg yolks
½ tsp cinnamon
Grated zest of 1 lemon
1 tsp baking powder

Mixture 3
2 lb/1 kg pitted sour cherries
4 egg whites
Oil to grease the pan
4 oz/100 g shelled almonds, finely chopped

Cut the bread rolls into thin slices, lay on a cookie sheet and dot with the butter. Bake in a preheated oven until golden yellow. Then place in a dish and pour over the milk. Using a hand whisk, beat the butter with the sugar and the egg yolk until fluffy. Stir in the cinnamon, lemon zest, and baking powder, and combine this mixture thoroughly with the bread mixture. Add the sour cherries. Beat the egg white until it is very stiff and fold in carefully. Grease an ovenproof baking pan, scatter the chopped almonds in the bottom and pour in the mixture. Bake in a preheated oven at 350 °F/175 °C for approximately 50 minutes. Serve from the pan.

Spitting cherry pits – a national sport

Where do cherries taste best? In a neighbor's garden? Perhaps. But it is certainly true that the luscious fruit tastes best of all where one is allowed to spit out the pits freely. And, this being the case, wherever cherries are found growing in any great quantity there seem to be competitions, of varying degrees of seriousness, to see how far people can spit cherry pits. The less serious competitions probably include the Cherry Pit Spitting Contest held every February in the American state of Minnesota, where the club's constitution requires its members to commit some nonsensical act or other at least once a month. In Germany – not surprisingly – the flight of a cherry pit propelled from the mouth is essentially taken more seriously. So it is also no surprise that the world record for this hard-core sport should have been won by a German on home ground: Horst Ortmann, from Langenthal in northern Hesse, set the record in August 1994 with an amazing 95 feet (28.98 meters). Even the Witzenhausen locals were unable to match this, although they hold all the other national records for cherries. Not for want of trying, however: each year at the cherry fair, anyone capable of action, rather than just talk, makes an attempt on the record. At the time of going to press, the Witzenhausen record remains a comparatively modest 61 feet (18.58 meters), but Witzenhausen people are absolutely determined that the 65-foot barrier will soon be broken.

Desserts

Frankfurter Kranz
Frankfurt ring cake

For the batter

½ cup/125 g butter
¾ cup/150 g sugar
Pinch of salt
Grated zest of 1 lemon
4 eggs
2 tbsp rum
1 cup/150g flour
2 tbsp cornstarch
1 tsp baking powder
Oil for greasing the pan

For the filling

1 cup/200 g sugar
5 egg yolks
4 tbsp rum
¾ cup/200 g soft butter
Cookie crumbs and glacé cherries to decorate

To make the batter, beat the butter and sugar together until fluffy. Stir in the salt, lemon zest, eggs, and rum. Gradually add the flour, cornstarch, and baking powder. Grease a tube pan and pour in the batter. Bake in a preheated oven at 350 °F/175 °C for about 45 minutes. Turn the cake out on to a rack and leave to cool. For the buttercream filling, make a syrup by boiling the sugar with 6 tbsp water. Whisk the egg yolk and pour in the syrup, stirring constantly. Stir in the rum and beat until the mixture has cooled. Beat the butter until fluffy and incorporate the egg mixture a spoonful at a time. Cut the cake horizontally into three layers. Spread each layer with buttercream and reassemble. Spread buttercream over the outside and sprinkle with the cookie crumbs. Place the remaining buttercream in a pastry bag with a star-shaped nozzle and pipe decorative whirls around the ring, topping each with a quarter of a cherry.

Brenten
Almond cookies

2½ cups/500 g ground almonds
2 tbsp rosewater
2½ cups/500 g sugar
Sugar for the cookie sheet
⅓ cup/50 g flour
1 egg white
Flour for the work surface

Mix the almonds with the rosewater and sugar in a pan. Heat gently, stirring constantly, until the mixture comes away from the sides of the pan. Sprinkle sugar into an earthenware bowl and pour in the mixture. Leave to stand for several hours in a cool place. Then knead in the flour and the egg white. Roll out the dough on a floured work surface to a thickness of just under half an inch (1 cm). Cut out shapes with a cookie cutter. Line a cookie sheet with baking parchment and bake the cookies at 300 °F/150 °C for about 15 minutes. Cool on a wire rack.

Bethmännchen
Marzipan cookies

2 cups/500 g marzipan
¼ cup/50 g confectioner's sugar
5 tbsp rosewater
1 egg white
Shelled almonds to decorate
Oil for greasing the cookie sheet

Knead the marzipan with the confectioner's sugar, 2 tbsp rosewater and the egg white to form a smooth dough. Roll the dough into balls the size of a walnut, and press 3 almonds into each with the tips pointing upward. Grease a cookie sheet and place the cookies on it. Bake in a preheated oven at 350 °F/175 °C until a pale golden color. When cool, brush the cookies with the remaining rosewater.

Bethmann and Rothschild

The fame of the Frankfurt banking family of Bethmann is not confined to the fields of economic history and – owing to Chancellor Theobald von Bethmann-Hollweg – political history. It is a name which is still on everyone's lips, at least in Frankfurt, thanks to the confectionery made from marzipan and known as "Bethmännchen" in honor of the Bethmann family. Another Frankfurt family, the Rothschilds, who founded the financial dynasty that was to span the globe, began by trading in wine, sugar, coffee, and other commodities, especially currency. Meyer Amschel Rothschild, born in either 1743 or 1744, founded his business in the "Hinterpfann," a backstreet house off the Judengasse in the Jewish quarter. His life was no bed of roses: even when the business expanded and the family moved to the famous "house with the green sign," the ten children were obliged to share a single bedroom. A common interest in numismatics had meanwhile brought Rothschild into contact with Wilhelm, the heir apparent and eventual Landgrave of Hessen-Kassel. The clever financier soon concluded some important financial deals for his ruler, to their mutual advantage. As a result Rothschild soon became financial adviser to a number of German princes.

The popular Frankfurt businessman's stroke of genius was to establish branches in London, Naples, Vienna, and Paris, and to make four of his sons responsible for these. The fifth son was to take charge of the main office in Frankfurt. And since the brothers had vowed to work together as closely as possible, they soon built up a financial network which was to serve all the great rulers of Europe. Today the Rothschilds are still a family with enormous influence, not confined to international banking. Thanks to a moderately profitable investment by the French branch of the clan, the family name is also well known in gourmet circles: *Château Lafite* and *Château Mouton Rothschild* are among the best and most expensive wines made in Bordeaux.

Butter, egg yolks, and sugar go into the filling for the Frankfurt ring cake.

The butter must be at room temperature so it can be beaten until it is light and fluffy.

Then the egg yolk and sugar mixture is gradually added.

The cooled cake is sliced horizontally into three layers.

The layers are spread with buttercream and the cake is reassembled.

A folded piece of baking parchment helps to give a smooth finish.

Cookie crumbs not only look pretty but taste good as well.

Each buttercream whirl is topped with a quarter cherry.

School: a sweet start

"I carried my *Tüte* like a flagstaff in front of me. From time to time I put it down on the pavement, groaning. From time to time my mother helped me. We were sweating like furniture removers. A sweet burden is a burden nonetheless." This is how Erich Kästner, author of the famous children's book *Emil and the Detectives*, remembers his first day at school and the traditional cone-shaped bag that was in his case evidently loaded with sweets.

The custom of sweetening the bitter pill of the first day at school, when life begins in earnest, has a long history in Germany and Austria (it is unknown elsewhere in Europe.) The bourgeoisie in Saxony at the beginning of the 19th century were the first to use *Tüten*, as the bags of delicious sweets are called, to make education more palatable to their offspring. However, the tradition is even older than that, and is rooted in superstition: originally the dried umbilical cord of the pupil, sewn into a little bag inside a breast pocket, was supposed to make the child more eager to learn. Later on, this relic was replaced by the root of an evergreen shrub, harvested between the feasts of the Assumption and the Birth of the Virgin Mary. Eventually the root was replaced, by an edible symbol: a sweet pretzel that was eaten on the way to school on the first day.

The legendary "Tütenbaum," a tree laden with goodies, has quite different origins. The teacher picked the crop of the tree (mostly fruit and cookies) for his new schoolchildren if they were good and worked hard. This custom, which is especially prevalent in southern Germany, probably began when parents left appropriately filled bags for the pupils in their teacher's charge. These were then hung on a branch in the classroom, well out of reach of umbrellas.

Today the bags of sweets, no longer home-made by parents, are something of a fashion accessory, which the manufacturers present at trade fairs in the fall – between 600,000 and 700,000 are sold every year. They are usually conical in shape and around 28 inches (70 centimeters) high, but in the former East German federal states the square *Tüten* that were customary in the days of the German Democratic Republic are still popular, perhaps because they are rather larger. With the passage of time, pretzels and fruit were increasingly displaced by candy, cookies, and chocolate bars, which led dentists and nutritional scientists to appeal each year for more healthy items, and even a toothbrush, to be packed in the *Tüten*. These appeals met with only limited success. However, for some years now doctors have been looking more favorably upon the contents of the bags. Although toothbrushes remain the exception rather than the rule, T-shirts, CDs and similar "cool" items are increasingly finding their way into the bags.

Proud recipients of Tüten in the 1950s (above) and today (below right.) Although the nature of the bags has changed, the pride, pleasure, and curiosity regarding the contents of other children's Tüten remain. And parents still manage to sweeten the shock to their offspring of life beginning in earnest.

This woodcut from 1880, "A Christmas Carol," copied from a painting by Hans Ströse shows the formal restraint in the family circle typical of the period.

The Christmas tree stands on a table laden with gifts. The tree did not become an indispensable part of Christmas until the end of the 19th century.

Particularly beautiful woodcarvings, like this Christmas pyramid, were produced in the Erzgebirge mountain region, where families had to earn extra money by working at home.

The Christmas tree

The meaning of the Christmas tree has been interpreted in countless different ways. It is supposed to be a primeval German symbol, Germanic to the tips of its clipped roots, the cult symbol of the midwinter festival.

Two natives of Hesse, the brothers Grimm, are responsible for these speculations. Following their investigations during the first half of the 19th century into heritage and tradition, research was carried out in the states of Germany according to the principle that everything of any cultural value must hark back to the mists of antiquity. This approach was very congenial to the Nazi ideologues, who celebrated Christmas as a "Germanic Yule festival."

Not until modern folklorists applied a scientific approach to the candlelit tree was it discovered that it has only existed since the time of the Reformation. At that time it was still not a Christmas tree in the modern sense of the word, but stood in the guild halls as a repository of gifts. The route from the guild hall to the home was a long one, leading first to the courts of European princes. The custom did not become widespread among the general population until after the war of 1870–71, when the Prussian king had Christmas trees put up in hospitals and shelters.

When Christmas became established as a festival that was celebrated at home, and hopefully in harmony, each family developed its own rituals, frequently handed down from generation to generation. The external framework is of course common to everyone, as is the tendency for people to overeat regularly during the Christmas period, starting with *Plätzchen*, traditional Advent cookies, and building up to an orgy of over-indulgence when the fat Christmas geese are cooked and eaten. Goose and carp are the traditional festive dishes of the two days of Christmas, while for Christmas Eve, interestingly enough, each family has its own preferred dish. This is usually something that can be prepared quickly – no one wants to spend time in the kitchen on Christmas Eve. And the dishes are usually chosen because the adults associate them with Christmas Eve in their own childhood, so that nostalgia sets in with the first bite.

Left: Crib scenes, such as this one in the Thuringian city of Erfurt, are built in the central squares of many cities in the period leading up to Christmas.

Christmas cookies

Ulmer Weihnachtssterne
Ulm Christmas stars

1½ cups/200 g flour
¾ cup butter
2 eggs, separated
1 small bottle rum flavoring
1 tsp cinnamon
Pinch of cardamom
½ cup/100 g sugar
Pinch of salt
Flour for the working surface
1 cup/300 g marzipan
Chopped candied fruit for decoration

Make a dough using the flour, butter and egg yolks. Mix in the rum flavoring, cinnamon, cardamom, sugar, and salt, and chill the pastry in the refrigerator for 30 minutes. Roll out on a floured work surface to a thickness of a little less than a quarter of an inch (½ cm) and cut out star shapes with a cookie cutter. Line a cookie sheet with baking parchment and place the cookies on this. Mix the marzipan to a smooth paste with 2 tbsp water and the egg white. Fill a piping bag fitted with a star-shaped nozzle with the mixture and pipe a ring on each star. Decorate with the candied fruit and bake in a preheated oven at 350 ºF/175 ºC for about 15 minutes.

Schwarz-Weiss Gebäck
Black-and-white cookies

1 cup/250 g butter, at room temperature
Scant cup/200 g sugar
2 eggs
2½ cups/350 g flour
1 cup/150 g fine rolled oats
4 tbsp cocoa powder
2 tbsp milk
Flour for the work surface
Egg yolk for glazing
Butter for greasing the cookie sheet

Beat the butter with the sugar and eggs until light and fluffy. Gradually add the flour and the rolled oats, and combine all the ingredients to form a smooth dough. Divide the dough into three. Blend the cocoa powder with the milk and mix into two portions of the dough. Roll the portions in foil and chill for at least 30 minutes in the refrigerator. Then roll out one light and one dark piece on a floured work surface and place briefly in the freezing compartment. Cut the dough into strips a little less than half an inch (1 cm) wide, brush with egg yolk and assemble in a chequerboard pattern. Roll out the remaining piece of dough thinly and brush with egg yolk. Lay the chequerboard block on this and wrap the sheet of dark-colored dough around it. Chill. Then cut thin slices from the block of dough and lay these on a greased cookie sheet. Bake in a preheated oven at 350 ºF/175 ºC for about 15 minutes.

Spitzbuben
Almond and oat cookies with blackberry jelly

¾ cup/200 g butter
½ cup/100 g sugar
5 egg yolks
1½ cups/200 g flour
1¼ cups/200 g fine rolled oats
½ tsp vanilla essence
½ cup/75 g ground almonds
Flour for the work surface
6 tbsp blackberry jelly
Confectioners' sugar for dusting

Beat the butter with the sugar and egg yolks until light and fluffy. Gradually incorporate the flour and rolled oats. Mix in the vanilla essence and almonds, and chill the dough for 30 minutes in the refrigerator. Then roll out thinly on a floured work surface, and cut out an equal number of circles and rings of similar size with a heart-shaped hole in the center. Lay on a cookie sheet lined with baking parchment and bake in a preheated oven at 350 ºF/175 ºC for about 10 minutes. Leave the cookies to cool and then brush the circles with blackberry jelly. Dust the rings with confectioner's sugar. Place a ring circle on top of a jelly-coated circle.

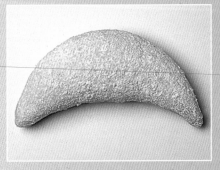

Vanillekipferl
Vanilla crescents

2 cups/250 g flour
¾ cup/200 g butter
½ cup/100 g ground almonds
¾ cup/150 g vanilla flavored sugar

Knead the flour, butter, almonds, and half the sugar together to form a dough and chill for 30 minutes in the refrigerator. Then form the dough into a roll. Cut slices from the roll and shape them into small crescents. Place on a cookie sheet lined with baking parchment and bake in a preheated oven at 350 ºF/175 ºC for about 15 minutes. Carefully coat the crescents with the vanilla sugar while they are still hot.

Zimtsterne
Cinnamon stars

3 egg whites
2 cups/250 g confectioner's sugar
1⅓ cups/250 g ground almonds
Grated zest of 1 lemon
2 tsp cinnamon
Sugar and flour for rolling out

Beat the egg whites until very stiff. Gradually add the confectioner's sugar. Set aside 4 tbsp of the egg white mixture for glazing. Mix in the ground almonds, lemon zest, and cinnamon, and knead the dough lightly. Dust the work surface with sugar and flour and roll out the dough. Cut out star shapes using a cookie cutter. Line a cookie sheet with baking parchment and place the stars on this. Brush with the glaze and bake at 300 ºF/150 ºC for 20 minutes.

Beat the egg whites until they are the consistency of snow.

Gradually pour confectioner's sugar into the stiff egg whites.

Remove 4 tbsp of the mixture and add the almonds to the remainder.

Add the cinnamon and lemon zest and form the dough into a ball.

Dust the work surface with confectioner's sugar and a little flour.

Roll out the dough on the prepared work surface.

Loosen the dough from the work surface before cutting out shapes.

Cut out small stars using a star-shaped cookie cutter.

Place the stars on baking parchment and brush with the egg white mixture.

The cinnamon stars are ready after baking for about 20 minutes.

Dough for a gingerbread house

1 cup/200 g sugar
4 tsp/20 g butter
4 cups/500 g flour
2 tsp baking powder
Grated zest of 1 lemon
½ tsp cinnamon
Pinch of ground nutmeg
Pinch of cardamom
Pinch of ground cinnamon
3 egg yolks
Flour for the work surface

Heat the sugar with the butter, stirring constantly, until the sugar has dissolved. Remove from the heat and leave to cool. Sift the flour and baking powder into a bowl. Gradually stir the flour into the sugar mixture. Stir in the lemon zest, spices, and egg yolks. Knead the dough lightly on a floured work surface, cover, and allow to rest for a while. Roll out the dough to form a square a little less than half an inch (1 cm) thick. Line a cookie sheet with baking parchment and bake the gingerbread in a preheated oven at 350 °F/175 °C for 15-20 minutes. Leave to cool on a wire rack. Depending on the design, a gingerbread house will require three or four sheets of gingerbread. The pieces are attached with sugar frosting made by beating 2 egg whites until they are frothy and adding 1½ cup (200 g) confectioner's sugar. The candy used to decorate the gingerbread house is also attached with sugar frosting.

Grimm's fairy-tale woman

"We now have a wonderful source, an old lady from Zwehrn, who knows an incredible amount and tells a very good story. She has a knowing look, and her wisdom and refinement distinguish her from most peasant folk ," wrote Wilhelm Grimm in 1813 in a letter about Dorothea Viehmann. Wilhelm and Jacob Grimm have her to thank for 19 of their best children's fairy tales. Ludwig Emil, the painter among the three Grimm brothers, who were natives of Hanau, drew the story-teller, and this picture adorns the second edition of the Grimm brothers' fairy tales. But Dorothea was also rewarded for her trouble in other ways. "On each occasion, the old woman is provided with coffee, a glass of wine and money into the bargain." Dorothea Viehmann was the daughter of the landlord of the "Knallhütte," an inn near Kassel on the route to Frankfurt. She often entertained the guests with tales from her vast repertoire. As the name of her father, Pierson, indicates, she was of Huguenot descent, and as a result themes from Provence and the French Jura found their way into the Grimm brothers' "genuine Hessian" fairy tales. There is, however, a clear distinction between the French tales and the corresponding German versions. While the French give detailed descriptions of eating and drinking, this only plays a minor role in the German stories. Bernhard Lauer gave an example of this, on the occasion of the exhibition in 1996 entitled "Food and drink in the fairy tale: a culinary journey through the fairy-tale world of the Brothers Grimm". A translation of the story of Rapunzel, translated from the French in 1790, refers to her eating "boiled and roast meat, marzipan and almonds, and little cookies," while this is missing from the Grimm brothers' later version. Occasionally, however, food does provide a backdrop for important scenes or ultimate reconciliation in the Grimm brothers' tales. The contrasts between rich and poor are also frequently symbolized by the food on the table.

Flour instead of cement – for a substantial gingerbread house.

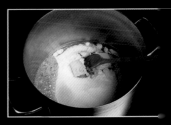

Sugar is also used in the construction, melted with butter.

The pan is taken off the heat and the flour and baking powder are added.

The lemon zest, egg yolks, and spices are added, stirring constantly.

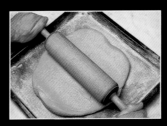

The dough is kneaded and then rolled out into a square.

Depending on the design, three or four such squares are required.

Templates are laid on the gingerbread and the shapes are cut out.

Window shutters are attached with sugar frosting.

Now the decorating can begin, also using sugar frosting.

The walls are also fixed together with sugar frosting.

Hamburg
Schwerin
Bremen
Hanover
Berlin
Düsseldorf
Magdeburg
Potsdam
Bonn
Erfurt
Dresden
Wiesbaden
Mainz
Saarbrücken
Stuttgart
Munich

UWE ANHÄUSER

The Rhineland-Palatinate

Two thousand years of good living are reflected –
metaphorically speaking – in the wineglasses and
cooking pots of the Middle Rhine and its tributaries.
The region was invaded by countless warrior hordes
from the time of Caesar onward, and almost all the
occupying forces left traces of their own cultures behind,
including many a Lucullan specialty. Most notably of all,
the Romans introduced winegrowing to the banks of the
Mosel (our grateful thanks to Emperor Probus!).

Even during the period of Roman colonization, Trier
and Mainz were urban centers at the heart of Europe,
and their influence extended over a wide area. The
Middle Ages saw other towns and cities such as Speyer,
Worms, and Kaiserslautern become historical focal
points, while the valley of the Middle Rhine between
Bingen and Koblenz, with its castles and churches,
assumed major cultural status.

There was famine in the area in the 19th century, and
those who did not emigrate had to sustain life on bread
and potatoes. But necessity is the mother of invention,
and many recipes for potato dishes date from that time.
During the decades when the local people had little to
eat, the Middle Rhine became a popular resort of
English and Prussian tourists, who were attracted by
the flourishing Romantic traditions of the Rhine.

Many great historical figures settled in the land of the
vine: Charlemagne, the Emperor Barbarossa,
Hildegard of Bingen. Later, famous people such as
Johannes Gutenberg (inventor of printing) and
Nikolaus August Otto (inventor of the internal
combustion engine) made their names. Carl Zuckmayer
is an outstanding literary figure of the 20th century, and
his rural comedy *Der fröhliche Weinberg* ("The Happy
Vineyard") is a celebration of his native land.

Although the banks of the Rhine and Mosel have such
a wealth of regional history, the Federal State of the
Rhineland-Palatinate, created in 1946, cannot really be
called a single entity. Nonetheless, in all the state's
geographical areas – the Westerwald, Eifel, Hunsrück,
Rhinehessen, and Palatinate regions – historical
connections and shared folk customs have united to
create both a cultural and a culinary identity.

Left: The Federal State of the Rhineland-Palatinate, created in 1946, consists
of five geographical regions. This is a view from the north of the Palatinate.

The transformation of the grapes into must and the must into wine is known as "vinification." During fermentation, warmth, carbonic acid, and alcohol develop.

Winegrowing

The journey of wine from the grape to the glass is a long one. It passes from the vineyard to the cellar, and thence to the bottle, and has many companions along its way: vineyard laborers, grape pickers, cellar masters, and oenologists.

The process begins with the planting of cloned vines: identical genetic copies of healthy and largely virus-resistant stock, which will not produce flowers for the first three years. It is around the flower panicles that those desirable objects, the grapes themselves, will form. An important factor influencing the quality of a wine is the location of the vines: the nature of the soil, the climate, the height of the vineyard above sea level. Other crucial factors are the way in which the vines are cultivated, the pruning of their bunches of grapes and foliage, the moment chosen for the harvest, and the number of vines grown per acre.

The transformation of the grapes into must and the must into wine is known as "vinification." In making red wine, the grapes are pressed after the vintage, that is to say, they are crushed, (usually having been removed from their stalks), and then the must, consisting of the juice and skins, is fermented in a stainless steel vat or large wooden barrel. During this fermentation of the must, which takes about three days for light wines and up to two weeks for a heavier wine, the sugar present in the must turns to alcohol through the action of the natural yeasts present. Today, computer-regulated temperatures usually aid the process too. The more alcohol that is created, the more color pigments and other substances in the skins are leeched out, and the wine becomes red, fruity, and rich in these extracts to a greater or lesser degree. It is then racked off, that is to say, it is pumped or siphoned out of the fermentation vat into a wooden barrel where it continues to ferment for several more weeks. Wine that has fermented out will re-ferment in spring, and the harsh malic acid turns to soft lactic acid in a process known as malolactic fermentation; the red wine, until now very rough in flavor, becomes smoother. It then goes into another vat where it clarifies, and the process of maturing begins. The wine matures in large wooden casks or barrels which allow it to "breathe," and it also becomes slightly concentrated through evaporation. After a period of time, it is put into bottles, where it goes through the final phase of maturation.

In making white wine, the grapes are pressed with their stems, the juice (with skins and stems removed) is clarified overnight, and slightly sulfured to counter the risk of oxidation. Controlled fermentation of the must is usually ensured by the addition of patent yeasts, although some winegrowers avoid them because of the uniformity of the end product. In order to make it sweeter, fermentation of white wine is often stopped before

Bunches of grapes ready for picking promise the winelover that his glass will be full next year.

Information on the sugar content of the grape juice is provided by the special areometer (a kind of hydrometer).

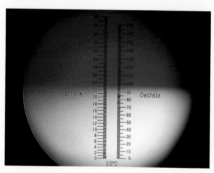
The degree on the Oechsle scale shows how many grams of alcohol per liter the wine contains.

the sugar has been entirely transformed into alcohol; either the yeasts are filtered out, or the temperature is lowered. Malolactic fermentation in white wine may be prevented or permitted, depending on the acidity content. The wine is lightly sulfured again after the first racking. Some particularly aromatic wines mature on the remains of the yeast left after fermentation, and these wines are described as "on the lees." Before bottling, usually in the spring following the vintage, white wines are lightly filtered again. However, top qualities of wine, with more fullness and complexity of flavor, are allowed to mature for a longer period.

Opposite: a wealth of fruits, the produce of a long summer, brims over its containers after picking.

The Palatinate and the Mosel

Although they are situated in the same state, the two winegrowing regions of the Mosel (with the Saar and Ruwer) and the Palatinate could not be more different. As the name tells us, the Mosel area lies on the banks of the River Mosel along a stretch of 143 miles (230 kilometers) between Perl and Koblenz, and this situation determines its character: the vines grow on precipitous slopes, on the northern bank of a watercourse that has made its way, winding endlessly, through the rugged mountain landscape for millions of years. The Palatinate, on the other hand, originally called the Rhenish Palatinate, does not in fact touch the Rhine anywhere. Instead, its vineyards, while always within view of the Rhine valley, extend over some 50 miles (80 kilometers) on the eastern flank of the forested Haardt area, on hillsides rolling gently from Wissembourg in Alsace to Worms.

With the Rheingau, the Mosel, which grows 54 percent of Germany's entire production of Riesling, is one of the two classic areas of cultivation of this most German of all grapes. "The Riesling of the Rheingau speaks with charm and dignity," runs a proverb, "and the Riesling of the Mosel with grace and wit." An unusually long growing season, lasting until well into the fall, brings plenty of sun, but also a good deal of cool, wet weather. This microclimate is the result of the stormy weather of the Eifel and the Hunsrück areas. The rather complex nature of the conditions affecting the Rieslings of the Mosel also includes the schist slopes on which the best vineyards grow, turning them into unique wines, with a softly intense bouquet, elegant acidity, and a subtle undertone of mineral flavors. The finely balanced harmony between these factors gives them outstanding individuality.

As in most cultivated areas of southern Germany, it was the Romans who introduced winegrowing to the country over 2000 years ago. The Elbling they preferred – which made rather thin, acid wine – was the dominant grape variety until the 18th century. Then Riesling was introduced because of its greater resistance to frost, and it has predominated from the early 19th century to the present day. Elbling is grown today only on the Upper Mosel, and in some parts of the Lower Mosel. It represents 9.1 percent of the winegrowing area of the entire Mosel region, which covers 29,000 acres (12,500 hectares). Wine made from Müller-Thurgau grapes (22 percent) and Kerner grapes (7.7 percent), also grown in the Mosel, along with smaller quantities of the Bacchus, Optima, and Spätburgunder varieties, is notable more for quantity than quality.

The Rhineland-Palatinate
Winegrowing regions

The 56,800 acres (23,000 hectares) of vineyards in the Palatinate grow on gently rolling hills with soils of shell limestone, loess, and clay, along with some sandy soils and volcanic slate marl. The southern "wine climate" is so warm and sunny that about two dozen grape varieties grow in the Palatinate, not to mention almonds, figs, and sweet chestnuts. The leading wine varieties are Riesling and Müller-Thurgau, each with 21 percent of production, followed by Kerner (11 percent) and Silvaner (7 percent). Scheurebe, Morio Muskat and Weissburgunder, Portugieser and Huxelrebe grapes are rare today, but Grauburgunder, Dornfelder and Spätburgunder are grown with increasing frequency.

The characteristic feature of the wine in the Palatinate has always been its superabundance. In the Middle Ages, when the geographical and political center of Europe lay between Worms and

Landau, the area was already being described as "the wine cellar of the Holy Roman Empire of the German Nation." It is said that Attila, King of the Huns, never reached France because he enjoyed the wine of the Palatinate so much. The two Heidelberg casks of the Elector Palatine held 76,000 gallons (350,000 liters). The wine cannot have tasted very good, for most of it came from the peasants' tithes. *Qualitätswein* began to be made in the Palatinate only at the end of the 18th and the beginning of the 19th century, when the extensive secularization of the monastic winegrowing estates by Napoleon encouraged the rise of middle-class culture in many areas, including winemaking. The vineyard owner Andreas Jordan (1775–1848), who in 1802 raised the first Riesling to come true to variety, is regarded as the founding father of winegrowing in the Palatinate.

Grapes are grown on an area of 12,500 hectares (29,000 acres) in the Mosel area.

The vintage is hard work on the steep slopes, but the wine made from the harvested grapes is of high quality.

The drinkers' war for Thurant Castle

Zorno was a robber knight, notorious throughout the valley of the Mosel. He was the scourge of the countryside, and a tyrant to the vintners, whom he kept in mortal terror by his constant demand of: "Your barrel or your life!" In fact Zorno made this brusque request so often that one day the bishops of Trier and Cologne felt obliged to settle their own differences for once and intervene. But when their army of mercenaries marched to the gates of the winegrowing village of Alken in 1246, the monster was standing high on the battlements of his castle of Thurant, mocking them as he looked down, and brandishing a tankard. "Well, clerics," he boasted, "God is on my side, for I have plenty to drink!" Storming the castle proved useless, and the bishops soon realized that Thurant could not be taken by force

of arms, but must be starved out – or rather, made to surrender for lack of drink. They and their army prepared for a long siege. But the mercenaries, eager for action, became restless and unruly when they had to wait around doing nothing (and just outside a winegrowing village at that). After the first deserters had been picked up in cellars and punished, the wise commanders decide that in order to raise the army's morale every man would have his daily wine ration. This kept the army quiet "for two intoxicated years," we are told, until Zorno finally ran out of wine and hoisted the white flag. But the bishops had a steep bill to pay: their 1500 mercenaries had cost them half a gallon (2.75 liters) of good Alken wine a day each, amounting in all to 3,000 tuns (a tun contained 220 gallons, or 1000 liters). It is said that directly after the surrender Thurant had to be mortgaged, as the only way the bishops could find of footing the bill.

Tasting wine

You do not necessarily need all five senses about you in order to taste wine, but you certainly need three of them. Good wine is assessed in three ways: by looking at it, smelling it, and finally tasting it.

First you look at the wine to see whether it is clear. Its color – golden yellow in a good sweet white wine, deep red in a good claret – is not only attractive, but provides information about the age and nature of the wine. Good, weighty red wines, for instance, are usually a dense, deep red at first, turning lighter in color with time; their bluish red takes on a more yellowish tinge, and they look lighter at the edge of the glass than in the middle. A wine is no longer fit to drink when it has turned brownish yellow.

The shape of the glass is important, not just for visual reasons. It should be bulbous, and wide enough for the bouquet to collect in it and rise to the nostrils in concentrated form. White wines need a rather narrower glass, and the more concentrated a red wine, the more voluminous the glass required. Take a glass filled to a maximum of one third and swirl it in circular movements, so that the bouquet can develop. Your sense of sight comes into play again here; the more "tears" that run down the sides of the glass, the more concentrated extracts the wine contains, and with luck it will have greater structure and body (although this may also mean too much alcohol and sugar).

Once your nose is over the top of the glass, it is best to take in the bouquet with one long breath. What you think you smell then is bound to be relevant, for impressions of smell are as subjective as they are imaginative. Apart from a few "objective" characteristics, such as the amount of alcohol (you will be able to tell from sniffing it whether too much has been left), or certain pleasing primary aromas such as lemon or apple, stinging nettle or chocolate, the wine lover can make up his own mind about the bouquet and whether it suggests chalk, or the flowers of an alpine meadow, or even – a notorious example of wine buffs' jargon – cat's pee.

The tasting process is much the same, although since we really register only four kinds of flavors – sweet, sour, salty, and bitter – we smell more than we taste: on its way through the mouth the wine passes the gums and the nasopharyngeal cavity, where olfactory sensors are waiting for it. It is advisable to take a fairly large sip and mix it with air in the mouth, so that the combination of smell and taste tells you about those attributes of the wine described by experts as "fruity," "bitter," "soft," or "dry," and gives you further impressions of its depth, body, and density.

Many winegrowing estates, such as that of Schloss Wallhausen on the Nahe, invite visitors to taste their produce. The vintner first offers the white wine.

A sample of red wine is removed with a pipette and put in a tasting glass. The expert can draw conclusions about the quality of the wine from its color.

The sweetness in the wine

The international reputation of Riesling wines, especially those of the Mosel-Saar-Ruwer and the Palatinate, has been damaged by the stickily sweet flavor of some mass-produced wines that make their way on to the market.

These artificially sweet wines are sweetened by the addition of sugar, by too much unfermented must (sugar reserves), or by artificially stopping the fermentation process by pressure or chilling, so that complete fermentation of the wine, and thus the entire transformation of its fruit sugar into alcohol, is prevented. This synthetic sweetness often conceals mistakes in the winemaking, and is intended to get inexperienced wine drinkers over the hurdle of the natural acidity which is "too sour" for them.

However, a certain sweetness in Rieslings can be delightful, provided it is natural. Many dry *Spätlese* wines have carefully calculated amounts of sweetening agent (unfermented grape juice) added to round off the flavor, or to add delicate emphasis to a fruity note already present. The international success now enjoyed once more by the leading vintners of the Mosel and Palatinate, after a long period when their products fell into disrepute, due not least to the practice of artificial sweetening, has popularized not only fresh, light *Kabinett* and *Spätlese* wines, but also *Auslese, Trockenbeeren-auslese*, and *Eisweine*, with their elegant, sometimes opulent, and even powerful natural sweetness.

This natural sweetness is created in the grapes while they are still on the vine. Botrytis, known in Germany as "noble rot," makes the skin of the grapes so thin that most of the water inside evaporates, and the grapes shrink to the size of raisins. Their contents are concentrated, and the fruit sugar in particular increases. For *Eisweine*, literally "ice wines," the grapes must be harvested at a temperature of at least minus seven degrees Celsius; frost congeals the water content of the grapes, concentrating the sweetness even more.

If you have a cold it is no use attending a wine tasting; the nose tells us a great deal about wine, both objectively and subjectively.

Cooking with wine

Moselaal in Riesling
Mosel eel in Riesling

1 Mosel eel or river eel, weighing about 2 lb/1 kg, prepared for cooking
juice of 2 lemons
2 cups/500 ml Mosel Riesling
salt
2 large onions, each studded with 3 cloves and 2 bayleaves
scant ½ cup/100 g melted butter
parsley and slices of lemon to garnish

Wash the eel, pat it dry, and sprinkle with lemon juice. Bring the wine to a boil in a fish kettle with 1 cup/250 ml water, salt, and the spiked onions. Put the eel in the liquid, and simmer gently over low heat, covered, for about 20 minutes. When the eel is cooked, put it on a prewarmed dish, pour the melted butter over it, and garnish with parsley and lemon slices. Serve with boiled potatoes.

The remains of fruit left after the grapes are pressed can be used on the land as a fertilizer, or distilled to make spirits. Those in the Mosel area who venture to call 38 percent proof spirits of this kind by the fashionable name of "grappa" will earn the scorn of the local people. On the other hand, someone ordering "Mosel whisky" shows that he is knowledgeable, and will be served a good measure, with an aroma and yellowish coloring that tell you the spirit was matured in oak casks.

Fasanengockel
Cock pheasants

2 young pheasants
salt and pepper
1 small red cabbage, cooked and chopped
scant 1 cup/100 g butter
1 cup/250 ml red wine
1 cup/250 ml stock
2 apples
2 tsp cranberry compote

Wash the pheasants, pat them dry, and season well inside and out with salt and pepper. Chop the gizzards, mix them with the red cabbage, and stuff the pheasants with this mixture. Melt half the butter in a roasting pan, and brown the pheasants on all sides. Roast in a preheated oven at 400 °F/200 °C for about 30 minutes, until the flesh is pink. Baste now and then with the red wine and stock. Peel, halve, and core the apples, and cook them in the remaining butter until they are tender but not too soft. When the pheasants are cooked, arrange them on pre-warmed platter. Put a spoonful of the cranberry compote in the center of each apple half, and arrange around the pheasants. Potato croquettes go well with this dish.

Winzeräpfel
Vintner's apples

For the apples
4 large apples
1 tbsp sultanas
1 tbsp chopped walnuts
½ tsp vanilla essence
½ tsp ground cinnamon
1 bottle/700 ml Riesling

For the sauce
1 vanilla bean
4 cups/1 liter milk
1 scant cup/150 g sugar
1 tbsp/25 g cornstarch
3 egg yolks

Peel the apples and scoop out the cores, leaving a large hollow area. Mix the sultanas with the chopped walnuts, vanilla essence, and cinnamon, and stuff the apples with this mixture. Place them side by side in an ovenproof dish, and pour the wine over them. Bake in a preheated oven at 300 °F/150 °C for about 30 minutes. Meanwhile, make the sauce: slit the vanilla bean lengthwise and scrape out the small inner seeds. Put the vanilla bean, its inner seeds, and the milk in a pan, and bring to a boil. Add the sugar, and dissolve it in the vanilla-flavored milk. Whisk the cornstarch with a little water, stir it into the milk, and bring to a boil again. Take the pan off the stove, and thicken the sauce with the egg yolks. Serve with the hot baked apples.

Food in the Middle Ages

Deplorable as it may seem to us today, medieval cooking in the many tiny states along the Rhine reflected a society deeply divided into two very different classes. Serfs, day laborers and farmhands had to fill their stomachs with cereals and mush, while prosperous aristocratic and merchant families, as well as a large proportion of clerics, monks, and nuns regularly ate meat or fish. Some scholars estimate that the amount of meat eaten during the Middle Ages, around 220 pounds (100 kilograms) per head a year, was considerably more than it is today. The theory has not been proved, but we may assume that up to the 16th century a great deal of meat was eaten in Germany in any case, and eaten more frequently than in the early 19th century.

Records of tithes, manorial dues, and the events known as "visitations" often make the detailed reconstruction of medieval menus possible. Meticulous lists of stocks and deliveries, such as those left by the cellarers of the many monastic vineyards of Trier, also provide useful information on the drinking habits of the feudal age. Similarly, the menus of chivalric banquets that have come down to us contain interesting details of culinary preferences in fortresses, castles, clerical refectories, and patrician houses.

Even in the poorest fortresses of remote mountainous regions overgrown with forests, plenty of game and preserved fruit and vegetables from the garden made up for seasonal shortages of fresh food. The gardeners, huntsmen, and guards employed by feudal lords usually benefited by their proximity to the court kitchen, and had "soup or vegetables in the morning, soup and meat at noon, with vegetables or milk, and at night preserved meat and milk again."

In the context of cultural history, the social contrasts in people's diet were not a matter of chance, but corresponded directly to the social hierarchy. Every rank of society had its own culinary standards, derived from and indeed conditioned by traditional laws. For instance, a shepherd boy who could be proved to have eaten a leg of lamb had to spend a week in prison for this "crime." And anyone who was caught poaching in the lord's game preserves in the forest could usually expect an immediate death sentence. All privileges and prohibitions in matters of hunting, stockbreeding, grazing rights, and tilling the fields were traditionally governed by strict regulations, which included the amounts of basic nourishment laid down by the authorities for the great majority of the population: serfs and tenants who owed dues to the lord of the manor. The archbishops of Mainz drew up extremely precise guidelines for the provision of flour, bread and drink to the men who tilled their fields and vineyards. In fact the rations allotted by these princes of the church were generous by comparison with those in other regions, and to this day, throughout the Rhineland-Palatinate, there is a proverbial saying: "Living is good under the [bishop's] crozier!"

The "medieval banquets" now offered as tourist attractions at various castles along the Middle Rhine and its tributaries imitate the lavish meals once reserved for the upper classes of the Middle Ages: salt meat, braised or boiled fresh meat, home-cured sausage and ham, together with sauerkraut, all kinds of vegetables, and stone-baked bread, followed by dried fruit, berries sweetened with honey, and plenty of beer and wine.

The real charm of these "medieval banquets," however, when they follow the originals faithfully, is in their "props" and eating implements: the food comes to table on well-scoured wooden boards, in shallow wooden dishes, or tall, barrel-shaped bowls, with stoneware pitchers holding soup and beverages. You eat with your fingers, as was still customary in some parts of Europe into the 20th century; even emperors ate with their fingers before the Italian fashion of using a fork came in. An eyewitness writes in 1547, of Emperor Charles V, that: "At several Reichstags, I saw the Emperor at meat ... He had nothing cut up for him, and did not use his own knife much, only to cut a number of little pieces of bread, of such a size that he could place one in his mouth with every morsel. And when he wished to eat of a dish, he cut it partly away at the corner he liked best with his knife, then broke off his portion with his fingers, placed the dish under his chin, and ate in so natural a fashion, yet so neatly and cleanly, that it was a pleasure to watch him."

However authentic today's medieval banquets claim to be, they are certainly not authentic in one aspect: the spicing of the food. The ruling class of the Middle Ages used spices in such large quantities that we would find their food inedible. The richer the host and the grander the occasion, the more pepper, saffron, nutmeg, etc. was used in preparing the meal. Medieval Europe was addicted to spices; they were extremely expensive, and were thus a status symbol, and they also conveyed the flavor of an exotic, fascinating culture discovered during the Crusades, the culture of the East (see also page 166).

Medieval recipes do not give quantities, but from the records we can form an approximate idea of the amounts of spices thought necessary for the entertainment of 40 guests: "A pound of powdered columbine ... half a pound of ground cinnamon ... two pounds of sugar ... an ounce of saffron ... quarter of a pound of cloves and Guinea pepper ... an eighth of a pound of pepper ... an eighth of a pound of ginger root ... an eighth of a pound of nutmeg ... an eighth of a pound of bay."

The kitchen of the medieval fortress of Marksburg, the only fortress along the Middle Rhine never to have been destroyed.

Opposite: this medieval illumination shows the festive banquet given by Duke Charles the Bold of Burgundy in 1474 in honor of Emperor Frederick III.

Vegetable dishes

Rote-Bete-Gemüse
Beets with sour cream and lemon
(Illustrated below, center)

6 beets
salt
1 tbsp lard
1 tbsp flour
1 small onion
5 cloves
1 tsp sugar
½ tsp cinnamon
white pepper
juice of half a lemon
2 tbsp sour cream

Scrub the beets well under running water, trim away the roots and leaves. Put into boiling salted water, and simmer for about 1½ hours, until tender. Take the beets out, run cold water over them, skin and cut into slices. Melt the lard in a heavy pan, cook the flour in it gently until pale yellow, and slowly add 1 cup/250 ml of water, stirring constantly. Peel the onion and grate it into the sauce, add the cloves, sugar, cinnamon, salt, and pepper. Allow the sauce to thicken for 5 minutes, stirring constantly. Add the beets, bring to boil again, and take the pan off the stove. Stir in the lemon juice and sour cream, taste, and adjust the seasoning if necessary.

Schnippelbohnesupp
Green bean soup
(Illustrated above, center)

2 lb/1 kg fresh green beans
2 potatoes
2 carrots
soup vegetables (carrot, celery stalk, leek, bunch of parsley)
6 cups/1.5 liters meat stock
salt and pepper
pinch of ground nutmeg
¾ cup/200 ml cream

Clean and wash the vegetables. Cut the beans into small pieces, dice the potatoes, carrots, and soup vegetables. Bring all to boil with the meat stock, season with salt, pepper, and nutmeg, cover, and simmer over a low heat for about 20 minutes. Serve the cream separately, stirring into the bowls of soup. Fresh yeast plum cake goes well with this green bean soup.

Zwetschgenkuchen
Yeast plum cake
(Illustrated left)

4 cups/500 g flour
½ cup/100 g sugar
pinch of salt
2 cakes compressed yeast
1 cup/250 ml lukewarm milk
⅓ cup/75 g butter
1 egg
butter for the baking pan
2 tbsp white breadcrumbs
4 lb/2 kg plums

Make a yeast dough with the flour, half the sugar, salt, yeast, milk, butter, and egg, and allow it to rise. Butter a baking pan, and roll the dough out on it, pulling it up at the sides. Sprinkle with the breadcrumbs, and allow to rise again for 10 minutes. Wash, halve, and pit the plums. Flatten the plum halves slightly, and place side by side close together on the dough. Bake for 30 minutes in a preheated oven at 400 °F/200 °C.

Yeast plum cake

Green bean soup

Beets with sour cream and lemon

Potatoes

The people of the Palatinate were ahead of their time in appreciating the potato. They recognized the nutritional value of this member of the Solanaceae plant family even earlier than the inhabitants of the Vogtland area, and the Palatinate was the first place on German soil to become true potato country. Waldensians from Piedmont first cultivated potatoes in 1665 in the parish of Germersheim, in the Electorate of the Palatinate. There are documentary records of this, and we may conclude that the potato was grown here as part of the staple diet even earlier. Rudolf Virchow, a doctor who studied the health of the poor in the middle of the 19th century, tells us that the village of Biberau in the Odenwald was the leading potato growing village of the time. In general it was the poor mountainous regions that became early centers of potato growing.

In the Hunsrück and Westerwald areas, the potato, known as the Grundbirne ("ground pear"), played so essential a part as the main source of nutrition, especially at times when food was short, that potato dishes feature prominently today on all menus typical of the region. After World War II, the potato again became a lifesaving item in the diet.

Kartoffelgulasch
Potato goulash

8 floury potatoes
salt
2 large onions, finely diced
2 tbsp butter
2 tbsp flour
3 cups/750 ml milk
1 lb/500 g boiled pork sausage, sliced
1 bunch of parsley, finely chopped
generous ⅓ cup/100 ml white wine
pepper
pinch of ground nutmeg

Wash the potatoes, and cook them in their skins until tender. Drain the potatoes, run cold water over them, peel, and slice. Sauté the onions gently in the butter until transparent. Dust them with the flour, brown slightly, and add the milk. Allow to thicken for 10 minutes, stirring constantly. Mix in the slices of sausage and potato, and reheat them in the sauce. Add the chopped parsley, and season to taste with the white wine, salt, pepper, and nutmeg. Serve a green salad with the potato goulash.

Kartoffelsuppe mit Zwetschgenkuchen
Potato soup with yeast plum cake

4 potatoes
salt
3 tbsp butter
1 onion, finely diced
3 scallions, thinly sliced
1 tbsp flour
3 cups/750 ml meat stock
2 cups/500 ml cream
pepper
2 tbsp croutons

Wash the potatoes, and cook them in their skins for 20 minutes, until tender. Drain, peel, and put them through the potato ricer. Melt 2 tbsp of the butter, and sauté the onions and scallions gently in it until transparent. Add the flour, stir until golden yellow, and then add the meat stock, stirring constantly. Mix in the potato purée, bring the soup to boil, and gradually stir in the cream. Divide the remaining butter into small pieces and add, season with salt and pepper. Serve the potato soup with croutons, and the yeast plum cake separately (recipe on opposite page).

Hunsrücker Kartoffelwurst
Hunsrück potato sausage

12 potatoes
salt
1½ lb/750 g uncooked pork belly
½ lb/250 g cooked beef
scant ⅓ cup/75 ml meat stock
white pepper
ground nutmeg
1 tsp dried marjoram
sausage skins

Wash the potatoes, and cook them in their skins for 20 minutes, until tender. Drain, peel, and put them through the potato ricer. Dice the pork belly and the beef, and put them through the grinder. Mix well with the potato and stock, and season well with salt, pepper, nutmeg, and marjoram. Put the mixture into sausage skins, and simmer for 1 hour at 175 °F/80 °C, until done.

√ w/ geschnetzletes instead of blood sausage

Kartoffelgugelhupf mit Blutwurstdipp
Potato gugelhupf with blood sausage dip
(Illustrated below)

8 potatoes
2 onions, finely diced
8 oz/250 g side bacon, finely diced
5 egg yolks
salt and pepper
pinch of ground nutmeg
6 tbsp/100 g flour
butter and white breadcrumbs for the mold
1¾ lb/800 g blood sausage
1 tbsp oil
1 tbsp each chopped parsley and chives

Peel the potatoes, wash, and grate coarsely. Put the grated potato in a dishcloth and squeeze out all the liquid. Thoroughly mix half the onions and bacon with the potatoes. Mix in the egg yolks, season with salt, pepper, and nutmeg. Gradually work in the flour until you have a smooth, firm dough. Grease a gugelhupf mold, and sprinkle with the white breadcrumbs. Put the potato dough in the mold, and bake in a preheated oven for about 1½ hours at 400 °F/200 °C. Turn the gugelhupf out of the mold, and cut into slices. Dice the blood sausage. Sauté the remaining onion gently in the oil until transparent, add the blood sausage, and sauté until it breaks up. Mix in the parsley and chives, and serve the blood sausage dip with the potato gugelhupf.

The Romans

When Caesar's legions were subduing the northern Gauls around 50 B.C. they had a particularly easy conquest of the land inhabited by the Celts on the Mosel, Nahe, Saar and Rhine. The Treveri, who lived in Luxembourg, Trier and Koblenz had in fact appealed to the Romans to protect them against the many wild hordes of Germanic freebooters who often crossed the river, looting and burning the countryside on the left bank of the Rhine. Julius Caesar was delighted when the Treveri appealed for help, and immediately sent in his troops. At the same time, however, he gave orders for the introduction of the laws and administrative regulations of the Roman Empire into the entire area between Trier, Mainz, and Cologne.

The arrival of the Romans in the land of the Treveri marked the beginning of a period of history lasting a good 500 years (until around A.D. 450), while the native Celtic culture had the culture of the far more advanced Romans superimposed on it, and was eventually entirely suppressed. In many ways, this comprehensive cultural transformation may be compared to the spread of the American way of life around the globe in the present day: the language, luxury goods, and technical achievements of the occupying power were imitated, imported, and finally adopted unreservedly. Within a few generations the Celts developed into a classic provincial Roman society.

The main centers on the Rhine and Mosel flourished, and their prosperity also benefited their rural surroundings. In particular, there was a great concentration of economic forces in the Treverian metropolis of Trier, which as Augusta Treverorum was even sometimes regarded as the capital of the entire *Imperium Romanum*. Mosel fishermen and fish farmers from the river valleys, farmers and cattle-breeders from the heights of the Eifel and Hunsrück, as well as carters, gardeners, vintners, artists, and craftsmen lived by supplying the markets, villas, and palace households of Trier.

Trier's trade relations extended throughout western and southern Europe: imported goods from all the Roman provinces between Britain, Asia Minor and North Africa found their way to the city on the Mosel. Archeologists studying the early history of Trier have found many burial sites from the Roman period containing evidence of these contacts: as well as grave goods – gold jewelry, coins, and glass goblets – many Etruscan bronzes reflect the former luxury of the city. Even Egyptian statuettes have been found in

Roman cuisine is experiencing a revival: this Roman meal was made from recipes taken from Apicius's cookery book.

the Mosel area, and the dates left over after a funeral feast are clear evidence that Trier had a flourishing trade in southern fruits.

Not only the finds of grave goods but also many ornamental tombstones present a lively picture of life in Roman times. The reliefs on dozens of huge funerary monuments, now on display in the Rheinisches Landesmuseum in Trier, may be regarded as a unique pictorial record of everyday life in the Roman empire. The scenes they show give us an insight into the private and professional lives of people of all classes. There is a highborn lady at the hairdresser's, for instance, and a legionary in full uniform. Farmers are shown at their various tasks, and paying the annual rent. Carters drive vehicles drawn by one or more horses, fishermen pull their nets aboard, boats are towed upstream, their crews hoist sails. The stone carvings of Mosel wine boats from Neumagen-Dhron are famous, together with their obviously hard-drinking sailors, and the "merry steersman," whose sunny expression makes him look like a Roman version of "Michel," the stereotypical if not very bright German of today. Apart from these wine boats, the Trier museum also has several stone reliefs with depictions of feasts in ancient times, giving us an excellent chance to examine what the indigenous Celts regarded as the quintessence of the Roman way of life.

Ave Apicius

Marcus Gavius Apicius, who left us a unique collection of over 300 recipes in his "Art of Cooking" of around A.D. 25, has gone down in history not only as a great gourmet but as an unusually logical one. It is said that he lived almost entirely for the pleasures of the table, and since he gave at least fifty lavish banquets a year, he ran through an immense fortune. The story goes that when Apicius discovered one day that his remaining property would not finance the next three dinners he planned to give, he decided to make his departure from this world of plenty in style, and immediately drank a cup of hemlock.

Apicius's "Art of Cooking" is evidence of the large quantities of herbs and the many different wines used in the Roman kitchen. Although the recipes give no indication of quantities, cooking them today shows that the chefs of the ancient world usually thought more of adding complex and indeed overpowering combinations of seasonings than of bringing out the natural flavors of fish, meat, or vegetables.

The universal seasoning was *liquamen*, extracted from anchovies, and as essential an ingredient in soups, meat, and vegetable dishes as in pastries and desserts. At dinner, which usually consisted of three courses, the Romans liked to start with salads, mushrooms, shellfish, and salted fish. A particularly popular hors d'oeuvre was stuffed dormice. The main course consisted of boiled or roast meat and poultry, accompanied by vegetables, while the dessert course usually featured fresh fruit or pastries sweetened with honey.

Men's work

Even beyond the Hunsrück and the countryside around the River Nahe, the people of Idar-Oberstein are known to be open-minded and tolerant. But tolerance stops short of any interference with their "national dish," spit-roasted meat. They certainly celebrate the town's *Spiessbratenfest* "spit-roast festival" every summer

Whatever the seasoning, it always includes onions.

as a huge, exuberant bit of fun, and do not even take it amiss if ignorant visitors are disrespectful enough to call the *corpus delic(a)ti* that gives the festival its name a "barbecue." And even the most diehard of these spit-roast artists do not really mind a few plain sausages being added to the roasting grid, along with pieces of sparerib, neck or loin that have previously lain in imaginative marinades. But when it comes to the actual preparation and cooking of their own specialty, the spit roast, they will tolerate no liberties.

Malicious tongues might call it machismo, since traditional spit-roasting is strictly men's work. Apparently, around 1850 some gemstone prospectors from Idar-Oberstein came home from the jungles of Brazil, bringing back the secrets of its preparation. Even today, when the fragrance of roasting meat wafts over the whole town and all the surrounding villages on warm weekends, you can see hundreds of husbands and fathers tending the fires of their grills in the gardens, while it is up to their wives in the kitchen to prepare the equally traditional accompaniments of boiled potatoes and radish salad. It is generally accepted that nothing will change this division of labor.

Generally the grill consists of a tripod or a kind of metal gallows, with a round grid of adjustable height hanging from it. The fire burns in a circle of stones or a round trough surrounded by a wall

similar to that of a well. Less frequently, oil cans cut in half lengthways contain the fire, and a rolled joint is turned constantly over it on a long spit. The more usual type of grid, on or inside which the meat is turned, is used to cook portions of meat weighing from half a pound to a pound (250 to 500 grams), which have spent at least a day and a half in between thick onion rings, salted, peppered, and rubbed with garlic. The more talkative possessors of secret recipes will sometimes refer to clever touches with dill, savory, thyme, mild paprika, nutmeg, borage, parsley, or vegetable stock.

Practical jokers have spread the tale that the "original Idar-Oberstein" spit roast can be properly cooked only over a fire made of beech logs stored in an upright position for seven years. In fact, any non-resinous wood from deciduous trees is suitable. The meat should be put over the fire only when a good quantity of glowing embers has formed, with flames licking up above it at least hand high. Just before the pieces of meat are ready (after being turned once or twice), a couple of juniper twigs may be thrown on the fire. A dash of beer helps to bring out the flavor too.

Below: the meat may be turned on the spit as a rolled joint, or cooked as portions on a grill and turned by hand during cooking. The seasonings are always important.

A rolled joint is tied up with kitchen string.

Now the meat must rest, covered with onions.

Two unfortunate pigs

For want of a wooden peg, the night watchman of Wittlich fixed the iron bolt of the Himmerod Gate in place with a chunk of rutabaga one evening. A stray pig came along and ate it. Meanwhile, thieves were lying in wait outside the gate, and they were now able to enter the town. They fell on the unsuspecting citizens, robbed them, and set their houses on fire. After this attack, the town councillors of Wittlich condemned the greedy rutabaga-eating pig to death by burning at the stake. Of course not even the executioner could resist the smell of roasting that wafted over the place of execution when the sentence was carried out. Ever since then, Wittlich has celebrated the "Pig Burners' Carnival," and to this day almost 100 unfortunate pigs are roasted on the spit every year.

In nearby Ebernburg, too, a harmless pig felt the full weight of destiny fall on it during a siege. Food was running out, but to persuade the enemy that the townsfolk had plenty of food, they led the animal out on the parapets every morning, and tweaked its soft parts hard. Its shrieks sounded as if it were being slaughtered. In fact it was their very last pig, and the besieged townsfolk were in danger of dying of starvation. But they continued the policy of pinching the pig and making it scream until their psychological warfare took effect, and the besiegers went away frustrated. Now, at last, the poor pig really could be slaughtered. As it was a male animal, the town was known thereafter as Ebernburg, from the word *Eber*, a boar.

Good and fat – not too thin

"Better fine and fat and wobbly, than thin and bony and all knobbly!" Nothing if not explicit, this proverb is known from the southern Palatinate to the high Westerwald, and sums up the local attitude to meat consumption in general. When pigs were kept not just on farms, but in the sheds or cellars of town houses, it was not as a kind of hobby, but as a necessity of life. And where the proverbial laboring man's cow was kept, as well as some goats, the description "good and fat" was a status symbol.

The festivities surrounding pig-killing were traditionally celebrated in villages before Christmas, when animals fattened up in summer would hang steaming in rows on the butchers' racks. Boiled pork, salted meat, and various homemade sausages were prepared, providing the staple diet for the long winter weeks to come. Many marinades typical of the region derive from that lean time of the year; they may contain vinegar, wine, onion, garlic, pepper, juniper berries, bayleaves, and celeriac.

A parade at the Wittlich Pig Burners' Carnival: although Wittlich is in the Eifel area, the cheerful attitude of the Mosel region is typical of the merrymaking.

Huge numbers of roast pork rolls are sold at the biggest popular festival in the Eifel – truly an occasion of great proportions (and large portions).

A national dish

Even people with an aversion to advertising slogans may admire the simple but brilliant German advertisement that runs, *Die Liebe zur Pfalz geht auch durch den Saumagen* (literally, "Love of the Palatinate comes by way of the pig's stomach," but with reference to both the expression that someone who has a *Saumagen* can stomach anything, and also to the local dish of stuffed pig stomach). Even critical gourmets must admit that other fossilized remains of the cooking of the Rhineland, some of them known for centuries beyond the borders of Germany, have been overtaken by stuffed pig stomach, now the national dish of the Palatinate. Sauerbraten (braised beef in vinegar), red cabbage, even sauerkraut hardly get a mention today in France, Great Britain or Russia. And since stuffed pig's stomach has been mentioned by so many international politicians, the region of its origin cannot disregard its ever-increasing efficacy in the matter of public relations.

Stuffing the stomach of an animal with a mixture of meats after slaughter, then cooking or drying it, is the very oldest form of sausage-making. Babylonian clay tablets of the 3rd century B.C. mentioned the technique, and in the *Odyssey* Homer several times speaks of blood sausage contained in the stomachs of goats or pigs. The stuffed pig stomach of the Palatinate is not as old as those examples, for what distinguishes it from other versions of the dish is the fact that it contains potatoes, and they were not introduced into the Palatinate until the 17th century. Precooked, diced potatoes form part of the stuffing, along with coarsely ground pork or sausagemeat, onions, and such seasonings as pepper, marjoram, and nutmeg. The stuffed stomach is simmered in water, and can be sautéed on all sides in hot oil before serving, to give it a crisp coating. It is then carved in slices, and eaten with sauerkraut and creamed potato.

Stuffed pig's stomach is one of the meat and sausage products of the Palatinate for which special quality guidelines were laid down in the years 1977–79. They also include Palatinate liver sausage, containing marjoram and 20 percent liver, Palatinate blood sausage or bacon blood sausage, which has diced bacon worked into it (amounting to 40 percent of the sausage in old recipes), and Palatinate collared brawn. Pressed head has also been known far beyond the Palatinate itself for a long time. Once a typical by-product of the home slaughtering of animals to provide food to last the winter, pressed head is made in several different versions, generally including meat from the pig's snout and calf's feet, and a variety of garden produce such as celeriac, leek, carrots, scorzonera, and onions.

Bacon, ham, assorted cold cuts, homemade sausages, brawn, and cheese should all be included on the nourishing platters offered as *Vesper* (a late afternoon or evening snack) all over the Rhenish Oberland and the Palatinate. In addition, traditional breads are now being revived. During the last two decades, historic parish bakeries have been restored in hundreds of villages throughout the region and are now in use again, baking and distributing local specialties. This new enthusiasm for good stone-baked bread, potato bread, *Kastenriewes* (a potato cake baked in a square pan), and *Quetschekuchen* (yeast cake with plums) has led to the introduction of a "bakery festival" in many places taking place at least once a year, with other items from the local village's culinary tradition also on offer.

In the old days, *Vesper* was usually eaten in the late afternoon by men working out in the fields or woods. Only in winegrowing areas is this early evening meal still common. Instead, you will find picnickers on vacation. A typical vintner's *Vesper* must naturally be chosen to suit the wine that, equally naturally, is drunk with it. But what kind of meal consisting of bread and pork, sausage or cheese would not go down well with a Riesling or Kerner wine?

Pfälzer Saumagen
Palatinate stuffed pig's stomach
(Illustrated right)

1 small, cleaned pig's stomach
(ordered in advance from the butcher)
5 shallots, finely diced
1 clove of garlic, crushed
1 tbsp butter
1 bunch of parsley, chopped
8 cooked potatoes
12 oz/350 g lean pork belly
12 oz/350 g pork
12 oz/350 g sausagemeat
2 bread rolls, soaked in milk
3 eggs
salt and pepper
1 tsp dried marjoram
½ tsp ground nutmeg

Soak the pig's stomach in water overnight. Next day drain it well, and sew up two of the three stomach openings with kitchen string. Sauté the shallots and garlic gently in the butter until transparent, add the parsley, and cook again briefly. Take the pan off the stove and allow it to cool slightly. Cut the potatoes and meat into small dice, and mix thoroughly with the sausagemeat, the soaked rolls (with the milk pressed out), the onion mixture, and the eggs. Season the stuffing well with salt, pepper, marjoram, and nutmeg, and put it into the pig's stomach. Sew up the opening. Bring plenty of water to a boil in a large pan, put the pig's stomach into it, and allow to simmer over low heat for about 2½ hours. Do not on any account let it boil. When the stomach is cooked, take it out of the water, drain it, and cut it into slices ½ inch/2 cm thick. Serve with sauerkraut made with wine, and wholemeal bread.

Liver dumplings and homemade sausage with wine sauerkraut.

Leberknödel
Liver dumplings

4 stale bread rolls
scant ⅓ cup/75 ml hot milk
1 onion, finely diced
1 tbsp butter
2 tbsp chopped parsley
1 egg
salt, pepper
pinch of ground nutmeg
½ tsp dried marjoram
½ lb/250 g calf's liver
4 slices bacon

Cut the rolls into thin slices, place in a bowl, and cover with the hot milk. Allow to soak for 15 minutes. Meanwhile, sauté the onion gently in the butter, until transparent. Add the parsley and cook for a moment longer. Take the pan off the stove and allow to cool. Stir the onion and parsley mixture and the egg into the soaked rolls. Season this dough with salt, pepper, nutmeg, and marjoram. Put the liver and the bacon twice through the fine disk of the grinder, and knead them into the dough. With wet hands, form the dough into dumplings. Bring a large pan of salted water to boil, place the dumplings in it, and let them simmer for about 25 minutes. Lift the cooked dumplings out of the water with a perforated spoon. Serve with home-made sausages and wine sauerkraut.

»Vice vinum«: Viez

Not only in the orchards of Merz on the Saar, but in "holy Trier" itself, the local cider has become something of a national drink. Its traditional name in the region is *Viez*, from the Latin *vice vinum*, meaning, roughly, "instead of wine" or "substitute wine." But such a definition of the term would infuriate many people who enjoy it, for their elixir is neither second choice nor a descendant of Norman cider, nor should it be confused with the "Eppelwoi" (apple wine) of Frankfurt. Viez is Viez, and Viez it will remain for the forseeable future, as the local patriots of Trier firmly state, for it tastes very different from ciders elsewhere. It is best drunk with a hearty *Vesper* platter (snack) containing cheese, ham, and home-style sausage. A pint glass (quarter of a liter) of Viez is also a traditional accompaniment to fried freshwater fish from the Mosel.

Palatinate stuffed pig's stomach

State hunts

Wooded ridges, dominating the landscape, rise above the valleys, hills, and high plateaux that are cultivated as vineyards or arable land all over the Rhineland-Palatinate. The Vosges mountains, the Wasgau, the Haardt in the Palatinate, the Donnersberg, Idarwald and Soon forests, the Hocheifel, the Linzer Höhe or the Köppel: these dark green wooded heights are a striking feature, marking off the geographical contours of the region. Forested regions richer in game than any others in West Germany, they lie just outside small conurbations, not far from many stretches of the autobahn.

In the Soonwald forest, where men from the Electorate of the Palatinate were hunting game in 1780, Count Walram of Sponheim was tracking down boar, deer, and village maidens as early as 1250, and the dukes of Pfalz-Zweibrücken and Pfalz-Simmern, following in his footsteps, stalked game on the heights of the Soonwald forest 250 years later. They converted the ruins of the old fortress into a hunting lodge, to which they invited guests from neighboring small states. Not, of course, without ulterior motives, for a jovial evening over a glass of wine was a good time to talk politics. Half a century ago Theodor Heuss, then president of the Federal Republic, remembered this tradition, and held the first Federal German state hunt. Since then politicians from Bonn and Berlin and foreign ambassadors have come to the quiet forests of the Soonwald annually in the fall, to stalk their prey in the undergrowth rather than along the corridors of power.

The hunter from the Palatinate

When Friedrich Wilhelm Utsch held the post of "mounted hereditary forester of the Great Soon" around 1780, this forest in the Hunsrück area belonged to the dukes of the Electorate of the Palatinate. Kaiser Wilhelm II thought it worth celebrating the activities of Utsch, a mighty hunter whose deeds were recorded in song. On August 13, 1913 His Majesty personally unveiled a putto-adorned memorial to Utsch as "supreme among German huntsmen" near the Waldweiler Entenpfuhl. It stands there to this day, reminding us of the Baroque pleasures of the hunt in the old days. A rather coarse tale is told in the villages on the outskirts of the Soonwald concerning the day when this memorial was unveiled: out of sheer respect (it is claimed), a dozen or so of the foresters invited to the Kaiser's reception soiled their green trousers. It seems more likely that an overseasoned dish of wild boar was the reason for this unfortunate incident. Historically, Friedrich Wilhelm Utsch (1732–1795) cuts a better figure than the robber chief Schinderhannes, the notorious "hero of the Hunsrück" who prowled this area two decades later, even if certain critics sought to annoy the Emperor by remarking that, "The fame of Friedrich Wilhelm Utsch, has suffered from a mighty putsch." Utsch is buried in the village of Auen; his gravestone explicitly calls him "huntsman of the Electorate of the Palatinate." Another hunter in the Soonwald has also entered German song, but as it has no melody Gottfried August Bürger's ballad of 1774, *Der wilde Jäger* (The Wild Huntsman) is little known despite its stirring opening lines:

"The Count of the Rhine, he blew his horn,
And went out hunting one fine day.
His stallion whinnied in the dawn,
His men went galloping away.
O'er hill and dale, o'er field and hollow,
Where the Count rode his men would follow."

Wildschweinrücken in Kruste
Saddle of wild boar in a crust
(Illustrated opposite)

For 8 people

1 saddle of young wild boar, with bones left in, weighing around 6½ lb/3 kg
salt and pepper
1 tsp thyme
1 tsp sage
1 tbsp lard
2 carrots, sliced
½ celeriac root, diced
1 onion, diced
2 cups/500 ml red grape juice
6 tbsp/100 g butter at room temperature
3 eggs
10–12 tbsp breadcrumbs
2 bunches of parsley, chopped
1 cup/250 g black grapes
generous ⅖ cup/100 ml cream

Wash the saddle of wild boar, pat it dry, and season well with salt, pepper, thyme, and sage. Melt the lard in a heavy pan, and seal the saddle of boar over high heat, meat side down. Turn it over, add the carrots, celeriac, and onion, and sauté. Pour in the grape juice, cover the pan, and cook over moderate heat for 1½ hours. Beat the butter and eggs until light and foamy, and gradually work in the breadcrumbs and parsley until you have a thick paste. Remove the meat from the pan, drain it, and coat it with the paste. Put it back in the pan, and bake in a preheated over for 15–20 minutes at 400 °F/200 °C, until the crust is golden brown. Put the saddle of boar on a carving board. Sieve the juices from the pan. Halve and seed the grapes, bring to a boil in the pan juices, season with salt and pepper, and stir in the cream. Remove the meat from the bones, carve into slices, and arrange on a pre-warmed serving dish. Serve the sauce separately.

Entenpfuhler Wilderersalat
Entenpfuhl poacher's salad

14 oz/400 g roast game (leftovers of roast hare, venison, or wild boar)
2 cooking apples
2 small oranges
2 tbsp white wine
⅔ cup mayonnaise
salt and pepper
4 tbsp brandy
1 tsp mustard

Cut the cooked game into narrow strips. Peel, quarter, and core the apples. Peel and quarter the oranges, and remove the white pith. Cut the apples and oranges into small pieces, and pour the white wine over them. Beat the mayonnaise, and season it with salt, pepper, brandy, and mustard. Put half the mayonnaise in a glass bowl, layer the apples, meat, and oranges on top, and cover with the rest of the mayonnaise. Allow to stand in the refrigerator.

Deer were not the only game to be shot by politicians. The forests of the Rhineland-Palatinate are very rich in game, including large herds of wild boar.

Süss-sauer eingelegte Moselfische
Sweet-sour marinaded river fish

12 small river fish, prepared for cooking
juice of 2 lemons
salt and pepper
flour for coating the fish
oil for frying
4 cups/1 liter wine
2 tbsp sugar
1 tbsp pickling spices
4 large onions, sliced
8 bay leaves

Wash the fish, pat them dry, and sprinkle with the lemon juice. Allow them to stand for 10 minutes, salt and pepper them, and coat them with the flour. Fry in batches in plenty of hot oil, remove with a perforated spoon, and drain well on paper towels. Bring the wine to a boil with 2 cups/500 ml of water, the sugar, 1 tsp salt, and the pickling spices. Arrange the fish, sliced onions, and bay leaves in a large dish, pour the marinade over them, cover, and allow to stand for 2 days. Serve with bread and cider.

River dwellers

Since the end of the 1980s the major cleaning operation carried out on the Rhine as a result of compulsory international conservation measures has been rewarded by an annual improvement in the quality of its water. Consequently, that great "German river," along with the Mosel, now harbors stocks of edible fish worthy of the name, and worth fishing for. There have even been sightings of small salmon. But it is no longer worth anyone's time to refurbish the pretty little fishing boats that until around 1960 used to throw out their nets and make a good catch. Despite the success of environmental policies, and declarations of intent going even further, there can be no return to the days of small-scale fishing on the Rhine. The freshwater fish farmed in thousands of pools around the country have taken over the home market, and leisure anglers seek their catches in countless woodland or country streams, or in the many reservoirs of the Palatinate, in Lake Laach, and some of the small lakes of the Eifel region – and not least in the Rivers Nahe, Lahn, and Ahr. Furthermore, there are countless "trout farms" in almost every valley that has a stream of any size running through it, inviting people to make excursions to them. Most of these properties once belonged to mills, and their ancient water rights ensure the present owners a good living. Millponds have been converted into fishponds from which the catch can be taken straight to the kitchen, and served up on the dining table guaranteed as fresh as nature made it.

Fish are served in the traditional manner at the Worms fried fish festival, which is held at the end of July every year; they are gutted, seasoned with salt, and fried in oil. The fishermen's mock battle in the harbor is all part of the fun (opposite).

Moselländische Hechtpfanne
Fried pike in the Mosel country style

1 pike, weighing about 2½ lb/1.2 kg, prepared for cooking
salt and pepper
juice of a lemon
flour to coat the fish
¼ cup/50 g butter
2 onions, diced
½ lb/200 g mushrooms, sliced
2 cups/500 ml Mosel wine
1 cup/250 ml cream
1 tbsp chopped parsley

Wash the pike, pat it dry, and season it inside and outside with salt and pepper. Sprinkle with the lemon juice, and let it stand for 15 minutes. Then coat the pike in flour, shaking off any excess. Heat the butter in a long fish pan, and brown the pike on both sides. Add the onions and mushrooms, fry them briefly with the fish, and pour in the wine. Let the pike simmer until done – about 20 minutes (do not let it boil). When it is cooked, take the pike out of the pan and keep it warm. Stir the cream and parsley into the cooking liquid, and reduce slightly. Serve the sauce separately. Boiled potatoes and a green salad go well with this dish.

"Fish must swim," says an old German proverb – so wine flows freely at the fried fish festival.

"The hosts of the scaly horde"

"Their many kinds, their slanting course in swimming, and those companies which ascend up against the stream, and all the offspring of their countless tribe, it is not lawful for me to declare … Do thou for me, O Nymph, dweller in the river's realm, declare the hosts of the scaly horde …" writes Ausonius (c. A.D. 365), and he goes on, in these lines from his poem *Mosella*, to list all the fish that still swam in the Mosel in his day. Ausonius sees the river with the eyes of a knowledgeable gourmet, not just a poetic observer of nature:

"Neither shalt thou, O Perch, the dainty of our tables, be unsung – thou amongst fishes river-born worthy to be ranked with the sea-bred, who alone canst vie on equal terms with the rosy mullet; for not insipid is thy flavor, and in thy plump body the parts meet as segments, but are kept apart by the backbone. Here, too, doth he, jestingly known by a Latin proper name – that dweller in the marshes, most deadly enemy to plaintive frogs – Lucius (the Pike), beset pools dim with sedge and ooze: he, chosen for no service at banquets, is fried in cook-shops rank with the fumes of his greasy flavor. Who shall not know of the green Tench also, the comfort of the commons, of Bleak, a prey for boyish hooks, of Shad, hissing on the hearth, food for the vulgar, and of thee, something between two species … not yet salmon, no longer trout, and undefined betwixt these twain …?"

Mineral water

There is no doubt that water is popular these days. Even in traditional citadels of brewing, where the mere mention of the word "water" might once have been expected to give rise to hilarity, if not to cause actual offense, waiters now show no surprise when someone orders mineral water. In top restaurants, a stylish designer bottle containing water from springs as far away as possible is a status symbol.

This is no storm in a water glass, as the statistics show. In recent decades, consumption of mineral and medicinal water has risen steadily. While it stood at 3.5 gallons (12.5 liters) a head in 1970, it is now approaching the 21 gallon (100 liter) mark. Growth rates of over 5 percent delight the 239 firms marketing German mineral waters, and they need not fear that supplies will run out. The country has around 550 officially recognized springs of mineral water, fed by rain, and everyone knows that Germany has plenty of that commodity. However, water deposits opened up by drilling wells, often to a depth of several hundred meters, do not consist of the snow or rain that fell yesterday. The process whereby the water trickles through strata of coarse or fine gravel and sand can take several hundred years. Not only does that process filter and cleanse the deep springs, it also helps the water to absorb minerals and trace elements from the strata through which it passes, and it is in these substances that the healthy properties of the water reside.

Depending on their situation, mineral springs have a greater or lesser mineral content. Water in areas where there were volcanic or tectonic disturbances some 70 to 200 million years ago is particularly rich in minerals. Such areas are found in the Eifel, the upper and central valley of the Rhine, and the stratified slopes of southwestern Germany. In these regions, the water runs through many different strata, absorbing a large quantity of minerals.

Mineral substances and trace elements, of course, give mineral water added value, and dieticians are pleased that it is in fashion at the moment – although there is no denying the proverbial saying that "Water may quench your thirst, but it does not teach you to sing." It is still true that only those beverages with alcoholic "trace elements" can move the Germans to song.

Below: water, the source of life. Natural mineral water contains valuable minerals and trace elements.

Different kinds of water

Medicinal water
has a medicinal effect because of the minerals and trace elements it contains, and it is classified as a medicine; the label must list its beneficial properties and any side-effects.

Natural mineral water
must come from an underground deposit, a natural or artificially drilled spring, and be bottled close to its place of origin. It may be marketed only after its purity and mineral content have been analysed.

Spring water
must come from an identified spring, may not be treated, and must be of drinking quality; however, it need not contain any minerals or trace elements.

Table water
is a definition allowing the manufacturer a free hand with the water which goes into his product, and lets him decide whether to enrich it with minerals or salt, and where and how he bottles it.

Tap water
is mainly drawn from groundwater, with the addition of river, lake, and small amounts of industrial water, chemically treated; it may contain 50 milligrams of nitrates per liter (about 3 grains per gallon) and up to 0.5 milligrams (about 0.03 grains per gallon) of pesticide.

Spas

Every spa in Germany, and there are around 220 of them, can look back on its own unique history. The development of the spa in general can be traced by studying Bad Ems, where people flocked to bathe in the medicinal springs of the Lahn valley and drink their waters even in Roman times. It was frequented not only by legionaries who had contracted bronchitis while standing guard on the nearby Roman border wall of the Limes, but by ladies of the highest social circles who went there to cure their ills. The fair Agrippina, wife of Germanicus, bathed at length in the "boys' spring" at Ems, and was duly brought to bed of a son, known as Caligula, although he was not a great success later as Emperor of Rome. Many augurs had muttered dark forebodings by his cradle, commenting that his conception had been along the lines of the old saying "For barren wives, a spa is best – if the spa doesn't do it, she may try a guest."

During the immediate post-Roman centuries, few of the spas of antiquity on German soil retained their reputation. In most places, the tradition of healing springs was either entirely lost, or turned into folktale fantasies of obscure thermal spas or "springs of youth," as in Hans Sachs's mention of "the spring of life, in which the old are made young again." On the other hand, there was a great boom in public bathing during the Middle Ages; crusaders in the East had encountered the habit of bathing in public before days of rest and festivals. On their return, many knights had a comfortable bathing chamber built into their rather uncomfortable castles, and soon such baths were to be found at all German princely courts and in many towns. They functioned in much the same way as Turkish steam baths, and sovereigns and town councillors alike appreciated the income derived from renting out such baths for the purposes of cleansing, sweating, and medicinal blood-letting.

Many historical documents also suggest an early concern with aspects of hygiene: "The spread of leprosy and syphilis, with the increased danger of infection, the wearing of linen underclothes, a fashion now adopted by the common folk, many changes in habits and customs, and particularly the dissolute conduct associated with the public baths, caused a gradual decrease in visits to them. The habit of frequent bathing was lost again. On the other hand, it then became fashionable in Germany to visit thermal spas and their springs as pleasure resorts." Ultimately, however, it was the natural scientists and doctors of the Renaissance who applied the precepts of classical writings and the beneficial effect of thermal springs and water to the human organism.

Around 1450 a great rise in the number of visitors to Bad Ems was recorded; they were mainly

people recommended by doctors in Koblenz and other towns along the Rhine to take a cure. Later, many spa visitors followed the plausible enough recommendation of the Frankfurt "physicus" Johan Helfrich Jüncken: "Drinking from the springs has done much good to many with a chill, or thickness on the chest, or with coughs and shortness of breath, and even those already coughing blood have often felt considerable relief, and lived many years longer." However, a number of physicians shook their heads over the extravagant conduct of visitors to the spas "who come to the baths at the wrong time, against reason and without the advice of a doctor, and while they are there they eat voraciously, drink, and sleep, to the ruin of their health." At the beginning of the 19th century, when Bad Ems –

"where all the world met in the baths" – was gradually assuming the rank of "summer capital of Europe," Johann Wolfgang von Goethe scratched a saying in the wall of his lodgings that was to serve all spa visitors as a motto: "Should you ask after us, we were here; and may you who come after us feel your blood at least as fresh, and be as pious, as good, and as happy as we were."

Above: the interior of the wellhouse at Bad Pyrmont, from a lithograph of 1861.

Strong tobacco

One of the last areas in Germany where tobacco is
grown is in the "Wittlich hollow," as the area is known.
There are famous and extensive plantations on the
plains of the southern Palatinate at Herxheim, Hayna,
Rülzheim, Bellheim and Hatzenbühl. Even visitors who
do not identify the plants in the fields as tobacco will
notice an agricultural peculiarity: the tall drying sheds
standing on the outskirts of all the villages. The parish
of Herxheim, which consists of five formerly
independent villages, prides itself on being the largest
tobacco-cultivating community in Germany. Tobacco
from the Palatinate is in demand as part of the mixture
for cigarettes made by international firms, and also
gives its characteristic aroma to several world-famous
cigar brands.

Southern fruits of the southern Palatinate

"The place of spring," "the little garden of the
nuns," "the maidens' dell," "the little well of love"
– many writers have risen to poetic heights in
describing parts of the landscape along the Rhine
and its tributary valleys. Perhaps the ultimate
example of such pretty sayings is the pet name for
the Bad Dürkheim district, described as "the
dimple in the cheek of the Palatinate." It is
certainly a place with a very mild climate, where
the almond trees often come into blossom at the
end of February.

The almond, originally a native of the
Mediterranean, was being grown in the Palatinate
one thousand years ago. As early as around 1140,
Hildegard of Bingen described the medicinal use
of Palatinate almonds. Around 1550 Sebastian
Münster, the famous geographer of Ingelheim,
said that "all Germany" could be fed with the
great quantities of almonds picked in the
Rhineland-Palatinate. During the 14th century,
profits from the sale of almonds were so good that
the Electors felt obliged (not least for reasons of
taxation) to strictly regulate their cultivation .

Only in the course of the 19th century did the
economic importance of the almond decrease.
When scarcely an almond tree along the Wine
Road of the Palatinate blossomed in the spring of
1900, the ingenious economist Councillor Buhl of
Deidesheim had new almonds planted along a
number of main roads near Gimmeldingen. Buhl
had foreseen that thousands of almond trees
would have a new economic importance, attracting
the tourist trade, and the often-quoted "sea of
pink blossom along the Wine Road of the
Palatinate" provided free advertising every year.

When local patriots claim that Paradise must have
been situated near Edenkoben, Landau and
Klingenmünster, they cite Eve's fig leaf as proof.
In fact genuine fig trees do grow in many sheltered
courtyards in this area, sometimes even by the
roadside. But it would be an exaggeration to call
figs a local crop; fully ripe fruits can be picked only
after mild winters and hot summers, and then from
fig trees growing in the most sheltered positions.
Under similarly advantageous climatic conditions,
some enthusiastic gardeners have also succeeded
in wresting a few fruits from their carefully
cherished lemon trees in the village of Haardt.
Another plant species from the south can be
admired in Ilbesheim, where saffron, then almost
beyond price, grew 550 years ago; since 1992 it has
been grown again beside the road to Landau-
Wollmesheim.

Lemons are of neither culinary nor economic importance to the southern Palatinate, but the fact that amateur gardeners
succeed in cultivating them is evidence of the extremely mild climate of this region.

Sweet chestnuts

The sweet chestnut (*Castanea sativa*) is regarded as "the most important southerner in the Palatinate." It does not, like other subtropical trees such as cedars, wellingtonias, paulownias, cypresses, and sequoias, grow in groups in the parks and gardens of the Palatinate, but covers huge expanses of woodland. Particularly in the shelter of the Haardt, ancient stands of trees cover the slopes of the southeast outskirts of the Palatinate forest, which reach down to the climatically mild low-lying plains of the Upper Rhine. Sweet chestnuts are typical of this landscape, with their densely leaved crowns and the long catkin blossoms that gleam like ornaments of gold brocade in June and July. The prickly cases of the fruits split in the fall, shedding two to four flat nuts each; they are very tasty, and delicious either roasted or boiled. Chestnut woods form a backcloth of dark green to dozens of winegrowing villages, from the Leininger Land near Bad Dürkheim, to Edenkoben and Dörrenbach, and on to Bad Bergzabern. The first young saplings were probably grown by monks in medieval tree nurseries; but it has also been claimed that the Romans brought chestnuts as well as vines into the Rhineland-Palatinate. While sweet chestnuts are generally known in Germany as *Maronen* (from the French *marron*), here they have always had the local name of *Keschte*. The castle of Hambach, famous as the destination of the 1832 freedom march organized by a revolutionary group, is called after them, bearing the name of the *Keschteburg* (chestnut castle).

In the fall the prickly fruits of the sweet chestnut burst open, shedding two to four nuts.

Kastaniencreme
Chestnut cream

1 lb/500 g chestnuts	
½ cup/100 g sugar	
½ tsp vanilla essence	
2 tbsp orange liqueur	
1 cup/250 ml cream	

Cut a cross-shaped slit in the chestnuts, and roast in a preheated oven at 350 °F/175 °C for 10 minutes. Take the chestnuts out of the oven, cool and peel them, carefully removing the inner skin. Simmer the chestnuts in water for 30 minutes, until soft. Drain and sieve. Mix in the sugar, vanilla essence, and orange liqueur. Whip the cream until stiff, and fold carefully into the chestnut mixture. Chill before serving.

Sweet chestnuts can be boiled or roasted, and make very good stuffings, for instance for poultry.

As Christmas approaches, roast chestnuts are sold in city centers and at markets.

Hildegard of Bingen

Even in her lifetime, Hildegard of Bingen (1098–1179) was known throughout the western world as *prophetissa teutonica* ("the German prophetess"). She was entrusted to the nuns of the convent of Disibodenberg for her spiritual education at the age of eight, and spent three decades in the nunnery studying, praying, and meditating, before the sisters chose her as their mother superior in 1136.

On the hill where the nunnery stood, high above the confluence of the rivers Nahe and Glan, Hildegard had visions in which she saw the universe as a place of constant battle between good and evil. The spawn of hell was everywhere: Satan himself, dreadful demons and monsters threatened all human souls. But amidst this cosmic chaos she also saw shining paths leading to a center where the divine Trinity appeared. Hildegard experienced these visions not in dreams but in her waking state, and immediately dictated an account of them to a monk, whose notes appeared in 1151 as *Scivias* ("know the ways"); this was Hildegard's principal literary and theological work. The *Liber vitae meritorum* ("Book of the Merits of Life") followed in 1163, and the *Liber divinorum operum* ("Book of the Works of God ") in 1174.

A quotation from *Scivias* runs: "The soul glides into the body, like sap into the tree. The sap causes the tree to put out leaves and blossom, and to ripen fruit, and so the body is ripened by the soul. How does the fruit of the tree ripen? Through the right amount of warmth in summer. And how is that performed? The sun warms it, the rain gives moisture, and it ripens in moderate warmth. What does this mean? Why, that the mercy of the grace of God shines like the sun on men, the breath of the Holy Ghost pours over them like rain, and a right measure in all things leads them, like moderate summer air, to perform good works. Acknowledge then, O Man, what you are in your soul, that you may not cast aside your reason and lower yourself to the level of the beasts of the field."

The present revival of interest in Hildegard has attracted an increasing number of traditional Christians and people with esoteric leanings alike. Some hope that the "magic show" described in her visions, with its hallucinatory starbursts and effects of light and color, will reveal the deep mysteries of Creation to them. In view of such spectacular notions, few stop to entertain the sober theory that the prophetess's "inspirations, images and messages" could also be diagnosed as classic symptoms of severe migraine. But critical sobriety was not much in evidence in 1998, the 800th

Hildegard of Bingen, seer and healer, was the only woman of the Middle Ages to travel on preaching tours.

anniversary of her birth, an emotionally and commercially highly charged occasion, when over 100 titles of books by and about the Sibyl of the Rhine appeared. Her words and melodies for songs have been recorded on CD, and she is even on the Internet:
www.diozesetrier.de/einrich/bingen/homepage.htm.

Practical aids to life rather than occult visions are offered in Hildegard's writings on medicine (*Causae et Curae*), the 513 chapters of her *Physica*, and her *Pharmacopoeia of Plants*, a compendium of medieval pharmaceutical lore that is well worth reading. A few quotations are given on the page opposite.

Ten medicinal herbs from Hildegard's *Pharmacopeia*

1 Stinging nettle *(Urtica urens)*
"If a man is forgetful and would be cured of it, let him crush out the juice of the stinging nettle, and add some olive oil, and when he goes to bed, let him anoint his chest and temples with it, and do this often, and his forgetfulness will be alleviated."

2 Bramble leaves *(Rubus fruticosus)*
"The bramble, on which blackberries grow, is warm rather than cold. If anyone suffers a disorder of the lungs, and has a cough from his chest, let him take root of sneezewort, bramble leaves, hyssop, and a little origanum, add honey, and boil it all in good wine, then strain it through a cloth, drink sufficient quantity of it after a good meal, and do this often, and his lungs will be restored to health."

3 Vervain *(Verbena officinalis)*
"If a man have any rotten flesh in him, then boil this herb in water, lay a linen cloth on his wounds, and when the water has been pressed out lay on the vervain too. Do this until all the rottenness is gone."

4 Fennel *(Foeniculum vulgare)*
"However fennel is eaten, it makes men merry, and gives them a pleasant warmth, and makes them sweat well, and causes good digestion."

5 Cloves *(Syzygium aromaticum)*
"And if anyone have a headache, and his head is buzzing as if he were deaf, let him eat often of cloves, and they will ameliorate the buzzing in his head."

6 Hart's tongue *(Phyllitis scolopendrium)*
"Hart's tongue is warm, and good for the liver and the lungs, and for pain in the intestines."

7 Mullein *(Verbascum thapsus)*
"If any have a weak and sad heart, let him cook mullein with meat or fish, or with other herbs, and eat of it often, and it will strengthen his heart and make it merry."

8 Poppy *(Papaver somniferum)*
"Its seeds, if they be eaten, induce sleep and decrease itching. They suppress the torments of lice and nits. They may be eaten boiled in water, but are better and more effective raw than cooked."

9 Marigold *(Calendula officinalis)*
"The marigold is cold and damp, it has strong powers of growth in it, and is a remedy against poison. If anyone eat poison, or if it be served to him, let him boil marigolds in water, and after the water is pressed out let him lay them directly on his belly, and they will soften the poison and make it depart from him."

10 Milfoil *(Achilles millefolium)*
"Milfoil is rather warm and dry, and it is a sovereign remedy for wounds. Wash the wounds with wine, and let plenty of milfoil cooked moderately in water be laid on the cloth, while still warm, and so bind it over the wound."

These quotations have been slightly abbreviated and edited.

DORIS MÜLLER
Saarland

Songwriter Jürgen Albers sang of the Saarland, describing it as the land of "flowers and gearwheels," and the "Garden with a chimney in it." He could not have put it better: the juxtaposition of agriculture and industry characterizes the hilly landscape on the border with France, where coalmining and metallurgy gained importance during the 19th century. The laborers, whether living in mining communities or agricultural settlements, grew their own fruit and vegetables. They were encouraged to build their own houses and grow the basics in their own gardens.

That is not to say that the soil was particularly fertile. Potatoes were the main feature on the daily menu, and are still a key item in the cuisine of the Saarland today. And there is another product that is equally simple and hearty, and famous far beyond the region's boundaries: the Lyoner sausage.

About one-third of the "Garden of the Saarland" consists of woodland and forests, and 45 percent of the overall agricultural area is used wholly or partly for agricultural purposes. As well as natural attractions, such as the Saar Oxbow near Mettlach, a number of industrial memorials are as much a part of the Saarland's cultural heritage as churches, castles, and palaces. One of these is the "Alte Völklinger Hütte," the old foundry, which in 1994 was declared part of the world's cultural heritage by the UNESCO, and is visited as much as the late-Baroque Church of St Louis in the state capital Saarbrücken.

The Saarland is the youngest of the old Federal states, having been created in 1959; with an overall area of 990 square miles (2564 square kilometers); it is also the smallest (not including the city states). The region has only been a political, economic, and cultural unit since 1920, when, after an interesting history closely connected to that of France, the "Saargebiet," or Saar district, was created. Politically, its fate lay in the hands of France. The region's relationship with its neighbors, now friendly and of tremendous benefit to all concerned, also characterized the cuisine in the state, which gained a lightness and freshness from the influence of French cuisine.

Left: The Saar Oxbow at Mettlach, seen from the Cloef vantage point. The peninsula, which is embraced by the Saar, has long been of strategic importance.

Kerschder & Dibbelabbes

In the Saarland, potatoes are also known as "Grombiere," "Grumbere," and "Grumbeere," all of which translate as "pears from the ground." It is believed that they were introduced around 1700 by Walloon steelworkers, and they soon became the main agricultural product of this otherwise poor region. Wheat, oats, rye, and barley performed badly in the soil here, but the potato thrived. The introduction of artificial fertilization meant that other crops could be cultivated, but the potato has remained the Saarland's main staple food product. It is simply a part of the region, and is still found in countless variations in the Saarland cuisine today. Housewives, who had little other than potatoes on which to feed their families, used their imagination and, over generations, developed a wide range of tasty potato dishes. These include *Kerschdscher* (sautéed potatoes), *Hoorische* (dumplings made from uncooked potatoes), *Stracke* (elongated Hoorische), *Grumbeerkiechelcher* (potato pancakes), *Ge-* or *Verheirate* (potatoes with flour dumplings), *Gefillde Knepp* (raw dumplings filled with ground beef), *Stupperte* (deep-fried dumplings), *Iwwer die Platt Geschmelzde* (boiled sliced potatoes with milk or cream), and finally, the favorite – *Dibbelabbes*. The latter is a potato gratin, made with dried or smoked meat and leek, which is baked in the oven in a cast iron "Dibbe," or gratin dish. *Dibbelabbes* is also often prepared on top of the stove, when it is turned frequently to encourage the formation of a good crust.

A few potatoes, a little fat or milk – *Kerschdscher* and *Plattgeschmelzde* were quick and easy to prepare, and so became a staple in the daily diet of the mining farmers, that is to say, those small farmers who were unable to eke out a satisfactory living from agriculture, and therefore, in the middle of the 19th century, had quite literally to "go underground." During the week, they spent their time as miners underground, sleeping in specially constructed dormitories close to the mine. These dormitories contained large stoves, which enabled the men to look after themselves. They brought the ingredients for their meals from their own gardens, which their wives tended.

Dibbelabbes

2¼ lbs/1 kg potatoes
2 large onions
2 tbsp oil
4 oz/100 g dried or smoked meat, diced
1 leek, cut into thin rings
1 egg, beaten
Salt and pepper
Generous pinch of ground nutmeg
1 tbsp chopped parsley

Peel and wash the potatoes, then coarsely grate them. Wrap in a clean tea towel, and squeeze well to remove the liquid. Peel the onion, and grate into the potato. Heat the oil in a skillet, and braise the dried meat. Stir in the sliced leek and simmer until translucent. Add the potato and onion mixture, and pour over the egg. Season with salt, pepper, ground nutmeg, and parsley. Combine the ingredients well. Cover, and bake in a preheated oven at 400 °F/200 °C for about 1 hour. Remove the lid 15 minutes before the end of the cooking time so that the top turns crispy. Dibbelabbes is delicious served with applesauce or an endive salad.

Kerschdscher
(Illustrated bottom left)

2¼ lbs/1 kg potatoes
4 tbsp clarified butter or oil
Salt

Peel and wash the potatoes, then cut them into dice. Heat the oil in a cast-iron skillet, and add the potatoes. Cover with a lid, and cook for 10 minutes. Remove the lid and carefully turn the potatoes over. Season with salt. Continue to cook, turning frequently, until they have turned brown and crispy.

Verheirate
(Illustrated bottom right)

1½ lbs/750 g potatoes
Salt
Generous 1 lb/500 g flour
2 eggs
7 oz/200 g bacon, cut into dice
½ cup milk

Wash and peel the potatoes, and cut into sticks. Boil in salted water for 20 minutes. Meanwhile, combine the flour, eggs, and ½ a cup of water to make a viscous dough for the *Mehlknepp* (flour dumplings). Bring plenty of water to a boil, and add 1 tbsp water. Drop tablespoonfuls of the dough into the boiling water, and simmer for about 5 minutes. Remove with a ladle, and keep warm. Fry the bacon in a skillet until the fat begins to run. Pour over the milk. Place alternate layers of potato sticks and dumplings in a preheated dish, and pour over the bacon milk.

Kerschdscher

Verheirate

Vegetables

The meadowland known as the Lisdorfer Au is the Saarland's main fruit and vegetable growing area. The area lies to the south of Saarlouis in a widening of the Saar valley. It is almost on the same level as the Saar, and vegetables thrive on this plain been created by the river, which tempers the climate and also provides the water for irrigation.

The vegetable garden was created at the same time as a fort, which was built by French King Louis XIV in Saarlouis in 1686. The French demanded a constant supply of fresh vegetables, and the farmers of Lisdorf fulfilled these wishes. An indenture of a lease with the Lisdorf farmers dated 1694 reveals the variety of available vegetables: red beet, yellow carrots, different varieties of cabbage, artichokes, peas, beans,

Brussels sprouts, asparagus, melons, strawberries, and onions. With a variety such as this, it was only a matter of time before people in the neighboring Lorraine also became customers, as did the royal court of Saarbrücken. The garrison latrines provided the means for fertilization. Another form of fertilizer typical in the Saarland was Thomas meal, a by-product from the steelworks.

Initially, market ships transported the vegetables to the customers. However, the expansion of the mining industry in the 19th century led to better transport connections, and soon the whole coalmining area and neighboring France were being supplied. In 1835, a pastor named Hansen established Prussia's first agricultural college in Lisdorf. The goods were sold directly to customers, to local wholesalers, and at the market in Saarbrücken. Due to the density of the newly created industrial conurbation, the demand for vegetables from the Lisdorfer Au increased steadily. As the result of wide distribution, the

available range was restricted to new potatoes, lettuce, rutabaga, cauliflower, savoy cabbage, cucumbers, and asparagus.

Growers in Wallerfangen and Beaumarais on the left bank of the Saar decided early to specialize in growing asparagus. Today the Lisdorf farmers concentrate on the cultivation of fine vegetables, and, thanks to innovativeness and flexibility, play a leading role in the market.

The vegetables grown in the small gardens of the Saarland soon found their way into the soups and stews of traditional Saarland cuisine, their main ingredient being – not surprisingly – the potato, which was also served with soup in the form of potato waffles. In the area around Saarbrücken and Zweibrücken, for example, *Löffelbohnensuppe* (green bean soup) is accompanied by *Quetschekuchen* (plum cake).

Löffelbohnensuppe
Green bean soup

2¼ lbs/1 kg fresh green beans
Generous 1 lb/500 g floury potatoes
1 onion, chopped
Soup vegetables (1 leek, 2 carrots, 2 celery stalks and parsley), chopped
1 tbsp butter
6 cups/1½ liters stock
Salt and pepper
2 shoots of summer savory
⅔ cup/150 g light cream

Trim the beans, and cut into small pieces. Peel and wash the potatoes, then dice. Melt the butter, and glaze the onion, and the soup vegetables. Add the beans and the potatoes, and pour over the stock. Season with salt, pepper, and savory, then cover with a lid and simmer gently for about 20 minutes. Finally, stir in the cream, and season again with salt and pepper. Serve with potato waffles or plum cakes.

Graupeneintopf
Barley stew

2 tbsp butter
1 small onion, chopped
1 clove of garlic, chopped
¼ tsp rubbed marjoram
¼ tsp dried summer savory
4 oz/120 g pearl barley, washed
1 medium carrot, diced
1 celery stalk, diced
1 medium potato, diced
Generous 8 cups/2 liters chicken stock
1½ oz/40 g smoked bacon rind
8 oz/240 g turkey meat
1 tbsp oil
Salt and pepper
1 leek, thinly sliced
1 scallion, sliced
3 tbsp roasted onions

Melt half the butter in a large pot, and glaze the onions and garlic. Add the marjoram, savory, barley, and the diced vegetables, and simmer briefly. Pour over the chicken stock, add the bacon rind, and bring everything to a boil. Cover, and simmer gently for about 10 minutes. Meanwhile, cut the turkey meat into small pieces, sauté in the oil, and add to the stew. Season to taste with salt and pepper, and simmer for another 10 minutes. Sauté the leek and scallion in the remaining butter. Add to the stew, and bring to a boil again. Sprinkle over the roasted onions before serving.

Mangoldsturzensalat
Beet greens salad

14 oz/400 g beet greens/spinach beets
Salt
4 eggs
6 tbsp oil
2 tbsp flour
1 small onion, finely chopped
1 clove of garlic, finely chopped
⅔ cup/150 ml vinegar
1 cup/ ¼ l stock
Pepper
4 tomatoes, each cut into 8 pieces
Seasonal salad leaves for garnish

Blanch the beet stalks in boiling salted water, then plunge into ice cold water. Strip the leaves from the stalks, and cut into 2½ inch/6 cm pieces, then into ¼ inch/½ cm lengths. Boil the eggs in salted water for 4–5 minutes, cool under cold running water, and peel. To make the sauce, heat the oil in a pot, stir in the flour, and sweat until brown. Add the onion, and the garlic, and brown lightly. Pour over the vinegar, and the stock. Simmer gently for 5 minutes, and season with salt and pepper. Strain, and cool slightly. Dress the beet greens, tomatoes, and salad leaves with the sauce. Arrange on plates, and garnish with the eggs.

Lyoner

Viewed objectively, the *Lyoner* is a sausage. A ring-shaped braising sausage that is made from lean meat, tasty bacon, salts, seasoning, and water. And that is how it is eaten: hot or cold, with plenty of mustard, and a freshly-baked bread roll, cut into slices for a breakfast sandwich; boiled or fried with sautéed potatoes and a green salad at midday; broiled and served with fresh bread and mustard in the evening.

However, viewed subjectively, the *Lyoner* is more than a sausage. It is a piece of the Saarland's national identity, and as such is comparable to Berlin's *Currywurst* or Munich's *Weisswurst*. Village and town festivals, private garden parties, and even official receptions hosted by the regional government are unimaginable without *Lyoner*. "Every Friday in the Saarland, every payday, every topping-out ceremony, is also a Lyoner festival," is how the Saarland writer Ludwig Harig puts it. And the city council of Saarbrücken went a step further in 1996, when its members seriously considered naming a street in the industrial area where the sausage factories were located, the "Lyonerring."

People like to ascribe the state's well-developed "Lyoner culture" to the mining industry, on which by far the greater proportion of the population of the Saarland depended for its livelihood. Because of the severity of their physical labors, the miners required a good quantity of concentrated protein while they were underground. This requirement was met by the Lyoner, which, compared with other meat products, was relatively inexpensive, easy to eat, and required little in the way of preparation. In the works canteen, known as the "Kaffeekisch," and where simple, inexpensive food and drink are still available today, any miners who worked an extra half-shift were given a piece of sausage, a bread roll, and a bottle of beer in addition to their overtime payment.

Lyoner sausage is made in a special machine that consists of a rotating bowl and rotating knives. These chop the lean meat, which is then combined with bacon, seasoning, and ice. Finally, the mixture is pushed into medium to large caliber (1½–1¾ inch/40–46 mm) sausage skins made from beef intestine. Only natural skins are used. The appropriate heat treatment is applied to ensure that the Lyoner cuts well, and then the sausage is smoked in the smoke of pure beech wood. The Lyoner sausage manufacturing process is one of the few processes that is the same for all of the manufacturers in the Saarland; the only differences being the proportions of the basic ingredients, and the seasoning. The manufacturers' biggest, and most closely guarded secret is the particular combination of seasonings. These could be: garlic, thyme, coriander, ginger, cinnamon, nutmeg, and pepper.

Saure Lyoner
Pickled Lyoner

1½ lbs/800 g Lyoner sausage
2 large onions
½ cup/125 ml water
3 tbsp vinegar
Salt and pepper, Pinch of sugar
4 tbsp oil
½ bunch of parsley, chopped

Skin the Lyoner and cut into slices. Peel the onions, and cut into thin rings. Make a marinade from the water, vinegar, salt, pepper, sugar, and oil. Place the Lyoner and the onion rings in a bowl, pour over the marinade, and leave to stand. Sprinkle with the parsley before serving.

Fleischsalat
Meat salad

14 oz/400 g Lyoner or similar smoked sausage
2 large pickled gherkins
4 tbsp mayonnaise
2 tbsp gherkin vinegar
Salt and pepper
Pinch of sugar

Cut the sausage into slices, then cut the slices into strips. Cut the gherkins into ¾ inch/2 cm strips. Combine the mayonnaise with the vinegar, salt, pepper, and sugar. Add the sliced sausage and gherkins, and stir well. Leave to stand for 1 hour. Serve the salad with fresh bread rolls, tomatoes, and hardboiled eggs.

Lyoner sausage, which is relatively inexpensive, provided a good amount of protein for the miners. The typical "miner's breakfast" consisted of Lyoner, bread rolls, and mustard.

Festivals above ground

If food is scarce, a festival with more richly laden tables than normal is extra special. The goat, for example, that was enjoyed at Easter, or a child's first communion or confirmation, made for a feast – especially for the laborers who were only rarely able to afford meat. One event that was hugely special in the lives of young people was the annual fair, the "Kirmes" or "Kerb," to which the whole extended family was invited. No expense was spared; endless cakes were baked, and often a pig was slaughtered as well.

The amount of food laid on the table for either a feast or an everyday meal depended on whether the table belonged to a miner or a settler. The mining farmers, who tended their own small vegetable gardens, had the basics such as potatoes, sausage, bacon, eggs, butter, sauerkraut, and pulses, and accordingly were able to eat reasonably well. Thus the miners from the northern Saarland were better off than their colleagues in the mining settlements, who were known as "colonists," and who had been farmers until they were no longer able to grow enough food to feed themselves.

Whereas the mining farmers were able to eat ham and eggs during the week, the miners' families in the "colonies" had to restrict their meat consumption to Sundays and holidays. If meat was served at all, it was most likely to be beef soup or fried pork belly with a sauce, and served with boiled potatoes and vegetables, or a salad. During the week, the "colonists" lived mainly on bread and potatoes in countless guises. Even when the miners went to work, their wives were often able to send them on their way with a sandwich consisting of two slices of bread and cold potato pancakes, which bore the somewhat euphemistic name of "ham sandwich." This was probably because they did not want to be regarded as inferior to the mining farmers, who invariably had the real thing in their sandwiches, and who, in the miners' eyes, were rich – rich enough, so they said, that when they returned home on Saturdays they brought with them bread rolls and sausage for their children.

Another feast for the children was when their fathers brought the legendary "rabbit sandwich" back from a shift. The bread, which was by now dry and curling at the edges, but was none the less a welcome extra portion for the children, was accompanied by a story of a bunny rabbit that waited by the wayside in order to give the miner this little treat …

Wambefäschd – a feast for the belly

Between 1817 and 1912, miners in the Saarland celebrated the now legendary mountain festivals, known in the local dialect as "Wambefäschd" or the "Miners' Ball." These events always followed the same sequence: after the church service, the miners, dressed in their Sunday best, set off on the mountain parade. The pit director first gave his talk (which always followed pretty much the same theme), and in which he swore "unity and solidarity" and "loyalty to King and Country."

Then the fun began. One of the main reasons for the popularity of the Summer Festival was the generous amount of food donated by the pit management, the main attractions being beef with rice and boiled hams. With free beer and cigars. Dancing for the adults, and games for the children provided exercise and amusement afterwards. Physical exercise must have been essential in view of the quantities of food served up, for example in the King's Mine. For the Mountain Festival in 1898, more than 3 pounds (1.5 kilograms) of ox were served per person, plus the same amount of bread, 5 liters of beer, and 12 cigars. The guests were allowed to take any leftovers home with them, and everyone had the next day off work to recover.

The Mountain Festivals did not take place during the strike at the end of the 19th century, which was when the legal protection association was founded. The "unity and solidarity" formerly sworn by the miners and the pit directors was probably reduced to a minimum during this time.

Ziegenbraten
Roast goat

3½ lbs/1½ kg saddle of goat
Salt and pepper
2 tbsp lard
2 cups/½ liter stock
Bunch of parsley, chopped
Bunch of chives, sliced
2 tbsp butter
¾ cup/200 ml light cream

Pour boiling water over the saddle of goat. Dry with paper towels, and rub in plenty of salt and pepper. Heat the lard in a large pot, and brown the meat on all sides. Roast the meat in a preheated oven (400 °F/200 °C) for just 1 hour, basting frequently. Melt the butter, and braise the parsley and chives. Remove the roast from the oven, and gash the meat several times. Spread the herbs into these gashes, and roast the meat for another 30 minutes. Remove the saddle of goat from the pot, then add the cream to the juices. Season the sauce with salt and pepper, and pass through a fine strainer. Serve the sauce separately.

The goat

The goat is still known as the "miner's cow" in the Saarland today. Keeping goats was closely linked to the development and expansion of the mining industry in the 19th century. At that time, a large number of poor farmers in the villages surrounding the high forest, the Palatinate, and the Hunsrück found work in the mines. In order to provide accommodation for the landless miners, the pit direction provided loans and premiums to enable the miners to finance their own homes, and at the end of the century the majority of the miners owned a red stone-built house in the newly created miners' settlements in the vicinity of the pits. These settlements were known as "colonies" in the Saarland, a name which is still used today. Unlike the mining farmers, the miners had no land to cultivate, but they did keep one or two working animals that played a large role in ensuring the physical wellbeing of the miners' families. From the middle of the 19th century, the goat become the "little man's cow," providing both milk and meat. During and just after the war, keeping a goat or two was essential for nutritional reasons. In 1950, there were still 80,000 goats, but by 1980 this number had dwindled to 300 goats, held by 100 people.

Apart from the sheep, the goat (which is very easy to look after) is one of the oldest domestic animals. Archaeologists tell us that they were kept during the Stone Age. The tender, aromatic flesh is considered a delicacy by connoisseurs, and it is still customary in the Saarland today to serve roast kid at Easter.

In 1994, UNESCO declared the "Alte Völklinger Hütte", the old foundry, part of the world's cultural heritage. It is a much-visited site, popular with tourists.

Steelworkers and lunchboxes

The traditional industry of the Saarland was for many years characterized by coal, iron, and steel. Miners and metallurgists worked extremely hard; their calorie requirement was very high, and their food wholesome. There is a saying in the Saarland, according to which "Anyone who works hard, needs to eat well."

After the Second World War, there was even a department that made sure the miners were provided with noodle soup with lots of meat before each shift so that the starving men would survive having to work so hard. Lots of men took the noodle soup home with them, where it was "stretched" by adding water and home-grown vegetables.

The second large group of workers in the Saarland, the steelworkers, carried their stew or a mixture of potatoes, carrots, and bacon or dried meat, to work with them in a tin lunchbox, known as a Henkelmann. Needless to say, these tin pots did not keep the food warm for long, and it was customary for wives or children to carry them to the mine gates at mealtimes so that the men could enjoy a hot meal.

Schwenk-braten

Saarbrücken-born writer Georg Seitz is responsible for the saying, "Der Mensch denkt, Gott lenkt, der Saarländer schwenkt," which loosely translates as, "Man thinks, God guides, the people of Saarland swing."

The object being "swung" by the people of Saarland is a roast, and you can smell it in every garden in summer, especially the garlic and thyme – the typical smell of the "swing roast." Some 8000 events take place in the Saarland throughout the summer, ranging from street parties to city festivals, and it is impossible to imagine them without the familiar "Schwenkbraten." Since its introduction in the early 1970s, this roast pork dish has quickly become the national dish.

It is generally believed that this so-called "new Saarländer" arrived a quarter-century ago from the Hunsrück mountains, where it is also known as "Schaukelbraten."

The home-made "swinger" is the pride of every garden owner in the Saarland.

Supposedly, German gem hunters working in Brazil in the 19th century brought the recipe back to Germany with them from the Brazilian jungle. The fact that this roast so quickly became such a firm part of this small federal state is probably due in large part to the Saarland people's legendary sociability, for which sociologist Gerhard Bungert has an interesting explanation. As the result of the regional coal and steel industry that flourished in the Saarland for 150 years, many private homes were built. Owning one's own home brings with it a certain amount of "immobility," and usually means that the residents stay in the same place for many years. This leads to increased involvement in local events, since the main part of one's leisure time is spent in one's own community.

Amateur carpenters like to construct their own three-legged "swing-roast stand" at home, and proudly present the end product to friends and family in their garden. If time and/or talent are lacking, there are numerous "DIY" establishments that come to one's aid at the beginning of the warm season with a wide range of "Schwenker" to make sure that any and every one in Saarland can "swing" when the summer comes.

The quality of the swing roast begins with the pork, which has to be marinated before cooking.

Each cook has a preferred recipe, which usually includes paprika and a particular combination of herbs.

The seasoned meat is covered with a thick layer of onions – and garlic.

The meat is now anointed with oil; any additional ingredients are the "chef's secret."

The meat is left to marinate overnight, often longer, to give the flavors more time to "develop."

A veritable "cholesterol bomb"

The egg

Just as any reference to "milk" is always taken to be a reference to cow's milk, an egg is generally taken to be a hen's egg. The perfect shape is protected on the outside by a thin calcium shell which allows air to penetrate. Inside, the yolk is suspended between two so-called chalaza, and surrounded by albumen. A thin membrane surrounds the yolk, in which the chick grows from the blastodisc and the blastula. The actual yolk provides the initial nourishment for the growing bird, and it is a powerpack of vitamins A, D, E, K, B1, B2, B6, and B12. The fat content is also high, with plenty of unsaturated fatty acids and lecithin, and a large amount of cholesterol. The egg yolk contains almost seven times as much energy as the white does, and far more protein. It also contains generous quantities of phosphorus, calcium, and iron. Egg protein is widely regarded as a measuring scale for biological nourishment, since its essential amino acids largely equate the proportion of human protein.

Overall, egg is a highly valuable food, not just for its essential amino acids, but also because of its wealth of vitamins and minerals. However, because of their high cholesterol content, eggs should be consumed in moderation.

Pfannkuchen
Pancakes

4 eggs
Generous 2 cups/½ liter milk
2 cups/300 g flour
Salt and sugar
Pinch of baking powder
Oil for frying

Whisk together the eggs and the milk. Gradually add the flour, and season the batter with 1 pinch each of salt and sugar. Stir in the baking powder, and a little water if required; the batter should be fairly thin. Leave to stand for 20 minutes, then whisk again thoroughly.
Heat the oil in a skillet, and pour in a ladle of batter. Fry the pancake until golden on both sides. Keep warm until all the pancakes are ready. Spread over a thin layer of jelly, roll into sausage shapes, and serve.

Eggs in the kitchen

Whole eggs
Whole eggs are used to bind all types of dough for breads and cakes, and they also help to lighten them. They are also used to bind the dough for pasta and dumplings, and dishes made with ground meat.

Egg white (albumen)
Egg white is used to clarify stocks and jellies. Beaten egg whites are used to lighten desserts and cremes, cake dough and cookie pastry, vegetable, fish, and meat concoctions.

Egg yolk
Egg yolk is used to bind soups and sauces, cremes and mayonnaise. It is also brushed onto surfaces to add gloss, and used as an "adhesive" in recipes containing grains, spices, nuts or raisins in breads, cakes, cookies, and pastries.

Desserts

Butterkuchen
Butter cake
(Illustrated bottom right)

Cake

4 cups/500 g flour
5 tbsp sugar, 2 eggs
2⅓ cakes of compressed yeast
½ tsp salt of hartshorn (ammonium bicarbonate), dissolved in a little milk
6½ tbsp/100 g butter
½ cup/125 ml lukewarm milk
Butter to grease the baking sheet
6 tbsp/100 g melted butter
⅔ cup/100 g almond slivers

Creme

Generous 4 cups/1 liter milk
6 tbsp sugar
4 tbsp corn starch
1 tsp. vanilla essence
1 cup/250 g butter
4 tbsp confectioner's sugar

Topping

1½ cups/200 g confectioner's sugar

Make a dough of the flour, sugar, eggs, yeast, hartshorn salt, butter, and milk, and leave to rise until it has doubled in volume. Grease a baking sheet, and press the dough onto it. Brush with the melted butter, and sprinkle over the almond slivers. Cover the dough, and leave for another 15 minutes. Bake in a preheated oven (430 °F/220 °C) for about 25 minutes.

When the cake has cooled, cut it in half lengthwise, and then widthwise. Make a custard from the milk, sugar, vanilla essence and corn starch, and leave to cool. Beat the butter and the confectioner's sugar until fluffy, and spoon into the custard. Use as a filling for the cake. To make the topping, beat the confectioner's sugar into a little hot water, and spread over the cake.

Kranzkuchen
Ring cake
(Illustrated bottom center)

2 lbs 3 oz/1 kg flour
2⅓ cakes of compressed yeast
10 tbsp/150 g butter
1 cup/200 g sugar
½ tsp vanilla essence
2 eggs
1¼ cups/300 ml lukewarm milk
1 tsp salt
Grated rind of 1 lemon
Flour for the work surface
Egg yolk for the glaze

Make a dough of the flour, yeast, butter, sugar, vanilla essence, eggs, milk, salt, and lemon rind. Leave to rise until it has doubled in volume. Divide the dough into three equal-size pieces, and roll each one out to a thin strand on the floured work surface. Braid the 3 pieces of dough together. Line a baking sheet with greaseproof paper, and place the braid on the paper in the shape of a ring, joining the two ends together. Brush the surface with beaten egg yolk, and bake in a preheated oven (400 °F/200 °C) for 1 hour.

Apfelwaffeln
Apple waffles
(Illustrated bottom left)

¼ cup/60 g butter, 1 tbsp sugar
½ tsp vanilla essence
2 eggs
½ cup/60 g flour
½ cup/60 g cornstarch
½ tsp baking powder
Generous ⅓ cup/100 ml milk
Grated rind of 1 lemon
1 apple
Oil for greasing

Make a thick batter of the butter, sugar, vanilla essence, eggs, flour, corn starch, baking powder, milk, and lemon rind. Refrigerate for 1 hour. Peel and core the apple; cut into eighths, slice thinly and add to batter. Heat your waffle iron, and grease with a little oil. Bake the waffles in the usual way. Serve with whipped cream or wine creme (recipe on page 252).

Orchards and strawberry fields

Fruit growing by command

Before politicians were able to utilize the mass media for campaigns such as "Eat more fruit," the powers-that-be usually had only one way of persuading the people to do as they said: punishment. This was the modus operandi of Prince Wilhelm Heinrich of Nassau Saarbrücken, who wanted to promote fruit growing in the 18th century. Every person who did not plant at least two fruit trees would be liable to punishment. Such draconian measures were no longer necessary a hundred years later, when fruit growing clubs and associations and private nurseries had achieved a high level of recognition. Fruit trees were everywhere to be seen in the state's gardens and thoroughfares. Today, the main fruit growing centers are the Merziger Becken, the regions of the high forests, and the Bliestal.

Apple growing has long been a tradition in the Merziger Becken, as has "Viez," a spirit that is brewed from the fruit. Here in this region, and on the plains to the left and right of the Saar River, is where the marvelous orchards are found, and in the spring delight the senses with masses of blossom, and in the fall with deep-red apples. Traditionally, apples were grown in the Saarland primarily for Viez and for domestic use. However, they are now also used for compotes, jellies, and cake toppings, as are pears, plums, rhubarb, and all kinds of berry fruit.

Strawberries are another traditional fruit of the Saarland, and one in which St Barbara, a tiny village on the way up to the Gau, specializes. People had already begun to grow strawberries as a replacement for the vineyards before the First World War. The bright, sunny terraces of the Saar Valley were ideal for the early varieties, which could be sold for a good price.

Between the wars, strawberry growing gained in economic importance, since the inhabitants of St Barbara, mainly laborers in the nearby stoneware factory at Wallerfangen, were badly affected by the closure of the works. More effort was put into strawberry cultivation, and the fruit was exported as far away as Cologne and the industrial area around the Ruhr.

The rha of the Barbarians

Many individual foods are both toxic and edible, and the question as to how long it must have been before man learned to differentiate between the two – and how many lives were lost before this achievement – is an interesting one.
Rhubarb must have claimed many lives, but despite that it also has a number of healing properties. The ancient Chinese have left us the first records (dating back to 2700 BC) of this member of the buckwheat family, from which we know that they used it as a laxative.
Rhubarb was introduced in Europe just before the birth of Christ. Roman writers described it as the "Rha of the Barbarians," Rha being the River Volga, on the banks of which the "Barbarians" (by which they meant the Tartars) cultivated the plants.
In Germany, rhubarb was grown only for medicinal purposes until the beginning of the 17th century. Then some British botanists had the idea of eating it – and promptly bit into the wrong parts: the leaves, which they prepared as spinach. However, the blades contain oxalic acid, which is not only bad for us, but also the reason why rhubarb leaves are only to be recommended as a last meal!

Right: Rhubarb is actually a vegetable, but for culinary purposes it is used like fruit. The stalks are used for desserts, jellies, and compotes, and it is also delicious as a cake topping.

Rhabarberkompott mit Quarkschaum
Rhubarb compote with quark mousse

9 oz/250 g rhubarb
½ cup/100 g sugar
1 tsp gelatin
½ cup/125 ml red wine
¼ cup/60 ml port
1 cinnamon stick
Juice of 1 lemon
3 oz/80 g raspberries

Wash and peel the rhubarb, and cut into 1½ inch/4 cm lengths. Sprinkle over ¼ cup/60 g of sugar, and leave to stand for 30 minutes. Soften the gelatin in some water. Bring the remaining sugar and the other ingredients to a boil in a saucepan, and reduce to ¼ of the original volume. Stir in the rhubarb with the juices, and bring to a boil. Remove from the heat. Squeeze the excess liquid from the gelatin, and stir into the contents of the saucepan. Add a little more sugar if required. Cool, then place in the refrigerator to chill.

Quarkschaum
Quark mousse

1 vanilla pod
½ cup/125 ml milk
1 cup/100 g confectioner's sugar
2 egg yolks
10 tbsp/160 g firm quark (smooth cottage cheese)
4 egg whites
8 scoops of vanilla or walnut ice cream
Mint leaves for garnish
confectioner's sugar for topping

Cut the vanilla pod open lengthwise, and remove the marrow. Add to the milk, and bring to a boil in a saucepan. Remove from the heat, and strain. Beat ⅓ cup/40 g confectioner's sugar with the egg yolks until fluffy, and stir in the vanilla milk. Continue beating over hot water until the mixture becomes stiff. Add the quark, and stir until smooth. Place the bowl in a large container of ice cold water, and continue beating the quark mixture until cold. Beat the egg whites with the remaining confectioner's sugar until very stiff, then gradually combine with the quark mixture. Divide the rhubarb compote between 4 chilled soup plates, place 2 scoops of ice cream on top, and cover with the quark mousse. Place in a very hot top-heated oven (510 °F/250 °C) until just golden. Garnish with mint leaves, and serve immediately.

Right: The tiny village of St Barbara has concentrated its efforts on the cultivation of strawberries, for which the conditions on the sun-drenched terraces of the Saar Valley are ideal.

Pflaumenkuchen
Plum cake

Dough
1½ cups/200 g flour
½ cake fresh yeast
2 tbsp/25 g sugar
Pinch of salt
2 tbsp/30 g butter
Scant ⅓ cup/75 ml milk
Flour for kneading
Fat for the mold

Topping
1 lb 10 oz/750 g plums
1 tbsp sugar
½ tsp cinnamon

Strain the flour into a bowl, and make a well in the center. Crumble in the yeast, and sprinkle over the sugar and a pinch of salt. Pour the milk into a small saucepan, add the butter, and heat gently until the butter has melted. Pour over the yeast. Use your hands to knead the ingredients until you have a smooth dough. Cover with a clean teacloth, and leave in a warm place for about 30 minutes until it has doubled in volume.
Knead the dough well on a floured surface, and roll out. Grease a springform pan, place the dough in it, drawing the sides up slightly. Wash the plums, then halve them and remove the pits. Arrange on the dough with the cut side facing up. Bake in a preheated oven (350 °F/175 °C) for a good hour. Combine the cinnamon and the sugar, and sprinkle over the hot cake. Leave to cool in the pan.

Fruit toppings on tarts

There are almost as many different toppings for a Sunday fruit tart as there are combinations of numbers for a lottery. Apples, gooseberries, pears, plums, cherries, apricots, grapes, blueberries, rhubarb, strawberries, blackberries, redcurrants, peaches – just about every variety of fruit can be used, either in splendid isolation or combined. However, unlike with the lottery, there is no loser. A fruit tart will always succeed. Anyone who is nervous about their yeast dough rising or worried that their shortcrust pastry could be too short, can buy the base in a supermarket or from a baker's shop, and just put on their own topping.

Of course, that course of action is not for the more ambitious bakers. They bake their own, and may even spread a layer of quark, custard, or other filling under the fruit, and will make the topping a veritable work of art: crumble crust, raisins, finely chopped nuts, and artistic pastry designs are as decorative as they are delicious. And if you prefer a plainer touch, just cover the fruit with a glaze. This too is available from a supermarket; all you have to do is add water.

Is the neighbor's fruit always sweeter?

Living close to a border can, at worst, mean war and strife, but at best, there are many advantages to be gained from another culture. The people who lived in the region of what is today called the Saarland have experienced the former in the Franco-Prussian war of 1870/71, and in two World Wars. On the other hand, the treaty of Versailles after the First World War led to the creation of the "Saargebiet," the Saar region, whose political affairs were in the hands of France. France owned the Saar pits, and the franc was the official currency. The Saarländer went "back home to the Empire" in 1935, and when their 1000-year history ended in 1945, American troops soon followed the French. In 1946, the border was drawn between the Saarland and the rest of Germany, and the franc was re-introduced as the currency. French products were available at good prices on Saarland's markets – products that were generally unobtainable "in the Empire," (the name still given to the Federal Republic in parts of the Saarland today) – special cognacs, for example, and coffee from French colonies in Africa. As the franc was not very stable, the people of Saarland made the most of their spending power after the hard years of the War, and this is how they came to be known as "pleasure-seeking." Finally, in 1959, the

Saarland was reintegrated with Germany. It became the youngest Federal state, and the people were quick to exchange their French "old crocks" for tax-free German cars.

The culinary influences which France had on the Saar region go back even further. Back in 1690, farmers emulated the French in their methods of vegetable cultivation in the Lisdorfer Au, and then supplied the produce to their neighbors. When the population increased as the result of industrialization, France became very important to the Saarland as a supplier of fruit, vegetables, and other produce. French fruit made a significant contribution to the Saarland market, since the state was unable to produce more than a third of its own requirements.

Today, the state's best and most respected restaurants have French-sounding names. "Amuse gueule" is a standard term in pubs offering good, plain cooking; the courses have French names, and lots of fresh products are used to make light dishes. Plain dishes are enhanced by the addition of salmon and other varieties of fish (the typical Saarland potato soup is served with strips of smoked salmon), garlic, and unusual herbs.

Mürbteigboden
Shortcrust pastry
For 2 springform pans

3 cups/400 g flour
1½ cups/350 g cold butter
2 eggs
⅔ cup/160 g sugar
Pinch of salt
Flour for kneading
Butter for the molds
Generous 1 lb/500 g pulses (dried)

Strain the flour over the worktop, and make a well in the center. Cut the butter into small pieces, and sprinkle over the edge of the flour. Put the eggs, sugar, and a pinch of salt in the well, and quickly make a smooth pastry. Shape the pastry into a ball, wrap in clear wrap, and place in the refrigerator for 1 hour. Then roll out thinly on a floured work surface. Line the greased baking sheet or springform with the pastry, drawing the sides up slightly. Cover the pastry with greaseproof paper, and place the pulses on top. Bake blind in a preheated oven (350 °F/175 °C) for about 10 minutes. Take out of the oven, remove the paper and the pulses, and leave to cool slightly. Then fill as required, and finish baking.

Schwäbischer Apfelkuchen
Swabian apple cake

Shortcrust pastry (see left)

Topping
1¾ lbs/750 g cooking apples
⅓ cup/50 g rum-soaked raisins
⅓ cup/50 g almond slivers

Peel and halve the apples, and remove the cores. Thinly slices the apple quarters, and spread over the pastry base. Brush the apple slices with the melted butter, and sprinkle over the sugar, raisins, and almonds. Bake in a preheated oven (400 °F/200 °C) for about 50 minutes.

Riemelestarte mit Birnen
Riemeles tart with pears

Shortcrust pastry (see left), pastry remnants

Topping
Generous 1 lb/500 g pears
4 oz/100 g melted butter
1 egg yolk
⅓ cup/50 g almond slivers

Cut strips from the pastry remnants using a zigzag pastry cutter. Peel and halve the pears, and remove the cores. Cut into thin slices. Brush the pastry base with melted butter, and arrange the pear slices to overlap. Brush with the remaining butter. Braid the pastry strips over the top, press the edges together, and brush with beaten egg yolk. Sprinkle with the almond slivers, and bake in a preheated oven (350 °F/175 °C) for about 30 minutes.

Stachelbeerkuchen
Gooseberry cake

Sponge shell (ready made)

Topping
1¾ lbs/750 g gooseberries
¾ cup/150 g sugar
Rind of ½ a lemon
2 tbsp fresh breadcrumbs
1 packet of glaze

Wash the gooseberries, then top and tail them. Put the sugar and the lemon rind in 1 cup/250 ml of water, and bring to a boil. Pour in the gooseberries, and simmer gently for 10 minutes. Do not boil them, as they will burst. Sprinkle the breadcrumbs over the cake base. Remove the berries from the cooking liquid using a ladle, and spread them over the sponge shell. Stir the glaze into the cooking liquid (or as directed by the manufacturer), bring to a boil, then spread over the berries.

Erdbeerkuchen
Strawberry cake

Sponge shell (ready made)

Topping
1¼ lbs/600 g strawberries
½ cup/100 g sugar
½ tsp vanilla essence
1 packet red glaze

Gently wash the strawberries, leave to drain, then remove the stalks. Cut any large ones in half. Place the strawberries in a bowl, then sprinkle over the sugar and vanilla essence. Mix gently, and leave to stand for 15 minutes. Arrange the strawberries over the sponge shell. Follow the packet instructions to make a glaze from the strawberry juice and water, and brush over the strawberries.

Rhabarberkuchen mit Eierguss
Egg-glazed rhubarb cake

Shortcrust pastry shell (see left)

Topping
Generous 1 lb/500 g rhubarb
⅔ cup/150 ml light cream
2 eggs, 2 tbsp sugar
2 tbsp corn starch
½ tsp. vanilla essence

Wash and peel the rhubarb, then cut into lengths of about 1¼ inch/3 cm. Spread over the pastry shell. To make the sauce, combine the cream with the eggs, sugar, and custard powder, stir until smooth, and then pour over the rhubarb. Bake in a preheated oven (400 °F/200 °C) for 25–30 minutes.

Kirschstreusel
Cherry streusel

Yeast dough base (see recipe for plum pie, page 313)

Topping
Generous 1 lb/500 g cherries, pits removed
4 oz/100 g butter
½ cup/60 g flour
4 oz/100 g sugar

Spread the cherries over the base. Combine the butter, flour and sugar with your fingertips, rubbing together until the mixture resembles fine breadcrumbs, and sprinkle over the cherries. Bake in a preheated oven (350 °F/175 °C) for about 30 minutes.

Viez and various spices are mixed together in a large pot (illustrated in the background) and heated.

Wine for the countryman

On the subject of "Viez," an interesting quotation that dates back to the 19th century speaks favorably of the advantages of this apple wine. "Consumption of the same causes less sweat than that of wine, the latter being also more expensive; beer deteriorates when carried into the fields during the summer months; it also soon goes off and loses its flavor; spirits consumed in summer to quench the thirst damage the nerves, and make the individual tired and sleepy. A good fruit wine, however, taken with a piece of well-baked black bread, is wonderfully fortifying, boosts the worker's energy during the day, and provides relief from the day's heat and toil."

As we said, this is most interesting, especially as the writer does not even stop to consider another thirst quencher: water. But that was hardly a realistic alternative at the time, since in highly industrialized areas such as the Saarland the water was frequently undrinkable, and in fact the source of much disease. So "Viez" was all that the fieldworker had to drink.

Viez is a dry to sweet apple wine that is brewed predominantly in the area around Merzig, and where it is generally regarded as a national drink. Mention is made of "puitz" in documents drawn up by the Abbot of Prüm in 1413. However, Viez was made much, much earlier; it is likely that the ancient Germans produced a tasty must from the fruit of the crab apple tree, which was intoxicating when fermented. Roman settlers and legionaries refined the drink by blending the fruit with apple varieties from their own homes, which they named "vice vinum," or "wine substitute."

Known to the Romans as a "substitute for wine," apple wine plays a pivotal role at the Merziger Viezfest.

Viez is intoxicating, and so it is a good idea to have something substantial to eat.

The end of the apple harvest is the time to celebrate and display the sheer variety of apple-based foods.

Potato pancakes, or *Reibekuchen*" swimming in hot fat – just the thing for a chilly fall day.

The Merziger Viezfest is held on the first Saturday in October. Most people drink their Viez hot.

JOSEF THALLER

Baden-Württemberg

"Let us flee to Swabia. We will live as is the habit of the country. God help us! There is sweet food there and an abundance of all good things," wrote Goethe in *Reineke Fuchs*.

An abundance of all good things – Goethe's words are still very true of this region bordered by the Rivers Rhine, Neckar, Danube, and Lech. They are equally true of Württemberg, and Baden, and all the fine foods they produce: fruit and vegetables from the area around Lake Constance, cattle from the rich meadows of the Hohenlohe region, pointed cabbage from the fields near Stuttgart, juicy asparagus from Schwetzingen in the north of Baden, and ham and kirsch from the Black Forest. The food eaten in both parts of Baden-Württemberg is dominated by solid, wholesome dishes, though there is greater refinement and delicacy in Baden, probably due to influences from the area's French neighbors. All the same, they have a good deal in common, and not just in the sphere of food and drink. For centuries the histories of Baden and Württemberg were both troubled and painful. Only a small stratum of the population profited from the riches the land provided in the Kingdom of Württemberg and the Duchy of Baden. The poor could not live off the beauty of the landscape in the idyllic Neckar Valley or the Markgräfler Land, which Johann Peter Hebbel called "a little garden of paradise."

In spite of these historical parallels, there was a great deal of skepticism in 1952 when the federal state of Baden-Württemberg was formed. There are certainly differences: the Swabians are regarded as less trusting, and stay faithful to their puritanism, the heritage of a land that has produced more than its fair share of great scientists and engineers, such as Johannes Kepler, Gottlieb Daimler, and Robert Bosch. The region has also been rich in poets and thinkers: Schiller, Hegel, Hauff, Hölderlin. The Badeners are regarded as people who enjoy life. However, both are capable of hard work and practicality. As a result, they have done together what no one dared to predict, building Germany's "model federal state," which is not just first among the states in terms of industrial exports, but also has the largest number of starred restaurants.

Left: One of the many wayside crucifixes that impress visitors to the Swabian Alb district.

Our
daily bread

In the Christian West bread is regarded as a gift from God, a link between the people and their Creator. Bread and wine incarnate the body and blood of Christ. Bread and salt are offered to guests and conquerors alike. Bread is seasoned with all the toil and pain of the people, but is also their greatest reward. Bread is never thrown away. No one jokes about bread. Bread is life. In many parts of Bavaria farmers still draw a cross on the loaf with their thumb before it is first cut. As they say in Swabian, the main dialect of the region, "Wo Fried ist, da ist Gott und Brot, wo Unfried ist, ist der Teufel und d' Not" (Where there is peace, there you will find God and bread, where there is no peace, there you will find the Devil and need).

The history of bread goes back almost as far as that of humanity. It begins about 10,000 years ago in the late Stone Age, when humans ceased to live as nomads and began to settle in one place and cultivate the land. The first bread is thought to have been made by accident when the remains of a porridge of ground or crushed grains were inadvertently left lying on a hot stone. The first deliberately produced breads were unleavened. Excavations near Lake Constance have shown that lake dwellers who lived in houses built on supporting piles in the water, crushed millet, barley, or wheat grains and mixed them with water to make unleavened bread 3000 years before Christ. Raising agents were unknown at that time, at least not in Europe.

Until the 18th century, when potato began to be grown on a massive scale, porridge and bread were the most important foods in Europe. The poor ate porridge, bread was available to those who could afford to buy it, or had an oven or access to a communal bakehouse. Fine wheat bread was particularly expensive and valuable, and was only affordable for the very rich.

Given the central importance of cereals and bread in the economy, times of shortage threatened the majority of the population with starvation. When the cereal harvest failed there was famine, and whole state systems have been destabilized by increases in the bread price. Even in Stuttgart, which was certainly not a hotbed of revolutionary fervor, one person was killed and many were injured in riots that followed an increase in the price of bread in 1847.

All civilized peoples have always been concerned to ensure that bread should be affordable for the very poorest. In Ancient Rome every citizen had a legal right to an allowance of bread called the *frugium*. The poor and rich were equally entitled to this benefit, but it was only a matter of life or death to the poor. In the early 14th century the city

Bread prices over the years

Year	White bread Marks per kg	Mixed bread Marks per kg
1905	0.33	0.26
1914	0.35	0.28
1921	8.40	3.50
1922	150	17–140
1923 (2/7)	7400	1250
1923 (16/10)	350 million	240 million
1923 (14/12)	440 billion	300 billion
1924 (2/1)	0.44	0.30
1925	0.52	0.33
1930	0.53	0.38
1939	0.47	0.34
1945	—	0.36
1949	0.59	0.45
1952	0.80	0.66
1955	0.90	0.68
1959	1.10	0.83
1962	1.20	0.90
1964	1.30	1.00
1965	1.40	1.05
1970	1.50–1.90	1.15–1.40
1975	1.50–2.40	1.80–2.30
1980	2.80–3.70	2.50–2.80
1986	3.80–4.60	3.20–3.50
1990	4.10–5.20	3.20–3.60
1994	4.60–5.20	3.90–4.20
1996	5.70–5.80	4.10–4.40

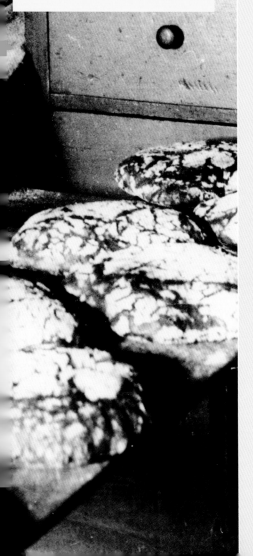

council of Frankfurt proclaimed that bread could only be sold for either one or two Hellers, "in order that every poor man may have what he needs to live." [p. 321] The price of bread was determined by the market price for corn. In most cities there was a set bread price, so that changes in the price of cereals could only bring about variations in the weight of a loaf. Almost everywhere the permitted weights were set by baking a standard loaf under the supervision of the local council. Changes required the permission of the council, which often led to conflicts between the bakers and their city elders. Bread inspectors played an important role up until the 19th century. Not only did they have to monitor quality regulations, it was also their job to check weights and measures.

Over 300 different varieties of bread and about 1200 other baked goods are made in Germany.

However, despite all this variety, the German bread trade is dominated by just four basic types: rye bread, wheat bread, mixed rye bread, and mixed wheat bread. Northern Germany has traditionally been the home of rye bread, and the largest area of land cultivated with rye is in Brandenburg. The south of the country is renowned for wheat bread. North Germans like their bread dark and heavy like the northern topsoil; in the south people prefer bread to be light and firm with a spicy, thick crust.

Until the second half of the 19th century bakers worked in small craft bakeries, just as they had done ever since the Middle Ages. Mechanization and then industrialization transformed the trade entirely. Large-scale bakeries dominate the scene today, though they are returning to traditional breads after years of dull uniformity on the bread market.

The lightness of wheat flour makes it particularly desirable. In the Middle Ages only the rich could afford it.

Wheat is difficult to grow. It only flourishes in nutrient-rich soil, and needs warmth and plenty of water.

Rye is the dominant bread cereal in Germany, not least because it can be used to make sourdough.

Rye is adaptable. It will grow perfectly well in rough, stony soil and even flourishes at high altitudes.

Oats are extremely healthy. Before the potato was introduced they were the staple food of the poor.

Oats are easy to grow. They do not need a great deal of sun or warmth and grow on poor soil.

The dough for a Musberg loaf consists of white and wholemeal wheat flour with sourdough.

Anne Reitz weighs out 2½ lb (1200 g) of dough for a 2 lb (1 kg) loaf (20 percent weight loss during baking).

The bread is kneaded so that it has an even crumb and no large air holes form.

Freshly baked every day

"Make sure you use your own stove, home-baked bread is the best food of all." This old German saying has taken on a new relevance, and not only on account of the Germans' increasing sense of uncertainty about the contents of their most important staple food. The trend for baking bread at home is also associated with a sense of nostalgia, a yearning for the food that grandma used to make. Not only is this good for the profits of Germany's health food shops, it has also resulted in many old bakehouses being opened again throughout the country.

Health-conscious home bakers only use high quality corn from organic farms and grind it themselves in their own home grain mills just before they use it. The manufacturers of cereals mills and automatic bread baking machines have reacted to this trend with ever improving products. As long as they follow the instructions, even the least proficient baker can make bread that is not just healthy, but tastes good as well, provided they have the patience and the stamina. Whether the bread is made with yeast or sourdough, the raising agents need plenty of time to aerate the dough, while stamina is required when kneading because the longer the dough is kneaded, the better the bread will be.

Opposite page: Master Baker Anne Reitz knows her craft. The dough is of just the right consistency.

The dough is placed in a little basket to rise for 15–30 minutes. This is called the second proving.

Once the dough has increased in volume by a third the basket is turned over and the bread goes into the oven.

The old wood-burning oven that is still used at the *Eselsmühle* does a good job, as can be seen from the finished loaf.

The bread is carried off to the *Eselsmühl* shop, where the customers are already waiting impatiently for their fresh loaves.

The rise of yeast and sourdough

The great difference between the unleavened breads of ancient times and modern leavened breads is the use of raising agents – yeast, sourdough, ammonium carbonate, potash, and baking powder – that aerate bread dough by producing carbon dioxide. Baking powder is a child of the food industry (see page 240) and first became a common household product at the end of the 19th century. Sourdough and brewer's yeast have a long history by comparison. They were known to the ancient Egyptians and Babylonians, who discovered their aerating properties when brewing beer. Baking and brewing have always belonged together. The Egyptians made bread out of wheat and beer out of barley. The oldest large-scale bakery and brewery we know of was excavated in 1988 in Upper Egypt and dates from the 4th millennium B.C. Wall paintings in the tomb of Ramses III, who died in 1165 B.C. show how bread was made in ancient Egypt, with the bakers kneading dough with their feet instead of their hands.

The art of making leavened bread spread from Egypt to ancient Greece and then throughout the Roman empire. In Germany the first bakeries were built by the Alemannic tribes before the arrival of christianity. Ekkehard the Elder, a 10th century monk, reports that at the time of Saint Gall, in the 7th century, there were ovens being used for baking in which a thousand loaves could be baked simultaneously. In ancient Greece sourdough, known as *zyma*, was made in two ways. After the grape harvest, bakeries would make large stocks by preparing a dough of millet and fermenting wine juice that served as the starter culture. For daily requirements sourdough was made just as it is now made in many households that place a premium on healthy food and bake their own bread. Cereals are mixed with water to make a paste that has to go through several stages of fermentation before it can be used as the basis for bread making.

Making sourdough at home

In Germany sourdough can be bought in health food or organic shops in pre-prepared or dry form. However, it is better to start your own sourdough. This should be done with good-quality flour. It is important to note that sourdough needs several stages of fermentation, so it should be started at least two days before you want to bake. The method is as follows:

1. Starter culture
Mix 2 oz (50 g) of rye flour with the same amount of tepid (95 °F/35 °C) water to a paste and leave it covered in a warm place for eight hours.

2. Refresher sponge
Measure out one third of the rye flour to be soured (when making a rye loaf this will be 40 percent of the rye to be used in the loaf; when making mixed bread 50 percent). Mix with the same amount of tepid water and combine with the starter culture. This "sponge" must likewise be covered and put in a warm place for a further eight hours.

3. Base leaven
Now mix another third of the flour to be soured with the same amount of water and combine with the refresher sponge. Cover and put in a warm place.

4. Full leaven
Finally, mix the last third of the rye flour to be soured with the same amount of warm water and add to the basic leaven. However, the full leaven can only be left for four hours before it is used to make bread. 4 oz (100 g) of a full leaven made in this way can be kept aside as the starter for the next sourdough. The sourdough will keep in a fridge for one or two weeks. If you want to store the dough for longer, add flour until it becomes crumbly. This crumbly dough can be kept in the fridge for several weeks.

Happy souls and fire riders

The renaissance of bread-baking has brought new honor to the communal bakehouses in many villages and towns. At the same time it has also ensured that a traditional bread specialty that used to be made at the end of every baking day has not been completely forgotten. Known as *Weihen*, *Deien*, or *Dünnet*, it is easy to make: leftover bread dough is pressed flat, topped with bacon, cream, or scallions, sprinkled with caraway, and baked until crisp in the heat retained by the oven. A simple delicacy, the rediscovery of which has added another treasure to the rich variety of bread and baked goods in the south of Germany.

This richness, which is particularly evident among the small baked goods of Baden-Württemberg, is to be explained not just by regional differences, but also has historical grounds. Most bakeries were located in the free cities and towns of the Holy Roman Empire, which were fiercely proud of their independence. These centers often developed their own specialties, such as *Aalener Prügel*, *Biberacher Knauzenwecken*, *Ravensburger Seelen*, *Reutlinger Kimmicher*, and *Ulmer Zuckerbrot*.

The *Reutlinger Mutschel* is a small, star-shaped loaf with eight points that was traditionally made in Reutlingen on the feast of Epiphany. According to legend, one year the people of the city allowed an apprentice craftsman to starve to death on this day, after which they were only allowed to bake the *Mutschel* on the Thursday after Epiphany.

Mutscheltag has been the most important festival in the city for hundreds of years – when Reutlingen was still a free city (1280–1803). The festival was associated with the recruitment of young men into the army and the *Mutschel* was given as the prize in target shooting competitions. Since the 19th century people have competed for the eight-pointed delicacy in games of dice. Even today it is possible to find merry circles of drinkers in the bars happily shaking dice. The dice combinations are known by quaint and curious names: *Kirchenfenster* (church window), *Bauernfenster* (peasant's window), *Der Wächter bläst vom Turm* (the watchman blows from the tower), *Nacket's Luisle* (Naked Louise), *Langer Entenschiss* (long duck dropping), *Einsame Filzlaus* (lonely louse), *Haar im Loch* (hair in the hole), and *Fünf Finger* (five fingers). The players certainly need to keep their five fingers agile if they want to win a large *Mutschel*, and anyone who has been out playing dice and drinking beer all night will certainly need a big one to nibble while they find their way home!

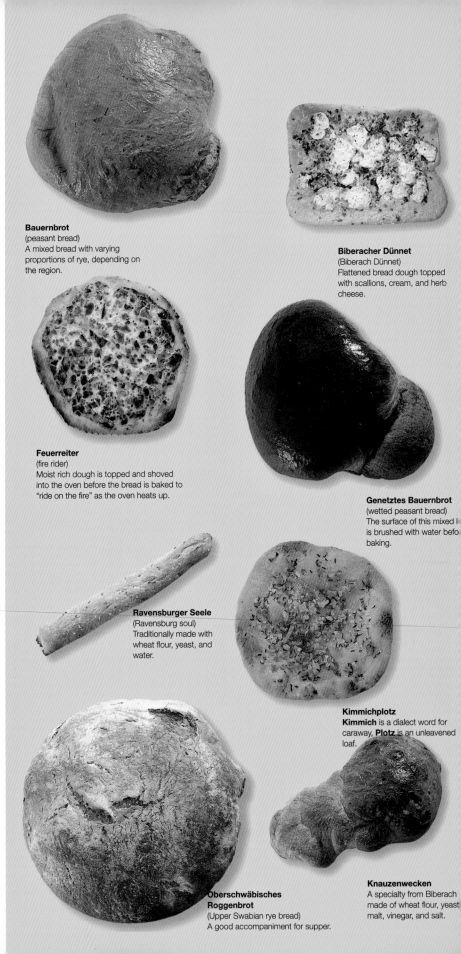

Bauernbrot
(peasant bread)
A mixed bread with varying proportions of rye, depending on the region.

Biberacher Dünnet
(Biberach Dünnet)
Flattened bread dough topped with scallions, cream, and herb cheese.

Feuerreiter
(fire rider)
Moist rich dough is topped and shoved into the oven before the bread is baked to "ride on the fire" as the oven heats up.

Genetztes Bauernbrot
(wetted peasant bread)
The surface of this mixed l[...] is brushed with water befo[...] baking.

Ravensburger Seele
(Ravensburg soul)
Traditionally made with wheat flour, yeast, and water.

Kimmichplotz
Kimmich is a dialect word for caraway, **Plotz** is an unleavened loaf.

Oberschwäbisches Roggenbrot
(Upper Swabian rye bread)
A good accompaniment for supper.

Knauzenwecken
A specialty from Biberach made of wheat flour, yeast malt, vinegar, and salt.

...efezopf
...east plait)
...aten with coffee or wine, and ...aditionally served after ...nerals.

Special baked goods are often eaten at festivals, such as the Filderkraut Festival in Echterdingen, where finely topped **Deien** are served.

Laugenbrezel
(salted pretzel)
The most typical example of the Swabian baker's craft, and is even served at political receptions.

Doppelwecken
(double roll)
Twin bread rolls for a slightly larger snack.

Mohnhörnle
(poppy seed croissant)
A crescent of rich, sweet bread covered with poppy seeds.

Holzofenbrot
(wood-fired oven bread)
Now that baking is enjoying a renaissance, bread is again being made in communal bakehouses with wood-fired ovens.

Fastenbrezel
(Lenten pretzel)
This traditional pretzel from Biberach is not dipped in brine before it is baked.

Reutlinger Mutschel
Traditionally made in Reutlingen on Epiphany and given as a prize in games of dice.

Ulmer Spatz
(Ulm sparrow)
This salt-coated roll is a reminder of the story about the sparrow that showed the people of Ulm how to push a beam through a narrow opening.

Ulmer Zuckerbrot
(Ulm sugar bread)
Traditional yeasted bun with sugar, fennel seeds, and rose oil.

Weisses Genetztes
(white wetted bread)
Upper Swabian white bread. Its crust is brushed with water before baking.

Ulmer Wasserweck
(Ulm water roll)
Small wheaten roll made with water instead of milk.

325

Bread

"there is no real bread in the States and I like eating bread, my main meal is in the evening, and it is bread and butter," wrote Bertolt Brecht (1898-1956) on October 4, 1941 in his journal. When they are abroad many Germans have exactly the same feelings as the poet from Augsburg, who spent the Nazi period in exile, some of it in the United States. Homesickness first makes itself felt in the desire for "real bread." There is no other country of the world that offers such an enormous variety of breads as Germany. Over 300 have been counted, and more are being added to the list all the time. There is no way of proving that the Germans are the world's champion bread eaters, but it is clear where they come in Europe – number one by a long way. Every German eats 179 pounds (81.4 kilograms) of bread and baked wheat goods a year. The Italians, who come second, consume 163 pounds (74 kilograms), and the Finns 161 pounds (73 kilograms).

This means that, on average, every German citizen eats one bread roll and four slices of bread every day of the year. Mixed breads, which make up 52 percent of bread sales, are most popular, followed by rye breads with 18 percent, multigrain breads with 12 percent, sliced breads with nine percent, wheat breads with seven percent, and other varieties with two percent. Mixed breads consist of a mixture of wheat and rye flour. Mixed wheat bread must contain at least 50 percent and no more than 90 percent wheat flour. The same applies to the rye flour content of mixed rye breads. "Specialty breads," such as pumpernickel and multigrain bread, are made with special flour, contain special ingredients, or are baked in a special way.

Moreover, the bread and butter that Bertolt Brecht so loved to eat is a German invention.

20 of Germany's 300 breads

1	*Sonnenblumenbrot* (sunflower bread)
2	*Malzkorn* (malted grain bread)
3	*Malzmehrkorn* (malted multigrain bread)
4	*Fränkisches* Krustenbrot (Franconian crusty loaf)
5	*Gutsherrenbrot* (lord of the manor bread)
6	*Vollwertbrot* (whole wheat bread)
7	*Bauernbrot* (peasant bread)
8	*Weissbrot* (white bread)
9	*Doppelback* (twice-baked bread)
10	*Schwarzbrot* (black bread)
11	*Dreikornbrot* (three grain bread)
12	*Eifelerbrot* (Eifel bread)
13	*Oberländerbrot* (Oberland bread)
14	*Schwarzbrot* (black bread)
15	*Dinkelbrot* (spelt bread)
16	*Paderborner* (Paderborn bread)
17	*Kosakenbrot* (Cossack bread)
18	*Graubrot* (gray bread)
19	*Vollroggenbrot* (whole rye bread)
20	*Grahambrot* (Graham bread)

Green spelt is harvested mechanically, then dried with hot air (opposite page, bottom right).

Green spelt is spelt harvested early at the "hard dough stage," when it is fully formed, but still green. It is dried and used mainly to thicken soups.

Spelt and green spelt

Spelt is an ancient cereal that developed out of the original wheat varieties, Einkorn and Emmer. As it will grow in even poor soil, is resistant to disease, and flourishes under the severest climatic conditions, it was widely cultivated in hilly areas. In Germany it was particularly popular in the "Swabian" areas of central Franconia and Württemberg. As a result, it was often called *Schwabenkorn* (Swabian corn).

However, as spelt yields are much lower than those attained by wheat and the removal of the husks is labor-intensive, and therefore costly, it has acquired a bad reputation in the 20th century. Apart from this, spelt reacts "negatively" to artificial fertilizers. In other words, they do not increase its yields. This characteristic made it ultimately unsuited to modern agriculture, and it has had to bow out in the interests of what is called "progress."

The 12th century abbess Hildegard von Bingen is famous for her mystic visions. She also wrote extensively on medicine, and believed that spelt was the best cereal of all. She praised its positive effects on the body, blood, and digestion, and claimed that, "it makes the spirit of man light and cheerful." Spelt has more essential amino acids than other forms of wheat. Its analytical values for seven of the eight building blocks of life are higher than normal soft wheat. It is also richer in many vitamins than other cereals. Spelt's high silicic acid content is unusual. This chemical is thought by some to have positive effects on the brain, as well as on the skin and hair. As far as the uses of spelt are concerned, it is particularly significant for its protein content. It has many excellent glutens, and, as a result, is perfect for baking. It makes light doughs and fine, easily digestible pastries. Its flavor is slightly nutty.

The renaissance of spelt may be a result of the fact that the cereal has a general reputation as a healthy food – in Hildegard's medicine book spelt diets are treated as a kind of panacea. At the same time, its culinary qualities have won it ever increasing numbers of enthusiasts. Demand for

spelt bread and baked goods is rising all the time. Spelt is also perfectly suited for combining with gluten-free cereals.

The fact that spelt is expensive has not stopped this development. In the end there are good reasons for its price. For one thing, yields tend to be rather low. However, what makes it really expensive are the husks. It comes as no surprise that the German word for "husk" is the cognate *Spelz*. Spelt grains are almost twice as large as wheat grains and sit firmly embedded in their husks. Threshing alone is not enough to loosen them. This has to be done by means of a special peeling procedure called hulling that can only be carried out by special mills or organic farmers who have their own hulling plants.

The husks make up one third of the weight of spelt, but there are medical uses for this waste. According to Hildegard, lying on spelt husks, or at least resting one's head on [p. 329] them, is enough to reduce pain, aid relaxation, and, many people benefit from the cereal's high silicic acid content.

Early harvested spelt has already developed fully, but is still green, and is called green spelt. The harvest must be timed perfectly to coincide with the hard dough stage, as it is known. Finally, green spelt is dried at 230 °F (110 °C) or higher. This stops it from sprouting and makes it suitable for milling. Green spelt has contributed greatly to the spelt revival.

Below: Green spelt is dried at a temperature of 230 °F (110 °C). Hot air from an oven burning beechwood logs is used to dry the grains.

Dinkelwaffeln
Spelt waffles

3½ tbsp/50 g butter
3 tbsp/100 g honey
2 eggs
2½ cups/300 g whole spelt flour
2 tsp cinnamon
1 tsp baking powder
2 cups/500 ml tepid milk
fat for frying
confectioner's sugar

Cream the butter, honey, cinnamon, and egg. The spelt flour should be freshly milled. Mix it with the baking powder and fold it into the creamed mixture gradually, adding first a little flour, then a little tepid water. Allow to rest for a little, then fry the waffles one at a time in hot fat. Use one small ladle of batter for each waffle. Sprinkle with confectioner's sugar and serve with coffee or stewed fruit.

Grünkernküchle
Green spelt patties

1 cup/100g green spelt flour
¼ cup/30 g whole wheat flour
salt
generous 1½ cups/375 ml water
1 small onion, finely chopped
1 tbsp chopped parsley
2 eggs
lard or vegetable fat for frying

Boil up the green spelt meal, flour, and chopped onion in the water with a pinch of salt. Stir thoroughly until the water has been absorbed, then allow to cool. Add the eggs and season with salt. Form small patties and fry in hot lard or vegetable fat. Serve with a green salad.

Green spelt ears: spelt harvested before it is fully ripe.

Green spelt shortly after threshing.

Green spelt that has been dried over beechwood.

Hulled green spelt.

Spätzle and Knöpfle

Spätzle – the very sound of the word puts a gleam in the eyes of Swabians and Badeners living abroad or "in exile in Prussia." *Spätzle* means home and security, memories of happy childhood days eating *Spätzle* served with sauce and – anything else would be unthinkable – potato salad. *Spätzle* form the cornerstone of cooking in Baden-Württemberg. They are the region's most unique contribution to German cuisine.

Like all real classics, Spätzle are amazingly simple: flour, eggs – the quantity can be varied according to taste – salt, and a little tepid water are mixed to a smooth, elastic dough. The dough is spread on a wet board and shaved off into bubbling water with a knife. The *Spätzle* are lifted out with a skimmer as soon as they float to the surface of the water, then turned in butter, and served with a variety of dishes. They go just as well with saddle of venison, roast pork, smoked shoulder of bacon, roast meat with cabbage, or lentils with sausages. The basic rule of *Spätzle* – one egg to every 1 cup (100 g) of flour – is merrily dispensed with in Baden, where people put in as many eggs as the dough will take, particularly on festive occasions. This can sometimes mean eight eggs or more to a pound (500 g) of flour.

It is not just the ingredients that vary, also the shape. At least, this used to be the case. Many eating places used to offer a choice between thick and thin *Spätzle* on Sundays, each prepared by a special *Spätzle* cook, usually a housewife from the neighborhood. The most remarkable versions are *Knöpfle* ("little buttons"). They are somewhat thicker than *Spätzle* and rounded because they are not shaved off with a knife or a special *Spätzle* cutter, but pushed into bubbling water through a strainer with more or less large holes. Although they are called "little buttons," *Knöpfle* do not have to be small. For example, *Hefeknöpfle* can be the size of a fist, or even a football. Before serving they are sliced using a wire. *Knöpfle* are eaten mainly in the Allgäu and Oberland districts, *Spätzle* in Württemberg and Baden.

Opposite: Whether as a side dish or as a meal on their own, one portion is never enough when the Swabians eat Spätzle.

Spätzle Grundrezept
Basic Spätzle recipe

4 cups/500 g flour
5 eggs
1 tsp salt and nutmeg
1 cup/250 ml tepid water
3 tbsp butter for the pan

Mix the ingredients to a smooth dough in a bowl. Beat the dough vigorously until it starts to bubble. Allow the dough to rest briefly, then beat again. Spread portions of dough onto a wet wooden board. Using a knife or a Spätzle cutter, shave off strips ¼ inch (0.5 cm) wide into boiling salted water. Keep dipping the knife into cold water as you shave off the Spätzle. When the Spätzle float to the surface of the water, take them out with a skimmer, rinse quickly with cold water, and drain. Melt the butter in a deep pan and reheat the Spätzle in it.

Kässpätzle
Cheese Spätzle

Spätzle dough according to basic recipe
7 oz/200 g grated Emmentaler cheese
butter for the dish
1 large onion, cut into rings
⅓ cup/80 g clarified butter

Make the Spätzle according to the basic recipe. Butter a shallow, heat-safe dish and layer the cheese and Spätzle in it. Bake for about 10 minutes in an oven preheated to 430 °F (220 °C). Brown the onion rings in the clarified butter, pour them over the cheese Spätzle, and serve immediately.

Hefeknöpfle mit sauren Bohnen
Yeasted Knöpfle with sour beans

Knöpfle
2½ cups/300 g flour
½ cup/125 ml tepid water
1 cake (15 g) of compressed yeast or 1 sachet (7 g) active dried yeast
1 tsp sugar, 1 pinch of salt
1 egg

Beans
1 lb/500 g green beans
a little savory
3½ tbsp butter
1 small onion, finely chopped
3 tbsp/50 g flour
salt and pepper, 1 pinch of sugar
1 tbsp vinegar
3 tbsp brown butter

Dissolve the yeast in the tepid milk. Sieve the flour into a bowl, form a depression in the middle, and pour in the milk and yeast. Mix well, cover, and leave in a warm place to rise. Then stir in the other ingredients and beat until the dough comes away from the spoon. Cover and leave to rise in a warm place for approximately 2 hours. Divide the dough into 4 large pieces and boil in a covered pan of salted water for 15 minutes. Boil the beans with the savory in salt water, but do not let them overcook. Meanwhile, cook the onion in the butter, dust with flour, and brown. Pour on a little of the bean water, season with salt, pepper, sugar, and vinegar, then stir in the beans. Take out the Knöpfle, cut into slices with a wire, top with brown butter, and serve with the beans.

Hefeknöpfle are very large, yeasted Spätzle. They are cut into slices with a wire and served with sour beans.

Spätzle variations

Krautspätzle (sauerkraut Spätzle)
Make the Spätzle according to the basic recipe. Put several layers ½ inch (2 cm) deep into a shallow, buttered dish, covering each layer with cooked sauerkraut that has been kept dry. Bake in a preheated oven. Serve topped with onion rings browned in clarified butter.

Spinatspätzle (spinach Spätzle)
Mix the Spätzle dough with 9 oz (250 g) minced raw spinach. Fresh herbs can be used in the same way.

Brägelte (geröstete) Spätzle (fried Spätzle)
Take Spätzle made the day before and fry slowly with butter in a skillet until golden and crispy. Serve as a simple summer dish with fresh green salad.

Leberspätzle (liver Spätzle)
Mix 2 cups (250 g) flour and 9 oz (250 g) raw, sliced liver to a smooth dough with two eggs, salt, a little marjoram, and 2 tablespoons of finely chopped parsley. Allow the dough to rest for an hour, then follow the basic recipe. Put the Spätzle into soup or serve fried with salad.

Saure Spätzle (sour Spätzle)
Make Spätzle according to the basic recipe. Make a sauce out of ⅔ cup (80 g) butter, 4 tbsp (60 g) flour, one finely chopped onion, one whole onion spiked with a bay leaf and two cloves, 2 cups (500 ml) of meat stock, 2 or 3 tablespoons of vinegar, sugar, salt, and pepper. Sweat the chopped onion in a little butter, add the rest of the butter and flour, then fry until brown. Pour on the stock, add the spiked onion, and cook slowly for 20 minutes. Take out the whole onion and season the sauce with vinegar, sugar, salt, and pepper. Add the warm Spätzle and serve with green salad.

Milchspätzle (milk Spätzle)
Make the Spätzle according to the basic recipe and serve in a sauce made of 3 tbsp (50 g) flour, 3½ tbsp (50 g) butter, 4 cups (1 liter) of milk, two eggs, salt, and pepper. Make a light roux with the butter and flour, add the milk, take off the heat, and mix in the eggs. Season with salt and pepper, and pour over the Spätzle.

Krautbaunzen (sauerkraut noodles)
Season 1 lb (500 g) raw sauerkraut, 3 cups (350 g) flour, and 2 eggs with salt and pepper, then knead to a dough. Cut off small pieces and shape into noodles about 1½–2 in. (4-5 cm) long. Cook for 15–20 minutes in bubbling salted water, remove, drain, and fry until golden in ⅓ cup (80 g) hot pork fat.

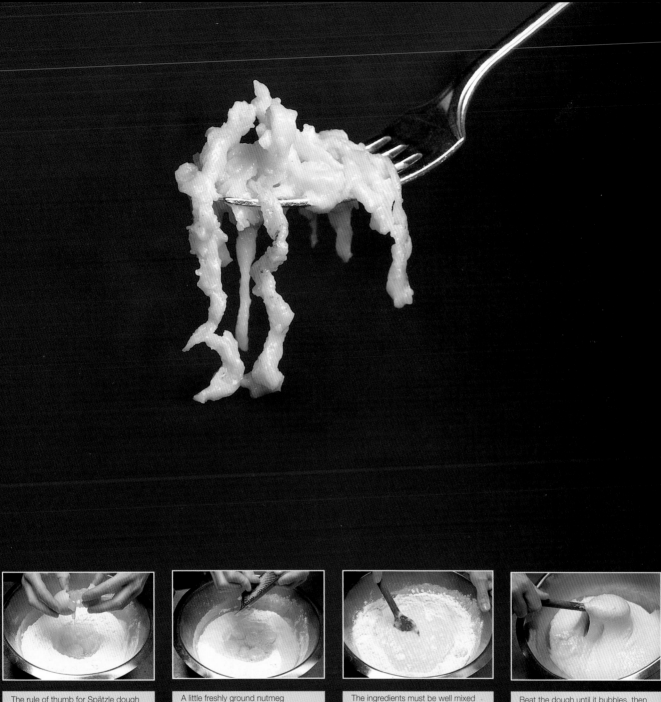

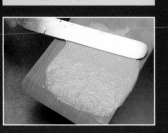

The rule of thumb for Spätzle dough is one egg to 100 g flour.

A little freshly ground nutmeg improves the flavor.

The ingredients must be well mixed with a wooden spoon.

Beat the dough until it bubbles, then leave to rest a little.

Spread a portion of dough onto a wet wooden board.

Shaving off Spätzle into boiling water tests the cook's skill.

Take the Spätzle out when they float to the surface.

Rinse the Spätzle and reheat in hot butter.

Maultaschen

For the local writer Thaddäus Troll, who died in 1980, they are the essence of all things Swabian: "This unprepossessing exterior conceals a delicious core. They taste 'hehlinge' good," explained the author of the bestseller *Deutschland deine Schwaben* ("Germany your Swabians"). *Hehlinge* is a dialect word that means secret, or concealed. It is oddly appropriate. The pale dough hides delicious riches: spinach, onions, egg, parsley, nutmeg, marjoram, sausage meat, ham, pork, or bacon! When it was explained to Thaddäus Troll's daughter that *Maultaschen* were a favorite Lenten food eaten on Good Friday, she said with outrage, "Do you think the Lord God is so stupid that He can't see through pasta dough?"

Maultaschen are made in two forms: some are like rather overgrown ravioli, others look like thick slices of strudel. The dough and filling are the same in both cases. The dough is a simple pasta dough rolled out as thin as possible. Every family has its own recipe for the filling, but all Swabians are united on one thing: *Maultaschen* are served in two courses; and both courses should only be eaten from one plate, a deep soup dish. First of all the beef soup is ladled from the tureen, then eaten with a couple of *Maultaschen*. The next course is a large bowl of potato salad and another couple of *Maultaschen*, which are topped with onion rings fried in butter. There is also a third variation: *Maultaschen* left over from the previous day are cut into small pieces and baked with whisked egg. This is served with green salad.

No one knows the origins of the word for this finest achievement of Swabian cookery. There may be a hint in a cookbook published in 1785, the *Neues Lexikon der französischen, sächsischen, österreichischen und böhmischen Kochkunst* ("New Lexicon of French, Saxon, Austrian, and Bohemian Cuisine"). Among the book's Austrian recipes we find "*Maultasche* or *Schlikkrapfen* made of fine flour." This suggests that, like the very drinkable Trollinger wine that has been produced in Württemberg for 250 years and was originally called *Tyrollinger* (Tyrolean), *Maultaschen* were introduced to Württemberg from the Tyrol. This is quite likely, because large parts of Württemberg were once ruled by Austria, but this is not the whole truth of the matter. *Maultaschen* have other relatives, such as Chinese *won ton*, Siberian *pelmeni*, Italian *ravioli*, and Jewish *kreplachs*, though it would never occur to a Swabian to see the similarities between them as anything but purely accidental.

Grundrezept Maultaschen
Basic Maultaschen recipe

Pasta dough

4 cups/500 g flour
4 eggs
a little water (depending on the size of the eggs)
flour for the pastry board

Filling

1 lb/500 g spinach
salt
2 onions
butter for frying
1 bunch of parsley, finely chopped
4 stale bread rolls, soaked in water
9 oz/250 g ground meat
9 oz/250 g cooked sausage, diced finely
2 eggs
pepper and nutmeg
1–2 tbsp breadcrumbs

Sieve the flour into a bowl. Break the eggs into the center and beat to a firm dough, working out from the center. Add a little water if necessary. Swabian cooks usually use about half an eggcup of water for each egg. Take the dough from the bowl and knead it fully on a floured pastry board. It must be firm and smooth. Form into a ball, cover, and leave to rest. While it is resting, make the filling. Blanche the spinach in salted water, press dry, and chop coarsely. Press the water out of the bread rolls. Chop the onions finely and fry in butter. Add the parsley and the soaked bread rolls, and mix well. Fry the ground meat in the butter. Put the spinach, ground meat, diced sausage, and the bread mixture into a bowl, beat the eggs and add them to the filling. [p. 333] Knead well and

The filling for herb Maultaschen is spread onto thinly rolled pasta dough.

The mixture must be distributed as evenly as possible. One edge of the dough is left free.

The free edge of dough is brushed with a little melted butter so that it sticks better.

Beginning with the unbuttered edge, the dough is rolled up like a strudel.

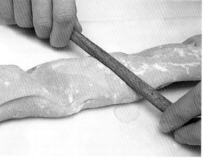

It is best to use the handle of a wooden spoon to divide the Maultaschen "strudel" into equal pieces.

The Maultaschen must now cook for 10–15 minutes in simmering water. They must not boil.

season with salt, pepper, and nutmeg. The mixture should be smooth and soft. Add a few breadcrumbs to adjust the consistency if necessary.

Cut the dough into 6 pieces and roll out each one as thin as possible. The filling can be spread thinly and evenly on the strips of dough, which are then rolled up diagonally into "strudels" about 3½–4 inches (8–10 cm) long. Alternatively, the filling can be arranged in small piles, then covered with a second strip of dough, which is cut into squares with a knife or a pizza cutter. Put the Maultaschen into simmering water and cook for 10–15 minutes, depending on size. The water must not boil. Serve in beef broth, or top with crispy onions and serve with potato salad. For the crispy onions, slice two large onions finely and fry very slowly in about ⅓ cup/80 g fresh butter over a low heat until they go golden brown. When the onions are done they brown very quickly, so make sure they do not over cook.

Kräutermaultaschen
Herb Maultaschen

Dough according to basic recipe

Filling
1 bunch of parsley
1 bunch of chives
1 bunch of scallions and seasonal herbs, such as borage, burnet saxifrage, etc.
½ cup/125 ml sour cream
9 oz/250 g leftover boiled meat

Chop the meat finely. Chop the herbs as finely as possible, then mix with the meat and sour cream to make a smooth, soft mixture. Add breadcrumbs if necessary. Make the Maultaschen according to the basic recipe.

Griebenmaultaschen
Dripping Maultaschen

Dough according to basic recipe

Filling
1 cup/240 g dripping
2 eggs
2 tbsp flour
2½ cups/125 g fresh breadcrumbs
2 tbsp finely chopped herbs (parsley, chives, etc.)
pepper and salt

Combine the ingredients to make a smooth mixture and make Maultaschen according to the basic recipe.

Opposite: Cooks can give free reign to their imagination when combining ingredients for Maultaschen fillings.

Dripping Maultaschen

Herb Maultaschen

Potato and flour

North meets south

Germany is divided into two culinary halves: the north and the south. Bavarians tend to divide the whole world into the areas where *Weisswurst* (white sausage) is eaten and those foreign lands where it is unknown. This serves mainly to keep a healthy distance between them and alien culinary influences, but the other dividing lines are real enough, particularly the one between flour and potato-based cooking. It is true that there are exceptions, such as massive balls of solid dough known in Schleswig-Holstein as *Mehlbüdel* that were once made with kidney fat and are regarded as the forerunners of the great English suet puddings.

Another region that does not follow the rule is Baden-Württemberg, where flour and potatoes are united in an unusual alliance. This is a result of the proverbial thriftiness of the Swabians. If there was not enough flour, the dough was padded out with potatoes, which were much cheaper. The consequence was the creation of wonderful potato-flour mixtures such as the little potato noodles called *Bubespitzle*, also known in the Franconian dialect of the Hohenlohe area as *Bauchstecherle*, *Kartoffelkratzed*, or *Nackete Mariele*. In Oberland one variation on this idea, *Kartoffelwurst*, is made with yeasted dough, like the *Kartoffelstrudel* (potato strudel) of the Ries area around Nördlingen, the *Kartoffelkuchen* (potato cake – see page 87) that is made in Grossbottwar, a small winegrowing center to the north west of Stuttgart, and, last but not least the patties known as *Aalener Schneiderfleck*.

There are a number of simple meals based on this combination: *Schnitz und Spatzen*, in which pieces of boiled potato float in a rich broth with Spätzle, and the famous *Gaisburger Marsch* (Gaisburg march), which is claimed to originate in a part of Stuttgart called Gaisburg. It is said that it was the favorite food of the volunteer soldiers who made the pilgrimage from their barracks to a tavern in Gaisburg every Sunday. The landlord is claimed to have invented this beef stew with potatoes and *Spätzle*, hence the name. Though it is unlikely to please the people of Gaisburg, it is much more likely that the Gaisburg march is nothing more than the Swabian version of an Austrian dish called *Grenadiermarsch* (Grenadiers' march), which was hugely popular in the 19th century, a filling beef stew in which pasta and potatoes were brought together in just as pleasing a manner as the *Spätzle* and potatoes in Gaisburg march.

Gaisburger Marsch
Gaisburg march

1 lb/500 g stewing meat, preferably brisket or neck of beef
9 oz/250 g soup bones, including at least one marrowbone
soup vegetables (2 carrots, 2 celery stalks, 1 leek, 1 bunch of parsley)
salt, a few peppercorns
1 bay leaf
1 tbsp finely chopped parsley

Potatoes and Spätzle

9 oz/250 g peeled potatoes
9 oz/250 g Spätzle
1 onion
1 tbsp butter

Rinse the bones, put them in a pan of cold water, and heat. As soon as the water boils, put in the beef. Skim off any foam that forms and reduce the heat. After half an hour add the soup vegetables and a little salt, and simmer gently for about 2 hours. While the stew is simmering, keep skimming off the foam. Dice the potatoes, boil in salt water, and drain. Make the Spätzle according to the basic recipe (see page 330) and keep warm. Slice the onions into fine rings and brown in the butter until golden. When the meat has cooked, remove it from the stock and dice into cubes, which should not be too large. Put the meat into a tureen with the Spätzle and potatoes. Sieve the beef stock and pour it over the meat, potatoes, and Spätzle. Sprinkle with parsley and serve with onion rings fried in butter.

Sweet potato noodles

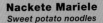

Potato noodles

Nackete Mariele
Sweet potato noodles
(Illustrated left)

7 oz/200 g flour
2 lb/1 kg potatoes
10 tsp/150 g soft butter
salt
cinnamon and sugar

Grate the potatoes finely and mix with the flour, 4 tsp (50 g) of the butter, and a little salt. Knead to a dough, which should not be too stiff, and form into noodles as thick as a thumb and as long as a finger. Fry gently in the rest of the butter – not too quickly as the noodles must not go brown. Sprinkle with cinnamon and sugar, and serve with apple sauce.

Bubespitzle
Potato noodles
(Illustrated bottom left)

2 lb/1 kg potatoes boiled the day before
3 eggs, salt
6½ tbsp/100 g flour
clarified butter for frying

Push the peeled potatoes through a sieve. Add the eggs, a pinch of salt, and as much flour as is needed until the dough is firm. Knead well, form into a long roll, and cut off small pieces about ½ inch (1 cm) thick. Roll on a floured board or between your hands to make small sausages the length of a finger. Put into bubbling salted water. When they start to float, take them out, drain, and fry in hot clarified butter. Serve as a side dish with meat or as a main dish with sauerkraut.

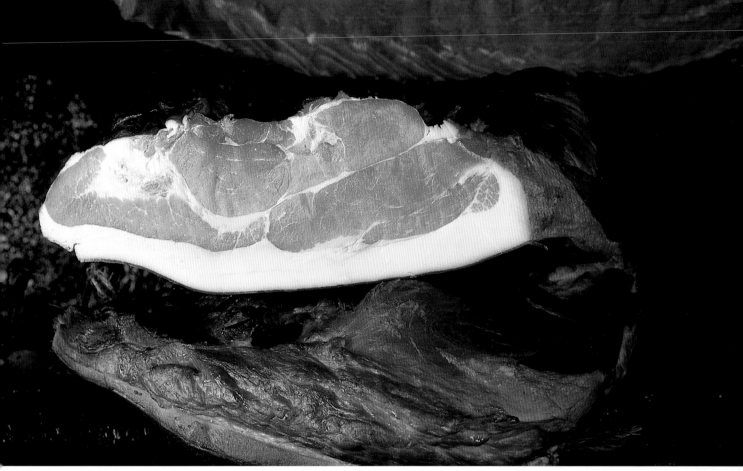

Black Forest ham the way the locals like it, with a thick layer of fat.

Dry cured, cold smoked

Ham

The people of the Black Forest love to eat local ham with a thick layer of fat. The farmers in the area never used to slaughter any pig that weighed less than 6 hundredweight (3 metric hundred weight), and many of them still maintain the custom, just as they still give their animals natural feedstuffs from their own farms – cereals, potatoes, and whey – because they know that what a pig eats is just as crucial to the quality of the ham as the care and patience exercised when it is cured.

Only boned rear-leg hams are used. Small butchers and other suppliers of top-quality products use traditional methods in which the ham is dry cured, in other words, salted by hand. Every butcher has his own combination of salt and spices. The salt draws the moisture out of the ham and forms a brine, which drains slowly away. Depending on the style of preparation, the ham may cure for several weeks or months. Injection salting, also known as "brine pumping," involves injecting a brine concentrate into the meat. It is used in large-scale production, but is regarded with contempt by manufacturers of quality ham.

The "curing time" is the time that the salt needs to penetrate to the center of the meat. When the curing process is completed, the ham is hung up to dry either in the pure air of the high Black Forest, or in light spruce smoke, which gives it a unique flavor that is truly unmistakable. The smoke must be cold (below 77 °F/25 °C), and the ham must not be allowed to "cook." The lower the temperature the longer the ham has to hang in the smoke. Cold smoking is the mildest and gentlest method, but also the most time consuming, and therefore the most expensive. When ham is dry cured and cold smoked, it loses 30 to 40 percent of its weight.

Another specialty from the Black Forest is bacon. Good bacon with plenty of fat running through it is salted in a spiced brine, then smoked over a small fire of resin-rich pine wood until it goes black on the outside. The farmers of the region and other connoisseurs particularly love Black Forest bacon for supper with a thick slice of home-baked bread and a small glass of kirsch.

Herr Jäckle's smoke oven is situated directly under the roof of his farmhouse, in the Black Forest.

The vegetable of princes

The vegetable of princes, the joy of spring, tender ivory – no other German vegetable has as many flowery names as asparagus – and no other vegetable enjoys such a high reputation. German asparagus is the most expensive in Europe by a long way. Nevertheless, although the market is now being swamped with cheap imports from neighboring countries and the Mediterranean, gourmets are more than happy to pay the price for German asparagus. They know that it tastes best "picked in the morning, eaten at midday," and that the product's flavor and consistency are dependent on its freshness.

Asparagus is cultivated in almost all the German federal states, but its historic roots are to be found in the area around Stuttgart. This is where asparagus was grown in Germany for the very first time during the 16th century. Until the 19th century the luxury vegetable was only intended for the tables of court. It was the vegetable of princes, after all. The consumer profile is now very different, but the amount of work required by asparagus cultivation is the same, and the vegetable is still harvested by hand.

Asparagus is a member of the *Liliaceae* family, grows in carefully tended, loose, sandy soil, and is usually planted in fields that face south. It takes three years for a plant to produce its first tips. The bleached asparagus favored in Germany has to be protected from sunlight with a knee-high bank of earth because the asparagus tips start to discolor if they are exposed to the rays of the sun. For this reason they are picked in the gray of early morning. Fine cracks in the earth show the picker where to dig. He uncovers the tip by hand and cuts it off just above the stem with an asparagus knife. A practiced asparagus picker can harvest 8 to 12 pounds (4–6 kilograms) in an hour. The date when the annual harvest begins depends on the weather. The asparagus first starts to sprout when the soil reaches a minimum temperature of 54 °F (12 °C). Usually the season extends from April to June 24, the birthday of St John the Baptist. However, asparagus also grows later in the north than in the south and earlier in Schwetzingen (Baden) than in Schrobenhausen (Bavaria) on account of the weather conditions.

Most asparagus farms in southern Germany are small family businesses. As a rule, asparagus is distributed through producers' wholesale markets. The freshly picked

Bleached asparagus must on no account be exposed to light as the tips will discolor.

Hard work: the tips are uncovered by hand and cut off with an asparagus knife.

Now the asparagus is carefully pulled out of the soil. Broken tips fetch a lower price.

tips are taken to collection points and sold in large halls. [p. 336] Curiously enough, when the first asparagus is traded at the beginning of the season the current price of veal is used as a guide, because there is no market price to work on.

You can tell fresh asparagus by the noise it makes when two sticks are knocked together; also the cut ends are light in color and juicy. Asparagus is always washed before it is peeled. When peeling large quantities it is advisable to cover the peeled sticks with a damp cloth so that they do not dry out. It is best to use a special peeler, and start just over an inch (about 3 cm) below the tip. Green asparagus is peeled from the bottom upward, and only the bottom third of the tip is peeled.

It is possible to buy special asparagus steamers with separate baskets in which the delicate vegetable is cooked gently and keeps more of its flavor. Cooking times are 12 to 15 minutes, depending on how thick the tips are. If a normal pan is used the tips should be tied together with a piece of thread. It is recommended that the water be flavored beforehand by boiling the discarded bits of the stem and peelings in it with a little butter, salt, and a pinch of sugar.

In order to allow the delicate flavor of the asparagus to come to the fore, serve it with melted butter and new potatoes. If cooking for dedicated asparagus eaters, allow about a pound (500 grams) per person, less if it is a side dish.

Background: Asparagus is shielded from the light by a knee-high square bank of earth. Asparagus is still picked by hand.

A cure-all and aphrodisiac

Asparagus officinalis L. is the botanical name for asparagus. *Asparagus* is a Latin word for the fat shoot of a plant before its leaves develop; *officinalis* indicates that asparagus was once used as a remedy by monastery apothecaries. The ancient Greeks and Romans thought that the plant could increase potency. According to a herbal written in 1563, "eating asparagus makes men feel lusty with desire." What is more, asparagus was used in traditional folk medicine as a remedy for practically everything, including toothache, rheumatism, liver problems, hip pains, hemorrhoids, and attacks of fever. Of course asparagus is neither an aphrodisiac nor a magic cure for all ailments, but it is a very healthy food. It is rich in vitamin C, calcium, and phosphorus. 93 percent of asparagus is water, and it has only 26 calories per 4 ounces (100 g). The aspartic acid and saponin it contains activate the kidneys and have an diuretic effect. Vitamin-rich green asparagus has an even higher nutrient content than bleached asparagus.

A rich harvest. A practiced asparagus picker will pick 8 to 12 pounds (4–6 kilos) in an hour.

Tips are cleaned with water. At the price they are paying shoppers do not want to pay for soil.

The vegetable of the kings is sorted by size and quality and sent to market the very same day.

Asparagus dishes

Spargel mit Salzkartoffeln, Butter und Schinken
Asparagus with boiled potatoes, butter, and ham
(Illustrated below)

4 lb/2 kg asparagus
14 oz/400 g cooked ham
1½ lbs/600 g new potatoes
13 tbsp/200 g melted butter

Prepare the asparagus according to the basic recipe. Serve the ham cold. Scrub the new potatoes clean and boil them in their skins.

Grundrezept Spargel
Basic asparagus recipe

4 lb/2 kg asparagus
1 tbsp butter
salt
1 pinch sugar

Wash and peel the asparagus, peeling down from the top of the tip to the thicker end. Cut off the ends. Bring plenty of water to a boil in a pan with the butter, a little salt, and sugar. Put the asparagus in the boiling water and cook over a low heat for 12–15 minutes. Lift out of the pan, drain, and serve on a warmed plate.

Spargel mit Kratzede
Asparagus with Kratzede pancakes
(Illustrated top left)

Kratzede is also known in Baden-Württemberg as *Eierhaber*, *G'fuhrlets*, *Rührum*, and *Stierum*.

4 lb/2 kg asparagus

Kratzede
2 cups/250 g flour
salt and nutmeg
1½ cups/375 ml milk
3 eggs, separated
butter for frying

Combine the flour with the salt and nutmeg. Stir to a smooth consistency with the milk and mix in the egg yolks. Whip the egg whites until stiff and fold into the batter. Heat the butter in a skillet and ladle portions of batter into the hot fat. Fry the pancakes until golden brown on both sides and tear to pieces with a fork. Keep warm in the oven until all the batter has been fried. Serve with cooked asparagus.

Asparagus with Kratzede pancakes

Asparagus with boiled potatoes, butter, and ham

Spargelsalat
Asparagus salad
(Illustrated bottom right)

2 lb/1 kg asparagus

Vinaigrette

1 tbsp white wine vinegar
1 shallot, finely chopped
1 bunch of chives, finely chopped
1 bunch of chervil, finely chopped
salt and pepper
2 tbsp extra virgin olive oil

Cook the asparagus according to the basic recipe until *al dente*. Cut into pieces about 5 cm long. Combine the vinaigrette ingredients to make a dressing and pour onto the asparagus while it is still warm. Serve with calf cheek, tongue, or sweetbread, according to taste.

Spargel mit Flädle
Asparagus with pancakes

4 lb/2 kg asparagus

Pancake batter

scant 3 cups/350 g flour
5 eggs
3 cups/750 ml milk
salt
butter or oil for the skillet

Beat the ingredients to make a thin pancake batter. Fry thin, crispy pancakes, using 2 pans, if necessary. Serve with cooked asparagus in a light butter sauce (melted butter) or Hollandaise.

Spargel mit Strübli
Asparagus with Strübli

Asparagus with Strübli is an old Baden specialty that has almost been forgotten. There are two versions of Strübli: the first made with beer batter, which is poured through a funnel into deep fat, where it twists into bizarre shapes; and the second made of choux pastry, which is either poured directly into the fat or piped into a ring shape on a board using a pastry bag and fried when it has set a little.

4 lb/2 kg cooked asparagus

Beer batter

2 cups/250 g flour
3 eggs
salt
nutmeg
1 cup/250 ml beer
½ cup/125 ml mineral water

Combine the ingredients to make a thick batter, if necessary adding a little more flour. Pour a stream of batter into hot, deep fat. As soon as the curls have turned golden, remove them and dry on paper towels. Keep warm until the batter is finished, then serve with cooked asparagus in a herb sauce.

Choux pastry

2 tbsp butter
1 cup/250 ml milk
1 cup/125 g flour
3–4 eggs
1 pinch salt
1 pinch sugar
clarified butter for frying

Boil up the butter and milk together, and mix in all the flour. Stir vigorously until the batter comes away from the sides of the pot. Remove from the heat and mix in the eggs, salt, and sugar. Allow the batter to cool. Pour the batter straight into the fat, or pipe it onto a floured board, then drop into the fat. Serve with cooked asparagus.

Classic sauces to go with asparagus

The classic accompaniment to fresh asparagus is melted butter, unless you prefer a light vinaigrette. For many asparagus lovers it is best eaten with melted butter, new potatoes, and smoked meat or cooked ham from the Black Forest.

The classic sauce for asparagus is Hollandaise. For each half pound (250 grams) of butter you will need 3 egg yolks, 3 tablespoons of water, 1 tablespoon of white wine vinegar, a pinch of salt, and a pinch of pepper. Heat the vinegar with 1 tablespoon of the water and a pinch of pepper, and reduce the fluid down to a teaspoonful. Add the 2 egg yolks and the remaining 2 tablespoons of water, then whisk the mixture until it is smooth and creamy. Now add the melted butter drop by drop. If the sauce becomes too thick, a little tepid water can be added and beaten in. At the end the sauce is seasoned with salt. Sauce Mousseline, or Sauce Chantilly, is airier than Hollandaise and made in the same way, but with one third whipped cream. Another excellent sauce for asparagus is Sauce Maltaise, in which the juice of blood oranges and a little grated orange rind are added to a Hollandaise.

Asparagus is excellent baked in Hollandaise or Sauce Mornay, a béchamel sauce thickened with egg yolk and mixed with parmesan and Swiss cheese.

Asparagus salad with tongue

Animals undergo less stress when they are slaughtered singly.

After the pig has been stunned its throat is cut and the blood drained.

The pig is scalded in a tub of hot water and roughly dehaired.

Now comes the fine work. The remaining bristles are scrubbed off.

The pig is hung up, then washed down and gutted.

The luxury of an individual death

Slaughter day

Eberhardt Friess is the only butcher in Luizhausen, a small town in the Swabian Alb district. Like many of his colleagues in the region he earns his living mainly by slaughtering animals on farms. The law says that this work can only be done by a butcher who is entered in the guild register, in other words, someone who has passed the examinations required of a master butcher.

This Saturday Eberhardt Friess drives to a small farm in Halzhausen to slaughter two young pigs. The work is done at the back of the yard, where it cannot be seen from the road. This location has been chosen for good reason: the public must not be able to see the animals being slaughtered, and children below 14 years must not be allowed to watch. The times are long past when the little ones would watch the show with rapt attention and wait to be given the pig's bladder, which they could fill with air and use as a ball.

There are many preparations to be made before animals are slaughtered at the owner's house or farm. The wooden scalding tub has already been softened the day before, so that it is watertight. The farmer's wife started heating up the old boiler early in the morning so that there is plenty of hot water to scald the pig with. Large logs of dried beechwood, which burns particularly slowly and strongly, are smoldering under the vessel in which the sausages will later be cooked.

Eberhardt Friess is known as "Stacho" due to his spiky hair (the German word for "spiky" is *stachelig*). He arrives early and sets up his equipment: the wooden stand, rather like a saw horse, on which the pig is dehaired, the frame from which it is hung to be split and gutted, and the buckets for cleaning the guts. The farmer's son brings the pigs from the stall one by one. They are in a familiar environment and are more hungry and curious than excited. They were not fed the day before because this makes it easier to clean the gut. Home slaughtering is regulated closely by the German laws on animal welfare. The animal must be stunned quickly, and, with the exception of rabbits, it is not allowed to kill an animal by striking it on the neck, stabbing it in the neck, or breaking its neck. The scalding, dehairing, cutting, and hanging of slaughtered animals can only begin once they are clinically dead.

Stacho stuns the pigs with a bolt pistol. What follows is performed with almost surgical precision. First the pig's throat is cut. The blood spurts out with some force because the heart is still beating, and is caught in a bucket. It is important to be quick bleeding the pig so that the blood does not absorb any germs from the gut. Now the pigs are scalded in hot water and dehaired with a scraper. This must also be done quickly. The longer it takes, the harder the work becomes.

He begins the gutting by removing the tongue. The pigs are hung up by their two rear trotters on the frame and the skin is stripped back to reveal the sinews and tendons of the rear legs. This is where the butcher's real work begins: cutting out the meat to be used for sausage, removing the fat from the bacon, loosening, cleaning, and tying the guts, dividing the meat for the two varieties of *Kochwurst* (boiled sausage) that are to be made straight away after the pigs have been slaughtered: *Leberwurst* (liver sausage), and *Blutwurst* (blood sausage). The sausage meat is mixed in two zinc-galvanized pans, which have been carefully cleaned and stand ready in the yard. All the sausages are seasoned with salt and pepper, but each variety has other ingredients that give it its unique character: allspice and marjoram in the *Blutwurst*, and onions spiked with spices, bay leaves, grated onions, and thyme in the *Leberwurst*. The meat for the sausages is still warm and sits steaming in a huge pail: the bacon and the fat, the cheeks and the snout, the fresh liver and the blood that was collected and stirred well in a bucket when the pig's neck was cut.

Eberhardt Friess makes the two sausage mixtures almost at the same time, seasons them, tastes them, and expresses his satisfaction. Almost every slaughterhouse in the country has a powered grinder for cutting up the meat. Friess does not own one, but his huge old hand grinder does the job perfectly well. The steaming sausage mixture is fragrant and appetizing. If you try it with your finger it tastes almost as good as the finished product. The filling and twisting of the guts is fast and routine. Within a very short time the two baths are half full of tied sausages, which finally go into a pot of simmering water. Any of the mixture that is not used is canned.

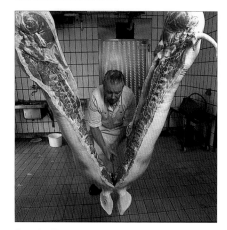

Opposite: The butcher comes to the farm to slaughter pigs. Top: A carcass being split correctly by a butcher at a local slaughterhouse. Even there the slaughtering is done individually and not in huge numbers.

After the slaughtering comes the sausage making. The fresh ingredients are made into *Leberwurst* and *Blutwurst*. The seasoning has to be just right.

The guts have been carefully cleaned and are now filled with liver sausage meat.

Now the sausages are tied. There are small sausages. . .

. . . and large ones. ISO standards are not observed closely here. Any leftover sausage meat is put into cans that are sealed and sterilized in hot water.

The feast after the slaughtering

During both the slaughtering process and the feast that comes afterward the center of attention is always the sausage pot. In the past all the neighbors would be invited round to eat belly of pork and *Metzelsuppe* (slaughter day soup). At the very least they would be given a couple of freshly made *Leberwurst* and *Blutwurst*. Today such gestures of neighborly consideration have become rare in the countryside, but the farmer's extended family still come on slaughter day to eat together. If he has no urgent business to take him away, the butcher will sit at the table and eat just as hungrily as the other guests.

The feast begins with *Wurstbrühe* (sausage soup), also known as *Metzelsuppe* (*Metzel* means "slaughter," or "butchery"), a strong broth with little lumps of fat floating in it. This is a great delicacy in spite of its bloodthirsty name. The belly of pork cooked in the soup makes it particularly warming and nourishing. Any sausages that have burst during the day are added and give the soup a wonderful, rich flavor. Then comes the meat course: the tail, ears, cheeks, and snout lie pink and white on a bed of sauerkraut. They are served with sausages fresh from the pot and still covered with steam. No wonder Ludwig Uhland was inspired to write a song to *Metzelsuppe*, in which he sang the praises of fresh sausages, making much play of the fact that the German words *Wein* (wine) and *Schwein* (pig) rhyme in the most enticing fashion, as do *Wurst* (sausage) and *Durst* (thirst). As these rhymes suggest, a successful slaughtering day is always celebrated in style!

Swabian sausage glossary

Bauernbratwurst
An uncooked sausage made of raw, smoked, and dried pork.

Gelbwurst
A scalded sausage made of an ordinary sausage meat mixture in gut dyed with saffron.

Griebenwurst (Blutwurst)
A boiled sausage made of pork fat with bacon, pig cheeks, snout, liver, and blood in pig's large intestine.

Landjäger
An uncooked sausage made of beef and pork and pressed flat. Also known as *rund Peitschenstecken*.

Leberwurst
A boiled sausage made of fresh pork, unsmoked bacon, and pig liver in pig gut or cow's small intestine.

Oberländer
A skinless sausage of veal and pork.

Presskopf
A boiled sausage made of pig tongue, heart, cheek, belly, and fat in a pig stomach. This mixture is often canned.

Rote
A scalded sausage made with a similar mixture of meat to that used in *Saiten*, but with skins made of pig gut.

Saiten
A scalded sausage made with a mixture of beef and pork in sheep gut.

Schwartenmagen rot
A boiled sausage made with blood, fat, and cheek or knuckle.

Schwartenmagen weiss
A boiled sausage made from pig head or knuckle with fat and onions.

Schwarzwurst
A boiled sausage made of pig blood, bacon, and fat.

Metzelsuppe and Schlachtplatte – these are the highlights of the slaughtering day.

Back to the old breeds

The pig

The pig is, and always has been, the number one provider of meat for Germany's kitchens. Some 60 percent of all meat eaten is pork, which is far more than any other variety.

In recent years, though, it has declined slightly in popularity due to the somewhat questionable fattening methods, which have been reason enough for more responsible farmers and breeders to rethink and return to the country's old breeds instead of the standard German pig. One of the guiding lights of this movement is Rudolf Bühler, who has been particularly active in promoting the re-introduction of the Swabian native pig. Although this pig does take a little longer to mature than its pedigree counterpart, it has retained its natural layer of fat and, most importantly, it tastes much better.

Two-hundred-and-sixty farms have now formed a producers' cooperative. Their Swabian pigs are free to roam, and feed on all-natural fodder that contains no chemicals but is enriched with a high-protein supplement of pea or bean meal. Their straw-lined stalls are spacious and comfortable, and the pigs have plenty of room to move around. It goes without saying that the meat from this fortunate minority amongst pedigree pigs is superb, and a tribute to the south-west's most popular Sunday roast: crispy roast pork in Swabia, and the spicy Schäufele (pork shoulder) in Baden.

Stuffed pork belly

Potato salad

Bietigheim "greenbacks"

Bietigheimer Laubfröschle
Bietigheimer "greenbacks"
(Illustrated opposite, bottom of page)

The standard stuffing for *Maultaschen* (ground beef, chopped onion, egg, finely chopped bacon, fresh breadcrumbs, spinach, and seasoning) can, of course, be used instead of this version. "Greenbacks" are the stuffed cabbage of springtime. They are usually served by themselves, just in the stock in which they were cooked, but they can also be served with a potato salad.

2 lb/1 kg spinach (large leaves)
4 oz/100 g smoked pork belly, diced
2 tbsp oil
1 finely chopped onion
4 oz/100 g cooked ham, finely chopped
bunch of finely chopped parsley
bunch of finely chopped chives
7 oz/200 g white bread cubes, crusts removed and softened in a little milk
4 eggs
salt, pepper, and nutmeg
oil for the dish
½ cup meat or vegetable stock

Wash the spinach, remove the stalks. Blanch 20 large spinach leaves briefly in boiling water, then drain. Continue with the remaining spinach, squeezing it well, and then finely chop. Fry the pork belly in oil until crisp, then add onion, diced sausage and herbs. Pour over the softened bread cubes, combine with chopped spinach and eggs, and season well. Open out the blanched spinach leaves, spoon filling into each and fold over. Oil a heatproof dish, place the rolled up leaves side by side in the dish, with the seam at the bottom. Pour over the stock, and cook on the middle shelf of a preheated oven (400 °F/200 °C) for about 15 minutes.

Gefüllter Schweinebauch
Stuffed pork belly
(Illustrated opposite, top of page)

Serves 6

3¼ lbs/1½ kg pork belly with rind on (ask your butcher to cut a pocket in the meat)
salt and pepper
1 chopped onion
5 tsp/25 g butter
4 oz/100 g fresh cooked ham, finely chopped
bunch of finely chopped parsley
7 oz/200 g mushrooms, sliced
1 bread roll, softened and cut into small dice
9 oz/250 g ground veal
1 egg, separated
grated lemon rind
clarified butter
2 cups/½ liter meat stock

Season the pork belly with plenty of salt and pepper. Sauté the onion in the butter until translucent. Combine the cold meat, parsley, mushrooms, the softened bread roll, ground veal, and egg yolk. Beat the egg white until stiff, and add to the mixture. Season with salt, pepper, and grated lemon rind. Fill the pork belly with this mixture, and sew up the opening. Brown the pork belly on all sides in hot oil, then, with the rind facing down, place in a preheated oven (400 °F/200 °C). Turn after 30 minutes, and roast for a further 1½ hours, basting frequently with the stock.

Badisches Schäufele
Baden pork shoulder
(Illustrated bottom right)

Serves 6

1 Schäufele (salted and smoked pork shoulder on the bone)
salt and pepper
1 carrot
1 onion
1 celery stalk
½ cup white wine from Baden

Season the meat with salt and pepper. Place it in a roasting pan with the fat layer facing upward (do not score), and add the coarsely chopped vegetables and water to a depth of two fingers. Place in a preheated oven (400 °F/200 °C), and roast for between 2 and 2½ hours, basting frequently. Pour over the wine for the last 15 minutes of the cooking time. Serve the meat with spätzle and cabbage.

Pork shoulder with spätzle

Vesper – Take a break

"No, net hudle," – loosely translated as, "No worry – no hurry," is the Swabians' creed, and expresses the desire to avoid any hectic and exaggerated activity either at work, or when taking a break. The reason why the word "Hudle" (it is derived from "Hudelwisch," which is the name given to the birch broom that is used to remove the ash from the oven before baking the bread) does not appeal to the Swabians, and probably not to the people of Baden either, is because of its suggestions of slovenliness. Whatever a person is doing, whether *schaffen* (working) or *vespern* (taking a break), it must be done properly. That is possibly why the break is also an occasion for silent reflection, rather than noisy sociability. At an event such as a festival or fair, a *Vesper* will be taken either to avoid drinking on an empty stomach, or else because it is simply a good time for one.

The *Vesper* is a break with food that is traditionally taken twice a day, once in the morning and once in the afternoon; occasionally in the early evening. The choice of hot or cold food is left to the individual – there is certainly a wide choice: cheese, cold meat, ham, pickled kidneys or liver, brawn, pork cracklings, pickled gherkins, salt pretzels, and so on.

In former times, when tradesmen still conducted much of their business in the taverns over a break, the morning *Vesper* was usually taken between 10 and 11. Today, it is usually only senior citizens who take a break at this time, provided they can find a suitable location that is open. Many workshops, construction sites, and factories take their break between 9 and 9.30 in the morning. Despite the freedom afforded by "flexitime," this "second breakfast" is hardly ever missed. This is also the time when butchers and bakers have their highest turnovers, since it is when apprentices and juniors everywhere are sent forth to fetch *Leberkäs*, sausage and cold meats, fresh bread rolls, pretzels, and so on. A Swabian bank even went as far as to state, in a recent job advertisement, that apprentices fetching the provisions for the Vesper would be able to pay by credit card.

One item that is essential for the Vesper is the pocket knife, which is used both for cutting and skewering the food and lifting it to the mouth. Even if cutlery is provided, a true *Vesperer* will prefer to use his pocket knife as a sign of freedom, of independence. The same freedom that allows him to give Götz von Berlichingen's "Swabian greeting" ("Go to hell!") to anyone, at any time …

Vesper choices

1 Bugblättle. The *Bugblättle* is a particularly tender piece of meat from the cow's shoulder.
2 Cheese from the Harz Mountains, marinated in oil and vinegar. A crusty pretzel is a good accompaniment.
3 Smoked ham and blood sausage are traditionally served for Vesper.
4 Gröscht's are made from veal and cattle organ meat.
5 Boiled pork knuckle, served with cabbage or sauerkraut.
6 Kräuterkäse – herb cheese – is bought ready-made, and blended with butter and cream.
7 Blood sausage salad, made with onions, vinegar, and oil.
8 Pork cheeks on lentil salad, a modern Vesper dish.
9 Luckeleskäs is a coarse-grained soft cheese, so named because it used to be fed to chickens (*Luckeles* is the local word for "chicken").
10 Veal head, boiled or roast, is a popular snack.
11 Fried *Peitschenstecken* were typically served with wine in factories and workshops where brooms were made.
12 *Backsteinkäse* is especially tasty if served with oil and vinegar.
13 *Landjäger* and *Peitschenstecken* are typical hard sausages, and very popular for the Vesper.
14 A salad of marinated veal head roulades is a modern Vesper dish.
15 *Leberle sauer* (soused liver) is an essential item on every Swabian menu – and an equally essential part of the Vesper.
16 *Saure Nierle* (soused kidneys) are one of the Swabians' favorite Vesper choices.
17 Red and white collared brawn, served with oil, vinegar, and onions.
18 Brawn is made from the gelatinous parts of the pig, such as the snout, ears, and trotter.
19 Another typical Vesper dish is a variety of cold meats and hams.
20 Not forgetting the vitamins: radishes and horseradish.

Be it the Swabian "Vesper" or the Bavarian "Brotzeit" – the snack is a fixed part of the day in the south of the country.

Fruit schnaps

The empire of distillates is a galaxy, a fascinating universe of astounding variety. The ABC of German varieties alone ranges from Swabia's "Apple water" and "Air water" from the Chemnitz to the "Zibärtle" from the Black Forest. The best of all are the berry spirits and the pomaceous fruit spirits of the south-west. This is also where most of the small distillers are found: almost every farm in the Baden region and many parts of Swabia has the right to distill. Their cherry brandies, also known as *Chriesiwasser*, their sloe, Mirabelle, plum and raspberry spirits are among the finest produced by German distillers. An incredible

Josef Heinzelmann standing in front of 80 tons of apples, collected from the orchards of the Deckenhausen valley.

The apples come from around Lake Constance.

First, the apples are washed in a large barrel.

Apples and quince (added to improve the flavor) are coarsely chopped.

The fruit is wrapped in cloths for protection.

The apples are pressed to release the juice, which is then collected.

The must matures after the juice has been 8 weeks in the barrel.

Fruit wine

Fruit wine is the classic accompaniment to Vesper, just as beer is to the Bavarian *Brotzeit*. Although the alcohol content is about the same as that of beer, it has the added advantage that is does not give the drinker a "pot belly." This fermented juice of apples and pears from the many orchards and allotments in the land should really be a fashionable drink. Taken in moderation, it not only aids the digestion, but also clears the head. Sadly, though, it does not appear to be in vogue any longer. Only the elderly appreciate its benefits as a "life-enhancing" tonic. Until a few decades ago, fruit wine was the national beverage of the Swabians. Back in the 1950s, every decent Swabian household had to have its barrels of fruit wine, in addition to the barrel of cabbage, meat preserved from its own animals, and the *Gsälz* (fruit preserves). The better barrels, which contained pear fruit wine (*Bieramoscht*) were usually stored behind the others to make them slightly less accessible. For centuries, fruit wine was the drink in every household. Beer and wine were drunk in inns and taverns, fruit wine at home. Every Swabian householder would have fetched two or three pitchers of fruit wine from the basement every day. And every Swabian householder would have greeted guests with the words, "Magsch Moscht?" ("How about a fruit wine?").

1   2   3   4

amount of raw material is required, which is hardly surprising when you think of the end product. In former times, cherry brandy was made only from the small, bitter-sweet rowanberry, which was crushed whole, including the pit. The noble Black Forest raspberry spirit is still made solely from wild raspberries. An amazing 66 pounds (30 kilograms) of fruit are needed for a single bottle of genuine raspberry schnaps, which becomes easier to understand when you consider than the fruit mash from 100 pounds (45 kg) of raspberries provide just 5½ gallons (25 liters) of juice. The situation is the same with the fruit brandies. Depending on the particular variety, 220 pounds (100 kilograms) of apples will give between 5 and 12 pints (3 and 7 liters) of pure alcohol, and the same weight in pears between 5 and 10 pints (3 and

6 liters). Pear brandies retain more of the typical fruit flavor than apple brandies.

Baden-Württemberg contains the basic products for these wonderful distillates, namely pomaceous and berry fruit, in abundance. Most fruit thrives in the 14,826 acres (6000 hectares) of growing areas around Lake Constance, followed by the Ortenau district with 8400 acres (3400 hectares), Ravensburg with 3950 acres (1600 hectares), and the districts of Constance, Heilbronn, Rems-Murr, Breisgau-Hochschwarzwald, Hohenlohe, Emmerdingen, and Lörrach (all under 2500 acres/1000 hectares arable area). The center of the fruit-growing area, Lake Constance and the districts of Ortenau and Ravensburg, combined represent 27,180 acres (11,000 hectares), or 55 percent of the total fruit-growing area of the Baden-Württemberg region.

1 **Wild black cherry**, August Kottmann, Bad Ditzenbach

2 **Black currant**, Edmund Marder, Albbrück

3 **Sloe gin**, Edmund Marder, Albbrück

4 **Quince schnaps**, Edmund Marder, Albbrück

5 **Topinambur**, Ewald Kopp, Sinzheim

6 **Mirabelle schnaps**, Klaus Schindler, Oberkirch

7 **Zibärtli-Wildpflaume**, Hermann Schwörer, Durbach

8 **Williams pear**, Wilfried Graf, Obersasbach

9 **Schnaps made from wine yeast**, Ewald Kopp, Sinzheim

10 **Old Plum**, Walter Hörner, Schallstadt-Wolfenweiler

11 **White raspberry brandy**, Bimmerle, Achern-Mösbach

12 **Black Forest mountain cherry brandy** (10-year-old), Theo Lettner, Kappelrodeck

13 **Apple schnaps**, Kammer-Kirsch, Karlsruhe

14 **Black Forest cherry brandy** (Jahrgang 1985), Alfred Schladerer, Staufen

15 **Haferpflaumenwasser**, Theo Lettner, Kappelrodeck

6   7   8   9   10   11   12   13   14   15

Goodness from inside

Offal does not really feature in the cuisine of the north. In southern Germany, however, it is an important item on the menu, although even here there are certain limits. The spleen (*Milz* in German), which in Bavaria is used to make *Milzwurst* (a type of sausage) and dumplings, is not used beyond Swabian Biberach, although there it is served in *Biberacher Milzle*, but that is a one-off. This "line" between Bavaria and Swabia is the only place where the spleen is used in Swabian cuisine.

Offal is popular in Vesper dishes (snacks) in the Swabian-Alemannian region. Tripe, the omasum of the cow, is served in a sauce made of flour and butter, stock, vinegar, and bay leaf. Liver and kidneys are also served "pickled." Brains and sweetbreads are very popular in soups. If the old adage that the cuisine that includes offal has to be a good cuisine is true – the cuisine of France, Italy, and China for example – then the cuisine of southern Germany is undoubtedly a force to be reckoned with.

Biberacher Milzle
Biberach spleen

Stuffing

4 oz/100 g calf sweetbreads, soaked and blanched
6 oz/150 g veal, passed through the fine disc of a meat grinder
4 oz/100 g of the scraped spleen
1 bread roll, cut into small pieces
2 eggs
1 tbsp finely chopped parsley
1 tsp chopped chives
2 finely chopped scallions
salt and pepper
marjoram

Use a sharp knife to cut open the end of the spleen, scrape out the contents, and turn inside out. Dice the sweetbreads, and combine with the meat, 4 oz (100 g) of the spleen, and the diced bread roll, eggs, onions, and herbs until you have a smooth mixture. Season with salt, pepper, and marjoram, and use to stuff the spleen. Sew up the end of the spleen. Place in simmering salted water (to which you can add a few soup vegetables) and cook at 175 °F/80 °C for about 30 minutes. Remove the spleen from the water, and cut into slices. In Biberach, this dish is served on *Nudelsupp* (noodle soup), but it can also be browned in butter and served with potato salad, or eaten cold for Vesper. *Biberacher Milze* can also be served just with a seasonal salad, "nouvelle cuisine" style.

The secret's in the stuffing, and the stuffing for *Biberacher Milzle* uses sweetbreads, ground veal, bread, and eggs.

The spleen is cut open at one end with a sharp knife, the contents removed, and the spleen turned inside out.

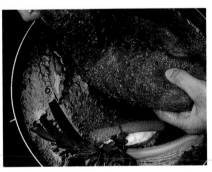

The stuffing ingredients are combined in a bowl and stirred until the mixture is smooth, and then seasoned.

A certain amount of dexterity and a spoon are required to get the filling inside the spleen.

The spleen is sewn up and placed in a pot of simmering salted water with a few root vegetables.

Biberacher Milzle can be eaten for Vesper, or fried in a little butter and served with a potato salad.

Biberacher Milzle

Saures Kalbsherz in Trollinger
Pickled calf heart in red wine

1¾ lbs/800 g calf heart
2 cups/1/2 liter dry Trollinger
dash of wine vinegar
1 large onion, chopped
1 carrot, sliced
1 small head of celery, chopped into small dice
1 bay leaf
3 cloves
10 juniper berries
10 black peppercorns
clarified butter for frying
1 tbsp tomato paste
2 cups/500 g sour cream

Separate the heart in the center, and wash. Make a marinade from the red wine, vinegar, and the root vegetables. Tie the spices in a piece of muslin, and place in the marinade. Soak the heart in the marinade for about 2 days. When ready to cook, remove the heart from the marinade and pat it dry with paper towels. Heat the clarified butter in a casserole, and brown the heart on all sides. Pass the marinade through a strainer, and reserve the liquid. When the heart has been browned on all sides, add the root vegetables and the tomato paste, and cook until a good color. Pour over the marinade (with the spices still in their bag), and cook the heart until it is soft. Remove when cooked. Stir the sour cream into the cooking juices, and season to taste. Serve with homemade spätzle, creamed potatoes, dumplings, plain boiled potatoes, small pasta, or any kind of salad or seasonal vegetables.

Saumagensalat
Salad of pig stomach

2–3 pig stomachs (order ready prepared from your butcher)
1 onion, spiked with a bay leaf and a clove
Salt

Salad
5 tbsp wine vinegar
1 tbsp mustard
salt and freshly milled pepper
pinch of sugar
water
4 tbsp oil
2 finely chopped onions
bunch of scallions
bunch of chives, finely chopped

Garnish
Radishes

Clean the stomachs, and place in a pot containing plenty of water. Bring to a boil, drain, and cover with fresh water. Season with salt, add the onion, then bring to a boil and cook for 1 hour. Remove from the water, leave to cool, then cut into slices. Make a salad dressing from the vinegar, mustard, salt, pepper, sugar, oil, and a little water. Combine with the chopped onions, the sliced onion greens, and the finely chopped chives. Add the sliced stomach, and leave to stand. Garnish with the radishes before serving.

Pancake soup

Sorrel soup

Hot stuff

A Swabian, so it is said, eats soup five times a day. His Alemannian cousin is equally fond of it, from the extremely modest flour soup (see page 379) to the more extravagant snail soup (see page 354). Soups have always played an important role in the cuisines of Baden and Swabia, for everyday as well as for special occasions.

Wedding soup has always been a specialty. This is a beef consommé that is noted for the abundance and variety of what goes into it: strips of shortcrust (plain) pastry, *Leberspätzle* (liver spätzle), marrow dumplings, meat dumplings, meat strudel, and pancakes, to name but a few. There is a good reason for this: centuries ago, the law governed the number of courses that could be served at a wedding. This was intended to prevent less wealthy citizens from over-extending themselves financially when feeding the invariably large number of guests attending a wedding. However, in order to ensure that there was still a certain level of opulence, the soup contained more than was usual. This satisfied the law, whilst still enabling the good burghers to demonstrate what they were able to afford.

Laugenbrezelsuppe
Pretzel soup

6 day-old bread rolls
4 cups/1 liter meat stock (cold)
2½ tbsp butter
4 egg yolks
salt and pepper
nutmeg
2 tbsp cream
1 bunch of chives, finely chopped

Cut the bread rolls into small pieces. Soak in the cold stock, then slowly bring to a boil. Combine the egg yolks with the cream. Pass the bread mixture through a strainer, then bring to a boil again briefly. Remove the saucepan from the heat. Add the egg mixture, and season with salt, pepper, and nutmeg. Garnish with the chopped chives before serving.

Riebelessuppe
Riebel soup

Riebelessupp, also known as "Lazy wife's soup," is found all over southern Germany, and it is highly popular in Swabia. This, however, is in no way a reflection on the domestic or culinary talents of the women of Swabia. Quite the opposite. Men have been known to make it too!

2 cups/250 g flour
2 eggs
1 egg yolk
salt
4 cups/1 liter meat stock
bunch of chives or parsley, finely chopped

Combine the flour, eggs, and salt to make a firm dough. Leave the dough to dry, then grate coarsely onto baking parchment. Heat the grated dough briefly in the hot stock, sprinkle over the finely chopped chives (or parsley), and serve.

Schwäbische Hochzeitssuppe
Swabian wedding soup
(Illustrated opposite)

4 cups/1 liter strong meat stock	
bunch of chives, finely chopped	

Optional ingredients

1. Meat dumplings

5 oz/125 g ground veal (from your butcher)	
2 tbsp cream or milk	
1 egg	
salt and pepper	
½ tsp grated lemon rind	
1 tbsp finely chopped parsley	
fresh breadcrumbs	

Combine the meat with the cream, egg, seasoning, lemon rind, a little finely chopped parsley, and enough breadcrumbs to make a firm, smooth mixture. Break off small portions, drop in lightly boiling salted water, and simmer gently. Do not boil.

2. Liver dumplings

3½ tbsp/50 g butter	
5 oz/125 g calf or chicken liver, very finely chopped	
2 eggs	
salt and marjoram	
2 stale bread rolls, softened in a little milk	
salt	

Beat the butter until creamy, then add the calf or chicken liver, eggs, seasoning, and the squeezed bread rolls. Using a spoon, scoop out fairly small portions, and cook in simmering salted water.

3. Shredded pasta

3 eggs	
2 cups/250 g flour	
pinch of salt	
½ cup tepid milk	
lard or oil for deep-frying	

Make a dough from the eggs, flour, salt, and milk. Grate through a coarse grater into the hot oil. Remove the pasta with a ladle when golden in color, and drain.

4. Pastry strips

2 eggs	
¼ cup/60 g butter	
2 tbsp milk	
¾ cup/100 g flour	
salt	
5 level tsp baking powder	

Separate the eggs. Beat the butter with the egg yolks until fluffy. Add the milk, flour, salt, and baking powder. Knead well, then fold in the beaten egg whites. Line a baking pan with parchment, and spread the dough out to a thickness of ½ inch (1 cm). Bake at medium heat. Cool, then cut into strips.

Place the ingredient of your choice into warmed soup plates, pour over the hot stock, and top with chopped chives.

Swabian wedding soup

Flädlesuppe
Pancake soup
(Illustrated opposite, top of page)

1 cup/125 g flour	
½ cup/125 ml milk	
2 eggs	
salt and nutmeg	
bacon for frying	
4 cups/1 liter of hot stock	
bunch of chives, finely chopped	

Combine the ingredients to make a smooth batter. Heat the bacon in a skillet until the fat begins to run, and cook thin pancakes with the batter. Leave the pancakes to cool. Cut into thin slices, and serve in a clear, strong meat stock garnished with chopped chives.

Badische Sauerampfersuppe
Baden sorrel soup
(Illustrated opposite, bottom of page)

9 oz/250 g sorrel	
1 tbsp butter	
salt	
4 cups/1 liter clear meat stock	
1 cup/250 ml cream	
2 egg yolks	
pepper	

Remove the leaves from the thick sorrel stalks, and wash thoroughly in several changes of water. Shake lightly, then sauté until soft in a little butter with a pinch of salt. Purée, or pass through a strainer. Combine the cream with the egg yolk. Bring the stock to a boil, stir in the sorrel, and remove from the heat. Thicken with the egg yolk and cream mixture, and serve immediately.

Snails

Escoffier, the leading exponent of nouvelle cuisine, named them Europe's "most imaginative appetizer," and they are one of the traditional dishes of Burgundy and Alsace. In Baden, they have long been regarded as "poor people's food," and in parts of Upper Swabia they were for a long time considered, understandably, to be nothing more than a salad-eating pest. A pest, however, that to everyone's amazement and general delight was first served in vicarages – "The preacher's eating snails!" they exclaimed – where French dining habits were frequently imitated.

As far as the season is concerned, ideas differ. Some people think that snails are a winter dish, and not edible until they have rid themselves of any toxins and sealed off the opening to the shell with a membrane, in anticipation of their winter hibernation. Others, however, believe them to be a spring treat, once they have awoken from their hibernation and gained a little weight after gorging themselves on fresh greenery.

The preparation is equally arduous in both cases. In the former, the membrane sealing the opening has to be removed. And whether sealed off or not, the snails have to be washed thoroughly several times. They are then placed in a mixture of cooking salt, vinegar and flour for a while to eliminate any remaining toxins and impurities. They are then washed again, before being blanched for five minutes in simmering water. When cool, the snail is removed from the shell using a small fork. The intestine, the dark part at the rear, is cut away, and the meat rubbed thoroughly with salt before being simmered over a low heat in a stock consisting of half white wine and half beef stock or water, soup vegetables, pepper, and whichever herbs are to hand. The empty shells are boiled in plenty of water to which a little bicarbonate of soda has been added, then rinsed and left to dry.

When the shells are completely dry, a little snail butter is pushed inside them, then the cooked snails, after which the shells are sealed with snail butter. Snail butter is made from fresh, ideally unsalted butter, finely chopped parsley, a few finely chopped shallots, a little salt, and crushed garlic. The shells are then placed in an ovensafe dish, and baked in a preheated oven.

Badische Schneckensuppe
Baden snail soup

24 snails (canned or prepared in the kitchen)
4 shallots
8 tsp/40 g butter
pinch of salt
1 cup/250 ml dry white wine
4 cups/1 liter meat stock (ideally veal)
julienne strips of carrot, celery, and leek, weighing about ¾ oz/20 g each
1 cup/250 ml cream
2 egg yolks
2 tbsp finely chopped parsley

Remove the snails from the can (reserving the liquid). Finely chop the shallots, and sauté in the butter with half the finely chopped snails. Season with salt, and pour over the white wine, the snail liquid, and the stock. Bring to a boil briefly, add the remaining halved snails and julienne vegetables, and simmer gently for 10 minutes. Finally, combine the cream and the egg yolks, and use to thicken the soup. Garnish with parsley before serving.

In winter, the vineyard owners use their vineyards as a source of protein: they collect snails from them.

It is not usually necessary to dig down farther than 12 inches (30 cm) to find the sealed snails.

The gourmet is especially pleased if the snails are large; there's not much to them at the best of times.

The membrane that seals off the shell must be cut away before preparation.

Before green cabbage can be used, the thick stalk needs to be removed. This is done using a so-called "cabbage-borer."

Cabbage grating contest at the annual "Filderkrautfest" in Echterdingen. The cabbage must be grated fast …

… and it should be finely shredded when it leaves the grater.

Deien (see page 324) or salt cake with a delicious topping are prepared for the festival, just like in times gone by.

Cabbage from the Fildern

The Fildern, a fertile high plain to the south of Stuttgart, is famous not just for the cultivation of cabbage, but also because it is where a Zeppelin airship caught fire and exploded in 1908. The Count and his airships have long been relegated to history, but cabbage from the Fildern is very much part of the present, and, after a temporary lull in the 1970s, is again becoming popular. According to numerous gourmets, the Fildern is where the world's best cabbage grows – fine veined, and far more delicate and tasty than other specimens. It is not just the locals who appreciate this delicacy; a large part of the region's non-native inhabitants, especially those from Greece, Turkey, and the former Yugoslavia, use it for their national dishes, as in *Filder cabbage à la grecque*, for example. However, they prefer to preserve the whole cabbage.

The history of Filder cabbage, the only white cabbage that is conical rather than round in shape, dates back to the 16th century. It was supposedly the monks from the monastery in Denkendorf

who first produced this special variety. In 1772, Berhaus priest Johannes Bischoff wrote of the cultivation on the Fildern: "The white cabbage is the only [cabbage] that is grown here."

Cabbage-growing is still the main crop in the rural communities of the Fildern today, ahead of other vegetables and cereals. The clay soil, which has a very high water content and a basic clay layer of between 16 and 20 feet (5 and 6 meters) and a fertility grade of 80, is one of the best soils in the world for growing cabbages. That is why it pained the farmers of Plieningen, Echterdingen, and Bernhausen, whose land adjoined the airport, when, in 1996, they had to hand over 500 acres (200 hectares) for the expansion of the airport and its motorway link. Today, cabbage is grown on just 570 acres (231 hectares) – in contrast to 1600 acres (646 hectares) in 1978.

Since the cabbage is highly sensitive to pressure, it is still harvested by hand. Most of the cabbage is made into sauerkraut at the seven small factories that remain in the Fildern.

Opposite: A prize example! Margit Kitzele has already removed the outer leaves.

For best results, the pastries are baked in a traditional oven.

The heat in the oven must be just right, as the thin pastry cakes burn easily.

Green cabbage for Paris

For centuries, cabbage was one of the Filder locations' main trade items, alongside cattle, cereal, fruit, flax, and linen. As recently as the 1930s, Filder farmers sold their wares on the markets in the villages and towns.

A horse, a carriage, and an alert terrier were the main requisites of these itinerant farmers. The dog watched over the carriage and the wares, while the farmer transported the cabbage into the customers' houses, sometimes cutting them as well. However, this task was also frequently performed by peripatetic "cabbage wives" or cutters, who, with their cabbage cutters, traveled the land as journeymen (or women).

Once roads and rail had been developed, it became

possible to sell further afield. The railroad opened in 1888, and cabbages were exported to Alsace and as far as Paris. Around the turn of the century, cabbages from Echterdingen and Möhringen were sent by the wagon-load to the French metropolis. Two or three men accompanied the wagons, and they were responsible for slicing the cabbage on arrival.

At the time, there were no specifically grown varieties, since each farmer grew his own. The only differentiation made was between early, mid-season, and the large and the smaller later varieties. Because of its excellent shelf life, the smaller late variety was the most suitable for export to distant places.

Topped Deien – a delicacy that visitors to the festival anticipate with pleasure.

Typically German? That's what you think!

Sauerkraut

According to a rhyme by Ludwig Uhland, sauerkraut is a typically German food – but he was mistaken. Sauerkraut is not a German invention. It's not even Germany's national dish, although most foreigners immediately associate the two. In fact, in World War II, the British referred to the soldiers of the Wehrmacht as "the krauts."

"Associating Germans with sauerkraut is a historical error," wrote Hans Hermann von Wimpffen in his "Big Book of Sauerkraut," going on to say that this "was the fault of the Alsatians, who are descended from the Alemannians. The Alemannians gave their name to an entire nation – in France, Germans are known as 'les Allemands.' And it's the Alsatians who added sausage and bacon to their sauerkraut and made it their national dish, and whom the Germans have to thank for their supposed favorite dish." Although the Alsatians were the first to pickle cabbage, which they did in 15th-century central Europe, they did not invent it, either. In fact, the ancient Greeks and Romans were already familiar with it.

The method of preparation has remained the same: finely sliced white cabbage is mixed with salt. How the cabbage is cut reveals where it is cut: southern Germans prefer it more thinly sliced than their fellow citizens in the north. However, there are no regional boundaries as to what happens after the cutting, salting, and weighting. This is where the lactic acid bacteria take over. Scientists did not discover them until the 18th century but, as we have already said, their effects were already known in antiquity. These bacteria, which were first discovered in curdled milk, are also present in the human body, and are programmed to destroy other bacteria. If they fail to do this, rot occurs rather than fermentation. Starch and sugar – in the case of cabbage, the fruit sugar – nourish the bacteria, and during the fermentation process they produce lactic acid and carbonic acid.

Today, some 80 percent of sauerkraut is sold in preserved form. Specially grown white cabbage weighing up to 15 pounds (7 kilograms) is used for industrial production. In the early 1930s, the Hengstenberg company became the first to can normal, barrel-fermented sauerkraut – with resounding success, quite literally. During the sterilization process, which is achieved by heating canned goods, the lids flew off. It was not easy to establish why this happened, but it is because carbonic acid, oxygen, and gases expand in heat. The problem was solved by heating the cabbage before it was canned to allow the gases to escape.

Fasan mit Rieslingkraut
Pheasant with Riesling sauerkraut

Pheasant
A brace of pheasant, each weighing 2 lbs/1 kg
10 juniper berries
salt and pepper
4 large slices bacon
1 coarsely chopped onion
sprig of thyme
8 tsp/40 g melted butter
1 cup/¼ liter dry white wine
1 cup cream

Riesling sauerkraut
1 small onion, finely chopped
1 apple, cut into small pieces
3½ tbsp/50 g goose or pork lard
1 cup/¼ liter Riesling
generous 1 lb/500 g sauerkraut
1 bay leaf, 2 cloves
salt and sugar

Wash the pheasants, and pat dry with paper towels. Season well inside and out with the crushed juniper berries, salt, and pepper, and lard with the bacon. Tie the drumsticks together. Brush a chicken brick with butter, and place the pheasants inside, together with the onion and thyme. Place the chicken brick in a preheated oven (400 °F/200 °C). Reduce the heat to 350 °F/180 °C after 10 minutes, and roast for 45 minutes, basting frequently. Remove the pheasants from the brick, and place inside the oven with the door open to keep warm.
Pour the wine into the roasting juices, add the cream, and bring to a boil. Season, and add a few pieces of cold butter to bind if liked. Serve the sauce separately.
To make the Riesling sauerkraut, sauté the finely chopped onion and the apple in the lard until translucent, then pour over the Riesling. Loosen the sauerkraut with a fork, and spread over the liquid. Cover with a lid, and simmer gently for 1 hour. Season with salt and pepper. Creamy mashed potatoes go very well with this dish.

White cabbage, of which there are many different varieties, is usually used for sauerkraut.

This is a green cabbage. The outer leaves are removed, and then the head is cut in half.

The cabbage is then cut into thin slices, either by hand using a knife, or with a special cabbage cutter.

Special sauerkraut containers are made of earthenware, and have a water channel. The sauerkraut is placed loosely inside.

Sea salt can be added if liked (salt is a good preservative), but is not necessary.

The sauerkraut has to be flattened, since the cabbage has to release enough liquid to cover it.

The cabbage is weighted, for example with a preserving jar full of water, so that it remains in the liquid during fermentation.

The lid is placed inside the water-filled channel. This prevents water from entering the jar.

Sauerkraut prevents scurvy

When Captain James Cook left on his voyage of discovery in 1772, he loaded 60 barrels of sauerkraut on board. This was not just to give his sailors something good to eat – it was also to prevent them from losing their teeth: there was a great risk of scurvy on long sea voyages.

Scurvy is caused by a vitamin deficiency that occurs if the body has to go without vitamin C for more than four weeks. Sauerkraut was the ideal prevention at that time. Not only did it keep well and for a long time – the last barrel on Cook's voyage was opened in 1775, two weeks before the ship returned to its English harbor – but it also contains good quantities of vitamins and minerals. It contains vitamin B6 (0.2 mg per 100 g), vitamin C (20 mg per 100 g), vitamin K (1.5 mg per 100 g), potassium (288 mg per 100 g), calcium (48 mg per 100 g), and iron (0.6 mg per 100 g).

Although nowadays it is possible to prevent a vitamin deficiency by popping a few vitamin pills, sauerkraut still has its health-giving merits: the lactic acid bacteria help to regulate stomach and intestinal activity, and kill bacteria. Raw sauerkraut is particularly beneficial, and is excellent for treating chronic constipation as well as stomach and digestive problems.

Of veal and beef

In view of the current controversy surrounding beef that is causing such unease amongst European consumers, what follows will sound like a fairy tale from the good old days. In Baden, calves were fed eggs in addition to their mother's milk. In order to improve the flavor of the meat, farmers started to fatten the animals a month before they were due to be slaughtered. They were fed one egg on the first day, two on the second, three on the third, and so on until the 15th day, when the numbers were decreased again, to end with one egg the day before slaughtering.

In "the good old days," when the world of beef was still in order, veal was considered the perfect food for invalids and people who wanted to lose weight, since, although it contains quite a lot of protein, it is low in fat. A lean calf contains 17 percent protein and only 1.5 percent fat, and calves were often lean since they invariably did not have enough time in their short lives to put down a layer of fat.

The youngsters should not be slaughtered too soon, though. At the age of two months, the meat is still fairly watery and quite weak; only at three or four months it has achieved the ideal consistency. After that, the meat fibers become a little coarser, and the flavor deteriorates with each passing month.

People from Baden and Swabia love their stuffed veal breast, roast veal, preserved veal, and Swabian roast. The flavor depends not just on the age of the cow, but also on the breed, and its diet. In Baden Württemberg, the best beef comes from the Hohenlohe region: pasture cattle of very high quality with a grainy, well marbled meat. Although Charolais cattle are now also bred here, the native Limburg (which is similar to the French Limousin, and the two types of meat are almost identical) is even better.

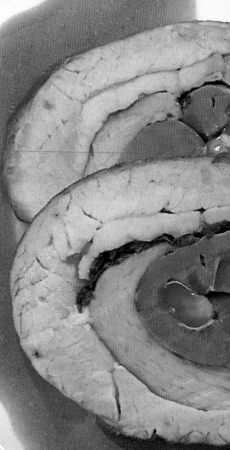

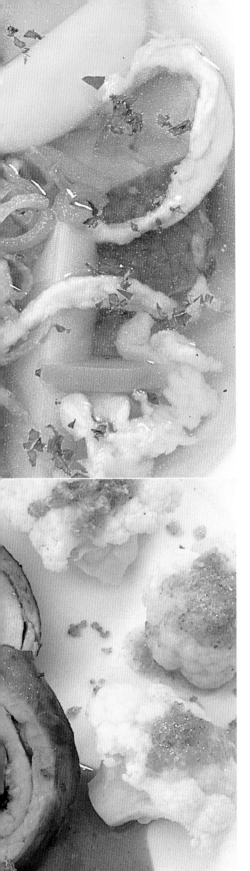

Roast veal is usually cut from the haunch, and is traditionally served on high days and holidays in Swabia.

Roast breast of veal. This dish can also be stuffed with breadcrumbs, and is served with a potato salad.

Preserved veal is made by first boiling the meat, then turning it in a roux. It is usually taken from the shoulder.

Kalbsvögele ("veal birds") are roulades stuffed with a mixture of mustard, pickled gherkins, onions, and bacon.

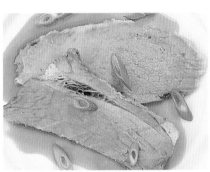

Boiled udder and meat from the breast or top rib are popular in the Schwäbische Alb.

Onion pot roast, a traditional Swabian dish. The meat should be at least the thickness of two fingers.

Braised tongue is one of many organ meat dishes popular in the south-west of the region.

The breast can also be boiled in a vegetable stock, and served with potatoes and vegetables.

It's early in a December morning, and the hunters are about to set off ...

Halali

Although it is early in a December morning, it is more like April. Just an hour ago, it seemed as if the day was going to be sunny; it was almost too mild for the season. Now, however, the cold is penetrating, and the bitter wind spatters the rain over the assembled hunters.

Once a year, always on the first Monday in December, Alfred Schweizer, innkeeper, butcher, and hunter of Sielmingen, invites a number of people to hunt. Some 30 hunters, and six or seven beaters, gather: friends and acquaintances from the neighborhood, and a few outsiders. A tractor and trailer are available for the elderly and sore-footed to spare them the arduous march across the loamy fields. Walter Schweizer, at 80 years of age the most senior member of the group, still drives himself around on these occasions. There will be four drives in the morning, and another four in the afternoon. In between, there will be a break for "Vesper," with beer, mulled wine, pretzels, bread rolls, and hot dogs provided. At the last hunt, 70 hares were caught; this time there will probably not be quite so many.

Baden-Württemberg boasts an abundance of game, more than just about any other region in the Federal Republic. The antlers in the state's coat of arms are an indication of the importance of the hunt here. However, stocks in the south-west of Germany have declined dramatically in recent decades. Some hunters remember that, just 20 years ago, great numbers of pheasant, partridge, and quail were shot within the Sielmingen boundaries, but they are rarely seen today. Quail in particular are now so rare that no hunter would even contemplate shooting them. The reason for the decline in wild poultry is the impoverishment of the landscape as a result of intense farming. The fields that once were the natural habitat of these birds, which afforded them protection and food while breeding, have disappeared, and the pesticides that are now used are also hazardous.

The hunting ground that Alfred Schweizer leases for the benefit of his guests is situated on the boundary of the parish of Sielmingen. The area is characterized by turnip fields, harvested maize fields, orchards, bushes, coppices, and tumbledown sheds.

After the obligatory greeting by the buglers and the master, the hunters are divided into groups. This is done quietly and without much fuss. Alfred Schweizer has everything under control, as he does every year. Hunters are economical people, and by nature pragmatic. Their habits and customs are usually practical in origin, and are marked by a respect for nature. Only the dogs are excited, anticipating the chase.

Hunters and beaters depart, spreading out over a distance of 65 to 100 feet (20 to 30 meters). This "shape" of hunt is called the "Bohemian strip." By

It's a big day for the hunters and their hounds, and they're all looking forward to it.

The happy and successful hunters – who have bagged 55 hares.

the time they have crossed a maximum of 325 feet (100 meters), there are at least 11 pounds (5 kilograms) of clay hanging from each boot. The more corpulent hunters – and there are usually plenty of them – are becoming increasingly red-faced. It's quiet for a while, but then suddenly – a burst of gunfire, then nothing for a moment, then another burst. Rabbits and hares break from their hiding places, and dart haphazardly through the fields. A brief command here, another one there, and the dogs retrieve the bag.

No one knows how great a distance the hunters will have covered by the end of the day. But one thing is for sure: it will not be as large or varied as a celebratory hunt that took place on 19 February 1763 in honor of Count Karl Eugene in the Degerloch forest: the bag consisted of 1211 deer, 30 fallow buck, 150 roe buck, 330 wild boar, 56 badgers, 270 foxes, 3002 rabbits, two chamois, two wolves, two lynx, 197 pheasant, 5302 partridge, 209 wild duck, and 400 wood pigeon. On one day!

Opposite: A pack of hounds spells death for the hare – as do the hunters and their guns.

Hasenpfeffer mit Lemberger
Jugged hare with red wine

1 hare, approx. 4–5 lbs/2 kg
2 cups/½ liter Lemberger
2 tbsp vinegar
1 chopped onion
2 carrots
½ a celeriac root, diced
1 leek
2 bay leaves, 2 cloves, 1 tbsp peppercorns, 3 juniper berries, 1 sprig of thyme
2 tbsp oil or lard
salt and pepper
2 tbsp tomato paste
1 cup/250 ml meat stock
½ cup/125 ml pig blood

Wash the hare, and divide it into 12 pieces. Make a marinade with the red wine, vinegar, onion, carrot, celery, and leek. Tie the bay leaves, cloves, peppercorns, juniper berries, and thyme into a bouquet garni. Place the pieces of hare in the marinade, and steep for 2 days. Pat the hare dry with paper towels, then fry until brown on all sides. Season with salt and pepper. Add the root vegetables from the marinade, and the tomato paste. Pour over the meat stock and 1 cup (250 ml) of the marinade, add the bouquet garni, and simmer gently for 1 hour. Remove the meat when cooked, and keep warm. Pass the juices through a strainer, and bring to a boil again briefly. Remove from the heat, and stir in the pig blood.
Serve with spätzle.

Rehrücken in Spätburgunder
Saddle of venison in red wine

2 cups/½ liter Spätburgunder
1 cup/¼ liter water
1 tbsp salt
1 onion, spiked with 1 bay leaf and 2 cloves
6 peppercorns, 6 juniper berries
1 carrot, cut in slices
2½ lb/1.2 kg saddle of venison, tendons and membrane removed
salt and pepper
4 juniper berries, crushed
4 shallots, coarsely chopped
6 tbsp/100 g clarified butter
2 tbsp tomato paste
1 cup/250 ml venison stock
½ cup/125 ml Spätburgunder
small sprig of thyme
1 tbsp blackcurrant jelly
1 cup/250 g sour cream
8 tsp/40 g cold butter

Boil up the water, salt, pepper, juniper and carrot. Leave to cool, then marinate the saddle of venison in this liquid for 1–2 days. Remove, pat dry with paper towels, and rub with salt, pepper, and juniper. Place in a roasting dish with the shallots, pour over some of the clarified butter, and place in a preheated (400 °F/200 °C) oven. Reduce the heat to 350° F/180 °C after 10 minutes, and roast the venison for about 30–40 minutes. Keep basting with clarified butter.
Remove the venison, and keep warm. Heat the tomato paste in the meat juices, and pour over some of the marinade. Add the venison stock, red wine, and thyme. Bring to a boil briefly, then pass through a strainer. Stir in the sour cream, season to taste, and bind with the cold butter. Remove the meat from the bones, cut into thick slices, and rearrange on the bone.

Wine

Baden-Württemberg wine buffs have always rated social gatherings as more than mere contemplative pleasure. Despite the excellence of the region's wines, they have always valued clean, fresh everyday wines. These are the ones that are seen in summer, the outside of the bottle moist with condensation, standing next to "Vesper" dishes on vine-shaded garden tables outside the inns and taverns – a sight that lifts and gladdens the heart (and the throat.) An onion traybake – *Zwiebelkuchen* – is served with the young, not fully fermented wine. The *Besenwirtschaften* ("broom inns"), which are found all over Baden-Württemberg and are recognized by the brooms that hang over the door, will open later in the year, in the fall. The brooms indicate that the innkeeper is serving last year's wines. There's a long tradition to these taverns: they were instigated by Karl the Great in 800.

In Baden-Württemberg, as elsewhere in Germany, it was the medieval monks' year-round need for communion wine that played an important part in the development of the wine culture. Extant documents confirm that vines were grown in the south-west of Germany toward the end of the 8th century. In the 16th century, according to an ancient chronicle, in this "main quaffing period of the

The food in a typical *Besenwirtschaft* is plain and simple: here, the landlady serves Fleischkäs with potato salad.

In the "Lotte" broom tavern, last year's wine is served from the barrel.

German people, in which between 130 and 150 liters [230 and 260 pints] of good, average or sour wine flowed down every single gullet every year," the vineyards of Württemberg covered an area of 111,195 acres (45,000 hectares). However, the Thirty Years War put an end to this initial "blossoming" of the region's viniculture. In 1652, 32,000 acres (13,000 hectares) either lay fallow or had gradually been reclaimed by forest and woodland. The grapevines of Württemberg and Baden did not recover until the 19th century, a change in fortune that was marked in 1868 by the opening of the first winegrowing school in Weinsberg.

Riesling vines grow on 25 percent of the arable area in Württemberg, which mainly consists of lime, heavy marlaceous and clay soils. Although there is a small group of top, classily elegant, fruity varieties, Riesling could be described as having an "understated elegance." Between Reutlingen and Künzelsau, more than 50 percent of the wines are reds, and typical of the region, such as the Dornfelder, Lemberger, or Samtrot ("red velvet"). The specialties include Schiller wines, a red made from white, blue, and red grapes, and the ever-popular Trollinger.

The people of Baden, although expert winemakers, grow mainly Müller-Thurgau grapes, which is an undemanding variety in both flavor and care. The crossing of Riesling and Silvaner was one of the countermeasures initiated against the catastrophe of 1860, when large areas of the central European

Vinifera vines fell victim to *phylloxera*, a blight that was brought over from the United States. The introduction of grafted vines played an important part in the reconstruction of the wine culture. As *phylloxera* has always existed in the United States, the vines are resistant to it. German winegrowers therefore imported North American vines into Europe, and grafted their resistant roots onto European Vinifera vines.

The warm, dry climate between the Black Forest and the Vosges Mountains, and the contrast in soil varieties, which range from chalk and loam to volcanic and granite soils, ensure that Baden always produces important German wines: excellent whites, "gray," and – remarkably for Germany – "blue" Burgundies that are a match for any international competitor, and some admirable Rieslings. Because it lies in the south of the country, Baden was the only one of 13 German winegrowing regions to be awarded the warm winegrowing zone "B" rating by the E.U. in 1970, meaning that requirements concerning growing and expansion are more stringent than in the northern "A" zone.

Some 80 percent of the entire harvest is processed by cooperative societies, which were set up in the middle of the 19th century, and which spread rapidly throughout Baden-Württemberg. Today, two cooperatives claim to have been the first. One is on the Ahr. The other, in the province of Württemberg, is the vintners' cooperative society in Neckarsulm.

Typical grape varieties from Baden and Württemberg

Baden

Müller-Thurgau
A cross between Silvaner and Riesling. Popular wine for the masses. The modern version (usually Rivaner) is also interesting; a fruity-spicy white. Grown on 32 percent of the winegrowing area, in terms of quantity it is the market leader.

Klingenberger
Grown on heavier soils, so less elegant than Rieslings from the Moselle or Rheingau, but the soils also make it more delicate in aroma, decidedly fruity, and above all else, refreshingly sparkling. A good position will produce an excellent wine.

Grauburgunder
A specialty of Baden, especially from the Kaiserstuhl district. Was formerly known as Ruländer, and was then sweeter and more densely grown. Modern Grauburgunder wines are fruity-soft, light (despite being 13 percent proof!), and often dry yet honey-sweet.

Weissburgunder
Its freshness, fruitiness and strength make it a slightly "snappier" alternative to the Grauburgunder.

Gutedel
The typical variety of the Markgräflerland; fizzy and light. Is crossed with Silvaner to produce Nobling.

Clevner
A mutation, presumably originating from the Spätburgunder, this Frühburgunder is a member of the Pinot family. Resembles the Spätburgunder in stature, but not in quality.

Spätburgunder
Grown on 27 percent of the winegrowing area, which puts it in second place. A full-bodied red with plenty of tannin, now imposing in structure, fruit, and depth. "Descendants": Spätburgunder-Weissherbst (made from blue Pinot grapes that are fermented like white wine without the grape skins) and Badisch Rotgold, a cross between Spätburgunder and Ruländer.

Württemberg

Trollinger
Württemberg's national vine: popular red wine, imported 250 years ago from the Tyrol, which is now, despite having produced some exemplary vintages, a rather more pale red wine.

Lemberger (auch Limberger)
Late ripening red wine variety, known as Blaufränkisch in Austria. Produces strong, fruity wines, some impressive in structure.

Samtrot
Something special from Württemberg, grown on less than 150 acres (60 hectares): a mutation of the Schwarzriesling (also Müllerrebe), which has nothing to do with Riesling, and a lot with the Pinot family (Pinot Meunier). A light red, deep and long-lasting as a Pinot Noir. Very good as a Spätlese, but still well balanced and full of life.

Kerner
A cross between Trollinger and Riesling, whose aroma and fine fruitiness it may also acquire. Best drunk young and chilled.

Clevener
Not to be confused with the Clevner from Baden. This is the name given to the (Gewürz-)Traminer in Württemberg. Spicy-aromatic white wine with an intense flavor and lots of character, especially if grown on a dry soil.

Baden-Württemberg
Winegrowing regions

0 — 20 km

Cooking with wine

Wine is an important ingredient in many traditional Baden dishes. From the well-known Schäufele, which is made with a good white wine, ideally a dry Weissherbst, to the saddle or ragout of venison, made with a Spätburgunder, and Mistkratzerle (chicken) in Riesling. Fish, whether trout or perch from Lake Constance, is also often cooked in wine. The wine that is drunk with the meal should also be used in the cooking, whatever the quality (and price). In Baden cuisine, the best is just about good enough.

By contrast, not many traditional Swabian dishes are cooked with wine, although two notable exceptions are tripe, and lentils with Trollinger. Wine is subtly combined with other ingredients – namely eggs and sugar – to make Chaudeau sauce from Swabia. This popular dessert sauce, which is not unlike Italy's Zabaglione, is often served with Pfitzauf (baked ramekins), baked apple and bread pudding, apple cakes (see page 380), and other traditional desserts.

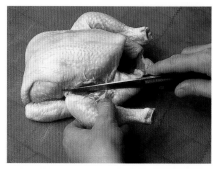

A sharp, pointed knife, ideally a boning knife, is needed for dividing the chicken into sections.

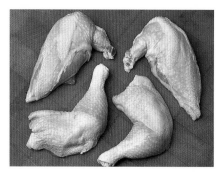

The drumsticks and breast pieces (not boned) are used to make "Chicken in Riesling."

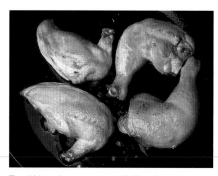

The chicken pieces are seasoned with salt and pepper, and then browned lightly on all sides.

Diced carrots and celeriac are important ingredients, and provide good flavor. Quartered mushrooms and thyme are also added.

Wildschweinschulter in Spätburgunder
Shoulder of wild boar in red wine

1¾ lb/800 g shoulder of wild boar
salt and pepper
6 juniper berries, crushed
clarified butter for frying
2 coarsely chopped onions
1 carrot, sliced
¼ of a celeriac root, diced
½ a leek, cut into rings
1 tsp tomato paste
1 bay leaf
1 clove
4 peppercorns
1 cup/¼ liter Spätburgunder
1 cup/250 ml venison stock
scant ½ cup/100 g cream

Rub the meat with salt, pepper, and the juniper berries. Heat the clarified butter in a casserole, and brown the meat on all sides. Add the onions, carrot, celeriac, leek, and tomato paste, and fry until the vegetables are just turning brown at the edges. Add the spices, and pour over the wine. Place in a preheated oven (350 °F/180 °C) and cook for about 45 minutes. At the end of this time, remove the meat from the dish and keep warm. Pass the cooking juices through a strainer. Add the stock and the cream, and season with salt and pepper. Cut the meat into slices, and pour over some of the sauce. Serve the remaining sauce separately.

Opposite page: A good white wine, served with the dish and used in the cooking, elevates the "Mistkratzerle" to "Chicken in Riesling."

Ochsenschwanzragout mit Lemberger
Oxtail ragout with red wine

2 oxtails, cut into pieces
salt and pepper
4 onions
2 carrots
¼ of a celeriac root
7 oz/200 g streaky bacon, smoked
⅓ cup/80 g pork lard
1 cup/¼ liter Lemberger wine
4 cups/1 liter meat stock
8 peppercorns, crushed
2 bay leaves
1 tsp cornstarch
½ cup/125 g sour cream

Wash the oxtails, and pat them dry with kitchen paper. Sprinkle with salt and pepper. Peel and finely chop the onions, carrots, and celeriac, and dice the bacon. Melt the lard in a large, heavy pot. Add the oxtail pieces, and brown well on all sides. Add the onions, carrots, celeriac, and the bacon, and cook until the vegetables are just turning color. Pour over the Lemberger and a little stock, setting the remainder of the stock aside. Add the peppercorns and bay leaves to the pot, and simmer the oxtails gently for 2–3 hours until cooked, adding stock as required. Just before the end of the cooking time, stir the cornstarch into a little Lemberger and bind the sauce. Season to taste, and add the sour cream just before serving. Place the oxtail ragout in a warmed dish to serve. Spätzle and homemade pasta go very well with this dish.

Lammhäxle mit Schwarzriesling
Lamb trotters in a light red wine

4 lamb trotters
salt and pepper
oil for frying
2 finely chopped onions
1 carrot, sliced
1 leek, cut into rings
¼ of a celeriac root, diced
2 tsp tomato paste
sprig of thyme
sprig of rosemary
3 cups/¾ liter Schwarzriesling
2 cups/½ liter lamb stock
2 cloves of garlic
1 bay leaf
1 clove
6 peppercorns

Remove the fat and the sinews from the lamb trotters, and season them with salt and pepper. Heat the oil in a casserole, and brown the trotters on all sides. Add the finely chopped vegetables, and cook until just turning brown. Add the tomato paste, thyme, and rosemary, pour over a little wine, and stir well. Then pour over the remainder of the wine, and lamb stock, and add the spices. Cover, and roast in a medium oven for 1½ to 2 hours. Then remove the trotters, pass the sauce through a strainer, and bind with cold butter if required (slowly beating it in with a whisk). Serve with fresh garden vegetables and Knöpfle.

Hähnchen in Riesling
Chicken in Riesling

1 oven-ready chicken, approx. 2½–3¼ lb/1.2–1.5 kg
salt and pepper
3 ½ tbsp butter
2 tbsp oil
1 onion, finely chopped
1 carrot, diced
¼ of a celeriac root, diced
1 cup/¼ liter Riesling from Baden
8 oz/200 g mushrooms, quartered
sprig of thyme
2 tbsp sour cream

Remove the breasts and drumsticks from the chicken, and season with salt and pepper. Heat the butter and oil in a casserole, and brown the chicken pieces on all sides. Remove, and keep warm. Place the onion in the casserole and heat, then return the chicken pieces to the pot, and add the root vegetables, Riesling, mushrooms, and thyme. Simmer everything gently over a low heat for 40 minutes. Remove the chicken pieces, and keep warm. Pass the cooking liquid through a strainer, and cook to reduce to half the quantity. Finally, stir in the sour cream, and season to taste. Heat the chicken pieces in the sauce (do not boil), and serve on warm plates with homemade noodles and a fresh green salad.

Freshwater fish

Brook trout or brook charr
Trout-like fish with a green-tinted back; requires good quality water; delicate, aromatic flesh.

Roach
Flat, high-backed body, large red eyes; numerous tiny bones; flesh of average quality.

Tench
Strong body, small eyes, and slimy skin; good breeder; tasty, slightly oily flesh.

Catfish
Scaleless predatory fish with typical "feathers" around its mouth. Can be up to 10 feet (3 meters) in length, and weigh 330 pounds (150 kilograms). Flesh almost without bones, highly aromatic, and oily.

Scaly or wild carp
Has an even, scaly skin; this original variety of the carp is a pond-dweller; tasty flesh.

Rudd
Gets its name from its red-tinted abdominal fins; lives in stagnant or slow-flowing waters; very bony, tasty flesh.

Mirror carp
High-backed farmed carp with few scales; oily, tasty flesh.

Common eel
Lives in rivers and lakes before swimming to the Sargasso Sea to spawn; flesh very oily and difficult to digest.

Salmon
Spawns in fresh water. This extremely popular desirable fish, the flesh of which is highly versatile, is now usually produced on salmon farms.

Pike
Predatory fish that stalks its prey in the murkiness of underwater plants. Sweet, firm flesh, and excellent for cooking.

Lake Constance whitefish
Slim fish belonging to the coregonus family, which also includes the European whitefish or lavaret. Pleasant tasting, and excellent for smoking. Prepared as trout.

River perch
High, prickly back fin; lives in rivers and lakes; flesh excellent, firm and low in fat.

Rainbow trout
Imported from the United States in 1880; tiny black dots on head, body and fins; easy to breed; flesh juicy and pleasant.

Bream
High-backed fish that is related to the carp; lives in lakes and slow-moving waters; flesh full of bones, but very tasty.

River trout
Home-loving relative of the sea trout; lives in cool, well oxygenated waters; flesh delicate and highly aromatic.

Fresh waters

Long ago, the Baltic Sea was known as the "mare suevicum." In the 3rd century, the Alemannians migrated from there to the region around the Neckar, the Danube, the Lech, and the Iller. Mare suevicum – Swabian Lake – is still the name for the 210 square miles (538 square kilometers) of Lake Constance, and the people of Bavaria, Austria, Switzerland, and not least Baden, devour with relish the whitefish, perch, burbot, char, pike, eel, and zander from its waters.

Baden-Württemberg, together with Mecklenburg Vorpommern and Bavaria, contains more fish than any other German state, despite the fact that countless varieties have become extinct as the result of water construction and pollution. Some of the fish to have suffered this fate are the shad, great shoals of which were found in the Neckar below Heilbronn and in the Rhine, and which were of great financial significance, as well as the sea lamprey and salmon.

There used to be great quantities of salmon in the upper Rhine, but interestingly it avoided the Neckar – unlike the shad. However, it also liked the Murg, and traveled as far as Baiersbronn. According to old guild reports, 36 tons of salmon were caught every year in the Rhine in southern Baden. By the 1930s, this figure had dropped to about 6½ tons a year, and by the 1950s, salmon-fishing had ceased altogether. However, there is now a campaign, "Salmon 2000," which is intended to reintroduce salmon to the waters of Baden-Württemberg. Whether the campaign will be successful remains to be seen.

Although some types of fish are now extinct, a wide variety is still found in Baden-Württemberg. A close look at the records and stock investigations reveals details of astonishing quantities of varieties that are virtually unknown to the non-expert. Although river lamprey, Danube lamprey, dace, Mediterranean chub (very large quantities), south-west European nase, ide, minnow, rudd (large quantities), nase, bleak, white bream, crucian carp, loach, and weatherfish (comparatively rare) tend to end up in the angler's own cooking pot, the fact that they even exist is a good indication of the quality of the waters here.

Further evidence of the improvement in water quality is provided by the river trout, which used to be the most common variety in Baden-Württemberg, and which is now once again found in most waters, thanks to strict measures. Stocks in Lake Constance are also increasing: in the middle of the 1990s, 960 tons of fish were caught in the upper part of the lake, and 240 tons in the lower part. Germany's proportion was 60 percent in the upper lake, and 66 percent in the lower lake.

Bodenseefelchen »Müllerin«
Lake Constance whitefish

- 4 Lake Constance whitefish, each weighing 7–9 oz/200–250 g
- juice of 1 lemon
- salt and pepper
- flour
- ¼ cup/60 g clarified butter or lard
- 8 tsp fresh butter
- lemon quarters and parsley to garnish

Gut the whitefish. Wash them inside and out, and dry with paper towels. Sprinkle over the lemon juice, salt, and pepper. Allow to absorb the lemon juice and seasoning. Then turn in the flour (shaking off any excess), and fry in the melted butter until golden on both sides. Remove from the skillet, and arrange on a warmed plate. Pour over brown butter (made from the 8 tsp of fresh butter), and garnish with lemon quarters and parsley. Serve with a warm potato salad or boiled potatoes with parsley, and a green salad.

Badischer Grashecht mit Speck gebraten
Baden pike with bacon

- 1 pike, weighing approx. 3¼ lbs/1½ kg
- salt and pepper
- flour
- clarified butter or oil for frying
- butter for the dish
- 4 oz/100 g streaky bacon, cut into strips
- 1 finely chopped onion
- 2 sprigs of thyme
- 3 cups/¾ liter dry Baden Riesling
- ⅓ cup/80 g butter

Gut the pike. Wash inside and out, and cut into fillets. Do not remove the skin. Use tweezers to remove any small bones. Season the fillets with salt and pepper. Coat on both sides with flour (shaking off the excess), and fry in the clarified butter over a high heat. Butter a flat dish, and place the fish, skin side up, in the bottom of the dish. Top with the bacon strips, and bake in a preheated oven (350 °F/180 °C) for about 20 minutes. Add the onion, thyme, and white wine after 10 minutes. Finally, remove the bacon strips, dot with the butter, and continue baking in the oven until the top of the fish is crispy. Remove, spoon over the cooking juices, and serve with boiled potatoes and seasonal vegetables, or with a fresh salad.

Kocheraal in Salbei
Eel with sage

- 2¼ lbs/1 kg oven-ready eel (skinned, gutted, and cut into large pieces)
- salt
- ¼ cup/60 g clarified butter
- 20 sage leaves
- ½ cup/125 ml white wine
- 8 lemon quarters to garnish

Season the pieces of eel with salt, and fry over a high heat in half the clarified butter. The eel should not give off water. Add the stalks of the sage leaves, and cook the eel for about 20 minutes over a medium heat. Meanwhile, fry the sage leaves in the remaining butter until crispy. At the end of the cooking time, arrange the eel on a warm plate. Add the wine to the cooking juices, and pour this over the fish. Garnish with the lemon quarters and the sage leaves. Boiled potatoes are the best accompaniment.

Early in the morning, the fishermen sail out onto Lake Constance.

The nets were spread out the previous day, and now they are brought in.

A good catch: there's a prize pike in the net.

The fish are already on the market when most people are just getting up.

Commercially available fruit

Apricot
Apricots grow in Germany. Europe's northern-most apricot region is Saxony-Anhalt.

Apple
This "fruit of paradise" is one of the most popular fruits in Germany's kitchens.

Raspberry
Raspberries are very nutritious, as they contain plenty of minerals. They are best eaten absolutely fresh.

Strawberry
Strawberries also grow in the wild, and their aroma is far superior to that of the cultivated varieties.

Quince
Quince must be cooked before they can be eaten. They are usually made into jelly, or else puréed.

Gooseberry, white
White gooseberries are more tart than the red ones, and they are ideal for cooking and preserving.

Victoria plum
Plums can be used on cakes, for purées or compotes, juice. They are also distilled.

Purple grape
Some people have never tried this variety of grape in any form other than pressed, and then consumed from a bottle … but they are also delicious when eaten fresh!

Jams, jellies, preserves, marmalade

The day will come when a hotel guest will ask a politically correct waiter for "marmalade" with breakfast – and be given a citrus fruit product in return, since that is the only thing that E.U. guidelines allow us to call "marmalade." Everything else is now either "preserve" or "jam," or, if it is made from fruit juice, "jelly."

Fortunately, not many German cooks care much for the E.U. and its guidelines, and those who still do their own preserving will continue to label their jars as desired, such as "Strawberry/rhubarb jam," "Red (or black) currant jam," or "Plum jam." The word "marmalade" used to refer to a product that was made from several different varieties of fruit, whereas "preserve" was made from just one.

The cooking method has not changed. Chopped fruit is boiled with sugar until it reaches the setting point. The only basic rule is to keep cooking times as short as possible, as otherwise the pectin in the fruit, which is a natural gelling agent, is destroyed. Also, the proportion of pectin, acid, and sugar must be right. Apples, red and blackcurrants, gooseberries, blackberries, and apricots all contain sufficient natural pectin, but a readymade gelling agent should be added to strawberries, raspberries, cherries, and morello cherries. Some good fruit combinations are: strawberries and rhubarb; strawberries and red or blackcurrants; red or blackcurrants and gooseberries; red or blackcurrants and cherries; red or blackcurrants and raspberries; raspberries and cherries; apples and cranberries; apples and blackberries; apples and elderberries; elderberries and plums.

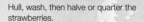

Hull, wash, then halve or quarter the strawberries.

Add 4 lbs strawberries (2 kg) and juice of 2 lemons to 3 lbs (1.5 kg) of sugar.

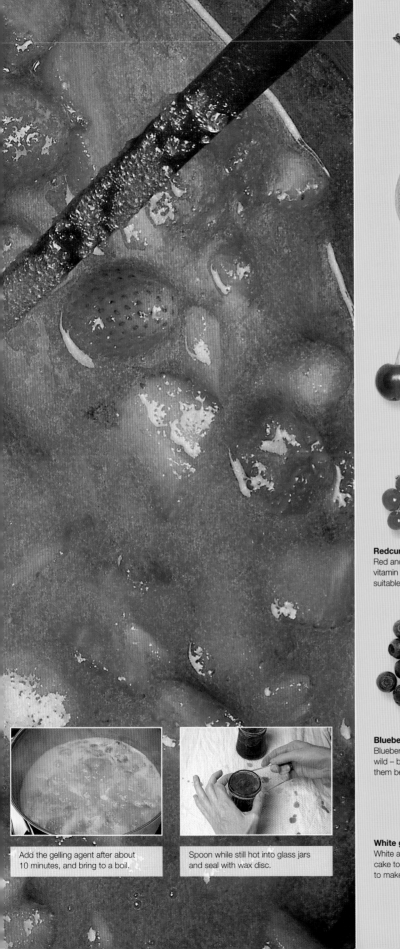

Add the gelling agent after about 10 minutes, and bring to a boil.

Spoon while still hot into glass jars and seal with wax disc.

Pear
Like apples and quince, the pear is a pomaceous fruit.

Cherry
Cherries add interest to a cake – just try to imagine a Black Forest cherry cake without them.

Purple (common) plum
A pit-fruit that dries successfully, and is used in a large number of sweet and sour dishes.

Redcurrants
Red and blackcurrants are full of vitamin C, and very acidic. They are suitable for preserves and compotes.

Gooseberry, red
Red gooseberries can be very sweet when they are absolutely ripe, and should be eaten raw.

Blueberry
Blueberries can be picked in the wild – but remember to wash them before eating.

Mirabelle
These round, yellow, sweet pit-fruits are a member of the plum family.

White grape
White and red grapes can be used as a cake topping, in fruit salads, for juice, and to make jelly.

Diet busters

The greatest threat posed to the health cure and weight loss programs of Black Forest clinics and spa resorts in Baden is not the healthcare reform, but the Black Forest cherry cake. This light, smooth, seductive concoction, which is made from eggs, sugar, flour, sour cherries, chocolate flakes, cream, and kirsch, is the fixed star in the firmament of Germany's cakes and gateaux, and at least as popular as Vienna's *Sachertorte*. Unlike the *Sachertorte*, though, no records of its origins exist, and no lawyers are retained to deal with copyright. Nor is its recipe kept locked away in a safe somewhere – anybody can bake a Black Forest cherry cake.

The other Alemannian and Swabian cakes and gateaux are also well worth breaking the diet for, even if they fail to match the Black Forest cherry cake in splendor and opulence. The Swabian *Träubleskuchen* (redcurrant cake), the *Käskuchen* (cheesecake), the Swabian-Alemannian *Apfelkuchen* (apple cake), for which the apples can be either grated or chopped, and *Rhabarberkuchen* (rhubarb cake), that other delicacy of early summer – these creations are all part of everyday Swabian-Alemannian cuisine.

Something that dates back to the Swabian Baroque and is well worth rediscovering is the *Brottorte*, or bread cake, which is made from butter, eggs, lemon, sugar, almonds, and black bread. Its fall from fame has to have been due to the vast quantity of eggs it calls for: 16 whole eggs, and 12 egg whites to ¾ pound of black bread. That is a shame, though. Were 16 people to share it, their cholesterol intake would not exceed that of a boiled egg at breakfast, and there is no reason why it should not be used in clinics and spa resorts as a dietetic food.

Träubleskuchen
Redcurrant cake

1 cup/250 g flour
2 eggs, separated
½ cup/125 g butter
¾ cup/200 g sugar
generous 1 lb/500 g redcurrants
8 tsp almond slivers

Make a smooth dough from the flour, egg yolks, butter, and 6 tablespoons of the sugar. Leave in a cool place for 30 minutes. Wash the redcurrants, and remove the stalks. Roll out the dough, and use to line a springform pan. Bake the shell (390 °F/200 °C) for about 25 minutes. Beat the egg whites until stiff, and add the remaining sugar. Stir the redcurrants into the beaten egg whites. Sprinkle the almonds over the pastry shell, and pour over the egg white and sugar mixture. Bake (320 °F/160 °C) for about 20 minutes until the surface has turned a light yellow.

Top: Children dressed for their First Communion. The girl is wearing the St George headdress.

Schwarzwälder Kirschtorte
Black Forest cherry cake
(Illustrated opposite)

Sponge base
6 eggs, separated
¾ cup/150 g superfine sugar
1 cup/125 g flour
3½ tsp grated hazelnuts
pinch of salt
2 tbsp cocoa powder
½ tsp vanilla essence

Shortcrust shell
1 cup/125 g flour
1 egg yolk
¼ cup/65 g sugar
pinch of salt
¼ cup/65 g butter

Filling
5 tbsp raspberry jelly
½ oz/15 g powdered gelatin
2 tbsp sugar
1 tsp vanilla essence
3 cups/750 g whipping cream
½ cup/125 ml Kirsch
2 cups/500 g sour cherries (from a jar)
¼ cup/60 g grated chocolate

Start by making the sponge base. Combine the egg yolks with the sugar and a little water, and beat until light and fluffy. Beat the egg whites, and spoon into the egg yolk mixture. Sieve the flour over the top. Then add the grated hazelnuts, salt, cocoa powder, and vanilla essence, and combine well. Line a springform pan (10 inch/26 cm diameter) with waxed paper, then spoon in the mixture and level off. Bake at 355 °F/180 °C for 30 minutes. Remove from the oven, and leave to cool.

Make a shortcrust (plain) pastry from the ingredients listed above, and leave in a cool place for 30 minutes. Roll out the pastry, and line the base of a springform pan. Bake at 430 °F/200 °C for 25 minutes.

To make the filling, pass the raspberry jelly through a strainer. Soak the gelatin in cold water. Add the sugar and vanilla essence to the cream, and beat until stiff. Stir the gelatin and a dash of Kirsch into the whipped cream. When cool, place the shortcrust shell in a cold springform pan. Cut the sponge base in half widthwise. Spread the

raspberry jelly over the shortcrust base. Sprinkle half of the Kirsch over one of the halves, and place on top of the raspberry jelly on the shortcrust base. Arrange all of the cherries except 14 over this sponge half. Spread ⅔ of the cream over the cherries. Top with the second sponge half, and sprinkle over the remaining Kirsch. Open the springform pan. Spread the remaining cream around the sides of the cake, and pipe 14 cream rosettes on top. Place a cherry on each rosette, and sprinkle the chocolate flakes over the center of the cake and around the sides.

Black Forest national costume

When asked what the German national costume is, most foreign visitors will undoubtedly reply: Bavarian Lederhosen – and the Black Forest Bollenhut, or "pompom" hat. The pompom hat is part of the cliché of the Black Forest – and that's to say nothing of the St George Schäppel (headdress), the Mühlenbacher Goldhaube (golden bonnet), the Markgräfler Hörnerkappe (horned hat), or the Furtwangener Strohzylinder (straw cylinder), the Kinzigtaler Rollenkranz (rolled hat), the Hanauer Kappenschlupf (cap), or the Schluppbacher Silberkäppe (silver cap). In fact, its correct name is the Schiltacher Bollenhut, since Schiltach is the only place where the pompom hat is found, in red for young girls and black for married women. People from the Black Forest do not waste much time wondering why that should be so; it is simply a part of their identity, and not just something that is worn at trade fairs or cultural events to entertain visitors. The *Schäppel*, *Kränze* and *Hauben* are still worn on high church days, such as Easter, Low Sunday, and Corpus Christi, at a First Communion and Confirmation, at weddings and church consecrations. So are other valuable garments: the hand embroidered bodice, the silk scarves, also hand embroidered, the fabric-backed chemisettes, which are made of tulle, the lace collars, and the wide skirts and dresses made of satin crepe. However, the elaborate headdresses require the most labor, and they are now prohibitively expensive. That is why they usually belong to a family's heritage, and are passed on from generation to generation, or else belong to the church and are lent out on special occasions.

The sponge and shortcrust bases for the Black Forest cherry cake are made separately.

Kirsch is added to the whipped cream, which has been combined with gelatin.

The shortcrust base is placed inside a cold springform pan, and the raspberry jelly sieved through a strainer.

It's looking good: the glistening red of raspberry jelly against the lighter background of the shortcrust base.

The sponge base is cut in half, then sprinkled with Kirsch. This is now placed on top of the layer of raspberry jelly.

The sour cherries are spread evenly over the sponge base, and then topped with a thick layer of cream.

Spoon on, smooth with a palette knife – but don't use all the cream; keep a little for later.

There must still be enough room in the springform pan for the second sponge layer.

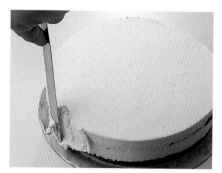

The springform pan is opened, and the whole cake is covered with the remaining cream.

Now for the finishing touches: a whipped cream rosette is piped onto each slice of the cake.

And just to make sure we're up to maximum calories: add chocolate flakes to the center and around the sides.

14 pieces of cake for 14 lucky people, and the crowning glory is a glistening cherry on top of each cream rosette.

Germany – the home of the gateau

Aidatorte (Aida gateau): pastry shell; chocolate cream between 3 sponge layers. Edge 3 or 4 layers of pyramid cake. Garnished with cream and chocolate.

Blueberry crumb: yeast dough base, then sponge. Filled with vanilla cream and fresh blueberries. Topped with blueberry crumb, sprinkled with confectioner's sugar.

Bohèmetorte (Bohème gateau): pastry shell, then a layer of vanilla cream with puff pastry rolls, and a layer of strawberry cream. Topped with filled puff pastry rolls.

Carolatorte: pastry shell, spread with jelly; coffee-flavored buttercream between layers of sponge, pieces of pyramid cake. Topped with marzipan and covertures.

Eierlikörsahne (egg liqueur cream): baked vanilla base with grated coconut and chocolate, topped with cream, and garnished with a truffle.

Fruit salad gateau: pastry shell, covered with a sponge layer. Vanilla cream, topped with various fruits. Clear glaze, edge garnished with toasted almonds.

The confectioner's pride: cakes and gateaux fresh from the bakehouse. These creations are among the specialties of German confectioners. Few domestic cooks have the skill (and time!) to make their own, and usually people visit a café to enjoy them.

Erdbeersahne (strawberry cream): pastry shell, then sponge layers, and a strawberry cream filling made from puréed strawberries, sugar, and lemon juice.

Erdbeertorte (strawberry gateau): pastry shell, then sponge, followed by vanilla cream topped with fresh strawberries, cut into quarters and a red cake glaze.

Flockensahne (cream flakes): several layers of choux pastry, then vanilla cream and cranberry jelly, topped with crumbled choux pastry.

Florentiner Kirsch (Florentine cherry): base made of butter, eggs, and hazelnuts, then a set cherry filling, topped with a honey and almond layer.

Frühlingstorte (spring gateau): pastry and sponge base, then vertical layers of pastry, sponge, and cranberry jelly. Topped with buttercream and redcurrant jelly.

Goethetorte (Goethe cake): pastry shell spread with jelly. Five layers of chocolate sponge, interspersed with chocolate cream and cherries; chocolate topping.

Herrentorte (gentlemen's cake): alternate layers of sponge and a light wine cream, made with beaten egg whites. Covered in marzipan, and topped with chocolate.

Glasierte Baumkuchentorte (glazed layered cake): layers of marzipan and rum, apricots, with a top layer of fondant. The cake is garnished with chocolate.

Pralinétorte (praline torte): pastry shell, then two layers of sponge with apricot jelly in between. Nuts, praline cream, chocolate topping, and garnished with praline.

Rhabarberstreusel (rhubarb crumb cake): yeast dough base, sponge layer, then a layer of a thick vanilla cream with rum, blanched rhubarb. Topped with sugar.

Sarah-Bernhardt-Torte (Sarah Bernhardt cake): 4 alternate layers of meringue and mocha butter cream. Topped with a layer of marzipan and mocha cream.

Stachelbeer-Vanille-Sahne (gooseberry and vanilla cream): A yeast base with a layer of sponge. The gooseberry filling is topped with vanilla cream and nuts.

Strawberry Charlotte: pastry shell with a layer of sponge. Layers of strawberry cream, made from puréed strawberries, then strawberry jelly and cream.

Pineapple layer cake: pastry shell. Seven layers of sponge, interspersed with pineapple jelly. Ganache topping, garnished with candied pineapple.

Mignontorte: pastry shell. Six alternate sponge layers and buttercream. Topped with glazed marzipan, and garnished with a profiterole.

Apfeltorte (apple cake): a yeast dough base, then a sponge layer. Fresh apples, almonds, and raisins, thickened with apple purée. Shortcrust topping with almond slivers.

Plum cream: pastry shell, then a layer of sponge. Plum cream applied in layers, topped with plum jelly, cream, and plums. Edged with ladies' fingers.

Alemannian carnival

An outsider would think that the masks and mummery of the Alemannian *Fasnacht* carnival celebrations belonged to the Andes or the Himalayas rather than central Europe. It is a spectacle that appears to be light years away from the "drilled steps" of Cologne's *Funkenmariechen* dancers, the informality of Munich's *Fasching*, or the precise choreography of the Mainz carnival. Even the gloomy monotony of Basle's *Morgenstreich* is not a patch on the *Fasnet*. One can almost feel the sorcery, the wildness of pre-Christian times.

Traditional events, such as the *Rottweiler Narrensprung*, "fools' leap," and the appearances of the old *Narrenzünfte*, fools' guilds, begin on "Dirty Thursday" before the Fasching weekend.

Above: The *Rottweiler Narrensprung* begins on the Thursday before the Fasching weekend. Brightly colored fools are carried through the town on "horses."

Below: Rottweil is populated by fascinating, almost archaic-looking creatures. The masks are often very old; the poles are used for fighting and for jumping.

They date back to the late Middle Ages. Over the course of the centuries, the style of the events has changed from rustic and rather coarse to occasions that are now more bourgeois, more "gentrified" – but no less coarse. The larger "fools' guilds" in particular are firmly rooted in the social life of the towns, and that explains why the key positions in the events are often held by the towns' dignitaries. This, however, makes no difference in the degree of ridicule that is piled on the heads of the "powers that be" at these events.

There is no special cuisine at these times, apart from the deep-fried doughnuts and beignets that are also available in Bavaria in the form of *Faschingskrapfen*. Flour soup is served in some areas, and dried fish in the Wolfach valley, which used to be available in every inn and tavern. Otherwise, the food is the same as for other social occasions, sausages and potato salad, for example. The main thing is to keep it simple.

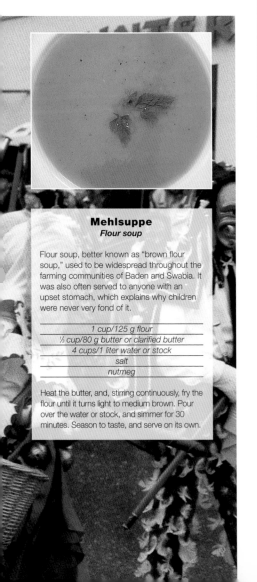

Mehlsuppe
Flour soup

Flour soup, better known as "brown flour soup," used to be widespread throughout the farming communities of Baden and Swabia. It was also often served to anyone with an upset stomach, which explains why children were never very fond of it.

1 cup/125 g flour
⅓ cup/80 g butter or clarified butter
4 cups/1 liter water or stock
salt
nutmeg

Heat the butter, and, stirring continuously, fry the flour until it turns light to medium brown. Pour over the water or stock, and simmer for 30 minutes. Season to taste, and serve on its own.

Deep-fried pastries

It is said that flour, eggs, milk, and fat are the four pillars on which the Swabian-Alemannian cuisine is based, especially in the Swabian Allgäu, the Oberland, and the Hohenlohe. Nowhere is the sheer variety of deep-fried products greater than in this part of the land; some of the more outlandish are *Hasenöhrle* (hare's ears), *Salbeiküchle* (sage biscuits), *Bubeschenkle* (baby's legs), *ausgezogene Küchle* (stretched cookies), and *Wespennester* (wasps' nests). The abundance of deep-fried pastries is closely linked to the agricultural structure. The Hohenlohe, Oberland, and Allgäu are primarily cattle regions. There, the farmsteads are the biggest, the farmers the wealthiest, and the cattle the fattest. This is because the old Württemberg custom of estate partitioning, according to which even the

tattiest item of clothing would be ripped up and divided equally between the beneficiaries of an estate, was not practiced here. In Upper Swabia and the Hohenlohe, the estate has always gone to the eldest descendant, which ensured that the estate remained intact. The farmers in Old Württemberg, where everything was divided up and shared out, have always been poor. They had too much to die with, and too little to live on.

Wealthy farmers meant a rich cuisine. Clarified butter remained a sign of affluence, right up until the 20th century. Deep-fried pastries were served on special occasions by the less well-off, for example at Fasnet, holy days, and at harvest time. People wanted to really fill up on buttered pastry at least a few times a year.

Above: Deep-fried pastries, in all their variety and glory – and with highly imaginative names: Zopfküchle (braided cookies), Bubeschenkle (baby's legs), Apfelküchle (apple cakes), G'wallete Küchle (rolled cookies), Fasnetsküchle (carnival cookies), Hasenöhrle (hare's ears), Salbeimäusle or Salbeiküchle (sage mice, or cookies), Wespennester (wasps' nests), and Ausgezogene (stretched cookies).

Desserts

Ofenschlupfer
Baked apple and bread pudding
(Illustrated right)

8 day-old bread rolls
12 slightly tart apples
butter for the dish
¼ cup/50 g sugar
2 tbsp raisins
4 cups/1 liter milk
6 eggs
¼ cup/50 g sugar
½ tsp vanilla essence
6 tbsp/100 g melted butter
3 tbsp/50 g butter, flaked
sugar for topping

Cut the bread rolls into slices. Peel and core the apples, and slice them. Butter an ovensafe dish. Layer the slices of bread and apples inside the dish, sprinkling some sugar and raisins over the apples. Finish with a layer of milk-soaked bread rolls (to prevent the crust from becoming too hard). Whisk the eggs with the remaining milk, sugar, vanilla essence, and the melted butter. Pour this mixture over the contents of the dish, making sure that the top layer of bread is well covered. Top with the flakes of butter and sugar, and bake in a preheated (400 °F/200 °C) oven.

Schneeballen
Snowballs
(Illustrated opposite)

4 egg yolks
3 tbsp/50 g butter
2½ tbsp/40 g sugar
3 egg whites
generous 1 cup/150 g flour
clarified butter for frying
confectioner's sugar

Beat the egg yolks, butter, and sugar, until fluffy. Beat the egg whites until stiff, and fold into the egg yolk mixture. Add enough flour to make a soft dough. Roll out as thinly as possible, and cut out circles using a wine glass or similar round object about 3 inches (7 cm) in diameter. Use a pastry wheel to cut 4 lines within the circles, ending about ½ inch (1 cm) from the edge. Insert a spoon handle through the two loops in the pastry you have just created. Hang the pastry by the handle in the hot butter to fry. Sprinkle with confectioner's sugar, and serve.

Variation: Cut the pastry into random lengths, and bundle them together loosely to make a "snowball," then deep fry. For a third version, roll out a length of pastry measuring 25–30 inches (60–70 cm) by 2½–3 inches (6–7 cm). Cut this length of pastry into finger-thick pieces, holding them in place at the top and bottom. Fold the strips in on each other to create a snowball shape.

Versoffene Jungfern
Tipsy maidens
(Illustrated below)

Red wine syrup
2 cups/½ liter strong red wine
½ cinnamon stick
grated rind of ½ lemon
3 tbsp sugar
pinch of ground cloves
lemon juice

Dough
¾ cup/150 g superfine sugar
3 eggs
generous 1 cup/150 g flour
3 tbsp hot water
2 tsp baking powder
½ tsp vanilla essence
finely grated rind of ½ lemon
oil for frying

Place the red wine, cinnamon stick, and the lemon rind in a pot and reduce for about 20 minutes. Then add the sugar, ground cloves, and lemon juice to taste. To make the dough, beat the sugar and eggs until fluffy, then gradually add the flour and the water, alternating between the two. Add the remaining ingredients, and combine well. Scoop out small dumplings with a spoon, and deep fry in hot oil. Pour over the red wine syrup, and sprinkle with confectioner's or superfine sugar if desired. Serve immediately.

Apfelmann
Baked apple pudding
(Illustrated opposite)

⅓ cup/80g raisins
5 tbsp rum
3 cups/150 g fresh breadcrumbs
5 tbsp chopped hazelnuts
¾ cup/150 g superfine sugar
10 tbsp/140 g butter
1 tsp grated lemon rind, cinnamon
4 large apples, butter

Soak the raisins in the rum for 30 minutes. Combine the breadcrumbs, hazelnuts, ⅔ cup/100 g sugar, melted butter, lemon rind, and the cinnamon, then add the rum-soaked raisins, and stir well. Peel and core the apples, and cut into thick slices. Sprinkle with a little sugar. In a bread pan, alternate layers of the breadcrumb mixture with layers of the apple. Dot the top with butter, and bake in a preheated (400 °F/200 °C) oven for 30–40 minutes. Combine the remaining sugar with the cinnamon, and sprinkle over the baked apple pudding before serving.

Baked apple and bread pudding

Tipsy maidens

Pfitzauf
Baked ramekins

2 cups/250 g flour
2 cups/½ liter milk
4 eggs
1 tsp salt
2½ tbsp melted butter
extra butter

Combine the first 5 ingredients, and use to half fill the Pfitzauf molds (ramekins). Bake in a preheated oven (350–400 °F/180–200 °C) for about 30 minutes. Serve with a fruit sauce.

Apfelküchle
Apple cakes

4 large, slightly sour apples
juice and grated rind of 1 lemon (unwaxed)
2½ tbsp sugar
1¾ cups/200 g flour
2 tbsp milk
2 eggs
1 egg yolk
4 tsp sugar
pinch of salt
butter or oil for deep frying
cinnamon and sugar

Peel and core the apples. Cut into slices, and combine with the lemon juice, lemon rind, and sugar, and set aside. Make a smooth dough from the flour, milk, eggs, sugar, and salt. Coat the apple slices in this mixture, and deep fry in hot oil. Dip in the sugar and cinnamon mixture, and serve while still hot, with fruit sauce or with coffee.

Baked apple pudding

Snowballs

381

Hamburg • Schwerin
• Bremen
Hanover • • Berlin
Magdeburg • Potsdam
Düsseldorf •
Bonn • • Erfurt • Dresden
Wiesbaden •
Mainz •
Saarbrücken •
Stuttgart •
• Munich

CHRISTINE METZGER
Verena von Funcke · Florian Mikorey
Ingeborg Pils · Barbara Schnabel

Bavaria

That famous inn the Hofbräuhaus, the Munich
Oktoberfest, lederhosen, liter-sized beer tankards,
romantic fairytale castles, Baroque splendor set off by
the imposing backdrop of the Alps – such is the
stereotyped idea of Bavaria. In fact, it has become
synonymous abroad with the popular image of
Germany in general. And of course there is some truth
in the image: enjoyment of the pleasures of life, a deep-
rooted sense of tradition, and simple piety are all
typically Bavarian, as is the pride of its inhabitants in
their beautiful homeland. But of course such an idea of
Bavaria also falls short of reality, particularly in
geographical terms. The largest state in the Federal
Republic of Germany, it embraces Lower Bavaria, the
Upper Palatinate, Upper, Middle and Lower Franconia,
and Swabia. The people of the Free State fall into three
groups: Bavarians, Swabians, and Franconians,
distinguished from each other by their dialect, history,
and customs. Franconia and Swabia did not become
part of Bavaria until the beginning of the 19th century,
and still feel some reserve toward the state capital.
"Munich was a shining light," wrote Thomas Mann, but
it is not the only fixed star in the Bavarian firmament.
The state can also boast Passau, Augsburg, Regensburg,
Nuremberg, Würzburg, and the Wagnerian town of
Bayreuth – to mention only a few of the centers that
have a wealth of history and culture behind them.
Architects, painters, musicians, writers, natural
scientists – Bavaria has produced them in such
numbers that to name any of them would seem unfair
to a great many others.

The cuisine of Bavaria is as rich as its landscape, and
the beer brewed in the state is famous all over the
world. Roast pork, the coarse-cut meat loaf known as
Leberkäs (literally, "liver cheese"), and the *Weisswurst*
("white sausage") made of veal are among its
specialties. The Bavarians have even used their famous
sausage to set frontiers – the "Weisswurst Equator"
divides the Free State of Bavaria from the land to the
north of it, inhabited by "Prussians," and the Bavarians
are anxious to distinguish themselves from the
Prussians in every possible way, even to the symbolical
construction of a "sausage wall."

Left: the monastery of Benediktbeuern is picturesquely set against the
backdrop of the Alps. This Benedictine abbey was founded in the middle of
the 8th century; the monastery church of St Benedict is a Baroque building
dating from 1681–1686.

Weisswurst and Leberkäs

No other item of food in the Free State is the subject of such taboos and rituals as the *Weisswurst* of Munich. The ritual begins even at the time of its purchase: Regensburg, *Landjäger*, and Viennese sausages are bought in pairs, but the *Weisswurst* comes singly. Anyone going into a butcher's and asking not for "four *Weisswurst* sausages" but for "two pairs" of them immediately reveals himself as a "Prussian." And if visitors from northern Germany venture to order potato

salad or even ketchup with their *Weisswurst* in a bar or inn, they may well find that the waiters simply refuse to serve them, remarking, "We're not in Prussia here." It may be news to the guests so brusquely refused service that they are Prussians – they may always have thought themselves natives of some Hanseatic town, or maybe the Rhineland, and were fairly sure they had nothing to do with the former great power of Prussia. But it is useless to draw such historical distinctions in Bavaria, where everything the other side of the *Weisswurst* Equator is Prussian, and that is that.

No one knows why the sole accompaniments of this particular sausage are bread rolls or pretzels, and mild mustard. The reason why the concoction – a mixture of veal, bacon, calf feet, bacon rind, onion, parsley, lemon zest, ground cloves, nutmeg, and pepper – is not supposed to hear the famous

"chimes of twelve o'clock" is more obvious. The prohibition dates from the time when the Munich *Weisswurst* was first invented, and as befits a national symbol, the day itself can be pinpointed: it was created by the butcher and innkeeper Sepp Moser on 22 February 1857. Since no preservatives were used in making sausage at the time, it did not keep long, quickly losing its flavor and aroma, so that it had to be eaten very soon after it was made. The tradition persists today: white sausage is eaten in the middle of the morning, with half a liter of beer or a *Weissbier*.

It must be admitted that there was a time when even the gastronomes of Munich experimented with their national treasure, but *Weisswurst* coated in breadcrumbs, deep-fried, grilled, served with side dishes, or even as part of a salad, simply did not catch on. Such deplorable attempts to inter-nationalize it failed because they deprived the sausage if its own unique flavor. It has to be heated slowly in hot water, nothing else, and the water must not on any account boil, or the sausage will burst and taste of nothing at all.

Leberkäs, "liver cheese," is less capricious. It contains neither liver nor cheese, but is a meat loaf made of beef and pork, bacon, spices, and crushed ice. Fifty-five pounds (25 kilograms) of ice goes into every 220 pounds (100 kilograms) of liver cheese, and malicious tongues have said that the major expense incurred in making it is the water bill. However, butchers do not add so much ice out of thriftiness, but because the ice prevents the protein from coagulating too quickly when the meat for the meat loaf is ground. If that happens the mixture will not be fine enough, and this Bavarian specialty, baked in a rectangular pan at a moderate temperature, has to be fine in texture. It was once eaten mainly by laborers or the lower middle classes, and was regarded as a cheap meal; today it is popular with all sections of the population, and has many variations. *Leberkäs*, cut into fairly thick slices, may be eaten fresh from the oven, where it has formed a slight crust, accompanied by mild or medium-hot mustard and a pretzel as a snack. A slice in a crusty white roll is the Bavarian answer to the all-conquering burger. For a complete, satisfying meal, *Leberkäs* is cut into slices as thick as your thumb and fried on both sides in a skillet, then topped with a fried egg and served with potato salad. Connoisseurs enjoy it cold in beer gardens and as a snack. Thinly sliced, it is eaten for breakfast, or as part of a platter of mixed sliced meats. And if you want to try something entirely different, cut slices of the meat loaf into thin strips or dice, add onions, pickled gherkins, and tomatoes, and dress with oil and vinegar.

Weisswurst sausages

Weisswurst etiquette

"There are four main groups of people: 1. Bavarians; 2. Swabians; 3. Prussians; 4. Foreigners," writes the author Herbert Rosendorfer in his *Königlich Bayerisches Sportbrevier* ("Guide to the Sports of the Kingdom of Bavaria"), describing the Bavarians' attitude to the rest of the world. The fourth group is easily summed up: it consists of Americans, Asians, Africans – people who, it may be assumed, never had contact with anything as noble as Bavarian culture, and must therefore be forgiven much. For instance, ordering sauerkraut with *Weisswurst*. *Weisswurst* and sauerkraut – imagine! A native Bavarian sitting nearby will either turn away in horror, or be quick to offer advice when, in addition, he sees the "foreigner" wielding a knife and fork, cutting the sausage up into small pieces. He will explain that the correct way to eat this sausage is to *zuzeln* it – a verb for which the foreigner, even if he is a German citizen, will search his dictionary in vain. It is a Bavarian dialect word meaning "suck," and describes the proper way to eat *Weisswurst*: you cut it in half with a knife, pick it up in your fingers, dip it in sweet mustard – no other kind will do – and suck it out of its skin. The experience is primeval and sensuous; it is no coincidence that "sucking" the sausage suggests associations with breast-feeding. If inhibitions acquired in childhood put you off the idea, then it is permissible to slit the sausage lengthwise, remove it from its skin, and eat it with knife and fork. But that lengthwise cut places a severe strain on the tolerance of true Bavarians.

Leberkäs with potato and endive salad

To make the sweet mustard so popular in Bavaria …

… mix finely and coarsely ground mustard seed together.

Add brown sugar and hot vinegar, stirring.

The mustard must be well mixed to a thick consistency.

Then let the mustard stand overnight to absorb the flavors.

Next morning it can be put into jars and labeled.

Not all mustards are the same.

Time for a snack

The state constitution may not actually say so, but a working man in Bavaria has the traditional right to stop for a break and eat a snack – *Brotzeit*, literally "bread time." Anyone employing a handyman in the house should be aware of that; otherwise, he will employ the methods perfected over many generations to make it known when he demands his rights. His repertory includes a spontaneous decline in productivity, accompanied by loud complaints about the heat and the dust, or – if he happens to be the introverted type – he may suffer in silence, mopping the sweat from his brow at frequent intervals. The symptoms speak for themselves: the man needs something to eat, and above all something to drink, for naturally a beer is part of his "bread time." Beer, after all, is liquid bread, and is regarded as a staple foodstuff in Bavaria.

Originally, this break for a snack was the kind generally described in Germany as "second breakfast." On farms, the first breakfast consisted of bread and milk, fare that would not keep a man hard at work on the land going for long. The farmer's wife or the maidservants would take something more substantial out to the fields in the middle of the morning – in both solid and liquid form. In the craft trades, it was always the apprentice's job to go and fetch the men's snack. The custom remained in force until the 1960s, when the trade unions finally asked whether it was really a sensible part of a lad's training to fetch rolls filled with *Leberkäs* from the butcher.

Today, *Brotzeit* is not confined to the morning. It may be eaten in the afternoon, and supper in a beer garden may also be described as *Brotzeit*. If you are asked to visit "just for a *Brotzeit*," there will be no hot food; instead, you will be served sliced sausage, cheese, radishes, *Obatzta* (made of Camembert cheese and onions), and of course bread, rolls, and pretzels. Butter does not feature on a genuine Bavarian *Brotzeit* platter, which itself ought to be made of wood. Unlike people farther north, where open sandwiches served on bread and butter were invented, the people of the south traditionally eat their bread plain. Students of folklore explain that bread is better flavored in the south, thus acquiring the status of an item of food in its own right, rather than being just something to support the topping.

Right: a snack tastes best shared with friends in an inn or beer garden, before or after a game of cards.

Bratensülze, made from cold roast pork in aspic.

Fleischpflanzerl, ground meat with bread rolls and onions.

Leberkäs, "liver cheese" can be eaten hot or cold as a snack.

Limburg cheese, a soft cheese related to Romadur, but larger.

Obatzta, made of ripe Camembert mixed with onions and raw egg.

Ox cheek salad, finely diced, with a piquant onion dressing.

Open sandwich with chives – a Brotzeit for vegetarians.

Roast pork is delicious when sliced and eaten cold.

Stockwurst is similar to Weisswurst, but has a firmer consistency.

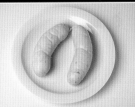

Weisswurst is eaten only before noon, with bread rolls and sweet mustard.

White Presssack sausage, cut into strips and eaten with mustard.

Red Presssack sausage has a more robust flavor than its white counterpart.

Regensburg sausage is nearly always eaten cold, in a salad.

Sausage salad, with a piquant onion and pickled gherkin dressing.

Simila et bracchium

The Bavarian word for a bread roll, either plain or topped with sesame seeds, is *Semmel*; it is a small, crisp white roll made from wheat flour. The flour in fact gives the roll its name; it derives from the Latin word *simila*, meaning "fine wheaten flour." The Romans first crossed the Alps in the year 15 B.C. Over the following centuries there was a great deal of traffic on the Via Claudia, the Roman road leading to Augusta Vindelicorum, modern-day Augsburg, and it was along this road that they imported wheat from Egyptian granaries into the country. It was a grain that grew well even north of the Alps, in the mild climate and rich soil of the area, and bread baked from wheat flour was still a part of the local diet after the Romans left.

The country that was once ancient Germania owes the modern German word is *Brezel*, from the Latin *bracchium*, meaning "arm" or more specifically "forearm," because the pretzel looks like intertwining arms, although the original Roman shape was a closed ring. The twisted shape of the pretzel did not appear until the 12th century, and to this day it is the official symbol of the baker's trade. Although pretzels were also traditionally baked in some north German cities, they are really natives of the south, since very fine wheat flour is still needed to make them.

The difference between German pretzels and Bavarian *Brez'n* or *Brezen* is that the Bavarians invented the salt-glazed pretzel – or so the story goes. The Swabians make similar claims, and tell their own tale of its invention. However, this is not the place for the Swabian legend, and the Bavarian version runs thus: on the morning of 11 February 1839, a baker called Anton Nepomuk Pfannenbrenner made a mistake. He was making pretzels in the Royal Munich Coffeehouse of Johann Eilles, supplier to the Bavarian court, and he brushed them with a salt solution, which was

The classic Semmel, a roll made of fine wheat flour.

Maurerloabl, cheap rye rolls for laborers.

Pfennigmuggel rye rolls – good value for money.

Maurerloabl with added caraway seeds.

standing around ready to clean the baking pans, and looked like the syrup generally used to glaze pretzels at the time. As you may have guessed, the salty glaze proved a great success, and the luckless baker became a hero of Bavarian legend.

If you hoped to make your name in the history of the pretzel today, you would need to invent a pretzel-twisting machine, for no such thing yet exists: pretzels must still be handmade. Up to the twisting operation, it is easy enough: the dough consists of fine wheat flour, water, and yeast, the little cookies are dipped in a three percent salt solution, and garnished with large salt crystals. Since pretzels taste best fresh, almost every beer garden today has its own pretzel oven.

In the past, pretzels were eaten only on fast days, at Easter, or on certain festival days. As shaped breads (see p. 444), they are firmly rooted in the cycle of seasonal customs. Depending on the particular region, a godfather might give them to his godchild, or a lover to his beloved, and they were supposed to bring blessings, good luck, and health. On St Martin's day, the time when farmhands changed their jobs, they and the other farm servants received a "St Martin's pretzel." The "All Souls' pretzels" still made in Augsburg and some other towns today remind us of the old custom whereby pretzels were also associated with the end of life, and were hung on gravestones and crosses.

Place one half of the pretzel over the other, twist, and press. A skillful baker performs the operation at speed.

To give them an attractive brown color, the pretzels are dipped in a salt solution, and sprinkled with coarse salt.

Bread rolls in the political arena

"Early in the morning, Maxl came out of the house, looking refreshed, and carrying a full basket. It contained gleaming oblong *Wecken* rolls, and crisp *Semmeln*. The villagers stood at their windows, looking at him in no very friendly way. He went down the rather steep slope of the village street, which led to the banks of the lake. 'Does that impertinent fellow plan to sell his paltry rolls to our king?' grumbled the suspicious locals. Their suspicions were misplaced. The king, who was only twenty-seven years old, had very bad teeth and ate nothing but soft white bread, brought from Munich every other day by a mounted courier. Maxl was off to the Schlosswirtschaft (palace tavern) opened about a year before by Karl Wiesmaier, and frequented by the lower ranks of palace servants …He had chosen his moment well, for they were just having their 'second breakfast' in the wood-paneled tavern. They all looked benevolently at the baker as he entered, each took several rolls from the basket he handed around, and Wiesmaier filled up the bread platters on the tables. 'Why, this is excellent! Delicious! Nicely crisp, and soft inside! Very good!' remarked the royal valet, eating a white roll, and he turned graciously to Maxl. 'This Starnberg baker knows his business, and though he may have had no luck so far, this bread can be recommended to His Majesty in person. Here's to you, master baker – your very good health!'"

This passage by Oskar Maria Graf (1894–1967), from his book *Das Leben meiner Mutter* ("My mother's life"), is an account of the early career of his father, the first master baker from Berg on Lake Starnberg, where Ludwig II, the "fairytale king" of Bavaria, had his official residence. Graf owed the success of his bakery in a rural area to his distinguished customers among the monarch's retinue, for the local farmers and their families made their own bread. Refined white flour was expensive, and was therefore the food of the rich people in high society.

The general public of Bavaria has not been able to afford fine white rolls of the *Semmel* type until the last few decades – when the rolls themselves entered the political arena. Under a headline running, "Our rolls are too small," the Munich evening paper of 28 October 1959 ran the following story: "Yesterday Dr Hildegard Hamm-Brücher, Free Democrat deputy in the Bavarian Parliament, brought a dozen rolls and a letter scale along to the meeting of the Agricultural Committee. In front of her fellow deputies, she weighed the rolls on her letter scale. The lightest weighed 36 grams (about 1¼ ounces), the heaviest 51 grams (about 1¾ ounces). Most of the rolls weighed around 40 grams (about 1½ ounces). 'The housewife expects to get a roll weighing 50 grams for her 8 pfennigs,' said Dr Brücher. 'An average weight of 40 grams defrauds the customer. The baker will be able to make 20 extra rolls out of the quantity that should be enough for 100, and he makes an extra profit too.'" Despite Dr Hamm-Brücher's valiant stand, however, there is still no set legal weight for small bakery items – bread products weighing less than 8 oz (250 grams) – but it seems that this no longer troubles anyone, never mind what the Free Democrat deputy said in the lean years of the 1950s.

Left: the pretzel is traditionally eaten on fast days and feast days. Of course it has to appear at the biggest popular festival in Bavaria, the Munich Oktoberfest, where it assumes gigantic proportions.

Beer gardens

It is said that the beer gardens of Munich and its surroundings alone can accommodate over 100,000 people in all, which is hardly surprising. Every landlord with the minimum equipment necessary – beer, and a garden area where he can set out chairs and tables – will erect a large board outside his establishment announcing "Beer garden." The Association for the Promotion of Munich Beer Gardens (and yes, such a body really does exist) encourages the practice, no doubt because it would not have many members if it were to confine itself to those few inns that really do deserve the name of beer garden! Strictly speaking, there are two criteria: first, a beer garden must provide somewhere for customers to sit under the shade of a group of old chestnut trees, and second, they must be able to bring their own food. Other establishments are simply inns with gardens, and they can be found anywhere else in Germany. Beer gardens, on the other hand, are a Munich institution with a long tradition behind them.

The beer garden owes its origin to the brewery regulations of 1539, which stated that no beer could be brewed between 23 April and 29 September, since brewing beer in summer meant an increased risk of fire. Faced with such a long period of drought, brewers were extremely active in March, making large quantities of a special brew known as "March beer," which kept longer but had to be stored in a cold place if it was not to go off. Since neither artificial ice nor modern refrigeration was around at the time, brewers resorted to other methods, and dug cellars. However, the high water table of Munich meant that these cellars could not go too deep, and ways of keeping the beer cool had to be added from above. Brewers tipped gravel into their cellars, and planted over them a large-leaved tree to provide sufficient shade – the chestnut.

Gravel, chestnut trees, tables and benches, fresh, cool beer from the cask: the summer was saved, and a way of bridging that dreadful stretch of time between April and September had been devised. Thirsty folk would go "to the beer cellar." The institution soon became so popular that inn landlords resented the competition, and demanded that brewers be forbidden to sell their beer direct. The people of Munich have always reacted violently to any threat to their beer supplies. There was a danger of rebellion, and King Ludwig I of Bavaria (who lived from 1786 to 1868, and is not to be confused with Ludwig II, the "fairytale" king) finally decided for the sake of peace, that the brewers could go on serving their own beer, but could not sell food with it. This was the origin of the custom whereby people going "to the beer cellar" took their own snacks with them. It is still usual to bring your own food to the "real" beer gardens of Munich. The classic accessory of a customer of the beer gardens is a small willow basket with room in it for sausage, cheese, radishes, salt, bread, cutlery, and a wooden platter – all the essentials for a satisfying snack. The traditional radish was cut into thin spirals, then salted until it "wept," so that it had a mild, delicious flavor when eaten. *Obatzta*, made of ripe Camembert, onions, and eggs, is a favorite in beer gardens, and today you can buy it there too. The dishes on offer will vary from one beer garden to another; the larger establishments have self-service areas providing everything you could find on the menu of a high-class inn: grilled chicken, *Leberkäs*, grilled or broiled sausage and sauerkraut, knuckle of pork, roast pork with dumplings. There are numerous vegetarian alternatives, such as open sandwiches of tomato, chives, and curd cheese. In some beer gardens you can also buy the famous *Steckerlfish*, charcoal-grilled mackerel wrapped in thick paper and served with as many little wooden forks as there are customers around the table. For a basic rule of good manners in the beer garden is that you share whatever you have to eat. If you buy food to take along, you add a little extra to your basket, and an extra place setting – you never know whom you might meet, and they might be hungry.

A pagoda in Munich

A typical Munich child visits a beer garden early in life, and there are playgrounds for older children, where their parents can keep an eye on them.

A cute little fellow like Benjamin here – a true Munich resident – enjoys the beer garden too, and has eaten many a bone there.

The Chinaturm (Chinese Tower), which can seat 7000 customers and is the second largest beer garden in Munich, takes its name from the emblem rising grandly in its midst, a wooden pagoda on five floors built here in 1790. Why there should be a Chinese pagoda in the "English Garden" area of a Bavarian city is a question one might well ask, except that the atmosphere of a beer garden has such a soothing, calming effect on customers that they are more likely to turn their minds to modern-day problems – such as the price of beer (a constant source of complaint every year), or the weather, so important for a pleasant visit to a beer garden, or what one is eating, and the sights to be seen. There are plenty of those in the Chinaturm: punks and tramps, mountain bikes and their riders with sturdy calves, tattooed male chests, rollerbladers gliding skillfully between baby strollers and dogs of indefinable breeds. And it is not just the various canine species that add color to the scene – humanity is so varied here that it surpasses every other Munich beer garden, and so many languages are spoken that on some days you might well take the pagoda for the Tower of Babel itself. Seven thousand people living close together in an area are enough to make it a small town, and the 7000 to be found sitting at the wooden tables of the Chinaturm on a fine day could indeed populate a town: they are of all ages, from all income levels, classes, family backgrounds, cultures, and culinary traditions. Although in theory anyone can sit next to anyone else, as in all beer gardens, in practice the majority of Munich customers have structured themselves into their own groups. Families with small children, for instance, sit at

the tables near the sandpits, where parents can keep an eye on their offspring over the rim of a *Masskrug* (the traditional liter tankard), getting to their feet only when a child falls over or demands to be taken to the carousel – an old one, with wooden animals, on which generations of Munich children have ridden off into life. Sun worshipers indulge themselves away from the shade of the chestnuts and close to the pagoda itself, where eccentrics wishing to attract attention also gather. Gays have their own areas, and so do ordinary families, clubs, and schoolchildren. Even people who do not belong to any of these groups like to have their usual places, since that makes social life in the beer garden easier. Who wants to scan 7000 faces before recognizing an acquaintance, or make elaborate arrangements by phone beforehand in order to meet in this vast area? Those inconveniences can be avoided if people stick to their customary places. What's more, you will know how to avoid people you do *not* want to meet …

The meteorological bureau claims that only 30 to 40 evenings a year are really warm enough for sitting in a beer garden, but the reality presents a different picture. Lovers of beer gardens will sit at their wooden tables in overcoats if necessary. As a result, in many years the beer garden season begins as early as February, and the taps of the beer kegs are open even when the buds on the chestnut trees are still tightly closed.

Typically Bavarian

The pig

"Bavaria feeds its swine on acorns and other forest fruits in such quantities that it can supply all the other countries of Europe with their meat," writes Örtel in his *Map of Bavaria* of 1570. It is hardly surprising that beyond the borders of the province, people spoke enviously of the *Saubaiern* (literally, "sowish Bavarians") who brought hundreds of thousands of gulden into the state every year with the sale of their fine-flavored animals, and enjoyed a great many themselves, as well as exporting them. The domestic pig (*Sus domestica*) was the ideal companion for a Bavarian farmer: undemanding, companionable, and fertile. It would eat kitchen scraps and chaff with relish, and every bit of it could be used, from its snout to its curly tail.

Even in the 19th century, Old Bavaria was famous for its stockrearing and production of piglets, while Franconia was known as a good region for fattening up the pigs. The distinction is explained by the fact that there were still meadows where pigs could forage in Upper Bavaria and Swabia, while the Franconians had already specialized in raising crops, and having fewer meadows went over to stall-feeding. At the time, the Bavarian and Swabian breeds were kept; the Bavarian pig must have been very like the Swabian-Halle breed, now experiencing something of a revival on many Bavarian farms turning to alternative methods of farming. Today, according to the statistics, only 3.5 million of the pigs in Germany, which amount to 24.3 million in all, are kept in Bavaria, putting it in third place behind Lower Saxony and North Rhine-Westphalia. The most popular breed for fattening is a cross between the German Landrace and the Pietrain pig. Although a third of all German agricultural holdings are located in Bavaria, its degree of self-sufficiency in the supply of pork products, at 70 percent, represents a backward step; nowadays pigs have to be imported for Bavarian consumption.

Yet over the centuries the Bavarians have always enjoyed the many culinary pleasures provided by the pig, and still do. Sucking pig, pork in beer, roast pork, knuckle of pork, stuffed breast of pork, *Wammerl* (smoked pork belly), pickled pork, brawn – the list of dishes provided by the pig is a long one, and every cook swears by personal recipes, handed down through the family. The best drink to go with pork of any kind is freshly drawn beer in the liter tankard peculiar to Bavaria, and the meat is served with cabbage and dumplings. Even in the language, the "sow" has assumed special significance as a kind of Bavarian comparative: a Bavarian wishing to say he felt really well would use the phrase *echt gut*, the word in Bavarian is *sauwohl*, literally "sowishly well," and conversely a bad-tempered person will quickly become *saugrantig*, "sowishly sulky," if something has put him into a bad mood.

This pig is a cross between an improved Landrace and the Pietrain breed.

The improved Landrace is larger and longer than the German Edelschwein.

The German Landrace puts on plenty of fat when well fed.

Roast pork, etc.

Roast pork and knuckle of pork have always been the best criteria of the quality of cooking in a Bavarian inn. In fact it is really quite simple to make these typical Bavarian dishes faultlessly, but in the kitchen, as elsewhere, simplicity is often difficult to achieve. Since both specialties are made only from the best cuts of meat, and served with a dark sauce that is not thickened, there is no room to disguise any mistakes in the cooking. If the meat is not top quality, the roast pork will be fibrous and tough, and the knuckle dry and hard.

To cook a juicy joint of roast pork, take a piece from the shoulder or neck of the animal, not too lean, so that plenty of fat will run out. The advantage of shoulder of pork is that its rind will provide delicious, crisp crackling, a kind of tasty byproduct. The rind of the joint is cut into diamond shapes with a sharp kitchen knife, and the meat is seasoned. It is roasted in a pan in a moderate oven, surrounded by diced root vegetables, onions, and veal bones, and basted from time to time with water, stock, or beer. Seasonings and ingredients for the sauce differ from region to region, but everyone agrees on the basic method of preparation.

Not so with knuckle of pork. No one has yet decided whether it should be boiled first, and then roasted, or just roasted. Both methods have their supporters, who appeal to ancient usage and traditional culinary secrets to back their claims. At any rate, the end product should be the same: a crisp knuckle of pork with a crunchy crust.

According to a Bavarian proverb, "It needn't be little so long as it's good." The experienced cook applies this rule of thumb in calculating the right amount of meat for roast pork and knuckle of pork – with the thought at the back of her mind that any leftovers will make a nice dish of roast pork in aspic.

Schweinshaxn
Knuckle of pork

2 pork knuckles (from the back legs of the animal)
salt and pepper
2 tbsp clarified butter
2 onions, diced
soup vegetables (4 carrots, 4 celery stalks, 2 leeks, large bunch of parsley), diced
2 cups/500 ml dark beer

Wash the pork knuckles, pat them dry, and score the rind into diamond shapes. Season well with salt and pepper. Melt the butter in a roasting pan and seal the knuckles well on all sides. Add the onions and soup vegetables, fry briefly, and add 1 cup/250 ml water. Braise in a preheated oven at 340 °F/175 °C for about 2 hours. While the meat is cooking, baste it several times with beer. Then raise the temperature to 430 °F/220 °C, and continue roasting the meat until it has a crisp crust. Put the knuckles on a warmed platter, and do not remove the meat from the bones until served. Boil up the juices in the pan with the rest of the beer, season with salt and pepper, and pass through a fine sieve. Serve with white bread dumplings, and potato and cucumber salad, and pass the sauce separately.

Kartoffel-Gurken-Salat
Potato and cucumber salad

2 lb/1 kg waxy potatoes
salt
2 onions, finely diced
¾ cup/200 ml hot meat stock
3–4 tbsp wine vinegar
pepper
3 tbsp oil
1 small cucumber
1 tbsp chopped parsley

Wash the potatoes, and boil them in their skins in salted water for about 25 minutes, until tender. Drain, run cold water over them, peel them, and allow them to cool. Cut them into thin disks, and place in a dish with the onions. Make a marinade of the hot stock, vinegar, salt, pepper, and oil, and pour it over the salad. Mix carefully and allow to stand for a good hour. Then peel and finely slice the cucumber, salt it, and press out its juice. Add the sliced cucumber to the potato salad. Add the chopped parsley, mix carefully, and serve.

Schweinsbraten
Roast pork

2 lb/1 kg shoulder of pork, with rind
salt and pepper
1 tsp ground caraway seeds
1 tbsp clarified butter
4 veal bones, 1 onion, coarsely diced
2 cloves of garlic, crushed
soup vegetables (carrot, celery stalk, leek, bunch of parsley), diced
2 cups/500 ml beer

Wash and pat dry the shoulder of pork. With a sharp knife, cut the rind into a diamond pattern, and season the shoulder well all over with salt, pepper, and ground caraway. Melt the butter in a large roasting pan and brown the veal bones in it. Add the onion, garlic, and soup vegetables, and brown them lightly. Lay the shoulder of pork on top of the vegetables, rind upward, add 1 cup/250 ml water, and roast the pork in a preheated oven at 340 °F/175 °C for 45 minutes. Then raise the temperature to 430 °F/220 °C and roast the meat for another 30–40 minutes. While it is roasting, pour some beer over it from time to time. Take the joint out of the pan when it is done, and allow it to rest for 10 minutes before carving. Add a little water to the juices in the pan, pour through a sieve, and season to taste with salt and pepper. Serve potato dumplings and coleslaw with the roast pork, and pass the sauce separately.

Krautsalat
Coleslaw

1 small white cabbage
salt
⅔ cup/150 ml vinegar
1 cup/250 ml meat stock
1 tsp caraway
white pepper
a pinch of sugar
7 oz/200 g smoked Wammerl (belly of pork)

Quarter the cabbage, and remove the stalk. Shred the cabbage finely, and blanch it briefly in salted water. Drain the cabbage thoroughly. Mix the vinegar, meat stock, caraway, pepper, and sugar together, and pour over the hot cabbage. Cut the belly of pork into small dice, melt it until the fat runs in a dry pan, and mix it and its fat with the cabbage. Allow to stand for at least 1 hour.

Pichelstein stew

When a Bavarian tells you he didn't get where he is today on *Brennsuppe*, he means that his family was not poor, and he was not brought up on the thin brown soup, thickened with flour, that bears that name, but had more substantial nourishment, for instance liver dumplings, pancakes, spleen sausage, beef with noodles, all cooked in good, strong meat broth, even if he didn't necessarily convey these dishes to his mouth with a golden spoon.

Beef soups with tasty garnishes are an important part of Bavarian cooking, but of course there were certain regions of this comparatively rich province where meat broth was a rarity, and liver dumplings were served only on special occasions. The traditionally poor regions of the Upper Palatinate, and parts of Lower Bavaria, have more recipes than the rest of the state for soups based on flour and milk; one of them, *Herbstmilch* "milk of the fall season," has gained fame beyond its own area,

At the Pichelstein festival in Regen, the rising generation of young cooks sings the praises of this nourishing stew.

thanks to a novel of the same name in which the author, Anna Wimschneider, who grew up on a farm, told the story of her life. That fame is literary rather than culinary, for the recipe is so simple that not even the trendiest of cooks have tried to imitate it. "*Herbstmilch* is sour milk to which you add more curdled milk almost daily. You then stir the milk, take out a liter, whisk it with flour in a liter of boiling water, and stir in some sour cream," writes Anna Wimschneider.

Another Lower Bavarian dish, on the other hand, a stew said to have been first served in 1823 or 1847 on the peak of the Büchelstein, and therefore known as Pichelstein, has established its place in German cuisine as a whole, and has even been ennobled by the chef Wolfram Siebeck. He makes Pichelstein with the finest fillet steak, and cuts the root vegetables to different thicknesses – slicing the carrots, which take longest to cook, "as thin as a breath, if you can tell how thin a breath is." Made in this way, the dish is on the stove for only 15 minutes in all.

Where it was invented, however, it does not aspire to such distinction. A true Bavarian *Pichelstein* is neither as exquisite nor as expensive as Siebeck's version, just a simple stew with vegetables. Its special feature is that it contains three kinds of meet: beef, pork, and either veal or mutton.

Pichelsteiner
Meat and vegetable stew

10 oz/300 g pork
10 oz/300 g veal
10 oz/300 g beef
1 tbsp clarified butter
1 lb/500 g potatoes, cut into cubes
2 leeks, sliced into rings
3 carrots, cut into disks
½ celeriac root
salt and pepper
4 cups/1 liter meat stock
1 tbsp chopped parsley

Cut the meat into small dice. Melt the butter in a large pan and add alternate layers of meat, potatoes, and vegetables. Season with salt and pepper, add the meat stock, bring to a boil, and simmer over medium heat, covered, for about 45 minutes, until done. Sprinkle with the parsley before serving.

Soups and stews

Allgäu cheese soup – this specialty is from the Allgäu, Germany's main cheese-making region.

Pretzel soup is made with toasted pretzels, meat stock, and a dash of cream.

Franconian wedding soup, with three garnishes: pancake strips, semolina dumplings, and liver dumplings.

Franconian cabbage soup is made with finely shredded white cabbage and fine strips of vegetables.

Semolina dumpling soup: small dumplings made of semolina and butter floating in clear beef broth.

"Milk soup of the fall season" is made with sour milk, and can have potatoes and cream added.

Brain soup is not to everyone's taste: it is made of cooked, puréed calf brains in a white soup.

Hofer Schnitz is a one-pot dish of root vegetables, which may have beef added.

Hop soup, a spring dish made with the delicious young shoots of hops, served with white toast.

Sweetbread soup contains sliced pancake roll filled with calf sweetbreads and sausagemeat.

Herb soup used to be a dish for fasting days. Herbs are added to a white soup.

Liver dumpling soup: the dumplings, made of ox or calf liver, are served in strong beef broth.

Lower Bavarian meat soup: bread soup in clear beef broth. Ideal for using up leftover bread.

Spleen soup: good beef broth garnished with fine strips of ox spleen on slices of white bread.

Upper Palatinate butter dumpling soup: the dumplings are made of butter, egg, and breadcrumbs.

Panada soup: the name of this white bread soup is from the Latin word for bread.

Pancake soup, a clear beef broth with finely sliced strips of pancake in it. Serve with finely chopped parsley.

Whisked soup: a dish eaten by the poor. The soup is thickened with a flour, egg, and water roux.

Saure Kutteln
Sweet-sour tripe

1¼ lb/600 g of cooked tripe
2 tbsp butter
1 onion, diced
1 tbsp flour
3 cups/750 ml stock
½ cup/125 ml wine vinegar
2 bayleaves, 5 juniper berries
sugar, salt, and pepper
½ cup/125 g cream

Cut the tripe into thin strips. Melt the butter and fry the onion in it gently until transparent. Stir in the flour and cook until golden yellow. Add the stock, vinegar, bayleaves, and juniper berries. Season with sugar, salt, and pepper, and add the tripe. Simmer gently for 10 minutes, then stir in the cream and adjust the seasoning to a piquant flavour with salt, sugar, pepper, and vinegar. White bread dumplings go well with this dish.

Saures Lüngerl
Pickled lungs

2 onions, diced
2 tbsp butter
2 tbsp flour
2 cups/500 ml meat stock
1½ lb/750 g pickled lungs, cut into thin strips
1 cup/250 g cream
1 tsp rubbed marjoram
salt and pepper
vinegar to season
1 tbsp chopped parsley

Soften the onions in the butter until transparent. Stir in the flour and cook until golden yellow. Pour in the stock, stirring, and simmer for 5 minutes. Then add the lungs, pour in the cream, and season with marjoram, salt, and pepper. Allow to simmer over gentle heat for 10 minutes. Adjust the seasoning before serving with salt, pepper, and vinegar. Bread or a white roll of the *Semmel* type will go well with this dish, or it can be served in a soup plate with white bread dumplings, sprinkled with parsley.

Paniertes Euter
Udder in breadcrumbs

4 slices of cooked udder, each weighing about 6 oz/150 g
salt and pepper
2 eggs
4 tbsp breadcrumbs
2 tbsp butter

Season the slices of udder with salt and pepper. Coat them first with beaten egg, then with breadcrumbs. Heat the butter in a skillet, and fry the slices of udder on both sides over moderate heat until golden brown.

Gespicktes Kalbsherz
Calf heart larded with bacon

1 calf heart, weighing about 1¼ lb/600 g
4 oz/100 g unsmoked bacon
salt and pepper
1 tbsp butter
1 onion, diced
soup vegetables (carrot, celery stalk, leek, bunch of parsley), diced
1 cup/250 ml red wine
2 cups/500 ml stock
1 tsp thyme
1 tsp rubbed marjoram
⅖ cup/100 g soured cream

Cut open the heart, wash it well, and remove the internal sinews and veins. Sew it up again, using kitchen twine. Lard with the bacon, and season well with salt and pepper. Melt the butter in a braising pan, and fry the heart over high heat, browning it on all sides. Add the onion and soup vegetables, and fry briefly with the heart. Boil up the juices in the pan with the red wine, add the stock, and season with thyme and marjoram. Braise for about 1½ hours, covered. At the end of this time, take out the heart and keep it hot. Put the liquid in the pan through a strainer, add the soured cream, and season the sauce to taste with salt and pepper. Carve the heart into slices, and serve with the sauce and boiled potatoes.

Offal

Traditionally, the Bavarians have always eaten in the way recommended by modern dieticians, taking several small meals spaced out through the day. Breakfast is followed by the mid-morning snack, and then there is room for a small *Voressen*, an appetizing hot dish, between the mid-morning snack and lunch. In the past, Bavarians went to the butcher's or the inn to eat one of the typical delicacies that now feature on the menu of a main meal too, made of the offal of veal, beef, lamb, and pork. The term *Voressen* originally applied only to tripe, the edible stomach lining of cattle or calves.

Offal is low in fat and easily digested, rich in minerals, vitamins, and trace elements (and today, unfortunately, in heavy metals as well), and it contains arachidonic acid, which is good for the heart and the circulation. Before gourmets developed a taste for it, offal had another great advantage – it was inexpensive, and just as nourishing as the far more expensive lean meat.

Classic French cuisine made veal offal a dish fit for the aristocracy, and it was then beyond the reach of the poorer classes. After B.S.E. and the other scandals surrounding meat, the brains of the animals at least are unsaleable, and are thrown away in today's crisis-ridden abattoirs.

Offal includes the brain, tongue, heart, sweetbreads (the thymus gland of calves and lambs), the diaphragm, lungs, liver, spleen, kidneys, tripe, and cows' udders. All these items find their way on to Bavarian plates, although visitors from the North may regard them with some suspicion. The spleen is used for spleen sausage, eaten broiled, coated with breadcrumbs, or in soup. Other specialties are calf sweetbreads, finely sliced lungs in a sweet-sour cream sauce, tripe soup, fried sucking pig, pork or ox liver, kidneys braised with onions, larded calf heart in sauce, sliced ox heart, and brains in breadcrumbs fried in butter.

Cooking with beer

Apfelkücherl in Bierteig
Apple fritters in beer batter
(Illustrated below left)

2 cups/250 g flour
1 cup/250 ml light beer
3 eggs, separated
a pinch of salt
4 small apples
fat for deep frying
2 tbsp sugar, 1 tsp ground cinnamon

Mix the flour, beer, egg yolks, and pinch of salt together, and allow to stand for 15 minutes. Whisk the egg whites until very stiff, and fold into the dough. Peel and core the apples. Cut them into slices about ⅓ in (1 cm) thick, dip the slices in the beer batter, and fry in batches in hot fat until golden brown. Take the fritters out of the fat, and drain briefly on kitchen paper. Keep them warm until all the fritters are cooked. Mix the sugar and cinnamon together, and sprinkle over the apple fritters before serving.

Karpfenfilets in Bierteig
Fillets of carp in beer batter
(Illustrated center)

4 fillets of carp, each weighing 10 oz/300 g
salt and pepper
the juice of 1 lemon
1 cup/150 g flour
⅓ cup/100 ml light beer
2 eggs, separated
flour to coat the fish
fat for deep frying

Wash the carp fillets, pat them dry, season with salt and pepper, and sprinkle with the lemon juice. Allow to stand for 15 minutes. Meanwhile, prepare the batter: mix the flour, beer, egg yolks, and a pinch of salt together, and allow to stand for 15 minutes. Whisk the egg white until very stiff, and fold into the dough. Coat the fillets of carp in flour, shaking off any excess. Dip the fillets in the batter. Deep fry in the hot fat until golden brown, drain briefly on kitchen paper, and serve with potato salad.

Münchner Biersuppe
Munich beer soup
(Illustrated right)

2 tbsp butter
4 cups/1 liter light beer
salt, pepper, and sugar
½ tsp ground caraway
a pinch of ground nutmeg
the juice of 1 lemon
2 egg yolks
⅓ cup/100 ml cream
4 tbsp croutons

Melt the butter in a pan. Add the beer, season with salt, pepper, a pinch of sugar, caraway, nutmeg, and lemon juice. Bring to a boil, and remove from the heat at once. Whisk the egg yolks with the cream, and stir into the soup. Serve with croutons.

Niederbayerisches Bierfleisch
Lower Bavarian beef in beer
(Illustrated below right)

1½ lb/750 g braising beef
2 tbsp butter
6 oz/150 g raw ham, cut in strips
2 onions, diced
2 tbsp flour
2 cups/500 ml dark beer
salt and pepper
1 tsp dried marjoram
1 bayleaf
2 tbsp chopped parsley
vinegar and sugar to season

Wash the beef, pat it dry, and cut it into cubes. Melt the butter in a casserole, and seal the meat in it. Add the ham and the onions, and brown briefly. Dust with the flour, fry briefly, and add the beer. Season well with salt, pepper, and marjoram. Add the bayleaf, cover the meat, and allow it to simmer for about 45 minutes, until tender. Just before it is done, stir in 1 tbsp parsley, and season with vinegar and sugar for a piquant flavor. Garnish with the rest of the parsley, and serve in the casserole.

Fillets of carp in beer batter

Munich beer soup

Lower Bavarian
beef in beer

Apple fritters in beer
batter

At the Oktoberfest, beer is served in a tankard known as a Masskrug. Those who do not like cold beer can order a beer warmer filled with hot water.

Snuff

"She kept a snuffbox in much state, 'Twas carved by Frederick the Great, Of walnut wood, a pretty toy, And it was all her pride and joy." So wrote the satirist Joachim Ringelnatz in a humorous poem. Whether Frederick the Great ever found time for woodcarving or not, he was certainly an enthusiastic snuff taker, and he was not alone in this habit. Noblemen, diplomats, clergymen, and even ladies never went out without their snuffboxes in the 18th century. Snuff went out of fashion among the upper classes in the 19th century, but the habit persisted for some time in country areas. Although only two firms out of the hundreds who used to manufacture this form of tobacco in Bavaria are still in business, to this day you may see men in an inn taking a pinch of the snuff they call *Schmalzer*. This name for snuff was coined because it used to be mixed with *Schmalz*, meaning in Bavarian *Butterschmalz*, melted butter, although that is no longer the custom. Snuff is now made from different tobaccos, fermented in various ways, dried and crumbled to a fine texture, and enriched with aromatic substances.

The inns of Bavaria

When summer comes, and with it the visitors who bring such prosperity to the Bavarians, quite a number of the people of Munich feel tempted to paint their arms with the word "Hofbräuhaus" – "Hofbräu" on the forearm, "haus" to complete the word on the upper arm. Then, when yet another Japanese or American visitor approaches to ask the way to that famous establishment, they only have to stretch out their arms and point.

In spite of all the city's other attractions, the most popular place in Munich for sightseers is an inn, even though it does not offer any culinary miracles, nor is it particularly comfortable, and it is certainly not frequented by a representative cross-section of the city's population. Critics claim that the Bavarians sitting there traditionally clad in lederhosen and hats with tufts of chamois hair are paid by the brewery as "extras."

In its early years, the Hofbräuhaus was not open to everyone. As the name suggests, it was the court brewery, serving beer only to employees of the court. This was in line with the decisions of Duke Wilhelm V, who feared the anger of the Munich brewers; they occupied a powerful position in the city, and were not keen to see competition. Beer-drinking had regained popularity in the 16th century, replacing expensive imported wine as the beverage of the upper classes. The upper classes of the time obtained their "barley wine" from Einbeck in Hanover, but that entailed considerable expense, since the Bavarian court consumed 442 casks of winter beer and 1443 casks of summer beer – a cask contained about 60 "measures."

A measure was 1 liter (4 cups) of beer. The idea that the Bavarians really do have a whole liter of beer served in a tankard, and drink it, and even order another, is certainly one of the attractions drawing foreigners on pilgrimage to the Hofbräuhaus. They may not be aware that Bavarian *Helle*, "light," a pale ale with an alcohol content of 2–3.5 percent, is not particularly strong, and the full measure is hardly ever served anyway. Of course that is illegal, and customers could protest, but hardly any do, for the drinker who insists on his rights must expect the waitress to slam down his beer and food so ungraciously that he will not enjoy his visit to the inn, which spoils the point of it. You go to a bar mainly for relaxation, you want something to eat, or just something to drink, you want to play cards, or talk to friends at your regular table, or *Stammtisch*. The *Stammtisch* is an even more popular institution in Bavaria than in the rest of Germany; 38 percent of the population frequent a *Stammtisch* in Bavaria, while in this respect Berlin comes last in the whole of Germany, scoring only 14 percent.

Art or kitsch? The tankards from which Bavarians drink their beer have always attracted attention. "The Bavarians cannot make their drinking cups large or strange enough. They drink to one another out of apes and clerics, monks and nuns, bears and owls, even the Devil himself," wrote a chronicler in 1589. Above: an attractive selection from the 20th century, including a Jugendstil tankard (below center).

Complaint of a tavern roll

"Not every roll has as difficult an existence as those of us sold in taverns. A private roll, for instance, is bought from the baker, taken home, and usually eaten at once. But we tavern *Semmeln*, along with our colleagues, the rolls known as *Weckerln* and *Loabeln*, and small household loaves, generally suffer a miserable existence before the guests consume us.

The city council did once spare a thought for our welfare, and put little notices up in every tavern reading: "No feeling the food before you purchase." But no one takes any notice of that now. As if it weren't bad enough to be put straight into the crematorium for baking as soon as we are shaped out of flour and water, once we are done we are carted away in delivery baskets by inexperienced bakers' boys, those baskets are flung roughly into vans, and we poor rolls race off at 60 km an hour to the restaurant or inn where, supposedly, we will be eaten the same day. ... The cashiers (who used to be waitresses) put us into bread baskets early in the day, and place us on the tables. Now comes the hygienic treatment to which we are subjected! The Bliemchen family arrives from Saxony, coming straight in from the railroad station for an early bite to eat. They all sit down, and Frau Bliemchen happens to take me out of the basket, pushes in my ribcage, says to her husband, 'Ooh, look at this, Gustav, just feel that roll, feel how soft it is! They don't bake nice crisp bread here in Bavaria, not like we bake it in Leipzig.'

Herr Bliemchen was unable to press me at once, since he was blowing his nose at the time, and only when he has put away his handkerchief does he pick me up, squeeze me until I almost resemble a pancake, and return me to the bread basket, remarking, 'You're quite right, Pauline dear, all the other rolls seem to be soft too' – for he is checking them, squeezing roll after roll. So there we lie in the basket, all our ribcages broken."

(Karl Valentin, from "Complaint of a Tavern Roll")

Green gold

In late September and early October, when visitors coming down from the north to the Oktoberfest drive to Munich along the A9 autobahn, they pass through a remarkably attractive part of the countryside about an hour before reaching the Bavarian capital. Hundreds of tall, thin poles tower into the sky here, as if to prevent a squadron of U.F.O.s from landing. Newcomers may assume they are for growing genetically mutated giant beans, until they realize that they are driving through the Holledau, the largest hop-growing area in the world. This "green gold" is grown in the Holledau on an area of around 965 square miles (2500 square kilometers). All other hop-growing areas, naturally, pale beside it, although they too contribute to Germany's reputation for growing hops of the finest quality, exported to over 100 countries. In Franconia, hops are cultivated to the south and east of Nuremberg, around Spalt and Hersbruck respectively; they flourish in Baden-Württemberg around Tettnang on Lake Constance, and there are smaller areas of cultivation in the Elbe-Saale region, and the Baden, Bitburg, and Rhineland-Palatinate area.

In the past a cup of hop tea was thought to be a sovereign remedy for gout. The healing power of hops was known in ancient times, and both the Babylonians and the Egyptians were already using them to brew beer. The first recorded mention of the growing of hops in Germany dates from 736, at Geisenfeld in the Holledau area, and a 13th-century document tells us that hops were then being grown in Spalt. At the time, it was townsfolk rather than country people who grew them, and found it a lucrative hobby. As a result, the term *Hopfengarten*, "hop garden," became established even for large hop plantations. Then Duke Wilhelm IV of Bavaria issued his decree regulating the purity of beer, and it gave hops an advantage over all the other aromatic plants that used to be added in brewing beer. Monks were the first to grow hops in the Holledau, where they found optimum conditions here for growing the important ingredient that went into their "liquid fare for fast days": deep soil for the roots, which can grow down 13 feet (4 meters), plenty of sun and rain, not too hot, and valleys offering protection from the wind. More and more hop gardens were laid out in the 19th century in poor areas of forest and marshland, where only sour grapes would grow; improvements in transport made it easier for crops to reach the trading center of Nuremberg. Growers could be sure of demand from the "beer capital" of Munich, and from the large number of Franconian breweries.

Hops improve the keeping quality of beer, clarify it, and give it a decorative, foamy head, its characteristic flavor (either more or less bitter), and a full aroma. Brewers distinguish between

A pleasing sight for beer drinkers: hop plants, seen here in their infancy, will grow and grow.

Hop shoots are a delicacy, but picking them is hard work, and as a result they fetch very high prices.

You need a "feel" for the right place to break off the shoots. Only the upper parts are used in cooking, usually briefly blanched and served as a salad.

Hop shoot salad is a treat that only hop growers can afford; sometimes called "hop asparagus," it is a good deal more expensive than real asparagus.

bitter hops and aromatic hops. The botanical name for the plant, a member of the Cannabaceae family, is *Humulus lupulus*. It is a perennial, potentially productive for up to 20 years, dioecious, and fertilized through dispersal by wind. Although beer is generally considered a man's drink, only female hop plants are used, but their umbels must remain unfertilized, so all male wild hop plants growing near the hop gardens are grubbed up. Propagation is vegetative, done by grafting. It is the substance known as lupulin that interests brewers; this golden yellow powder is shed from glands at the base of the umbels.

Hops used to be grown up poles, but they are cultivated on a larger scale today. Wire netting is stretched over wooden posts 23 feet (7 meters) tall, 165 of them to 2½ acres (1 hectare). This structure is anchored to the ground at the side with steel cables, for it must withstand not only wind and storms but also the weight of the hop plants, which can amount to 40 tonnes per hectare (16 tons per acre) just before harvest.

Until then, however, there is an agricultural saying to the effect that "the hop likes to see its master daily." The work of cultivation begins in March, when the tops of last year's plants are cut down and cleared away (mechanically these days). It becomes very labor-intensive from the end of April, when training wires have to be fixed to the netting above and anchored to the ground below. Each plant may put out up to 60 shoots, and only two or three are trained to twine clockwise up the wires. This work still has to be done by hand, and a Polish labor force is often employed. The other shoots are pruned away, also by hand. The soil is frequently hoed and fertilized over the following weeks, and the plants sprayed against disease and pests.

Toward the end of August, the hops are at their best for the brewers' purposes: the wires, with their heavy load, are cut from underneath, pulled away from the netting at the top of the structure, and taken off to the hop-picking machine that carefully separates the leaves and stems from the precious umbels of flowers. The high water content of the hops is then reduced to about twelve percent during a period of some six hours in the drying kiln. They will now keep well, and can be put into sacks, to await further treatment.

Long-term agreements with buyers give the hop-growing firms in the Holledau security, and they have a certain percentage not ordered in advance with which they can speculate. However, growers do not pray just for good prices, but to be spared hailstorms. Insurance is expensive. Their prayers are addressed to the Virgin Mary, and to the martyr St Castulus, revered as the patron saint of the Holledau. In the old days, his aid was also requested by the famous (or notorious) "Hallertau horse thieves" in whom the locals take secret pride today, celebrating their deeds in song – this was at a time when the people of the Holledau were still described as paupers, and long before the green gold of hops brought them prosperity.

Hop pickers

The Holledau region is still full of the strong fragrance of the hops at harvest time, as it was in the past, and the roads are livelier than usual, for the landscape changes daily as the luxuriant hop bines wither, gradually falling from the bare poles.

But there is something missing from this picture: hop pickers. Once picking machines came into general use in the Holledau at the end of the 1950s, they became superfluous. There were still around 140,000 seasonal workers picking hops in 1953, but by 1958 only 6000 were required. For almost a century they had come from near and far, from big cities, from as far away as the Ruhr, sometimes in whole families. They worked hard for a bare three weeks, getting free board and lodging in return for a chance to earn something on the side, laboring from dawn to dusk, seated on stools in the middle of the harvested bines in the hop gardens, constantly picking the umbels into a basket. Shelters often had to be erected to protect them from the weather, the rough texture of the plants made their hands sore, their cramped backs ached, and at night all they could do was fall into bed. We may doubt whether,

after a day of such hard labor, they made as merry in their improvised communal quarters as legend would have us believe. Experienced hop pickers like to recall how someone would sometimes play the concertina, before they were all overcome by weariness. And before going to bed they were paid their day's earnings in the form of metal tokens for each *Metzen* – a container of umbels holding a volume of 60 liters (13 gallons). The tokens were exchanged for cash at the end of the hop harvest. Then, holding the last bine aloft on a pole, they went merrily off to the farm, the girls and draft animals often crowned with hops.

Once payment had been made, the women of the house served a lavish harvest festival meal, usually roast pork and cabbage, and there would be great celebrations, with music, singing, and dancing. An average agricultural region in the Holledau, with a hop-growing area of about 19 acres (7.86 hectares), can bring in the harvest within about ten days, with the help of machines and only four or five workers – it would take twice as long with 120 manual workers as hop pickers. Immigrant laborers, mainly from Poland, are in demand today only to train the young shoots up their wires in spring, for this work still has to be done by hand.

At hop festival time, the bines are torn down from the wires as they were in the old days …

… when hop pickers removed the umbels. Today, machines do the same work in a fraction of the time.

This is the precious substance, lupulin, a golden yellow powder formed in the female umbel.

Holledau hops are exported worldwide. A special seal guarantees their quality and place of origin.

Liquid bread

There are two important dates in the history of German beer: the years 1516 and 1987. Both mark events connected with the purity regulations that make German beer famous all over the world and guarantee its quality. These regulations originated in Bavaria, the land of beer *par excellence*. In Ingolstadt in 1516, Duke Wilhelm IV issued a decree stating that: "It is our express desire that from henceforth, in our towns, our markets, and in the country, nothing should be used in the making of beer except barley, hops, and water alone."

Barley, hops, and water: these were to be the sole ingredients of beer made in Germany. So it is still, and so it will remain, despite the judgment of 12 March 1987 reversing the ruling, when German brewers took their case to the European Court of Justice – and came away defeated. The goddess Justitia and the E.U. had poured scorn on their beer, and Germany was told that imports of beer not brewed according to the purity regulations in force in the Federal Republic itself must be permitted.

Heated discussions at many a *Stammtisch* in German inns ended with general agreement that anyone drinking "this imported rubbish" – for instance, Belgian beers made with cherries, strawberries, coriander, sugar, or honey! – had only himself to blame for any ill effects. The 28

gallons (127.4 liters) statistically consumed by every German in 1998 came as a rule from the beer drinker's own locality, and few of the country's breweries (over 1300 in all) distribute outside their local areas. Most of the country's breweries (about 700) are in Bavaria anyway, and Franconia occupies a special position, with around 500 private breweries there, 250 of them still family firms. The region around Bamberg has a denser concentration of breweries than anywhere else on earth. As for tastes in beer, the nation is clearly divided: Pils dominates the north of Germany, while light, dark, and export brews are preferred in the south. The strongholds of top-fermented beers are in Berlin (*Berliner Weiss*), Düsseldorf (*Alt*), Cologne (*Kölsch*), Leipzig (*Gose*), and Bavaria (*Weissbier*, "white beer").

Weissbier, "white beer," is a Bavarian specialty. It is a top-fermented brew made from malted wheat and barley, and served in special *Weissbier* glasses.

Kölsch, brewed by the top-fermented method, is drunk from tall glasses called *Stangen*, literally "sticks," served from a *Kranz* (literally "garland"), a special tray.

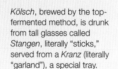

Düsseldorf is famous for the brew known as *Altbier*, "old beer," a top-fermented, dark, bitter beer, with a strong hop flavor. It is drunk from thin glasses.

The return to small-scale brewing

Germany has 1283 commercially registered breweries; in 1998 they produced the considerable quantity of 2457 million gallons (111.7 million hectoliters) of beer. However, the quantity is decreasing; the figure in 1997 was 2525 million gallons (114.8 million hectoliters). Only 51 of these firms brewed over half a million hectoliters; 715 produced less than 110,000 gallons (5000 hectoliters).

The number of these small breweries has been steadily increasing in recent years; the figure in 1994 was 625.

This figure illustrates an obvious trend. In many parts of Germany small-scale breweries operating in the old style have been set up, and the process continues. Sometimes they even use the old vats and traditional implements. Specialties of small local breweries include "eco-beer," made with organically grown hops and malt, and natural, unclarified beer. Some small breweries combine both kinds. An example is the Rathsbräu of Wiesbaden where, as in many other similar small breweries, beers to suit the season are brewed over a couple of months or so. The fine particles of yeast and protein left behind by the brewing process of natural, unclarified beer give a full and satisfying flavor.

Are there disadvantages? Well, the yeast residue can start a secondary fermentation, particularly in the bottle, which would impair flavor, and there is a danger that the beer will go off or be too fizzy. Unclarified beer does not keep well, either, and must be drunk within two weeks, preferably on the premises where it was brewed. Filtered beer, on the other hand, will keep for four to six weeks, and filtered and pasteurized beer will keep for a year.

Pilsner (or Pils) is one of the most popular beers in Germany. This fine bitter must be drawn very carefully into a tall, narrow glass.

The beer tankard known as a Masskrug holds a liter of beer – the usual quantity in which it is drunk in Bavaria.

For those who cannot drink quite so much, the Bavarians also have a half-liter glass in which they serve '"light" beer, which is a pale ale.

405

Hops (left) give the beer its aroma. The barley must be malted before brewing begins.

The quality of the beer also depends on the water in which the crushed malt is slowly heated.

The art of brewing

The Bavarians would like everyone to assume that the art of brewing beer actually originated under the blue and white flag of the Free State of Bavaria. But there is archeological evidence to the contrary; finds from ancient Mesopotamia show that beer already existed in around 4000 B.C. Traces of mash have been found in the remains of pottery vessels. Very probably this great liquid discovery was made by the Babylonian civilizations, and with even greater probability the discovery was made by chance, when someone was baking bread and the flour or the bread became damp, at some point beginning to ferment – so it is really quite appropriate to call beer, brewed as it is from barley, "liquid bread."

It is a long way from the pottery vessel to computer-operated brewing, but the principle has hardly changed. The brewing process still consists of starting fermentation by mixing hops, yeast, malt, and water together, and stopping the fermentation again at the right moment. So much for the theory; the practice is much more complicated. A high degree of expert knowledge and craftsmanlike skill is necessary for the brewing of good beer.

First, the crushed malt has to be mixed with water in the brewing room, and then heated to various temperatures in the mash tub. In the process the components of the malted mash liquefy, and their enzymes are activated. The malting and mashing of the grain exposes its starchy part, and at around 140 °F (60 °C) the malting enzyme begins to break the starch down, producing sugar which will ferment.

Now the mash is put in the clarifying vat, containing a kind of sieve on which the insoluble particles, or "draff," are deposited. They act as natural filters through which the beer wort passes, clarifying it. The wort now runs off into the brewing vat, where it is boiled with the addition of hops. The more hops, the more bitter the flavor; the fewer hops, the sweeter and maltier the beer will taste.

After boiling the wort for one or two hours, the brewer is left with the right concentration of extracts, the "original wort." These extracts are the maltose and protein substances. Then the wort runs through a hop sieve, and is clarified and cooled. The cooled wort now runs off into the fermentation vats, and only at this point is the

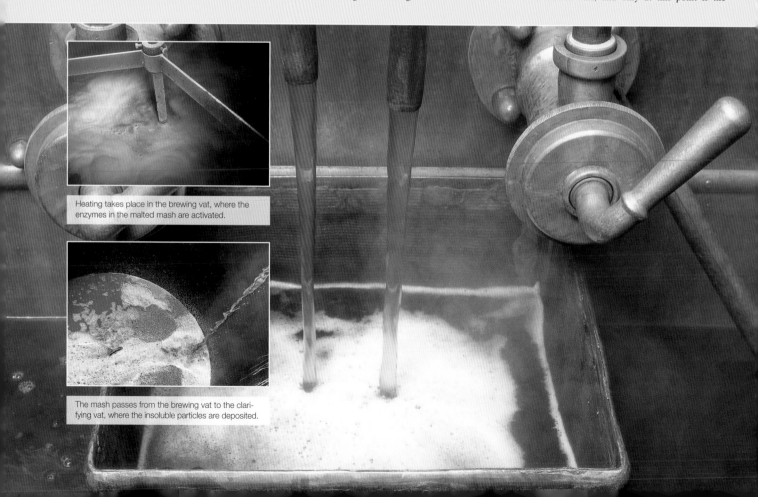

Heating takes place in the brewing vat, where the enzymes in the malted mash are activated.

The mash passes from the brewing vat to the clarifying vat, where the insoluble particles are deposited.

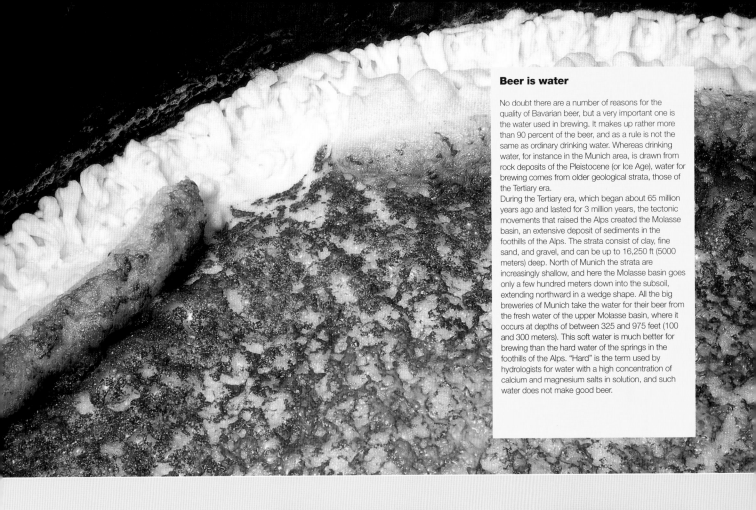

yeast added. Its function is to turn the maltose into alcohol and carbon dioxide.

In the process, the carbonic acid peculiar to beer develops; it is this carbonic acid that creates the head in the beer glass. Fermentation with bottom-fermenting yeast (which settles on the bottom of the vessel, hence the name) takes about eight days, and with top-fermenting yeast that rises to the top, fermentation lasts about five days. The young beer must now be stored and continue fermenting for some weeks to mature.

All breweries follow this basic method today, and they all make beer in the same way, but no one brewery's beer is exactly like another – and that is where the art of brewing lies.

A sample is taken during clarification, to test the content of the beer wort.

A buoyant gauge shows the content of the original wort (the amount of maltose and protein substances in it.)

Opposite: after clarification, the filtrate is returned to the brewing vat and boiled up with the hops.

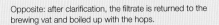

Above: yeast working on the beer in an open wooden vat in the Rathsbräu in Wiesbaden.

Cooling: the wort is cooled to 43 °F (6 °C), and then fermented in fermentation vessels in the cellars.

The equipment of the Rathsbräu in Wiesbaden: cooler at the back, filtration vat in the middle, brewing vat in front.

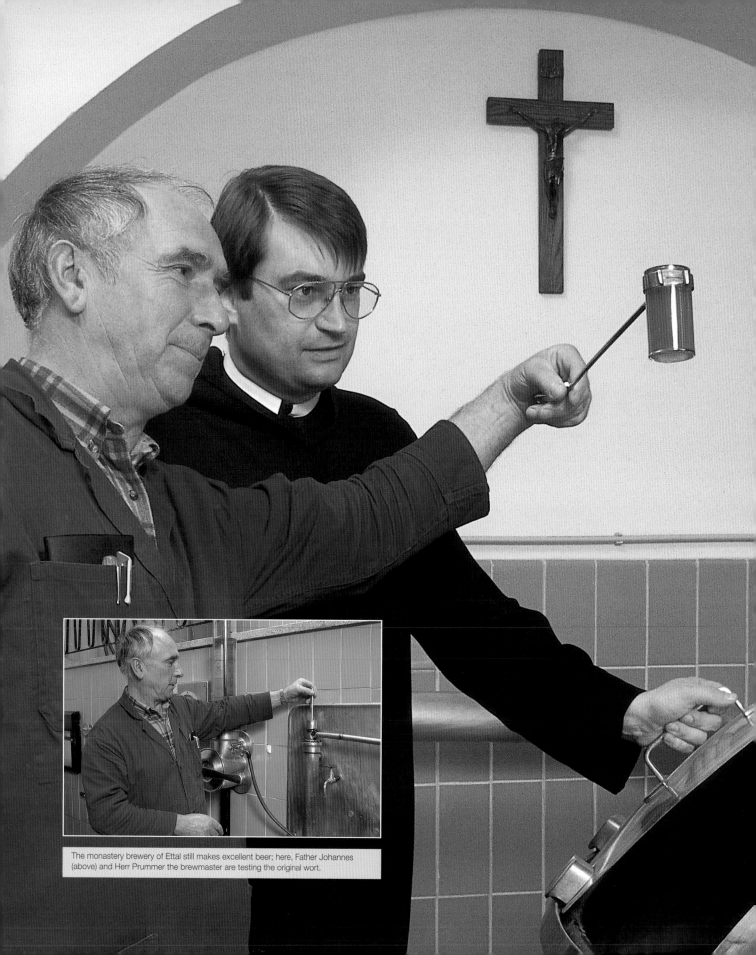

The monastery brewery of Ettal still makes excellent beer; here, Father Johannes (above) and Herr Prummer the brewmaster are testing the original wort.

Brewing and fasting

The art of brewing beer has very close connections with the monasteries in Bavaria. The first Bavarian breweries were run by monks, particularly monks of the Benedictine order. Brewing rights belonged to the sovereign, who granted them first to the church, later to the nobility as well. The first brewery of which there are official records was at the Benedictine monastery of St Gall, which began making beer in the middle of the 9th century. The oldest monastery brewery to make beer commercially was at Weihenstephan, for in the year 1040 the bishop of Freising granted the pious brothers of that establishment not only the right to brew beer, but permission to sell their products. Soon after this date more and more monasteries acquired brewing rights; one was the monastery of Benediktbeuren, granted such rights in 1048. The oldest brewery still in business under monastic management is at the monastery of Weltenburg, founded in the year 1050.

Beer, regarded today as the monastic beverage *par excellence*, one that could be enjoyed even on fasting days as "liquid bread," was not always the usual drink of the devout brethren. The Benedictine Rule at any rate – and it is the oldest of the rules of the various orders – speaks not of beer but of wine. At the time it was drawn up, wine was as natural a part of the daily diet of the servants of God as salt in their soup. Beer probably gained ground as the staple monastic drink because wine became too expensive. Transport costs in particular were high, and the quality of the wine itself suffered from long journeys.

The monastery beers rightly esteemed today were not particularly strong and intoxicating in the early history of brewing. Far from it: the monks made their beer almost exclusively from oats, which produces a rather poor, weak brew. Not until the 13th century did barley become established, leading to an improvement in the quality of beer, but also to a temporary decline in the fortunes of the breweries. Yields of barley were small, prices shot up, and beer sales declined sharply. Viticulture profited from this development, and again it was the monks who were the viticulturists. They grew grapes and made wine partly on their estates on the Danube between Kehlheim and Regensburg, and on the Isar at Landshut, partly on their estates in winegrowing areas such as Franconia, Austria, and the Tyrol.

Only when winegrowing began seriously to suffer from the depredations of war and from climatic change, and imports became too expensive, was there a revival in the brewing of beer (i.e. from the 15th century onward).

The rulers of states, who made a profit from charges on beer, also took an interest in the way it was made and what went into it. This was the background to the famous purity regulations of the year 1516, when Duke Wilhelm IV of Bavaria decreed that beer must contain nothing but barley, hops, and water.

Monastic liqueurs

One tends to associate liqueurs with elderly ladies who enjoying a little nip or so with their afternoon coffee – or by the fireside in the evening, if they happen to be characters in an English detective story. It is rather difficult to imagine those more masculine figures the monks sipping such sweet confections, their lips pursed. Yet liqueur making, like brewing and fish farming, was an art developed and perfected in the monasteries. Monks and nuns were educated people; they knew how to grow herbs and use them medicinally. They also knew that the ethereal oils of plants will dissolve in pure alcohol, so that their medicinal effects will develop, and they had mastered the art of distillation. Herbal essences in alcohol were used in homeopathic dosages at the time – and at some point, to make the bitter medicine palatable, sweetening must have been added, and the liqueur was created. Even today a special mixture of herbs, such as the monk in the picture below is expertly putting together, is the mark of a good monastic liqueur – and of course the devout brothers keep it a strict secret.

The monastery of Ettal was founded in the 14th century. During the Baroque period it was renovated, and then rebuilt after a fire. The church is among the finest Baroque buildings in Bavaria.

The holes in the cheese

"Ma, how do the holes get into the cheese?" A little boy in a revue sketch by Kurt Tucholsky sets a whole evening party in uproar with this question. "Well, the holes in the cheese, that's to do with the way it's made," claims the boy's father. "People make cheese out of butter and milk, and it ferments, and then it gets damp." The child's uncle says the holes are due to the casein, someone else says the cheese stretches too fast in the warmth of fermentation, yet another guest thinks that "the cheese shrinks during fermentation."

The company, now engaged in lively argument, goes to look up the question in an encyclopedia, but the page with the entry on cheese happens to be missing. The ensuing disputes lead to protestations that certain members of the party have been insulted, and people threaten to change their wills. "No one is left on stage but a sad Emmental cheese and a little boy raising his plump arms to heaven and, in a tone that seems to accuse the universe itself, shouting out loud, 'But Ma! How *do* the holes get into the cheese?'"

Let us answer that question straight away: the holes in Emmental cheese are made by propionibacteria added to the cheese, which create

gas during the maturing process. However, this is only one of the many possible methods of making rennet cheeses. Rennet cheeses are those which, unlike cheeses made with sour milk, have rennet, a substance usually derived from the stomachs of calves, added as a starter to curdle the milk. There are four main stages in the making of rennet cheeses:

Stage one is to curdle the milk. In the process, the protein casein contained in the milk coagulates by the action of acids. This spontaneous coagulation is controlled by adding rennet to the warm milk. Coagulation can begin at 68 °F (20 °C), and the subsequent curdling will take between 30 minutes and 36 hours, depending on the cheese.

The result is a coagulated mass, which is cut into small pieces with a cutter, the "cheese harp," to make the curd. The harder a cheese is to be, the smaller the pieces must be. Now the whey, which has not been skimmed, is drawn off, and the curd is ground or milled. The process of draining can be accelerated by pressing. If soft cheese is to be made from the mixture of curds and whey, it is treated very carefully; if the end product is to be a hard cheese, the mixture is heated and milled. Then the cheese is poured into molds, pressed if necessary, and regularly turned, together with the mold.

The third stage is the salting and washing of the cheese. Salting, whether brine or dry salt is used, accelerates the drying process, helps to form the rind, and intensifies the aroma. Since salt inhibits

attack by harmful microorganisms, the cheese will keep better when salted. Depending on the kind of cheese, the process takes between two and four days. Again depending on the cheese, the salt content of brine used will vary between 9 oz (250 g) and 12 oz (350 g) per 4 cups (1 liter) of water. In the last stage, the cheese rests in drying rooms, and any liquid evaporates through the rind. The cheeses are turned regularly. The maturing process itself takes place in cellars at a constant temperature of about 54 °F (12 °C), with a humidity of 75–78 per cent. Again, the length of time maturing takes varies according to the kind of cheese.

Depending on the way they are made, rennet cheeses are subdivided into soft cheeses, semi-soft cheeses, and hard cheeses. Soft cheeses have a high water content and a smooth consistency. They are nearly all small in size, and do not usually take long to mature. Soft cheeses have a characteristic rind, subdivided again into white mold cheeses and washed-rind cheeses. In semi-soft cheeses, the water content is much lower, and their consistency is the result of more whey being pressed out. Hard cheeses spend a long time maturing and thus lose much of their liquid. During the maturing process, hard cheeses can absorb a number of different aromatic substances.

Making cheese in the Alm; morning and evening milk are mixed together.

The milk is gradually heated in the cheese pan to 122 °F (50 °C).

Rennet powder, dissolved in milk, is added to curdle the milk.

Once the coagulated milk has set, it is cut with a "cheese harp."

The curd hangs above the pan to let some of the whey drain off.

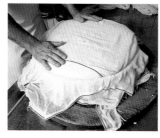
The cheese is wrapped in several large cloths.

The draining of the whey is accelerated in the cheese press.

The cheese is dated, and is left in brine for several days to salt it.

Say "cheese"

The history of cheese goes back to ancient times: presumably someone once left milk in a warm place, and it turned into a solidified curd of sour milk cheese. And at some point, a hunter will have discovered about the action of rennet from observing the stomach of a young ruminant that had just been suckling its mother's milk. There is evidence that cheese was made over 5000 years ago in Mesopotamia, the Land of the Two Rivers. The Greeks and Romans enjoyed cheese, and the Celts, who were knowledgeable cattle breeders, already had a well developed tradition of cheesemaking. Cheese was eaten regularly at the court of Charlemagne, and the Gelchenwang alpine pasture in the Gunzesried valley was supplying cheese to the Franconian court at Kempten as early as 820. Payment of dues in kind, in the form of cheese, was made for centuries to ecclesiastical or noble lords of the manor.

Monastic life had a great influence on the development of cheese making, particularly in Germany. Old monastery accounts and cellarers' records show exactly how important a part cheese played in the diet. Village cooperatives made cheeses that began to differ from valley to valley at an early date. In the Alpine regions, the monasteries hired out cheese-making pans to the mountain peasants, and were paid in an agreed quantity of cheese. In 1400, the monastery of St Gall received 5000 cheeses on this basis, and developed their cheeses into a considerable industry. Under Duke Wilhelm V (1579–1597), "cheese in the Parmesan style" was already being made in Bavaria. Maximilian, Elector of Bavaria, even brought cheese experts from Switzerland and Lorraine to Bavaria.

Often, influences from outside helped the cheesemakers of Germany to develop their methods. Dutch cheesemakers were involved in creating what is probably the best known of German cheeses, Tilsit. It owes its name to the town of Tilsit on the Memel, founded by the German Order in 1406. Limburg cheese too has a long tradition behind it; even in the time of Charlemagne, it was an established item on German menus. A cheese with a milder flavor is the Romadur red cheese. In Bavaria *Weisslack* cheese is very popular; it is a strong-flavored, rectangular cheese with a hard rind, also known as "beer cheese."

Bavaria is the biggest cheese producing region in Germany. The major dairy farming region of the Allgäu, sometimes called "the cheese-making dairy of Germany," produces about 11,000 tons of cheese a week. Since total production in the Federal German Republic is around 30,000 tons a week, this is a good third of it. Lower Saxony comes second, with about 7000 tons a week. The hills and pastures of Upper Bavaria and the Allgäu offer ideal conditions for dairy farming – and a cheese is only as good as the milk that goes into it. In turn, the quality of the milk depends on the grass eaten by the cows. Up to 50 plant species can grow in a meadow left in its natural condition, and an old pasture will give cheese a fuller flavor and aroma. In addition, pastures containing many plant species provide milk for cheese that keeps well, and the Emmental cheese of the Allgäu is famous for its quality. A whole Emmental (a hard cheese) weighs 176–198 pounds (80 to 90 kilograms). Its little brother, Allgäu mountain cheese, weighs only 44–66 pounds (20–30 kilograms), and is made exclusively of summer milk, which gives it its pure, mild flavor.

The curds are lifted out of the cheese pan in a cloth.

A year-old cheese stored in a cellar on the Mitterhaus alpine pasture.

411

Farming in the mountain pastures

The mountain huts set so picturesquely in this landscape, offering hospitality to walkers and skiers, might be taken for the inspired idea of some clever promoter of the tourist industry. Not so: alpine farming is thousands of years old, and originally must have been the only way that human beings could survive in the Alps. Some of the mountain dwellers in their remote farms were self-sufficient until well into the 20th century, and to be self-sufficient they had to use a very short growing season to produce all the food they would need for the winter – a very long one in this area. They worked on several levels: crops were grown in the small, intensively farmed valleys, while the wide slopes higher up were used for stock rearing and dairy farming. Some of the farmhands would take the cattle up to the high pastures and stay there with them for 100 to 120 days in summer, before returning to the farmstead.

Until the end of the Middle Ages the mountain farmers mainly kept sheep and goats, animals that cope well with the bleak climatic conditions of the Alps. There were only a few cattle. Milk was processed up in the pastures, usually in the form of sour milk cheese, which can be easily and profitably made from small quantities of milk.

The 14th and 15th centuries brought change into the traditional methods of mountain farming. At this time the population was increasing, towns were growing, and the agricultural areas around them concentrated on arable crops. Stock breeding and dairy farming were banished to more remote areas, which in turn restricted their own arable farming in order to supply increased demand for cheese. However, only rennet cheeses would keep and travel well, while maintaining their high quality, and equipment in addition to expert knowledge were needed to make such cheeses. As a result, it was mainly the alpine pastures owned by noblemen and monasteries that turned to commercial production.

In the Allgäu, now the major cheese producing area of Germany, cheese-making on a large scale began relatively late. The farmers there practiced arable farming and cattle rearing mainly to supply their own needs, and to pay their rent. For centuries, the major source of income was growing flax and making linen, but this epoch ended in the late 18th century, with the invention of mechanical looms. The region would have lapsed into dire poverty had not certain forward-looking minds imported experts from Switzerland and Holland, to produce Limburg and Emmental cheese. Within 50 years much arable land had been put down to grass, particularly in the south Swabian region, and dairy farming became the leading agricultural industry. The experts were men – typical wherever rennet cheeses were produced for sale – and consequently they took over the dairy work that had traditionally belonged in the women's domain. Even today, men predominate as *Senner* (the local word for dairymen and stockmen) on the alpine pastures of the Allgäu, but in Upper Bavaria two thirds of the 700 or so mountain farms are run by women.

A characteristic feature of the old mountain huts is the open fireplace in the living room, with a movable wooden arm over it from which the big cheese pan hangs. Hay was stored in the loft, in case of early snowfalls, and the cowherds often slept there. When they brought the cheese down from the mountains at the end of the season, they carried it over difficult terrain on stretchers; otherwise, the cheeses were brought down on a "snail," a cross between a sleigh and a cart.

Until the end of the 18th century and the beginning of the 19th, cheese was only made up in the mountain pastures, but later, when clover and lucerne were introduced, there was a huge increase in the growing of fodder crops in the valleys. More cows could now be kept on the same area, milk production rose, and the milk had to be processed. Cheese-making firms were set up in the valleys in the middle of the 19th century. In the end, the cheesemakers of the mountain pastures could not stand up to the competition, and most of the *Sennalpen* became *Galtalpen*, alpine pastures grazed mainly by young cattle.

Although cheese made in the mountains may have lost its economic importance, mountain farming is still an important agricultural industry in Upper Bavaria, particularly in the Allgäu. In the southern Upper Allgäu, over half of all agricultural land is mountain pasture. The highlands of the Upper Allgäu extend from 2000 feet (622 meters) on the northern state border to a height of 8690 feet (2649 meters) at the Hochfrottspitze. Every year in the summer months, about 25,000 head of young cattle, 2900 cows, 1000 ewes and 100 horses are driven up to 610 alpine pastures in all, to spend some 100 days there. In the area itself, people distinguish between low-lying pastures, up to 3280 feet (1000 meters), medium-lying pastures at 3280–4595 feet (1000–1400 meters), and high-lying pastures at over 4595 feet (1400 meters), which are grazed progressively upward as the summer proceeds.

There are good reasons why the animals are still driven up to the mountain pastures: the higher the grass grows, the better its quality. The plants of the upper meadows have a higher protein and fat content, and are more nourishing and more easily digested. Alpine animals do not grow as fat as those kept in the valleys, but young animals that have grown up on the mountain pastures develop more resistance to disease, and are in general fit and strong: on the open meadows where cattle can move about freely, an animal will walk about 6 miles (10 kilometers) a day as a rule. It has been calculated that during grazing over a period of 100 days in the Friederalm area, on the southern slopes of the Kauner range, animals will cover a distance of 745 miles (1200 kilometers). So it is not surprising that on the colorful occasion of their return to the valleys, the cattle may look lean but will be bursting with vitality.

Mountain pastures like the Mitterhaus still have an important part to play in the Allgäu and Upper Bavaria.

Opposite: the cows are decorated to be driven down from pasture.

The flax flower pattern in this butter mold, which is almost a hundred years old, reminds us that the Allgäu was once mainly devoted to growing flax and making linen.

Cabbage and root vegetables

"Bavaria goes its own free way, spooning in cabbage twice a day, two a day, all through the year, make seven hundred and thirty, I swear!" wrote the poetic cobbler Hans Sachs of Nuremberg in the 16th century. Whether the Bavarian love of cabbage really has anything to do with the freedom of the Free State itself is questionable. More probably, in Bavaria as in other parts of Germany, cabbage and turnips were the staple vegetables of the poor before the introduction of the potato. "Cabbage" usually means sauerkraut, and it needs the addition of something to enrich it, often smoked belly of pork (*Wammerl*), pork, or fried sausages. With such accompaniments, cabbage in the form of sauerkraut is the one vegetable that Bavarians will traditionally tolerate on their plates.

Unterpleichfeld, north of Würzburg, has long been the leading producer of the Bavarians' favorite vegetable – 321 acres (130 hectares) of white cabbage are grown and prepared for sale here, and almost as much "blue cabbage," as red cabbage is known locally. Among other specialties of the region are the *Kümmerli*, also grown in Lower Bavaria: these small gherkins are pickled from July onward, and can also be made into a favorite cold summer soup. Onions are grown on a large scale around Landshut, and Forchheim on the western border of Franconian Switzerland (a region in the north of the Franconian Jura) is a center for the growing of horseradish, which the Franconians like to eat with their fried sausages as an alternative to mustard. Franconian *Krenweiberl*, horseradish women, still come to Munich today to supply the state capital with horseradish. It is obvious around Schweinfurt that parsley, in the Franconian dialect *Peterla*, adds something extra to dishes other than just boiled potatoes and soups. In this part of the country, Schwebheim in particular finds a market for its culinary and medicinal herbs, and *Petersilienplootz* (parsley tart,) a variant on the ever popular onion tart, was created here.

Beside such everyday pleasures, the Bavarian countryside can provide for more sophisticated tastes: Schrobenhausen in the west of the hop-growing Holledau area is famous for its asparagus, and at Volkach, where the Main describes a large curve, its tender spears occupy around 680 acres (275 hectares). It goes well with the wine produced on the nearby slopes. The "garlic country" near Nuremberg, Dürer's native city, also provides Fürth and Erlangen with asparagus, and has always been a region for growing almost all vegetable varieties, although the nickname "garlic country" is rather misleading, for the aromatic bulb itself is mainly imported today. Nor must Kitzingen be forgotten as an area where vegetables have long been grown both in the open and under glass; traditionally, it supplies not only Munich, but also Berlin, and even sends vegetables as far as Sweden. Every other radish of the many eaten for *Brotzeit*, the classic Bavarian snack, has been grown in Kitzingen.

Scorzonera
(Illustrated right)

Franconia has a long tradition of the intensive cultivation of special crops: even in the 12th century, writers referred to it as a market gardening area. At quite an early date the mild climate here, particularly in the valley of the Main, enabled market gardeners to harvest two or three crops of different vegetable species a year from the same land. Several varieties were grown in the same bed. A favorite vegetable was, and indeed still is, scorzonera, which will keep well stored in a winter bed. Scorzonera, sometimes called "winter asparagus," has an aromatic, astringent flavor, and is very rich in protein. However, preparing it is tedious: you have to scrape or peel the roots to remove the dark brown outer layer. The juice that oozes out oxydizes very quickly, and if the roots are not immediately put into water to which vinegar has been added, they will discolor and turn brown.

Home-grown and imported vegetables are always in season in the Munich Victuals Market.

Scorzonera can be grown in your own garden. It likes deep, rich soil.

Stored in a winter bed, scorzonera will keep very well in the winter.

Cleaning scorzonera is tedious, and stains the hands brown.

Put the peeled roots in vinegar water to keep them white.

Schwarzwurzeln in Béchamelsauce
Scorzonera in béchamel sauce

1 tbsp vinegar
1 tbsp flour
a generous 2 lb/ 1 kg scorzonera
salt
2 tbsp butter
2 tbsp flour
1 cup/250 ml hot stock
¾ cup/200 ml cream
white paper
a pinch of ground nutmeg
2 tbsp white wine
1 tbsp chopped parsley

Mix the vinegar and flour in a bowl with 4 cups/1 liter of water. Scrub the scorzonera under running water, peel, and cut into pieces 1¼ inch/3 cm long. Put them into the water and vinegar at once, to keep them white. Blanch the scorzonera in lightly salted water for 15–20 minutes, until just tender. Then drain them well. Melt the butter in a pan, and fry the flour in it gently until golden yellow. Add the hot stock, stir in the cream, and simmer the sauce for 10 minutes, stirring. Adjust the seasoning with salt, pepper, mustard, and wine, and reheat the scorzonera in the sauce. Sprinkle with parsley before serving.

Above: this is the correct way to prepare radishes of the large type for snacks: cut thinly in a spiral and then salted until it "weeps." Cutting it this way is an art, but luckily there are special gadgets to help you.

Wirsingkraut
Savoy cabbage

1 head of savoy cabbage
salt
1 small onion, finely diced
2 tbsp butter
pepper
a pinch of ground nutmeg
2 cups/500 ml meat stock
⅖ cup/150 ml cream
1 tsp cornstarch

Clean the savoy, cut it into quarters, and remove the stalk. Blanch for 2 minutes in lightly salted water, then drain well and cut the cabbage into strips. Fry the onion gently in the butter until transparent, add the strips of cabbage and fry briefly. Season with a little pepper and nutmeg, add the meat stock, cover, and cook for 20 minutes. Whisk the cream with the cornstarch, and stir into the cabbage. Cook for a few more minutes, adjusting the seasoning if necessary with salt and pepper. Put the cabbage into a prewarmed dish, and serve with fried sausages and mashed potato.

Franconian sausages

Franconia and Thuringia are linked not only by their shared border – they both have a generally acknowledged weakness for fried or broiled sausages. Nuremberg sausages, in particular, have achieved international fame: these delicacies, made of pork sausagemeat, should be no longer than a little finger, and weigh ¾ ounce (23 grams) each; they are cooked to a nice brown color over open beechwood fires, and are served half a dozen or a whole dozen at a time. Those who dislike horseradish as an accompaniment can choose coleslaw or potato salad. Nuremberg has records of the consumption of sausagemeat cakes ever since the 14th century, and in 1658 the butchers' journeymen of the town made a sausage 658 ells long (about 1300 feet) for the needy citizens. A cookbook of 1721 recommended sausage soup with a piquant seasoning of ginger, pepper and mace – and the Franconians even invented a recipe for sausages in dark beer.

Coburg, with its mighty fortress, the Veste, known as the "Franconian Crown," also has its local sausages; Coburg sausages are the thickness of a thumb, a hand's breadth in length, and acquire their unforgettable aroma from pine or fir cones in the fire over which they are cured. Originally, sausages from the triangular area bordered here by the curves of the river Main were 3 feet (1 meter) long, and came neatly rolled up in an impressive coil; you can try them at the wine festival held on the first weekend of August in Sulzfeld, south of Kitzingen. The local people are particularly proud of the *Blaue Zipfel* or "blue tip," which in spite of its rather indelicate name (*Zipfel* can also mean a penis in German) is ordered and eaten without a blush even by the most modest Franconian girls: raw sausages are cooked in a liquid containing vinegar (hence the "blue" element), onions, bayleaves, and a dash of Franconian wine, and are served in this broth.

Nackerte, raw sausagemeat seasoned with onions, salt, pepper, and paprika, served on black bread and butter, is a particularly popular snack in the Nuremberg area. A slice of *Pressack*, "pressed sausage," will also help to fill the gap until lunch – it gets that name because the basic mixture of finely ground rind and chunks of cooked pork, and offal, is "pressed" into the skin through a funnel. *Pressack* may be white or red; in the latter case blood is added. Morning and evening alike, the thick Nuremberg sausage sold in a continuous ring make a popular snack. It consists of pork, cut sometimes finely, sometimes rather coarsely, and because of its shape one expert on Franconia has compared it to the walls surrounding old towns. Another specialty is the *Knäudele*, a short blood sausage or liver sausage.

Franconian liver Pressack – a Pressack sausage may be either red or white.

Kulmbach sausages are longer than the little Nuremberg fried sausages.

Each region of Franconia has its own sausage specialties. Coburg sausages taste particularly good eaten in the pretty market place of Coburg.

Nuremberg fried sausages, eaten half a dozen or more at a time.

Saura Knöchla: brawn in aspic, made from head, snout, and trotters.

Saure Zipfel: raw sausages cooked in a broth containing vinegar.

Roter Gelegter includes offal and meat from the pig's head.

R.Boseckert
Brat- und Bockwürste

Not so much a sausage …

Not so much a sausage, more a way of life … everything revolves around the sausage in Germany. It is served at breakfast and for a snack, it is eaten hot or cold for the main meal of the day, or made into sausage salads, and it is available wherever people in a hurry want fast food: at the railroad station, in gas stations, in urban malls, at popular festivals. This particular form of fast food has a long tradition behind it: the first sausage stall was set up in Regensburg when the Stone Bridge of that town was being built between 1135 and 1146. The laborers who came to work on the bridge had no wives or cooking stoves with them, and were ideal customers when the idea of selling them hot sausages was first thought up.

Sausages are usually made of meat, bacon, offal, salt, and seasonings. The ingredients are chopped, well mixed, and stuffed into sausage skins. The manufacture of sausage is subject to strict legal regulations, which stipulate, for instance, the minimum quantity of lean meat that each kind of sausage must contain. However, every butcher has a free hand in seasoning and the other niceties of preparation, so that as a result every region and every family of butchers has its own recipes.

One writer has counted 1700 different varieties of sausages in Germany, another has come up with the figure of 1564. Never mind how many there really are – it is certain that no other country has such a wide range of sausages. It is rather odd that with the essential meaning the product has here, people say something is einem *Wurst*, literally, "a sausage to one," meaning they couldn't care less about the subject of conversation. *Wurstigkeit* ("sausageness"), meaning indifference, has entered the language too. Etymologists have no explanation for these terms except to say: "Origin uncertain." Obviously they couldn't care less about sausages!

A small selection from the wide variety of sausages

1	Tongue sausage
2	Cervelat sausage
3	Pâté sausage
4	Salami
5	Blood sausage
6	Ham sausage
7	*Feldkieker* ("spyglass sausage")
8	Paprika sausage
9	*Mettwurst*, smoked pork and beef sausage
10	*Weissgekochte*, "white sausage"
11	Mushroom pâté sausage
12	Tongue pâté sausage
13	Fine smoked liver sausage
14	Thuringian red sausage
15	Coarse *Leberkäse*
16	Children's sausage
17	Beer sausage
18	Beer sausage with ham

Sausage dishes

Blut- und Leberwürste
mit Sauerkraut
Blood sausage and liver sausage with sauerkraut
(Illustrated below left)

2 onions, diced
7 oz/200 g smoked Wammerl (belly of pork), diced
2 tbsp clarified butter
2 lb/1 kg fresh sauerkraut
½ cup/125 ml stock
1 bayleaf
5 juniper berries
1 tsp ground caraway
4 blood sausages
4 liver sausages
1 large potato
salt and sugar

Fry the onions and the belly of pork gently in the clarified butter, until transparent. Add the sauerkraut, and pour in the stock. Season with the bayleaf, juniper berries and caraway, cover, and cook over moderate heat for about 40 minutes. Meanwhile, put the sausages in cold water and heat them up gently (do not let them boil). Peel the raw potato, and grate it into the sauerkraut. Bring to a boil again, and continue simmering for a few minutes until the grated potato is cooked. Adjust the seasoning with salt and sugar. Arrange in portions on prewarmed plates, with 1 blood sausage and 1 liver sausage to each plate, and serve with creamed potatoes.

Milzwurst in aufgeschmalzter
Brotsuppe
Spleen sausage in bread soup with fried onions
(Illustrated center)

4 cups/1 liter meat stock
1 clove of garlic, crushed
1 small carrot, finely grated
salt and paper
1 tsp rubbed marjoram
a pinch of ground nutmeg
1 tsp ground caraway
4 slices spleen sausage, each weighing about 4 oz/120 g
3 tbsp lard
3 tbsp butter
8 oz/250 g onions, sliced into rings
14 oz/400 g stale bread, cut into thin slices
2 tbsp chopped parsley or chives

Bring the meat stock to a boil with the garlic and the finely grated carrot. Season well with salt, pepper, marjoram, nutmeg, and caraway. Add the slices of sausage, and warm them in the soup over low heat (do not boil again). Melt the lard and butter in a deep pan, and fry the onions until they are dark brown. Put the bread in a deep tureen, and pour the soup and the sausage slices over it. Cover and allow to stand, then mix in the onions and the fat. Sprinkle with parsley or chives, and serve immediately.

Regensburger Wurstsalat
Regensburg sausage salad
(Illustrated above right)

1¼ lb/600 g Regensburg sausage
2 large onions, thinly sliced into rings
3 tbsp vinegar
salt and pepper
3 tbsp oil
2 shallots, finely diced
radishes, chives, and pickled gherkins to garnish

Skin the sausage, and cut it into thin slices. Arrange on a large serving platter, with the onion rings. Make a dressing of the vinegar, 3 tbsp water, salt, pepper, oil, and shallots, and pour it over the sausage. Garnish with radish, chives, and gherkins, and serve with wholemeal bread.

Wollwürste
"Wool sausages"
(Illustrated below right)

12 Wollwürste
1 cup/250 ml milk
1 tbsp melted butter

Soak the sausages (which of course contain no wool!) in the milk for 5 minutes, turning them now and then. Take them out, pat them dry, and fry in hot melted butter on both sides for about 3 minutes until golden yellow. Serve with potato salad.

Chickens

"The chicken holds pride of place among the fowls of the earth," wrote Magister Elsholtz in his *Diaeteticon*. His high opinion of chickens is rather curious, for the hen does not feature with much dignity in colloquial German – the expression *dummes Huhn* ("silly chicken") is echoed in English by "dumb cluck," and English, like German, speaks of a helplessly confused person "running around like a headless chicken." Nor have natural scientists thought very highly of the chicken. In his *Naturstudien* ("Studies in Natural History") of 1865, Hermann Masius wrote that the chicken is "a faithful but prosaic fowl, in which all the romanticism of ornithological nature and indeed every flash of understanding are extinguished. The chicken is of limited intelligence, and submissive by nature."

We may assume that Magister Elsholtz was referring to the bird's culinary rather than its moral or ethical qualities. Even so, it is hard to share his opinion today. The dry, fibrous chicken breasts on the standard menu of every airline, the battery-reared broilers turning on the spits of snack bars and restaurant chains, are not exactly calculated to make one sing the praises of the chicken. It is a different matter if you are lucky

Max and Moritz, the naughty boys in Wilhelm Busch's classic 19th-century comic verses, appreciated good food. Busch lived in Munich for many years, and contributed to local newspapers and journals.

enough to eat a free-range chicken reared on a traditional farm, one that has grown up with its own kind and probably a flock of ducks, geese and turkeys too, free to run about and scratch in the dust to its heart's content, and fed on grain, pieces of eggshell, and vegetable peelings. For not only does the quality of the eggs depend on what the chicken ate – buyers have realized how much the bird's food affects the flavor of its meat ever since chickens were marketed after being fed so much fishmeal that even the strictest of Bavarian Catholics could consume them on Fridays without a pang of conscience.

Backhendl
Fried chicken

1 fresh broiling chicken, weighing about 2½ lb/1.2 kg
salt and pepper
5 tbsp flour
3 eggs
5 tbsp white breadcrumbs
oil for frying

Wash the chicken, pat it dry, and cut into portions. Season with salt and pepper. Dip the chicken pieces first in flour, then in beaten egg, and finally in the breadcrumbs; press the coating of breadcrumbs in well. Heat the oil in a deep fryer to 345 °F/175 °C, and deep fry the chicken portions for about 20 minutes, until golden brown. Drain briefly on kitchen paper before serving.

The chickens who end up in chain restaurants are not free-range, but battery-reared fowls.

Sad to say, happy hens who can scratch in the dust to their hearts' content are a small and privileged group.

The lacteous agaric is a good mushroom for frying.

The rough-stemmed boletus turns gray when cooked, and is unsuitable for drying.

Green russula. Not many people are familiar with this tasty mushroom.

Honey mushroom is excellent as a vegetable, and in soups and sauces.

Mushrooms

In Bavaria mushrooms are called *Schwammerl*, from the word *Schwamm*, "sponge," and it is a very good description, since mushrooms will absorb water like dry sponges. Every mushroom hunter knows that a warm day after rain is the best time to fill your basket. And anyone preparing mushrooms, and wondering whether to serve them as soup or a delicious vegetable, should not forget their affinity with liquid: use only the minimum of water in cleaning them. It is best to remove earth and evergreen needles with a knife, and dip the mushrooms briefly in water only if they are very sandy; that way they will retain the special flavor and aroma that make fresh wild mushrooms such a delicacy.

Schwammerlgemüse
Stewed mushrooms
(Illustrated below left)

1 lb/500 g fresh mushrooms, for instance red boletus, chanterelles, chestnut boletus
1 small onion, finely diced
2 tbsp butter
1 cup/250 ml strong veal stock
1 bunch of parsley, finely chopped
salt and pepper
a pinch of ground nutmeg
⅔ cup/150 ml cream

Clean and slice the mushrooms. Soften the onion in the butter until transparent, add the mushrooms, and let them cook in their own juices for 5 minutes. Add the veal stock, mix in the parsley, and season with salt, pepper, and nutmeg. Add the cream, and let the mushrooms simmer for another few minutes.

Reherl mit Rührei
Chanterelles with scrambled egg
(Illustrated below right)

12 oz/350 g chanterelles
1 small onion, finely diced
2 tbsp butter
4 eggs
4 tbsp cream or milk
salt and pepper
2 tbsp chopped parsley

Clean the chanterelles, and halve any that are very large. Soften the onion in a skillet in the butter until transparent, add the chanterelles, and let them cook in their own juices for 7 minutes. Whisk the eggs with the cream, season with salt and pepper, and pour over the chanterelles. Allow to thicken over gentle heat, stirring lightly. Sprinkle with the parsley and serve at once.

Red boletus grows under birch trees, and turns black when cooked.

St George mushroom or May mushroom grows in May and June.

Chestnut boletus: an excellent flavoring for sauces when dried.

Blusher mushroom makes excellent eating, but is not suitable for drying.

Chanterelles: cleaning them is tedious, but the flavor is worth it.

Wrinkled rozites: almost too good to use in mixed mushroom dishes.

Velvet foot: grows on deciduous trees even in mild winters.

Shaggy cap: despite its unattractive appearance, it tastes very good.

Morels are suitable for all dishes, and for drying.

The cep is the king of mushrooms, firm-fleshed, productive, and delicious.

The little cluster fungus adds flavor to soups and sauces.

Goat's lip mushroom: a boletus species that can be stewed, fried, or dried.

Cattle country

Although the pig may be the most popular animal in the Bavarian kitchen, in purely economic terms the Free State of Bavaria is cattle country. The statistics record over 100,000 farmers in the state who keep cattle. There are 4.2 million animals in Bavaria, including 1.6 million dairy cows. The farmers of Bavaria can boast of being 200 percent self-sufficient in beef, and only 12 percent of fattening bullocks are kept in farms with over 100 animals, while over half of them are on farms with less than 29.

Large areas down to grass favor cattle-raising in the Free State, and the soil and climate are just right to grow corn for winter fodder. The breed most commonly kept is the dual-purpose type with a particolored coat, which can provide both beef and dairy products. Charolais and German Angus cattle are now popular in areas of pure beef farming.

Boiling or braising is the most popular Bavarian method of cooking beef, first because it brings out the flavor, and second, because the by-product is a good strong beef broth, delicious with liver dumplings, semolina dumplings, spleen dumplings, or pancake strips.

Bófflamott
Marinaded braised beef
(Illustrated below)

½ leek
1 large carrot
1 root of Hamburg parsley
¼ celeriac
a generous 2 lb/1 kg beef from the shoulder
2 oz/50 g bacon, to lard the beef
1 onion, spiked with a bayleaf and 2 cloves
5 juniper berries, crushed
½ cup/125 ml wine vinegar
4 cups/1 liter red wine
salt and pepper
2 tbsp clarified butter
2 tbsp sugar
¼ cup/75 ml cream

Clean the vegetables, and dice them. Place in a dish with the meat, spiked onion, and juniper berries, and pour the red wine and vinegar over them. Add water just to cover the meat. Let it marinade in a cool place for 2–3 days, turning from time to time. Take the meat out of the marinade. Lard it with the bacon, pat it dry, and rub salt and pepper into it. Pass the marinade through a sieve. Melt the clarified butter in a braising pan and seal the meat on all sides. Add the vegetables from the marinade, fry briefly with the meat, and add a dash of red wine. Add the marinade and braise the beef over low heat for about 2 hours. Remove the meat from the pan, pass the sauce through a sieve. Remove the spiked onion and juniper berries, and purée the vegetables. Add the residue from the bottom of the pan to the sauce, adjust the seasoning with sugar, salt, and pepper, and stir in the cream.

Every part of the animal is used: favourite beef and veal dishes

1 Calf sweetbreads: the outer skin and inner tubes must be removed before cooking. Toss the sweetbreads in flour, and fry in butter for a bare ten minutes. Season with salt, pepper, and lemon juice. Potatoes and a green salad are good accompaniments.

2 Breast of veal is stuffed with white bread dumpling dough, particularly in the Allgäu. It is then roasted in the oven for about 1½ hours, carved into fairly thick slices, and served with potato salad and a green salad.

3 Knuckle of veal is either roasted in the oven like knuckle of pork, or broiled and eaten with dumplings or a potato and gherkin salad. Braised in a pan with potatoes and vegetables, knuckle of veal is a delicious dish that is easy to prepare.

4 Calf head is popular in Bavaria, particularly fried. Simmer half a calf head in salted water for two hours, with root vegetables, then remove the meat, coat it in breadcrumbs, and fry in hot butter until golden brown. Calf feet can be prepared in the same way: halved, boiled, then coated in breadcrumbs, and fried for five minutes in plenty of hot fat.

5 Calf kidneys: can be either cooked in a sweet-sour sauce or, as shown here, eaten as roast loin of veal with kidneys. The rolled loin, complete with kidneys, can be bought ready prepared by the butcher. Seal it by frying quickly on all sides, and put it in the oven with some water, an onion, and a carrot. Carve into fairly thick slices, and serve with potato salad.

6 Calf or ox liver is used to make liver dumplings in Bavaria; they are eaten either in soup, or with sauerkraut, bacon, and pork dishes. Sweet-sour liver can also be made with pig liver. Cut the liver into strips, fry with onions, add stock, vinegar, and cream. The Bavarians like to eat this dish with creamed potatoes rather than salad.

7 Kronfleisch ("crown meat") is the Bavarian term for the meat from the diaphragm, because it crinkles up like a crown when it is cooked. It is simmered gently with soup vegetables for about 30 minutes, and served with freshly grated horseradish and wholemeal bread, or boiled potatoes.

8 Calf or ox tongue is simmered with root vegetables for a good hour, skinned while still hot, cut into finger-sized slices, and served with caper or chive sauce. The pickled ox tongue shown in the illustration is served with gravy.

9 Oxtail – makes tasty dishes in Bavarian cookery; it can be served boiled, with horseradish sauce, or if braised will make a good ragout with the meat either removed or left on the bones, as shown here.

Root vegetables, onion, bayleaf, cloves, vinegar, and red wine: a good marinade for braised beef.

The marinaded beef, larded with bacon, is sealed quickly in hot fat.

After the vegetables from the marinade have been fried with the meat, add a dash of red wine and the marinade.

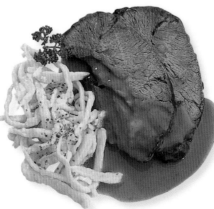

The Oktoberfest

The giant wheel is motionless, towering in the Bavarian sky. The carousels too are as still as the cast-iron figure of Bavaria presiding over the festival area known as *die Wiesn* ("the meadow"). The little cars of the roller coaster are parked on the level, at their stations. But the visitors to the biggest popular festival in the world have already arrived. The "Child of Munich" in the shape of a pretty young girl has already dismounted from her horse, and the handsome, heavy horses have pulled the brewery drays with their beer barrels, and the heads of the big Munich breweries, safely to the festival site. There are only minutes to go.

Then, on the dot of twelve noon on this last Saturday in September, twelve cannon shots ring out across the *Wiesn*, and a cry goes up of "*Ozapft is!*" At once the funfair rides begin moving, you hear the first shots from the rifle ranges, and beer flows from the taps.

"*Ozapft is!*" means that the first barrel of Oktoberfest beer has been broached, the tap driven home by the wooden mallet is safely in the bung, and beer is on its way into tankards. Since 1950 the ceremony has been performed by the Lord Mayor of Munich. Every year, local political interest centers on the number of blows it takes him to broach that first barrel. If a Lord Mayor does it with only three blows, as Christian Ude did, the local papers applaud his record-breaking feat, and it does more for his reputation than many a clever decision taken in the Town Hall.

During the 16 days of the festival, the whole life of the Bavarian capital centers on the great event. Firms invite their employees to the beer tent, or at least hand out tokens to be exchanged for beer and fried chicken; regulars of particular inns move to the festival tents instead; and the children of Munich give their parents no peace until they have been taken to the Oktoberfest at least once. And their parents or grandparents are glad to oblige, for all true natives of Munich treasure memories of visits to the Oktoberfest in their own childhood, even though there are complaints today that it is too crowded and over-commercialized. Business is certainly good: in 1998 around 1200 million gallons (55 million hectoliters) of beer went down the throats of the thirsty visitors, over 600,000 chickens turned on their spits, 84 whole oxen were roasted, and about 15 tons (280 hundredweight) of fish ended up over the charcoal grill. Some seven million people from Germany and abroad throng the beer tents, "where loud brass bands their music vent through smoke and beer fumes in the tent," as Eugen Roth commented in rhyme. "This is the cheerful festive season; Munich makes merry, with good reason, for every table's occupied; all differences are swept aside."

The waitresses who make their way through the tumultuous tents, balancing trays of half chickens or roast beef with virtuoso skill, are the true matadors of the occasion. Their earnings are so good that many girls take holidays from their usual jobs at this time in order to work at the Oktoberfest. Of course only experienced, expert waitresses will be hired, women able to manage eight to twelve liter tankards at once, and with

Brass bands, groups in Bavarian costume and marksmen's clubs as well as magnificently adorned drayhorses arrive for the Oktoberfest.

People of all classes and all ages come together in the beer tents – united by the beer.

There is a band playing in every tent. People sing along to the music, and enjoy a drink.

A famous institution is that of the "Fisherwoman Vroni," whose establishment sells char-grilled mackerel.

Whole oxen are roasted on the spit. About 80 oxen are eaten at every festival.

strong nerves that can stand up to hearing the band shout hundreds of times a day, "One, two, three – down the hatch!," inciting the cheerful crowd to consume ever more beer.

The beer sold at the Oktoberfest comes exclusively from Munich breweries – they have successfully repelled competitors from the countryside around. Prince Luitpold of Bavaria is particularly irate over this monopoly on beer; he is a brewer himself, but does not own a brewery in the capital, and has mounted several spectacular campaigns to point out that the people of Munich owe the Oktoberfest to his family; the first was held in 1810 on the occasion of the wedding of Crown Prince Ludwig of the house of Wittelsbach. At the time, a horse race was arranged outside the city, "at the Sendlinger gate, along the side of the road to Italy." It was a huge public success, and was repeated the following year for political reasons: the young monarchy could present itself in an attractive light at a popular festival, and receive the plaudits of its subjects. The horse race has not been held since 1938, but the "Central Agricultural Festival" still occurs every three years. Although the Oktoberfest has changed fundamentally during the course of its existence – it has been canceled only twenty-four times because of cholera, war, or inflation – to the people of Munich it is still "their" festival.

A wedding breakfast for the people

When Bavaria became a kingdom in 1806, it did so largely through the agency of a self-proclaimed emperor, Napoleon. In the previous year, Bavaria had decided to side with France in the Napoleonic wars, instead of joining a coalition with Austria against the French, and the ruler of the state received the rank of king as a reward. There was never any ceremonial coronation of Maximilian Joseph, so the first great event that the Wittelsbachs could hold in celebration of their royal dynasty was the wedding of Crown Prince Ludwig to Therese Charlotte Louise of Saxe-Hildburghausen.

The wedding was on 12 October 1810, and the celebrations were to last five days. Munich was magnificently adorned, ordinary citizens and nobles vied with one another to decorate their houses gaudily, and people flocked into the city from all around to hail the happy couple, see the festivities, and enjoy the public hospitality, which was particularly lavish, in keeping with the occasion: tables and benches had been prepared in the inner city for "the many people who came streaming in," and on 13 October the royal house served its subjects 32,065 "loaves of white bread," 3992 pounds of Swiss cheese, over 80 hundredweight of mutton, 8120 cervelat sausages, and 13,300 pairs of smoked sausages. There was beer to drink, of course, over 5000 gallons (232 hectoliters) of it, and just under 88 gallons (4 hectoliters) of Austrian white wine. Even the prisoners in jail had reason to celebrate, since they were given a specially good meal on the wedding day.

The fifties

"Prosperity for all," was the slogan of Ludwig Erhard. Even in his appearance, he embodied the idea of success in the early Adenauer era: well fed, a round face with a cigar in the middle of it. There were no anti-smoking campaigns then: an ashtray was as much a standard item of furnishing as the kidney-shaped tables of the fifties, and "dieting" was an alien notion at a time when Germans in general were glad to have something to get their teeth into, after years of near starvation following the war.

The store windows were suddenly full again after the currency reform of 20/21 June 1948, and the official abolition of rationing in the Allied Western zones at the beginning of 1950 was a mere formality. The "economic miracle" and a "wave of gluttony" were characteristics of West Germany in the 1950s, along with the reconstruction of the bombed cities and an attitude of optimism about the future on the one hand, and anxiety about the Cold War and latent fears of the nuclear bomb on the other.

Cars were a luxury. People rode bicycles, sometimes motorized, and tradesmen like bakers, who had to deliver goods, used three-wheeled floats. When the motor industry brought reasonably priced products on to the market – Volkswagens, Isettas, Goggomobiles, the Messerschmitt bubble car – some of the more prosperous citizens of Germany started driving south on holiday, and here they came into contact with Mediterranean cuisine for the first time. Television began transmitting in Germany for Christmas, 1952. Few people could afford the expensive sets, veneered in oak in the old German style, but those who could placed them in the

A real luxury:
stuffed trout

Toast Hawaii

Bananas with ham
on rice

Herring in aspic

1953: the displays of goods for sale were tempting, but many people, like these boys in Munich, could only look at Paradise and dream of a couple of oranges.

Cocktail snacks

Cheese nibbles

Mayonnaise was a must, even in horseradish sauce

Stuffed eggs

Ham and asparagus rolls

Ludwig Erhard, Minister for Economic Affairs and "father of the German economic miracle," with his recently published book *Wohlstand für Alle*, "Prosperity for All."

middle of the living room hung with drapes, so that neighbors and friends could gather to enjoy TV together, an experience enhanced by the consumption of cubes of cheese speared with grapes on toothpicks. Among the stars of the new medium was the television cook Clemens Wilmenrod, who introduced German housewives to the delights of sophisticated cookery with such recipes as Papal Chicken, Italian Omelette, and Anonymous Chicory. He warmly recommended the use of the *Heinzelkoch* ("Brownie Cook") in preparing these dishes: it was a small oven with a grill that "could be plugged into any convenient power point" and according to Wilmenrod "is part of the future, because it guarantees the future."

In fact not many housewives had electrical appliances, and chicken, whether papal or heretical, was still regarded as a dish for special occasions, just as Toast Hawaii brought a breath of luxury to the table through the agency of canned pineapple. Rich dishes were very popular for entertaining: cakes and tarts filled with fresh cream or buttercream, tomatoes or cucumbers stuffed with salad ingredients in mayonnaise. No buffet party was without its plastic toothpicks for nibbles; along with nylon, plastic was the material of the fifties. It was hygienic, and could be effectively disinfected with Sagrotan, another fifties product widely used in Germany. The popular non-iron shirts for men were made of Nyltest, and there were expensive nylon stockings for ladies. A pair of nylon stockings was considered a perfectly acceptable gift for a guest to take his hostess, and she would be very happy to receive them. Many hosts were delighted to be given a briquette for the stove; it ensured that they and their guests would not have to spend the evening shivering.

Dumplings

Life without dumplings? Impossible!

Caspar von Schmid of Schwandorf, an influential figure at the court of Munich in the second half of the 17th century, must have had the welfare of the bodies and souls of the state's subjects at heart. "The people of Bavaria," he wrote, "should be spared banishment from the country wherever possible, because then they would be deprived of dumplings."

So there it is, down in black and white: long before the *Weisswurst* and its "equator" dividing Bavaria from the north existed, the state was embodied in a dumpling – or rather, in many kinds of dumplings. The Bavarian range comprises semolina, bacon, liver, plum, potato, and above all white bread dumplings. The Bavarians themselves have even put their dumplings into orbit on occasion. Helmut Winter, from Pasing near Munich, made international headlines in 1967 for firing dumplings from a home-made catapult at the Starfighters roaring over his home. He succeeded in his aim, too: not literally, for he brought down no Starfighters (they were well able to ground themselves without Helmut Winter's assistance),

To make white bread dumplings, slice 10 oz/300 g of day-old rolls, and soak them in ¾ cup/200 ml hot milk.

Add two eggs, a finely diced, fried onion, fresh parsley, salt, and a little nutmeg.

Different sorts of dumplings

1 Pretzel dumplings are made with soaked pretzels rather than rolls.

2 Bohemian dumplings, a gesture from the neighboring state, made with yeast.

3 Crackling dumplings, with crackling added to the bread dumpling dough.

4 Upper Bavarian crackling dumplings; the crackling is wrapped in little coats of dough.

5 Semolina dumplings, little oval semolina shapes, mainly served in soup.

6 Fifty percent dumplings, made of half raw, half cooked potatoes.

7 Cheese dumplings, made of a dough of flour, salt, and water, with cheese added.

8 Potato dumplings are good with almost any meat dish in sauce.

9 Uncooked potato dumplings also go well with meat dishes in sauce.

10 Spleen dumplings, bread dumplings made like liver dumplings, but using spleen instead.

11 Liver dumplings taste good in soup, or with sauerkraut and pork dishes.

12 Ham dumplings: the bread dumplings contain snippets of ham.

Bread dumplings for weekdays, liver dumplings on Sundays

"Even at other times, [Grandfather] was often to be found in the kitchen, helping Grandmother peel turnips or cut up white rolls for our dumplings, which had to be served every day. There were dumplings even on Sundays, although much larger and darker, in the form of liver dumplings. We never threw away the water used for cooking the dumplings – which were not only tasty but cheap – it was brought to the table too, in a large, patterned dish. Grandmother would also serve a small pan of onions browned in hot fat, and in summer a little dish of chives. Grandfather would take the big home-baked loaf of bread from a cupboard – it was surrounded by ringshaped impressions made with our large doorkey – and begin slowly and carefully slicing little pieces into the broth. Then he would pour the fat over the bread and broth, season it all well with salt and pepper, and stir it with his spoon several times. After that, he would say, 'There, Mother, now it tastes better.'

We ate meat only on very special occasions. Even on Sundays my grandparents were content with liver dumplings, eaten with the *Tauch*, a vegetable dish made of root vegetables or kohlrabi. Only Grandfather had a piece of boiled beef fat with his Sunday dinner, and he ate it salted and peppered, with a slice of bread."

From Lena Christ, *Erinnerung einer Überflüssigen* ("Memories of a Superfluous Girl"), 1912

Pound the mixture well, and then add a little flour, until the dough is the right consistency.

Form it into neat balls with wet hands, slide into boiling water, reduce the heat, and cook until done.

but as a result of his eccentric one-man protest, the flight paths of these low-flying aircraft were moved away from the area.

The people of Deggendorf can also look back on the militant past of their dumplings: a story relates that the town once defended itself against the troops of King Ottokar of Bohemia with dumplings. The old recipe for Deggendorf dumplings was reconstructed at the Lower Bavarian Festival of 1961, and was a particularly elaborate one: a dough made of flour, egg, strong meat stock, and a little milk, was mixed with fine black breadcrumbs. This dough was then wrapped around a roll minus its crust, softened in milk, and simmered in water until done.

The white bread dumpling, which the people of Old Bavaria claim to have invented, is regarded as the Bavarian dumpling *par excellence*. Potatoes have never enjoyed a high reputation in those prosperous areas where grain grew in abundance, and even the servants ate dumplings made of rye: an inferior grain, but still, it was grain. Rottal dumplings are famous for being so hard that you could throw them over the roof of a house and they would not break up when they came down the other side – or so they say in the Rottal area. Dumplings do seem to have become airborne quite frequently in Bavaria.

Poaching and game

Although by no means all the people of the Free State of Bavaria live in the mountains, the stereotype of the Bavarian presents him as *Homo alpiniensis* wearing short or knee-length lederhosen, held up by embroidered leather suspenders, with a hat on his head, and in the hat – very conspicuous, its wearer's pride and joy – a large tuft of chamois hair.

The hat with its chamois tuft can be bought today in stores selling Bavarian costume, and even newcomers can go around wearing an attribute once reserved for experienced hunters in the high mountains, who would have to shoot several animals to acquire that genuine tuft of chamois hair. It comes only from the hairs growing on the nape of the neck and along the back of a mature male chamois, which are particularly long in winter. Another sign of a man's hunting skill, one that was also supposed to protect its wearer from danger, was the *Charivari*, a silver pendant, usually in the shape of a watch chain, with the teeth of an animal, or sometimes the claws or beak of a game bird, shot by the wearer worked into it.

Naturally only a man of high social rank could wear such insignia, since only the nobility had game rights, and game was the food of the court. At fine banquets, such as the funeral banquet held on the death of Albrecht IV of Bavaria in 1509, or the wedding of Duke Wilhelm V of Bavaria to Renata of Lorraine in 1568, game featured prominently on the menu. The wild boar's head was a showpiece at these magnificent banquets, and it had to be the head of a male. Although the flavor had a rancid aftertaste, imparted by the animal's sex hormones, male animals took precedence as a status symbol. The head was skinned and cooked, with the tusks still in place. Then the prepared skin was put back over it, and the head was served up. It cannot have been the best of eating, but it was undoubtedly impressive as a display of virility.

People of lower rank, who could enjoy a hare or a deer only if they had been poaching, had rather more appetizing ways of cooking game. Erna Horn, in *Bayern tafelt* ("Bavaria at Table") describes the *Brotzeit* of workers in the porcelain factories: "The porcelain workers of northeast Bavaria had their own specialty. Poor as they were, and remote from easily accessible sources of nourishment, they sometimes provided well for themselves, and had a real "porcelain worker's *Brotzeit*." Bread did not have much to do with it, but if they came by a young wild boar, a deer, a hare caught in a snare, a rabbit or a fat goose that was just begging to be taken, it was a notable occasion. The whole operation had to be a swift one, in order to pass undetected. Gutted, skinned or plucked, salted, and packed in mud or porcelain clay, the "*Brotzeit*" found its way into the firing kilns. No sizzling sounds or cooking aromas gave it away, for the hard crust of clay kept its secret until it was done."

The chamois is not hunted for its meat alone; the older bucks provide the hair for the chamois tufts that are in great demand as hunting trophies.

Marinaded venison Ruhpolding style

Criminal folk heroes

"I am the prince of the forests, and no one is equal to me. My realm is as wide as the blue sky above. The game on God's earth is free to all, so I will let no one stand in my way, and those who shoot no game are fools." This is a translation of the Bavarian dialect song of "Bavarian Hiasl," or rather one of the many songs written to glorify him. Matthias Klostermeyer, born in 1736, was the most famous poacher in the Bavarian Alps, and a thoroughly shady character. Although a legend reminiscent of Robin Hood has grown up around him, he was in fact a criminal, a robber, and murderer who did not confine his activities to poaching. None the less, he could count on the sympathy and active support of the peasants. One reason was their dislike of seeing their fields devastated by the lord of the manor's game, and another was the mere fact that the poacher was a man who opposed authority. Only the nobility had hunting rights, and they imposed harsh penalties on anyone who took their game. Minor offenses were punished with forced labor, imprisonment, or the loss of the offender's right hand; "hardened criminals" like Matthias Klostermayer were subjected to even more draconian penalties. In 1771 Klostermayer was executed in Dillingen by being wrapped in a cow's skin, dragged through the town, strangled, and broken on the wheel. He is said to have commented on his sentence with the words: "You'll all be gone too in fifty years, and so will the Elector."

"Bavarian Hiasl" was the most famous poacher of his time, but certainly not the only one: poaching was so widespread in the hill country of Bavaria in the 18th and 19th centuries that more game was probably killed illegally than legally. The people were poor, and the lords' woods were full of game – and if a man provided himself with meat from the forests, not only did it seem right to the forthright popular mind, even the priest in the pulpit said that God had made game as nourishment for all men. The poacher was a folk hero, a rebel, who took from the rich only what they had in superfluity. As such, he appeared in popular plays and in literature – a just and simple man, in constant danger of being taken by the lord's henchmen or shot by the lord's huntsmen, but always one step ahead of the gamekeepers. The lawyer and writer Ludwig Thoma of Dachau (1867–1921) described a poacher, the "man from Niederegg," in his story *Der Wilderer* ("The Poacher"): "A pair of cunning gray eyes look out from the weathered face, to which the prominent, sharply contoured nose gives an almost martial expression, and those eyes and something around the mouth betray a quick wit. He studies the policemen with a brief, keen glance, then looks boldly at them, and not for a moment does he show the least surprise." The police search his house, of course find nothing, and go away. There stands the man from Niederegg "in his yard, with a satisfied grin," and he goes straight off to set another couple of snares.

Rehragout

Ragout of venison

(Illustrated below right)

- *a good 1½ lb/750 g haunch of venison, boned*
- *2 tbsp lard*
- *2 onions, diced*
- *1 carrot, finely diced*
- *1 leek, cut into thin rings*
- *salt and pepper*
- *½ cup/ 125 ml red wine*
- *½ cup/ 125 ml meat stock*
- *¼ cup/60 ml pig blood*
- *a pinch of sugar*
- *1 tbsp wine vinegar*
- *½ cup/ 125 ml soured cream*

Wash the meat, pat it dry, and cut it into cubes. Melt the lard and brown the meat in it on all sides. Add the onions, carrot, and leek, and continue frying for another 5 minutes. Season with salt and pepper, add the wine, stock, and pigs blood. Cover, and allow to braise for 1 hour over medium heat, stirring now and then. Adjust the seasoning with sugar, vinegar, salt, and pepper, stir in the soured cream, and put the ragout in a prewarmed serving dish. Serve with bread dumplings or noodles, and celeriac salad.

Wildschweinfilet in Rotweinrahmsauce

Fillet of wild boar in cream and red wine sauce

(Illustrated center)

- *a good 2 lb/1 kg fillet of wild boar*
- *1 large onion, coarsely diced*
- *1 large carrot, diced*
- *½ leek, cut into rings*
- *4 oz/100 g Wammerl (smoked pork belly), diced*
- *¾ cup/200 ml game stock*
- *salt*
- *1 cup/250 ml red wine*
- *1 cup/250 ml cream*
- *1 tbsp oil*
- *pepper*
- *⅓ cup/100 ml sherry*
- *⅓ cup/100 ml crème fraîche*

Remove all skin and sinews from the wild boar fillet, fry the skin and sinews with the root vegetables and pork belly, add the game stock, and simmer. Season with a little salt, add the red wine and cream, bring to a boil, and then pass the sauce through a sieve. Seal the fillet well on all sides in a skillet in oil, then reduce the heat and continue frying, covered, until done. Season with pepper, simmer for a few more moments, then add the sherry. Pour in the red wine sauce, and bring to a boil. Take the fillet out of the sauce and carve into slices. Stir the crème fraîche into the sauce, and serve it separately from the fillet. Serve spätzle noodles and pears stuffed with cranberries as accompaniments.

Ruhpoldinger Hirschziemer

Marinaded venison Ruhpolding style

(Illustrated left)

Marinade

- *2 small onions, diced*
- *2 carrots, cut into small dice*
- *1 Hamburg parsley root, diced*
- *¼ celeriac root, diced*
- *3 cups/750 ml red wine*
- *salt and pepper*
- *½ tsp rubbed marjoram*
- *1 bayleaf*
- *5 juniper berries, crushed*

Meat

- *a good 3 lb/1.5 kg saddle of venison, on the bone, prepared for cooking*
- *2½ oz/75 g dried mushrooms*
- *5 oz/150 g fat bacon*
- *salt and pepper*
- *3 juniper berries*
- *2 tbsp butter*
- *3 small onions*
- *2 carrots, cut into pieces*
- *¾ cup/200 ml soured cream*
- *1 tbsp black breadcrumbs*

To make the marinade, bring the onions, carrots, parsley root, and celeriac to a boil with the red wine, herbs, and seasonings, and simmer for 10 minutes. Take off the heat and allow to cool. Put the venison in a dish, pour the marinade over it, cover, and allow it to stand in a cool place for 3–4 days, turning it now and then. Before cooking the meat, soak the mushrooms for 20 minutes in lukewarm water. Take the saddle of venison out of the marinade, drain well, and pat dry. Cut the bacon into narrow strips and use them to lard the meat, taking the larding needle well into the venison and following the grain of the fibers. Rub the meat with salt, pepper, and the crushed juniper berries. Melt the butter in a roasting pan, and seal the meat quickly on all sides. Skin and halve the onions. Add to the meat, with the carrots and the drained mushrooms, and fry briefly. Add the soured cream, and pour the marinade in through a very fine sieve. Cover, and cook in a preheated oven for about 1½ hours at 430 °F/220 °C. When the meat is done, take it out of the pan and keep it hot. Stir the breadcrumbs into the juices in the pan, and simmer for a few minutes. Season with salt and pepper. Remove the meat from the bones, and rearrange it on the bones, on a warmed serving platter. Serve the sauce separately. Potato dumplings and red cabbage go well with this dish.

Fillet of wild boar in cream and red wine sauce

Ragout of venison

Ludwig II of Bavaria

The romantic fairytale king, the fanatical builder, a ruler who was shy in company, the platonic admirer of Sissi, wife of Emperor Franz Joseph of Austria – many myths and legends have accumulated around Ludwig II of the house of Wittelsbach, the "one true king of our age," as the French poet Paul Verlaine described him, and they are still alive today. His mysterious death certainly contributed to the legend: on the night of 13 June 1886 the king, who had been deposed for his "paranoia," and his companion Dr von Gudden were found dead in Lake Starnberg. Had he drowned? He was an excellent swimmer. Was he murdered? The mystery remains unsolved to this day.

When Ludwig came to the throne in 1864 at the age of 18, Bavaria had four million inhabitants. They welcomed the accession of a young and handsome king who, in the century of the Biedermeier style and Bismarck, was a fervent admirer of the music of Richard Wagner, and considered the absolute monarchy of the King Louis XIV of France, the Sun King, the highest form of kingship. In the course of his twenty-two-year reign he built three castles – Neuschwanstein, Linderhof, and Herrenchiemsee – spending over 6 million marks on them in 1883 alone. They brought him to the brink of personal financial ruin. (At this time a family of five, with the father and mother working in a factory, had to make do on 1100 marks a year.) Although Ludwig's minister of finance and the Bavarian parliament did not look kindly on his passion for architecture, the people loved him, perhaps not least because his dreams, located outside the political realm, did not cause a drop of blood to be shed on the battlefields to which other rulers dispatched their subjects.

Fantastic and magnificent as his buildings were, sophisticated and sensitive as were his feelings for poetry and music – with the best will in the world, even a local patriot could not have numbered Ludwig II among the ranks of royal gourmets. Very much in the Wittelsbach tradition, meals at court during his reign were subject to strict ceremonial etiquette. But unlike his father, who had set little store by mealtimes, Ludwig II took them as the occasion for magnificent demonstrations of his regal status. A whole retinue of servants had to transport valuable silver, porcelain, and other tableware within a few hours from one of the restless ruler's castles to another, even to remote mountain huts, and they had to be ready to prepare and serve an extensive range of dishes at any time. A complete menu might, for instance, contain chicken soup with rice, Rhine salmon cooked in the Dutch style, braised beef and vegetables, mutton chops with cabbage

King Ludwig II of Bavaria, (1845–1886). Schloss Neuschwanstein is in the background.

A royal menu from the year 1878. The king valued magnificence more than good cooking.

Entenleberpastete (duck liver pâté), featured on King Ludwig II's menu for 10 May 1866.

Bayerisch Crème (Bavarian cream), a delicious creation of the royal kitchen, although rather expensive to make.

Brussels style, capon with noodles, goose liver pâté, roast pheasant, chestnut pancakes à la Lyon, Prussian tart, and frozen whitecurrants in champagne.

The menus, table services, and clothes were always adapted to the court's present location. In the Moroccan House in the park of Schloss Linderhof, the style was Arab, and in "Hunding's hut" (a building modeled on an episode in Wagner's Ring cycle) it was rustic. However, the king set little store by the actual contents of the serving dishes, so long as the food was hot. In his royal residence in Munich, the kitchen was so far from the royal apartments that, as the supervisor of the royal kitchen staff wrote in 1884, the food was always cold by the time it reached his Majesty's antechamber, had to be heated up again, and often stood about for hours on the anteroom stove, losing much of its goodness. In his castles at least, Ludwig wished to cut the journey between kitchen and table down to a minimum, and in Neuschwanstein he had an elevator for food built down through three floors. In Linderhof, at his wish, one of the first electricity stations in Bavaria was constructed, and the display of the first elevator to carry people at the World Exhibition in Paris inspired him to have his own "magic table" installed, so that he need not have servants around him while his dinner was served. The dining table was completely laid on the floor below, and then rose by electricity to his dining room.

Entenleberpastete
Duck liver pâté

Pastry
1 lb/ 500 g flour
1 egg
1 tsp salt
2 tsp brandy
1 scant cup/225 g cold butter

Filling
2 large duck livers
salt and white pepper
1 tsp pâté spice
2 canned truffles
½ lb/250 g lean veal
½ lb/250 g unsmoked bacon
2 oz/50 g smoked bacon, diced
2 shallots, diced, 6 mushrooms, sliced
1 tsp chopped parsley, ½ tsp dried Provençal herbs
2 oz/50 g cooked ham, finely diced
2 tbsp brandy
1 egg yolk, whisked with 1 tbsp cream
¾ oz/20 g powdered gelatin
1 cup/250 ml Madeira

To make the pastry, knead the flour, egg, ½ cup/125 ml water, salt, and brandy together, and roll out thinly. Place one-third of the butter, thinly sliced, on the pastry, fold it over and roll it out again. Repeat this process twice more. Let the pastry rest overnight in the refrigerator. Sprinkle the duck livers with salt, pepper, and pâté spice, spike with some slices of truffles, and leave in the refrigerator overnight. Next day put the veal and fresh bacon through the grinder twice, fry the smoked bacon in a dry skillet until the fat runs, soften the shallots, mushrooms, and parsley in the skillet, season with salt and Provençal herbs, and mix with the ground meat. Add the cooked ham and the brandy. Roll out the pastry to a finger's thickness, and use it to line a pâté mold, letting the pastry overlap the sides. Fill with one-third of the meat mixture, a halved duck liver, and slices of truffle. Add another third of the mixture, place the second halved liver and slices of truffles on it, and then cover with the remaining mixture. Make a lid of the remaining pastry and cover the pâté with it, pressing the edges of the pastry well together, and make a small hole in the middle. Glaze with the egg and cream, and bake for about 1½ hours in a preheated oven at 350 °F/180 °C. Turn the pâté out of the mold and allow to cool. Soften the gelatin in a little water, warm the Madeira, and dissolve the gelatin in it. Pour a little of the mixture into the opening in the pastry, and put the rest in a shallow dish. When it has set, dice it and serve with the pâté.

Bayerisch Creme
Bavarian cream

1½ oz/40 g powdered gelatin
2 cups/500 ml milk
1 vanilla bean, split open
6 egg yolks
1 cup/125 g sugar
2 cups/500 ml cream

Bring the milk to a boil with the vanilla bean, take off the heat, and allow to cool slightly. Beat the egg yolks with the sugar until light and foamy, and slowly stir in the hot vanilla milk. Pour into a pan, and stir over moderate heat until the custard thickens. Dissolve the gelatine in it, take it off the heat, and allow to cool, stirring from time to time. Whip the cream until very thick. When the custard begins to set, carefully fold in the whipped cream. Allow to set in the refrigerator for at least 3 hours.

The Bocksbeutel and its contents

Franconian wine

In Bavaria, the land of beer, good and indeed often excellent wine is made from the grapes grown on the varied Triassic soils of the northern area of Franconia, where the River Main meanders in convoluted shapes as it flows toward the Rhine. The best German Silvaner comes from this region, and so does a whole range of outstanding variants on the Riesling x Silvaner cross: a soft, flowery, pleasing Müller-Thurgau, with vines covering 47 percent of the agricultural area of Franconia, around 11,600 acres (4700 hectares) in extent; a lively, fruitily elegant Rieslaner, which used also to be known as Main-Riesling; a spicy Bacchus, and a fresh, aromatic, late-ripening Scheurebe – all of them popular and suitable for making table wines of good strength and quality.

Riesling, of which only four percent of Franconian wine is made, is one of the least grown grapes in the area; the reason lies in the continental climate of Franconia. Such a climate, with hot summers and cold winters, a short growing period, and early or late frosts that can take the winegrower by surprise, does not really suit the most successful of all German grapes. Only in the microclimate south of Würzburg does a Riesling grow that can compete with the best German representatives of the variety in its breeding, elegance and refinement. It has been famous as *Steinwein* since the 18th century, together with the other wines of the region, and owes its name to the Würzburg *Lagen*, or vineyard areas, of Stein and Steinharfe, which are among the largest undivided areas of vineyards in Germany. It was in the Stein vineyards of Würzburg, in the Rococo period, that the German custom arose of labeling a bottle with the name of the vineyard area where the grapes had grown rather than the name of the grower or a wine-growing estate. After 1718, Steinwein was sold in a bottle that differed from the customary German kind in its unusual shape and interesting name: it is known as the *Bocksbeutel*, literally, "goat's bag," apparently from the shape of a male goat's scrotum. It was the cellarers of the Würzburg Bürgerspital, a wine-growing estate founded as a charity in 1309, who hit upon the idea of the unusual shape of the bottle. To this day, the vineyard, with 346 acres (140 hectares) of vines, is one of the largest in Germany. The idea was to protect its product from the many pirated versions of the popular Franconian wine by giving the bottle its typical design; the seal of the hospital was contained in the glass as well.

The dates of foundation of the long-established Bürgerspital, the Staatlicher Hofkeller and the Juliusspital with its huge cellar vaults, underneath the hospital of the same name built in 1576 by Prince-Bishop Julius Echter of Mespelbrunn – with 395 acres (160 hectares) of vines, it is the third largest German vineyard estate – are evidence of the long and honorable tradition of Franconian winegrowing. The center, Würzburg, was among the most famous winegrowing cities of Germany in the 18th century, with its magnificent Residence Palace and the river Main, which was extended to provide the main transport route. In the 17th century, the vineyard areas north and south of the River Main as it winds its way through Bavaria, comprising some 99,000 acres (40,000 hectares) of vineyards in all, made up the largest wine-growing area in the whole of the German Reich of the time. The popularity of Franconian wines is their earthy strength and a certain informal charm.

Excellent wine is grown in the valley of the Main. The Silvaner wines in particular are of outstanding quality.

Buying wine

The first and only point of reference in buying wine (at least in the supermarket and most wine stores) is the label. Anyone can see what it says, but not by any means everyone knows what it actually means. European, Federal, and provincial German authorities determine the content of a label. By law, it must state the group to which the wine belongs (for instance *Tafelwein*, *Prädikatswein*), the maker's name and the business address of the firm, the amount the bottle contains – and for a *Qualitätswein* the year, the official number it has scored in testing, the region where it was grown (for instance, Franconia, the Palatinate), and the alcohol content. The label must also state the area of origin, i.e. the region where the wine was grown (for instance Markgräfler Land, Hochheim), the community or vineyard area (for instance Geisenheim, Gutes Domtal), or the name of a single vineyard (for instance Assmannshäuser Höllenberg). Not obligatory, but desirable information that is often given, is the grape variety (for instance Riesling, Spätburgunder,) and some indication of flavor, for instance dry, medium sweet.

The information on labels should be carefully read. Famous names of vineyard areas such as Ürziger Schwarzlay or Wehlener Sonnenuhr do not really say much about the quality of the wine, since many leading areas were greatly extended after the passing of the new German wine law of 1971, and sometimes now comprise certain areas much less suitable for viticulture than the old single vineyard that once gave the area its name. Prefixes such as *Kabinett*, or *Trockenbeerenauslese*, do not indicate anything about the real quality of the wine except in connection with the quality of the grapes used; for instance, a *Kabinett* made from a good Riesling may be a good deal better than a *Trockenbeerenauslese* made from an uninteresting Silvaner. And the assurance *Gutsabfüllung*, "estate-bottled," tells you only that a wine was actually put into bottles on a certain estate, but not where the grapes came from. Anyone who wants to know whether a wine is dry, medium, or sweet should look at the alcohol content; the higher it is, the more sugar will have fermented out, and consequently the drier the wine will be – always assuming no further sweetening has been added later. A showy bottle or a flamboyant label can often be misleading too: for instance, a Rheingau Riesling from an old traditional bottle with a family crest and Gothic lettering will very probably taste more elegant and modern than a thin Chardonnay from an ultra-chic designer bottle. Buying a bottle of wine on outward appearance alone, although it is often the only option, is always risky. To be sure of a good buy one needs competent advice, preferably combined with a chance to sniff the bouquet of the wine in the glass and then taste it.

Harvest time above the Lower Franconian city of Würzburg on the Main, which was one of the most famous wine-making areas of Germany in the 18th century.

Shapes of wine bottles usual in the German wine trade. On the left, the famous and unique Franconian Bocksbeutel.

Bavaria
Wineproducing areas

HESSE

THURINGIA

Östheim

Bad Neustadt

Coburg

Hammelburg
Fränk. Saale

Haßberge

Lichtenfels

Aschaffen-burg

Loh

Schweinfurt

Zeil am Main

Bamberg

Spessar

Markt-heidenfeld

Main

Volkach

Steigerwald

Hessenthal

Würzburg

Wertheim

Iphofen

Höchstadt an der Aisch

Miltenberg

Ochsenfurt

Erlangen

BADEN-WÜRTTEMBERG

Aisch

Neustadt an der Aisch

Fürth

Nuremberg

N
0   10 km

Rothenburg ob der Tauber

The Nuremberg Christmas fair

Glühwein and Lebkuchen

Special trains are laid on, countless buses run, people even charter planes to get to the Christkindlmarkt (literally, the "Christ Child Market"), Nuremberg's Christmas fair, an event running from the Friday before the first Sunday in Advent until Christmas, and one that makes the old imperial city even more of a tourist attraction than in the summer vacation. The first mention of a *Kindlesmarck* occurs in the records in 1628, and a history of the city dating from 1697 calls the pre-Christmas fair the *Christkindleinsmarck*. Its origin and name date from the time of the Reformation, when the upper classes of Nuremberg, which became a Protestant city quite early, emulated the reformers in teaching their children about the "holy Christ Child" rather than the figure of St Nicholas. Around the middle of the 18th century, 140 persons had permission to offer their wares for sale at the market; all the crafts of the city were represented – of course including those that had made Nuremberg a center for the making and sale of toys ever since the 15th century. When family festivities around the Christmas tree became increasingly popular in the late 19th century, assuming the status of the year's high point, the result was a boom for the Christkindlmarkt, previously a comparatively modest affair.

Many of the features typical of the occasion today go back to the time of the Third Reich, when Nuremberg had a Lord Mayor who brought the fair back to the city's main market place, after its venue had been changed several times. Ever since the first post-war fair in 1948, the *Christkindlein* and the Christ Child's Prologue have stood in the balcony of the Frauenkirche (Church of the Virgin), a focal point of the opening ceremony: the Child was first impersonated by the very popular local actress Sophie Keeser, who was succeeded by a colleague, and today a pretty girl is chosen "from the people" to be the Christ Child for two years. All the girls who have so far filled the role at the fair have had their wardrobes provided by a large firm specializing in the manufacturing of *Lebkuchen*, the famous German spicy ginger cookies sweetened with honey.

Those who have made their way along the festively decorated streets, and have reached the main market with its impressive "Schöner Brunnen" ("Beautiful Fountain"), are standing on historically interesting ground, for this was once the city's Jewish quarter. It was destroyed in a pogrom in 1349 and the Gothic Frauenkirche now stands on the site of the synagog. The stalls, adorned with evergreen branches and Christmas lanterns, entice visitors to buy Christmas tree decorations, art and craft items, little figures made of dried plums with walnut heads, and gilded angels; the first of these is said to have been made about 300 years ago, for a mother whose child had died during Advent. The smell of grilled sausages fills the air appetizingly; in some places the aroma of burnt almonds is overpowering, but subtler scents can be made out as well – the smell of brightly painted shapes of *Eierzucker* ("egg sugar"), soaked in aniseed liqueur, or of the *Spekulatius* (in the shape of a human figure, and spiced with cardamom), of *Hutzelbrot*, a fruit loaf, and of course the famous Nuremberg *Lebkuchen*. Having made your purchases, if you then relax over a glass of *Glühwein* – mulled wine flavored with cinnamon and cloves – all these fragrances will leave something of the scent of Nuremberg's past in your nostrils, for spices have played a considerable part in the city's history. Major trade routes met here, and it was the merchants of Nuremberg whose families made up the powerful "patriciate" for hundreds of years, and whose word counted for most in the city council.

Sweet things from the Christkindlmarkt

"Eisenlebkuchen" ("iron" spice cookie) covered with chocolate, a Nuremberg specialty.

Sometimes the famous Nuremberg Lebkuchen have almonds and sugar frosting.

A fruit loaf, also called a "Kletzenbrot" in Bavaria, contains dried fruit and nuts.

Coconut macaroon – these cookies are seasonal to Christmas, and are on sale at the Christmas fair.

The first German rail train ran between Nuremberg and Fürth in 1835.

"Magenbrot" ("stomach bread"), a delicious cookie containing fine spices said to be good for the digestion.

Large nut Lebkuchen are made without any frosting, and decorated with nuts.

Prune man and prune woman – a perfect couple, made of dried fruit.

You can stock up with Christmas decorations such as straw stars at the Christmas fair.

Prune men and prune women – partners who "won't cause domestic strife," as the sign says.

Their power was increased by the fact that the craftsmen of the city had little influence: after a revolt in 1348, they were forbidden by imperial degree to form gilds. The spice trade was the backbone of many mercantile businesses. Before the sea route to India was discovered in 1499, the Arabs earned a fortune as middlemen trading with the "spice countries," and the seaports of Venice and Genoa then transported the spices on into the rest of Europe. The precious cargo was taken in covered wagons from those ports over the Alps, and after weeks of traveling, passing through such places as Salzburg, Linz, Passau, and Regensburg, finally reached Nuremberg. After journeys of thousands of kilometers overland, staggering prices were paid for something we use today in baking and cooking without a second thought. The Nuremberg patrician, Tucher, offered his services as an astronomer to speculators, claiming to have discovered a system for forecasting the market value of certain spices. Where large sums of money were concerned, total ruthlessness was the rule; during Dürer's time Nuremberg was a center of the saffron trade, and in 1444 a citizen was burnt to death there for adulterating saffron, along with his substandard wares, although the practice of adulteration was not particularly unusual.

A display of great wealth was made in the lavish use of expensive spices – as in the case of Anton Fugger of Augsburg, whose family rose to princely rank as the "Emperor's bankers," and who himself engaged in the spice trade. He had cinnamon burnt on an aromatic fire on his hearth in 1535.

The actual spices and other ingredients that go into the *Lebkuchen* of Nuremberg today are kept a closely guarded secret by every manufacturer. Although they have long been claimed to be inimitable, the name has been legally protected only since 1927. But even at the end of the 14th century it seems that some bakers were specializing in making these spice cookies, and the nearby Reichswald with its *Zeidler* (forest beekeepers) provided plenty of honey for the sweet *Lebkuchen*. Wherever a round *Lebkuchen* tin with a picture of Albrecht Dürer or a view of the castle on its lid may end up today after its purchase in the *Christkindlmarkt* – on the family table of Christmas gifts, or in the home of relatives in distant Australia – whenever you open it, even if it has long been emptied of its original contents and is now used as a place to keep postage stamps, something of the cosy aroma of the anticipation of Christmas will still cling to it.

Above: the Nuremberg Christkindlmarkt is held in the main square, in front of the Frauenkirche. Visitors come from all over the world to buy Christmas decorations and enjoy the unique Christmas atmosphere over Glühwein and Lebkuchen.

The sentimental story of a gilded angel

Many hundreds of years ago, "a very poor couple lived in Nuremberg. The husband was a woodcarver, but since he could not practice his craft, he kept the wolf from the door by carving wooden spoons … He and his wife had one great treasure, their little daughter Marie. The child was so pretty and delicate that people in the street used to say she ought to be living up in the proud imperial citadel, not in the poor carver's home." Then the plague came, and "one day the carver and his wife had to stand by and watch" as their little daughter died. "Now there was no joy in their poor lives at all, they sat at home grieving, and the mother wept quietly without ceasing. As for the father, he could carve no more spoons … In the end he took a piece of linden wood and tried to carve the head of a child, giving it his daughter's features." This is how the story of the gilded angel is told in a book of 1956 entitled *Für Dich. Ein Jahrbuch für Mädchen* ("For You. A Girls' Annual"). To tell the rest of the story in the rather briefer style of the 1990s: the mother showed everyone the likeness of her child, and they were all moved to tears and to generosity: the wigmaker provided little Marie's blond curls, other craftsmen gave the mother gold leaf, silk, ribbons, and lace, so that the poor carver's wife could clothe the little doll like a Nuremberg patrician's daughter. And as the child was now an angel, she gave her little wings and a crown, and the gilded angel was finished. End of sentimental story.

Gugelhupf
Fruit bread

4 cups/500 g flour
¼ cup/60 g sugar
a pinch of salt
2 cakes compressed yeast (or 1 envelope active dried yeast)
1 cup/250 ml lukewarm milk
¼ cup/60 g butter
2 eggs
⅔ cup/100 g raisins
flour for the work surface
fat to grease the mold
confectioner's sugar to dust

Make a dough with the flour, sugar, milk, salt, yeast, butter, and eggs, and leave to rise until it has doubled in size. Knock down briefly on a floured work surface. Add the raisins and knead them in. Place the dough in a greased Gugelhupf mold (a fluted ring mold), and allow to rise again, covered, for 20 minutes. Then bake for about 1 hour in a preheated oven at 400 °F/200 °C. Turn the Gugelhupf out of the mold on to a cake rack, allow to cool, and dust with confectioner's sugar before serving.

Glasierter Apfelkuchen
Glazed apple cake

| 2 cups/250 g flour |
| ½ cup/100 g sugar |
| ½ tsp vanilla essence |
| a pinch of salt |
| ¾ cup/200 g butter |
| 1 egg |
| 12 medium apples |
| flour for the working surface |
| fat to grease the pan |
| 2 tbsp breadcrumbs |
| ½ cup/125 g melted butter |
| 5 egg yolks |
| 2 cups/500 ml cream |
| 2 tbsp cornstarch |
| 1 packet of clear glaze |
| 2 tbsp chopped almonds |

Make a plain pastry with the flour, sugar, vanilla essence, salt, butter, and egg, and allow it to rest in the refrigerator for 30 minutes. Meanwhile peel, quarter, and core the apples, and cut them into thin slices. Line a greased spring-form pan with the pastry, prick the bottom of the tart shell several times with a fork, and sprinkle with breadcrumbs. Place the apple slices on top, and paint with the melted butter. Whisk the egg yolks, cream, and cornstarch together, and pour over the apples. Bake in a preheated oven for about 1 hour at 400 °F/200 °C. Mix the tart glaze according to the packet instructions, and pour over the apple cake while it is still warm. Decorate the edge of the cake with the chopped almonds.

Dobostorte
Layered chocolate tart

| **Dough** |
| 6 eggs, separated |
| ¾ cup/150 g superfine sugar |
| ½ tsp vanilla essence |
| ¾ cup/100 g flour |
| 2 tbsp cornstarch |
| fat to grease the pan |

| **Filling** |
| 4 oz/125 g dark block chocolate |
| 1 cup/250 g butter, at room temperature |
| ⅔ cup/125 g superfine sugar |
| 2 egg yolks |

| **Caramel** |
| 1 tbsp butter |
| ¾ cup/150 g superfine sugar |

Beat the egg yolks with the sugar and vanilla essence until light and foamy. Whisk the egg whites very stiff. Mix both in a basin, sieve the flour and cornstarch over the mixture, and fold in. Put ⅙ of the mixture in a greased spring-form pan, and bake in a preheated oven for about 7 minutes at 400 °F/200 °C. Remove the layer of cake from the pan. Bake 5 more layers in this way, and allow them to cool. To make the cream filling, melt the chocolate, beat the butter, sugar, and egg yolks until light and foamy, and stir in the melted chocolate. Spread 5 layers of cake with the cream, and place them on top of each other. Melt the butter for the caramel in a pan, and caramelize the sugar in it. Spread over the remaining layer of cake, and cut it into 16 portions. Place them on top of the tart, and chill it in the refrigerator.

Prinzregententorte
Prince Regent tart

| **Dough** |
| 1¼ cups/250 g butter |
| 1 cup/250 g sugar |
| 4 eggs, separated |
| 1⅔ cups/200 g flour |
| 2 tbsp cornstarch |
| 1 tsp baking powder |
| fat for the pan |

| **Filling** |
| ½ cup/125 ml milk |
| 7 oz/200 g semi-sweet chocolate |
| ¾ cup/200 g butter |
| 1¼ cups/150 g confectioner's sugar |
| 1 packet/125 g chocolate glaze |

Beat the butter, sugar, and egg yolks together until light and foamy. Whisk the egg whites until very stiff, and fold into the egg yolk mixture. Sieve the flour, cornstarch, and baking powder over the mixture, and fold in. Grease a spring-form pan, and put ⅕ of the batter into it. Bake in a preheated oven for about 7 minutes at 400 °F/200 °C. Remove the layer of cake from the pan, and bake 4 more layers in the same way. Allow them to cool. To make the filling, heat the milk and melt the chocolate in it. Allow to cool, stirring frequently. Beat the butter until foamy, mix in the confectioner's sugar and chocolate. Spread 4 layers of the tart with the chocolate cream, and place them on top of each other. Place the final layer on top, and paint with the chocolate glaze.

Prepare the starter dough with some flour, yeast, sugar, and lukewarm milk.

When the starter begins to work, add the rest of the ingredients.

Knead the dough well, add the raisins, and work them into the dough.

Allow the Gugelhupf to rise again in the pan, and then put in the oven.

The Schmalznudel café in Munich, where night owls gather early in the morning, serves only pastries made with clarified butter, the Bavarian form of *Schmalz*.

The cooking fat of the rich

When Bavarian recipes mention *Schmalz*, they do not mean melted lard, the usual German meaning of the word, but clarified butter: pure butter fat obtained by melting and straining the butter. Its advantage is that it will keep much longer than unclarified butter, and indeed can even keep for several years at temperatures of up to 40 °F (5 °C). Clarified butter was important for conserving food in the peasant kitchen, and so it was particularly valuable in Bavarian cooking. There are various different kinds of pastry dough for items fried in clarified butter, and some of the pastries that are the end product contain raisins or nuts; they may be sweet or not, filled with preserves, or plain. Flowers may be cooked in a batter, for instance as elderflower fritters, made in spring when the elders are in bloom; the flower clusters are picked from the elder bush, rinsed well, dipped in a pancake batter, and fried in hot clarified butter.

All the pastries fried in clarified butter are a closely linked custom. For instance, doughnuts are eaten at Carnival time all over Bavaria, and in some Catholic areas of Franconia it is still usual to make *Küchla*, "little cakes," for a child's first Communion; they are given away to friends and neighbors who come to offer their congratulations. It was once usual to eat pastries fried in butter on Sundays, and the farmer's wife would serve them after harvest or flax-beating – much to the delight of the farmhands and maidservants, since butter was by no means available in every kitchen. Only rich farmers with enough grazing for cattle, and a couple of dozen cows, could afford to make butter from their cream and then clarify the butter – and make such lavish use of it.

Opposite: doughnuts are fried until golden yellow in hot clarified butter. They must be turned.

Butter-fried pastries and doughnuts are made of yeast dough enriched with eggs.

In the Schmalznudel restaurant, they still use their old scales to weigh the dough.

The portions are placed on a board and the dough is left to rise.

Today, it is mechanically divided into small portions.

This is how the dough reaches the bakers working in the restaurant kitchen.

Ausgezogne, flat, round pastries, must be thin on the inside, and thick at the edges.

The dough for the oval Stritzerln is notched at the sides.

In front, an Ausgezogne, behind, some Stritzerln, swimming in hot clarified butter.

Doughnuts, still pale, as they are placed in the hot butter.

Before the next step in the process, the doughnuts must cool on a baking tray.

Then they are placed in pairs on a gadget that fills them with preserves.

These doughnuts are always dusted with sugar.

Shaped breads

Ever since human beings gave up the nomadic life and took to agriculture, bread has been a symbol of life and survival, so it is not surprising that it figures prominently in old customs. Heavy with significance, symbolizing fertility in itself, a magic charm against witches and demons, bread structured the course of the year and the course of human life alike. Christmas bread was thrown into the first furrow plowed in spring; bread was thrown into the water of a turbulent river to calm it. There were special breads for special festivals, and they were often distributed to the poor as well.

Specially shaped breads with a symbolic meaning connected with seasonal customs and the stages of human life are called *Gebildbrote*, literally, "shaped breads." They were baked in spring, at Easter, or at the New Year. Even today it is usual in Bavaria to take bread shaped like an Easter lamb to church on Easter Sunday and have it blessed, along with other foodstuffs. On birthdays, godparents used to give their godchildren shaped bread, often with money baked into it. Special breads were given away at weddings and christenings. Bread in the shape of a plait features among the more common forms, and has a symbolic function: instead of cutting off their own plaits of hair as a sacrifice when they were in need, women would offer a baked plait of bread instead. A whole range of pretzels, for Lent, weddings, Palm Sunday, blessings in general, and All Souls' Day, were intended to bring good luck, and the wheel, also interpreted as the wheel of the sun turning through the year, was a New Year symbol.

Few of these old customs survive today. If you go to the baker to buy a salted plait-shaped pretzel, you are probably not thinking of offering up your own hair as a sacrifice instead. And if you cut up a loaf marked into four quarters for breakfast, you no longer see it as a symbol of the passing of time, even if time is running out and you really ought to be in the office by now.

Double plait

Wedding anniversary pretzel

Birth of spring

Easter lamb

Mother's Day heart

New Year wheel

Wheel of the sun

Sign of the sun

Desserts

While Bavaria has used all means at its disposal to maintain its boundaries to the north – a place inhabited, as everyone knows, by "Prussians" – it has no problems at all with its southern neighbors. The state has historical, linguistic, and cultural links with Austria. Large parts of modern-day Austria, for instance Styria, the Tyrol, and Salzburg, were in Bavarian hands at some point in their history. The Bavarians and Austrians literally understand one another: almost all Austrian dialects are forms of Bavarian. A Munich taxi driver, who greeted a visitor from Linz with the words, in broad Bavarian, "Mia Bayern und d' Österreicha gemma zam, und d' Schweiz nehm ma ois Kolonie," illustrates this neighborly Alpine relationship, for in standard German the man was suggesting no less than a union of the two states, with the simultaneous colonization of Switzerland. Of course such sympathies are also felt in the kitchen, particularly in the matter of desserts. Strudel, popular in Bavaria as *Apfelstrudel*, cream cheese strudel, or cream strudel – the last two have a filling of Quark (curd cheese) – comes from Austria, where it is said to have been introduced by the Turks. The art of making strudel pastry is to stretch the dough of flour, egg, water, and oil out as thinly as possible. Steamed dumplings of yeast dough are made in both Bavaria and Austria, and so is the famous dessert *Kaiserschmarrn*, pancake pieces with sugar and raisins or sultanas. Originally, these dishes were not desserts for the end of a meal, but main dishes with which families had to fill their stomachs, for in the old days meat was very seldom eaten.

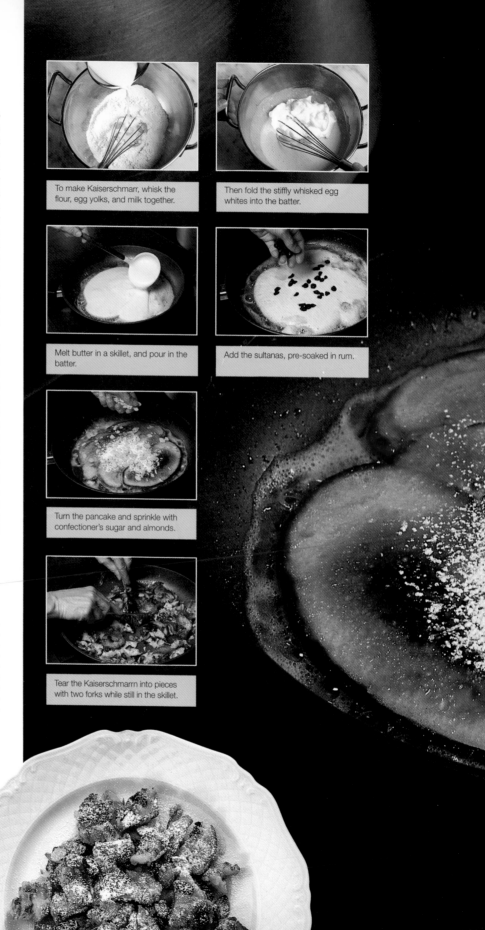

To make Kaiserschmarr, whisk the flour, egg yolks, and milk together.

Then fold the stiffly whisked egg whites into the batter.

Melt butter in a skillet, and pour in the batter.

Add the sultanas, pre-soaked in rum.

Turn the pancake and sprinkle with confectioner's sugar and almonds.

Tear the Kaiserschmarrn into pieces with two forks while still in the skillet.

Kaiserschmarrn
Pancake pieces with sugar and sultanas

⅔ cup/100 g sultanas
3 tbsp rum
8 eggs, separated
2 cups/250 g flour
1 cup/250 ml milk
salt and sugar
butter for frying
confectioner's sugar and flaked almonds, to finish

Wash the sultanas, drain well, and soak in rum for 30 minutes. Beat the egg yolks with the flour, gradually stir in the milk, and season the dough with 1 pinch each of salt and sugar. Allow to stand for 30 minutes. Whisk the egg whites until very stiff, and fold carefully into the batter. Melt a generous amount of butter in a large, heavy iron skillet, and pour in the batter. Add the sultanas. Fry over low heat until the underside is golden brown. Turn, and fry the other side golden brown. Sprinkle with the confectioner's sugar and then the flaked almonds. Tear the pancake into fairly large pieces with two forks while it is still in the skillet, then turn the *Kaiserschmarrn* out to on a prewarmed dish, and serve immediately.

Curd cheese dumplings, made of a yeast dough containing Quark, fried in clarified butter.

Plum dumplings are made with a potato batter. Each contains half a pitted plum.

Millirahmstrudel, a thin strudel pastry filled with curd cheese flavored with vanilla.

Fried plum sandwiches: sliced white rolls filled with plum purée, coated in egg and flour.

Regenwürmer: made with noodle batter, cooked in milk, and served with a cream sauce.

Tubular pastry noodles with custard: made of yeast batter and stuffed with pitted plums.

Rupfhauben: made of noodle dough formed into the shape of little hats, and cooked slowly in milk.

Scheiterhaufen consists of slices of rolls soaked in milk, with pieces of apple and raisins.

Topfenpalatschinken, pancakes filled with Topfen, the curd cheese known as Quark elsewhere.

447

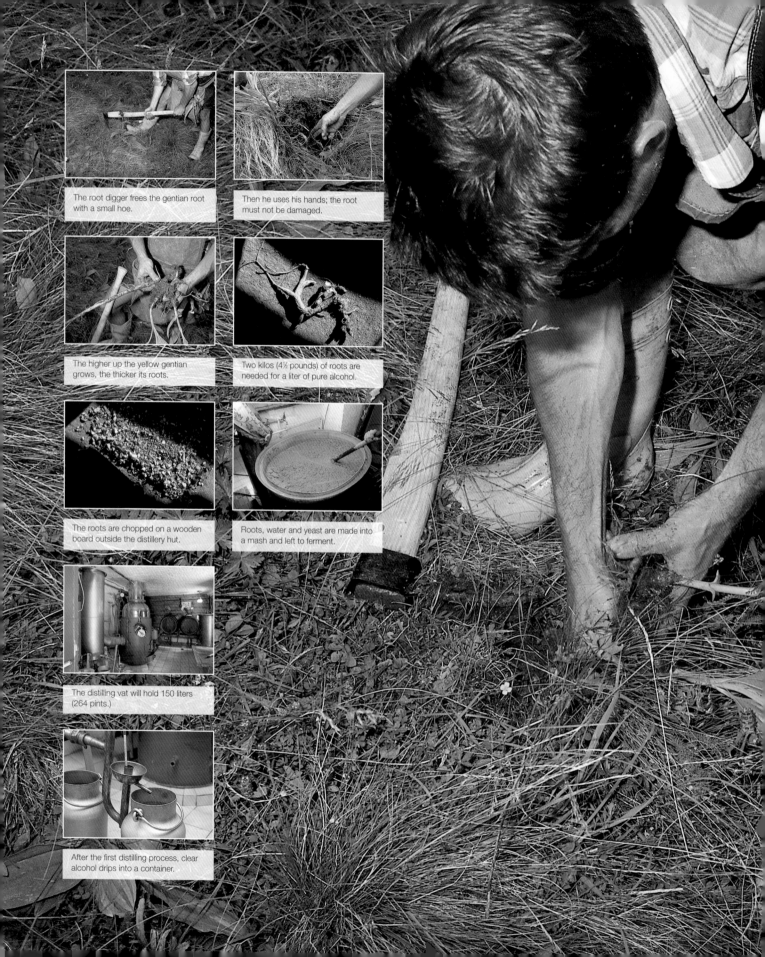

The root digger frees the gentian root with a small hoe.

Then he uses his hands; the root must not be damaged.

The higher up the yellow gentian grows, the thicker its roots.

Two kilos (4½ pounds) of roots are needed for a liter of pure alcohol.

The roots are chopped on a wooden board outside the distillery hut.

Roots, water and yeast are made into a mash and left to ferment.

The distilling vat will hold 150 liters (264 pints.)

After the first distilling process, clear alcohol drips into a container.

Clear mountain water, and the roots of yellow gentian, are the ingredients of gentian spirit.

Spirits made from roots

"Blue, blue, blue grows the gentian," is the song heard in all the alpine skiers' huts, and the hut wardens pour it out lavishly: a clear, high-proof spirit from a bottle adorned with the romantic blue flower of the mountains. Most people stop briefly and shiver after the first sip, but the locals know all about that. They assure the newcomers, with slightly injured local patriotic pride, that it is "good for you" and perfectly "natural," and furthermore, no one likes gentian until the second glass, but after the third you just can't stop. A hut warden of the old style keeps on pouring, and the skiers do not leave the hospitable hut until evening is drawing on, racing down the piste in a state of total intoxication. The doctors are already mixing plaster down in the valley hospitals …

When you are lying there in traction, there is no point in reflecting, ruefully, that you fell for a fraudulent label: mountain gentian spirit is not made from blue gentian at all, but from the roots of the yellow gentian (*Gentiana lutea*). It grows much larger than its blue-flowered cousin, and its flowers are nothing like as decorative, but it has bigger, sturdier roots, and the roots are what matter.

Today, yellow gentian is grown in fields down in the valleys; in the past you could find it only at heights above 3300 feet (1000 meters). The higher the plant grows, the thicker its roots, so that from early August to the first snowfall root diggers would make their way up the mountains to heights of up to 5000 feet (1500 meters) or even more. To make transport easier, the roots were processed on the spot, and distilleries were built where the root diggers and distillers spent the summer.

For reasons of tradition rather than economy the firm of Grassl, the oldest gentian distillery in Germany, founded in 1602, still keeps its distilleries on in the Berchtesgaden area, and while the most modern technology is used down the valley, up here they continue to work as they did hundreds of years ago.

The diggers bring the roots to the hut – a good man can dig 176 pounds (80 kilograms) a day – and they are coarsely chopped and made into a mash with yeast and water. After three to five weeks, the alcohol has formed, and then the furnace is heated and distilling begins. After the second distillation process, the distillate is taken down to the valley, where it is diluted with spring water, and stored in ashwood casks for up to five years. Ash is used because it imparts hardly any color, and gentian has to be a perfectly clear spirit when it is put into the bottles bearing the blue flower.

Besides gentian, which is made throughout the Alpine area, the people of Berchtesgaden have another specialty using roots: masterwort. However, masterwort, like the "bearwort" of Lower Bavaria, does not have enough fruit sugar to produce fermentation, and is added to the pure alcohol only as a flavoring.

Opposite: Today, yellow gentian is grown agriculturally down in the valley. In the past, root diggers climbed to heights of between 3300 and 5000 feet (1000 and 1500 meters) in summer.

A well-cooled nip of spirits is ready for travelers who happen to drop into the gentian-distilling hut.

Credits and Copyright

The cooperation of Oda Tietz, Leipzig, in the organization of the chapters on Thuringia, Saxony, and Saxony Anhalt is gratefully acknowledged.

Thuringia
P. 15: "Mutton stock and cucumber juice" from: Thomas Mann, Essays, Goethe als Repräsentant des bürgerlichen Zeitalters, S. Fischer Verlag, Frankfurt
P. 15: Recipe for "Red cabbage parcels," CMA Bonn

Saxony
P. 33 "Poor Prussia…," Christa Wachenfeld, Berlin
P. 37: Recipe for "Strawberry meringue gateau" Oda Tietz: Der Sächsische Küchenkalender, Südwest Verlag Munich
P. 39: "A Dresden childhood" from: Erich Kästner, Als ich ein kleiner Junge war, Atrium Verlag, Zürich

Saxony Anhalt
P. 53: "A surfeit of Baumkuchen" from: Hans Fallada, Damals bei uns daheim, Büchergilde Gutenberg, Frankfurt

Brandenburg
P. 82: "All about potatoes," Christine Metzger, Munich
P. 84: "Tubers at a glance," Christine Metzger
P. 86: "Potato salad," Christine Metzger

Mecklenburg
P. 114: "The festive goose," Christine Metzger
P. 119: "Herring products," Christine Metzger

Schleswig-Holstein
All texts apart from the following are by Justus Steidle:
P. 126: "Fishing grounds," Christine Metzger
P. 130: "Prawns from Büsum," Verena von Funcke, Munich
P. 131: P. 131: Recipe for "Heligoland lobster with vegetables in a cream sauce" from: Joseph Thaller, Die Meisterküche Schleswig-Holsteins, Mattaes Verlag, Stuttgart
P. 133: Recipe for "Stuffed cabbage," CMA, Bonn
P. 135: Recipes for: "Loin of lamb…" and "Salt meadow lamb…," Ministerium für ländliche Räume, Landwirtschaft, Ernährung und Tourismus des Landes Schleswig-Holstein
P. 139: "Ham – a cottage industry," Verena von Funcke
P. 140: "Game birds," Christine Metzger
Pp. 142–143: "A gas station…" and "Canola," Verena von Funcke
Pp. 146–147: "Food for the intellect," Renate Schober, Munich
P. 150: "Rum," Verena von Funcke
P. 151: "Rumtopf," Christine Metzger; "Rum terminology," Verena von Funcke

Hamburg
Pp. 158–159: Recipes by Obermeister Bernd Besch, Konditoren-Innung Hamburg

Bremen
Pp. 172–173: Schaffermahl recipes, Küchenmeister Ernst August Rotter, Bremen

Lower Saxony
P. 193: "Bregen, Pinkel: sausage lore," Christine Metzger
P. 196–7: "A tale to tell" and "Tales of Baron von Munchausen," Christine Metzger: recipe for Rat tails, Rattenfängerhaus, Hameln
P. 201: Recipe for Stuffed knuckle of heath lamb, CMA, Bonn

North Rhine Westphalia
P. 221: "The bread of those early years" from: Heinrich Böll, Das Brot der frühen Jahre, Kiepenhauer und Witsch Verlag, Cologne
P. 223: "Dining to music," Stefan Siegert, Hamburg
P. 224: "The open sandwich," Christine Metzger
P. 240: "Ready-made and convenient," Christine Metzger

Hesse
P. 250: "Riesling," Stefan Siegert
P. 268: "The Christmas tree" Christine Metzger

Rhineland-Palatinate
P. 277: "Winegrowing," Stefan Siegert
P. 278: "The wines of the Palatinate and the Mosel," Stefan Siegert
P. 280: "Tasting wine" and "The sweetness in the wine," Stefan Siegert
P. 296: "Mineral water," Christine Metzger; "Different kinds of water," André Dominé, Culinaria Organic and wholefoods – naturally delicious cuisine, Könemann Verlag, Cologne

Saarland
P. 310: "The egg," André Dominé, Culinaria Organic and wholefoods – naturally delicious cuisine, Könemann Verlag, Cologne
P. 312: "The rha of the Barbarians," Christine Metzger
P. 314: "Fruit toppings on tarts," Christine Metzger

Baden-Württemberg
P. 327: "Bread," Christine Metzger
Pp. 328–329: "Spelt and green spelt," André Dominé, Culinaria Organic and wholefoods – naturally delicious cuisine, Könemann Verlag, Cologne
Pp. 364–365: "Wine," Stefan Siegert
P. 372: "Jams, jellies, preserves, marmalade," Christine Metzger

Bavaria
All texts apart from the following are by Christine Metzger:
P. 384: "Weisswurst and Leberkäs," Ingeborg Pils, Munich
P. 389: "Bread rolls in the political arena" from Oskar Maria Graf, Das Leben meiner Mutter, Paul List Verlag, Munich 1994
P. 392: "The pig," Ingeborg Pils
P. 394: "Roast pork, etc.," Ingeborg Pils
P. 398: "Offal," Ingeborg Pils
P. 401: "Complaint of a tavern roll" from: Karl Valentin, Klagelied einer Wirtshaussemmel, Piper Verlag, Munich 1985
Pp. 402–403: "Green gold" and "Hop pickers," Barbara Schnabel, Arnstein
P. 405: "The return to…," Klaus Viedebanttt, Frankfurt
Pp. 406–407: "The art of brewing" and "Beer is water" Florian Mikorey, Munich
P. 409: "Brewing and fast days," Florian Mikorey
Pp. 410–411: "The holes in the cheese" and "Say cheese," Verena von Funcke
P. 412: "Farming in the mountain pastures," Verena von Funcke
P. 414: "Cabbage and root vegetables," Barbara Schnabel
P. 416: "Franconian sausages," Barbara Schnabel
P. 424: "Cattle country," Ingeborg Pils
Pp. 426–427: "The Oktoberfest," Ingeborg Pils
P. 431: "Bread dumplings…," from: Lena Christ, Erinnerungen einer Überflüssigen, Süddeutscher Verlag, Munich
Pp. 434–435: "Ludwig II of Bavaria," Ingeborg Pils
P. 436: "Franconian wine" and "Buying wine," Stefan Siegert
Pp. 438–439: "Glühwein and Lebkuchen," Barbara Schnabel

Bibliography

Abraham, Hartwig/ Thinnes, Inge: Hexenkraut und Zaubertrank. Unsere Heilpflanzen in Sagen, Aberglauben und Legenden, Greifenberg 1996
Ahrends, Martin: Allseits gefestigt. Stichwörter zum Sprachgebrauch in der DDR, Munich 1989
Anhäuser, Uwe: Sagenhafter Hunsrück, Band I und Band II, Briedel 1994 und 1995
ders.: Hunsrück und Naheland, Cologne 1996
Arens, Detlev: Sauerland mit Siegerland und Wittgensteiner Land, Cologne 1994
Arnim, Bettina von: Dies Buch gehört dem König, Berlin 1920
Binder, Egon M.: Knödel, Klöße und andere runde Sachen, Passau 1994
Bäumler, Susanne/Ottomeyer, Hans/Zischka, Ulrike (Publ.): Die anständige Lust, Munich 1994
Becker, Christiane: Das Schinderhannes-Kochbuch, Münster 1985
Arnim, Elizabeth von: Elizabeth auf Rügen, Frankfurt 1996
Behnke, H.: Ein Buch der Hamburger Küche, Hamburg 1910
Bericht zur Lage der Land-, Ernährungs- und Forstwirtschaft des Landes Brandenburg 1996, publ. vom Ministerium für Ernährung, Landwirtschaft und Forsten des Landes Brandenburg. Potsdam 1996
Bleuel, Hans Peter: Café en vogue. Munich, 1988
Börde-Museum Burg Ummendorf: Neulich sah ich … Aus dem Leben in der Börde vor mehr als einem halben Jahrhundert. Veröffentlichungen zur Geschichte von Natur und Gesellschaft vol. 9, Ummendorf 1995
Boldt, Klaus-Jürgen: Kochbüchlein Berlin und Mark Brandenburg, Leipzig 1995
Bowles, Edmund H.: Musikgeschichte in Bildern, Musikleben vol. 3, Leipzig 1987
Braungart, Margarete: Gekocht und gebacken in Südthüringen, Leipzig, 1989.
Braungart, Margarete: Und Mutter kocht die Klöß´, Erfurt 1995.
Buchholz, F.H.: Rathgeber für den Menagebetrieb bei den Truppen, Berlin 1882
Bungert, Gerhard/ Lehnert, Charly: Hauptsach – es schmeckt. Essen und Trinken und Feiern im Saarland, Saarbrücken 1995
Bungert, Gerhard, Mallmann Klaus-Michael: Bergmannsgeschichten von der Saar, Saarbrücken 1979
Bungert Mallmann: Kaffeekisch und Kohleklau, Saarbrücken 1980
Bungert Mallmann: Mit Mussik unn Lyoner, Saarbrücken 1981
Chronik der Deutschen, 3., überarbeitete und aktualisierte Auflage, Gütersloh/Munich 1983/1995
Clevely, Andi/ Richmond, Catherine: DuMont´s großes Kräuterbuch, Cologne 1995.
Das Filderkraut, publ. Stadt Filderstadt/ Stadt Leinfeld – Echterdingen
Das war die DDR. Eine Geschichte des anderen Deutschland. ed. Wolfgang Kenntemich, Manfred Durniok and Thomas Karlauf, Berlin 1993
Der Feldkochunteroffizier. publ. as vol. II of Der Unteroffizier,. Berlin 1943
Der Goldene Faden, Bienenleben, Imkerei, Naturhaushalt und Menschenwerk, publ. Niedersächsisches Minsterium für Ernährung, Landwirtschaft und Forsten
Die Akte Pommes Fritz. Geschichten um die Brandenburger Kartoffel, publ. Ministerium für Ernährung, Landwirtschaft und Forsten des Landes Brandenburg. Potsdam 1996
Dissertation on: Wurstarten in der Bundesrepublik Deutschland, Eine vergleichende Untersuchung über regionale Spezialitäten, submitted to Ralf Abel and Prof. Werner Kübler (Institut für Ernährungswissenschaften der Justus-Liebig-Universität Gießen)
Dippel, Horst (ed.): Das Weinlexikon, Frankfurt 1993

Dörner, Klaus S./Dörner Ilse S.: Das Hamburg Kochbuch, Husum 1993
Donderski, Manfred: Berliner und Brandenburger Küche. Berlin 1993
Drummer, Kurt/Muskewitz, Käthe: Kochkunst aus dem Fernsehstudio, Leipzig (DDR) 1981
Drummer, Kurt/Muskewitz: Von Apfelkartoffeln bis Zwiebelkuchen. Volkstümliche Gerichte aus der DDR, Leipzig (DDR) 1984
Dietze, Gudrun: Die schönsten Gerichte aus Thüringen, Leipzig 1994
Dobbertin, Hans: Quellensammlung zur Hamelner Rattenfängersage, Göttingen 1970
Einige Hamburgische Hausfrauen: Hamburgisches Kochbuch – Anweisungen zum Kochen für angehende Köche, Köchinnen und Haushälterinnen, Hamburg 1830
Eiselen, Hermann: Brotkultur, Ulm, Cologne 1995
Englert, Klaus: Spargel, Düsseldorf 1990
Familie v. Ribbeck und "ihr" Birnbaum, publ. Evangelische Kirchengemeinde zu Ribbeck, Ribbeck (no date)
Fontane, Theodor: Sämtliche Werke IV, Die Poggenpuhls, Munich 1959
Fontane Theodor: Sämtliche Werke V, Stechlin, Munich 1956
Franke, Gunther, and others: Früchte der Erde, Frankfurt am Main 1989
Freudenberg, Frank P.: Bier-Metropole Berlin, Nuremberg 1996
Freudenberg: Das Buch vom Stollen, Leipzig 1995
Fronius, Dagmar: Buletten & Co. Die besten Rezepte aus Berlin und Brandenburg, Munich 1995
Gehlen, Claudia von: Geschichte der Frauenbewegung erfahren, Berlin 1988
Geo 6/ 1997, Aale
Gerlach, Edith: Spreewald. Reiseskizzen und Rezepte aus der grünen Küche, Weil der Stadt 1992
Goethe, Johann Wolfgang von: Dichtung und Wahrheit. Frankfurt, 1993
Golz, Reimar und Schulz, Erhard: In Werder a./H. zur Blütezeit, Berlin (no date)
Goullon, Francois le: Der neue Apicius oder die Bewirtung vornehmer Gäste Neudruck des Buches aus dem Jahre 1829. ed. von Manfred Lemmer. Klassische Kochkunst, vol. 8, Munich
Gorys, Erhard: Das neue Küchenlexikon. Von Aachener Printen bis Zwischenrippenstück, Munich, 1995
Grimmelshausen, Hans Jakob Christoph von: Der abenteuerliche Simplicissimus, Klagenfurt 1973
Gutmann, Hermann/Mönch, Jochen, Hollanders, Sophie: Bremer Speisen, Bremen 1993
Habermas, Jürgen: Strukturwandel der Öffentlichkeit: Untersuchungen zu einer Kategorie der bürgerlichen Gesellschaft, Frankfurt, 1995
Hamm-Brücher, Hildegard: Freiheit ist mehr als ein Wort, Cologne 1996
Harndt, Ewald: Französisch im Berliner Jargon, Berlin 1990
Heise, Ulla: Kaffee und Kaffeehaus. Eine Bohne macht Kulturgeschichte, Leipzig 1996
Hendricks, Bernd/ Kowski-Kawelke, Hartmut: Der Pott à la carte, Munich 1994
Henseleit, Felix/Bickel, Walter: Berlin à la carte, Berlin 1972
Herrmann, Klaus: Pflügen, Säen, Ernten. Landarbeit und Landtechnik in der Geschichte, Reinbek bei Hamburg 1985
Heuß, Theodor: Vorspiele des Lebens, Tübingen 1953
Hildebrandt, Irma: Zwischen Suppenküche und Salon, Achtzehn Berlinerinnen, Cologne 1987
Höllhuber, Dietrich/Kaul Wolfgang: Die Biere Deutschlands, Nuremberg 1993
Hoerder, Dirk/Knauf, Diethelm (eds.): Aufbruch in die Fremde, Bremen 1992
Hoffmann, Reinhard: Brandenburg. Kleine Landeskunde, Berlin 1993
Horn, Erna: Bayern tafelt, Munich 1980

Hornickel, Ernst: Die Spitzenweine Europas, Stuttgart 1977
Integrierter Gemüseanbau im Land Brandenburg. publ. Ministerium für Ernährung, Landwirtschaft und Forsten des Landes Brandenburg. Potsdam 1996
Jagd. publ. VEB Tourist Verlag, Berlin/Leipzig 1983
Johnson: Der große Johnson, Stuttgart 1994
Johnson: Atlas der Deutschen Weine, Stuttgart 1995
Jordan, Peter/ Wheeler, Steven: DuMont´s großes Pilzbuch, Cologne 1996
Jung, Peter (ed.), Mark Brandenburg, Berlin 1991
Keller, Franz: Alemannisch angerichtet, Rombach 1986
Kisch, Egon Erwin: Razzia auf der Spree, Berlin 1986
Kluge, Friedrich: Etymologisches Wörterbuch der deutschen Sprache, völlig neu bearbeitet von Elmar Seebold, Berlin/New York 1989
Knoche, Andrea: Traditionelle Bräuche und Feste im Jahreslauf. Schriften des Museums für Thüringer Volkskunde Erfurt 8/1996. ed. von Marina Moritz, Erfurt 1996
Knuth, Detlef; Mieth, Olaf: Verbreitung, Gefährdung, Gewässeransprüche und Erhaltung des Edelkrebses Astacus astacus in Brandenburg, in Naturschutz und Landschaftspflege in Brandenburg, Heft 2/1993
Kölner Brauhaus Wanderweg, Cologne 1995
Kosler, Barbara/ Krauß, Irene: Die Brez'n, Munich 1993
Krift, Willi: So kochten wir in Westfalen, Münster 1996
Kux, Auguste: Die Feldküche. Gründliche Anleitung für Jedermann, Berlin 1878
Lämmel, Reinhard: Kulinarische Audienz am sächsischen Hof, Berlin 1991
Lappe, Werner/ Lauer, Alfred: Burger Brezeln und die Bergische Kaffeetafel, Remscheid 1995
Lau, Katja/ Schütterle Renate/ Roscher, Ernst: Speisen wie ein König, Munich (no date)
Lehnert, Claudia: Aus Dibbe & Pann, Saarbrücken 1995
Lestrieux, Elisabeth de/ Belder-Kovacic de: Der Geschmack von Blumen und Blüten. Eine kulinarische Entdeckungsreise, Cologne 1995
Lindau, Paul: Briefe aus der Neuen Welt, Berlin 1884
Linke, Wolfgang: Bünde, Münster 1994
Lossau, Manfred Joachim (ed.): Ausonius, Darmstadt 1991
Mager, Johannes/ Just, Rüdiger: Kulturgeschichte der Halleschen Salinen. vol. 4, Schriften und Quellen zur Kulturgeschichte des Salzes. publ. vom Technischen Halloren- und Salinemuseum, Halle (Saale) 1995
Meissner Porzellan. Das Erste in Europa. Reprinted from: Die Vitrine. No. 174. Juni 1993, Vienna; Zürich
Mendelssohn, Peter de: Der Zauberer, Frankfurt 1975
Merk, Gerhard/Sieber, Hannes: Das Münchner Bier, Freising 1991
Mollenhauer, Hans P.: Von Omas Küche zur Fertigpackung, Gernsbach 1988
Möller, Michael: Nassauer Rezepte aus Großmutters Kochbuch, Nassau 1993
Müller, Kai Ulrich/ Knabe, Hubertus: Berlin, Hamm 1996
Muus, B. J./Dahlström: Meeresfische, Munich 1985
Nerée, Av.: Die Militär-Dampfküche und Bade-Anstalt, Berlin 1880
Ohff, Heinz: 2mal Berlin, Munich 1985
Paczensky, Gerhard von/ Dünnebier, Anna: Leere Töpfe, volle Töpfe. Die Kulturgeschichte des Essens und Trinkens, Munich 1994
Pieszczek, E., and Ziegelmayer (eds.): 1. Tagungsbericht der Arbeitsgemeinschaft "Ernährung der Wehrmacht," Dresden and Leipzig 1942
Pomplun, Kurt: Pomplun's Großes Berlin Buch, Berlin 1985
Richter Louise/Hommer, Sophie Ch.: Illustriertes Hamburger Kochbuch, Hamburg 1879
Rössing, Roger: Wie der Hering zu Bismarcks Namen kam: Unbekannte Geschichten zu bekannten Begriffen, Leipzig 1995

Root, Waverly: Das Mundbuch, Frankfurt 1994
Rüdiger, Gerd: Currywurst. Ein anderer Führer durch Berlin, Berlin 1995
Rümpler, Theodor: Erfurt's Land- und Gartenbau in seinen wichtigsten Entwickelungs-Momenten, Erfurt 1865
Sächsisches Staatsministerium für Landwirtschaft, Ernährung und Forsten (publ.): Regionale Küche in Sachsen. Ein gastronomischer Führer, Leipzig, Dresden
Sattler, Peter W./Schnur, Horst/Reutter, Rolf/Weckbach, Willi: Odenwald, Künzelsau, 1994
Schall, Sybille: Bier is ooch Stulle, Berlin 1976
Scherr, Johannes: Illustrierte deutsche Kultur- und Sittengeschichte. Von den Anfängen bis zum Jahre 1870. Revised edition in 2 vols. by Alexander Heine, 1984
Schivelbusch, Wolfgang: Das Paradies, der Geschmack und die Vernunft, Frankfurt 1995
Schmidt, Gérard/ Römer, Joachim: Kölsch Kaviar un Ähzezupp, Cologne 1990
Scholze, Dietrich (ed.): Die Sorben in Deutschland. Sieben Kapitel Kulturgeschichte, Bautzen 1993
Schultz, Uwe (ed.): Speisen, Schlemmen, Fasten. Eine Kulturgeschichte des Essens, Frankfurt 1995
Seidel-Pielen, Eberhard: Aufgespießt. Wie der Döner über die Deutschen kam, Hamburg 1996
Stadtgeschichtliches Museum Leipzig/ Sammlung Eduscho, Bremen (publ.) Süße muß der Coffee sein! Drei Jahrhunderte europäische Kaffeekultur und Kaffeesachsen. (Catalog of the exhibition in the Stadtgeschichtliches Museum, Leipzig), Leipzig 1994.
Stein, Bernhard: Schwetziger Spargelbuch, Schwetzingen 1992
Stegmann, Friedrich H.: Der Pfefferkuchenbäcker und Lebküchler oder Anweisung, alle Sorten feiner und ordinärer Pfeffer- und Honigkuchen zu fertigen: nebst genauer Angaben des Verfahrens. Reprint of the original edition Weimar 1875, Leipzig 1989
Stutzer, Dietmar: Geschichte des Bauernstandes in Bayern, Munich 1988
Teuteberg, H.J./Wiegelmann, Günter: Unser täglich Brot, Münster 1986
Thaller, Josef: Die neue schwäbische Küche, Weil der Stadt 1984
Thaller: Original schwäbisch – Schwäbische Originale, Weil der Stadt 1987
Thaller: Schwäbische Vesper, Weil der Stadt 1986
Thiel, Paul: Lokal-Termin in Alt-Berlin, Berlin 1989
Tietz, Oda: Der thüringische Küchenkalender. Kochen und genießen im Laufe der Jahreszeiten. Munich 1996
Top No. 5. Mai 1997: Berlin International – Ein Informationsforum, Senatsverwaltung für Gesundheit und Soziales, Die Ausländerbeauftragte, Berlin
Troll, Thaddäus: Deutschland deine Schwaben, Hamburg 1967
Unsere Landwirtschaft. Eine Zwischenbilanz, publ. Deutsche Landwirtschaftsgesellschaft e.V., Frankfurt am Main 1985
Unsere Landwirtschaft im Wandel, publ. Presse- und Informationsamt der Bundesregierung. Bonn 1994
Vollmann, Rolf: Anna Amalia und die klugen Männer. In: Merian Weimar, Hamburg 1994, S. 82 – 90.
Wat wi äten. Uckermärkische Rezepte aus Angermünde, publ. Rat der Stadt Angermünde, Eberswalde 1990
Weber-Kellermann, Ingeborg: Die deutsche Familie, Frankfurt 1996
Werner-Künzig, Waltraut: Schwarzwälder Trachten, Karlsruhe 1991
Wilmenrod, Clemens: Es liegt mir auf der Zunge, Hamburg 1954
Wimpffen, Hans Hermann von: Das Große Buch vom Sauerkraut, Wien 1992
Zeltner, Renate: Kochen und Backen wie im Westerwald, Montabaur 1994

Acknowledgements

The publishers would like to express their thanks to everyone who has given their kind support and assistance, including those individuals and institutions who are not known to the publishers by name, but who have contributed to the project.

Aicha Becker, Cologne, for her devoted assistance in the coordination of the 1999 edition, photographer Christian Pompetzki, Berlin, Josef Thaller, Leinfelden, for picture research on Baden-Württemberg.

Bavaria
Hans Bader, Burgberg
Bäckerei Manfred Franzen, Cologne
Bäckerei Rischart, Munich
Benediktinerabtei Ettal, Pater Johannes, Frater Nikolaus und Braumeister Josef Prummer
Cafe Schmalznudel, Munich
Maria Christ, Nuremberg
Hannelore Ditter, Marktheidenfeld
Irina Ditter, Bayreuth
Enzianbrennerei Grassl, Berchtesgaden-Unterau
Hans Fischer, Nuremberg
Ludwig Freisinger, Munich
Gasthof Waller, Reisach
Werner Hedler, Küchenchef vom Hotel Eisvogel, Bad Gögging, Holledau
Maria Hörning, Marktheidenfeld
Fa. J. + R. Kiefhaber, Senfherstellung, Mammendorf bei Fürstenfeldbruck
Christoph Oberle, Erlangen
Firma Pöschl, Landshut
Gusti Schwarz, Munich
Charlotte Stegmüller, Munich

Baden-Württemberg
Robert Baur, Restaurant Posthalterei, Gammertingen
Besenwirtschaft Lotte, Stuttgart-Obertürkheim
Roland Böhler, Reichenau
Hartmut Böhner, Lichtenau
Cafe-Konditorei Fromme, Cologne
Deutsches Brotmuseum Ulm, Doris Schäfer und Inge Bachmaier
Alfons Eckart
Eberhard Fries, Lonsee
Karl Gebhard
Werner Hafendörfer, Bäckerei, Stuttgart
Hans Hartmann, Gasthof-Restaurant Bahnhof, Leinfelden-Echterdingen
Karl Hauser
Lena und Josef Heinzelmann, Trochtelfingen
Walter Höfling, Forellenhof, Lohr
Hans und Friedel Jäckle
Katholische Kirche St. Peter, St. Peter/Schwarzwald
Karl und Margit Kizele, Leinfelden-Echterdingen

Georg Mayer, Bermaringen
Karl Reich, Villingen-Schwenningen
Paul Rinderle
Alfred Schweizer, Restaurant Hahnen, Filderstadt
Hubert Treyer, Stadtverwaltung Pfaffenweiler/Breisgau
Erika Wiedmann, Amstetten

Hesse
Fa. Asbach GmbH & Co., Frau Behrens und Herr Claßen, Rüdesheim/Rhein
Herr Berger, Restaurant Dippegucker, Frankfurt/Main
Thea Büschel, Gronau/Leine
Cafe-Konditorei Fromme, Cologne
Kelterei Fink, Ehrenberg/Rhön
Metzgerei Pröscher, Schotten
Restaurant Pöttgen, Cologne
Restaurant Zum gemalten Haus, Frankfurt/Main
Sektkellerei Schloß Vaux, Eltville
Wiesbadener Rathsbräu, Braumeister Herr Holz und Herr Finke, Wiesbaden

Rhineland-Palatinate
Deidesheimer Hof, Deidesheim/Weinstraße
Herr Kost, Gleisweiler
Landhotel Hunsrücker Faß, Kempfeld
Marksburg, Braubach/Rhein
Prinz zu Salm-Dalberg'schen Weingut, Herr Eckes, Wallhausen/Nahe
Restaurant in der Kauzenburg, Bad Kreuznach
Weingut Dieter Sünner, Winningen/Mosel
Weinstube zum Domstein, Trier

Saarland
Margarete Bacher, Neunkirchen-Kohlhof/Saar
Alfons Kratz, Metzgerei, Merzig-Brotdorf

Index of photographs

Agentur für Presse- und Öffentlichkeitsarbeit, wpr communication, Königswinter: 84/85 (except large illustr. center)
© aid Bonn: 393 (3 small photos)
© aid Bonn / Dittrich: 201 (above, l)
© Architektur Bilderservice Kandula, Witten: 46/46
© Archiv für Kunst und Geschichte, Berlin: 42 (below, r), 104 (above, l), 146 (above, r) 197, 223, 268 (below), 283, 409 (below, r)
© Archiv Gebhardt / Photo: Rudi Dix, Munich: 267 (above), 428 (below, left)
© Archiv der Stiftung Deutsche Kinemathek Berlin / Photo: ringpress-Brünjes / Filmaufbau / Europa: 146/147 (large illustr.)
© argus-Fotoarchiv GmbH / Reinhard Janke: 179 (below)
© Atelier Osterholz, Bremen: 170/171
© Franz Bagyi, Weil der Stadt: 292
© BAV-Helga Lade Fotoagentur, Frankfurt / Main: 269 (above)
© Bayerisches Hauptstaatsarchiv, Geheimes Hausarchiv, ref. III/233/93/1 No. III/22/97, Munich: 434 (below)
© Bayerische Verwaltung der staatlichen Schlösser, Gärten und Seen, Ludwig II Museum, Herrenchiemsee: 434 (above)
© Benediktinerinnenabtei St. Hildegard, Rüdesheim / Rhein: 300
Bildarchiv Halloren und Salinemuseum Halle: 52/53, 56/57
© Bildarchiv Preussischer Kulturbesitz, Berlin, Lutz Braun: 83 (below, l)
© Bilderberg, Hamburg / Reinhart Wolf: 376 (background) and 382/383; H. & D. Zielske: 444/445 (large photo); Wolfgang Kunz: 154/155 (large illustr. above); 154 (below, r)
© Sonja Büschel, Cologne: 190 (background)
© Das Kartoffelmuseum, Munich Stiftung Otto Eckart: 83 (background)
© Deutsches Historisches Museum, Berlin (DHM): 121 (above, l)
© Deutsches Schiffahrtsmuseum, Bremerhaven: 179 (below)
© Fackelträger Verlag GmbH, Hanover, from: Das dicke Zillebuch: 69 (above, r)
© Peter Feierabend, Cologne: 267 (below, r)
© Astrid Fischer-Leitl, Munich: illustrs. 12, 30, 46, 58, 62, 78, 102, 122, 152, 168, 182, 210, 244, 250, 274, 278, 302, 318, 365, 382, 437
© Fotolia: 301 (1, 2, 4, 8, 9)
© Getty Images /Alex Mares-Manton: 301 (5)
© Gerald Grosse, Halle: 44 (below)

Recipe Index

Recipes with illustrations have page numbers in **bold** type.

General Index

Illustrations have page numbers in **bold**.